Crystal Reports™ 7: The Complete Reference

About the Author ...

George Peck is a software trainer, consultant, and developer with more than 20 years of experience in the computer industry. He purchased his first personal computer (a Radio Shack TRS-80) in 1978 and taught himself to program in one of the earliest versions of Microsoft BASIC. When Microsoft shipped Visual Basic 1.0, he drove to the shipper's warehouse to pick it up, rather than waiting the extra day for delivery.

After more than ten years as an internal consultant and trainer in a large corporation, George founded his own consulting and training firm, The ABLAZE Group, in 1994 (**www.AblazeGroup.com**). He started with a large Visual Basic/Crystal Reports project for a major West Coast bank, and since then he has trained, consulted, and developed custom software for large and small clients throughout the United States and Canada.

George is certified by Seagate Software as both a trainer and consultant for Seagate Crystal Reports 7. He was awarded *Training Partner of the Year* by Seagate for 1998-1999.

Prior to his computer career, George was a broadcaster, and his voice may still be heard in various national radio and TV commercial and promotional campaigns.

Crystal Reports™ 7:
The Complete Reference

George Peck

Osborne/**McGraw-Hill**

Berkeley   New York   St. Louis   San Francisco
Auckland   Bogotá   Hamburg   London   Madrid
Mexico City   Milan   Montreal   New Delhi   Panama City
Paris   São Paulo   Singapore   Sydney
Tokyo   Toronto

Osborne/**McGraw-Hill**
2600 Tenth Street
Berkeley, California 94710
U.S.A.

For information on translations or book distributors outside the U.S.A., or to arrange
bulk purchase discounts for sales promotions, premiums, or fund-raisers, please
contact Osborne/**McGraw-Hill** at the above address.

Crystal Reports™ 7: The Complete Reference

1234567890 AGM AGM 90198765432109 *

ISBN 0-07-211978-0

Seagate and the Seagate logo are registered trademarks of Seagate Technology, Inc.
Seagate Crystal Reports, Seagate Crystal Info, and Seagate Analysis are trademarks of
Seagate Technology, Inc.

Publisher
  Brandon A. Nordin

**Associate Publisher and
Editor-in-Chief**
  Scott Rogers

Acquisitions Editor
  Wendy Rinaldi

Project Editor
  Janet Walden

Editorial Assistant
  Monika Faltiss

Technical Editor
  Kern Pegg

Copy Editor
  Andy Carroll

Proofreader
  Stefany Otis

Indexer
  David Heiret

Computer Designers
  Ann Sellers
  Jani Beckwith

Illustrators
  Robert Hansen
  Beth Young

Series Design
  Peter Hancik

For Denise.
Thanks for your understanding,
your encouragement,
your keen eye, and your undying faith in me.
Now we can get back to living and loving again.

Contents at a Glance

Part II   Developing Custom Window Applications

Part III   Crystal Reports 7 on the Web

Part IV   Appendixes

Contents

Part I

Crystal Reports 7 Introduced

6   Analyzing with Advanced Selection Criteria   123

7   Making Your Reports Visually Appealing   139

8   Using Sections and Areas   155

Part II

Developing Custom Window Applications

Part IV

Appendixes

Acknowledgments

Perhaps it's not surprising that you can gather a rather large list of people to thank when undertaking a project of the magnitude of this book. Even though neither Billy Crystal nor Whoopi Goldberg is here to cut me off when I get too long-winded, I'll try my best to keep it just below the "boring" threshold.

Enough thanks can't go to my friends at Osborne/McGraw-Hill, whom I hope to actually meet in person some day. Wendy Rinaldi is an encouraging, but firm, collaborator who kept me focused and politely listened to my whining when things got behind. While Monika Faltiss' weekly e-mail nudges weren't enough to exactly keep me on track, I must commend her for keeping me "less off track." And, heartfelt thanks go to Janet Walden and Andy Carroll for moving me relatively close to proper sentence structure and for gently reminding me that there's no category in the *Guiness Book of World Records* for "the most illustrations and figures in a single chapter."

Folks at Seagate Software deserve some recognition as well. Kern, your insights were invaluable; thank you. Thanks to Phil Walston for the encouragement and help, and for believing in this book. And, Cathy, I hope you think that "making due without me" for all those months is now worth it.

To Janna Proulx: I still remember the day several years ago when you asked, "Do you know Crystal Reports?" I must admit to you now that I lied when I said "Yes." But, it was great motivation to learn. I trust you're pleased with my progress.

Then, there's K-PIG, 107-oink-5, the best Internet radio station on the planet (**www.kpig.com**). Thanks for keeping me company during those all-nighters.

On a more personal note, what can I say to Dad, who I think has always hoped that I'd follow in his writing footsteps. I hope you're proud of me. And, Mom, I truly wish I could thank you now for the appreciation for language that you've instilled in me, despite all my energy to fight your efforts.

—George Peck, July 1999–

Introduction

Some time before I started this book, I received a call at my office from a potential client who wanted some custom Crystal Reports designed. He was in somewhat of a hurry (what client who calls me isn't?) and I informed him that I was currently engaged and wouldn't be able to approach his project until a few weeks later. He didn't seem all that concerned, simply replying, "Oh well, any monkey or moron can create Crystal Reports."

I managed to hold my tongue and not tell him what that said about him and his company (since, despite his statement, he was *still* calling a consultant for report design). I did tell him, though, that he obviously didn't know the tool very well. While it was easy to create a simple report very quickly, I explained, there were an untold number of ins and outs that he would face when his reports began to get complicated. He'd be able to tap into his corporate databases in many new and innovative ways, and he could design his reports so they looked just like a page-publishing program created them. I described the whole Crystal Reports formula language, and the capability he'd find to design his own Windows programs and Web sites with Crystal Reports built right into them.

But, alas, he was unconvinced. This "Crystal Reports" thing, he retorted, was really simple, and he needed these reports created now. He hung up, presumably going on to the next person in his "monkey and moron listing" to find a report designer. But he left me with an idea. How about writing a book that would really dig into the meat of Crystal Reports? "There are so many things that people can do with it," I thought, "if there were just a good text that goes beyond the basics. One that offers lots of tips and tricks, exposes the 'gotchas,' that concentrates on the intermediate to advanced stuff, and delves into the tool's great Visual Basic and Web integration features." Well, here you go!

You'll find that this book goes beyond the basics—sometimes well beyond them. Chapter 1 will get you started quickly. Although reading the chapter certainly isn't mandatory, you'll probably feel even more comfortable with Crystal Reports if you've had some exposure to it already, or you at least have a good fundamental knowledge of database concepts or other query or reporting tools. Then it's on to the rest of Part I, where you'll learn intermediate to advanced techniques for formatting your reports, creating formulas, setting up sophisticated grouping, and using cross tabs, OLAP grids, and charts to expose your data in new and unique ways. You'll also learn how to use multiple report sections and conditional formatting to garner flexibility that you probably thought wasn't possible, shy of a programming language. And you can have a look at all the new features that have been added to Crystal Reports 7, such as the Document Import Tool, Geographic Maps, and Field Mapping. Then you owe it to yourself to look at Chapter 18 while you work a little with Seagate Analysis, Seagate Software's new (and absolutely free) query, reporting, and OLAP tool that was released after Crystal Reports 7. Seagate claims to have shipped this new tool to more than 1 million information technology professionals around the world, so you may already have a copy of it. If not, it's on the CD that accompanies this book (more information on which can be found in Appendix B in Part IV).

If you're a VB programmer, you'll want to dive right into Part II, the Visual Basic integration section. You'll see how to integrate a report you've designed right into your applications. You'll be able to control virtually all aspects of the report's behavior at run time, right from within your code. Design your user interface any way you like, design your report any way you like, and then make the two work seamlessly together to provide a great package for your application's audience.

Maybe you're one of the thousands of Web masters who's putting together your company's intranet or extranet. Or you might be a Web developer charged with designing yet another e-commerce site to open up a whole new market for your products. You'll want to look at Part III, where you can learn how to use the Crystal Web Reports Server or Microsoft's Active Server Pages, to add that great presentation-quality report you create right into your Web page, and control it completely based on your viewer's interactions.

To help you along, there's an accompanying CD on the inside back cover of the book (see Appendix B for more information). Put this in your CD-ROM drive and enjoy the packages that Seagate Software has thrown in for free. The new Seagate Analysis query, reporting, and OLAP tool is there for you, along with Seagate Info 7, the enterprise tool for Crystal Reports automated scheduling and distribution, as well as multi-dimensional OLAP analysis. And, if you're a VB programmer who hasn't installed

Crystal Reports 7 Professional yet, you can install the Report Designer component Version 6, which is also included on the CD. In addition, you'll find many of the reports that are demonstrated in the book, sample Visual Basic applications for each integration method discussed in the book, and a complete sample Web site that customizes a Crystal Report right in a Web browser based on user input.

If that's not enough, I've set up a Web site just for *Crystal Reports™ 7: The Complete Reference*. Point your browser to **www.crtcr.com**. You'll find some sample chapters in searchable electronic form, some additional samples and examples, any corrections to material that may have been discovered after printing, and a host of great links and information about Crystal Reports. If you have thoughts or suggestions about the book, or you have an idea or a tip for the next edition, click the e-mail link on the home page. I'd love to hear from you.

So, I hope the gentleman that I spoke to before I started *Crystal Reports™ 7: The Complete Reference* just happens to pick up a copy. I'm sure he'll find it enlightening as he explores all the hidden power and sophistication of this wonderful reporting tool, Crystal Reports 7. If he even reads just a little, he should be designing great-looking, functional reports in no time. He can probably impress his boss with the great in-depth information he'll come up with about the intricacies of his company's operations. Hey, he might get a raise, or maybe even get promoted to a management position (although hopefully not a politically sensitive one).

I hope you'll benefit from this book as well. If you can use Crystal Reports to make your life easier, improve the bottom line, or get promoted, this book will have served its purpose: you will have achieved *reporting independence*.

And, besides, you can never find a monkey or moron when you need one.

The Complete Reference

Part I

Crystal Reports 7 Introduced

Chapter 1

Common Ground: Creating a Simple Report

In the fast-paced information-technology community, a company that hasn't converted its mainframe and minicomputer applications to PC-based client/server systems is the exception rather than the rule. These new PC-based systems all have one thing in common at their core: an industry-standard database program to manage the data. But once thousands, or often millions, of pieces of data have been put into these databases, how can you extract the right data in a meaningful form? Enter the *database report writer*.

Introducing Crystal Reports 7

Seagate Crystal Reports has been the market leader and de facto standard for business and corporate report writing. In 1984, a Canadian shipping company wanted to produce custom reports from their accounting system. When the vendor said "We can't help you," the company created "Quick Reports," the precursor to Crystal Reports. Crystal Reports' first "bundle" was with that vendor's next version of their accounting software.

Seagate Crystal Reports is now bundled with over 150 leading software packages, from vendors including ACCPAC International, Great Plains Software, PeopleSoft, and is included with Microsoft's BackOffice and Visual Studio packages.

Crystal Reports is aimed at three general types of users:

- Casual business users, such as data analysts, executive assistants, or marketing directors, who will design reports around their corporate data to make intelligent business decisions.
- Information technology professionals, who will use Crystal Reports to integrate sophisticated reporting right inside their own Microsoft Windows programs.
- Webmasters, who will use it to provide print-quality reports and graphics over their intranets or the Internet.

Figure 1-1 shows the Crystal Reports 7.0 screen when the program is first started. Note the standard Windows user interface, including different toolbars, pull-down menus, and the Welcome dialog.

Tip   *You may turn the toolbars and status bar on and off from the View menu. In the 32-bit version of Crystal Reports, you may "undock" the toolbars from their default positions and place them anywhere you want. Just click on a blank part of the toolbar and drag it to the desired location. It will become its own "window." If you place it near the edge of the Crystal Reports screen (or back near its original position), it will snap into place along the edge of the screen.*

When you first start the program, the only two main functions that you'll usually want to perform are creating a new report and opening an existing report. Like most functions in Crystal Reports, these functions can be accomplished in several ways. If

Creates a new report

Opens an existing report

Pull-down menus

The Format toolbar is used to change the appearance of report objects.

The Standard toolbar contains the most frequently used Crystal Reports functions.

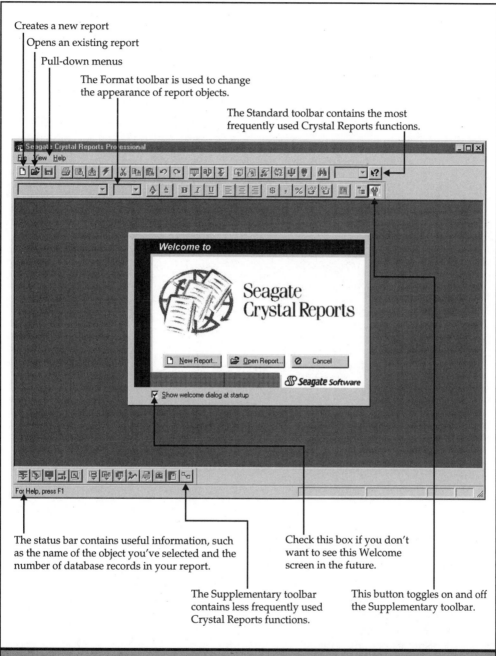

The status bar contains useful information, such as the name of the object you've selected and the number of database records in your report.

Check this box if you don't want to see this Welcome screen in the future.

The Supplementary toolbar contains less frequently used Crystal Reports functions.

This button toggles on and off the Supplementary toolbar.

Figure 1-1. *The Crystal Reports 7.0 screen*

the Welcome dialog screen appears, you can choose either function from it. If you've closed the Welcome dialog screen, you may use a pull-down menu option, a keyboard shortcut, or a toolbar button.

To open an existing report, select File | Open, use the shortcut key combination CTRL-O, or click the Open button in the Standard toolbar.

To create a new report, click the appropriate button on the Welcome dialog screen, or if you've closed it, use similar methods to those for opening an existing report. Choose File | New, the keyboard shortcut CTRL-N, or the New Report button in the Standard toolbar.

When you create a new report, the Report Gallery appears.

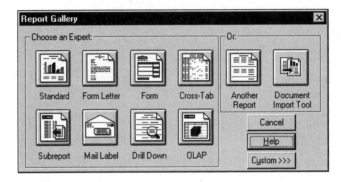

There are four general options you can choose from the Report Gallery:

- Create a report using one of eight report experts
- Base the new report on another existing report (the same as opening an existing report, but not keeping its filename)
- Create a new report from an ASCII text file using the Document Import Tool (covered in Chapter 16)
- Use the Custom option for precise control when designing a new report

Using the Report Experts

The eight standard *report experts* allow you to create "quick and dirty" reports with minimal effort. They're helpful when you want to create a simple report or put together the beginning elements of a more complex report. Choose the button that most closely matches the type of report that you want to create.

To create a simple, general purpose report (for example, an employee phone list or your last year's sales totals), click Standard to use the Standard Report Expert

(Figure 1-2). The Standard Report Expert presents a type of dialog box that's probably familiar to you if you've used other office suites or productivity products. You build your report by choosing options from the different tabbed pages in the dialog box. You advance to the next tab by clicking the tab itself or by clicking the Next button at the bottom of the dialog box.

To create a report with the Standard Report Expert, follow these steps:

1. In the Data tab, choose the type of database you want to base the report on. You will see different options in this tab, based on other software that's installed on your PC. For PC-style databases that reside on your hard disk or on a shared network drive, such as Microsoft Access, click the Data File button. To connect to client/server databases, such as Oracle or Informix, through open database connectivity (ODBC), click the SQL/ODBC button.

   You may also be able to connect to a client/server database directly, without using ODBC, if you have that database's client software loaded on your PC. Crystal Reports recognizes "native" drivers for such popular client/server databases as Microsoft SQL Server, Oracle, Informix, and IBM DB2. Additional buttons will appear in the Data tab if Crystal Reports detects these drivers.

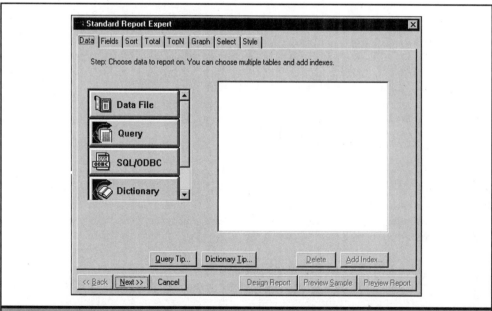

Figure 1-2. *The Standard Report Expert*

2. If you choose the Data File option, a Choose Database Files dialog box appears. Navigate to the drive and folder where your database is stored, and select it. If you choose a database that contains more than one table (for example, the XTREME.MDB sample Microsoft Access database that's included with Crystal Reports), you'll see the Select Tables dialog box.

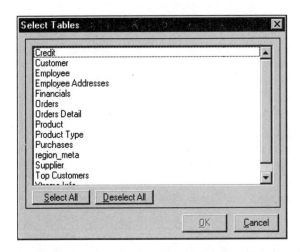

3. You may choose one table by simply clicking it. To select multiple tables, hold down the CTRL key while clicking the tables you wish to select. To select a range of tables, click the first table, and then hold down the SHIFT key while clicking the last table. Both tables, and all tables in between the two, will be selected.

When you've finished selecting tables, click OK to accept your selections and return to the Choose Database Files dialog box. You may choose additional database files in the Choose Database Files dialog box, or click Done to close the dialog box.

In case you didn't know it, the CTRL and SHIFT functionality just mentioned holds true for most other Windows programs, including Windows Explorer. If, for example, you'd like to copy multiple files between your hard disk and a floppy disk, you can select them the same way in Explorer before dragging them to the floppy disk icon.

4. If you chose more than one table, you'll be taken to the Links tab automatically. (Note that you won't see the Links tab unless more than one table is chosen.) This will show you the tables you've chosen in a visual format, allowing you to *link* the tables together, based on common fields. Crystal Reports will *Smart Link* the tables automatically, showing you lines indicating the fields and tables that are linked. If these links are correct (in the real world they rarely are), you may leave them as is.

If you need to delete a link Crystal Reports added, click the line that connects the tables, and press the DELETE key to remove the existing link. You may then create your own link by dragging from the "from" field and table and dropping on the "to" field and table. A line will appear, indicating your new link. Once you've linked the tables correctly, click Next or the Fields tab.

> **Note** *There are quite a few fine points to linking tables. Look for more information in Chapter 14.*

5. Here you choose the database fields you actually want to appear on your report. Select the fields you want included by using the click, CTRL-click, and SHIFT-click methods described earlier. Then click the Add button to move them to the Report Fields box.

   If you'd like to change the order in which the fields will appear on the report, or the column headings that will appear above them, you can make those changes in the Report Fields box. When you're finished, click Next or the Sort tab to move on.

6. Choose one or more fields to sort or group the report by. *Sorting* simply rearranges the order in which report items appear on your report. You may want an employee list sorted by employee last name, for example. *Grouping* sorts report items, but additionally puts them in groups that can have subtotals, counts, averages, or other summaries at the end. Grouping is covered in more detail in Chapter 3. When you have added your sort or group fields, click Next or the Total tab.

7. On the Total tab you can choose fields you want subtotaled or summarized at the end of groups, or grand-totaled at the end of the report. Within the Total tab, you'll see an additional tab for each field you chose to sort or group by. In each of these sub-tabs, Crystal Reports will have already added any numeric or currency fields to the Total Fields box and chosen to sum them.

   If you wish to subtotal the pre-chosen fields, you can leave them as they are. Otherwise, you can remove them from the Total Fields box by selecting them and clicking Remove, change their summary function from "sum" to something else (for example, average or count), or add new fields to summarize by using the Add button. There are a large number of mathematical and statistical functions available for use with numeric and currency fields, and a reduced number of summary functions available for other field types.

> **Note** *What you choose in the Total tab determines whether the report is sorted or grouped by the fields you chose in the Sort tab. If you add any total fields for a sort field, a group will be created on the report for that field with the summary information placed at the end of the group. If you eliminate any total fields for a sort field, report items will only be sorted by that field and no group will be created.*

8. Usually, any groups on your report are presented in alphabetical order (for example, Arizona precedes California, and both are followed by Oregon, Texas, and Wyoming). However, if you want to see the "top five states in order of sales," use the TopN tab to reorder the report groups by one of the subtotal or summary amounts, rather than by the name of the group.

   The TopN tab in the Standard Report Expert will show sub-tabs for each group on the report. Choose the group you want to set up TopN reporting for, and select TopN in the Sort All scroll box to see groups from highest to lowest, or BottomN to see groups from lowest to highest. Then, in the second scroll box, choose the summary or sum field that you want the TopN function to use to sort your groups. Choose what you want "N" to be—how many groups you want to appear on the report. Finally, click the Others check box if you want to include the rest of the report items that aren't in the TopN or BottomN. They will be placed in one last group with the name you specify.

9. The Graph tab lets you show your report data graphically in a bar, pie, or other form of chart. Four sub-tabs show up below the Graph tab that take you through creating a chart step by step.

Note   *Chapter 10 explains how to create graphs and charts in detail.*

10. To limit your report to meaningful database records, use the Select tab. It's doubtful that you will ever want to include every record in the database tables in your report. Many tables contain large numbers of records, and your reports will be much more meaningful if they only contain the relevant set of records.

    Choose one or more fields to select upon, and move them to the Select Fields box by clicking the Add button. When you select a field in the Select Fields box, two additional scroll boxes appear below. The Is scroll box can be changed to Is Not once you've chosen a comparison operator other than Any Value in the second scroll box. You can choose the comparison operator you need in the second pull-down list (including Equals, Less Than, Greater Than, One Of, and Between). Then choose the value you want to compare against in the additional scroll boxes that will appear. You may enter a comparison value directly, or you can click the down arrow in the scroll box to choose from a sample of data that will be read from the database field.

Note   *More detailed information on selecting records is contained in Chapter 6.*

11. The Style tab lets you determine the general appearance of your report and add a report title and bitmap graphic (such as a logo) to your report. When you

choose one of the available styles, a thumbnail image shows the general appearance of that style.

12. There are three choices in the Standard Report Expert dialog box that you can use when you are ready to complete the report. Click the Design Report button to create the report and proceed immediately to the Design tab, where you can see or change the database fields and other objects the Expert has laid out. Click Preview Sample to see a preview of the entire report, or just a subset of the report's records, based on a number you supply. Click Preview Report to apply the selection criteria you supplied in the Select tab and show the entire report in the Preview tab.

Once you have created the report using the Standard Report Expert, you can print it on a printer, export it to another file format, save it to the Crystal Reports .RPT file format, or use any other function that Crystal Reports provides. You can click the Design tab to make any manual adjustments to the report that you wish. You can also rerun the Standard Report Expert to make changes to the report, as well.

Saves the report

Sends the report to a printer   Reruns the Report Expert

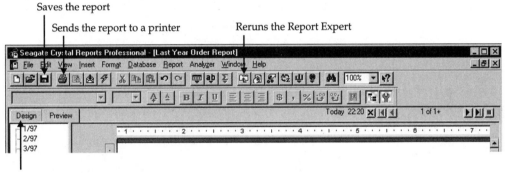

Click the Design tab to make manual
adjustments to the report.

Using the Custom Option

While the report experts simplify the report design process by presenting a step-by-step approach, they limit your flexibility to create a report exactly as you'd like it to look. You are required to accept the fonts, colors, and layout that the expert chooses. Group total and summary fields are not labeled, and group fields are repeated over and over again in every report line within the group.

Although it's initially more labor intensive, using the Custom option to create a report gives you absolute control over what you put on your report, where you put it, and how it looks. Even if you use the report experts, it's important to understand the concepts involved in the Custom option, as you'll want to use them to refine most reports that the report experts create.

To use the Custom option, click the Custom button on the Report Gallery dialog box when first creating a new report. When you do, the Report Gallery expands to show two additional choices you must make, the report type and data type.

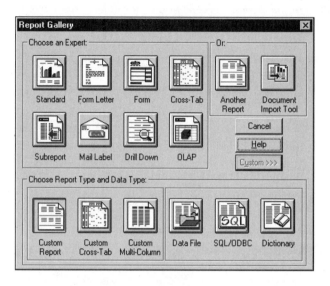

For most reports, you'll use the Custom Report report type. This option prompts you to choose and link tables, and then simply presents you with a blank Design tab for designing the report as you see fit. The Custom Cross-Tab option does essentially the same thing, but it runs the Cross-Tab Expert once tables have been chosen and linked (cross-tab reports are discussed in detail in Chapter 9). The Custom Multi-Column option also performs essentially the same steps, but sets a report option for multiple columns (such as those used in newspapers or phone books) and displays the multicolumn options for you in the Design tab.

The data type selections indicate the type of database or data source you want to base your report upon. Clicking Data File will display the Choose Database File dialog box. This option is used for PC-style databases that reside on your hard disk or on a shared network drive, such as Microsoft Access .MDB files, dBASE .DBF files, Paradox .DB files, and Btrieve .DDF files. Clicking the SQL/ODBC button will display a list of all ODBC data sources that have been defined on your computer, as well as "native" database drivers or custom file structures that Crystal Reports understands. Clicking the Dictionary button will create a report based on a Crystal Dictionary (discussed in Chapter 20) or a Crystal SQL Designer file (discussed in Chapter 19).

Tip   *Several unique report data sources can be selected if you click the SQL/ODBC button. To create a report based on the contents of one of your PC hard disks or a network disk drive, choose Local File System. To report on your Microsoft Outlook database, including your e-mail folders and your calendar, choose Outlook.*

Once you've chosen and linked tables, Crystal Reports will display the Design tab, along with the Insert Fields dialog box, as shown in Figure 1-3. Begin designing your report by simply dragging fields from the Insert Fields dialog box and dropping them on the report where you want them to appear.

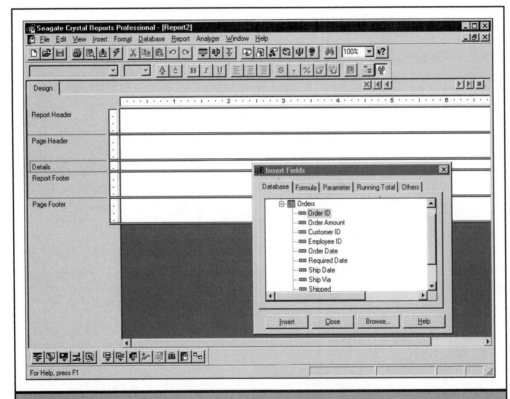

Figure 1-3.   *The Design tab and Insert Fields dialog box*

Report Sections

When you first create a new report, Crystal Reports will show five default sections in the Design tab. Table 1-1 outlines where and how many times each section appears in a report, and the types of objects you may want to place in them.

To place objects on the report, make sure the Database tab is selected in the Insert Fields dialog box. Then simply drag and drop the database fields you want included on the report to the report section where you want them to appear. You can use the multiple-selection tricks using the SHIFT and CTRL keys that were described earlier.

If you drag a database field into the Details section, Crystal Reports will place a field title in the Page Header automatically and align it with the database field. If you drag a database field into any other section, no field title will be inserted, even if you

Section	Where It Appears	What to Place in the Section
Report Header	Once only at the beginning of the report	Title page, company logo, introductory information that you want to appear once only at the beginning of the report, charts or cross-tabs that apply to the whole report
Page Header	At the top of every page	Field titles, print date/time, report title
Details	Every time a new record is read from the database	Database fields and formulas that you want to appear for every record
Report Footer	Once only at the end of the report	Grand totals, closing disclaimers, charts, or cross-tabs that apply to the whole report
Page Footer	At the bottom of every page	Page numbers, report name, explanations for figures in the report

Table 1-1. *Crystal Reports Default Report Sections*

drag the field into the Details section later—automatic field titles are only created if you drag a field directly into the Details section.

Previewing the Report

When you see objects depicted in the Design tab, Crystal Reports is only displaying "placeholders." You'll see the names of fields and objects and an outline, indicating how wide and tall they are. You won't ever see actual data in the Design tab. To see the report containing real data as it might appear when printed on a printer or exported to a Web page, you need to preview the report.

There are several ways of previewing a report. Choose File | Print Preview or click the Preview button on the Standard toolbar to preview the entire report. To preview a limited number of records, you can choose File | Print | Preview Sample and specify the number of records you wish to see.

When you preview a report, the Preview tab will appear next to the Design tab, as shown in Figure 1-4. You can scroll up and down through the report, use the Zoom control to change the zoom level of the report, and use the page navigation buttons to move through various pages of the report. You can easily move back and forth between the Design and Preview tabs by clicking them.

Moving and Sizing Objects

Once you've placed objects on your report, you will probably want to move them around the report as your design progresses. Crystal Reports uses the maximum length of string database fields to determine how wide to make them. Quite often this results in very wide string fields on the report. Based on the size of the data that these display, you'll probably want to shrink the size of these fields. Also, if you change the font size of an object, you'll usually have to adjust the object size accordingly.

The first step in moving or sizing an object is to select the object. Simply click it. A shaded outline and four blocks will appear around the object, indicating that it is selected. Now you can move or size it.

Pointing inside the selected object will cause your mouse pointer to turn into a 4-way pointer. You can then click and drag the object to a new location with the mouse. If you point at one of the four blocks, the *sizing handles*, at the top, bottom, left, or right of the object, your mouse pointer will turn into a 2-way size pointer. Clicking and dragging these handles will stretch or shrink the object. Sizing objects requires very precise accuracy with your mouse! Laptop users with trackpads will probably opt for an external mouse after trying this a few times.

Point inside a selected
object to move it.

Point at the desired sizing
handle to resize an object.

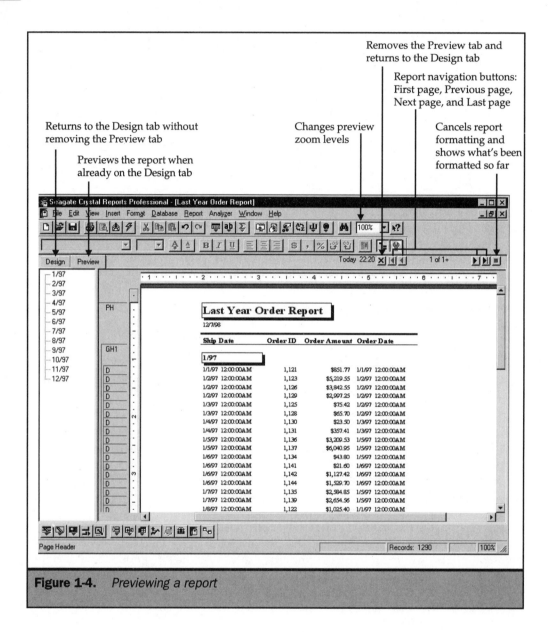

Removes the Preview tab and returns to the Design tab

Report navigation buttons: First page, Previous page, Next page, and Last page

Returns to the Design tab without removing the Preview tab

Changes preview zoom levels

Cancels report formatting and shows what's been formatted so far

Previews the report when already on the Design tab

Figure 1-4. *Previewing a report*

You're not limited to moving or sizing one object at a time. You can select multiple objects before moving or sizing them. CTRL-click or SHIFT-click to select more than one field or field title. You can also surround multiple objects with an elastic box. Before you start to draw the elastic box, make sure you de-select any already-selected objects by clicking an area of the report where there are no objects.

Using Guidelines to Move Objects

When you insert a database field into the Details section, Crystal Reports inserts two other things automatically. The first, the field title, appears pretty obviously above the field in the Page Header. What might not be so obvious is the *vertical guideline*. You'll notice a little "upside down tent" in the ruler above the report. Crystal Reports automatically placed this in the ruler, and it attached the field in the Details section and the field title in the Page Header to the guideline.

You may move objects as a group by dragging the vertical guideline left or right inside the ruler. All objects attached to that guideline will move at the same time. If you've placed a database field in the Details section and an associated field title in the Page Header, and inserted several group subtotals in groups and grand totals in the Report Footer, they will typically all be attached to the same guideline. Just move the guideline left or right to move all the objects together.

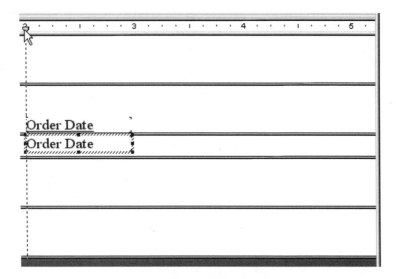

With a little experience, you'll probably quickly develop a love-hate relationship with guidelines. If you have lots of smaller objects positioned closely together on a report, you'll probably give up on the guidelines and just move them by CTRL-clicking or using an elastic box. If you have fewer objects spaced a little farther apart on your report, or lots of aligned objects in several report sections, you'll probably like using the guidelines to rearrange objects. Table 1-2 shows some of the guideline "gotchas" that may crop up in your report-design process, along with ways of solving the problems.

If you created the report with a Report Expert, you'll see that Crystal Reports put horizontal guidelines in on the left side of the Design tab. You can add these yourself if you use the Custom option. Just click in the side ruler to add a horizontal guideline. Then attach objects to them on the top, bottom, or middle. Move the guideline to move whole lines of objects up or down at the same time.

What Happened	How Is It Fixed?
You mistakenly dragged a guideline off the ruler when you just wanted to move it left or right. The objects attached to it haven't moved, and the guideline is now gone.	Click the Undo button on the Standard toolbar, or choose Edit I Undo. This will bring the guideline back. If you notice the missing guideline after you've completed other tasks, and you don't want to Undo, just add a guideline back into the ruler by clicking in the ruler; reattach the objects by dragging them to the new guideline.
You selected and moved an individual object or objects with your mouse, but the guideline didn't move with them. Now, when you move the guideline in the ruler, the objects don't move.	You detach an object from a guideline when you move the object in the Design tab. You cannot reattach guidelines to objects by moving the guideline in the ruler. You have to reattach *objects to guidelines* by moving the objects until they snap to the guidelines. You can tell when an object has been reattached to a guideline by looking at the very small red marks on the edge of the object where it's attached to the guideline.
You've resized or moved objects and they appear to now be attached to two guidelines: one on the left and one on the right. When you move either guideline, the objects stretch instead of move.	Resize the objects away from the guideline you don't want them attached to. By resizing, you detach them from one guideline while leaving them attached to the other.
You notice that when you delete objects from the report, the guidelines stay and clutter up the ruler. When you move other objects around on the report, they're always snapping to the stray guidelines.	Remove any unwanted guidelines by just dragging them off the ruler.

Table 1-2.   *Guideline "Gotchas"*

Formatting Objects

When you place objects on your report, Crystal Reports applies default font faces, sizes, colors, and formatting to the objects. You'll usually want to change some, or all, of this formatting to suit your particular report style or standards. There are several ways of formatting objects. As you use Crystal Reports, you may find that one way suits you better than another. Also, all formatting options aren't available with every method, so you may need to use a certain one to perform a specific kind of formatting.

Using the Format toolbar is the quickest way to apply standard formatting. The Format toolbar is like toolbars you may have used in word processors or spreadsheet programs. To format using the Format toolbar, first select the object or objects you want to format, and then change the formatting of them by clicking Format toolbar buttons or choosing items in scroll boxes.

Some formatting options, such as changing font color or formatting a date field to print in a long date format, aren't available on the Format toolbar. These formatting options, along with all the options available on the Format toolbar, can be chosen in the Format Editor, shown in Figure 1-5. To use the Format Editor, first choose the object or

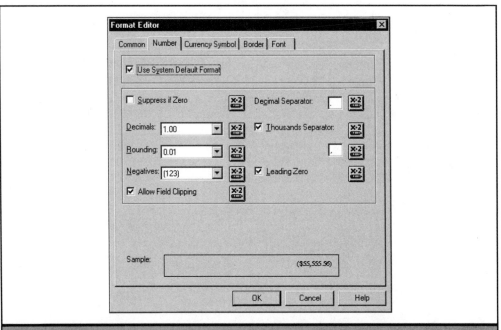

Figure 1-5.   *Formatting an object with the Format Editor*

objects that you wish to format. Then click the Object Properties button on the Supplementary toolbar, choose Format Field, Borders and Colors, or Font from the Format menu, or right-click on the object and choose Format Field, Change Border, or Change Font from the pop-up menu. All these options display the Format Editor. The only difference is the tab that will be chosen on the Format Editor when it appears.

Choose the desired tab on the Format Editor, and make formatting selections with the scroll boxes or check boxes. Click OK on the format editor to apply all the formatting you chose and close the Format Editor.

 You can add new objects, or move, size, and format existing objects, just as easily in the Preview tab as in the Design tab. Be careful, though, that you move or size objects accurately in the Preview tab. You may inadvertently move an object from the Details section to the Page Header, or make some similar undesirable move, without realizing it. Formatting objects in the Preview tab is great, but it may be better to size or move them in the Design tab.

Customizing Crystal Reports Behavior

When you first install Crystal Reports, it behaves in a certain way that should serve most users. However, you will probably want to customize the behavior of some Crystal Report options. Other software typically has a "Preferences" or "Options" menu item to accomplish this. Crystal Reports has two options that work together to control how the program behaves: Options and Report Options, both chosen from the File menu.

Most often, you will use the Options dialog box, shown in Figure 1-6, to change the default behavior of Crystal Reports. For example, to change the default font face and size from Times Roman 10 point to something else, you would click the Fonts tab in the Options dialog box and choose a different font or size. To change the default format of date fields from "mm/dd/yy" to "mm/dd/yyyy," you would click the Fields tab in the Options dialog box, and then click the Date button.

Note *Many options you choose here don't change items already placed on your report—they will only affect new items added to the report. For example, if you change the default font to Arial 8 point blue, only new objects that you add to the report from that point forward will take on that new formatting.*

There are a number of options that benefit the new user and make report creation a bit easier:

■ **Show Guidelines in Design**   almost always on; the majority of report designing should occur in the Design tab, and guidelines can be useful

■ **Show Guidelines in Preview**   almost always off; guidelines detract from the WYSIWYG view most people are used to

■ **Show Short Section Names in Design**   usually on to give you more design and preview area

■ **Show Section Names in Preview**   usually on to help troubleshooting sectional problems when you're in preview mode

■ **Snap to Grid**   great to turn off when you want to be able to truly use free-form placement of objects

■ **Show Grid in Design**   a very small grid size (under 0.5 inches) can be very distracting in Design (millions of dots on the screen), especially when zooming out to full-page view

■ **Show Grid in Preview**   almost always off to improve clarity

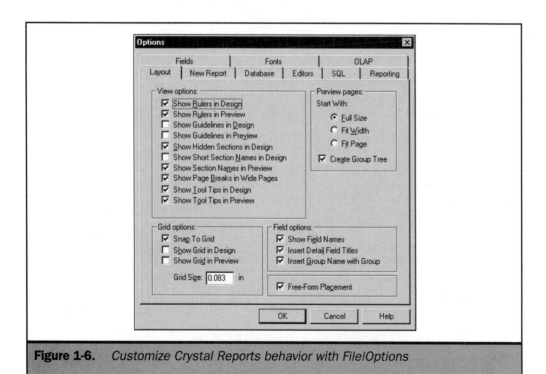

Figure 1-6.   *Customize Crystal Reports behavior with File|Options*

A subset of items from the Options dialog box appears on the Report Options dialog box, shown here:

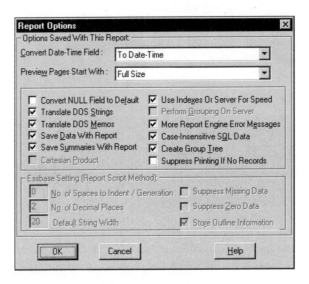

When you create a new report, Report Options are set based on what's chosen in the Options dialog box. Later, though, these options can be set differently than the corresponding Options dialog box item. When the report is saved, these options are saved along with the report. The next time the report is retrieved, they will *supersede* the corresponding Option item.

Chapter 2

Enhancing Appearance with Text Objects

There are many times during the report designing process that you need to just drop some *literal text* into your report. This could be a report title that you place in the Report Header, a label next to a subtotal in the Group Footer, or a whole paragraph explaining the methodology of the report that you place in the Report Footer. You can accomplish this with *text objects*.

To insert a text object, choose Insert | Text Object or click the Text Object button on the Standard toolbar. You'll see the text object attached to your mouse pointer. Position the mouse where you want the text object to go, and click. The text object will be dropped at that location, and you'll be immediately placed in *edit mode*. You'll always know you're in edit mode when you see a flashing cursor inside the text object and a small ruler at the top of the Design or Preview tab, as shown here:

Design		
Report Header		
Page Header		
Details		
Report Footer		
Page Footer		

Now, just start typing! The material you type will appear inside the text object. When you're finished, just click outside the text object to save your changes.

There are several ways to edit the contents of an existing text object. To use the "long way," select the text object and then choose Edit | Text from the pull-down menus, or right-click the text object and choose Edit Text Object from the pop-up menu. The "short way" is a simple double-click—double-clicking a text object will place you in edit mode. Once in edit mode, use the cursor keys, BACKSPACE key, and DEL key to move around and edit the text.

It's commonplace to attempt to exit edit mode by pressing the ENTER key. Not only will this not end editing, but it will start a new line in the text object. This can often cause the contents of the text object to partially or completely disappear. If you want to put line breaks in your text object, go ahead and press ENTER, but make sure you resize the text object when you're finished so you can see all your text.

Combining Database Fields

Simply typing literal text into text objects is a waste of their capabilities! Text objects are powerful elements that can help you create very attractive reports. Consider Figure 2-1, the beginning of a form letter that uses the Customers table from XTREME.MDB (included with Crystal Reports 7). Note the spacing problems with the contact name, city, state, and zip code. These lines are composed of separate fields from the Customers table. No matter how you try or how creative you get with sizing and moving these fields, they will not line up properly for every customer. They appear in the same horizontal location in every Details section, no matter how wide or narrow the fields are sized.

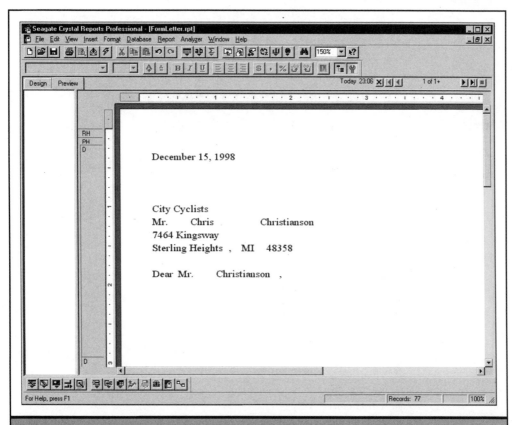

Figure 2-1.   *Spacing problems using database fields*

This type of problem is a dead giveaway that this is a computer-generated letter. Although most consumers are savvy enough to assume that a computer had something to do with the form letters they receive, you don't want to make it obvious. Crystal Reports gives you a better way with text objects.

In addition to containing literal text, text objects allow you to combine database fields with literal text. When the text object appears, it automatically sizes the contents of the database fields so that there is no extra space. Figure 2-2 shows the same form letter as Figure 2-1, but text objects are used to combine the database fields with literal text and spaces.

To combine database fields inside a text object, follow these steps:

1. Insert a text object as described previously. If you need to include any literal text, you may type it now or after you've inserted the database fields. It doesn't matter whether you leave the text object in edit mode or end editing.

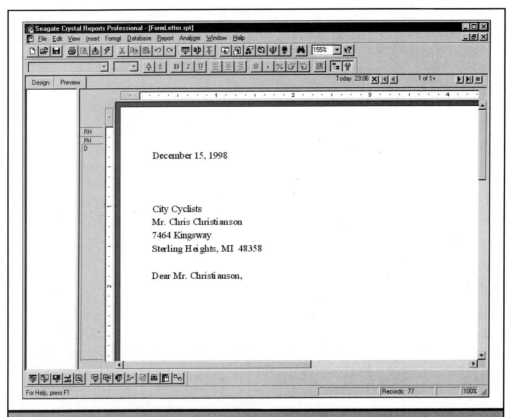

Figure 2-2. *Spacing problems solved with a text object*

2. From the Insert Fields dialog box, choose the field or fields you want to combine in the text object. Drag them from the Insert Fields dialog box into the text object. Note that your mouse cursor will change when you move over the text object and a blinking cursor will appear in the text object at the same time, as shown here:

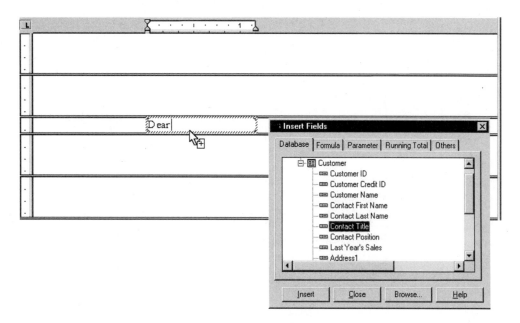

3. Before dropping the database field or fields in the text object, look very carefully at the location of the blinking text object cursor. Wherever the cursor is located is where the database field or fields will go when you release the mouse button. Release the button when the cursor is in the proper position.

4. The text object will go into edit mode if it wasn't already. You may now type more literal text or add another database field if you need to.

5. When you're finished combining database fields and literal text, end editing by clicking outside the text object.

Combining Special Fields

You're not limited to combining database fields inside text objects. You can use *special fields* as well. Special fields are system-generated fields, such as the Print Date, Print Time, Page Number, and Total Page Count. You may place them directly on the report, just like database fields. And, like database fields, you'll encounter spacing problems if you try to place them near literal text.

To combine special fields with literal text inside text objects, perform the same steps as for database fields, but instead of dragging and dropping fields from the Insert Fields dialog box, drag them from the Insert | Special Field pull-down menu option and drop them inside the text object.

Figure 2-3 shows the benefits of combining special fields with literal text in a text object.

There are several pointers that will help you as you combine fields and literal text inside text objects.

■ If you place a database or special field in the wrong location inside the text object (say you place the Last Name field in between the letters "a" and "r" in the word "Dear"), you can simply use your cursor keys, and the BACKSPACE or DEL key to make the correction. In this case it is easier to just delete the text following the special field, and re-enter it before the special field. You may also use CTRL-C to cut text and CTRL-V to paste text inside the text object.

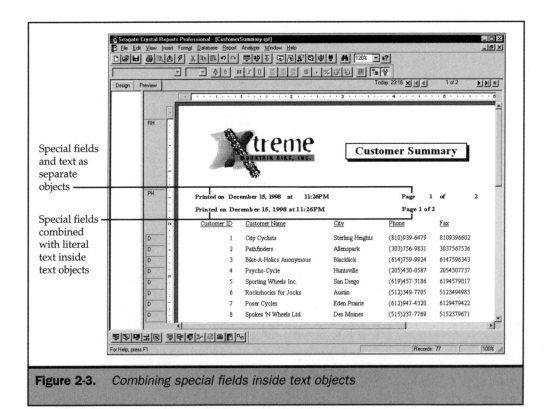

Figure 2-3. *Combining special fields inside text objects*

■ If you inadvertently drop a subtotal, summary, database field, etc., inside a text object by mistake (it's pretty easy to do, even if you're careful), you have two choices. If you catch the problem immediately, you can choose Edit | Undo, or click the Undo button on the Standard toolbar. The field will move back where it was before. However, if you notice that you accidentally dropped a field inside the text object after it's too late to reasonably undo it, edit the text object, highlight the field that was mistakenly added by clicking on it, and press the DEL key. The field will be removed from inside the text object. You will then need to recreate it again and place it in its correct position on the report.

The Can Grow Formatting Option

When you combine database fields or special fields inside text objects, Crystal Reports turns on the Can Grow formatting option automatically. You can turn it back off or change the Maximum Number of Lines option from the Format Editor. To display the Format Editor, use one of these options: select the text object and then select Format | Format Text from the pull-down menus; right-click on the text object and choose Format Text from the pop-up menu; or click the Object Properties button on the Supplementary toolbar. The Can Grow option is found on the Common tab of the Format Editor.

With Can Grow turned on, the text object will automatically grow taller to show all the text inside it. You can specify the maximum number of lines that the text object will grow, or leave the number set to zero for unlimited size. When Can Grow is turned on, the text object will only display as wide as it appears on the report. However, it will word-wrap at spaces in the text, creating additional vertical space up to the maximum number of lines.

This automatic behavior lets you size a text object to only one line high. If the contents of the text object can be displayed in one line, the text object will remain one line tall. If it needs more lines, it will expand only by the amount of vertical space necessary to show the material inside the text object (limited by the maximum number of lines).

Can Grow is helpful for other types of objects as well, not just text objects. You can set the Can Grow formatting option for string fields and memo fields. This is particularly helpful for "description" or "narrative" types of fields that could contain as little as a few characters and as much as several paragraphs of text. Can Grow isn't available for any type of object other than a text object, string field, or memo field.

Formatting Individual Parts of Text Objects

You can format a text object as you would any other object, using the Format toolbar or Format Editor. When you select a text object and change the formatting, such as setting a color or font size, the entire text object takes on that format. This may be the behavior you want.

However, there are other times that you may want certain characters or words in a text object to take on different formatting than the rest of the text object. Even more prevalent is a situation where you need to format individual database fields or special fields that reside *inside* a text object.

For example, when you insert the Print Date special field inside a text object, it will take on the default formatting from File I Options, perhaps a "mm/dd/yy" format. If you select the text object and display the Format Editor, there is no Date tab in which to choose an alternate date format—this is a text object you're formatting! Similarly, if you've placed a number field inside a text object, you may want to change the formatting to show no decimal places or to add a currency symbol.

To accomplish these types of formatting tasks, you must format individual parts of the text object. This is actually quite simple. Start editing the text object by double-clicking it. You are then free to select individual characters or words by dragging over them with your mouse or holding down the SHIFT key while using the cursor keys. You can then use the Format toolbar or Format Editor to change the formatting for just those selected characters.

To change the formatting of a database or special field inside a text object, edit the text object and then click the field you wish to format. You'll know you've selected the field when it becomes highlighted. You can then use the Format Editor (either from the Format menu or by right-clicking—the number formatting buttons on the Format toolbar won't work here) to change the format of the object.

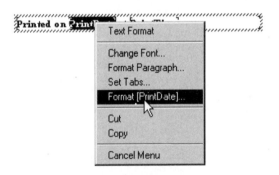

Performance Considerations

Text objects provide a powerful, flexible way to improve the appearance of your reports by combining fields and literal text. However, the cost of that flexibility is performance. Crystal Reports must perform a lot of internal calculations to combine and resize text objects on the fly. The result is performance degradation when you view the report in the Preview tab.

The degradation depends on a great number of factors, such as the processing speed of your machine and the overall complexity of the report. The problem is most acute when there are more than just a few text objects that combine fields, and when those text objects are located in the Details section. This requires Crystal Reports to perform the text object manipulation every time it prints another database record.

The following points will help you minimize performance problems related to combining fields inside text objects.

- Use them sparingly, particularly in the Details section. You'll notice much less performance degradation if you only use these techniques in headers or footers, because Crystal Reports won't have to perform the text object manipulation as often.

- If you do have a large number of items that need to be combined inside the Details section, consider using formulas instead. Formulas are much better optimized in Crystal Reports, so you won't notice nearly as much performance degradation. Formulas are covered in Chapter 5.

- Avoid using the Total Page Count special field or Page N of M special field on the report (for example, "Page 1 of 182"). Using this in combination with text objects that combine fields can be a performance "kiss of death" for your report. Not only does Crystal Reports have to perform all the text object manipulation before it can show you a report page, but it has to format *every page of the report*, as well. This combination will often have you clicking the Stop button (remember, it's next to the Last Page navigation button) on a regular basis.

Tip   *These performance issues only arise when you're viewing a Crystal Report online— when the report is being viewed in the Preview tab or as a compiled report (covered in Chapter 13). If you're going to print the report on a printer or export it to another file format (also covered in Chapter 13), you needn't worry about these performance issues. They won't affect you.*

The
Complete
Reference

Chapter 3

Sorting and Grouping

W hen you first create and preview a report, the report will show Details sections in *natural order*. That is, the records will just appear in whatever order the database sends them to Crystal Reports. This order can vary widely, depending on what database you are using, how you link tables, and other variables.

You'll probably want to control the order in which information appears on your report. An employee listing, for example, isn't very useful if it isn't in alphabetical order. A sales breakdown is probably more helpful if you see your sales figures in a particular order. You're probably interested in highest to lowest sequence of order quantities if you're about to send out boxes of Godiva chocolates at the holidays. On the other hand, lowest to highest sequence is probably more appropriate if you're about to send Vito from your marketing department to talk to certain customers.

Sorting Your Report

If you simply want to reorder your report's Details sections into a particular order, you need to *sort* the report. Sorting is useful for simple reports that need to present information in a certain order. To sort a report, choose Report I Sort Records from the pull-down menus, or click the Sort button on the General toolbar. This will display the Record Sort Order dialog box.

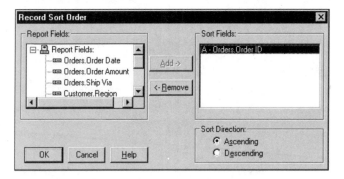

The left Report Fields box shows all the report fields that you've placed in the Details section of the report. You may choose one or more fields to control how you want your report sorted. Simply double-click the field you wish to sort on, or select the field and then click the Add button. Either method will move the field to the Sort Fields box on the right. You may then choose between the Ascending and Descending radio buttons to choose the sort order.

An *ascending* sort will order the records alphabetically A to Z; if the records start with numbers, these will appear before any letters, sorted 0 through 9. In a *descending* sort, the order is reversed. Records will appear in Z to A order, followed by any numbers in 9 to 0 order.

You may sort by as many fields as you'd like—you're not limited to one. This is handy, for example, if you want to sort your customers by state, and within state, by customer name. Just add the additional sort fields to the Sort Fields box and choose the sort order. When you click OK, Crystal Reports will sort by the higher fields first, then the lower fields.

Here are a few points that will help you sort your reports more effectively:

- Note that the Record Sort Order dialog box only shows report fields. You can't choose a field that's not actually on your report. If you wish to sort on a field that's not on the report, you have two choices. You can add the field to the report, choose it as a sort field, and then delete it from the report. If you do this, the report will print in the desired order, but the field won't appear. The second option is to add the field to the report, but format the field to be suppressed (on the Common tab of the Format Editor). Then choose the field as a sort field.

- You can't reorder the sort fields in the Sort Fields part of the Record Sort Order dialog box. If you want to change the order of the sort, you'll need to use the Remove button to remove fields and use the Add button to add them again in correct sort order.

- You can sort just as easily on Formula fields (covered in Chapter 5) as you can on database fields. This is often required if you want to customize some aspect of the way records are sorted. Just remember that if you're using a SQL database, such as SQL Server or Oracle, sorting on a Formula field will make Crystal Reports sort the records instead of having the database server do the work, which may affect the performance of your report. This is covered in more detail in Chapter 14.

Grouping Records

Sorting records is handy for lists or other simple reports that just need records to appear in a certain order. It's more common, however, to not only want to sort your report by certain fields, but to also have subtotals, counts, averages, or other summary information appear when the sort field changes. In order to accomplish this, you must use Crystal Reports *groups*.

When you create a report group, you not only sort the records on the report, but you create two additional report sections every time the group field changes. You may place subtotals, averages, counts or many other types of summary information in these sections. In addition, grouping your report enables the *group tree*, an Explorer-like window on the left side of the Preview tab. The group tree not only gives you a quick overview of the organization of your report, but also allows you to navigate directly to a particular group that you want to see.

There are several ways to create a report group. You may choose Insert | Group from the pull-down menus or click the Insert Group button from the Supplementary toolbar. The Insert Group dialog box will appear.

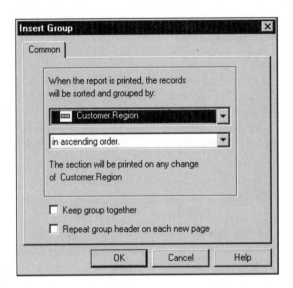

There are two drop-down lists and two check boxes that you use to insert a group. Follow these steps to complete the dialog box:

1. Click the top drop-down list to select the field you want to group on. The list will display fields on your report, as well as other fields in the tables that the report is using. You can group on a field already on the report or on a database field that you didn't put on the report. You can also group on a formula field.

2. Click the second drop-down list to select the order in which your groups will appear on the report. There are four options: ascending order shows the groups in A to Z order alphabetically; descending order shows the groups in Z to A order; specified order lets you create your own groups (described later in this chapter), and original order groups records in the order in which they appear in the database. (The latter is an interesting feature, but probably not useful in most reports.)

3. Click the Keep Group Together option if you want Crystal Reports to try to keep your groups from breaking at the end of a page. If you don't click this option, the beginning of a group and just a few detail records in the group may print at the bottom of a page, while the rest of the group's detail records and its subtotals may appear at the top of the next page.

4. Click the Repeat Group Header on Each New Page option if you don't use Keep Group Together or if you know you will have large groups that will span more

than a single page. This option will print the Group Header section (described later) at the top of each page where a group continues. This allows you to look at Details sections on subsequent pages and know which group they belong to.

Caution *Clicking Keep Group Together can cause odd behavior if the first group in your report won't fit on a page by itself. In this case, Crystal Reports will detect that it can't fit the group on the first page of the report and will start a new page before it starts printing the group. The result will be a blank first page.*

Figure 3-1 shows the two new sections that are added to the Design tab, the Group Header and Group Footer. These sections appear at the beginning and end of every group. Note that Crystal Reports places an object in the Group Header section

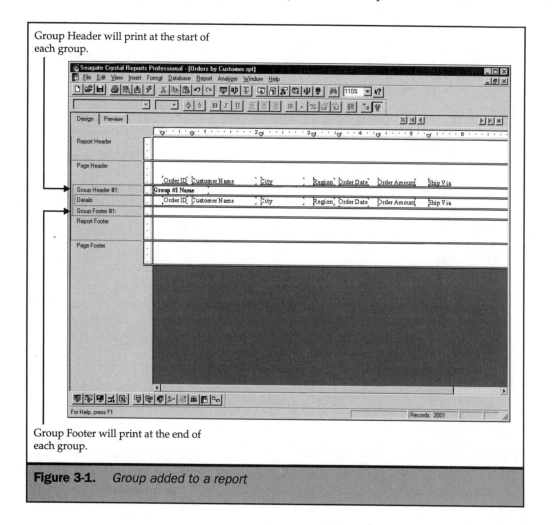

Figure 3-1.   *Group added to a report*

automatically. This *group name* object will automatically print the contents of the field on which the group is based in each group header. The Group Footer section is empty.

You may turn off the Insert Group Name with Group option in File | Options if you don't want Crystal Reports to automatically insert a group name object in the Group Header when a group is created. If this is turned off, or if you inadvertently delete a group name object, you can insert a group name by choosing Insert | Group Name Field from the pull-down menus or drag and drop a group name object after clicking the Others tab in the Insert Fields dialog box.

Figure 3-2 shows the Preview tab with the now-active group tree. You can see your groups in an outline form and navigate directly to the beginning of one of the groups

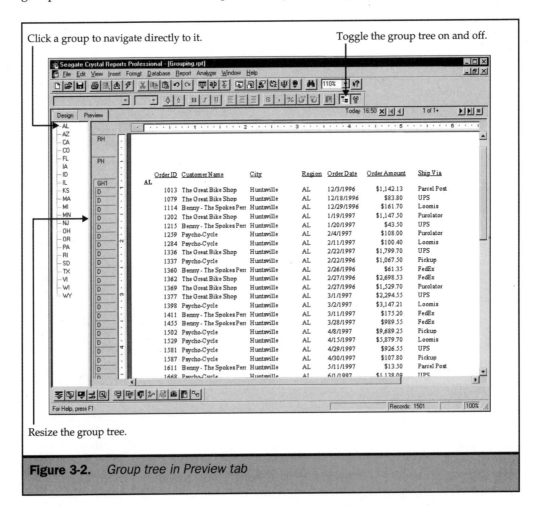

Figure 3-2. *Group tree in Preview tab*

by clicking on the group in the group tree. You can also turn the display of the group tree on and off by clicking the Toggle Group Tree button on the Format toolbar.

Manipulating Existing Groups

After you create a group, you may wish to delete it so just detail records print again without grouping. Or, you may wish to change the field that the group is based on, change the order of the groups from ascending to descending, or choose one of the formatting options to control the way Crystal Reports deals with page breaks inside groups.

There are two different ways to delete an existing group. The first is to choose Edit | Delete Group from the pull-down menus. You'll be presented with a list of groups (or only one, if that's all there is on the report). Choose the group and click OK.

The second way is to return to the Design tab and point your mouse to the gray section names on the left side of the screen. You must point to the Group Header or Group Footer for the group you wish to delete, and then right-click and choose Delete Group from the pop-up menu.

Deleting a group is a permanent operation, and you will be so warned. The Group Header and Group Footer sections will be removed from the report, along with any objects in them. You can't undo this: the Undo button on the Standard toolbar and Undo option in the Edit menu will be grayed out. It's not a bad idea to save the report before you delete a group. If it turns out to be a mistake, you can close the changed report (*without* saving changes), and go back to the saved version.

There are also two ways to change existing groups by redisplaying the dialog box that appeared when you created the group. You may change the field that the group is based on, change the order of groups (ascending, descending, specified, original), or select the Keep Group Together or Repeat Group Header on Each New Page options. The first way is to choose Report | Change Group Expert from the pull-down menus. Though not really an "expert," this option will present you with a list of groups that are defined on the report. Choose the group you want to change and click Options.

The second way to change a group is to return to the Design tab and point to the Group Header or Group Footer section of the group you want to change. Then, right-click and choose Change Group from the pop-up menu. The Change Group Options dialog box will reappear, allowing you to change group settings and click OK when you're finished.

Adding Subtotals and Summaries

So, what's the difference between just sorting the report and creating a group? Not only is the group tree useful with grouped reports, but you now have a section available for subtotals, averages, counts, and other summary functions at the end of each group. Although the Group Footer is empty when first created, you can insert subtotals and summary functions into it with ease.

There are several steps to inserting subtotals or summaries in your report:

1. Select the field in the Details section that you wish to subtotal or summarize.

2. Choose Insert | Subtotal or Insert | Summary from the pull-down menus, or right-click the field you've chosen and choose Insert Subtotal or Insert Summary from the pop-up menu. To insert a summary, you can also click the Summary button on the Standard toolbar.

   Subtotals can only be inserted for numeric or currency fields, whereas summaries can be inserted for any type of field (although not all summary functions will be available for nonnumber fields).

3. If you are inserting a summary, choose the Summary function (sum, average, etc.) that you wish to use. Then, choose the group in which you wish to place the subtotal or summary. The first (or only) group you've created is displayed in the drop-down list by default.

4. Click OK to place the subtotal or summary in the Group Footer directly below the detail field that you're summarizing.

5. Since Crystal Reports doesn't label group summaries for you, you should add text objects next to the summaries to indicate what they display. For example, a subtotal won't be confused with an average if you place a text object containing "Subtotal:" next to the subtotal object.

Here are a few pointers to keep in mind when inserting subtotals and summaries:

■ Although Crystal Reports places subtotals and summaries in the Group Footer by default, you don't have to leave them there. If you move them to the Group Header, they'll print the same information, but at the beginning of groups.

■ Once a summary or subtotal has been created, you don't have to delete it and insert a new summary if you want to change its function (for example, to change a subtotal to an average). Simply click on the subtotal or summary. Then choose Edit | Summary Field from the pull-down menus, or right-click the summary and choose Change Summary Operation from the pop-up menu.

■ You can actually create a group and a subtotal or summary in the Group Footer in one step. Simply select the field in the Details section that you want summarized, and insert a subtotal or summary as outlined previously. If there are no groups yet on the report, the Insert Subtotal or Insert Summary dialog box will, in essence, turn into a dialog box for inserting a group. If there are already existing groups and you want to create a new one, choose the field that you want to create the group on instead of an existing group. Again, the dialog will turn into an "insert group" dialog box. Once you choose the appropriate options and click OK, a group will be created and the subtotal or summary will be placed in the Group Footer all at the same time.

Table 3-1 shows the different summary functions that are available in the Insert Summary dialog box and what each does.

Function	Results
Sum	Returns the subtotal of the chosen field. This is only available for number or currency fields. Choosing a summary with the Sum function is exactly the same as inserting a subtotal.
Average	Returns the average of the chosen field. This is only available for number or currency fields.
Maximum	For number or currency fields, returns the highest number in the group. For string fields, returns the last member of the group alphabetically. For date fields, returns the latest date in the group.
Minimum	For number or currency fields, returns the lowest number in the group. For string fields, returns the first member of the group alphabetically. For date fields, returns the earliest date in the group.
Count	Simply counts the records in the Details section and returns the number of records in the group. Although you are required to choose a database field before selecting this option, the Count function will return the same number no matter which field you choose (with the exception of fields that contain null values).

Table 3-1. *Summary Functions*

Function	Results
Sample Variance Sample Standard Deviation Population Variance Population Standard Deviation	For number or currency fields only, these functions return the chosen statistical function for all the detail fields in the group. For details of how these values are calculated, refer to a statistics text.
Distinct Count	Similar to the Count function, but only returns the distinct number of occurrences of the field. As opposed to Count, the field you choose in the Details section before choosing Distinct Count is very significant. For example, if five records contain the following strings: "Los Angeles", "Chicago", "Vancouver", "Chicago", and "Miami", the Count function would return 5, whereas Distinct Count would return 4.
Correlation Covariance Weighted Average	For number and currency fields only. When you choose these functions, an additional drop-down list will appear letting you choose another numeric or currency field to use in the function. These functions vary in use and are explained in standard statistics texts. Crystal Reports online Help has good descriptions of some of these functions.
Median	For number and currency fields only. Returns the median, or middle, number in the group. If there is one number in the group, it is returned. If there are two numbers, their average is returned.
Pth Percentile	For number and currency fields only. When you choose this function, an additional box appears in which you can enter a number between 0 and 100 for P. This function returns the number that indicates what the percentile is for P, based on all the numbers in the group.

Table 3-1.   *Summary Functions* (continued)

Function	Results
Nth Largest	Returns the third, fifth, or tenth (etc.) largest value in the group, depending on the value you enter for N. For example, Nth largest with N equaling one will return the largest value in the group. When you choose this function, an additional box appears in which you can enter the value for N. For numeric fields, this function returns the Nth highest numeric value. With string fields, it returns the Nth value alphabetically (for example, if there are three records containing FedEx and two records containing UPS, Nth largest when N equals 2 will be UPS and Nth largest when N equals 3 will be FedEx).
Nth Smallest	Returns the third, fifth, tenth (etc.) smallest value in the group. For example, Nth smallest with N equaling one will return the smallest value in the group. When you choose this function, an additional box appears in which you can enter the value for N. This function behaves similarly to Nth highest with both numeric and string fields.
Mode	Returns the most frequently occurring value from all the detail records in the group. For numeric fields, the Mode function returns the most frequently occurring number. For string fields, Mode returns the most frequently occurring string (for example, with detail records containing five occurrences of FedEx, three occurrences of UPS, and eight occurrences of Parcel Post, Mode would return Parcel Post).
Nth Most Frequent	Returns the third, fifth, tenth (etc.) most frequent occurrence in the group. This is similar to Mode, except that you're not limited to just the *most* frequent occurrence.

Table 3-1. *Summary Functions* (continued)

If the details field that you summarize contains null values (a special database value where the field actually contains nothing, as opposed to a zero or empty string), the summary function won't "count" that record. For example, a Count or Average won't figure the null record into its calculation. If you wish to avoid this problem with the current report, you can convert database null values to zero or empty string values by choosing File | Report Options and clicking Convert NULL Field to Default. If you wish this to be the default option for all new reports, you can choose the same option on the Reporting tab from File | Options.

Grand Totals and Summaries

When you choose to insert a summary or subtotal, the object is placed in a Group Footer and shows the subtotal or summary for that group. You'll probably also want grand totals to appear at the end of the report, showing the overall totals, counts, or averages.

You can select the field in the Details section that you wish to summarize, and select Insert | Grand Total from the pull-down menus. You can also right-click on the field you wish to summarize and choose Insert Grand Total from the pop-up menu. In either case, the Insert Grand Total dialog box will appear.

The name Insert Grand Total is really a misnomer—the function should be called "Insert Grand Summary." You're always asked to choose a calculation. Choose from any of the functions described previously and click OK. The grand summary will be automatically placed in the Report Footer, where it will summarize all records on the report. Don't forget to include a text object in the Report Footer, too. Otherwise, the grand summaries will appear with no explanation as to what they are.

Tip	*If you create the same summary or subtotal for a group as well as a grand total, the object that Crystal Reports creates is actually the same object but in different report sections. You can simply copy a subtotal or summary object from a Group Footer to the Report Footer and get the same result.*

Multiple Groups

Crystal Reports does not limit your report to just one level of grouping. In fact, many powerful reporting features can be provided to your report viewer by creative use of multiple groups. The key to many sophisticated reporting requirements lies in creative use of formulas (covered in Chapter 5) in conjunction with multiple levels of grouping.

Multiple groups form a report hierarchy, with increasing levels of detailed information being presented by inner groups. For example, a report might be grouped by country first. Within the country group, there would be a geographic region group (Northwest, Southwest, etc.), then a group by state, a group by township, a group by city, and finally detail records showing individual customers or orders within that city. Each group has its own Group Header and Group Footer sections, and subtotals and summaries can exist for each group.

The group tree handles multiple levels of grouping very elegantly, following the general style of Windows Explorer. Plus signs (Expand buttons) are displayed next to groups that can be expanded to display other groups; minus signs (Collapse buttons) are shown beside expanded groups that can be collapsed. Figure 3-3 shows a report with multiple groups. Notice that you can navigate through the group tree by clicking the plus and minus signs to open and close group levels. When you find the group you want to see, click on the group name in the group tree to go directly to the beginning of that group in the report, no matter how deep the group is in the hierarchy.

To create additional levels of grouping, simply repeat the process described previously for inserting a group. The groups will appear in the order that you create them. You can use the Insert Subtotal/Summary options to add subtotals and summaries to the Group Footer and Group Header sections.

Tip	*If you click on a subtotal or summary in a Group Footer and look in the status bar, you'll notice that the summary is simply called "Sum of," "Average of," etc., followed by the name of the field that's being summarized. The name of the group that the summary is being calculated for isn't specifically included in the subtotal or summary. This allows you to copy the subtotal or summary object to other Group Footer sections to summarize those groups, or to the Report Footer to summarize or subtotal for the entire report. Use Edit	Copy and Edit	Paste from the pull-down menus to copy and paste the summaries, or select the summary and CTRL-drag to copy the object to another section.*

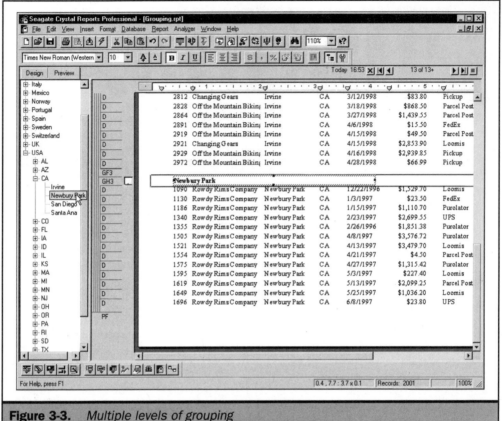

Figure 3-3. *Multiple levels of grouping*

You may inadvertently create groups in the wrong order. For example, if you wish to have your report grouped by state, then by city, make sure to create the groups in that order. If you create the city group first, followed by the state group, you'll have one group for each city with whatever state that city is in as a lower-level group. You'd have, for example, a group for Los Angeles containing a California group. Below that, you'd have a group for San Diego containing another California group.

This isn't as much of a problem as it might seem. You don't have to delete groups and reinsert them in the desired order—moving them around is surprisingly easy.

Simply return to the Design tab and point to the gray Group Header or Group Footer area on the left side of the screen. Point to the group that needs to be moved, and hold down the left mouse button—you'll notice that the mouse cursor turns into a hand symbol.

You can now simply drag and drop the Group Header or Group Footer on top of the group that you wish to swap it with. When you release the mouse button, the groups will swap locations. Don't be confused by the fact that the groups stay numbered in sequential order—the groups have been moved. In the preceding example, simply dropping the state Group Header (Group Header #2) on the city Group Header (Group Header #1) will swap the groups. The state Group Header will become Group Header #1 and the city Group Header will become Group Header #2.

Tip   *Although Crystal Reports does not impose any limit on the number of groups you can insert, the report will definitely be confusing if the number of groups reaches double digits. Sophisticated reporting should rarely require more than ten levels of grouping.*

Specified Order Grouping

There may be times when you need data grouped on your report in a special order that the database doesn't offer. For example, the database may contain a state field, but not a field indicating what geographic location the record belongs to (Northwest, Southwest, Midwest, etc.). While you can create a formula and base the group on that, *specified order grouping* is often more straightforward, allowing you to create customized groups without having to know the Crystal Reports formula language.

Specified order grouping lets you use a dialog box similar to the Select Expert (discussed in Chapter 1) to create your own groups, based on an existing database field. In the geographic location example used previously, you could create a Northwest group, consisting of Washington, Oregon, Idaho, and Montana. The Southwest group could include Nevada, California, Texas, and Arizona. The Northeast group could consist of New York, Maine, Vermont, and New Hampshire. Southeast could include Florida, Alabama, Louisiana, and Mississippi. All the other states not in these four groups could either be ignored or lumped together in a final group given a name of your choice, such as Midwest.

To specify your own groups, choose Specified Order in the Insert Group dialog box instead of Ascending or Descending order when you create a new group or change an existing group. (Don't forget, the quickest way to change an existing group is to point at the correct Group Header or Group Footer in the Design tab, right-click, and choose Change Group from the pop-up menu.) When you choose Specified Order, a Specified Order tab will be added to the Change Group Options dialog box.

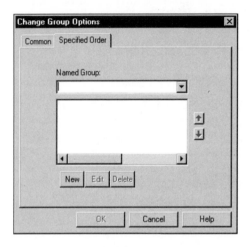

Note   *The title of this dialog box changes depending on whether you are inserting a new group or changing an existing group. The dialog boxes are identical (including Specified Grouping) except for the dialog box title.*

Click the New button to create a new named group. This will display the Define Named Group dialog box, shown next. Type the name the group should have on the report, such as Northwest. Then, using the tab below, indicate which records will be included in the group. For example, you may want the Northwest group to include records where Customer.Region is one of BC, OR, and ID.

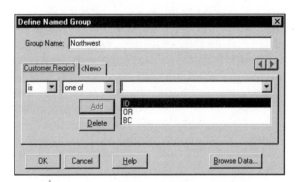

If you need to use several different criteria for the named group, you can click the <New> tab and add additional criteria for the group. When you're finished, click OK on the Define Named Group dialog box. The named group will be created and will appear in the list of named groups in the Change Group Options dialog box. You can now click the New button again to add additional named groups (for example, Southwest, including AZ, CA, and TX).

Tip   *Remember that clicking the <New> tab to create more than one selection tab will still only allow you to select based on one field—the field your group is created on. The criteria on the tabs will be joined using a logical "or" operation—this is different from the Select Expert.*

As you add new named groups, they will appear in the Specified Order tab of the Change Group Options dialog box in the order that you created them, *not* alphabetical order. If you wish to change the order in which the named groups appear on the report, select a named group and use the up or down arrows next to the list of named groups to change its position. The Other group, however, will always be last, no matter what you name it or how you position named groups with the arrow buttons.

Once you've created at least one named group, the Others tab will appear in the Group dialog box. You use this tab to deal with any records that haven't been caught by your specific named groups. You can discard the remaining records, place them in one "catch all" group with the name of your choice, or leave them in their own groups based on the database field. In the geographic example, Northwest, Southwest, Northeast, and Southeast have all been created as named groups. The Others tab is used to lump any regions that weren't otherwise specified into a Midwest group.

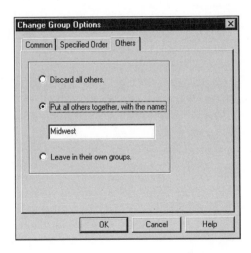

You might have noticed the Named Group drop-down list on the Specified Order tab. This list will browse the database, showing you samples of the actual field you're grouping on. If you choose one of these samples, Crystal Reports will create a named group with the same name as the actual database field. There are probably few instances when this will be the way you want to create named groups, so you'll usually want to click the New button and give the groups your specified names.

Once you create your named groups and click OK on the Change Group Options dialog box, the report will reflect your new grouping. Figure 3-4 shows a list of orders grouped by the five geographic areas described previously. If you wish to change any of your specified grouping options, or remove them altogether so that records appear in their own groups, just use the steps mentioned previously to change an existing group. The Change Group Options dialog box will open, and you can edit your specified groups or change grouping to ascending or descending order, which will remove specified grouping.

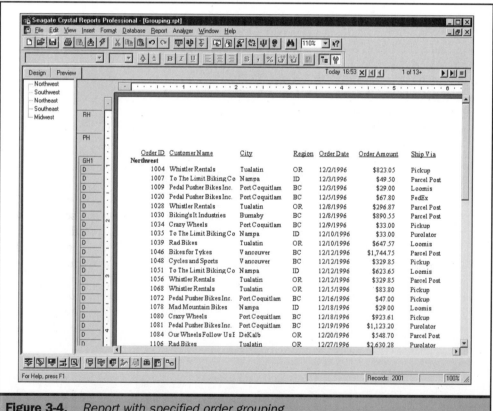

Figure 3-4.   *Report with specified order grouping*

Drilling Down on Data

One of the most powerful features of Crystal Reports is its online reporting capability. Although you can print reports on a printer and export them to other file formats, such as Word or Excel, the real power of many reports only becomes available when users can view and interact with them *online*. This means that the user directly views the .RPT file that Crystal Reports creates. This affords two benefits:

- A user can rerun the report whenever they want, seeing an updated view of the database at that moment.

- A user can interact with the report by using the group tree and drill-down capabilities.

The Crystal Reports Professional version offers online interactive reporting to users in three ways:

- Giving users their own copy of Crystal Reports, letting them open, view, and modify reports at will

- Creating Compiled reports, which allow a user to run a report without owning Crystal Reports (covered in Chapter 13)

- Reporting with a Web browser and a Crystal Smart Viewer (covered in Part III, starting with Chapter 29)

All three interactive methods allow a user to *drill down* on data in the report. This technique, a feature that has been carried over from early PC-based decision support system software, allows a report viewer to initially look at higher-level data. For example, a report might start at the country level. If the viewer sees a subtotal or summary number (or an element in a pie chart or other chart) for a particular country that interests them, they can double-click on that number. This will drill down to the next level in the report, possibly the region or state level, where they can see summary numbers for each of those states or regions. If the report is designed with several levels of drill-down ability, the user could then double-click a region that piqued their interest to display all the cities in that region. The drilling down could progress further, allowing users to drill down on cities and finally zip codes, where individual detail items at the zip-code level would appear.

Crystal Reports automatically sets up a drill-down hierarchy when you create groups. Every group you create can be drilled into, exposing the lower-level group and finally the Details section. So, for our drill-down example to work, you would create multiple groups on the report in the following order: zip code, city, region (state), and finally country.

Once you've created groups, you can drill down on the group name (automatically placed in the Group Header), or any summary or subtotal that you place in a Group Header or Group Footer. When you point at these objects, you'll notice that the mouse pointer changes from an arrow to a magnifying glass. This indicates that you can drill down on the group by double-clicking this object. When you double-click, a *drill-down tab* appears next to the main Preview tab, containing the lower-level group or detail data. Every time you drill down, a separate drill-down tab appears.

If you drill down enough times, there won't be enough room to see all the drill-down tabs, along with the main Preview and Design tabs. In this situation, two small arrows will appear next to the last drill-down tab. You can click these arrows to move back and forth among the tabs to see tabs that may have disappeared off the screen. You can also close any drill-down tab by clicking the red X button next to the page navigation buttons. This will close the current tab and display the tab to the left. You can close every tab this way (including the Preview tab), except for the Design tab.

Tip	*If you wish to print the report to a printer or export it to another file format, only the material appearing in the current tab will print or export. If you're displaying the Preview tab at the time, the whole report will print or export. If, however, you have a drill-down tab selected when you print or export, only the material in that drill-down tab will be included.*

Figure 3-5 shows a report with several drill-down tabs visible. Notice that there isn't enough room to show all the tabs, so small arrows appear to the right of the last drill-down tab. Also notice that the mouse cursor has changed to a magnifying glass because it is over a summary/subtotal object.

You can drill down on any report that has at least one group on it, even if all the Details sections are showing up already. Drill-down ability is really helpful with summary reports that start out showing only high-level data. A viewer will only want to see the lower-level groups and the detail when they drill down. Therefore, you'll want to hide the Details section, as well as the lower-level Group Headers and Group Footers, to create a truly useful drill-down report. You'll see how to hide or suppress sections in Chapter 8.

Caution	*If you have one or more drill-down tabs appearing alongside the Preview tab, there are very few report-design modifications you can make without receiving a message indicating that you won't be able to keep the drill-down tabs. Don't worry about this—just make the modifications and drill down again to redisplay the drill-down tabs.*

Grouping on Date Fields

When you create report groups based on date fields, you probably don't want a new group to appear every time the date changes from one day to another. You may only want a new group for every week, month, or calendar quarter. You could create a complicated formula that breaks down groups in this manner and group on the formula, but Crystal Reports provides a much easier way.

When you select a field to group on, Crystal Reports automatically adds an additional drop-down list to the Insert Group dialog box.

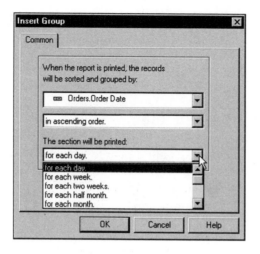

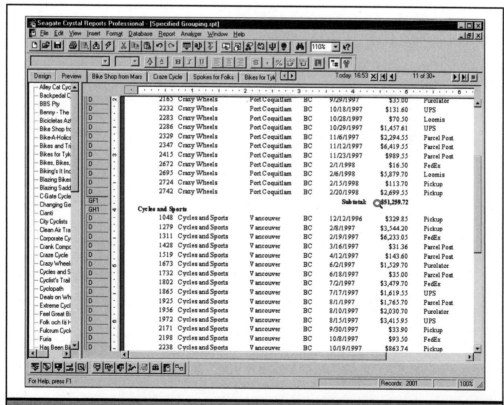

Figure 3-5. *Drill-down report*

You can choose how often a new group will be created by selecting the appropriate item from the list. Then click OK. The groups will now appear in the group tree for every month, quarter, year, or whatever period was chosen. The group name in the Group Header will indicate the beginning date for each group (the first month of the quarter, the first day of the week, etc.).

Formatting Group Name Fields

The group name field takes on the Crystal Reports default format for the data type of the group field. For example, the default format for date fields is mm/dd/yy. A group name for a calendar quarter group, then, will show up as 1/97, 4/97, etc. What if you'd prefer the group names to appear as "January, 1997" and "April, 1997?"

You can format a group name field just like any other field or object. Click on the group name field, and then format it just like any other object (by using the Format menu or right-clicking and using the pop-up menu). For a group name based on a date field, for example, you can choose how to have the month and year appear, as well as what character should be used as the separator between them. Figure 3-6 shows orders grouped by calendar quarter. Notice that the group name has been reformatted to make the quarter groups more meaningful (in this example, "January, 1996"). Notice also that a text object has been placed next to the group name ("Quarter starting") to indicate that the groups are based on calendar quarters.

Tip *You may notice that the group tree does not take on the formatting of the group name fields. In Figure 3-6, the group tree still shows dates formatted as mm/yy. The group tree takes its formatting from the formatting defaults on the Fields tab of File | Options. To change the appearance of the group tree, change the default formatting in File | Options and then refresh the report by pressing F5 or by clicking the Refresh button on the Standard toolbar. Don't forget, though, that every new object of the same data type that you add to the report will take on the new formatting. If you want to avoid this formatting issue, create a formula field that formats the data exactly as you'd like it to look and group on the formula field (as discussed in the following section).*

Grouping on Formula Fields

As your reports become more sophisticated, you'll find more and more often that you won't be able to create the groups you need just from database fields. You may be able to use Specified Order grouping, but even it is limited by its simple Select Expert-like approach. For the really tough grouping jobs, you'll need to create formula fields and group on them. Creating formula fields is covered in Chapter 5.

Grouping on a formula field is very simple (at least the grouping is, once you've created the formula). The formula will appear at the end of the list of report fields in the Insert Group or Change Group Options dialog box. Simply choose it as the field you wish to group on.

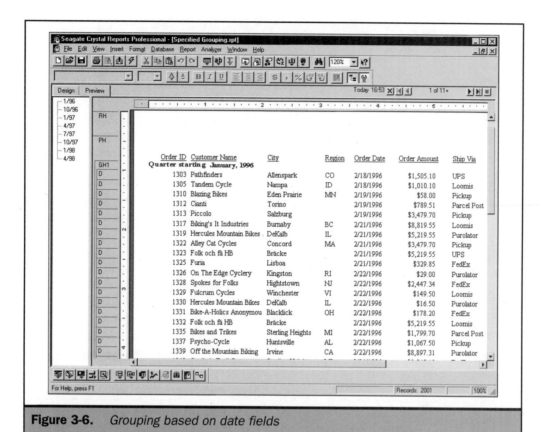

Figure 3-6.   *Grouping based on date fields*

A good example of when you might need to group on a formula field is the geographic grouping case mentioned earlier in this chapter. Suppose you want to first group by geographic location (Northwest, Southwest, etc.), and then within these groups you want to group on individual states or regions. That way, you'll be able to see group totals for both individual states and the higher-level geographic regions.

The problem is this: after you've created the specified-order grouping based on the Customer.Region database field for the geographic groups, Crystal Reports won't let you create a second group on the same database field in ascending order for the state groups. If you try to choose a database field that's already been grouped on, the OK button in the Insert Group or Change Group Options dialog box is disabled.

To solve this problem, here's a formula field called @Region that simply returns the Customer.Region database field.

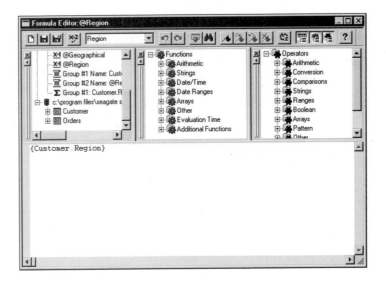

The @Region formula field can now be used instead of the database field to create the second group. Figure 3-7 shows the resulting report.

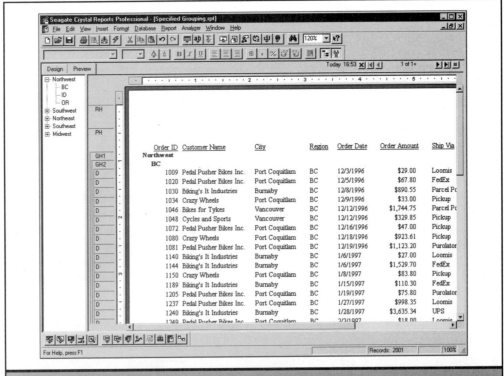

Figure 3-7.   *Multiple levels of grouping accomplished with a formula field*

Caution   *Although you gain great flexibility when you group on a formula field, you may lose a little performance along the way. When you group on a database field, Crystal Reports can have the database server (SQL Server, Oracle, etc.) sort records in the proper group order before sending them to Crystal Reports. When you group on a formula field, the server won't be able to sort the records in advance, leaving that for Crystal Reports to do once the records begin to arrive from the server. You may or may not notice any performance degradation, depending on the size of the report and the speed of your computer.*

Top *N* Reporting

Figure 3-8 shows a typical order summary report by customer name. This is a great drill-down report example—the Details section is hidden and only the summary information for each customer is showing (remember, hiding sections is covered in Chapter 8). This is a good report for the sales manager who is asked, "How did Clean Air Transportation Co. do last year?" All the viewer has to do is click Clean Air Transportation Co. in the group tree to go directly to its summaries.

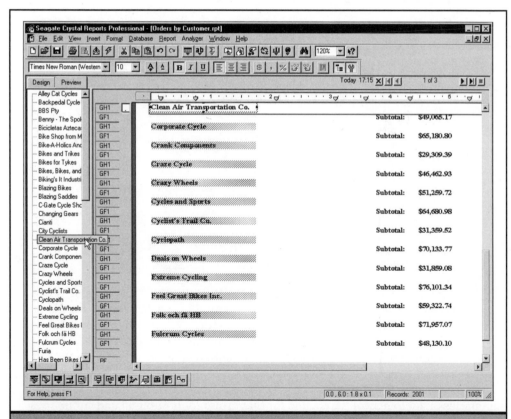

Figure 3-8.   *Order summary report by customer name*

However, what if the sales manager has ten boxes of Godiva chocolates that she wants to send to her ten best customers. Then, there's Rocko, the new sales associate, who needs to find the 15 worst performing customers so he can pay them a friendly visit. The report shown in Figure 3-8 is not very useful if you want to find the top ten or bottom 15 customers. The sales manager and Rocko would be much happier with a Top N report.

A Top N report lets you sort your groups by a subtotal or summary function (subtotal of order amount, for example), instead of the name of the group. That way, your groups will appear, for example, in order of highest to lowest sales or lowest to highest sales. In addition, Top N reporting allows you to only see the top or bottom N groups, where you specify the N.

Crystal Reports uses the Top N/Sort Group Expert to reorder your groups by a subtotal or summary. Choose this option from the pull-down menus by selecting Report | Top N/Sort Group Expert. You can also click the Top N Expert button in the Supplementary toolbar. Or, finally, if you select a summary or subtotal in a group footer and click the Sort button on the Standard toolbar, the Top N/Sort Group Expert will appear instead of the Record Sort Order dialog box.

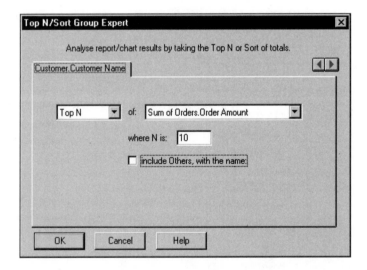

The Top N/Sort Group Expert (again, not really an "expert," just a dialog box) will present a tab for every group you've created on your report. Click the tab for the group that you want to reorder. When you first open the Top N/Sort Group Expert, the default setting for the first drop-down list is Sort All and the second drop-down list is empty. This simply indicates that this group initially will not be a Top N group and that groups will appear in the order you chose when you created the groups.

When you click the down arrow of the second drop-down list, you'll see all the summaries or subtotals you've created for that group (only subtotal and summaries you created with Insert Subtotal or Insert Summary will be there—you won't see any formulas or other fields). Choose the one that you want the Top *N* report to be based on. For example, if you want to see the top ten customers according to last year's sales, you'd choose Sum of Customer.Last Year's Sales. If you leave the first drop-down list set to Sort All, all groups will remain on the report, but will be sorted in ascending or descending order, based on the radio buttons at the bottom of the dialog box. If you want the groups sorted by more than one summary (for example, first by sum of order amount, then by count of order ID), select additional summaries from the drop-down list and choose an ascending or descending sort for each.

If you are only interested in the Top *N* or Bottom *N* groups, change the first drop-down list from Sort All to Top N or Bottom N. Top N sorts the groups from the highest to lowest value and Bottom N sorts from lowest to highest. The second pull-down list will allow you to select one summary or subtotal to use for Top *N* or Bottom *N*. Choose the summary you want to use. Once you've done that, a text box appears in which you can type the value of *N*. You also have a check box and text box that let you choose whether to include other groups not in the Top or Bottom *N* in the report. If you do include them, they will be lumped together in one other group with the name you type.

Using the Godiva and Rocko example earlier:

■ The sales manager's Godiva chocolate report would be Top N of Sum of Orders.Order Amount, where *N* is 10 and others are not included.

■ Rocko's friendly visit report would be a Bottom N of Sum of Orders.Order Amount, where *N* is 15 and others are not included.

The following Top *N* report shows who will be getting chocolates this year.

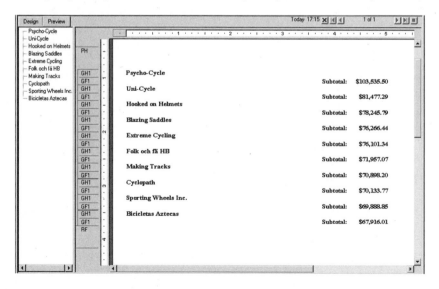

If you wish to change the report from Top *N* to Bottom *N*, change the value of *N*, or remove the Top/Bottom *N* sorting altogether and show all your groups sorted in the order you originally chose, simply redisplay the Top N/Sort Group Expert and change the values. Remember that a group will be sorted in its original ascending or descending order if you set the first drop-down list to Sort All and the second drop-down list to blank.

If you create a Top N report and don't include others, any grand totals you place in the Report Footer will still include all records on the report. If you want to include accurate grand totals in a Top N report, either include others or use a running total instead of grand totals (explained in Chapter 5).

Chapter 4

Creating Geographic Maps

New to Crystal Reports 7 is geographic mapping, the capability to create graphical maps that appear right in your report. You can now not only include textual information (for example, states, cities, and sales totals) but also a colorful map that plots the sales totals by state. Using maps, you can display information in a whole new way that helps analyze geographical data more easily.

Once you create a map, you can view it on the screen in the Preview tab or launch the Crystal Reports Analyzer, another new feature of Crystal Reports 7. The Analyzer tab appears next to the Preview tab, giving you access to specific functions for analyzing maps and charts.

 Mapping is only available in the 32-bit version of Crystal Reports. If you're using the 16-bit version with Windows 3.1, you won't be able to create maps.

Different Map Types

Crystal Reports provides five different types of maps. The type you choose depends on the data that you'll be depicting in the map and the way you wish to show it. Table 4-1 discusses the different types of maps and their uses.

Map Type	Description	Uses and Comments
Ranged	Assigns different colors to *ranges* of numbers. For example, a state that contains over $500,000 in sales would be bright red, a state that contains between $250,000 and $500,000 in sales would be orange, and a state that contains less than $250,000 in sales would be a deep magenta.	Useful for comparing different regions or countries to each other by shade or color. There are four ways to choose how the ranges are colored: (1) *Equal count* evenly divides the number of map ranges so that an equal number (or as close as possible to an equal number) appear in each range. (2) *Equal ranges* divides the map ranges by the summary numbers being shown on the map. This option will assign equal ranges of summary values, regardless of how many groups or regions make up each range. (3) *Natural break* also uses the summary numbers to determine map ranges, but bases range breakdowns on the average amounts of the ranges. (4) *Standard deviation* divides the map ranges such that the middle interval breaks at the average of the summary values. The ranges above and below the middle break at one "standard deviation" above or below the middle.

Table 4-1.   *Crystal Reports Map Types*

Map Type	Description	Uses and Comments
Dot density	Displays a dot on the map for every occurrence of the item being mapped. You'll notice a higher concentration of dots in areas of the map where there are the most occurrences.	Used to show a concentration of activity (for example, quantities or subtotals) in certain states or countries.
Graduated	A circle, or other symbol, is shown to represent data, with the size of the symbol being based on the concentration or level of the amount. This is a combination between a ranged and dot density map.	Will show just one symbol per country, state, etc., but will show a different size, depending on the number the map is based on. You can choose from any character in a large symbol font, as well as applying special effects (for example, drop shadow, halo) to the symbol.
Pie chart	Displays a pie chart over the related geographic area.	Only useful when comparing multiple related data points for the same geographic area. A pie chart is better for comparing items against each other, where all items total 100 percent. For example, if you're graphing sales by account rep, grouped by state, you would see a pie chart on each state showing how much of the "state pie" each rep has.
Bar chart	Displays a bar chart over the related geographic area.	Only useful when comparing multiple related data points for the same geographic area. A bar chart is better for comparing items over time, or other comparisons that aren't "piece of the pie" oriented. For example, if you're graphing sales for the past five years, grouped by state, you would see a bar chart on each state comparing the sales for the past five years.

Table 4-1.   *Crystal Reports Map Types* (continued)

Caution   *Crystal Reports 7 contains a limited number of maps. If you use a field that Crystal Reports can't resolve to an existing map, the map will show up as a blank area on your report. Check the Seagate Software Web site at* http://www.seagatesoftware.com/crystalreports *for information on additional maps that are available. Choose Technical Support and then look for Files and Updates. You may also get more information from MapInfo (the company that supplies the mapping component) at* http://www.mapinfo.com.

You have several ways of choosing the data that will populate your map:

- A *Group* map requires you to use existing groups with their subtotals and summaries for the map. A report grouped by country, for example, can be used to show the concentration of customers by country if you include a summary function that counts customers for each group.

- A *Detail* map allows you to create a map based on data in the report's Details section. You may have a detail report containing a sales figure for each customer. If you include the state each customer is in, you can create a Detail map based on the state and the amount of sales for that state. The map will show how sales compare by state. In effect, the map will group and subtotal your records by state, even if no state group exists on the report. You also would use a Detail map when you need to map multiple values per geographic region (as in the pie chart and bar chart explained in Table 4-1).

- A *Cross-Tab* map will plot data from a cross-tab object (covered in Chapter 9). The cross-tab must have at least one row or column field that's based on a geographic item, such as country or state. Because cross-tabs can contain multiple summary fields, you can use a cross-tab to create pie chart or bar chart maps.

Caution *Even though documentation and Help files indicate the capability, the first release of Crystal Reports 7 (7.0.x.192) does not allow creating maps from OLAP grids. This may be enabled in later maintenance releases of the product. (Refer to Chapter 17 for more on OLAP grids.)*

Adding a Map

To insert a map on your report, choose Insert | Map from the pull-down menus, or click the Map button on the General toolbar. The Map Expert appears, containing three main tabs: Data, Type, and Text.

The Data Tab

The Data tab is where you choose the type of map you wish to create, as well as the fields and summaries from the report that you want to base your map on.

Group Maps

To create a Group map, click the Group button on the Data tab, as shown here:

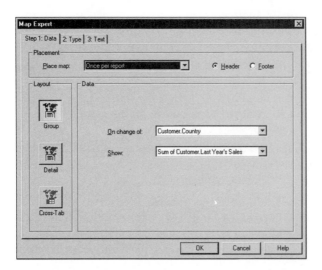

This map will include data based on an existing group on your report. The group needs to be based on some kind of geographic field, such as a country or state. The map will depict your chosen subtotal or summary field (or fields) for each group.

The Place Map drop-down list lets you choose how often you want the map to appear on the report. The options in this list will vary according to how many groups you have on your report. If you only have one group on your report, the only option available in the drop-down list is "Once per report." If you have more than one group, you will also have "For each *group field*" options for every group, *except for the top level group*. This is because you must always place a map at least one level higher in your report than the group your map is based on.

For example, if you only have a state group on your report, the only option for a group map is "Once per report," as you must have the map at a level higher than the group. However, if you have a country group and a region group within the country group, the drop-down list will allow you to choose "For each Customer.Region" (or whatever the field the region group is based on). If you choose this lower level, you'll have a map appearing in every country group, showing the geographic breakdown *by region* for that country.

You can then choose whether to have Crystal Reports initially place the map in the group or report header or footer, by clicking the desired radio button. After the map has been created initially, you can drag the map object from the header to the footer, or vice versa.

Use the On Change Of drop-down list to choose the geographic group that you want the map to be based on. Choose the summary or subtotal field you want the map to depict from the Show drop-down list.

Detail Maps

To create a Detail map, click the Detail button on the Data tab, as shown here:

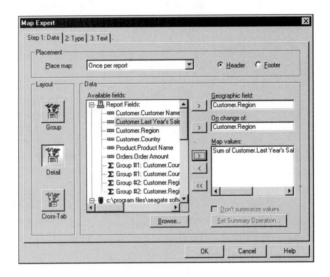

This map will include data based on detail lines on your report. One of your detail fields needs to be a geographic field, such as a country or state. The map will summarize one or more other detail fields and depict them on the map for each geographic field.

The Place Map drop-down list lets you choose how often you want the map to appear on the report. The options in this list will vary according to how many groups (if any) you have on your report. If there are no groups, the only option available in the drop-down list is "Once per report." If you have one or more groups, you will also have "For each *group field*" options for every group.

You can then choose whether to have Crystal Reports initially place the map in the group or report header or footer, by clicking the desired radio button. You are also free to just drag the map object from the header to the footer, or vice versa, after the map has been created initially.

The Available Fields list contains all the report, database, and formula fields available for the map. Choose the geographic field that you wish to have your map use. Then click the right arrow next to the Geographic Field box to choose the field. The same field will also automatically be placed in the On Change Of box. If you wish to just summarize values for the geographic field (for a range or dot density map, for example), just leave the same field in the two boxes. If, however, you wish to show a pie or bar chart on the map for another field (for example, you want to show a pie chart in each country comparing states), then choose the field you want to "compare" in the Available Fields list and click the right arrow next to the On Change Of text box. Finally, click one or more fields (using CTRL-click or SHIFT-click) in the Available Fields list that you want summarized in the map. Use the right arrow next to the Map Values box to add them. If you wish to remove a Map Value field or fields, click it in the Map Values box and click the left arrow. If you wish to remove all the Map Value fields, click the double left arrow.

Caution   *Crystal Reports mapping is very particular about the geographic field you base your map on. For example, if the field contains "USA," the map will recognize it. If it just contains "US," it won't. The same holds true for state names. Two-letter abbreviations should be recognized, while spelled-out state names may not. Sometimes you'll need to experiment and, in some cases, you may need to create a formula (discussed in Chapter 5) that changes the way the geographic data is presented. You can then base the map on the formula field.*

Even though this is a Detail map, Crystal Reports will still summarize values by default, as though report groups exist for the fields you've placed in the Geographic Field and On Change Of boxes. You can choose the summary function (Sum, Average, Count, etc.) you would like the map to use when summarizing the detail fields you've added to the Map Values box. Select a field in the box, click the Set Summary Operation button, and choose the function (Sum, Average, Count, etc.) that you wish to use. If you check the Don't Summarize Values box, the map won't summarize the values like a grouped report, but will just depict the *first* value in the details section.

Tip   *If you add a nonnumeric field to the Map Values box, it will automatically be summarized with a Count function. This cannot be changed.*

Cross-Tab Maps

To create a Cross-Tab map, click the Cross-Tab button on the Data tab, as shown here:

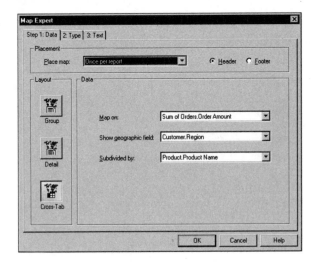

This map will depict data contained in a cross-tab object already on your report. The Cross-Tab button will only be enabled if you already have a cross-tab object selected on your report before you start the Map Expert. The row or column of the cross-tab must be a geographic field, such as a country or state. Because cross-tabs can have multiple summarized fields, you can create pie chart and bar chart maps from cross-tabs. Creating cross-tab objects is covered in Chapter 9.

The Place Map drop-down list lets you choose how often you want the map to appear on the report. If there are no groups on the report, the only option available in the drop-down list is "Once per report." If you have one or more groups, you will also have "For each *group field*" options for every group. Normally, you'll want to just match the location of the cross-tab—if there's one cross-tab on the report, choose "Once per report." If you are mapping a cross-tab in a group, then choose "For each *group field*" for the matching group.

You can then choose whether to have Crystal Reports initially place the map in the group or report header or footer, by clicking the desired radio button. You can also drag the map object from the header to the footer, or vice versa, after the map has been created.

In the Map On pull-down list, choose the summary field from the cross-tab that you want depicted. If you have multiple summary fields, you'll have multiple options here. Choose the row or column of the cross-tab that contains the geographic field the map will be based on from the Show Geographic Field drop-down list. If you want the cross-tab to be mapped as a pie or bar chart map, choose the other row or column in the Subdivided By pull-down list.

The Type Tab

Once you've chosen the data elements for your map, click the Type tab to choose the type of map you want to display.

- Clicking the Ranged button will present options for a ranged map, including how many intervals the map will contain, how the intervals are broken down, the beginning and ending color for the intervals, and whether the map should show empty intervals.

- Clicking the Dot Density button will allow you to choose large or small dots for the map.

- Clicking the Graduated button will present the symbol used for the graduated map. A circle symbol is chosen by default, but you can click the Customize button to change the symbol and color and to add special effects to the symbol, such as a halo or drop shadow.

- Clicking the Pie Chart button will present options for a pie chart map. You can choose small, medium, or large pies. If you click the Proportional Sizing check box, the pies will be sized according to the quantities contained in the data being mapped: larger quantities will create larger pies and smaller quantities will create smaller pies.

- Clicking the Bar Chart button will allow you to choose the size of the bars: large, medium, or small.

Tip   *You will be restricted to either the first three or the second two buttons, depending on how many data elements you've chosen for your map. If you've chosen only one data element to map, you will only be able to use the Ranged, Dot Density, or Graduated options. If your map contains multiple elements from a detail or cross-tab report, you will only be able to use the Pie Chart or Bar Chart options.*

The Text Tab

The Text tab lets you customize textual elements, such as the title and legend, that appear with the map. Type the title you wish the map to display in the Map Title box. Crystal Reports will automatically create a legend for the map. You can choose whether to display a full legend, a compact legend, or no legend at all by clicking the appropriate radio button. If you choose to include a legend, you can display the map-generated legend or specify your own by using the radio buttons and text boxes in the Legend Title section.

Once you've chosen all the necessary options, click OK. Crystal Reports will create the map and place it in the report or group header or footer that you specified. To modify an existing map, simply click the map to select it in either the Design or Preview tabs. Then choose Format I Map Expert from the pull-down menus, or right-click the map and choose Map Expert from the pop-up menu.

If you change the geographic item that a group is based on, you'll probably need to delete and recreate the map. Maps automatically choose their geographic field when first created, but don't re-choose a different field if the group they're based on changes. For example, if you create a ranged map based on a Country group, you'll see the world appear with different colors inside the countries. If you then change your group to State and add record selection to only include the USA, your map will still show the world. You'll need to delete and re-create the map to have it show just the USA with different colors for the states.

Drilling Down on Maps

Crystal Reports lets you drill down on maps, just like on group names and summaries (discussed in Chapter 3) and on charts and graphs (covered in Chapter 10). When you view a map in the Preview tab, just point your mouse to the geographic region you wish to look at in more detail. The mouse cursor will turn into a magnifying glass. Double-click on the desired area of the map to open up a drill-down tab next to the Preview tab. This drill-down tab will contain just the information for the report group represented by that map segment.

To close a drill-down tab, just click the red X that appears next to the page navigation buttons on the right side of the preview window. The current tab will be closed and the next tab to the left will be displayed.

Because a Detail map is already mapping the lowest level of information on your report, you cannot drill down on this type of map.

The Analyzer Tab

In addition to just viewing a map in the Preview tab, Crystal Reports 7 includes a new feature called the Analyzer tab. The Analyzer tab displays a map (or chart, as discussed in Chapter 10) by itself in a separate tab next to the Preview tab. The Analyzer tab lets you concentrate on the map by itself—no other report data is displayed. Also, the Analyzer tab lets you actually look at two maps at a time, one on top of the other. This may be helpful for comparing map breakdowns for different countries or regions, for example.

To display the Analyzer tab, select the map you want to analyze in the Preview tab. Then, right-click and choose Map Analyzer from the pop-up menu, or choose Analyzer | Launch Analyzer from the pull-down menus. The map will be displayed in the Analyzer tab.

If you have multiple maps on your report (different maps or the same map in different groups), you can show two maps in the Analyzer tab at the same time. Just choose the other map you want to display, and follow the same steps. The Analyzer tab will show both maps, separated by a movable border. If you try to add a third map to the Analyzer tab, you'll receive a message indicating that the Analyzer is limited to two maps. You'll have the choice of replacing the top or bottom pane with the new map you've selected.

Once you've displayed the Analyzer tab, you can choose options from the Analyzer pull-down menu, right-click in the Analyzer tab and choose options from the pop-up menu, or use the Analyzer toolbar. You can zoom in and out on the map, pan the map up, down, left, or right, or center the map on the screen. You can also change the type of map (ranged, dot density, etc.) as well as the order in which map "layers" are displayed.

Figure 4-1 shows the Analyzer with two maps displayed on top of each other. Notice the functions available on the pop-up menu, as well as the Analyzer toolbar.

Tip   *You don't have to launch the Analyzer to perform many of the Analyzer functions. You can right-click on the map right in the Preview tab and choose the Zoom or Pan options from the pop-up menu. You can also display the Analyzer toolbar by selecting it from View | Toolbars in the pull-down menus. From this toolbar, you can select Zoom and Pan functions while displaying the Preview tab. Note that the Change Map Type and Change Map Layers buttons will only work when the Analyzer tab is being displayed. And, although you can click the Drill Down button in the Analyzer tab, it will only function in the Preview tab.*

The Analyzer toolbar is available from the View | Toolbars pull-down menu.

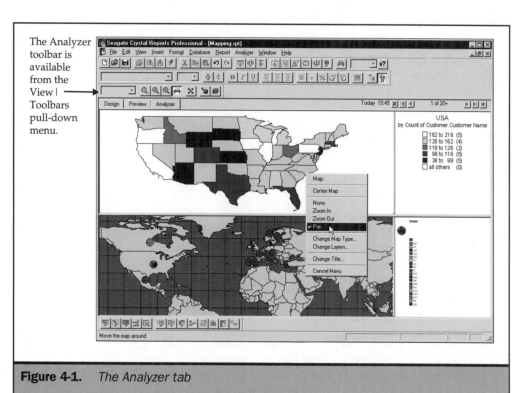

Figure 4-1.   *The Analyzer tab*

Map Layers

A map is displayed in the Analyzer tab using *layers*. If you are looking at a USA map, for example, the map may be composed of layers consisting of USA, US Highways, and US Major Cities. You can think of a map layer as a transparency containing just that layer's information that lies on top of the lower layers, which lie on top of the map. By using layers, the map can be displayed showing different levels of detail, usually determined by how far in the map is zoomed. If you are fully zoomed out on the map, you'll only see the states. As you zoom in, you will eventually see highways showing up across the states. And, as you zoom in even further, you will see dots and the names of cities within the states.

Although maps include layers in a default order with default settings, you can choose which layers to display, hide, include, or not include. You can also change the order in which the layers "lie" on the map, and change the zoom level at which layers become visible. To work with map layers, click the Change Map Layers button on the Analyzer toolbar, right-click in the Analyzer, and choose Change Layers from the pop-up menu; or choose Analyzer | Change Layers from the pull-down menus. The Layer Control dialog box is displayed.

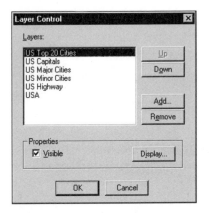

You will see all the layers included in the map by default. You can change the order in which the layers appear by selecting an individual layer and then clicking the Up or Down buttons to change the order of the layers. If you want to hide a layer so it doesn't show in the map, select the layer and turn off the Visible check box. If you decide you no longer want the layer at all, select it and click the Remove button.

If you decide you later want to redisplay a layer you removed earlier, or you want to add a new layer not already on the map, click the Add button. A File Open dialog box will appear. Additional layers are located in \PROGRAM FILES\MAPINFO\MAPS. Point to that folder and look for the appropriate .TAB file. Once you've chosen it, it will appear in the Layer Control dialog box.

To change the zoom level at which a layer will appear, select the layer and click the Display button. The Display Properties dialog box for that layer will open.

If you uncheck Display within Zoom Range, the layer will appear in the map at all times, regardless of the zoom level. If you leave it checked, you can set the minimum and maximum zoom levels at which the layer will become visible. Once you have made your choices, you can zoom in or out on the map to see the layer changes.

 If you are displaying two maps in the Analyzer, you must perform a zoom or pan operation inside the appropriate map to select that map. You can then use the Layer Control dialog box to work with map layers.

Figures 4-2 and 4-3 show the same map at the same zoom level with different settings for the US Highway layer.

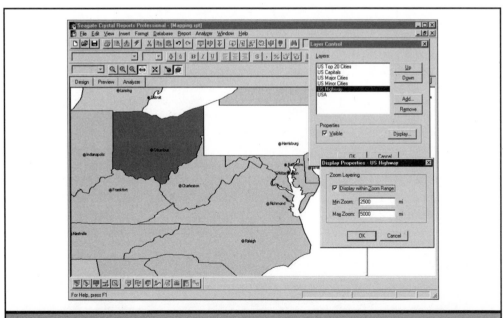

Figure 4-2. *Map with US Highway layer set for highways invisible*

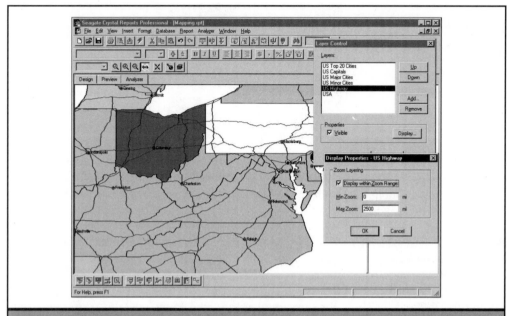

Figure 4-3.   *Map with US Highway layer set for highways visible*

The
Complete
Reference

Chapter 5

Using Formulas

When you first start using Crystal Reports, you'll be able to write some simple reports using data that comes entirely from the database. You simply drag fields from the Insert Fields dialog box onto the report, and away you go. However, it won't be long until you find that you want some information to appear on your report that isn't contained in the database. Or, you may find that you want to display a field differently on the report than it appears in the database. For these, and many similar situations, use Crystal Reports *formulas*.

A formula can be thought of as a math calculation or a small piece of computer programming code. If you're not used to them at first, creating formulas can appear to be very complicated. They may seem to be too much like programming (but then, maybe you *like* programming!). Formulas can be as simple or as complex as you want to make them—you can start with simple math computations and, as you get more comfortable, graduate to nested if-then-else formulas that use variables. Formulas bring the ultimate power and flexibility to Crystal Reports.

You can create formulas with either the Design or Preview tab displayed, although creating them in the Design tab is probably better, because you will have a more accurate idea of where the formulas will really end up when you place them on your report. All formula work begins at the Formula tab on the Insert Fields dialog box. Even if you choose Insert | Formula Field from the pull-down menus, all that will show up is the Insert Fields dialog box with the Formula tab selected.

Click the New button to create a new formula. You'll be asked to supply a formula name. Remember, you're *not* creating a file on disk when you add a formula, so you don't need to worry about file-naming conventions—the formula is just stored inside the .RPT file of your report. Your formula names can contain upper- and lowercase letters, spaces, and anything else that makes them descriptive. Use an easy-to-understand formula name—not only so that you'll be able to understand what they are when you look at the list of formulas you've created, but because the formula name is used for the field title when you place a formula in the details section. When you click OK, the Formula Editor is displayed.

The Formula Editor

Figure 5-1 shows the Formula Editor, which you'll use to create all your new formulas, as well as to edit any existing formulas. The Formula Editor has been completely redesigned in Crystal Reports 7. It may look a little foreboding at first, but don't worry—it will soon become second nature to you as you create and edit more formulas.

If you wish to customize the font face, size, and colors and the other appearance options that the Formula Editor uses, select File | Options on the pull-down menus and make your choices on the Editors tab of the dialog box that opens.

CRYSTAL REPORTS 7
INTRODUCED

Field Tree box contains a hierarchical tree of database fields, other formula fields, group subtotals, etc.

Toolbar provides access to the most common Formula Editor functions

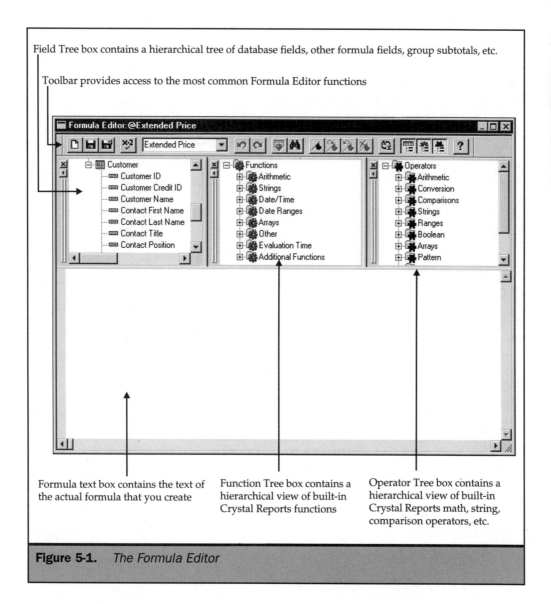

Formula text box contains the text of the actual formula that you create

Function Tree box contains a hierarchical view of built-in Crystal Reports functions

Operator Tree box contains a hierarchical view of built-in Crystal Reports math, string, comparison operators, etc.

Figure 5-1.   *The Formula Editor*

Before you actually create a formula, familiarize yourself with the layout of the Formula Editor. Notice that the toolbar, as well as the Field Tree, Function Tree, and Operator Tree boxes, can be closed, resized, moved, and undocked (detached from the main window and put in their own windows). You have a great deal of flexibility in customizing the way the Formula Editor looks.

Figure 5-2 shows the Formula Editor with the toolbar and Operator Tree box undocked.

If you mistakenly undock and then close the toolbar, you can get it back by right-clicking anywhere in the Format Editor and choosing Show Toolbar from the pop-up menu. You may also press ALT-T.

When you're working with the Formula Editor, you'll want to familiarize yourself with the toolbar, as you'll need to use it on a regular basis. There are buttons to create new formulas, save the formula you're working on, edit another formula, manipulate

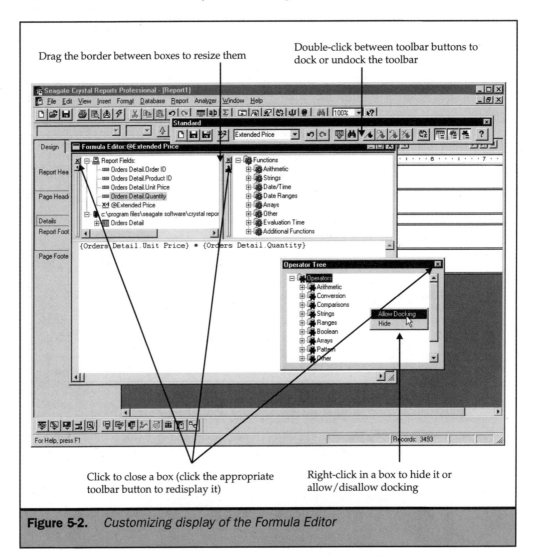

Figure 5-2. *Customizing display of the Formula Editor*

bookmarks, and on and on. Table 5-1 shows the functions of the Formula Editor's toolbar buttons.

Tip   *There are many other shortcut keys you can use while in the Formula Editor. Search Crystal Reports online Help for "Formula Editor Key Controls."*

Button/Key Combo	Name	Function
or CTRL-N	New	Creates a new formula. You'll be asked to give the formula a name.
	Save	Saves the current formula and leaves the Formula Editor displayed.
or CTRL-S	Save and Close	Saves the current formula and closes the Formula Editor.
	Check	Checks the syntax of the formula and reports any errors.
Customer Address	Name	Lets you choose another formula to edit, without closing and reopening the Formula Editor.
or CTRL-Z	Undo	Undoes the latest action.
or CTRL-SHIFT-Z	Redo	Redoes the latest action.
	Browse Data	Displays sample data from the database for the selected database field.
or CTRL-F	Find/Replace	Allows searching and replacing for specific characters in the current formula.
or CTRL-F2	Toggle Bookmark	Places a bookmark at the current line of formula text. If a bookmark is already there, removes it.

Table 5-1.   *Formula Editor Toolbar Buttons*

Button/Key Combo	Name	Function
or F2	Next Bookmark	Moves the cursor to the next bookmark in the current formula.
	Previous Bookmark	Moves the cursor to the previous bookmark in the current formula.
	Clear All Bookmarks	Removes all bookmarks from the current formula.
	Sort Trees	Sorts the contents of the three Tree boxes alphabetically, instead of in the default logical order.
	Field Tree	Displays/hides the Field Tree box.
	Function Tree	Displays/hides the Function Tree box.
	Operator Tree	Displays/hides the Operator Tree box.
	Help	Displays Formula Editor Help.

Table 5-1. *Formula Editor Toolbar Buttons* (continued)

There are two general approaches to building a formula: typing in the parts of the formula directly or double-clicking in the tree boxes. Once you become more familiar with the Crystal Reports formula language, you will probably create at least some parts of your formula by typing the formula text right into the Formula text box at the bottom of the Formula Editor. For example, it's often easier to just type in an asterisk when you want to multiply numbers, instead of clicking around in the Operator Tree box to find the multiplication operator.

Other parts of your formula, however, are best created automatically by double-clicking elements in one of the three tree boxes. For example, to include a database field as part of your formula, just find the field you want to include in the Field Tree box and double-click it. The field will be placed at the cursor position in the Formula text box, using proper formula language syntax.

Using the trees is easy. Simply find the general area of the tree that you are interested in, and click the plus sign next to the category that you want to use. All the functions or operators within that category will appear. Just double-click the one you want to use. It will be placed at the cursor position in the Formula text box. If you click a function that requires *arguments* (or parameters), such as an UpperCase function that needs to know what you want to convert to upper case, the function name and parentheses will be placed in the formula, with the cursor positioned at the location of the first argument. You can either type it in, or move to another tree (the Field Tree, for example) and double-click the field you want to add as the argument. After a while, you'll be able to find the functions or operators you're looking for quickly and create fairly large formulas by just pointing and double-clicking.

Notice the syntax that Crystal Reports uses when it places objects in the Formula text box (the small formula illustrated in Figure 5-2 is a good example). If you decide to type material into the formula yourself, you'll need to adhere to proper formula language syntax. Table 5-2 identifies special characters and other syntactical requirements of the formula language.

Character	Uses
. (period)	Used to separate the table name from the field name when using a database field. You must always include the table name, a period, and the field name—the field name by itself is not sufficient.
{} ("curly" or French braces)	Used to surround database fields, other formula names, and parameter fields. The formula won't understand fields if they're not surrounded by curly braces.
// (two slashes)	Denotes a comment. These can be used at the beginning of a line in a formula, in which case the Formula Editor ignores the whole line. You can also place two slashes anywhere in a formula line, in which case the rest of the line will be ignored.

" " or ' '
 (quotation marks or apostrophes)
	Used to surround string or text *literals* (fixed-string characters) in formulas. You can use either one, as long as they're used in matched pairs. For example:
	 `If {Customer.Country} = "USA" Then "United States"`
	 `Else 'International'`

( )
 (parentheses)
	Used to force certain parts of formulas to be evaluated first, as in the following:
	 `({Orders.Amount} + {Orders.Amount}) * {@Tax Rate}.`
	 Also used to denote arguments or "parameters" of built-in functions, as in this example:
	 `UpperCase({Customer.Customer Name}).`

Table 5-2.   *Formula Editor Special Characters*

Character	Uses
@ (at sign)	Used when including one formula in another formula. Crystal Reports automatically precedes formula names with the @ sign. Make sure you include it in the Formula Editor. (Don't forget the curly braces either!)
? (question mark)	Used when including a parameter field in a formula. Crystal Reports automatically precedes parameter field names with the question mark. Make sure you include it and the curly braces in the formula.
# (pound sign)	Used when including a running-total field in a formula. Crystal Reports automatically precedes running-total field names with the pound sign. Make sure you include it and the curly braces in the formula.

,
(comma)
	Used to separate multiple arguments in functions. For example:
	`ToText({Orders.Amount},0," ")`
	Don't add a comma as a thousands separator when using a numeric constant in a formula. For example:
	`{Orders.Amount} + 2,500`
	will cause a syntax error.

; (semicolon)	If your formula contains multiple statements, you must separate them with a semicolon.

ENTER key	You may press ENTER to start a new line in your formula anywhere between a field or function and an operator (don't put new lines or spaces in the middle of field or function names!). Long formulas are more readable on multiple lines. For example:
	`If {Order.Amount} > 5000 Then`
	`    "Qualifies for bonus"`
	`Else`
	`    "Not eligible for bonus"`

:=
(colon followed by equal sign)
	Used for variable assignment, such as:
	`NumberVar Quota := 1`
	Don't confuse this with just the equal sign, which is used for comparison:
	`If {Customer.Region} = "BC" Then`
	`    "Canadian Customer"`

Table 5-2. *Formula Editor Special Characters* (continued)

Data Types

As you begin to work with formulas, it's very important to understand the concept of *data types*. Every database field has a certain data type, and every formula you create will result in a single data type. These concepts are important because the formula you create must deal with data types properly, or you'll get errors when you try to save the formula, or the formula won't give you the result you're looking for. You can't, for example, add the contents of a number field to the contents of a string field with a plus sign—both fields have to be numbers. You can't convert a date field to uppercase characters, only a string field can be converted to uppercase.

By default, Crystal Reports doesn't display objects in the Design tab by their data types. It shows their names instead. You may prefer to see the data type representation instead of the field name. To do this, choose File | Options from the pull-down menus, and turn off the "Show Field Names" check box in the Field Options section of the Layout tab. Notice the difference between showing field names and showing data types:

Order ID	Order Amount	Order Date	Ship Via
-5,555,555	($55,555.56)	12/27/00 1:23:45AM	XXXXXXXXXXXX

You may want to turn off Show Field Names when you first start working with formulas. Seeing the data types can help you determine the type of operators and functions that will work with the database fields you're including in your formulas. Also, whenever you *browse* database fields in the Formula Editor, the data type shows up in the browse dialog box. In the preceding illustration, the fields have the following data types:

- Order ID is a *number* data type, which can contain only numbers (along with a period to indicate a decimal point and a hyphen or minus sign if it's a negative number). You can add, subtract, multiply, divide, and perform other math operations on number data types.

- Order Amount is a *currency* data type (only available from certain databases). This is similar to a number data type, but it avoids rounding errors that sometimes occur when performing math operations on number data types.

- Order Date is a combined *date-time* data type (again, only supported by certain databases). This can contain a date, time, or a combination of both. Other databases have date-only data types, and some have time-only data types.

- Ship Via is a *string* (or text) data type. The string data type allows any combination of characters to be placed in the field. However, because letters and punctuation marks can reside in the field, you can't normally perform mathematical calculations with the field.

There are other data types that you may encounter in your databases that aren't shown in this example:

- *Boolean* data type, which represents data that can only have a true or false value.

- *Memo* data type, which is designed to contain large amounts of text (much larger than the 255-character string limit), like narratives and comments.

- *BLOB* data type (an acronym for Binary Large Object), which can contain photos, graphics, or large amounts of plain ASCII text.

Memo and BLOB fields can only be placed on the report for display. They cannot be used or manipulated inside formulas. They won't even show up in the Formula Editor Field Tree box. Also, Crystal Reports does not include a "Rich Text Format" decoder—if a BLOB field contains RTF text, all the formatting codes and extra characters will appear on the report.

Creating a New Formula

Creating a simple math calculation is easy. Using the Orders Detail table of the sample XTREME.MDB database included with Crystal Reports, you can calculate the extended price of each order-line item with the following formula:

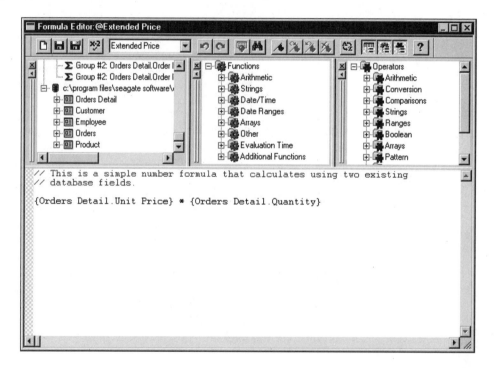

To create this formula:

1. Create a new report using the XTREME.MDB Microsoft Access sample database included with Crystal Reports. Choose the Orders Detail table from this database.

2. Click the New button on the Formula tab of the Insert Fields dialog box.

3. When asked to name the formula, call it Extended Price, and click OK or press ENTER.

4. When the Formula Editor appears, double-click the Orders Detail.Unit Price report field in the Field Tree box to add it to the Formula text box. If the field you want to add has already been placed on the report, you will actually find it in the Field Tree under both the Report Fields section and the Database name— there is absolutely no difference if you choose the field from either area.

5. Click the plus sign next to Arithmetic in the Operator Tree box to see all the arithmetic operators that are available. Double-click the multiply operator. (You can save yourself some mouse clicks by just typing an asterisk directly in the Formula text box, if you'd like. Although you don't have to put a space before or after the asterisk, the formula is easier to read if you do.)

6. Double-click the Orders Detail.Quantity field in the Field Tree box to place it after the asterisk.

When you have finished with the formula, you have several ways to save it and close the Formula Editor. When you first start to use formulas, you'll probably want to check the *syntax* of the formula before you save it. This will ensure that Crystal Reports can at least understand the different parts of the formula and how they are supposed to be calculated or manipulated. Check the formula's syntax by clicking the Check button in the Formula Editor toolbar, or press ALT-C. If Crystal Reports can understand all parts of the formula, a dialog box will appear indicating that no errors were found. (If you've ever written computer programs or used spreadsheet formulas before, though, you know that correct syntax doesn't guarantee that the formula will return the right answer!)

If there is a syntax error in the formula, Crystal Reports will display an error message and place the cursor at the point in the formula where it stopped understanding it. Sometimes these messages may be very descriptive

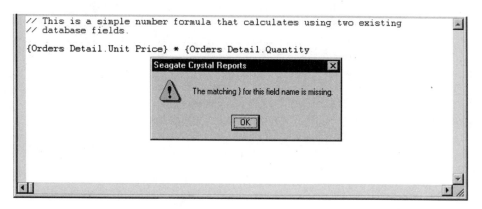

or very cryptic

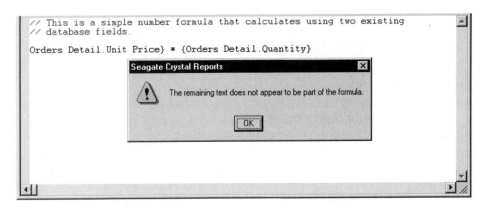

```
// This is a simple number formula that calculates using two existing
// database fields.

Orders Detail.Unit Price} * {Orders Detail.Quantity}
```

Seagate Crystal Reports

The remaining text does not appear to be part of the formula.

OK

even though both of these examples result from simply forgetting curly braces. You'll learn over time what most error messages indicate and how to resolve them.

 Even though you may not get any syntax errors when you check the formula when you first create it, you may still get an error when the report runs, depending on the actual data in the database. This may happen, for example, if you create a formula that divides two fields, but the "divided by" field returns a zero during a certain record. You'll then get a "Can't Divide By Zero" syntax error in the middle of the report process. If there's a chance that this type of error may occur based on the data, you'll probably want to add some type of "If <field> > 0 Then…" logic to ensure these types of "run time" syntax errors won't occur.

Once you've determined that there are no syntax errors, it's time to save the formula. You may either save the formula and remain in the Formula Editor, or save the formula and close the Formula Editor. There are two toolbar buttons for this, or CTRL-S will save the formula and close the Formula Editor.

If you choose to skip the syntax check and immediately save the formula, Crystal Reports will check the syntax anyway. If there is an error, you'll be given the opportunity to save the formula with the error. This makes little sense, as Crystal Reports will stop as soon as you try to run the report and display the error message in the Formula Editor. If you try to save and get a syntax error, correct the error and try to save the formula again. If there are no errors, you'll no longer get a syntax error message and the formula will be saved.

Once the formula has been saved and the Formula Editor closed, you will see the formula name under the Formula tab of the Insert Fields dialog box. You can simply drag and drop the formula on the report, just like a database field. In the case of the Extended Price formula, you'll notice that the formula has taken on the currency data type. This is because we multiplied a currency field by a number field. The resulting formula will be a currency formula.

Editing, Renaming, or Deleting an Existing Formula

Once you've created a formula, you may wish to change its calculation or add to its function. You can *edit* the existing formula by selecting the formula you wish to change in the Insert Fields dialog box and clicking the Edit button. This will redisplay the Formula Editor with the formula in it.

An even quicker method of editing is available after you've placed the formula on your report. In either the Design or Preview tab, click the formula. Notice in the status bar that the formula name is preceded by the @ sign. Crystal Reports automatically adds this symbol to the beginning of all formulas you create. Now that you've selected the formula, simply right-click and choose Edit Formula from the pop-up menu. The formula will reappear in the Formula Editor, ready for you to modify.

If you wish to *rename* a formula, you must do so from the Formula tab of the Insert Fields dialog box. Click the formula you want to rename, and click the Rename button. Type in the new name and click OK. If you've used this formula inside other formulas or elsewhere on your report, Crystal Reports will change the name there too.

If you select a formula on the report and click the DEL key, you will remove that particular occurrence of the formula from the report. However, the formula will still remain in the Insert Fields dialog box and take up memory and storage space when you save the report. If you're sure you no longer need the formula at all, delete it entirely. This must be done from the Formula tab of the Insert Fields dialog box. Select the formula you want to delete and click the DEL button. The formula will be removed from the dialog box.

Tip   *You won't be able to delete the formula if it's being used anywhere else on the report or in another formula. You'll need to remove any occurrences of the formula from the report and modify any other formulas that contain it (including the Select Expert or record-selection Formula) before you can remove it from the Insert Fields dialog box.*

Number Formulas

Probably the most common type of formula is a number formula, such as the Extended Price formula discussed earlier. Number formulas can be as simple as multiplying a database field by 1.1 to increase its amount by 10 percent, or as complex as calculations that include sophisticated statistical math. There is no special procedure required to declare a formula as a "number formula"—the formula simply takes on that data type based on the fields and operators that you use in the formula. As the Extended Price formula, shown here, demonstrates, multiplying a number field by a currency field results in a currency formula.

```
{Orders Detail.Unit Price} * {Orders Detail.Quantity}
```

Many number formulas will use a mathematical *operator*, such as a plus sign, a hyphen or minus sign, an asterisk for multiplication, or a slash for division. You will also need to use built-in *functions* that Crystal Reports supplies. You'll find all the built-in functions listed in the Function Tree box. By double-clicking a function, the function name will be placed in the Formula text box with the cursor located in between the opening and closing parentheses. You can then either type in the function's *arguments* or parameters, or double-click other fields or formulas in the Field Tree box to add them as arguments to the function.

For example, if you have a group on the report and you wish to include a group subtotal in a formula, you would use the Sum function. You'll actually find that three Sum functions are available, with one, two, or three arguments. Here are some examples:

```
Sum({Orders.Order Amount})
```

will return a total of all order amounts for the entire report.

```
Sum({Orders.Order Amount},{Customer.Region})
```

will return a total of just the order amounts in the region group where the formula is evaluated. If the formula was evaluated in the Wyoming group, the formula would return the order amount subtotal for Wyoming only.

```
Sum({Orders.Order Amount},{Orders.Order Date}, "weekly")
```

will return the order amount subtotal for the current order date group, calculating the subtotal based on a week of orders. Note that this third argument corresponds to the time periods that are available when creating a group based on a date field. Refresh your memory about date-field grouping by looking at Chapter 3.

So, you could calculate each order amount's percentage of the region subtotal by using the percentage operator and the Sum function as follows:

```
{Orders.Order Amount} % Sum({Orders.Order Amount},{Customer.Region})
```

There are built-in functions to calculate all the summary-type information discussed in Chapter 3, such as average, subtotal, *P*th percentile, and on and on. By opening up the Arithmetic category of functions in the Function Tree box, you'll also find functions to calculate remainders, absolute value, and to round numbers.

Order of Precedence

You'll sometimes find situations where you're unsure of the order in which Crystal Reports evaluates a formula's operators. For example, if you wish to add sales tax to an extended price, you might use the following formula. It is supposed to add 8 percent sales tax to the extended price of an order (already calculated in the @Extended Price formula):

```
{@Extended Price} + {@Extended Price} * .08
```

The question of how Crystal Reports calculates this is crucial. Does it calculate the addition operator first, then the multiplication operator, or does it calculate the multiplication operator first, then the addition operator? The results will vary dramatically based on the calculation order. Consider an Extended Price of $100 with addition performed first:

```
100 + 100 = 200
200 * .08 = 16.00
```

or with multiplication performed first:

```
100 * .08 = 8.00
100 + 8.00 = 108.00
```

While your customer might be very pleasantly surprised by the first calculation showing up on their invoice, the second calculation is certainly the correct one. But, looking at the formula, you'll notice that the multiplication operator is the second operator. Will it be evaluated second?

The answer is no, based on the *order of precedence*. Although it may sound like a computer concept, order of precedence is actually a concept that you should recall from your 9th grade math class. Simply stated, multiplication and division are evaluated first from left to right across the formula; then addition and subtraction are evaluated from left to right across the formula.

Based on this, the formula to add tax to the Extended Price shown earlier will work just fine. But, what if, for some reason, you want the addition performed first, not the multiplication. Again, thinking back to 9th grade math, you surround the part of the formula you want evaluated first with *parentheses*. The formula that will perform the addition before the multiplication is:

```
({@Extended Price} + {@Extended Price}) * .08
```

If you use one formula inside another formula, as in this example, Crystal Reports will calculate the embedded formula first (using the order of precedence), and then calculate the second formula.

String Formulas

Many times, the database will contain string or text data that is insufficient for your reporting needs. For example, you may want to sort a report by zip code, but the database only contains zip code as part of a City_State_Zip field. Or, you may want to make your reports Year 2000 compliant, but the database keeps dates in a string field with a two-digit year. Or, you may want to write a report to print checks, spelling out the dollar amount in words, using a number or currency field in the database. All of these are applications for a formula that either manipulates or creates string data.

Strings can be *concatenated*, or "tacked together," using the plus sign. Although the operator is the same one used to add numbers, the results will be very different depending on the data type. For example, this formula

```
25 + 7 + 100
```

will return a numeric result of 132. Because all the elements of the formula are numbers, the plus sign will add the numbers together and return a numeric answer.

Contrast that with this formula:

```
"25" + "7" + "100"
```

which will return a string result of 257100. By enclosing the numbers in quotation marks, Crystal Reports interprets the values in the formula as strings, not numbers. When you use a plus sign operator with strings, the result is the concatenation of the individual string elements.

This is very useful for many situations you'll encounter when reporting against databases. The following illustration shows the beginning of a form letter that simply uses database fields on the report.

January 12, 1999

Pathfinders
Miss   Christine   Manley
410 Eighth Avenue
Allenspark   , CO   80510

Dear Miss   Manley   ,

Notice the spacing problems for the contact name, city-state-zip line, and the letter's salutation. While you may be able to improve the appearance of this report slightly by resizing and moving the individual database fields, you'll never achieve a perfect result. By placing the database fields on the report in fixed locations, the report will never be able to accommodate varying widths of first names, last names, cities, and so on.

The next illustration shows the same report using formulas to concatenate the database fields together.

January 12, 1999

Pathfinders
Miss Christine Manley
410 Eighth Avenue
Allenspark, CO 80510

Dear Miss Manley,

The results are obvious: no matter how wide or narrow names or cities are, they are placed right next to the other items (with a space in between).

But why use formulas to achieve these results instead of just combining the database fields inside text objects? (Look back at Chapter 2 if you forgot about text objects.) For one thing, text object manipulation is much slower than formulas. Also, formulas give you a lot more flexibility in how your report looks. For example, you can just display the first initial of a contact name on the report using a formula. You can't do that with a text object.

Concatenating string fields is as simple as using the plus sign operator, as in

```
{Customer.Contact Title} + " " + {Customer.Contact First Name} + " " +
{Customer.Contact Last Name}
```

Notice that a space is "hard coded" into the formula using a *string literal*. String literals are simply fixed strings surrounded by quotation marks or apostrophes. You'll use them often in concatenation formulas and If-Then-Else formulas (discussed later in this chapter). So, the literal space in this formula will separate the title from the first name, and the first name from the last name.

You could create a salutation line using several string literals as follows:

```
"Dear " + {Customer.Contact Title} + " " +
{Customer.Contact Last Name} + ","
```

Notice that the word Dear and a space precede the title, a space separates the title from the last name, and a comma follows the last name.

There are many situations where you may want to use just certain parts of strings in a formula, not the whole string. For example, you may want to only use a first initial as part of the contact name on a form letter. By following a string field with a number or range of numbers enclosed in square brackets (known as a *subscript*), you can extract certain characters from the string field. For example:

```
{Customer.Contact Title} + " " + {Customer.Contact First Name}[1] +
". " + {Customer.Contact Last Name}
```

Notice that only the first character from the first name will be included in the formula, and a period has been added to the space literal between the first and last names.

Many older database systems contain date information in string fields. This is because earlier versions of mainframe systems or older database systems did not include a date data type. And, as many companies and programmers have found out in recent years, these dates often only include two digits to represent the year. To allow dates to sort correctly, the year needs to precede the month and day in these fields as well. So, it is very common to find January 10, 1999 coded into a string database field as 990110.

If you want to display the date in an "mm/dd/yyyy" format to make the date more readable, you could use string subscript operators to pick out the individual parts of the date, add some string literals, and rearrange the date's appearance. Assuming that the hire date in a "legacy" database is a six-character string field in the form "yymmdd," this formula will redisplay it as "mm/dd/19yy":

```
{EMP.HIRE_DATE}[3 to 4] + "/" + {EMP.HIRE_DATE}[5 to 6] + "/19" +
{EMP.HIRE_DATE}[1 to 2]
```

Notice that the subscript operator can also return a *range* of characters, not just one.

Caution   *No, this is not a Year 2000-compliant formula! If your database contains these types of string date fields, you'll need to make other accommodations for Year 2000 compliance, such as using an If-Then-Else statement (described later in the chapter) to check the year, and a "sliding scale" routine to place the year in the proper century.*

In addition to the subscript operator, there are many built-in string functions that you can use in your formulas. There are functions to return characters from the left of a string, the middle of a string, and the right of a string. Using these, the preceding date formula could be rewritten as follows:

```
Mid({EMP.HIRE_DATE},3,2) + "/" + Right({EMP.HIRE_DATE},2) + "/19" +
Left({EMP.HIRE_DATE,2}
```

The Mid function takes three arguments: the field or string to use, the starting position in the string to start reading, and the number of characters to return. The Right and Left functions take two arguments: the field or string to use and the number of characters to return.

Caution   *Crystal Reports doesn't deal well with formulas that may include a database field containing a null value (a special database value equating to empty, as opposed to zero for a number field or an empty string for a string/text field). If any part of the formula that you're using contains a null, the entire formula will return null. Use an If-Then-Else formula, along with the IsNull built-in function (described later in the chapter), to deal with potential null situations.*

The ToText Function

There is a crucial built-in function that you will use very often in string formulas. *ToText* is used to convert other data types to a string data type so you can use them in concatenation or comparison formulas. You can use ToText to convert numbers, dates, times—virtually any other data type—to strings. You need this functionality to avoid the type of problem shown here:

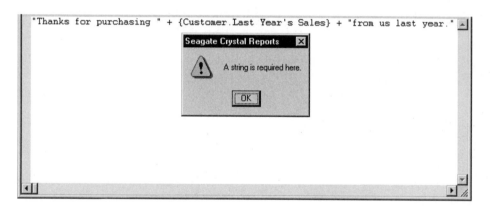

This problem occurs because you can't concatenate a currency field onto a string literal (or any other combination of mismatched data types). To convert a number or currency field to a string, such that you can concatenate it to another string, use ToText. The following will solve this problem:

```
"Thanks for purchasing " + ToText({Customer.Last Year's Sales}) +
" in products last year."
```

That formula will return

```
Thanks for purchasing $32,421.27 in products last year.
```

If you look in the Function Tree box under Strings, you'll see several permutations of ToText, with anywhere from one to five arguments. While the best place to look for all the ToText details is Crystal Reports online Help, here are a few additional ToText examples.

- Determine the number of decimal places.

  ```
  "Thanks for purchasing " + ToText({Customer.Last Year's Sales},0) +
  " in products last year."
  ```

  will return

  ```
  Thanks for purchasing $32,421 in products last year.
  ```

A second number argument to ToText determines how many decimal places Crystal Reports uses when it converts the number or currency field to a text string.

■ Determine the thousands separator.

```
"Thanks for purchasing " + ToText({Customer.Last Year's Sales},0,"") +
" in products last year."
```

will return

```
Thanks for purchasing $32421 in products last year.
```

A third string argument to ToText determines what thousands separator Crystal Reports uses when it converts a number or currency field to a text string. In this example, the two quotation marks side by side indicate an empty string, so ToText doesn't use a thousands separator.

■ Format date fields.

```
"Your order was placed on " +
ToText({Orders.Order Date},"dddd, MMMM d, yyyy.")
```

will return

```
Your order was placed on Monday, January 11, 1999.
```

This version of ToText uses a *format string* as the second argument. The format string (sometimes referred to as a "mask") uses special characters, such as pound signs, zeros, decimal points, the letters *d*, *m*, *y*, etc., as placeholders to indicate how data should be formatted when converted to a string. In this example, the "dddd" characters specify the day of the week to be spelled out fully. "MMMM" specifies a fully spelled month, "d" specifies the day of the month without a leading zero, and "yyyy" specifies a four-digit year. Any characters included in the format string that can't be translated into placeholders (such as the commas and periods) are simply added to the string as literals.

| Tip | *It's important to remember that the case of the placeholder characters is significant. When formatting time fields, for example, lowercase h characters indicate hours with a 12-hour clock, while uppercase H characters indicate hours with a 24-hour military clock. Or, if you use placeholder characters of the wrong case, Crystal Reports will just include the characters in the resulting string as literals.* |

Another built-in function, ToWords, comes in handy when writing checks with Crystal Reports. Consider the following formula:

```
ToWords({PAYROLL.NET_CHECK_AMT})
```

When placed on the report, this formula will return the following for an employee record with net pay of $1,231.15:

```
one thousand two hundred thirty-one and 15/100
```

Date/Time Formulas

There are many reporting situations where you need to manipulate date, time, or date/time data types. Most modern PC and SQL databases support some or all of these data types. Although date and time fields don't appear on the report as pure numbers (they often include other characters and words, depending on how they're formatted), they are actually stored by the database and Crystal Reports as numbers. Therefore, it's possible to do mathematical calculations on date fields. There are also built-in date and time functions that return just parts of date and time fields and that convert other data types to date or time fields.

Number of Days Between Dates

By default, when Crystal Reports performs math on date fields, the result of the calculation is in days. So, determining how long it took to ship an order is as simple as creating the following formula:

```
{Orders.Ship Date} - {Orders.Order Date}
```

Even though both the database fields in this formula are dates, the result of the formula will be a number—the number of days between the two dates.

Tip *This formula will return the number of calendar days between the two dates. If you wish to exclude weekends from this calculation, it becomes a bit more complicated, but can be done with some additional math calculations or by incorporating the DayOfWeek function. If you wish to exclude company holidays as well (holidays that might be stored in a database table), this could very well become a candidate for a User Function Library (discussed later in this chapter and in Chapter 28).*

You can calculate a date in the future. If, for example you wanted to create an accounts receivable report that showed the actual due date of an invoice, the date itself could be calculated by using invoice date (a date field) and terms (a number field), as follows:

```
{AR.INV_DATE} + {AR.TERMS}
```

Although you don't explicitly define this formula as a date formula, it will return a date data type showing the date on which the invoice is due, provided the terms field contains the number of days required for payment (30, 45, etc.).

Number of Hours and Minutes Between Times

You can also perform mathematical functions directly on time fields. When you calculate two time fields together, the result is in seconds. For example, the following formula will return the elapsed time, in seconds, between a starting time and ending time field in a college database's course table:

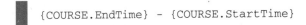

```
{COURSE.EndTime} - {COURSE.StartTime}
```

You may not want the time returned as seconds, but perhaps hours and minutes, minutes and seconds, or any combination separated with colons. To accomplish this, you have a bit more work to do, but not as much as you might think. Examine the following:

```
Time(0,0,0) + ({COURSE.EndTime} - {COURSE.StartTime})
```

You'll notice that parentheses force the time calculation to be performed first, resulting in the number of seconds between the two times. The Time built-in function is also being used to return a time data type, using three arguments: hour, minute, and second. The particular time being returned by the Time function is midnight. By adding the seconds between the two times to midnight, you in essence have the number of hours, minutes, and seconds that have elapsed since midnight.

When you place this on your report, you'll see hours, minutes, and seconds, followed by AM or PM (AM if the time difference is less than 12 hours, PM if more, assuming that you're using Crystal Reports' default "hh:mm:ss AM/PM" date format). Now it's simply a matter of using the Format Editor to suppress the AM/PM indicator by choosing 24-hour time display. You can also suppress any combination of hours, minutes, and seconds to show the elapsed time the way you wish.

Month, Day, Year, Hour, Minute, Seconds Functions

There are many built-in functions to help you use date and time fields. You can use the Month, Day, and Year functions with a date field as an argument to return just the month, day, or year of the date as a number. Conversely, with the Hour, Minute, and Seconds functions, you can supply a time field as a single argument and have just the hour, minute, or second of the time field returned as a number.

Date Function

A very important built-in function is Date. The Date function requires three numeric arguments: year, month, and day. You will use the Date function to create a date data type value to use in comparison formulas or other formulas that work well with dates.

This function will come in very handy if you want to convert dates contained in string fields to actual date data types. For example, if your legacy database contains dates in string fields formatted as "yyyymmdd," you can use a combination of string manipulation, the ToNumber function, and the Date function to turn them into dates. Examine the following formula:

```
Date(ToNumber({EMP.HIRE_DATE}[1 to 4]),
     ToNumber({EMP.HIRE_DATE}[5 to 6]),
     ToNumber({EMP.HIRE_DATE}[7 to 8]))
```

The subscript operator picks out the individual year, month, and day parts of the date string. Then, ToNumber converts them to numbers from strings, as Date requires numeric arguments. Then, Date turns the three numeric arguments into a date data type. When this formula is placed on the report, you have complete date-formatting capabilities. You can also use this formula in other formulas to perform date math.

Notice that this formula has been intentionally placed on three lines by pressing ENTER *after the commas that separate the function arguments. Don't forget that you can do this anywhere you want between different operators or parts of functions. This makes the formula much easier to read.*

If-Then-Else Formulas

If you don't consider yourself a computer programmer, then look at this section of the chapter carefully, and reconsider your career options! Crystal Reports allows the use of If-Then-Else logic in formulas. This logic is the cornerstone of much computer programming code, so once you learn If-Then-Else concepts, you'll be on your way to new heights! Even if you're not contemplating a career change, you'll need to use If-Then-Else formulas to perform really sophisticated report customization.

If-Then-Else formulas perform a test on a database field, another formula, or some combination of them. Your test can be as simple or complex as you need it to be—perhaps just checking to see if a sales figure exceeds the $1,000 bonus threshold. Or, you may want to check the number of days a product took to ship, in conjunction with the carrier who shipped the product and the sales level of the customer, to determine if a shipment met your company's shipping goals. If the test passes (returns *true*), the formula will return a certain result. If the test fails (returns *false*), a different result will be returned.

If-Then-Else formulas are created with the following syntax:

```
If <test> Then <result if true> Else <result if false>
```

The test portion of an If-Then-Else formula must use comparison operators found in the Operator Tree box. You'll find a Comparisons section of the box that, when opened, will show operators that test for equal, less than, greater than, and other combinations of conditions. These can be used in conjunction with And, Or, and Not *Boolean* operators to combine multiple conditional tests together. Here's a simple If-Then-Else formula that will return a string based on an order amount:

```
If {Orders.Order Amount} > 5000 Then "Bonus Order" Else "Regular Order"
```

The Order Amount database field is tested to see if its value is greater than 5000. If the test is true, the formula returns the "Bonus Order" string. Otherwise, the formula returns the "Regular Order" string.

Boolean operators can also be used to combine multiple comparisons together. You can use And, Or, and Not Boolean operators. The preceding formula has been slightly enhanced here, using a Boolean operator to combine two comparisons:

```
If {Orders.Order Amount} > 5000 And Month({Orders.Order Date}) = 12 Then
    "Holiday Bonus Order"
Else
    "Regular Order"
```

Here, the order amount has to exceed 5000 *and* the order must have been placed in December for the formula to return "Holiday Bonus Order." Orders over 5000 in other months will still be regular orders. If you change the "And" to an "Or" in the preceding formula, then *all* orders in December will be bonus orders, regardless of amount. Orders over 5000 will also be considered bonus orders the rest of the year.

Data Types in If-Then-Else Formulas

While creating If-Then-Else formulas, you must pay special attention to the data types that you're using in the formula. In the If test of the formula, make sure you use similar data types in each individual comparison operation. For example, if you want to test whether Customer.Country is "USA," the test will be:

```
If {Customer.Country} = "USA"
```

Since Customer.Country is a string field, you need to compare it to a string literal, enclosed in quotation marks or apostrophes. If the field you are testing is numeric, you need to use a number constant, as in the Orders.Order Amount sample shown previously. If you mismatch data types such as these:

```
If {Orders.Order Amount} > "5000"
```

you'll receive an error.

If you use multiple comparisons separated by Boolean operators, each comparison can have a different data type. For example, if you want to combine the two tests mentioned previously, your formula would start out as:

```
If {Customer.Country} = "USA" And {Orders.Order Amount} > 5000
```

In this case, the different data types in the If part of the formula are fine, as long as each "side" of each comparison is of the same data type.

For example, you may have an existing formula on your report, @Ship Days, that calculates the number of days it took to ship an order. But, since @Ship Days is a numeric formula, it will display a zero on your report if the order was placed and shipped on the same day. You would, therefore, write the following If-Then-Else formula to show the words "Same Day" on the report if @Ship Days is zero, or just the contents of the @Ship Days formula if it is not zero.

```
If {@Ship Days} = 0 Then
    "Same Day"
Else
    @Ship Days
```

But, if you use the Check button in the Formula Editor to check the syntax of this formula, you'll receive an error:

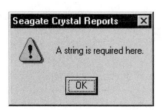

The problem is that Crystal Reports doesn't know what data type to assign to the formula. If the test returns true, the formula will return a string for the words "Same Day." However, if the test returns false, the formula will return @Ship Days, which is a number. Crystal Reports must assign a data type to a formula when it's first created—it can't wait until the report is running. Therefore, even though the "If" part of a formula can contain various data type tests, the "Then" and "Else" parts must contain the same data types.

Remember the function that converts other data types to strings? The following will solve this problem:

```
If {@Ship Days} = 0 Then
   "Same Day"
Else
   ToText(@Ship Days,0)
```

This result is better, as it doesn't show zero as the number of ship days. But, we want to take it a step further to make the report more readable. Look at the enhanced version of this formula:

```
If {@Ship Days} = 0 Then
   "Shipped Same Day"
Else
   "Shipped in " + ToText(@Ship Days,0) + " days"
```

This looks better on the report, particularly if the report isn't a straight columnar report. You might want to put this in a group header for an order, before the individual line items for the order show up in the details section. But, there's just one more problem. What will this formula return if it only took one day to ship the order?

```
Shipped in 1 days
```

While this probably won't mean your dismissal from the report development team, why not go one easy step further to make the report look even better? Try the following:

```
If {@Ship Days} = 0 Then
   "Shipped Same Day"
Else
   If {@Ship Days} = 1 Then
      "Shipped in " + ToText({@Ship Days},0) + " day"
   Else
      "Shipped in " + ToText({@Ship Days},0) + " days"
```

This is an example of a *compound* or *nested* If-Then-Else statement. Notice that you're not limited to one If, Then, or Else clause in a formula. You can make another If statement the result of the first Then, or the result of the first Else, and on and on. There is no specific limit to how many levels you can nest these, but obviously the formula becomes hard to follow after only one or two levels. Also, don't forget that the Else clause isn't required, so when you nest these, you won't have to always have a matching Else clause for every If.

If you've programmed in a language that uses If-Then-Else logic, you may be used to an End If statement that closes off an If statement. In those situations, you can include many statements between a Then and Else, or between an Else and the End If. Crystal Reports does not use an End If statement, so you can't include multiple statements in this manner.

If you need to have multiple things happen as the result of an If-Then-Else statement, you can include multiple statements, separated by semicolons, inside parentheses. *Or, you can repeat the statement several times in the formula, following each If-Then-Else statement with a semicolon to separate it from the next statement. This is particularly helpful when setting variables (discussed later in this chapter).*

Helpful Built-In Functions for If-Then-Else Formulas

If you look in the Function Tree box of the Formula Editor, you'll notice an Other category. Opening up this category will show you a variety of built-in functions you can use in If-Then-Else (and other) formulas to enhance your reporting flexibility. For example, all the "Special Fields" that were discussed in Chapter 2, such as Page Number, Total Page Count, Print Date and Time, Record Number, Group Number, and others, are available. There are other special functions that you can use to test for a null database value in the current, next, or last record; to check to see if the current database record is the first or last; or to see if the formula appears in a repeated group header. By using these special built-in functions, you can create formulas that make your reports more intuitive and easier to read.

Here are some examples:

- IsNull function

```
If IsNull({Customer.Region}) Then
    ""
Else
    ", " + {Customer.Region}
```

This formula checks to see if the region field contains a null value. If so, the formula will return an empty string (denoted by the two sets of quotation marks). Otherwise, the formula will return a comma, a space, and then the region name. This formula can then be concatenated with City and Zip database fields in another formula to form a City-State-Zip line. If the region in the database is null, the other formula won't become null.

Several factors determine whether or not the database will contain null values. In many cases, this is determined by the way the database is initially designed. If you would prefer to avoid null values appearing on the report, Crystal Reports allows you to convert them to a "default" format (typically a zero for number fields and an empty string for string fields). To do this for all new reports in the future, check "Convert NULL Field Value to Default" on the Reporting tab of the File | Options pull-down menu. If you want to set this for just the current report, check "Convert Null Field to Default" on the File | Report Options pull-down menu.

■ Next function

```
If ({Customer.Customer Name} = Next({Customer.Customer Name}) Then
   {Customer.Customer Name} + " continues on next page..."
```

The Next function reads a field in the next record of the database. This formula compares the field in the next record to the same field in the current record. If the values are the same, you know that the same customer will appear in the first record on the next page and you can note this with a text message. This formula would typically be placed in the page footer.

Notice that there is no Else clause in this formula. Crystal Reports doesn't require an Else clause in an If-Then-Else formula. If you leave the Else off and the test returns false, the formula will produce an empty string.

■ InRepeatedGroupHeader function

```
If InRepeatedGroupHeader Then
   GroupName ({Customer.Customer Name}) + "   - continued -"
Else
   GroupName ({Customer.Customer Name})
```

If you place this formula in the group header of a group with the "Repeat Group Header on Each New Page" option turned on (this can be set when you create or change a group—see Chapter 3), "- continued -" will only appear when the group header is repeated. This also uses the GroupName function to return the group name field for a particular group.

Boolean Formulas

There is one remaining type of formula that you may need to create—the Boolean formula. A Boolean formula can return just two values, true or false. You can think of a Boolean formula as just the "test" part of an If-Then-Else formula. When the formula is evaluated, it will ultimately just return one of the two states.

Here's a simple Boolean formula:

```
{@Ship Days} > 3
```

In this formula, the existing @Ship Days formula (a number formula) is tested to be greater than three (indicating a shipping exception). It either is or it isn't! If it is, the formula returns a true value—if it's not, the formula returns a false value.

When you then place this formula on your report, it will appear with a Boolean data type. If you have "Show Field Names" turned off in File | Options (discussed earlier in the chapter), then you'll see the formula show up with the word "True" in the Design tab. If you format the field, you'll notice a Boolean tab in the Format Editor that lets you choose how you want the true/false values to appear on the report.

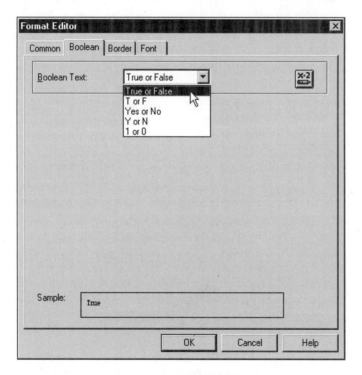

Although you may occasionally find Boolean formulas helpful when actually placed on the report, you'll probably use them much more often as a cornerstone for other formulas. For example, the Boolean formula shown previously indicates that Xtreme Mountain Bikes considers orders that took longer than three days to ship as exceptions. But Xtreme really wants to break down the shipping exception rule based on Last Year's Sales. If the customer purchased more than $50,000 in merchandise last year, then the three-day shipping exception will apply. However, if a customer purchased less, then a six-day shipping exception applies. This requires a *compound* Boolean formula, such as:

```
({@Ship Days} > 3 And {Customer.Last Year's Sales} > 50000)
Or {@Ship Days} > 6
```

This uses a combination of And and Or operators, along with the comparison operators, to create a more complex Boolean formula. What's important to remember, though, is that the ultimate result will still be just true or false. You can make a Boolean formula as complex as you want, using combinations of comparison operators along with And, Or, and Not operators. And in the end, only true or false will result.

Notice the parentheses around the first part of this compound Boolean formula. They ensure that both @Ship Days is less than three and Last Year's Sales is greater than $50,000 before "Oring" the @Ship Days greater than six test. Although this may make the formula more understandable, it is optional. Crystal Reports considers all Boolean operators (And, Or, and Not) equally in the order of precedence (discussed previously in this chapter). That is, it evaluates them equally as it travels through the formula from left to right.

There are several benefits to creating Boolean formulas in this fashion:

■ Once you've created a complex Boolean formula, you can include it in other formulas as the test part of an If-Then-Else, as in:

```
If {@Shipping Exception} Then
    "*** Shipping Exception ***"
Else
    "Shipped Within Goal"
```

This makes the second formula much easier to read and understand.

■ By using the Boolean formula throughout the report, you eliminate the need to retype the complex Boolean test over and over again, reducing the chance of errors. Even more important, you have one formula to change should the report requirements change down the road. For example, if you've used the @Shipping Exception formula as the cornerstone for 50 other formulas in your report, and you later decide to reduce the Last Year's Sales qualification from $50,000 to $35,000, you only have *one* formula to change on your report, not 50. All the rest will follow the change.

■ You can use the Boolean formula in advanced record selection (covered in Chapter 6) and conditional formatting (covered in Chapter 7) to limit the report to certain records or have certain objects on the report appear with different formatting.

Crystal Reports online Help is a wealth of wisdom on formula concepts and built-in functions. You'll find samples of every built-in function and many sample formulas that you can use as building blocks for your reports. Make use of this great resource as often as possible.

Variables in Formulas and Evaluation Times

As a general rule, formulas contain their value only for the duration of one database record. If you put a formula in the details section, it will evaluate every time a new record is processed and put its result in the details section. If you put a formula in a group footer, it will be evaluated when each group footer prints. In every case, the formula will not "remember" anything from the previous record or previous group footer. Once the next record or footer comes along, the formula evaluates completely "from scratch."

There are times, though, when you need a formula to remember material from record to record or group to group. You may want to accumulate some value as the report progresses so that you can print a total in a group footer or report footer. You may want to check the value of a subtotal in a group footer. If it exceeds a certain threshold, you want to increment a counter so you can show how many groups exceeded the threshold at the end of the report.

In order to accomplish this, you will need to somehow store information from record to record or group to group. This can be accomplished by using *variables*. A variable is simply a "placeholder" that Crystal Reports sets aside in the computer's memory. As the report progresses from record to record or group to group, your formula can refer back to the variable or change its contents. You can then use the variable in other formulas or display its accumulated contents in a group or report footer.

Declaring a Variable

The first step in any formula that uses a variable is to *declare* the variable. This sets aside a specific amount of memory for the variable, based on its data type. You'll find variable declarations listed in the Operator Tree box of the Formula Editor under Variable Declarations.

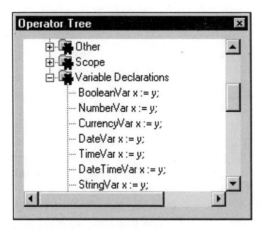

Notice that a different variable declaration statement exists for each Crystal Reports data type. You must consider in advance what kind of data your variable is going to hold and declare the correct type of variable. If, for example, you want to keep track of a customer name from record to record, and the customer name field in the database is a string data type, you'll need to declare a string variable to hold the information.

You must also give each variable a name. You can give it any descriptive name you wish, provided it doesn't contain spaces or conflict with another Crystal Reports formula language *reserved word*. You can't, for example, use variable names like Date, ToText, or UpperCase—these are reserved by the formula language for its own built-in functions.

To declare a variable, type the variable declaration followed by the variable name, such as this example:

```
NumberVar BonusAmount;
```

This declares a number variable called "BonusAmount" that can later be assigned a numeric value. The semicolon at the end of the statement separates this statement from the next one in the formula (presumably a statement to assign or test the contents of the variable). If you wish to use more than one variable in the formula, you may declare them together, again separated by semicolons. For example:

```
NumberVar BonusAmount;
StringVar BonusCustName;
DateVar DateBonusReached;
```

You may be used to assigning variables in other programming languages. Remember that Crystal Reports treats them differently. You must *declare a variable in each formula where you want to refer to it. However, even if you declare and assign it a value in one formula, and then declare it again in a formula that appears later in the report, it will retain the value from the first formula. Unlike many other languages, declaring a variable more than once* does not *reset its value to zero or empty (with the exception of Local variables, as described in the following section).*

Variable Scope

The whole idea and benefit of variables is that they retain their values as the report progresses from record to record or group to group. So, for variables to be of real benefit, they need to keep their values throughout the report process. And, because you may have several formulas that you want to refer to the same variable, you need to be able to refer to a variable in one formula that was already declared and assigned a value in another.

Exactly how far and where a variable keeps its value is determined by the variable's *scope*. If a variable has a narrow scope, it will only retain its value in the formula where it is initially declared—any other formula that refers to a variable with the same name will be referring to a brand new variable. If a variable has a wide scope, its value will be retained not only for use in other formulas, but even subreports within the main report. (Subreports are covered in Chapter 11.) There are three additional words you can place in front of your variable declarations to determine the variable's scope:

Local   The variable only remains in scope for the formula in which it is defined. If you declare a variable with the same name in another formula, it won't use the value from the first formula.

Global   The variable remains in scope for the duration of the entire main report. You can declare a global variable in one formula, and another formula will be able to use the contents placed in the variable by the first formula. Global variables, however, will not be visible in subreports.

Shared   The variable not only remains in scope for the duration of the entire main report, but can also be referred to in formulas in subreports. Not only can you use shared variables to pass data around the main report, you can use shared variables to pass information back and forth between the main report and subreports, as well as from subreport to subreport.

Add these keywords in front of variable declarations to determine their scope as follows:

```
Local NumberVar BonusAmount; //will only be visible in this formula
Global StringVar BonusCustName; //available to the whole main report
Shared DateVar DateBonusReached; //available to main and subreports
```

 If you leave off the variable scope keyword, the default scope for a variable will be global—it will be available to other formulas in the main report, but not to subreports.

Assigning a Value to a Variable

Once you've declared a variable, it won't do you much good if you don't assign a value to it. You may want to use it as an accumulator, to "add one" to it each time some condition is met for the database record. You may want to assign a string value to it, concatenating additional string values onto the variable as records progress. You then might display the value of the accumulated variable in the group footer, and assign the variable an empty string in the group header to start the whole process over again for the next group.

 If you declare a variable, but don't assign a value to it, it takes on a default value based on its data type. Numeric and Currency variables default to zero, string variables default to an empty string, Boolean variables default to false, and Date variables to a "0/0/00" date. Date/Time and Time variables have no default value.

There are two ways to assign a variable a value: you may assign it a value at the same time as it's declared, or you can assign a value on a separate line later in the formula. In either event, you must use the assignment operator, consisting of a colon followed by an equal sign, to assign a value to a variable. This is important—it's easy to get confused and just use the equal sign by itself. The equal sign only works for comparison—you must place a colon in front of the equal sign to make assignment work properly. Here's an example of assigning a variable a value on a separate line:

```
NumberVar CustomerCount;
CustomerCount := CustomerCount + 1
```

Here the CustomerCount variable is declared on the first line (terminated with a semicolon) and assigned on the second line. In this particular formula, the CustomerCount variable will keep its value from record to record, so it will be incremented by one every time the formula executes.

If you want to reset the value of the CustomerCount variable in a group header, you need to reset it to zero. Here's an example of how to declare and assign a variable at the same time:

```
NumberVar CustomerCount := 0;
```

Here the variable is declared, followed by the assignment operator and the value to assign the variable. In this example, placing this formula in the group header will reset the CustomerCount variable at the beginning of each group.

Tip   *Notice that a semicolon doesn't have to appear in the last line of a formula, as it is used to separate one statement from another. If all your formula does is declare and assign a variable, you don't need the semicolon at the end of the declaration/ assignment statement.*

You don't have to assign a value to a variable every time the formula executes. Nor do you need to assign the same value every time. Creative use of If-Then-Else formulas, along with variable assignment, makes for report flexibility that rivals that of many programming languages. Look at the following formula, which declares and conditionally assigns several variables.

```
CurrencyVar BonusAmount;
StringVar HighestCustName;
DateTimeVar DateBonusReached;

If {Orders.Order Amount} > BonusAmount Then
    HighestCustName := {Customer.Customer Name};
If {Orders.Order Amount} > BonusAmount Then
    DateBonusReached := {Orders.Order Date};
If {Orders.Order Amount} > BonusAmount Then
    BonusAmount := {Orders.Order Amount}
```

Look at this formula closely. Assuming it's placed in the details section, it keeps track of the highest order amount as the records progress. When an order exceeds the previous high amount, the customer who placed the order and the date the order was placed are added to variables. Then, the new high order amount is assigned to the bonus amount. There are several important points to note about the formula:

- There are multiple If-Then-Else statements (minus the Else—remember it's not required), separated by semicolons. They will all execute, but only the last statement will determine how the formula appears on the report. In this example, the last statement uses a currency data type, so the formula will appear on the report as currency.

- The sequence in which you place the statements is crucial. If you placed the If statement that assigns the BonusAmount variable as the first statement of the formula, the other two If tests would never evaluate to true because then the Order Amount would never be greater than the Bonus Amount variable.

- If you are keeping track of the bonus amounts, dates, and customer names for a certain group, such as region or country, you would want to make sure to reset the variables in the group header. If you fail to reset the variables and the next group doesn't have an order as high as the top value in the previous group, the previous group's values will appear for the following group as well.

- If you want to keep track of quotas or similar values for both group and report levels (you want to see the bonus customer for each region and for the entire report), you'll need to assign and maintain two sets of variables: one for the group level that is reset in the group header, and one for the report level that's not reset.

Displaying a Variable's Contents

In the preceding example, you saw how to accumulate values in variables in the details section, and how to reset them by assigning them a value of zero in the group header (or in another area of the report). You also need to have a way to show just what's contained in a variable on the report, or to use the variable's value in a formula some other way.

To show the contents of a variable, all you need to do is declare it. If the formula contains no other statements, declaring the variable will also return it as the formula value. For example, you might place the following formula in the group footer to show the customer who reached the bonus in the region group:

```
StringVar HighestCustName
```

Not only do you not need to place any other statements in the formula to show the value of the variable, you don't even need the semicolon at the end of the declaration line. It's the last line in the formula.

You may have situations where you want to show the contents of a variable, but you are using other statements to assign the variable in the formula. In that case, just declaring the variable won't display it, as the declaration statement won't be the last line in the formula. In this case, just add the name of the variable as the last line of the formula. This will then display the contents of the variable when the formula executes. Here's an example:

```
CurrencyVar BonusAmount;
StringVar HighestCustName;
DateTimeVar DateBonusReached;

If {Orders.Order Amount} > BonusAmount Then
    HighestCustName := {Customer.Customer Name};
If {Orders.Order Amount} > BonusAmount Then
    DateBonusReached := {Orders.Order Date};
If {Orders.Order Amount} > BonusAmount Then
    BonusAmount := {Orders.Order Amount};

HighestCustName
```

This formula will perform the test and variable assignments as before. But, the last line of the formula simply shows the HighestCustName variable, a string variable. So, this formula will show up with small *x*'s in the Design tab (if Show Field Names is turned off in File | Options) and the contents of the HighestCustName variable will be shown whenever the formula executes.

You can even go one step further, testing and assigning variables and then using them later in other calculations or concatenations. Here's another permutation of this formula:

```
CurrencyVar BonusAmount;
StringVar HighestCustName;
DateTimeVar DateBonusReached;

If {Orders.Order Amount} > BonusAmount Then
    HighestCustName := {Customer.Customer Name};
If {Orders.Order Amount} > BonusAmount Then
    DateBonusReached := {Orders.Order Date};
If {Orders.Order Amount} > BonusAmount Then
    BonusAmount := {Orders.Order Amount};

"As of this order, the amount to beat is " + ToText(BonusAmount) +
" set by " + HighestCustName + " on " + ToText(DateBonusReached, "M/d/yy")
```

This formula not only declares variables, it conditionally assigns them, and then concatenates and displays them, converting them to text as necessary.

Evaluation Times and Report Passes

As you probably have gathered by this time, formulas that contain variables are affected by where they are physically placed on the report. If you want to check values and assign variables during record-by-record processing, you must put the formula in the details section. If you want to show the accumulated totals for each group, you place a formula to show the total variables in the group footer. And to reset the variables for the next group, you need to place the formula that resets them in the group header.

However, just placing the formulas in these sections doesn't necessarily guarantee that they will actually evaluate in that section or during the logical "formatting" process of the report (where a group header prints, then the detail sections for that group, then the group footer, and so on). Consider the following example. Figure 5-3 contains a report that calculates a "running total" using a variable. The variable accumulates the order amounts in each detail section as the report progresses.

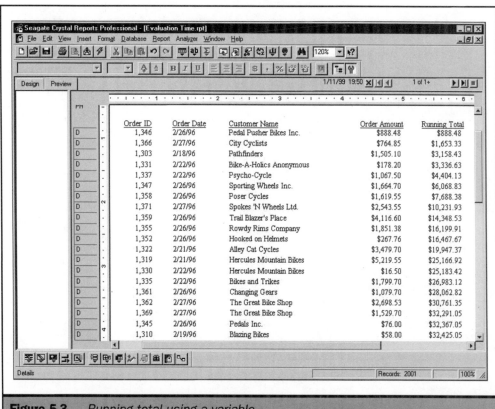

Figure 5-3. *Running total using a variable*

As you can see, the report is a simple detail report—there are no groups. In Figure 5-4, the report is grouped by Month. Look what happens to the running totals.

Why does adding a group result in the oddity with the running total? This happens because the formula is accumulating the running total at a different time than it's actually displaying it on the report. The formula is calculating while records are being read from the database, not when records have been grouped and are actually being printed or formatted. The formula is said to be calculating in a different *report pass* than the pass that actually formats the report. So, the running total has already been calculated for every record before Crystal Reports sorts the records to be placed in groups.

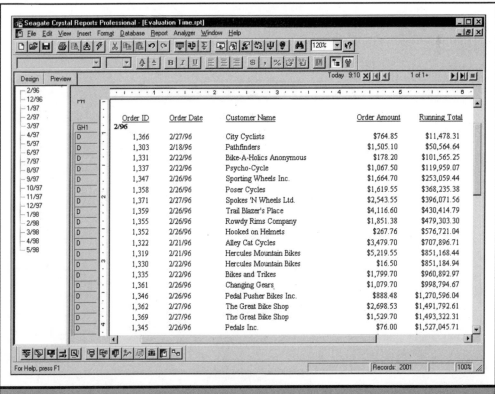

Figure 5-4. *Running total report after grouping*

This behavior may not be repeatable with a SQL database. When using a PC-style database, like Microsoft Access, Crystal Reports actually reads and sorts the data itself, creating the two-pass concept. With a SQL database, the data may be selected and sorted by the database server before it is sent to Crystal Reports. In that case, you won't see this odd behavior.

Crystal Reports generally breaks down its report processing into three passes. Certain types of formulas automatically evaluate during these passes:

Before Reading Records	This pass occurs before any records are read from the database. If formulas don't include any references to database fields or summary functions, they calculate in this pass.
While Reading Records	This pass occurs as records are being read from the database, but before any record selection, sorting, or grouping is performed. Formulas that include references to database fields, but don't contain any subtotal or summary functions, are calculated in this pass. These formulas are often called *first pass* formulas.
While Printing Records	This pass occurs after records have been read and are being formatted for display or printing. Sorting and grouping occurs during this pass. Formulas that include sum, average, or other summary functions, are included in this pass. These formulas are often called *second pass* formulas.

In most cases, you can trust Crystal Reports to accurately determine which pass it needs to evaluate a formula in. The glaring exception, however, is when a formula uses variables. If a formula simply declares a variable, or declares the variable and assigns it a literal or constant value, Crystal Reports will evaluate that formula in the Before Reading Records pass, as it makes no reference to database fields or summary functions. If you assign a variable a database value, it will evaluate that formula in the Reading Records pass (the formula will become a first pass formula). Only if you have some type of summary or subtotal function in the formula will Crystal Reports automatically evaluate the formula in the While Printing Records pass (the formula will then become a second pass formula).

This default behavior causes very strange results, as the previous running total example illustrates. When you use variables in your formulas, you may need to force the formula to evaluate in a different pass than it would by default. You do this by changing the formula's *evaluation time*. To do this, add an evaluation time statement as the first statement in the formula. Look in the Formula Editor Function Tree box, and you'll notice an Evaluation Time section. Open that section to see several evaluation-time statements that should now be mostly self-explanatory.

To force the formula that accumulates the running total to the second pass, where it will calculate the running total correctly after the records have been grouped, add the WhilePrintingRecords evaluation-time statement to the formula, as follows:

```
WhilePrintingRecords;
CurrencyVar RunningTotal := RunningTotal + {Orders.Order Amount}
```

Don't get confused if you can't insert a subtotal, summary, or grand total on a second pass formula. When you click this type of formula in the details section, no subtotal, summary, or grand total options will be available on the pull-down or pop-up menus. This is because subtotals, summaries, and grand totals are calculated in the While Printing Records pass. If the formula is already evaluating in that pass, you can't create a summary or grand total on it.

The one evaluation time function that may not be self-explanatory is EvaluateAfter. EvaluateAfter takes one argument: the name of another formula. This will force one formula to evaluate after another formula when they evaluate in the same pass and are in the same section of the report. Because Crystal Reports automatically evaluates formulas that contain other formulas in the proper order, you'll use this function very rarely. However, it may be necessary to use it with formulas that contain variables.

When Crystal Reports evaluates two formulas that contain the same variable in the same section of the report, it's not predictable as to what order it will evaluate them in. One example is if you place two formulas in a group footer. The first shows the values of the variables.

```
WhilePrintingRecords;

CurrencyVar BonusAmount;
StringVar HighestCustName;
DateTimeVar DateBonusReached;

"The highest order of " + ToText(BonusAmount) +
" was placed by " + HighestCustName + " on " +
ToText(DateBonusReached, "M/d/yy")
```

The second resets the variables to zero or empty to prepare for the next group.

```
WhilePrintingRecords;

CurrencyVar BonusAmount := 0;
StringVar HighestCustName := "";
DateTimeVar DateBonusReached := DateTime(0,0,0);
```

Because there's a chance that the formula that resets the variables will evaluate before the formula that shows them, you have two choices. First, and probably most logical, is to just move the formula that resets the variables to the group header. That way, the variables will be reset when a new group begins, after they have been displayed in the previous group footer. Or, if there is some logical reason that both formulas must exist in the group footer, you can use EvaluateAfter in the formula that resets the variables, as follows:

```
EvaluateAfter ({@Bonus Show});

CurrencyVar BonusAmount := 0;
StringVar HighestCustName := "";
DateTimeVar DateBonusReached := DateTime(0,0,0);
```

By placing EvaluateAfter as the first statement in the formula, you force the reset formula to evaluate after the display formula. Because you are forcing this formula to evaluate after a formula that's in the second pass, there's no need to include WhilePrintingRecords in this formula.

Tip *As you begin to add formulas that calculate and reset variables, you may find quite a few instances of things appearing in details and group header sections that show zeros or other unnecessary information. You can't delete the formulas from these sections, because then they won't evaluate properly. To hide them, just click Suppress on the Common tab of the Format Editor. You'll then see them on the Design tab, but not on the Preview tab or any other report output.*

When Not to Use Variables

It's fairly common to learn how to use certain "spiffy" features of a tool, and then to use them to excess! Variables have that potential. While they are fast and, if used judiciously, don't consume significant extra memory or resources, they can sometimes be "overkill." Look closely at your report if you find a use for variables. There may be an easier, quicker way to accomplish the same task.

Figure 5-5 is an example of a report that counts orders that exceed a $1,000 bonus level. Not only does the number of orders need to be shown at the group level, but at the end of the report, too.

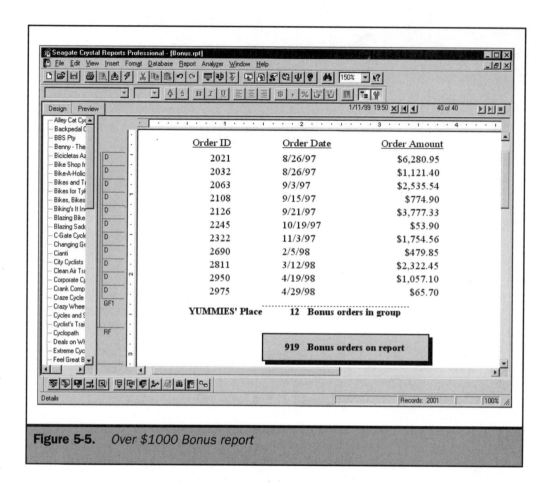

Figure 5-5. *Over $1000 Bonus report*

Using variables to accomplish this requires that several formulas be created. Two variables are also required: one to accumulate the bonus order count for each group, and one to count for the whole report. Here are the formulas.

@Bonus Calc is placed in the details section and suppressed:

```
WhilePrintingRecords;
NumberVar CountCustomer;
NumberVar CountReport;
If {Orders.Order Amount} > 1000 Then
    CountCustomer := CountCustomer + 1;
If {Orders.Order Amount} > 1000 Then
    CountReport := CountReport + 1
```

@Show Group Bonus is placed in the group footer:

```
WhilePrintingRecords;
NumberVar CountCustomer;
"This customer had " + ToText(CountCustomer,0) + " bonus orders."
```

@Reset Group Bonus is placed in the group header and suppressed:

```
WhilePrintingRecords;
NumberVar CountCustomer := 0;
```

@Show Report Bonus is placed in the report footer:

```
WhilePrintingRecords;
NumberVar CountReport;
"This report had " + ToText(CountReport,0) + " bonus orders."
```

While this will work, there is a much simpler way to accomplish the same task with just one formula using no variables. Create a single formula, place it in the details section, and suppress it. It will simply consist of:

```
If {Orders.Order Amount} > 1000 Then 1
```

When you place this in the details section, it will return a number constant of one when an order exceeds $1,000. If an order is under $1,000, the number formula will return zero (because the formula is numeric and there is no Else clause, it will return zero if the If test fails). You then need to simply insert a group subtotal and a report grand total on the formula to calculate group and report totals.

Voilà! The same result with much less effort. This simple technique of assigning a formula a value of 1 if a test is passed can become the cornerstone for a whole lot of statistics-type reports you may have to write.

You may also be able to save time by using running total fields instead of formulas with variables. The running total report earlier in the chapter that illustrates evaluation times is a perfect example. In this type of report, there's no need to create formulas to calculate the running total. Running total fields are covered later in this chapter.

Many of the types of formulas illustrated in this chapter are included in a report on the accompanying CD. Open FORMULAS.RPT to see how these, and similar formulas, are implemented.

User Function Libraries

Crystal Reports has been designed as an *"extensible"* reporting tool. As far as formulas are concerned, that means that you can develop your own functions to add to the

Function Tree box if Crystal Reports doesn't provide one you need. Look at the built-in functions that appear under the Additional Functions category.

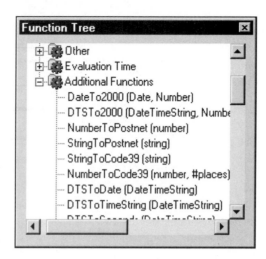

Every function in this category isn't really "built-in." These functions are being supplied to Crystal Reports by *User Function Libraries*, or UFLs for short. The UFL is supplied to Crystal Reports by an external Dynamic Link Library developed in another programming language. You can write your own custom functions using a Windows programming language, such as C++ or Visual Basic, and have them appear in this section of the Function Tree box. You could write, for example, a function that calculates the number of business days between two dates you supply, excluding any weekends and company holidays. You might write a function that converts a text string to proper case (that is uppercase letters at the beginning of the string and after every space, lowercase letters otherwise).

You can learn how to write your own UFLs in Visual Basic in Chapter 28.

Running Total Fields

Prior to Crystal Reports 7, you had to always use variables and multiple formulas to calculate "running totals." New to Version 7 is the *running total field*. A running total field can be inserted just like a database field. It gives you great flexibility to accumulate or increment values as the report progresses without the need for formulas or variables.

Figure 5-6 shows a Top *N* report (discussed in Chapter 3) that shows regional subtotals for the top five regions in the USA. This particular Top *N* report does not include "Others." As mentioned in Chapter 3, this causes the report grand totals not to agree with the sum of all the group totals. The grand totals are based on all report records, not just those that fall into the top five groups. Running total fields are the perfect answer to this problem.

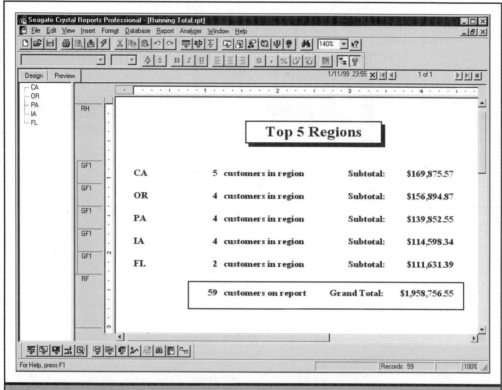

Figure 5-6. *Grand total problem with Top N report and no "Others" group*

All new running total fields are created from the Insert Fields dialog box. Just click the Running Total tab to begin. If you select Insert | Running Total Field from the pull-down menus, the Insert Fields dialog box will appear with the Running Total tab already selected. Click the New button to create a new running total field. The Create Running Total Field dialog box appears, as shown in Figure 5-7.

Start by giving the running total field a name. It can contain mixed case characters and spaces and won't conflict with formula or database field names. Crystal Reports will precede the running total field name with a pound sign (#).

Choose the report, database, or formula field that you want to use to calculate the running total by selecting the field in the fields list and clicking the right arrow next to the Field to Summarize box. Choose the type of calculation you want to use from the Type of Summary pull-down list. If you just want to increment the running total by one for certain records, use the Count or DistinctCount summaries (depending on how "unique" the field you are summarizing is), along with any field from the report that won't contain null values. Nulls don't increment counts.

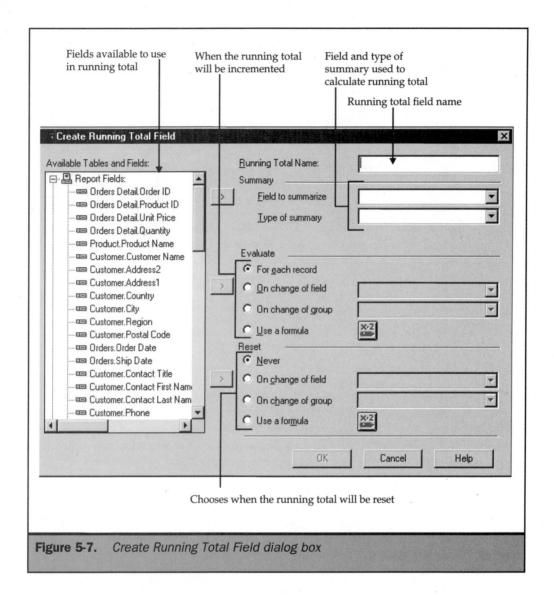

Fields available to use
in running total

When the running total
will be incremented

Field and type of
summary used to
calculate running total

Running total field name

Chooses when the running total will be reset

Figure 5-7.   *Create Running Total Field dialog box*

Choose when you want the running total to increment by making choices in the
Evaluate section. Choose when you want the running total to reset by making choices
in the Reset section. If you select a field in the Available Tables and Fields list and then
click the arrow next to the On Change of Field box, the running total will increment or

reset every time a new value appears in that field. If you click the On Change of Group radio button, you can then choose an existing report group in the pull-down list. The running total will increment or reset every time the chosen group changes. If you click the Use a Formula radio button, you can then click the Formula button next to it. The Formula Editor will appear, where you can enter a Boolean formula that will trigger when the running total field is incremented or reset.

Click OK when you've completed the Create Running Total Field dialog box. The running total will now appear in the Insert Fields dialog box and can be dragged and dropped on the report just like a database field. If you'd like to edit, rename, or delete the running total field, you have these choices on the Insert Fields dialog box. You can also right-click a running total field in the Design or Preview tabs and choose Edit Running Total from the pop-up menu.

To solve the problem with the Top *N* report without "Others," simply create two running total fields: one to calculate the number of customers

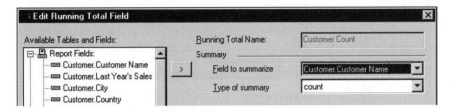

and one to calculate the sale grand total.

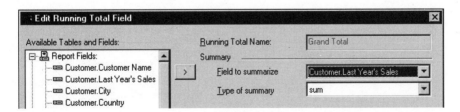

Place these running totals in the report footer instead of grand totaling the fields from the details section. As running totals only evaluate during the While Printing Records pass, the extra records in the "Others" group won't be included in the report footer. Figure 5-8 shows the correct totals now displayed on the Top *N* report.

Because running total fields are calculated in the While Printing Records pass of the report, you cannot create running total fields based on second pass formulas. For the same reason, you also can't base charts or maps on running total fields.

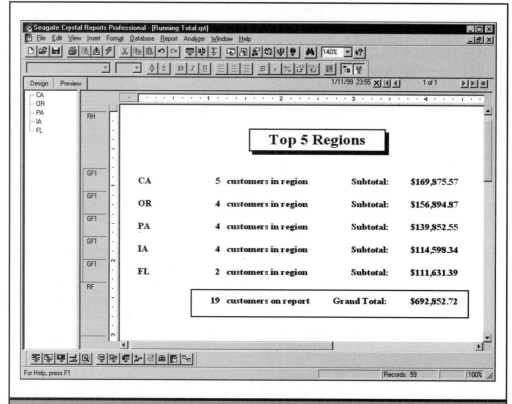

Figure 5-8. *Correct Top N report using running total fields*

The
Complete
Reference

Chapter 6

Analyzing with Advanced Selection Criteria

123

Creating a simple report is as quick as choosing tables, dragging and dropping fields on the report, and clicking the Preview button. However, if you only perform those few steps, you may have a much larger report show up than you bargained for! One important step missing from these is *record selection*. If you don't enter some sort of record-selection criteria, every record that exists in the tables you choose will appear on the report.

In the case of a small PC-type database with, say, 1000 records, this won't be terribly time or resource intensive. However, if you're connected to a large SQL database with potentially millions of records, the consequences of not including record selection will probably be felt on your network, and will certainly be felt on your desktop PC. Since Crystal Reports needs to store the data that makes up a report somewhere, you may run out of memory or temporary disk space in such a situation. Regardless of these concerns, your report will be terribly slow, and probably not very useful, if you have that many records on the report.

Virtually all reports will need some form of record selection criteria. You may want to limit the report to only USA customers, only subtotal orders placed in 1998, or only invoices that are more than 30 days past due. Record selection criteria can be used to limit your report to any of these sets of records. In any event, it's very wise to apply your record selection criteria early on in your report-design process—certainly *before* you preview or print the report!

The Select Expert

Crystal Reports includes the *Select Expert* to help you create useful record-selection criteria. You can use the Select Expert for simple, straightforward record selection, and as a starting point for more sophisticated record selection. The Select Expert can be run from within the Select tab on any of the report experts, or after you have chosen and linked tables using the Custom option. In either case, you'll want to make sure to use it before you preview the report.

To use the Select Expert while using one of the report experts, choose at least one table on the Data tab, and, if necessary, link the tables on the Links tab (table linking is covered in more detail in Chapter 14). You can then either progress through the other tabs until you reach the Select tab, or go to it directly. When you click the Select tab, the Select Expert will appear inside the report expert, as shown in Figure 6-1.

If you are using the Custom option to create a report, you must initially select and link tables. Once the Insert Fields dialog box appears, you can immediately run the Select Expert, or add fields to the report before running the Select Expert. Again, you'll want to run the Select Expert before you preview the report.

Run the Select Expert by clicking the Select Expert button in the Standard toolbar. You can also choose Report | Select Expert from the pull-down menus. If you have already added fields to the report and want to use one of them from the Design or Preview tabs for record selection, select the field on the report before you start the

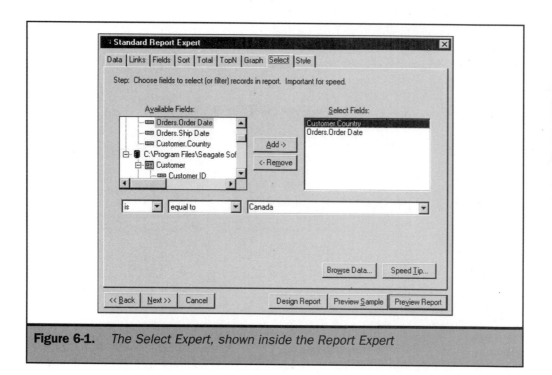

Figure 6-1.   *The Select Expert, shown inside the Report Expert*

Select Expert. You can also right-click your selected field and choose Select Expert from the pop-up menu. In each case, the Select Expert will start with a tab already created for the chosen field.

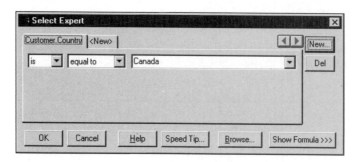

You may use this feature unintentionally. If you start the Select Expert and see a tab for a field that you don't want to select on, just click the Del button on the right side of the expert to delete the current tab. Then click the <New> tab or the New button to choose the correct field to select.

If this is the first time you've run the Select Expert, and you haven't chosen an existing report field, you'll see a Choose Field dialog box listing all report and database fields. You'll also see this dialog box if you are already displaying the Select Expert, and you click the <New> tab or New button to add additional criteria.

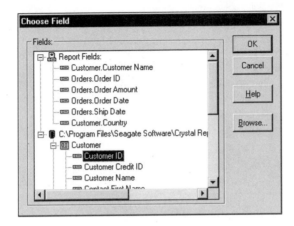

Click on the report or database field that you want your record selection to be based on. If you want to see sample data from the database for that field, click Browse. Once you're satisfied with the field you want to use for record selection, select it and click OK. The Select Expert will appear with a tab for that field.

Once you've chosen a field to select on, you'll see two additional pull-down lists with defaults of Is and Any Value. You will use these two lists to choose the comparison operation you want to use for your record selection. Initially, the first pull-down list will only contain the word Is. The second pull-down list will reveal all the comparisons you can use to select records. This second pull-down will vary, based on the type of field you have chosen for record selection. Table 6-1 explains the different operators that may appear in the second pull-down list.

Once you've chosen a comparison operator in the second pull-down list, the Select Expert will change, based on the selection you've made. If you've chosen an operator

Operator	Description
Any Value	This is the same as having no selection criteria at all. Is Any Value means it doesn't matter what's in the field—all records will be included in the report.
Equal To	The field must be exactly equal to what you specify.

Table 6-1. *Select Expert Comparison Operators*

Operator	Description
One Of	You can specify more than one item to compare to by adding multiple comparison items to a list. If the field is exactly equal to any of them, the record will be included.
Less Than	The field must be less than the item you're comparing to. If you are comparing numbers, the field must be smaller numerically. If you are comparing dates, the field must be an earlier date. If you're comparing strings, the field must be lower in the alphabet. If you check the Or Equal To check box, the field can be equal to or less than what you're comparing to.
Greater Than	The field must be greater than the item you're comparing to. If you are comparing numbers, the field must be larger numerically. If you're comparing dates, the field must be a later date. If you're comparing strings, the field must be higher in the alphabet. If you check the Or Equal To check box, the field can be equal to or greater than what you're comparing to.
Between	Allows you to select two items to create a comparison range. The field must be between, or equal to, the two items. The same type of comparison is used as with less than and greater than: numbers compare numerically, dates compare chronologically, and strings compare alphabetically.
Starting With	Allows you to specify "leading" characters to compare to. If the first characters in the field equal the specified characters, the record will be returned. If you want to perform several "starting with" comparisons, you can add multiple criteria to a list. This operator will only appear when you are using a string field.
Like	You can look for partial text matches using wildcard characters to search for records that contain particular characters or groups of characters. When you specify your comparisons, you can use a question mark to indicate that one character in the field at that position can contain anything. You can use an asterisk to indicate that the rest of the field from that point on can contain anything. If you want to perform several Like comparisons, you can add multiple criteria to a list. This operator will only appear when you are using a string field.

Table 6-1.   *Select Expert Comparison Operators* (continued)

Operator	Description
In the Period	Allows you to compare a date field to a group of built-in date ranges, such as the last week, last month, last quarter, current year, etc. This operator will only appear when you are using a date field.
True	Includes records where the field equates to true. This operator will appear only when you are using a Boolean field.
False	Includes records where the field equates to false. This operator will appear only when you are using a Boolean field.
Formula	Allows you to enter any Boolean formula using the Crystal Reports formula language. Similar to the Show Formula button in the lower right of the Select Expert.

Table 6-1.   *Select Expert Comparison Operators* (continued)

that only compares to one item (such as Equal To, Less Than, or Greater Than), one additional pull-down list will appear. If you've chosen an operator that can compare to multiple items (such as One Of, Like, or Starting With), a pull-down list will appear, along with a multiple-item box. You can add and remove items from the multiple-item box by clicking the Add and Delete buttons that appear next to the box.

The new pull-down list allows you to choose the item you want to compare the field to in two ways: typing it in directly or choosing it from the pull-down list. You can simply type the literal item you want to compare to directly in the pull-down list.

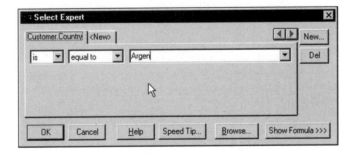

If you click the arrow on the pull-down list, the Select Expert will browse the database and list a few sample items from that database field. You may choose one of the items in the pull-down list for comparison.

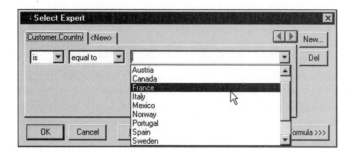

If the comparison operator you've chosen allows multiple entries, you can add an item you've typed to the multiple-item box by clicking the Add button. If you choose a browsed database item from the pull-down list, it will be added to the multiple-item box automatically. In either case, you can remove an item from the multiple-item box by selecting it and then clicking the Delete button.

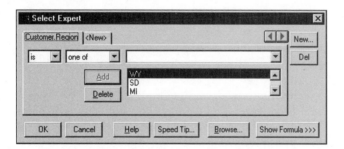

Once you've chosen any comparison operator other than Any Value (which you'll want to do right away—Any Value is the same as no selection at all), you can change the first pull-down list from Is to Is Not. This will, in essence, *reverse* the selection criteria you've chosen. If, for example, you chose a country field, an Equal To operator, and specified "USA" as the item to compare to, changing Is to Is Not will now include records for every country *except* the USA.

The Select Expert does not limit you to comparing just one field. Once you have added one database field, you can click the <New> tab or the New button. This will redisplay the Choose Field dialog box where you can pick another field to compare to. Once you pick this field, a new tab will display in the Select Expert where you can create another comparison. You may create as many tabs and comparisons as you need.

Crystal Reports applies a logical "and" to all the tabs in the Select Expert—they all have to be true for a record to be selected. If you would rather have a logical "or" applied to some or all of the tabs (so if any one of them is true, but not all of them, a record is returned), you must manually edit the selection formula created by the Select Expert. This is discussed later in this chapter in "Manipulating the Record-Selection Formula Directly."

Refreshing the Report Versus Using Saved Data

When you preview a report on the screen for the first time, Crystal Reports has to actually read the database and perform record selection, and only thereafter can it format and display the report. To enhance future performance while you work with the report, Crystal Reports creates a set of *saved data*. This saved data is the records that were retrieved from the database, and they are kept either in memory or in temporary files on your hard drive. If you perform simple formatting changes, move fields around, or make other minor modifications that won't require the database to be re-queried, Crystal Reports will use the saved data every time you preview the modified report, thus improving performance. If you add new fields to the report, Crystal Reports knows it has to re-query the database and does so without prompting. You may notice a bit of a wait while it runs the new query.

But, when you change record selection criteria, Crystal Reports doesn't know whether or not it needs to re-query the database. You will be given the option to Refresh or Use Saved Data. The choice you make is dependent upon whether you widened or narrowed the selection criteria. If you *narrowed* your selection criteria so that the new selection criteria can be completely satisfied with the existing saved data, you can choose to use the saved data. Since the database doesn't have to be re-queried, the changes will appear very quickly in the Preview tab.

If, however, you *widened* the selection criteria so that the saved data won't contain all the records you're specifying, you need to refresh the report so that the database can be re-queried. Choosing to use saved data in this situation will result in your report showing too few (if any) records, even though they actually exist in the database. However, the re-query will take time to perform. If you make the wrong choice and end up with too few, or no, records, you can refresh the report manually by clicking the Refresh button in the Standard toolbar, pressing the F5 key, or choosing Report | Refresh Report Data from the pull-down menus.

When you save a report, you have the option to store the saved data in the .RPT file. If you include the saved data, the report will immediately display the Preview tab showing the saved data the next time you open the .RPT file—no database re-query will be required. However, this will also make the .RPT file larger (sometimes significantly so), since it has to keep the saved data along with the report design.

Even if you open a report with saved data, the saved data will be discarded and only the Design tab will appear if the Discard Saved Data When Loading Reports option is checked on the Reporting tab of File | Options.

To choose whether or not to save data, check or uncheck File | Save Data with Report from the pull-down menus, and then re-save the report after making your choice. You can also make the choice with the appropriate check box on File | Report Options. If you wish to set default behavior for this for all new reports in the future, turn on or off the Save Data with Report option on the Reporting tab of File | Options.

Record Selection with Date Fields

Many reporting requirements can be satisfied by creatively using date fields in record selection. Crystal Reports provides a good selection of built-in date ranges you can use to compare to, or you can use other operators to compare date fields. When you choose a date field in the Choose Field dialog box, the Select Expert makes the In the Period comparison operator available. If you choose this operator, another pull-down list containing Crystal Reports built-in date ranges appears.

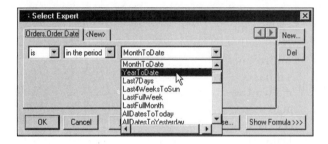

By using these built-in ranges, you can create a report that will return, say, only orders in the previous month by comparing to the LastFullMonth. What's particularly appealing about using built-in date range functions is the "self-maintenance" of the report. When you use the LastFullMonth range, for example, the report will always include orders from the previous month, no matter when the report is run. You don't have to manually change the date range every month.

There may be times, however, when you have to manually enter a date range for record selection. If, for example, you want to see all orders for 1995, you'll need to specify those dates manually. There is no built-in *X* Years Ago date range. In this case, you will choose the date field you want to select on (for example, Order Date), and use a Between comparison operator to indicate orders between January 1, 1995 and December 31, 1995. You'll need to enter the dates using the proper Crystal Reports formula syntax, which is Date(yyyy,mm,dd). Simply entering "1/1/95" and "12/31/95" in the Between pull-down lists will result in an error when you click OK.

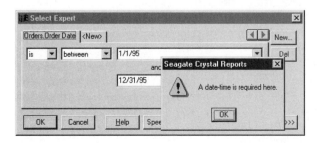

To correct this problem, enter a beginning date of Date(1995, 1, 1) and an ending date of Date(1995, 12, 31).

If you're selecting on a Date/Time field, supplying just a date will work fine. However, the Select Expert will not be able to interpret the Date function sufficiently to remember the comparison operator. The next time you open the Select Expert, it will have replaced the operator for the date field with a formula including the Date function.

Manipulating the Record-Selection Formula Directly

When you create record-selection criteria with the Select Expert, it actually creates a formula using the Crystal Reports formula language behind the scenes. For most simple record-selection criteria, you won't have to worry about manipulating this formula directly. Also, by using the Select Expert directly and not manipulating the actual formula that it creates, you will often maximize performance, particularly when using SQL databases.

However, there are times when the Select Expert itself won't provide enough flexibility for the record selection you need to accomplish. Consider the following two scenarios:

■ You have two fields on their own tabs included in the Select Expert: Region Is Equal To CA, and Order Amount Is Greater Than 2500.

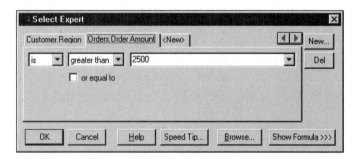

Since the Select Expert performs a logical And between the tabs, what do you do if you want to see all orders from California, regardless of the order amount, as well as orders from any other state over $2,500?

■ You are using a PC-style database, such as Microsoft Access or Btrieve. You wish to select on a country field, where the countries are fully spelled out. You select the following in the Select Expert:

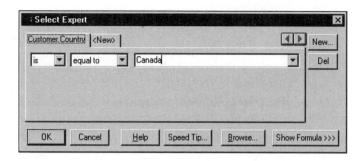

What happens if the data in the database can potentially be stored in various forms of upper- and lowercase letters. For example, records may exist with a country of "CANADA," "canada," or "Canada." Will they all be included on the report?

In either case, the Select Expert doesn't provide sufficient flexibility to create these types of special record selections. You must use a *record-selection formula*. The Select Expert creates a record-selection formula automatically as you add tabs and selection criteria. You can modify the formula it creates in one of two ways: by clicking the Show Formula button on the Select Expert itself, or by choosing Report | Edit Selection Formula | Record from the pull-down menus.

If you know you'll need extra features that the Select Expert doesn't provide, you can skip it entirely and create your record-selection formula right in the Formula Editor. Choose Report | Edit Selection Formula | Record from the pull-down menus to create the formula this way.

In the first scenario previously mentioned, you need to change the relationship that exists between the two criteria from an And to an Or. This is a simple process that you can apply right from the Select Expert or using the Formula Editor. To use the Select Expert, simply click the Show Formula button.

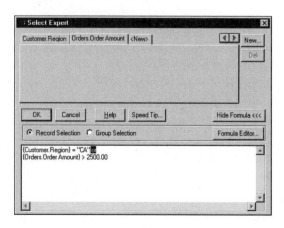

You can now modify the formula created by the Select Expert to show you all California orders, regardless of amount, and other orders over $2,500. Notice that the Select Expert has placed the And operator between the two parts of the selection formula. Simply position the cursor in the formula and change the And to Or, and then click OK.

If you click Show Formula in the Select Expert and then decide you want to use the full-featured Formula Editor, just click the Formula Editor button in the expanded Select Expert dialog box. The formula will be transferred to the Formula Editor where you can modify or enhance it.

In the upper- and lowercase scenario, you are faced with an initial question: Is record selection in Crystal Reports *case sensitive*? Does it matter in what case the fields are stored in the database? In the case of a PC-style database (such as the Microsoft Access or Btrieve examples listed in this scenario), the answer is a resounding *Yes*! If the database contains various cases, your record selection will need to accommodate that or all the records you expect to be retrieved for the report won't be.

Since you will ultimately be using the Crystal Reports formula language for your record selection, most of the features of the language are available for record selection. In this situation, it may be preferable to edit the selection formula in the Formula Editor so that you can see and use all the built-in functionality. The formula that the Select Expert created will appear when you choose Report | Edit Selection Formula | Record from the pull-down menus.

You can modify this formula to your heart's content, provided that the ultimate finished formula is a Boolean formula—it will ultimately just return true or false (refer to Chapter 5 for more information on Boolean formulas). The formula will be evaluated for each record in the database. If the formula evaluates to true, the record will be included in the report; otherwise the record will be ignored.

The case sensitivity issue can be resolved by using a built-in function to automatically convert the database field to uppercase before it's compared. By comparing this converted field to an all uppercase literal, you solve the case-sensitivity problem. Here's the modified selection formula shown in the Formula Editor:

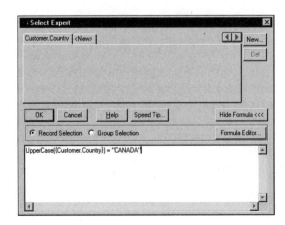

Case Sensitivity with SQL Databases

Case sensitivity can vary when using SQL databases or PC databases via ODBC. You may prefer that Crystal Reports not consider case sensitivity when performing record selection with a SQL or ODBC database. Although this is the default behavior "out of the box," be sure to check Case-Insensitive SQL Data on File | Report Options to affect the current report, or the same option on the Database tab of File | Options to set the default for all new reports you create in the future.

Even if this option is checked, some databases and ODBC drivers may not support case insensitivity with Crystal Reports. It's best to run a test with your own database to make sure you're retrieving all desired records with your record selection.

Tip *If you modify the formula the Select Expert created, or create your own, running the Select Expert again is fine. However, if the Select Expert is unable to fully interpret the formula you created, you'll see slightly different behavior for one or more tabs. You may see a tab with a field set to Is Formula and part of the selection formula showing in the third list box. You may also see a message indicating that the formula uses a "composite expression" and prompting you to edit the formula directly.*

Limiting Data with a Group-Selection Formula

When you use the Select Expert or create a record-selection formula with the Formula Editor, you affect the way Crystal Reports initially selects data from the database. Record selection occurs during the first pass, before data has been sorted or grouped. Because of this, you can't use record selection to limit your report, say, to groups where the total sales exceeds $100,000—the record selection occurs before these totals are calculated. (See Chapter 5 for a discussion of report passes.)

You may also want to use an existing report formula in record selection. However, if you use WhilePrintingRecords or a summary function to push the formula to the second pass, the formula won't show up in the Field Tree box when you create a record-selection formula. Again, the record selection occurs during the first pass, and second-pass formulas can't be used.

If you want to limit the report based on group subtotals or summaries, or somehow limit the report using second-pass formulas, you must use a *group-selection formula* instead of a record-selection formula. Create a group-selection formula from the Select Expert by clicking the Show Formula button and then clicking the Group Selection radio button (trying to select a group summary field directly from the Choose Field dialog box without clicking Show Formula and selecting Group Selection won't work). You can also select Report | Edit Selection Formula | Group from the pull-down menus. You can now create a Boolean formula to limit records using group summaries or second-pass formulas.

One word of caution: group selection occurs *after* the group tree, subtotals, and grand totals have been calculated. This can lead to apparent inaccuracies on your report. Look at the report shown in Figure 6-2.

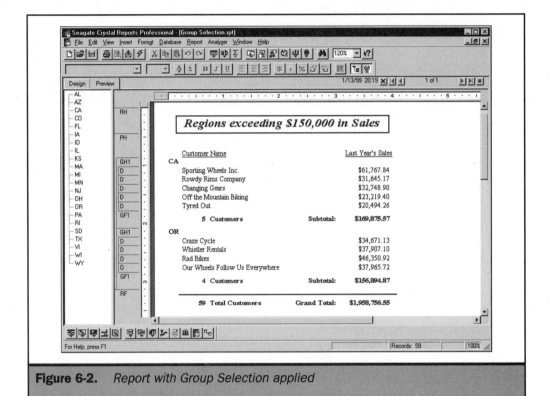

Figure 6-2. Report with Group Selection applied

You'll notice that the group tree shows many more regions than actually appear on the report. And, it doesn't take a math degree to see that the grand total doesn't quite add up.

This report applies a group-selection formula to limit the report to groups where the sum of Last Year's Sales exceeds $150,000. This group selection is applied after the group tree and grand totals have been created. Although there is no way to change the group tree in this situation, you can correct the totaling problem by using running totals instead of grand totals. Look at Chapter 5 for information on running total fields.

Performance Considerations with Record Selection

In many cases, record selection is the most time-consuming portion of the report process, particularly with larger databases. If you're using a PC-style database located on a local or network hard drive, Crystal Reports performs the record selection itself, reading every record in the database and only keeping those that match.

In this situation, performance considerations dictate using *indexed fields* for your record selection if at all possible. Indexed fields are fields that are specially designated when the database is designed. The field's index stores all the values in the field in a presorted state that makes it much faster to select records based on the field. To determine if a field is indexed, you may wish to consult the database designer.

You can also see which fields are indexed by using the Visual Linking Expert. Click the Visual Linking Expert button on the Supplementary toolbar, or choose Database | Visual Link Expert from the pull-down menus.

With PC-style databases, fields with a "tent" character are indexed.

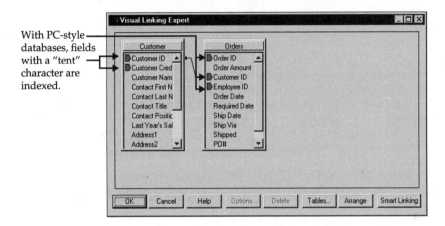

You'll notice a small "tent" character appearing next to every indexed field (the different colors you may see are generally insignificant to record selection, as long as you select on a field with the symbol). Make note of the indexed fields and attempt to use them in record selection. If the field you need to select on is not indexed, and record selection appears very sluggish, you may wish to consult the database designer about adding an index for that field.

Finally, double-check the setting of the Use Indexes or Server for Speed option. To check the option for the current report, look in the File | Report Options dialog box. If you wish to check the option for all new reports in the future, look for the option on the Database tab of File | Options. If this is turned off, Crystal Reports won't make use of field indexes at all.

Crystal Reports behaves a little differently when basing record selection on Date or Date/Time fields with PC-style databases. In these situations, you must ensure that Use Indexes or Server for Speed is turned off if the Date or Date/Time field is indexed. Otherwise, the report will actually perform more slowly and potentially not even include the correct set of records. This is not a consideration with SQL or ODBC database access.

SQL databases (or PC-style databases accessed via ODBC) present a different set of performance considerations. As a general reporting rule, you want to always have the SQL Server perform the record selection if at all possible. This can typically be accomplished by only using the Select Expert to create selection criteria—using the Formula Editor makes it entirely too easy to introduce functions that Crystal Reports can't move to the SQL Server. And, making changes to what the Select Expert creates with an Is Formula operator or the Show Formula button may also seriously degrade SQL Server record-selection performance. As with PC-style databases, make sure the Use Indexes or Server for Speed option is turned on in File | Report Options.

More in-depth discussion and examples of performance issues, including record selection, are found in Chapter 14.

Chapter 7

Making Your Reports Visually Appealing

Crystal Reports, as a Windows-based report writer, has many features that help you create eye-catching, visually effective reports. You can often use Crystal Reports to create reports right from the database that you formerly had to use a word processor or page publishing program for. The next time you're tempted to export database records to a text file and merge them in a word processing or page publishing document, come back and have a look at this chapter!

Chapter 4 discusses geographic maps. Chapter 10 discusses graphs and charts. But, even using just the textual elements of Crystal Reports can be very creative. Not only can you use any font installed on the "target" computer in your reports, you can set object foreground and background colors, choose unique borders on all four sides of objects, add drop shadows, and use other graphical features. You can include bitmap pictures on your report, either directly from the database (if the database contains BLOB fields) or added right into a report section. And, you can draw lines and boxes around the report to highlight important portions.

One of the first features of Crystal Reports that you'll want to make use of is *conditional reporting*. Conditional reporting lets you change the appearance of objects based on their contents or the contents of other fields, objects, or formulas. Some immediate uses of conditional reporting that may come to mind are:

- Showing sales figures in red if they fall below a predefined level
- Adding a border around an invoice number if it's past due
- Showing a report title that's different on the first page than the rest of the pages
- Graphically indicating with file-folder icons whether a case file has been opened or closed

The Highlighting Expert

The *Highlighting Expert* is a new feature of Crystal Reports 7. It lets you change the appearance of number and currency fields based on their contents. If a sales figure falls below a preset goal for the department, you can have it stand out with a white font color on a red background. Or, you can change the border on a Days Overdue formula that exceeds, say, 60 days.

To highlight a number or currency field, select the field you want to change. Start the Highlighting Expert by clicking the Highlighting button on the Format bar, choosing Format I Highlighting Expert from the pull-down menus, or right-clicking the object and choosing Highlighting Expert from the pop-up menu. Figure 7-1 shows the Highlighting Expert.

The key to using the Highlighting Expert is the conditions you declare for the field's contents. Begin by choosing a comparison operator in the Value Is pull-down list. You'll find most of the standard comparison operators you've used in formulas or in the Select Expert, such as Less Than, Greater Than, Equal To, Not Equal To, and so forth. Then, enter a constant number to compare to in the text box below (you can also

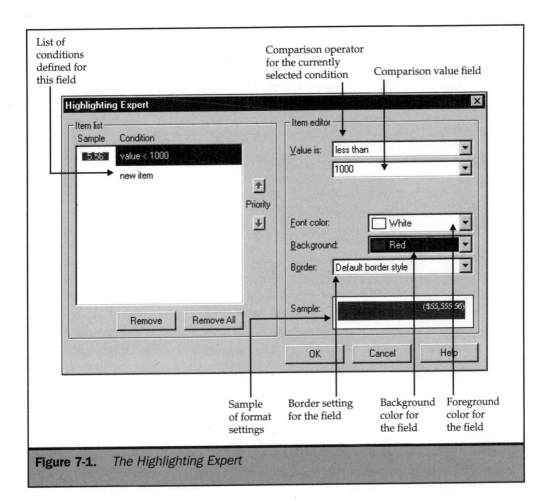

List of
conditions
defined for
this field

Comparison operator
for the currently
selected condition

Comparison value field

Sample
of format
settings

Border setting
for the field

Background
color for
the field

Foreground
color for
the field

Figure 7-1.   *The Highlighting Expert*

click the pull-down arrow and choose a value from the sample data in the list). Finally, choose any combination of font and background colors and border styles you want the field to have if the comparison is true.

To format the sales figure to show up as white text on a red background if it falls below the preset sales figure of $1,000, choose a comparison of "Less Than," type in the number 1000, and then choose a Font Color of White and a Background Color of Red. You will see a sample in the Sample box in the lower right of the Highlighting Expert, as well as to the left of the now-created condition in the Item List box on the left. When you click OK, the field will show white text on a red background for any sales figures less than $1,000.

You may want to set up multiple conditions if you want more than one formatting option displayed. To expand on the previous example, suppose you want to show bonus sales (over $5,000) in blue, in addition to the existing red background for those that fall below $1,000. Just click "New Item" in the Item List box. You can enter a new condition and another set of formatting options. Both will apply to the field.

You may have two conditions that conflict with each other. For example you could have a condition that formats field contents over $1,000 in red, and another that applies blue formatting for contents over $5,000. Since both conditions would satisfy the over-1000 condition, will everything over $1,000 (including anything over $5,000) be in red? It depends on the *priority* you assign the conditions. If the over-1000 condition is higher in the Item List box, everything over $1,000 will be in red. However, if the over-5000 condition is set higher, then it has priority—everything over $5,000 will be in blue. Then, the second item in the list (the over-1000 item) will be tested, placing anything over $1,000 in red. To change priority, click the condition you want to move and click the up or down Priority arrows.

Conditional Formatting Formulas

The Highlighting Expert is a "quick and dirty" way to format fields, because you don't have to know the formula language to use it. However, the tradeoff is in flexibility. As your reports become more sophisticated, there will be times when the Highlighting Expert won't provide all the flexibility you need. You may need to conditionally format fields other than number or currency fields. You may want to apply formatting other than just color and borders. For these situations, you need to use *conditional formatting*. Conditional formatting uses the Formula Editor to create one or more conditional formatting formulas that determine how the object appears.

Absolute Versus Conditional Formatting

Before you learn how to set formatting conditionally, it's important to have a fundamental grasp of *absolute formatting*. Absolute formatting is simply applying normal formatting to objects with the Format Editor. If you choose an object, right-click, and choose Change Font from the pop-up menu, the Format Editor will appear with the Font tab selected. If you change the color of the font to Red, *all* occurrences of the object on the report will be red. If you click the Border tab and check the Drop Shadow check box, *all* occurrences of the object will have a drop shadow. This is the process of absolute formatting.

As you approach conditional formatting, it's important to distinguish between two types of formatting properties: *multiple-choice* properties and *on-off* properties. On the Font tab, Color is a good example of a multiple-choice property. You can click a drop-down list and choose from any one of several colors. However, if you look at Drop Shadow on the Border tab, you'll just notice a check box: it can only be turned on or off. Whether a formatting property is multiple choice or on-off determines the type of formula you'll use to set it conditionally. Multiple choice properties are conditionally formatted with If-Then-Else formulas, while on-off properties are conditionally formatted with Boolean formulas.

Tip

You will need to be familiar with the Crystal Reports formula language to use conditional formatting effectively. To refresh your memory, look for information on If-Then-Else and Boolean formulas in Chapter 5.

To set formatting conditionally, click the Conditional Formula button that appears on the Format Editor next to the property that you want to format.

This will display the *Format Formula Editor* (essentially the same Formula Editor discussed in Chapter 5, but with a new title), shown in Figure 7-2. If you are formatting a multiple-choice property, you'll notice that all the available options for the property appear at the top of the Function Tree box. If, for example, you're conditionally formatting the Color property, you'll see all the available colors listed. If you're formatting a border, you'll see the different available line styles.

Use an If-Then-Else formula to determine the formatting of the object. Your formula can be as simple or complex as you need. For example, you may have a formula to set font color as simple as:

```
If {Customer.Last Year's Sales} > {@Bonus Level} Then Blue Else Black
```

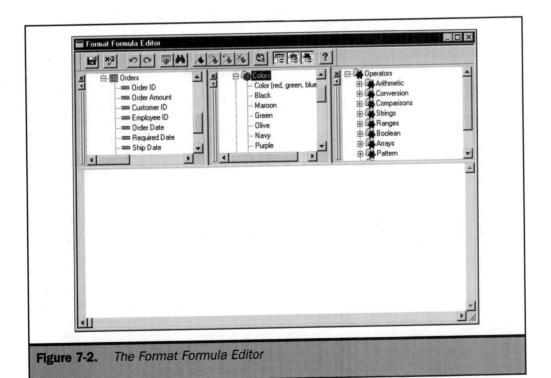

Figure 7-2. *The Format Formula Editor*

or a formula to set a bottom border as complex as:

```
If {Orders.Order Amount} > 5000 And {Orders.Ship Via} = "Fedex" Then
    DoubleLine
Else
    If {Orders.Order Amount} > 1000 And {@Ship Days} < 3 Then
        SingleLine
    Else
        NoLine
```

You can use any type of simple or compound If-Then-Else formula, as long as the results of every Then and Else are one of the available formatting properties in the Function Tree box.

When you are finished with the formula, you can use the Check button to check the syntax of the formula, or save the formula and close the Format Formula Editor with the Save button. The Format Editor will remain on the screen. Notice that the Conditional Formula button will change from blue to maroon, and the pencil character inside the button points at a different angle. This indicates that a conditional formula is set for this property.

To change the existing formula, click the Conditional Formula button again, and change the formula that appears in the Format Formula Editor. To delete conditional formatting and return to absolute formatting (or none at all), just highlight and delete the whole conditional formula. Then, click the Save button. You'll notice that the Conditional Formula button has returned to a blue color with the pencil pointed in its original direction.

If you're formatting an on-off property, the general procedure for conditional formatting is the same, but when you click the Conditional Formula button next to the property you won't see any additional functions in the Function Tree box of the Format Formula Editor. This is because you can't use an If-Then-Else formula to format this property. As the property can only have two states, on or off, you must format it with a Boolean formula that can return only one of two results: true or false.

To add a drop shadow to Customer Names who have last year's sales greater than $100,000, start by right-clicking on the Customer Name field. Choose Change Border from the pop-up menu, and click the Conditional Formula button next to the Drop Shadow property. When the Format Formula Editor appears, type in the following Boolean formula:

```
{Customer.Last Year's Sales} > 100000
```

The Boolean formula will evaluate to only one of two states: true or false. If the formula returns true, the formatting property will be turned on and the field will have a drop shadow around it. If the formula returns false, the property will be turned off and the field won't have a drop shadow.

You may be curious about how conditional formatting and absolute formatting interrelate. Consider the following scenario: You choose an absolute color of Red on the Font tab of the Format Editor and click OK. Of course, every occurrence of the field will be red. You then return to the Format Editor and, without changing the absolute formatting, click the Conditional Formula button next to the Color property and add the following formula:

```
If {Customer.Last Year's Sales} > 50000 Then Blue
```

Note the missing Else clause. Remember that Crystal Reports does *not* require an Else clause in an If-Then-Else formula. In a regular formula, if the If test fails and there's no Else clause, the formula returns a null value. But, what color will the font take on if there's no Else clause and absolute formatting is set to Blue?

Contrary to what might seem logical, when the If test fails in this case, the font will show up in black type, despite the absolute formatting of Blue. This is by design—if conditional formatting is applied, then absolute formatting is ignored! If the conditional formula fails (and there's no condition to "catch" the failure, like an Else clause), the Windows default color or format for that type of object will be used. Be careful with this if you don't use Else clauses, especially if you're formatting background colors. A font color of black isn't necessarily problematic, but a background color of black will often cause your report to look like someone plastered electrical tape all over it!

The exception to this rule, and a way to combine absolute and conditional formatting together, is to use the DefaultAttribute function. You'll notice this in the Function Tree box in the Format Formula Editor. If you use this with the Then or Else clause, the formula will use the setting from the absolute formatting property. Hence,

```
If {Customer.Last Year's Sales} > 50000 Then Blue Else DefaultAttribute
```

will show sales figures over $50,000 in blue and others in red. If you change the absolute color, then figures over $50,000 will still show up in blue, but the rest will take on whatever color you specified as absolute.

Note *If you've applied conditional formatting to a field that's also being formatted with the Highlighting Expert, the Highlighting Expert will take precedence. Only if it doesn't change the formatting of a field will conditional formatting be visible.*

Creative Use of the Suppress Property

If you search through the Format Editor, you'll notice that most (but not all) formatting properties can be set conditionally. One of the most flexible is the Suppress property on the Common tab. You may consider that absolutely setting the Suppress property is of limited usefulness. (Why even bother putting the object on the report if you're just going to suppress it?) There are some good reasons; for example, a formula that sets a variable to zero in a group header has to be in the header to work properly, but you don't want zeros showing up in every group.

But there are many more situations where *conditionally suppressing* an object can be useful. Here are some examples, and the corresponding Boolean formulas you will apply to the Suppress property.

- **Placing the word "continued" in a repeated group header**   In Chapter 3, the repeated group header was introduced. If you check this option in the Group Options dialog box, a group header section will repeat at the top of a page if a group continues from the previous page. It adds readability to your report if you can indicate that this group continues from the previous page.

  Place a text object that contains the word "continued," or something similar, in the group header close to the Group Name field. You must now suppress it if it is *not* in a repeated group header. Conditionally suppress the text object with the Boolean formula:

  ```
  Not InRepeatedGroupHeader
  ```

> **Note**   *When you conditionally suppress an object, you'll be using a Boolean formula, and when your formula returns true, the object will be* suppressed, *not shown. So you may have to think "backwards" when conditionally suppressing.*

- **Showing a bonus message only for certain records**   You may wish a report to indicate that a certain record (for example, a certain order or a certain sales person) has exceeded a pre-defined goal amount. Simply create a text object something like "Congratulations! You've exceeded the sales goal." Again, you have to think about when you *don't* want the text object to appear, not when you do. Assuming a $10,000 sales goal, conditionally suppress the text object with the following Boolean formula:

  ```
  {AccountRep.Sales} <= 10000
  ```

- **Showing a different heading on page 2 and later**   You may want to have a larger report title, perhaps including the company logo and a large font, on page 1 of the report. However, every other page needs to contain a smaller title without the logo, and perhaps include the word "continued." If you put the large title in the report header, you'll only see it at the beginning of the report. But putting the smaller title in the page header will result in it showing up on every page, including page 1.

  Create the text object that contains the smaller title and place it in the page header along with any column headings or other objects you want to appear on every page. But, conditionally suppress the text object containing the title with the following Boolean formula (PageNumber is a built-in function that returns the current page number):

  ```
  PageNumber = 1
  ```

You can also create formulas that provide roughly the same functionality of these examples. However, to minimize potential "formula clutter," it sometimes may be preferable to just create text objects and conditionally suppress them.

Special Fonts, Graphics, and Line Drawing

As mentioned at the beginning of the chapter, Crystal Reports is a true Windows report writer. This means that it can make use of most of the fonts and graphical capabilities of Windows.

Using Special Fonts

Don't hesitate to make use of symbol fonts that are installed on your computer. In particular, the Symbol and Wingdings symbol fonts are included as part of Windows and should be available to most "target" systems that will be running your report.

Don't forget that any fonts you use when designing your reports must also be present on the machine that runs your reports if you expect the report to look identical on both machines. You can be pretty safe using Times Roman, Helvetica, Symbol, and Wingdings fonts at a minimum, as they are installed by default on all Windows systems.

Both Symbol and Wingdings fonts contain typographical symbols instead of letters and numbers. Although you type letters and numbers into a text object or formula formatted with a text font initially, you'll see them replaced with the symbol characters once you change the font from a text font to one of the symbol fonts. You'll either need a font table (typically available from Windows Control Panel) or a little extra time to experiment and figure out what symbols display when you type certain letters, numbers, or special characters.

Figure 7-3 shows a report using the Wingdings font. In this example, the following formula is being displayed on the report next to the order amount, formatted using the Wingdings font:

```
If {Orders.Order Amount} < 1000 Then
    "L"
Else
    If {Orders.Order Amount} > 1000 And {Orders.Order Amount} < 2500 Then
    "K"
Else
    "J"
```

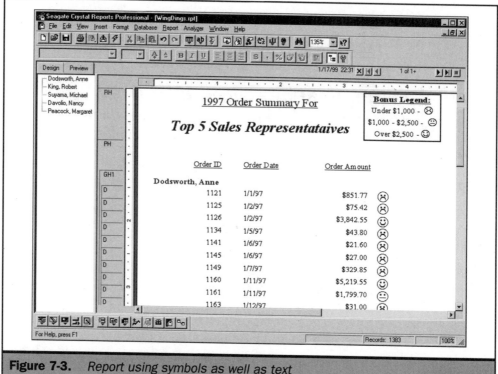

Figure 7-3.   Report using symbols as well as text

Crystal Reports includes built-in functions to convert text into barcodes appropriate for common barcode scanners and United States Postal Service address coding. Figure 7-4 shows product labels from the Product table in the XTREME.MDB sample database included with Crystal Reports. The Product ID field has been converted to barcode text using the following formula and then formatted with an appropriate barcode font:

```
StringToCode39 (ToText({Product.Product ID},0))
```

If you are using a version of Crystal Reports earlier than 7.0, or you upgraded from an earlier version, you may have barcode fonts that are included with earlier versions already installed on your computer. Check the list of fonts in the Format Editor to see if they are available. If you are just using version 7.0, there is a "crippled" barcode font package in the \UFL\UF5BCODE folder on the program CD.

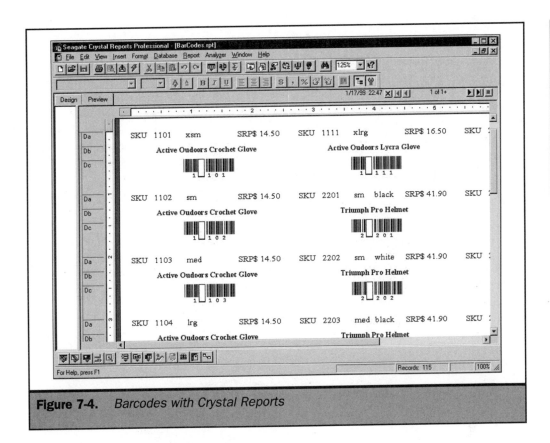

Figure 7-4. *Barcodes with Crystal Reports*

Using Bitmap Graphics

If you are planning on creating reports that approach the quality of output from page publishing programs, you'll soon have a need to use *bitmap graphics* in your reports. Bitmap graphics are common graphics files most often associated with the World Wide Web (such as .JPG files) or Windows paint program files (such as .BMP and .PCX files). You may have a company logo that you want included on the title page of the report. Or, you may want to add a smaller graphical element, like an icon, to another section of the report.

To insert a bitmap graphic, first make sure you are displaying the Design tab. Adding a graphic while viewing the Preview tab is risky, as you won't always be sure which report section the graphic will end up in. Click the Insert Picture button on the Supplementary toolbar, or choose Insert | Picture from the pull-down menus. A familiar "file open" dialog box will appear asking you to choose a bitmap format file. Navigate to the necessary drive and folder, and the dialog box will show any files at that location that can be added to the report. Choose the correct file and click OK.

An outline will appear alongside your mouse cursor. Drag the outline to the section of the report where you want the graphic to be placed, and click the left mouse button to drop it there. If the graphic happens to cover more than one report section, it will be dropped in the section where the upper-left corner of the outline is when the mouse is clicked. Once you drop the graphic, you'll see it appear in the Design tab.

You have complete control over how the graphic is sized and cropped. You can simply drag the graphic to a new location on the report, or resize it using the sizing handles on the sides and corners. You can also position the graphic (or any other object on the report, for that matter) with the Object Size and Position dialog box. Select the object that you want to position, right-click, and choose Object Size and Position from the pop-up menu. You can also choose Format | Object Size and Position from the pull-down menus.

To format the graphic more precisely, you can use the Format Editor. Make sure the graphic is still selected. Then click the Properties button in the Supplementary toolbar, right-click the graphic and choose "Format Graphic" from the pop-up menu, or choose Format | Format Graphic from the pull-down menus. The Picture tab, shown here, allows you to specify exact cropping and scaling specifications:

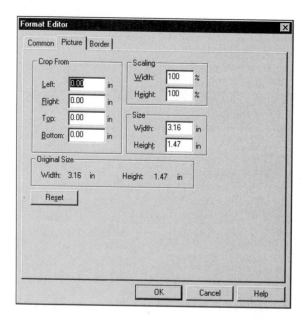

| Caution | *Only common bitmap graphic formats are supported in Crystal Reports. It will not recognize specialized formats (such as Adobe Photoshop) or any vector formats, such as those from CorelDRAW or Adobe Illustrator. If you wish to use these graphics in a report, you'll need to convert them to common bitmap formats with another program before adding them to your report.* |

Although using symbol fonts, such as Wingdings, is very powerful, you are limited to what is included in the font itself. Also, the symbols are generally simple two-dimensional images and can only be displayed in one color. Wouldn't it be nice if you could use smaller bitmap files, such as icon-like graphics that look more three-dimensional and include several colors, on your report?

Because you can suppress bitmap files conditionally, just like other objects, you have real power and flexibility in creating visually appealing and interesting reports using bitmap graphics. Figure 7-5 shows a report with unique icons indicating the status of an order. Orders that have been shipped (or are "closed") have a closed file folder next to them. Open orders (not shipped) have an open file folder next to them.

This report uses a technique that might be called *mutually exclusive suppression*. There are two different bitmap files on the report: an open-file bitmap and a closed-file bitmap. They are placed right on top of each other in the details section. They are conditionally suppressed in such a way that only one will ever be displayed at a time. In this case, they are suppressed using the Shipped field (a Boolean field) from the XTREME.MDB Orders table.

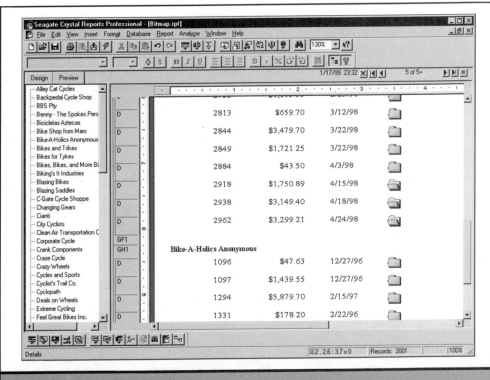

Figure 7-5.   *Using bitmap files*

The open-file bitmap is conditionally suppressed using the formula:

```
{Orders.Shipped}
```

while the closed-file bitmap is conditionally suppressed using the formula:

```
Not {Orders.Shipped}
```

Because of this, only one will ever be visible at a time.

The success of this technique depends on Crystal Reports allowing multiple objects to be placed right on top of each other. You have the ability to do this with any text or graphic object whenever and wherever you choose. Just make sure you implement some technique similar to this to prevent them from just splattering all over each other. You can also use the Move to Back, Move Backward, Move Forward, and Move to Front options from the Format pull-down menu or by right-clicking an object and choosing those options from the pop-up menu. These options will determine which objects have "priority" when they are placed on top of each other.

Line and Box Drawing

You can use the Border tab on the Format Editor to control lines on all four sides of individual objects. While this lets the individual objects stand out by having lines or boxes appear around them, you may want more flexibility to have groups of objects be highlighted with boxes or to have lines stretch partially or completely across sections.

Crystal Reports lets you use line and box drawing tools to create these boxes and lines. To create a line or box, ensure that you have the Design tab chosen. Inserting lines or boxes in the Preview tab may give you undesirable results if you don't put them in the right section.

1. Click the Insert Line or Insert Box button in the Supplementary toolbar. You can also choose Insert | Line or Insert | Box from the pull-down menus.

2. When you make either of these choices, your mouse cursor will change to a pencil. Point the pencil to where you want to begin the line or box, and hold down the left mouse button.

3. Drag the line or box to its ending position and release the button. Notice that you can only draw perfectly vertical or horizontal lines—diagonal lines can't be drawn.

The line or box will appear on the report, complete with sizing handles. You can now drag or resize the line or box just like any other object. You may also format the line or box with the Format Editor (using options from the Format pull-down menu or by right-clicking the line or box and choosing Format from the pop-up menu). You can choose the color, size, and style of the line or box, along with other options. Figure 7-6 shows a report that uses a horizontal line to delineate group footers and a filled box with a drop shadow around report totals.

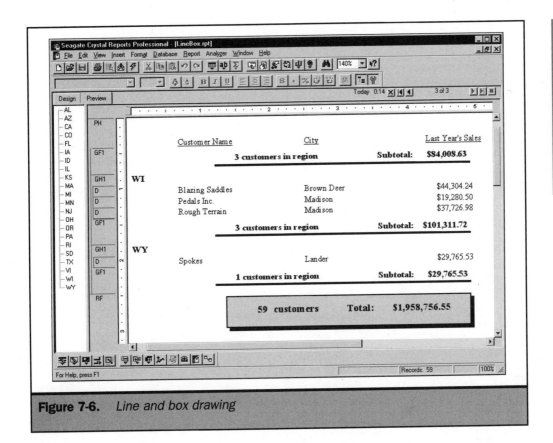

Figure 7-6.   *Line and box drawing*

You can draw lines and boxes that traverse multiple report sections. This is handy if you want to have a single box enclose a column starting in the page header and ending up in the page footer, including all the sections in between. However, this can sometimes result in odd behavior if, for example, you start a line in the page header, but end it in the details section or a group footer. If your lines or boxes traverse sections, make sure you preview the report to make sure you get the desired results.

The
Complete
Reference

Crystal
Reports
7

Chapter 8

Using Sections
and Areas

155

In previous chapters, you've learned how to change the appearance of individual objects on the report, such as changing the color of a field or adding a drop shadow to a text object. However, you also have the ability to format *entire sections* of your report. You can:

- Add a gray background to every other detail section
- Format a group header so every group starts fresh on its own page
- Create multiple columns in your detail section for labels
- Add a light-colored watermark graphic in its own page header section that appears behind the rest of your report

Formatting Sections with the Section Expert

There are several ways to change the appearance of an entire report section. You'll often just want to change the *size* of a section. Consider this "single-spaced" report:

Customer Name	City	Region	Last Year's Sales
City Cyclists	Sterling Heights	MI	$19,426.76
Pathfinders	Allenspark	CO	$42,601.14
Bike-A-Holics Anonymous	Blacklick	OH	$18,708.52
Psycho-Cycle	Huntsville	AL	$66,791.39
Sporting Wheels Inc.	San Diego	CA	$61,767.84
Rockshocks for Jocks	Austin	TX	$41,443.97
Poser Cycles	Eden Prairie	MN	$21,812.40

Notice the details sections appearing very close to each other. Maybe you'll just want to "double-space" the report. However, there is no double-space, space-and-a-half, or any similar function available in Crystal Reports. Instead, you choose how tall you want a section to be by using one of several techniques.

The simplest is to just drag the bottom border of a section down to make the section taller. Point to the line at the bottom of the section you want to resize—the mouse cursor will turn into two lines with up and down arrows. This section-sizing cursor indicates that you can drag the section border down to make a section taller, or drag the border up to make a section shorter.

By simply making the details section taller, the white space that's exposed becomes the "double-space" when you re-preview the report, as shown here:

Customer Name	City	Region	Last Year's Sales
City Cyclists	Sterling Heights	MI	$19,426.76
Pathfinders	Allenspark	CO	$42,601.14
Bike-A-Holics Anonymous	Blacklick	OH	$18,708.52
Psycho-Cycle	Huntsville	AL	$66,791.39

Although this is the most straightforward way to resize a section, you have other options available as well. By right-clicking in the gray section name on the left side of the Design tab, you will display the section pop-up menu. For example, right-clicking Details brings up this menu:

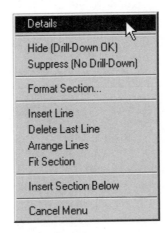

This pop-up menu contains four additional features for resizing sections, as listed here:

Insert Line	Adds an additional horizontal guideline to the section ruler on the left side of the section. If the section isn't tall enough to show the additional guideline, the section grows taller.
Delete Last Line	Removes the bottom guideline in the section and shrinks the size of the section proportionally. If you choose this option and there is no more room to shrink the section because of the objects in the section, you'll receive an error message.
Arrange Lines	Rearranges any horizontal guidelines in an even fashion. If there aren't enough horizontal guidelines to fill the section, additional guidelines will be added.
Fit Section	Automatically shrinks the size of the section to the bottom-most object in the section. If there are any horizontal guidelines below the bottom object, they are removed before the section is resized.

Although there may be times when you'll make use of the Insert Line, Delete Last Line, or Arrange Lines options from the section pop-up menu, you'll most likely find Fit Section the only useful option. It's particularly useful if the section is very large (perhaps you've deleted a large map, chart, or picture from the section and all the white space it took up is still there) and you want to shrink it without having to scroll down to find the bottom section border.

The Section Expert

While the Format Editor is used to format individual objects, you'll use the *Section Expert*, shown in Figure 8-1, to format entire sections of your report. There are a surprising number of options in the Section Expert for formatting individual report sections. Using them provides a new level of flexibility for your reports.

The Section Expert can be displayed in several ways. You can click the Section Expert button in the Standard toolbar, choose Format | Section from the pull-down menus, or right-click in the gray area of the section you wish to format and choose Format Section from the pop-up menu. If you choose the toolbar button or menu

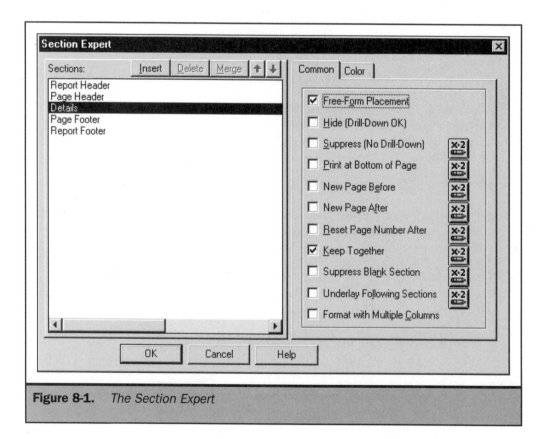

Figure 8-1.   *The Section Expert*

options, the first section will be highlighted in the Section Expert. If you right-click in the gray area of a section and use the pop-up menu, that particular section will be highlighted.

By selecting different sections of the report in the Section Expert, you can view and set formatting properties for the section. Note that the properties will vary slightly, and some won't be available, depending on which section you select. For example, the New Page Before property doesn't make much sense for a page header section, so it will be grayed out when a page header is selected. Table 8-1 explains the different section formatting properties available in the Section Expert Common tab.

Property	Function
Free-Form Placement	Allows objects to be moved freely throughout the section without snapping to horizontal guidelines. If turned off, horizontal guidelines are added to the left of the section and objects snap to them when moved.
Hide (Drill-Down OK)	Hides a section and all objects in it. However, if the section is within a higher-level group and that group is drilled into, this section *will* appear in the drill-down tab.
Suppress (No Drill-Down)	Suppresses a section and all objects in it. If the section is within a higher-level group and that group is drilled into, this section *will not* appear in the drill-down tab, even though a drill-down tab will appear.
Print at Bottom of Page	Prints the section at the bottom of the page. Typically used for invoices, statements, or other similar reports that require a group footer with a total to print at the bottom of the page, regardless of how many details sections print above it.
New Page Before	Starts a new page before printing this section. Useful in a group header if you want each group to start on its own page.
New Page After	Starts a new page after printing this section. Useful in a group footer if you want the next group to start on its own page.

Table 8-1.   *Section Expert Common Tab Formatting Properties*

Property	Function
Reset Page Number After	Resets the page number back to one after printing this section. Useful in a group footer if you want each group to have its own set of page numbers, regardless of the total number of pages on the report. Also resets the total page count field.
Keep Together	Prevents Crystal Reports from putting a page break in the middle of this section. For example, this would avoid having the first few lines of a multiple-line detail section appearing on the bottom of one page and the last few lines appearing on the next page.
Suppress Blank Section	Will suppress the entire section if all the objects inside it are blank. Useful in situations where you want to avoid white gaps appearing in your report if all the objects in a section have been conditionally suppressed or suppressed "if duplicated."
Underlay Following Sections	Will print the section, then all following sections will print right on top of the section. Useful for printing maps, charts, or pictures alongside data or underneath the following sections.
Format with Multiple Columns	Will create multiple newspaper or phone-book style columns. The Layout tab will appear when this property is checked. This is only available when the details section is chosen.

Table 8-1. *Section Expert Common Tab Formatting Properties* (continued)

Caution *Don't confuse the Keep Together section property and the Keep Group Together group property in the Change Group dialog box. Keep Together in the Section Expert just prevents the particular section from splitting over two pages, whereas Keep Group Together will attempt to keep the group header, all details sections, and the group footer for the same group from printing across multiple pages.*

You'll also notice Conditional Formula buttons for many properties on the Common tab. These properties can be set conditionally with a Boolean formula, if necessary. There are many uses for both absolute and conditional properties on the Common tab. Here are some common examples.

STARTING A GROUP ON ITS OWN PAGE   Checking New Page Before in a group header, or New Page After in a group footer (but not both) will cause each group to start on a new page. There is one problem with setting this property absolutely—you can end up with "stranded" pages. If you set New Page Before on a group header, you'll often encounter a stranded first page because the report header will print and Crystal Reports will skip to the next page before printing the first group header. Conversely, if you set New Page After on a group footer, you'll often encounter a stranded last page because the last group footer will be followed by a page break before the report footer prints.

To avoid these pitfalls, you can set the New Page Before or New Page After properties conditionally. To avoid a stranded first page, you can use a conditional formula to only set the New Page Before property on the second and subsequent groups—the first group will stay on the first page with the report header. Since the first group header will print at the same time the first record is printing, you can use the following Boolean conditional formula for New Page Before:

```
Not OnFirstRecord
```

To avoid a stranded last page, you want a new page after every group footer, *except the last one*. Since the last group footer will only occur on the last record of the report, you can use this conditional formula for New Page After:

```
Not OnLastRecord
```

PRINTING AN INVOICE TOTAL AT THE BOTTOM OF THE PAGE   You may be creating invoices grouped by invoice number, or statements grouped by customer number. You want the invoice or statement total, located in the group footer, to print at the bottom of the page, regardless of how many detail records print. Crystal Reports normal behavior is to print the group footer immediately following the last detail record. If there are only a few invoice items or statement lines, the total will print high up the page, right after the last detail line. If you want the total to print at the bottom of the page in this situation, check the Print at Bottom of Page property for the group footer.

STARTING PAGE NUMBERS OVER FOR EACH NEW GROUP   You might have a large report grouped by department that you want to "burst" apart and distribute to each individual department. Initially, you'll want to make sure to use the New Page Before property with the group header or the New Page After property with the group footer so you won't ever have the end of one department appearing on the same page as the beginning of the next.

However, you also don't want to confuse those who may look at page numbers on later groups in the report. Even though a page may be the first one for the IT department, it will probably have a much larger page number than 1. Simply check the Reset Page Number After property for the department group footer. Page numbers will then start over at 1 for each department.

The Color tab on the Section Expert, shown in Figure 8-2, lets you change the background color for an entire section, separate from any color formatting that individual objects in the section may have.

If you check the Background Color property, you can then choose from various colors in the pull-down list below. This will set the background color for the entire section. This lets you highlight entire sections with different colors, if you choose—for example, a report with the group footer section showing a different background color:

D		2805	Rad Bikes	Tualatin	OR	3/9/1998	$1,739.05	UPS
D		2839	Craze Cycle	Tualatin	OR	3/21/1998	$1,739.85	Pickup
D		2866	Whistler Rentals	Tualatin	OR	3/28/1998	$845.55	FedEx
D		2894	Our Wheels Follow Us Ev	DeKalb	OR	4/6/1998	$32.73	FedEx
D		2914	Rad Bikes	Tualatin	OR	4/14/1998	$373.35	Pickup
D		2939	Whistler Rentals	Tualatin	OR	4/18/1998	$2,084.59	Loomis
D		2940	Our Wheels Follow Us Ev	DeKalb	OR	4/18/1998	$161.70	UPS
D		2959	Craze Cycle	Tualatin	OR	4/21/1998	$959.70	Parcel Po
D		2968	Craze Cycle	Tualatin	OR	4/25/1998	$43.44	FedEx
D		2989	Craze Cycle	Tualatin	OR	5/1/1998	$238.63	FedEx
GF2								
GF1						Subtotal:	$617,204.64	
GH1		Southwest						
GH2		CA						
D		1026	Tyred Out	Santa Ana	CA	12/7/1996	$33.00	Pickup
D		1059	Off the Mountain Biking	Irvine	CA	12/12/1996	$364.67	Pickup
D		1065	Tyred Out	Santa Ana	CA	12/13/1996	$1,275.70	UPS

Notice the Conditional Formula button on the Color tab. This lets you set the background color conditionally. This can be helpful if you want to base a background color on some particular condition.

The location of the Conditional Formula button on the Color tab may confuse you. Since it's located next to the Background Color check box, you may think it requires a Boolean formula to set the Background Color property. In fact, it conditionally sets the background color itself with an If-Then-Else formula.

CREATING A "BANDED" REPORT   Mainframe reports often were printed on "green bar" or "blue bar" paper with alternating shades of color and white. This was designed to make columns of numbers easy to follow across the page. Now that many PC-based reports are printed by laser printers on plain paper, you must create your own "banded" reports if your reports would benefit from this kind of look.

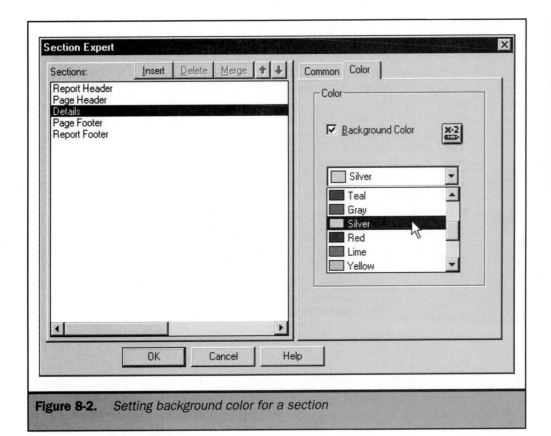

Figure 8-2.   *Setting background color for a section*

Simply giving the details section a silver background color isn't visually appealing, as shown here:

D	2712	Alley Cat Cycles	Concord	MA	2/12/1998	$1,619.74	Parcel Post
D	2735	Alley Cat Cycles	Concord	MA	2/19/1998	$8,819.55	Parcel Post
D	2753	Alley Cat Cycles	Concord	MA	2/24/1998	$1,619.55	UPS
D	2788	Alley Cat Cycles	Concord	MA	3/5/1998	$1,085.40	Loomis
D	2797	Alley Cat Cycles	Concord	MA	3/7/1998	$959.70	UPS
D	2898	Alley Cat Cycles	Concord	MA	4/9/1998	$1,000.96	Parcel Post
GF1	31 orders				Subtotal:	$54,565.39	
GH1	**Backpedal Cycle Shop**						
D	1222	Backpedal Cycle Shop	Philadelphia	PA	1/23/1997	$6,116.82	UPS
D	1327	Backpedal Cycle Shop	Philadelphia	PA	2/22/1997	$3,479.70	Pickup
D	1429	Backpedal Cycle Shop	Philadelphia	PA	3/16/1997	$2,294.55	Parcel Post
D	1498	Backpedal Cycle Shop	Philadelphia	PA	4/7/1997	$49.50	Pickup
D	1550	Backpedal Cycle Shop	Philadelphia	PA	4/20/1997	$973.98	Parcel Post

However, setting every other detail section to silver provides a good way to help report readers follow columns of material across the page. You can set the background color conditionally to accomplish this. Use the following conditional formula:

```
If Remainder(RecordNumber,2) = 0 Then Silver Else NoColor
```

This uses several built-in Crystal Reports functions. The Remainder function takes two arguments, the numerator and denominator. It divides the numerator by the denominator, but returns the *remainder* of the division operation, not the result of the division. The RecordNumber built-in function simply counts records consecutively, starting at 1. Therefore, *every other* record number, when divided by 2, will return 0 as the remainder. This will alternate the details section background color for every record.

2712	Alley Cat Cycles	Concord	MA	2/12/1998	$1,619.74	Parcel Post
2735	Alley Cat Cycles	Concord	MA	2/19/1998	$8,819.55	Parcel Post
2753	Alley Cat Cycles	Concord	MA	2/24/1998	$1,619.55	UPS
2788	Alley Cat Cycles	Concord	MA	3/5/1998	$1,085.40	Loomis
2797	Alley Cat Cycles	Concord	MA	3/7/1998	$959.70	UPS
2898	Alley Cat Cycles	Concord	MA	4/9/1998	$1,000.96	Parcel Post
	31 orders			**Sub total:**	**$54,565.39**	
	Backpedal Cycle Shop					
1222	Backpedal Cycle Shop	Philadelphia	PA	1/23/1997	$6,116.82	UPS
1327	Backpedal Cycle Shop	Philadelphia	PA	2/22/1997	$3,479.70	Pickup
1429	Backpedal Cycle Shop	Philadelphia	PA	3/16/1997	$2,294.55	Parcel Post
1498	Backpedal Cycle Shop	Philadelphia	PA	4/7/1997	$49.50	Pickup
1550	Backpedal Cycle Shop	Philadelphia	PA	4/20/1997	$973.98	Parcel Post

You can make modifications to this formula to shade more than just every other line. If you want *every two* lines shaded, you could change the formula slightly.

```
If Remainder(RecordNumber,4) In [1,2] Then Silver Else NoColor
```

This divides the record number by 4 and checks for remainders of 1 or 2. This will be true for every two records. The result is shown here:

2735	Alley Cat Cycles	Concord	MA	2/19/1998	$8,819.55	Parcel Post
2753	Alley Cat Cycles	Concord	MA	2/24/1998	$1,619.55	UPS
2788	Alley Cat Cycles	Concord	MA	3/5/1998	$1,085.40	Loomis
2797	Alley Cat Cycles	Concord	MA	3/7/1998	$959.70	UPS
2898	Alley Cat Cycles	Concord	MA	4/9/1998	$1,000.96	Parcel Post
	31 orders			**Sub total:**	**$54,565.39**	
	Backpedal Cycle Shop					
1222	Backpedal Cycle Shop	Philadelphia	PA	1/23/1997	$6,116.82	UPS
1327	Backpedal Cycle Shop	Philadelphia	PA	2/22/1997	$3,479.70	Pickup
1429	Backpedal Cycle Shop	Philadelphia	PA	3/16/1997	$2,294.55	Parcel Post
1498	Backpedal Cycle Shop	Philadelphia	PA	4/7/1997	$49.50	Pickup
1550	Backpedal Cycle Shop	Philadelphia	PA	4/20/1997	$973.98	Parcel Post

You probably get the general idea of how this works. You can now modify formula in any number of ways to change the way background shading works.

*When setting the background color of a section, as well as background colors for
individual objects, you may want to use NoColor instead of White to indicate a
normal color. By using White, you will have solid white colors that can sometimes
look unpleasant in combination with other solid colors. If you use NoColor, you often
achieve a certain amount of transparency that will look preferable when mixing
colors on the report.*

Creating Summary and Drill-Down Reports

A *detail report* shows every individual detail record in the database. This may often be
preferable for certain listings or smaller transaction-type reports. Oftentimes, however,
a viewer will only want to see subtotals, counts, averages, or other summary
information for certain groups on the report. The detail information used to arrive at
those summaries isn't as important. This calls for a *summary report*.

In its simplest form, a summary report will simply be a report with one or more
groups with the details section hidden or suppressed. Consider Figure 8-3, a detail
report of orders, grouped by customer.

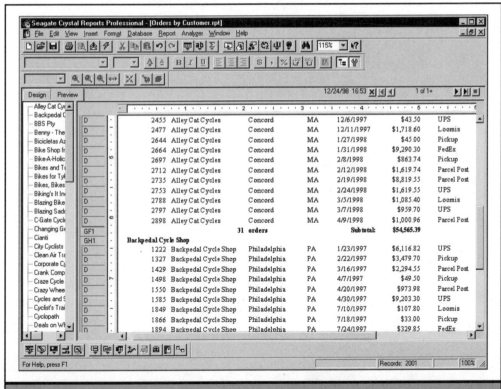

Figure 8-3.   *Orders detail report*

This shows every order for the customer, with an order count and order amount subtotal appearing in the group footer. While this may be useful for a report viewer concerned about individual orders, the sales manager or account rep may often just be interested in the summary information for each customer. All the order details just get in the way of their analysis.

In this case, simply hiding or suppressing the details section will create a much more meaningful report for these viewers. You can hide or suppress the details section from the Section Expert. As a shortcut, there are Hide and Suppress options available right in the section pop-up menu, as well. Just right-click the gray details section name at the left of the Design tab and choose Hide (Drill-Down OK) or Suppress (No Drill-Down) from the pop-up menu.

The details section will simply disappear from the Preview tab, while the group header and footer still show up. Figure 8-4 shows the resulting summary report, which is much more succinct and meaningful to a viewer looking at the big picture.

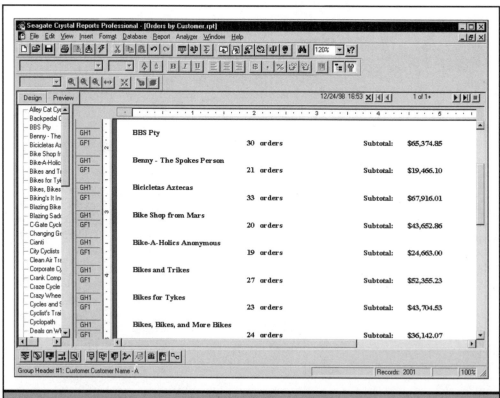

Figure 8-4.   *Orders summary report*

If you later want to change your report back to a detail report, you need to have the details section reappear. Just display the Select Expert with the toolbar button or pull-down menu option. Select the details section and turn off the Hide or Suppress property. You can also display the Design tab and right-click the gray area to the left of the screen where the details section is hidden or suppressed. To redisplay the details section, choose the opposite of the Suppress or Hide option you initially set.

You can choose how a hidden or suppressed section appears in the Design tab. Choose File | Options from the pull-down menus and look for the Show Hidden Sections in Design option on the Layout tab. If this is checked (the default), hidden or suppressed sections will still appear in the Design tab, but they will have gray shading through them. If you turn this option off, they will only show the bottom border of the hidden or suppressed section in the Design tab.

Choosing whether to hide or suppress a section determines whether or not you want a report viewer to drill down into the section (discussed next). Also, note that the Suppress property can be conditionally set in the Section Expert, while the Hide property cannot.

Drill-Down Reports

One of the most powerful features of an online reporting tool like Crystal Reports is interactive reporting. You may be creating a report to distribute to a large audience as a Compiled report (discussed in Chapter 13), via a Web page (covered in Part III), or as part of a custom Windows application (covered in Part II). A truly useful report will initially present viewers with higher-level summary or total information. If the viewer sees a number or other characteristic of the report that interests them, you want them to be able to drill down into just that particular area.

Drill-down is an interactive feature only applicable to viewers looking at a Crystal Report in its "native" format. Drill-down isn't available in any reports exported to another format, such as Word or Excel. And, obviously, drill-down isn't a feature that applies to reports printed on paper!

In its simplest form, a drill-down report can be created by hiding the details section (hence the Drill-Down OK notation alongside the Hide property) in a report that has one or more groups. When you point at any object in a group header or footer, you'll notice your mouse cursor change to a magnifying glass, or *drill-down cursor*. When you double-click, a separate drill-down tab will appear, showing the group header, footer, and details sections for that group. You can then navigate to the main Preview tab to see the summary report, or back to individual drill-down tabs to see the detail information. You can double-click in the Preview tab as many times as you want in order to create additional drill-down tabs.

More complicated drill-down reports can be created by using multiple levels of grouping, along with creative use of section hiding. Figure 8-5 shows a drill-down report containing a details section and three groups: country, region, and city. Initially the report just shows countries and their totals. If you drill down on a country, you'll

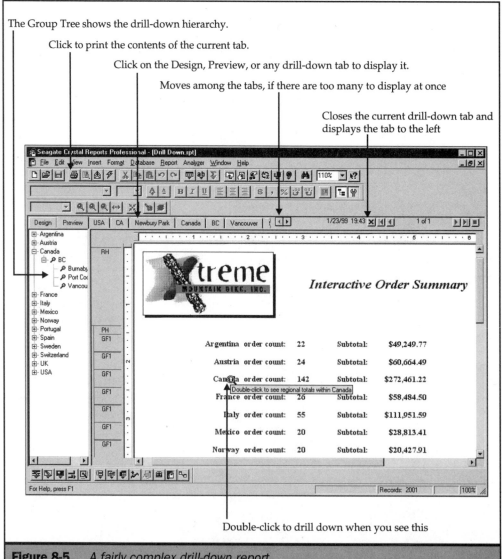

Figure 8-5. *A fairly complex drill-down report*

find region subtotals for that country. Drilling down on a region will show city totals. And finally, drilling down on a city total will show individual orders placed from that city.

You will probably want to move the column headings from the page header to a group header to make the drill-down tabs more readable. You may also want to move the Group Name object from a group header into a group footer and hide the group header along with the details section. This way, the summary report will just show one line per group until you drill down. Then, the group header (containing the column headings) will appear inside the drill-down tab, along with the details sections.

If you're interacting with a report, it's important to remember what will print or export if you click the Print button in the Standard toolbar, or choose File | Print from the pull-down menus. Only what's in the current drill-down tab (or Preview tab) will print or export. If you want to just print one drill-down tab, choose the drill-down tab and then click the Print button. If you want to print all the summary information in the main Preview tab, make sure it's selected before you print or export. If you want to print or export both summary and detail information *in the same report*, you must either display the details section and print from the Preview tab or create a separate report more appropriate for printing.

Using Tool Tip text can help a viewer determine what will happen when they double-click an object. By creating a string formula with the Tool Tip text Conditional Formula button on the Format Editor, you can give a viewer more information about what the object contains. The tool tip illustrated in Figure 8-5 comes from the following Tool Tip text Conditional Formula added to the GroupName field in the Country group footer.

```
"Double-click to see all regions in " + GroupName ({Customer.Country})
```

Look at the DRILLDOWN.RPT sample report on the Companion CD to see examples of innovative drill-down techniques.

Multiple Column Reports for Labels and Listings

Crystal Reports is designed to replace much of the repetitive printing you may have used a word processor for in the past. Immediate uses include form letters and mailing labels. You can also use the multicolumn feature of Crystal Reports to create newspaper-style columns in your reports. If you have just a few fields that you'd like to print in columnar form, the Section Expert provides the necessary section formatting.

In order to create mailing labels in Crystal Reports, click the Mail Label Expert button in the Report Gallery when first creating a new report. This brings up the Mailing Labels Report Expert, shown in Figure 8-6, which takes you step-by-step through the process of choosing the table and fields that make up your mailing label, and choosing from a predefined list of continuous-feed and laser printer labels.

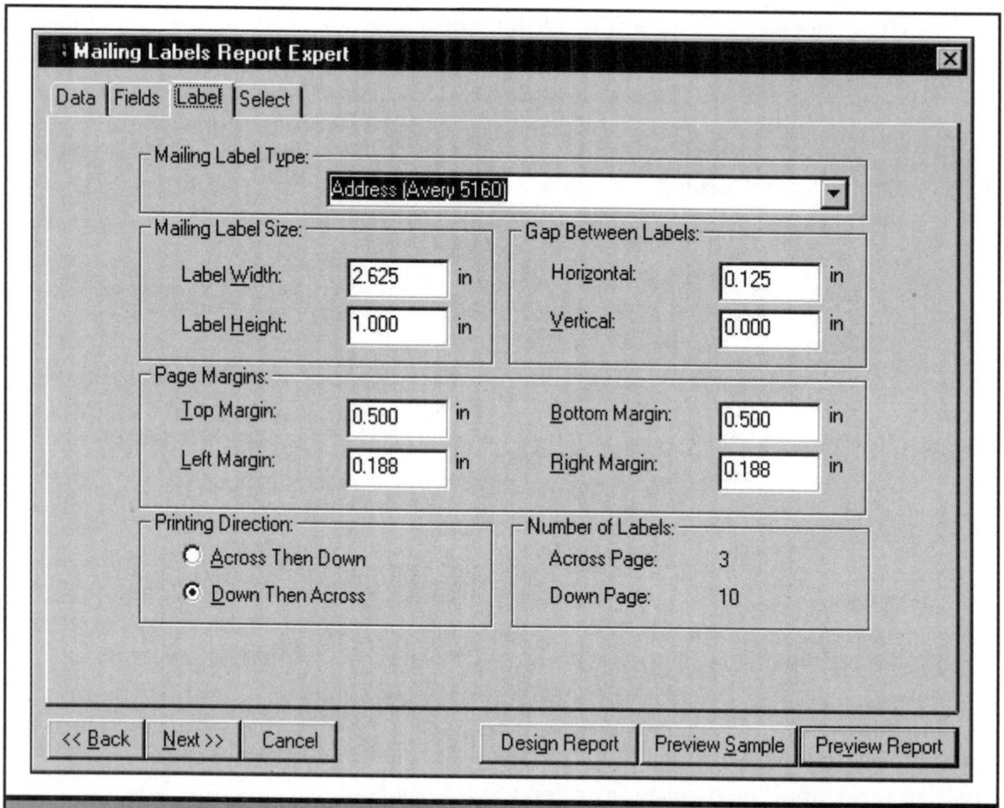

Figure 8-6. Creating mailing labels with a report expert

Since there is no similar expert for creating newspaper-style reports, you'll have to create such reports using the Custom option and the Section Expert. Recall one of the Section Expert's formatting properties, Format with Multiple Columns. This property is only available for the details section—it won't even appear in the Section Expert if you have any other section selected. Once you check this property, the Layout tab appears in the Section Expert, as shown in Figure 8-7.

Here you determine the specifics of the columns you want to create. Although you might expect to see a "number of columns" setting, this is actually determined by page margins (set with File | Page Setup), the width of the details section, and the horizontal gap between details. For example, if you have quarter-inch margins with standard letter-sized paper in portrait orientation, you'll have 8 full inches of printable space. If you choose a detail size width of 2.5 inches and a horizontal gap of a quarter inch, you'll have three evenly spaced columns with a quarter inch on all sides.

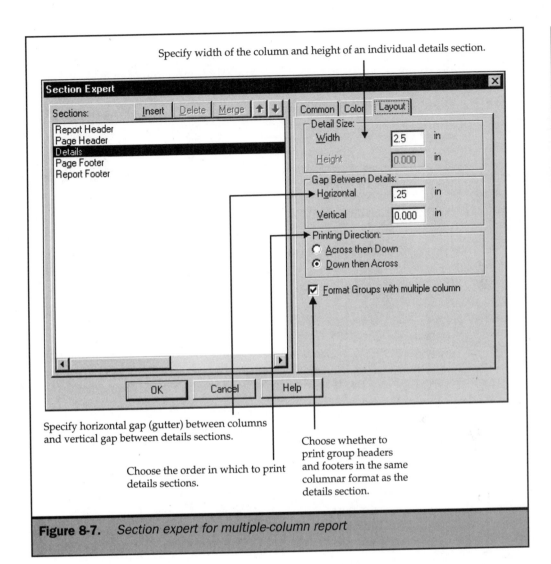

Specify width of the column and height of an individual details section.

Specify horizontal gap (gutter) between columns and vertical gap between details sections.

Choose the order in which to print details sections.

Choose whether to print group headers and footers in the same columnar format as the details section.

Figure 8-7.   *Section expert for multiple-column report*

CRYSTAL REPORTS 7 INTRODUCED

When you choose to format the details section with multiple columns, the Design tab changes slightly. You'll notice that the details section bottom border shrinks to equal the width you set in the Layout tab. The other sections of the report retain the full width of the page.

The exception to this rule occurs when you check the Format Groups with Multiple Column check box on the Layout tab. In this case, all group headers and footers will take on the same width as the details section. This can make a marked difference in the appearance of your report, depending on the size of your groups. As a general rule, not formatting groups with multiple columns will cause smaller groups to only print in one column on the left side of the page. Usually the only small groups that will print across multiple columns will be ones that start at the bottom of the page. Figure 8-8 shows the difference. You'll typically experience more predictable behavior by formatting groups with multiple columns.

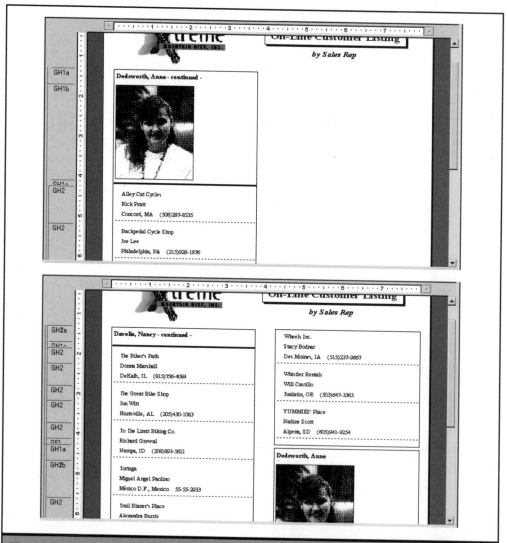

Figure 8-8. Report groups formatted without and with multiple columns

Multicolumn reporting works fine when previewing your report online or when printing to a printer. However, multiple columns will be lost when you export any reports.

Using Multiple Sections

To be precise, the five default sections that first appear in a new report, and any additional group headers and footers that are added later, are referred to as *areas*. This is because Crystal Reports lets you create multiple occurrences of the same area, and each of these occurrences is called a *section*. Creating multiple sections can be accomplished from the Section Expert by using the pop-up menu that appears when you right-click in the gray area on the left side of the screen.

To insert an additional details section, for example, right-click in the details gray area on the left side of the Design tab and choose Insert Section Below from the pop-up menu. Or, from the Section Expert, select the area that you wish to duplicate and click the Insert button. You'll see the details area split into two sections: Details a and Details b. Once you've created multiple sections in an area, the pop-up menu, shown next, and Section Expert, shown in Figure 8-9, take on a great deal of additional capability.

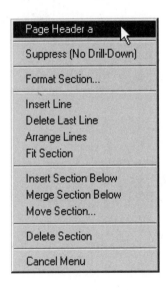

 You can also rearrange the order in which sections appear right in the Design tab. Simply click and drag the section you wish to move—the mouse cursor will change to a "hand." Drop the section in its new location in the same area. Although the section contents will swap, the consecutive lettering will not change—the first section will still be lettered "a," the second "b," and so on.

Creates a new section directly below the currently selected one

Deletes the current section, and all objects in it

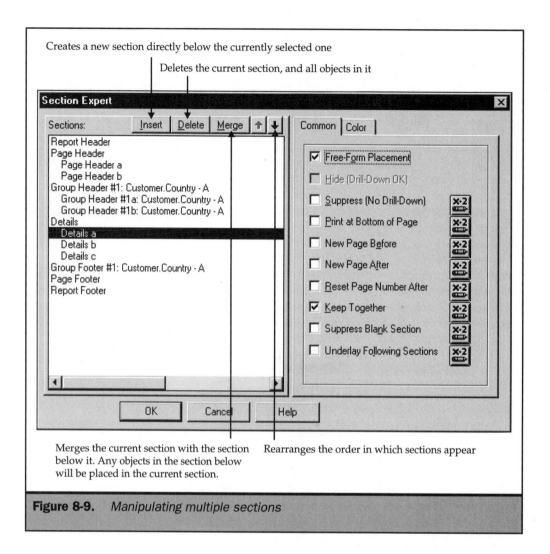

Merges the current section with the section below it. Any objects in the section below will be placed in the current section.   Rearranges the order in which sections appear

Figure 8-9.   *Manipulating multiple sections*

You can insert as many sections in an area as you wish—there can be Details a, b, c, d, and on and on. Any area can be comprised of multiple sections. There's nothing to prevent you from having three report headers, five details sections, two group footer #1s, or any other combination.

Once you've created the multiple sections, you can add objects to any of the sections. You can even add the same object to some, or all, of them. When the report prints, they will simply print one right after the other, with the objects showing up one below the other. Probably the biggest comment you have right now is "What's the benefit of multiple sections anyway? Everything just prints as though it were in one bigger section!"

Figure 8-10 is a great example of the benefit of multiple sections. This shows a form letter based on the Customer table from the sample XTREME.MDB database included with Crystal Reports. Notice that the letter consists of three different details sections. Details a contains the Print Date, Customer Name, and Address 1, Details b contains

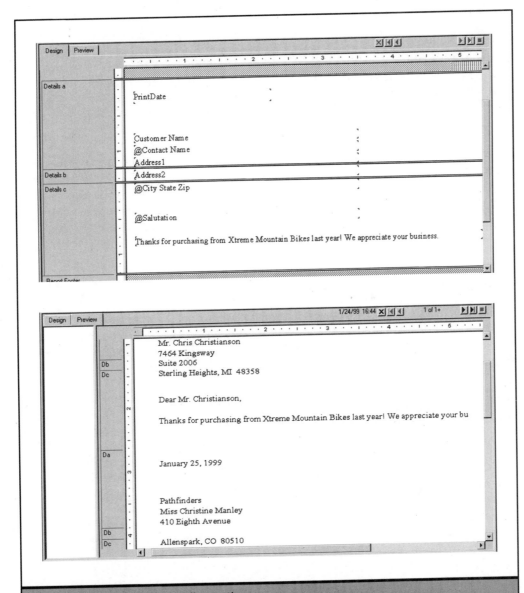

Figure 8-10. *Multiple details sections*

Address 2, and Details c contains the rest of the letter. When you preview the report, it just shows the details sections one on top of the other, as though everything is in one big details section.

But look at the letter for "Pathfinders." Notice the empty line that appears when there is no Address 2 database field. This behavior, again, is identical to what you'd expect if you had put all the objects in one tall details section.

Here's the benefit: you may *conditionally suppress* individual sections, in this case Details b, so that they appear or disappear according to your specifications. To eliminate the blank line that appears when there's nothing in Address 2, format Details b with Suppress Blank Section. If the objects contained in it all return empty (as is the case with Pathfinders), the section will not appear at all. You can also use the Conditional Formula button next to the Suppress property to suppress based on any condition you need.

 The more you work with areas and sections, the more you may notice the large amount of space the area and section names take up on the left side of the Design tab. If you wish to have more space for actual report objects, you can change the way Crystal Reports shows section names. Choose File | Options and check Show Short Section Names in Design on the Layout tab. "Report Header" will now be abbreviated "RH," "Page Header a" will become "PHa," and so on. You'll now have more room to work with actual report objects.

Conditionally Suppressing Sections

Not only do multiple sections become beneficial with conditional suppression, but even when you use single sections, there may be times you want a section to appear and others when you don't. Using the Conditional Formula button next to the Suppress property lets you supply a Boolean formula to determine when the section appears or doesn't appear. Consider the following examples.

PRINTING A BONUS MESSAGE FOR CERTAIN RECORDS   You are designing a list of orders by salesperson. You want a bonus message and a "lots o' money" graphic to appear below the order if it exceeds $2,500. However, if the order doesn't exceed the bonus level, you *don't* want the large blank space to appear where the graphic and message are located. If you just use the Format Editor to conditionally suppress the graphic and text object containing the message, they won't appear, but the empty space still will.

Simply create a Details b section and place the graphic and text object in it. Then, suppress Details b when the bonus isn't met, using the following conditional formula for the Suppress property:

```
{Orders.Order Amount} < 2500
```

Figure 8-11 shows the result.

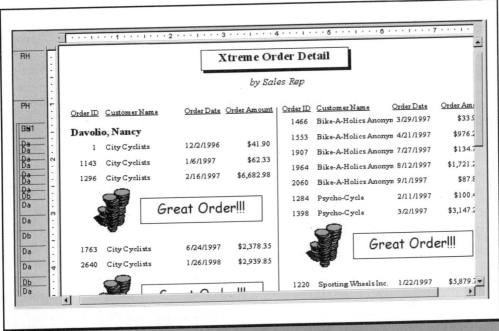

Figure 8-11.   *Multiple details sections with conditional suppression*

PRINTING A DIFFERENT PAGE HEADER ON PAGE 2 AND LATER   You may wish to print a title page or other large page header on page 1 of the report, perhaps containing a logo and large formatted title. However, on subsequent pages of the report, you want a less flashy header with smaller type and no graphic. You want column headings and the print date and time to show up on all pages of the report, including the first.

This presents a special reporting problem. The flashy page header can simply be put in the report header section. It will only, then, appear on the first page. However, if you put the smaller report title in the page header along with the column headings and other information, it will appear on page 1 along with the report header. You can use the Format Editor to suppress the object containing the smaller header, but then extra white space will appear on page 1.

The solution is to create a second page header section. Put the smaller report title in Page Header a and the column headings and print date/time in Page Header b. Then, conditionally suppress Page Header b so it won't show up on page 1. Here's the conditional formula, which uses the PageNumber built-in function:

```
PageNumber = 1
```

PRINTING "ODD" AND "EVEN" PAGE HEADERS OR FOOTERS   You may be printing your report on a "duplex" laser printer that can print on both sides of the paper. Or, you may want to photocopy your report from one to two sides and place it in a three-ring or other bound format. Crystal Reports lets you create separate "odd" and "even" page headers and footers to add a real page-published look to your report.

Simply create separate Page Headers a and b (and, perhaps, Page Footers a and b). Place the appropriate material in each section and position it properly for odd/even appearance. Now, conditionally suppress the sections. The sections containing the material for odd page numbers will be suppressed for even page numbers with the following conditional formula:

```
Remainder(PageNumber,2) = 0
```

And, the sections containing the material for even page numbers will be suppressed for odd page numbers with the following conditional formula:

```
Remainder(PageNumber,2) = 1
```

These formulas make use of the PageNumber built-in function described in the previous example. In addition, they use the Remainder function, which will indicate whether a page number is even or odd (even page numbers divided by two will return a remainder of zero, odd page numbers will return a remainder of one, as explained earlier in the chapter).

Underlaying Sections

The Section Expert includes the Underlay Following Sections property. As described in Table 8-1, this property will print the underlaid section in its usual position, but will print the following sections right over the top. Initially, this may seem of limited usefulness. How readable will a report be if sections are printing right over the top of earlier sections?

Look at Figure 8-12 to get an idea. This report includes a large, light "Draft" graphic that has been placed in the page header. When Underlay Following Sections is checked for the page header in the Section Expert, all the other sections will print right over the top of the page header, creating the watermark effect.

If you want to include column headings in the page header, along with the watermark, you experience a problem. The watermark will be underlaid as you desire, but so will the column headings! The solution, as you might expect, is to add a Page Header b. Place the watermark graphic in one page header section and format it to Underlay Following Sections. Place the column headings in the other page header section and don't underlay it. Which page header you place the objects in will

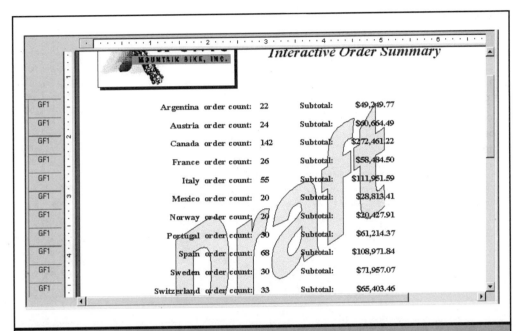

Figure 8-12.   *Using Underlay Following Sections to print a watermark*

determine whether the column headings are underlaid or not. If you put the watermark in Page Header a (which is formatted to Underlay Following Sections) and the column headings in Page Header b (not underlaid), the watermark will underlay the column headings. If you choose the other way around, the column headings won't be underlaid.

> **Tip**   *When you underlay a section, all sections will print over the top of it, until Crystal Reports comes to its "companion" section, which will not underlay it. For example, if you underlay a page header, all sections will print on top until Crystal Reports gets to the matching page footer. If you underlay Group Header b, all other sections will print on top until the report hits Group Footer b, which will not be underlaid.*

You can also use the Underlay Following Sections feature to place maps or charts beside the data they refer to, rather than on top or bottom of the related data. Figure 8-13 shows a report containing a map. Notice that the map appears alongside the data that the map refers to, rather than above. The map is still contained in the group header, but the map object has been moved to the right of the section and the group header section is formatted to Underlay Following Sections.

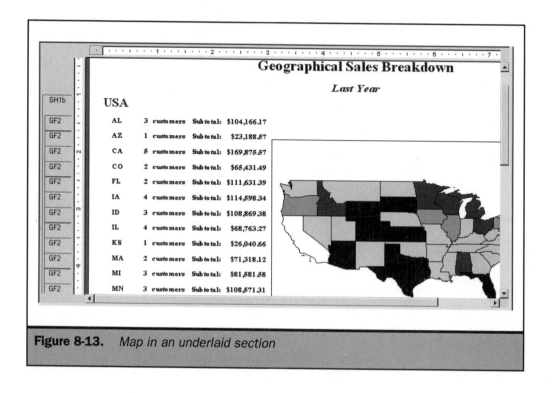

Figure 8-13.   *Map in an underlaid section*

Again, so that the USA Group Name field isn't also underlaid along with the map, it has been placed in a second group header, which is not underlaid.

The
Complete
Reference

Chapter 9

Analyzing with Cross-Tabs

Database report writers and spreadsheet programs are typically considered to be two completely separate products. The database report writer sorts and selects data very well, while the spreadsheet is great for analyzing, totaling, and trending in a compact row and column format. Crystal Reports provides a tool that, to a limited extent, brings the two features together. This tool is the *cross-tab object*. A cross-tab is a row and column object that looks similar to a spreadsheet. It summarizes data by using at least three fields in the database: a row field, a column field, and a summarized field. For each intersection of the row and column fields, the summarized field is aggregated (summed, counted, or some other type of calculation is performed).

Consider two common summary reports: The first summary report shows total sales in dollars for each state in the United States. The second report shows total units sold by product type. If a marketing analyst wanted to combine these two reports together to more closely analyze sales in dollars by state and units sold by product type, you would be limited in what you could offer with the standard grouped summary report.

You can create a report, similar to that shown in Figure 9-1 (initially grouped by state, and within state grouped by product type), that would provide the information the analyst desires. But if the analyst wanted to compare total mountain bikes sold in the country with total kids bikes sold in the country, this report would make the process very difficult. Product type is the inner group, so there are no overall totals by it. Also, comparing Alabama totals with Wyoming totals would be difficult, because they would be several pages apart on the report.

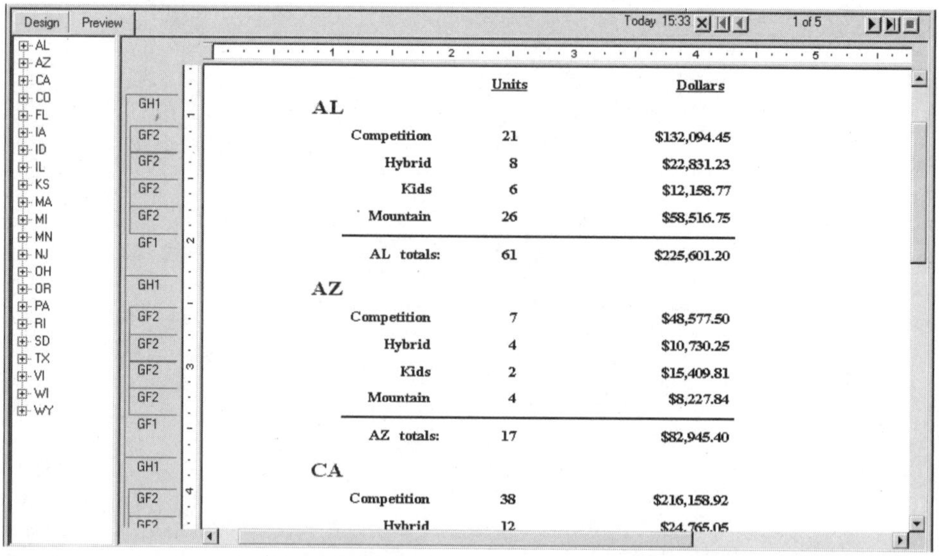

Figure 9-1. *Standard summary report with two groups*

This scenario is a perfect example of where a cross-tab object would be useful. A cross-tab is a compact, row and column report that can compare subtotals and summaries by two or more different database fields. Whenever someone requests data shown by one thing and by another, it's a cross-tab candidate. Just listen for the "by this and by that" request. Figure 9-2 will probably be much more useful to the analyst.

Creating a Cross-Tab Object

When you look at a cross-tab, it's tempting to think of it as an entire report unto itself, much like an Excel spreadsheet is entirely independent. In fact, a cross-tab is just an object that resides in an existing report section. Even when you choose the Cross-Tab Expert from the Report Gallery, Crystal Reports just creates a cross-tab object and puts it in the report header. You can create more than one cross-tab per report, if you wish. In fact, you can even copy an existing cross-tab and put it in several different sections of the same report. It's just an object, like a text object, map, or database field.

A cross-tab can exist by itself on a report (as evidenced by the Cross-Tab Expert), or can be placed on a report that already contains fields in the details section, as well as one or more groups. The report can be completely functional in every respect before the cross-tab is added—it just gets dropped in.

The first step in creating a cross-tab is ensuring that the tables you've chosen and linked for your report contain enough data to populate the cross-tab. If, for example,

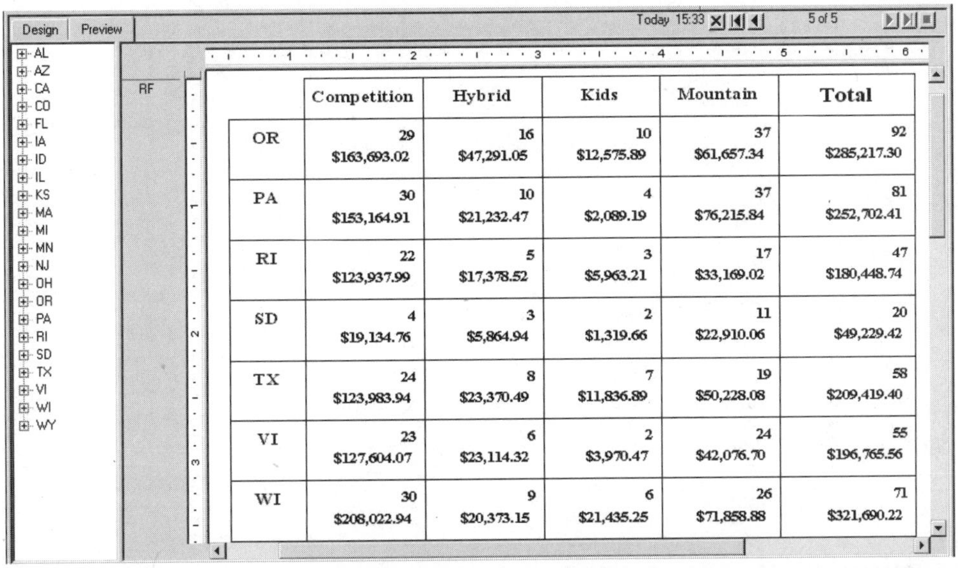

	Competition	Hybrid	Kids	Mountain	Total
OR	29 $163,693.02	16 $47,291.05	10 $12,575.89	37 $61,657.34	92 $285,217.30
PA	30 $153,164.91	10 $21,232.47	4 $2,089.19	37 $76,215.84	81 $252,702.41
RI	22 $123,937.99	5 $17,378.52	3 $5,963.21	17 $33,169.02	47 $180,448.74
SD	4 $19,134.76	3 $5,864.94	2 $1,319.66	11 $22,910.06	20 $49,229.42
TX	24 $123,983.94	8 $23,370.49	7 $11,836.89	19 $50,228.08	58 $209,419.40
VI	23 $127,604.07	6 $23,114.32	2 $3,970.47	24 $42,076.70	55 $196,765.56
WI	30 $208,022.94	9 $20,373.15	6 $21,435.25	26 $71,858.88	71 $321,690.22

Figure 9-2. *Cross-tab showing units/dollars by region and by product type*

you want to look at order totals for the years 1995, 1996, 1997, and 1998 by state, make sure you choose tables that include the order amount, the year the order was placed, and the state of the customer that placed the order. While this may seem rather obvious, you may not have enough data to adequately populate your cross-tab if you don't think ahead carefully.

You may or may not want to use actual report fields as cross-tab fields. If the fields are already on the report, you can add them to the cross-tab object. Or, if you've added completely different fields to the report, you can still base the cross-tab on other fields that exist in the tables you chose when creating the report.

You can use the Cross-Tab Expert from the Report Gallery, or add a cross-tab to an existing report you've already created. To use the Expert, just choose it from the Report Gallery when creating a new report. Once you've chosen and linked the tables you want to make up your cross-tab report, click the Cross-Tab tab. A rearranged version of the Cross-Tab dialog box will appear inside the Expert.

If you've already created another report using another Expert or the Custom option, you may insert a cross-tab object whenever you'd like. To create a cross-tab object, it's best to select the Design tab first. Although you can place a cross-tab on the report in the Preview tab, you may not be able to accurately tell where it's being placed. In the Design tab, there's no question. Click the Insert Cross-Tab button on the Supplementary toolbar, or choose Insert | Cross-Tab from the pull-down menus. The Cross-Tab dialog box will appear, as shown in Figure 9-3.

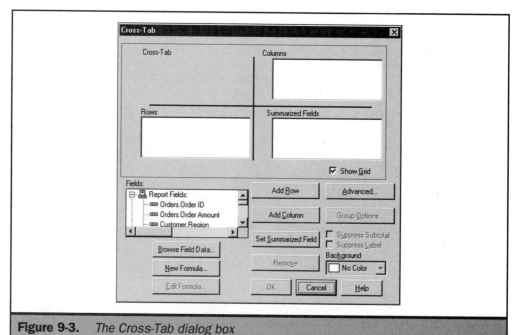

Figure 9-3.   *The Cross-Tab dialog box*

Look through the Fields box to find the fields you want to use for the cross-tab's row and column. Just drag your chosen field from the Fields box and drop it on the Rows or Columns box. You can also select the field in the Field box and click the Add Row or Add Column buttons.

Then, choose the field you want summarized in each *cell* (the intersection of each row and column). This will typically be a number or currency field, such as Quantity Sold or Order Amount, but doesn't have to be. If you choose a number field, Crystal Reports will subtotal the field for each cell. If you choose a field with another data type, a count of the number of occurrences of the field for each row/column combination will be shown. Drag the field to be summarized from the Fields box to the Summarized Fields box, or select the field and click the Set Summarized Field button.

If you'd like to use an existing formula for a row, column, or summarized field, just select the formula in the Fields box. If you'd like to create a new formula or edit an existing formula before using it in the cross-tab, click the New Formula or Edit Formula button, which will launch the Formula Editor where you create or edit the formula. The formula will then appear in the Fields box where you can drag it to the Row, Column, or Summarized Fields box.

There are several other options you can set before clicking OK that affect the appearance of your cross-tab. You can turn off or on the gridlines between cells with the Show Grid check box (the default is to show the gridlines). Also, you can set the background color for a row or column by selecting the row or column field and choosing a color from the Background pull-down list. The Advanced and Group Options buttons, along with the Suppress Subtotal and Suppress Label check boxes, will be discussed later in the chapter.

Once you have specified all your cross-tab options and clicked OK on the Cross-Tab dialog box, you'll be returned to the report with a small object attached to your mouse cursor. You can drop the cross-object in the report header or footer, or in a group header or footer. Cross-tabs can't be placed in the details section or in a page header or footer—you'll get a "no-drop" cursor if you try to position the cross-tab in these sections.

Drop the cross-tab below any other objects in the section, such as summaries, group names, or text objects. Although the cross-tab will appear relatively small in the Design tab, when you actually preview or print the report, it will grow both horizontally and vertically to accommodate all its rows and columns. If there are other objects below or to the right of the cross-tab, it will print right over the top of them. When you drop the cross-tab, the small object on the mouse cursor will turn into a larger cross-tab object, showing a layout of the row, column, summarized field, and row and column totals.

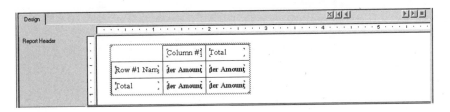

When you preview the report, Crystal Reports will cycle through the database several times to properly calculate the totals for all row and column combinations—you'll note the extra time required to do this. The cross-tab will then appear in the section where you placed it.

	Argentina	Austria	Canada	France	Italy	Mexico
Competition	$57,616.33	$55,339.27	$233,640.81	$60,971.15	$79,756.29	$34,992.6
Gloves	$12,744.29	$5,425.03	$29,347.18	$7,019.81	$9,972.65	$5,999.6
Helmets	$27,136.42	$14,536.93	$55,633.80	$16,160.25	$28,640.44	$2,707.5

The section in which you place a cross-tab is critical in determining the data that the cross-tab will encompass. If you place a cross-tab in the report header or footer, only one occurrence of the cross-tab will appear on the report (remember, the report header and footer only appear once at the beginning and ending of the report, respectively). This cross-tab will encompass all the data on the report. If you place a cross-tab in a group header or footer, you get as many cross-tabs on your report as there are groups.

Figure 9-4 shows a cross-tab using the XTREME.MDB sample database included with Crystal Reports. This cross-tab includes product name as the row, and city as the column. Notice that all cities in all states show up in the cross-tab.

Contrast this with Figure 9-5, which is the exact same cross-tab object that's just been moved to a state group footer. Now there will be a cross-tab on the report for every state group, but each cross-tab will only contain data for that particular group. If you choose to, you can copy the cross-tab object between a group header or footer to the report header or footer and actually see cross-tabs for individual groups, as well as an all-encompassing cross-tab for the whole report.

Editing an Existing Cross-Tab

Once you've created a cross-tab and dropped it on your report, it's easy to make changes to it. You must first select the entire cross-tab object, not just one of the objects that makes it up. Accomplish this by clicking either in the small white space in the upper-left corner of the cross-tab (above the first row and to the left of the first column) or by clicking on the gridlines between cells. You'll know you've selected the entire cross-tab if the status bar displays Cross-Tab: You can select the cross-tab in either the Design or Preview tabs.

Once you've selected the cross-tab that you want to modify, choose Format I Cross-Tab from the pull-down menus, or right-click and choose Format Cross-Tab from the pop-up menu. This will simply redisplay the Cross-Tab dialog box, allowing you to change row, column, or summarized fields.

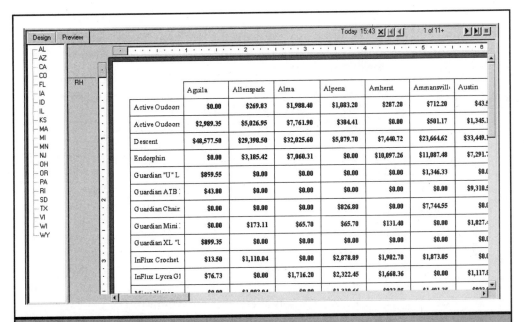

Figure 9-4. Cross-tab in report header

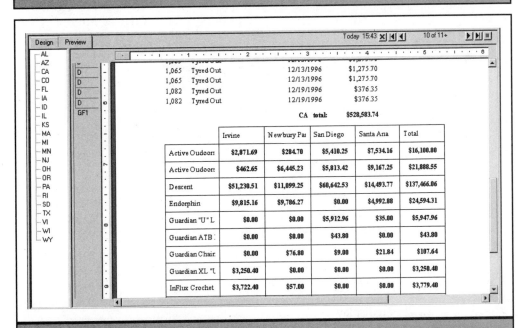

Figure 9-5. Cross-tab in group footer

You can also *pivot* the cross-tab. Pivoting the cross-tab is simply swapping the rows and columns around, so that what used to be the row will now be the column, and vice versa. Choose Format | Pivot Cross-Tab from the pull-down menus, or right-click on the selected cross-tab object and choose Pivot Cross-Tab from the pop-up menu.

Creative Use of Grouping and Formulas

As discussed previously, Crystal Reports chooses a default calculation for the summarized field when it creates the cross-tab. If you choose a number or currency field for a summarized field, Crystal Reports will use the Sum function to subtotal the numbers in each cell. This will typically be what you want for this type of field (for example, the total sales figure for Green Bikes in the USA). If you use any other type of field (string, date, Boolean, etc.), Crystal Reports will automatically use the Count function to count the occurrences of the particular summarized field for each row/column combination.

You are, however, completely free to change the function that Crystal Reports assigns to the summarized field. If you want to see the average sales figure in each cell, instead of the total figure, it's easy to change. In either the Design or Preview tabs, just click the object in the cell (the intersection of the row and column). The status bar will indicate that you've selected Sum of <summarized field>. Change the summary operation from Sum to Average (or any other available summary) by choosing Edit | Summary Field from the pull-down menus, or right-clicking and choosing Edit Summary Operation from the pop-up menu. This brings up the Change Summary Operation dialog box, shown here:

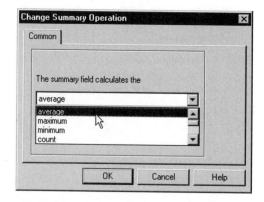

If you've used a nonnumeric field for the cross-tab summarized field, you can change the summary operation from Count to Minimum, Maximum, Distinct Count, or any other summary functions that are available for nonnumeric fields. This is similar to how you can change the summary operation with existing group summaries and subtotals, as discussed in Chapter 3. In fact, the cross-tab, in essence, groups database records for every row/column combination, creating the summary or subtotal field for each cross-tab "group." Chapter 3 has more information on available summary functions and what they calculate.

No matter how hard you try or how creative you might be, cross-tab cells cannot contain anything but numbers created from summary functions. Reports like calendars, schedules, or other row/column reports may look like potential cross-tabs. However, if there is to be some textual information at the intersection of the rows and columns, you'll need to design the report using other techniques. Cross-tabs are strictly for numeric analysis.

Changing Cross-Tab Grouping

Because Crystal Reports uses a procedure to create cross-tabs that's similar to its procedure for creating groups, you have some of the same flexibility to change the way the cross-tab is organized. You can change a cross-tab "group" when first creating the cross-tab or formatting an existing cross-tab. In the Cross-Tab dialog box, select the row or column field you want to change, and then click the Group Options button. The Cross-Tab Group Options dialog box appears.

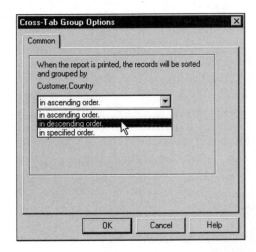

For a nondate field, there are three available options: ascending order, descending order, or specified order. Ascending order will show the cross-tab row or column in A to Z order. Descending order will show the cross-tab row or column in Z to A order. Specified grouping will let you create custom rows or columns, based on the contents of the database field you chose for the row or column. This works identically to Specified Order Grouping discussed in Chapter 3.

If the row or column field is a date field, time field, or date/time field, the Cross-Tab Group Options dialog box has additional options that give you even greater flexibility, similar to creating report groups with similar fields.

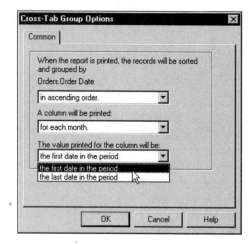

The A Column Will Be Printed pull-down list gives you a choice of how often you want a new row or column to appear in the cross-tab. Choices include every day, every week, every two weeks, every hour, every minute, and so on. Again, these are identical to the date/time grouping choices discussed in Chapter 3.

The The Value Printed for the Column Will Be pull-down list gives you two choices: the first date in the period and the last date in the period. If you choose the first-date option with, say, a quarterly date period for 1997, the cross-tab will show 1/97, 4/97, 7/97, and 10/97. If you choose the last-date option, the cross-tab will show the exact same data in the cells, but the dates will be 3/97, 6/97, 9/97, and 12/97.

To give you a better idea of the flexibility date group options provide, look at Figures 9-6 and 9-7, both showing cross-tabs based on the same date field. Figure 9-6 shows weekly date grouping with the first-date option, and Figure 9-7 shows quarterly grouping with the last-date option.

Using Formulas in Cross-Tabs

Even with the powerful grouping options and ability to change the summary function used to calculate cell values, you may not always be able to display material in a cross-tab exactly the way you want with just the database fields in the Fields box. You are completely free to use formulas in your cross-tabs as a row, column, or summarized fields. You can create the formulas in advance with the Formula Editor, or click the New Formula button right in the Cross-Tab dialog box to display the Formula Editor. Once you've created the formula, it will appear in the Fields box under the Report Fields category. Simply drag it to the Rows, Columns, or Summarized Fields box.

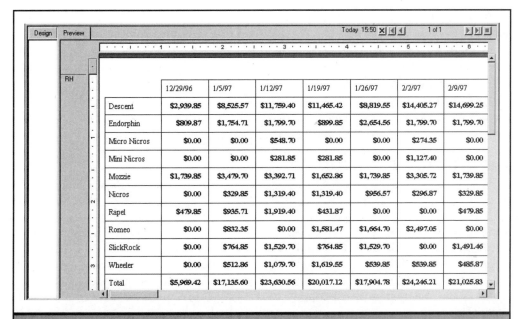

Figure 9-6. Cross-tab date field with weekly first date group options

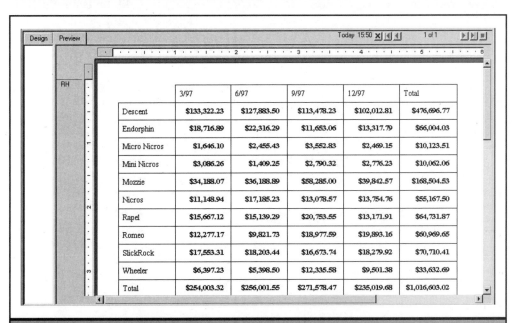

Figure 9-7. Cross-tab date field with quarterly last date group options

Because cross-tabs are calculated during the second report pass (WhilePrintingRecords), you cannot use second-pass formulas in cross-tabs. You can only use formulas that calculate during the first pass. However, you can base a chart or a map on a cross-tab, as cross-tabs are processed before charts and maps in the second pass. See Chapter 5 for a discussion on report passes.

Multiple Rows, Columns, and Summarized Fields

It's not too hard to see that the Rows, Columns, and Summarized Fields boxes in the Cross-Tab dialog box are more than one field tall. Yes, that means that you can add more than one database field or formula to any of these cross-tab sections. It's important to understand, though, how this will affect cross-tab behavior and appearance.

Probably the simplest place to start is with multiple summarized fields. If you add more than one field to the Summarized Fields box, the cross-tab will simply calculate the additional summary or subtotal in each cell. You could, for example, use Product Name as the row, Region as the column, and *both* Quantity and Price as summarized fields. The cross-tab would simply include two numbers in each cell—the total quantity and total price for that particular product and region.

You can even add the same field to the Summarized Fields box more than once and choose a different summary function for each occurrence. You could, for example, add both the Quantity and Price fields to the Summarized Fields box again. However, you might choose an Average summary function instead of a Sum for the second occurrence of the fields. The cross-tab would then show four numbers in every cell: total quantity, total price, average quantity, and average price.

Adding multiple fields to the Rows or Columns boxes causes a little different behavior that you need to understand. Whereas multiple summarized fields simply calculate and print in the same cell, multiple row or column fields don't just print over and over, side-by-side. When you add multiple fields to these boxes, you create a *grouping relationship* between the fields. Consider a cross-tab in which you add the Product Type field as the first row field, and the Product Name field as the second row field. Crystal Reports will create a group hierarchy by Product Type, and within that, by Product Name. The resulting cross-tab would look like Figure 9-8.

Notice that there are rows created for both the "inner" and "outer" groups—each product name has its own row within its product type, as well as each product type having its own subtotal row. And, at the end of the cross-tab, there is a grand total row for everything.

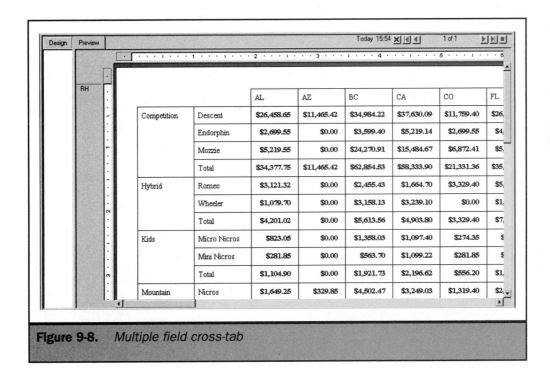

		AL	AZ	BC	CA	CO	FL
Competition	Descent	$26,458.65	$11,465.42	$34,984.22	$37,630.09	$11,759.40	$26,
	Endorphin	$2,699.55	$0.00	$3,599.40	$5,219.14	$2,699.55	$4,
	Mozzie	$5,219.55	$0.00	$24,270.91	$15,484.67	$6,872.41	$5,
	Total	$34,377.75	$11,465.42	$62,854.53	$58,333.90	$21,331.36	$35,
Hybrid	Romeo	$3,121.32	$0.00	$2,455.43	$1,664.70	$3,329.40	$5,
	Wheeler	$1,079.70	$0.00	$3,158.13	$3,239.10	$0.00	$1,
	Total	$4,201.02	$0.00	$5,613.56	$4,903.80	$3,329.40	$7,
Kids	Micro Nicros	$823.05	$0.00	$1,358.03	$1,097.40	$274.35	$
	Mini Nicros	$281.85	$0.00	$563.70	$1,099.22	$281.85	$
	Total	$1,104.90	$0.00	$1,921.73	$2,196.62	$556.20	$1,
Mountain	Nicros	$1,649.25	$329.85	$4,502.47	$3,249.03	$1,319.40	$2,

Figure 9-8. *Multiple field cross-tab*

You can set up this multiple field group hierarchy for either rows or columns. And, you can include as many fields as you want in the Rows or Columns box (although it won't make much sense if you go beyond two or three levels).

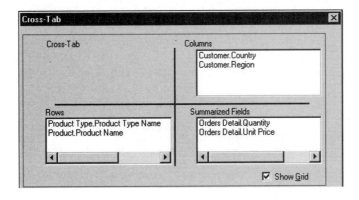

And, here's a portion of the resulting cross-tab.

		Canada		USA	
		BC	Total	AL	AZ
Competition	Descent	38.00 $55,269.19	38.00 $55,269.19	30.00 $38,071.06	12.00 $20,137.98
	Endorphin	13.00 $4,499.25	13.00 $4,499.25	5.00 $2,699.55	0.00 $0.00
	Mozzie	31.00 $27,750.61	31.00 $27,750.61	12.00 $8,699.25	0.00 $0.00
	Total	82.00 $87,519.05	82.00 $87,519.05	47.00 $49,469.86	12.00 $20,137.98

Note *What section of the report you place the cross-tab in is particularly important when you are using multiple row or column fields. If you create a cross-tab that's based on Country, and then Region, you'll have different behavior depending on where you put the cross-tab. If you put it in the report header or footer, you'll have rows or columns for each country, and all the regions within those countries. However, if you have already grouped your report by country, and you place the cross-tab in a country group header or group footer, you'll then have one cross-tab for every country. However, that cross-tab will only have one country row or column in it, followed by any regions within that country. If you find cross-tabs at group levels with only one high-level row or column, there's not a great deal of benefit to using multiple fields in that cross-tab.*

What's crucial if you plan on using multiple row or column fields, is that you choose fields that have a logical groupable relationship with each other. You may think of this relationship as being *one-to-many*. The Product Type/Product Name relationship is a good example—every one product type has many product names. Country/Region is another good example—every one country has many regions.

Placing two fields in the Rows or Columns boxes that don't have this relationship will cause an odd-looking cross-tab. For example, if you add Customer Name and Address fields to the same row or column box, you'll simply see the customer name row or column, immediately followed by a single address row or column. The summaries in each will be exactly the same. This is because there's no logical one-to-many relationship between the fields. (The exception would be if a single customer had more than one office location—then this would be a valid multiple-field cross-tab example).

Note *You may yearn for a cross-tab that allows multiple row or column fields that don't act as groups. You might, for example, want to see Actual $, Budget $, Variance $, and Variance % all as separate column fields that just calculate and print side-by-side. Sorry, but any time you add multiple fields to the Row or Column box, Crystal Reports will display the fields in a grouping hierarchy from top to bottom.*

Reordering Fields in the
Rows, Columns, or Summarized Fields Boxes

Not only do the multiple fields you add to the Rows or Columns box have to have a logical relationship, but they need to appear in the box in the right order as well. Using the previous Country/Region example, Country must be the first field in the box, followed by Region. If they're added the other way around, then each region will appear first, followed by a single row or column containing numbers from the country the region is in.

If you happen to add fields to the Rows, Columns, or Summarized Fields boxes in the wrong order, you can use the long way or the short way to fix the problem. The long way: delete the fields from the boxes and add them again in the proper order. The short way: simply drag and drop them in the right order right inside the box. You can select a field in any of the boxes, hold down the mouse button, and drop it in a different location in the box.

You can't drop a field above the existing top field in a box to make it the new top field. You must drag the top field down in the list to make it appear lower.

Suppressing Subtotals and Labels with Cross-Tab Groups

Look back at the multiple-row cross-tab in Figure 9-8. You'll see that it is first "grouped" by Product Type in ascending order, then by Product Name in ascending order. Notice that there are subtotals for each product type as well.

There may be situations where you want some additional grouping in your cross-tabs, but don't want to show the subtotals for an outer-level group. You also may want to have a cross-tab grouped logically by the outer level, but you don't even want the outer level to appear on the cross-tab. The Suppress Subtotal and Suppress Label check boxes on the Cross-Tab dialog box (shown earlier in Figure 9-3) are used to accomplish this.

First, you must select a higher-level field in the Rows or Columns box—selecting the lowest-level field (or the only field if there's just one) will disable these options. Once you've selected the higher-level field, you can click Suppress Subtotal. This will still include the multiple levels of grouping in the cross-tab but will eliminate the subtotals for the row or column you chose. Notice the effect on the cross-tab depicted in Figure 9-9.

Once you choose to suppress the subtotals, you are then also allowed to check the Suppress Label check box. Checking this option will completely eliminate the field you chose from the row or column. However, the rows or columns below it will stay grouped by it—the higher-level group just won't show up. Look at the results of Suppress Label, shown in Figure 9-10.

		Canada		USA			
		BC	Total	AL	AZ	CA	CO
Competition	Descent	$34,984.22	$34,984.22	$26,458.65	$11,465.42	$37,630.09	$11,
	Endorphin	$3,599.40	$3,599.40	$2,699.55	$0.00	$5,219.14	$2,
	Mozzie	$24,270.91	$24,270.91	$5,219.55	$0.00	$15,484.67	$6,
Hybrid	Romeo	$2,455.43	$2,455.43	$3,121.32	$0.00	$1,664.70	$3,
	Wheeler	$3,158.13	$3,158.13	$1,079.70	$0.00	$3,239.10	
Kids	Micro Nicros	$1,358.03	$1,358.03	$823.05	$0.00	$1,097.40	$
	Mini Nicros	$563.70	$563.70	$281.85	$0.00	$1,099.22	$
Mountain	Nicros	$4,502.47	$4,502.47	$1,649.25	$329.85	$3,249.03	$1,
	Rapel	$6,046.13	$6,046.13	$2,351.27	$479.85	$4,774.51	$1,
	SlickRock	$10,707.90	$10,707.90	$5,315.71	$764.85	$3,786.01	

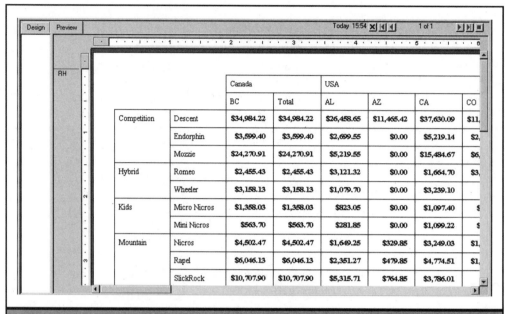

Figure 9-9. *Multiple row fields with subtotals suppressed*

	Canada		USA				
	BC	Total	AL	AZ	CA	CO	FL
Descent	38.00 $55,269.19	38.00 $55,269.19	30.00 $38,071.06	12.00 $20,137.98	39.00 $51,741.38	12.00 $14,699.25	$29,25
Endorphin	13.00 $4,499.25	13.00 $4,499.25	5.00 $2,699.55	0.00 $0.00	23.00 $7,918.69	9.00 $4,499.25	$5,35
Mozzie	31.00 $27,750.61	31.00 $27,750.61	12.00 $8,699.25	0.00 $0.00	26.00 $18,964.37	8.00 $6,872.41	$5,21
Romeo	10.00 $4,120.13	10.00 $4,120.13	13.00 $3,870.44	6.00 $2,497.05	12.00 $4,161.75	11.00 $4,994.10	$5,82
Wheeler	26.00 $5,317.53	26.00 $5,317.53	5.00 $1,619.55	3.00 $539.85	15.00 $3,778.95	0.00 $0.00	$2,15
Micro Nicros	10.00 $1,358.03	10.00 $1,358.03	9.00 $1,097.40	0.00 $0.00	9.00 $1,371.75	5.00 $548.70	$82
Mini Nicros	6.00	6.00	5.00	3.00	9.00	6.00	

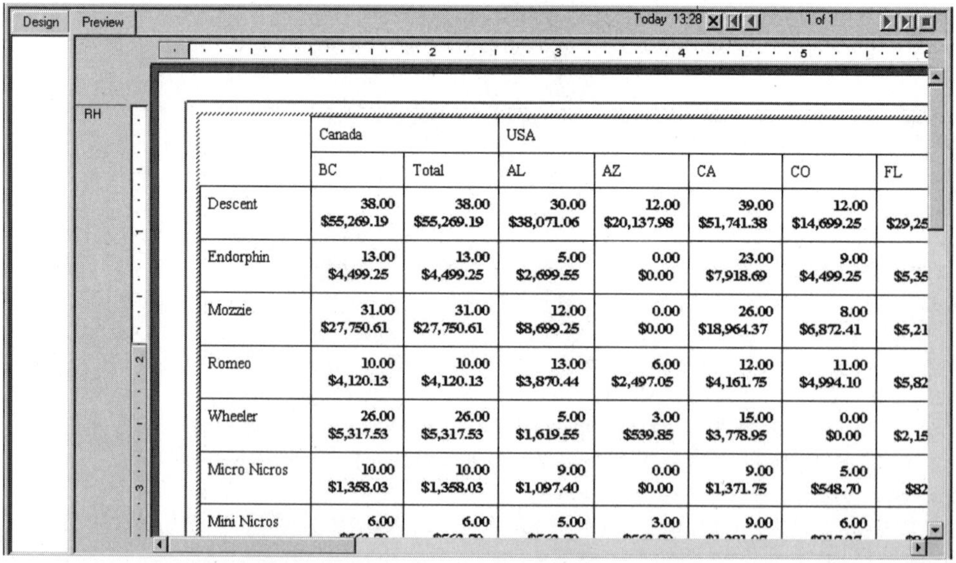

Figure 9-10. *Cross-tab with the Suppress Label option checked*

Improving the Appearance of Cross-Tabs

Although the formatting options on the Cross-Tab dialog box may look limited, you have lots of flexibility to control the way cross-tabs look. The first group of formatting options for cross-tabs lies in the individual cross-tab objects themselves. A cross-tab actually consists of a series of individual objects. The best way to see this is to look at a cross-tab in the Design tab.

	Column #1	Total
Row #1 Name	ail.Quantity	ail.Quantity
Total	ail.Quantity	ail.Quantity

Here you'll notice the row and column name fields. These are similar to group name fields in a regular report—they display the database fields that make up the row and column headings. You'll also see the Total text objects that indicate the subtotal and total rows and columns. These are standard text objects—you can just double-click them to change their contents if you wish. And, in the actual cells you'll notice the subtotal or summary functions that calculate the cross-tab totals.

Each of these individual objects can be resized or formatted to change the appearance of the cross-tab. For example, if a column in the cross-tab isn't wide enough to show its contents, the contents will just be cut off, or truncated. Examine the following cross-tab:

	1/96	10/96	1/97	4/97	7/97	10/97	1/98
Descent	########	########	########	########	########	########	######
Endorph	$3,651.08	########	########	########	########	########	######
Micro N	$0.00	########	$5,651.36	########	########	########	######
Mini Nic	$7,300.90	########	########	########	########	########	$9,983
Mozzie	########	########	########	########	########	########	######

Notice that the row labels are being truncated. Also, note that many of the cells contain pound signs, indicating that the cells aren't wide enough to show all the data in them (Allow Field Clipping is turned off in the Format Editor for the summary field). Although you may be tempted to look in the Cross-Tab dialog box for some sort of column width setting, you simply need to select the individual object that makes up the column, and resize it. This can be done in either the Design or Preview tab. Simply select the object, noting that all other similar cells are selected as well. Then, point to the *sizing handle* (the small blue blocks on all sides of a selected object) until the mouse cursor changes to the two-way sizing cursor. Then just resize the object to its desired width.

	1/96	10/96	1/97
Descent	#############	#############	#############
Endorphin	$3,651.08	#############	#############
Micro Nicrc	$0.00	#############	$5,651.36
Mini Nicros	$7,300.90	#############	#############

Tip *Allow Field Clipping is an option available for numeric fields on the Number tab of the Format Editor. If you check Allow Field Clipping, the contents of the field will simply be truncated if the field is not wide enough to display them. This is potentially dangerous, though, as the report may present inaccurate numbers if their full width is not displayed. Turn off Allow Field Clipping to have Crystal Reports show a series of pound signs when the field is not wide enough to display its entire contents.*

You can format the individual pieces of the cross-tab just like any other text object or number field, using either the Formatting toolbar or the Format Editor. You can change the object's color, font face and size, horizontal alignment, or any other standard formatting option. If you choose one of the summary or subtotal objects in the middle, you can specify the number of decimal places, whether to include a thousands separator or currency symbol, or any other formatting option available to numeric or currency fields. If you base a row or column on a date or time field, you can choose how the field is displayed—month/year, month/day/year, hour:minute, hour:minute:second, or any other variation provided by the Format Editor.

Tip *You can select multiple objects in a cross-tab by using CTRL-click. You can then format them all at the same time with the Formatting toolbar or the Format Editor.*

The Cross-Tab dialog box also provides some formatting flexibility. You can select a field in the Rows or Columns box and choose a background color for the entire row or column from the Background pull-down list. New to Crystal Reports 7 is the Advanced button in the Cross-Tab dialog box. Clicking this button will display the Advanced Cross-Tab Options dialog box, shown in Figure 9-11. The various options are explained in Table 9-1.

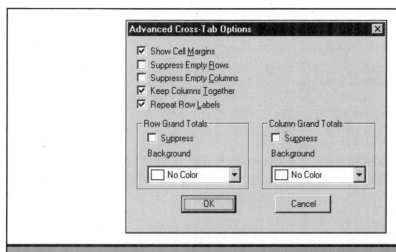

Figure 9-11. *Advanced Cross-Tab Options dialog box*

Option	Description
Show Cell Margins	Pads cells with white space on all sides. Turning this option off will place cells right next to each other.
Suppress Empty Rows	Rows with no data will not appear in the cross-tab.
Suppress Empty Columns	Columns with no data will not appear in the cross-tab.
Keep Columns Together	Prevents columns from being cut in half when a cross-tab exceeding the width of the page is printed.
Repeat Row Labels	If Keep Columns Together is checked, this option will repeat the row labels when a cross-tab exceeding the width of the page is printed on two or more pages.
Suppress	Prevents row or column grand totals from appearing in the cross-tab.
Background pull-down lists	If row or column grand totals are not suppressed, these pull-down lists set the background color for the grand total row or column.

Table 9-1. *Advanced Cross-Tab Options*

Many of the options in the Advanced Cross-Tab Options dialog box dictate how a cross-tab appears when printed on paper. This is significant, as Crystal Reports displays cross-tabs differently in the Preview tab than it will print them on a printer. Even if the cross-tab width exceeds the width of the page, the Preview Tab will show the entire cross-tab across the screen. You can continue to scroll farther right to see the rest of the cross-tab.

When it prints the cross-tab on paper, however, Crystal Reports must add page breaks if the cross-tab exceeds the width of the printed page. You can control how Crystal Reports formats the cross-tab across multiple pages with the options in the Advanced Cross-Tab Options dialog box. Figure 9-12 shows the printed results of the Keep Columns Together and Repeat Row Labels options being turned on. If these options were not turned on, the cross-tab would be broken right in the middle of a column, and the second page would not show any row titles.

Adding Legends to Cross-Tabs

If you add multiple summarized fields to a cross-tab, it may not be clear to your viewer what the numbers mean. Consider the following cross-tab that contains multiple summary fields:

		Canada		USA			
		BC	Total	AL	AZ	CA	CO
Competition	Descent	38.00 $55,269.19	38.00 $55,269.19	30.00 $38,071.06	12.00 $20,137.98	39.00 $51,741.38	$14
	Endorphin	13.00 $4,499.25	13.00 $4,499.25	5.00 $2,699.55	0.00 $0.00	23.00 $7,918.69	$4
	Mozzie	31.00 $27,750.61	31.00 $27,750.61	12.00 $8,699.25	0.00 $0.00	26.00 $18,964.37	$6
	Total	82.00 $87,519.05	82.00 $87,519.05	47.00 $49,469.86	12.00 $20,137.98	88.00 $78,624.44	$26

There are several summarized fields in each cell. However, it's not apparent to the viewer what these numbers are—they may be totals, averages, or counts. While Crystal Reports does not have a legend capability for cross-tabs, you can create your own

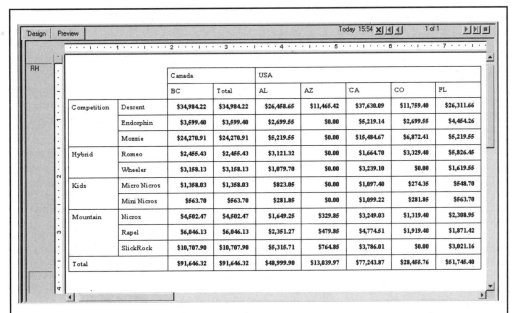

Page 1

		USA						
		IA	ID	IL	KS	MA	MI	MN
Competition	Descent	$26,164.67	$20,137.98	$8,819.55	$8,819.55	$14,258.28	$20,578.95	$31,603.40
	Endorphin	$3,509.42	$1,799.70	$4,454.26	$1,799.70	$1,799.70	$2,699.55	$2,699.55
	Mozzie	$10,352.11	$9,830.17	$3,479.70	$0.00	$5,219.55	$6,959.40	$3,305.72
Hybrid	Romeo	$2,497.05	$1,664.70	$4,869.25	$1,664.70	$3,329.40	$0.00	$2,497.05
	Wheeler	$539.85	$2,699.25	$2,645.27	$0.00	$2,159.40	$1,079.70	$1,619.55
Kids	Micro Nicros	$548.70	$823.05	$260.63	$0.00	$0.00	$274.35	$0.00
	Mini Nicros	$281.85	$281.85	$831.46	$0.00	$281.85	$549.61	$563.70
Mountain	Nicros	$4,601.41	$329.85	$3,282.01	$296.87	$1,962.61	$3,892.24	$2,308.95
	Rapel	$4,270.67	$6,669.92	$2,783.14	$0.00	$2,807.13	$2,351.27	$3,790.82
	SlickRock	$4,589.10	$1,529.70	$2,294.55	$764.85	$1,529.70	$4,550.86	$1,529.70
Total		$57,354.83	$45,766.17	$33,719.82	$13,345.67	$33,347.62	$42,935.93	$49,918.44

Page 2

Figure 9-12.   *Cross-Tab with Keep Columns Together and Repeat Row Labels
turned on*

legends using text objects, and optionally, with filled-box drawing. Here is the multiple-summary cross-tab with a legend:

		Canada		USA			C(
		BC	Total	AL	AZ	CA	
Competition	Descent	38.00	38.00	30.00	12.00	39.00	
		$55,269.19	$55,269.19	$38,071.06	$20,137.98	$51,741.38	$.
	Endorphin	13.00	13.00	5.00	0.00	23.00	
		$4,499.25	$4,499.25	$2,699.55	$0.00	$7,918.69	$
	Mozzie	31.00	31.00	12.00	0.00	26.00	
		$27,750.61	$27,750.61	$8,699.25	$0.00	$13,964.37	$
	Total	82.00	82.00	47.00	12.00	88.00	
		$87,519.05	$87,519.05	$49,469.86	$20,137.98	$78,624.44	$

(Legend: Quantity ■, Price ■)

Text objects have simply been placed in the same report section as the cross-tab, so that they appear in the upper left-hand corner of the cross-tab. The small white area in the cross-tab above the first row and to the left of the first column can be placed right over the top of the text objects. The summary fields have been formatted to show in a different color, and small filled boxes of the same color have been drawn with the box drawing tool (discussed in Chapter 7).

Conditionally Formatting Cross-Tabs

You may wish to conditionally format cross-tab cells, depending on their contents. Conditional formatting (discussed in more detail in Chapter 7), is the process of changing the appearance of a cross-tab cell based on its contents. You may wish to highlight certain cells that exceed a certain sales goal or shipping level; you can change the color, shading, or border of just those cells.

Select the summary or subtotal object that you wish to conditionally format. Then, choose Format | Highlighting Expert from the pull-down menus, or right-click on the cell and choose Highlighting Expert from the pop-up menu. You can choose Highlighting Expert conditions and formats to highlight certain cells.

You can also use conditional formulas if you choose. After selecting a summary or subtotal object in the cross-tab, display the Format Editor by choosing options from the Format pull-down menu or right-clicking and choosing options from the pop-up menu. You can click a Conditional Formula button anywhere on the Format Editor to set that formatting property conditionally.

What is CurrentFieldValue?

When you choose to use conditional formulas instead of the Highlighting Expert, you must be careful about the tests you use to conditionally format cross-tab summaries. Since the summaries are calculations based on database fields, but are not actually the database fields themselves, you can't just test a database field to conditionally format the cross-tab. And, contrary to what you see if you've placed subtotals or summaries in a group footer, you won't see the summaries or subtotals that make up the cells in the field list of the Formula Editor.

You must test the built-in CurrentFieldValue function when conditionally formatting cross-tabs. CurrentFieldValue, as its name suggests, returns whatever the field being tested contains. You can, therefore, use a conditional formula similar to the following to apply a silver background color to cross-tab subtotals that exceed $25,000.

```
If CurrentFieldValue > 25000 Then Silver Else NoColor
```

Figure 9-13 shows a cross-tab with this formatting.

 As much as you might like to, you cannot *drill down on a cross-tab object. If you include a cross-tab in another summary report, you can drill down on the summary report groups, but not on the cross-tab.*

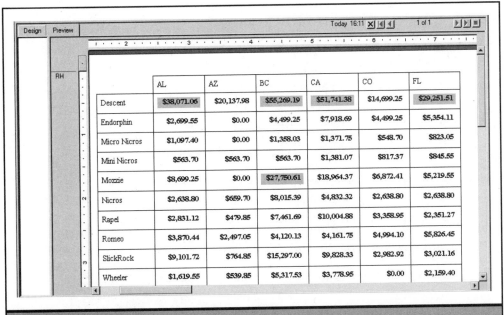

Figure 9-13. *Cross-tab conditional formatting*

The
Complete
Reference

Crystal
Reports
7

Chapter 10

Creating Charts

Crystal Reports isn't just for text! Not only can you create attractive, meaningful text-based reports, you can present the information graphically as well. Using Crystal Reports charting and graphing capabilities, you can see your database data presented in colorful bar charts, pie charts, three-dimensional area charts, and in many other ways. These charts can be seen in the Preview tab right inside Crystal Reports, on Web reports, included in reports exported to Word, Excel, or other word processing and spreadsheet formats, or printed on a black and white or color printer.

You should ask yourself (or your reporting audience) a couple of questions before you start to create a chart. "Will my viewer really benefit from a graphical representation of the data? And what kind of chart best matches the information to be shown?" While it's tempting to create lots of pretty, colorful charts, they aren't always an appropriate way to get across the "message" of the report. But for the many instances when a chart will add value to a report, you have a great number of charting options available to you.

Types and Layouts of Charts

Once you've decided to use a chart, you have two general choices to make about how you'll create your chart: what type of chart to use, and how the chart will be laid out. The *chart type* refers to what the chart will look like, showing data in bars, lines, a pie, or some other graphical representation. The *chart layout* refers to the data that will be used to make up the chart, whether it comes from the details section, from group summaries, or from a cross-tab or OLAP grid (OLAP reporting is discussed in Chapter 17).

Chart Type

The next choice to make is which type of chart best represents the data to be charted. While some types may be prettier than others, you will again need to consider what type of chart will add real meaning to the data, allowing the viewer to get the most benefit from the report. Table 10-1 discusses the main types of charts available in the Crystal Reports Chart Expert and where they are best used. When you begin to use the Chart Expert, you'll notice that there are actually several variations on each of these main chart types.

Chart Layout

In addition to the type of chart, you have a choice as to what data the chart will represent. *Cross-tab charts* and *OLAP charts* are fairly easy to understand—they graph data in existing cross-tab objects or OLAP grids on your report. A *Group chart* graphs data contained in subtotal or summary fields in existing group headers or footers. A *Detail chart* graphs data in the details section. Your choice of which to use will be based on your individual report design and the way you want to graphically display the data.

Chart Type	Usage
Bar 	A bar chart shows a series of bars side by side on the page. These are effective for seeing how items compare to each other in terms of volume, size, dollars, etc. They may also be effective in plotting growth over time.
Line 	Line charts show trends over time, particularly for multiple groups of data.
Area 	An area chart is similar to a line chart, except that the area below the line is filled in with a color. Like the line chart, it is helpful for showing trends over time, but for just one or a few groups of data.
Pie 	Pie charts, the circle with colored slices for each item, are good for seeing which item is the biggest "piece of the pie." They represent percentages for each item, and are effective for small to moderate numbers of items.
Doughnut 	A doughnut chart is similar to a pie chart—it shows who has the biggest bite of the donut. The only difference from a pie chart is that the doughnut has a hole in the middle, where the grand total for the chart is displayed.
3-D Riser 	The 3-D riser chart is a three-dimensional version of the bar chart. You can choose what shape you want for the bars—a cone, pyramid, etc. Because this chart is three-dimensional, it can show multiple groups of data side-by-side.
3-D Surface 	The 3-D surface chart is a three-dimensional version of the area chart; it shows multiple groups of data in a three-dimensional view.
XY Scatter 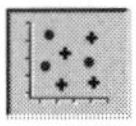	The XY scatter chart plots data as points on two axes, allowing you to see if a correlation exists between the individual items.
Radar 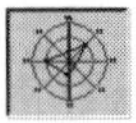	The radar chart looks a little like a radar screen, with concentric circles expanding from the center. Each group of data is drawn as a line from the center to the outside of the chart, with the subtotal of that group being displayed on the line in its relative location.

Table 10-1.   *Crystal Reports Chart Types*

Chart Type	Usage
Bubble	The bubble chart is very similar to an XY scatter chart, plotting individual points within two axes. However, the bubble chart provides more quantitative information by varying the size of the plotted points as well.
Stock	A stock chart is similar to a bar chart in that it displays side-by-side bars. However, all the bars don't start at the bottom of the chart. Both the top and bottom of the bars are based on data supplied. This chart is helpful for viewing minimum and maximum financial data, such as stock prices.

Table 10-1.   *Crystal Reports Chart Types* (continued)

It's particularly important to understand the difference between a Group and Detail chart, and to know where they can be placed on a report. Look at the following illustration:

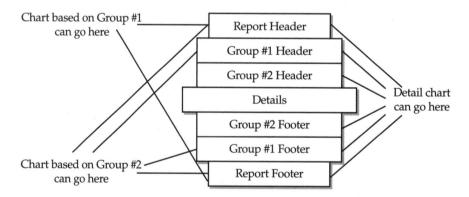

In essence, a chart must always be placed *at least one level higher* than the data it's graphing. A Detail chart must be placed in a group header or footer or the report header or footer. A Group chart must be placed in a group header or footer of a higher-level group (if there is one), or the report header or footer. You can *never* place a Detail chart, Group chart, or Cross-tab chart in the details section. And, even though Crystal Reports will allow you to place an OLAP chart in the details section (probably an oversight by the program's designers), it will never show any data.

Cross-tab and OLAP charts don't have the "one level higher" requirement, although they don't make much sense if they are placed at a lower level in the report. If, for example, you have a cross-tab object placed in the report header, it will only appear one time: at the beginning of the report. You can create a chart based on the one-time-only cross-tab and place it in group headers or footers. It will simply show the same information over and over again for each group.

Where you place a chart determines the data that it depicts. If you create a Detail chart and place it in a group header, it will depict just the details sections for that group—a different chart will appear for each group. If you place the same Detail chart in the report header or footer, it will depict data for the entire report. You'll see the same behavior for a Group chart. If you place it in a higher-level group, it will only graph data for subgroups within the group where it is located. If you place the Group chart in a report header or footer, it will include data for all groups on the report.

Creating Charts with the Chart Expert

You can create a chart either by using one of the report experts from the Report Gallery, or by using the Chart Expert after you've created a report with the Custom option. If you're using one of the report experts, clicking the Graph tab will display the Chart Expert right inside the report expert. If you've already created a report with an expert and want to just add a chart to it without re-running the expert, or if your report is designed with the Custom option, you can display the Chart Expert in one of two ways. Either click the Insert Chart button on the Standard toolbar, or choose Insert | Chart from the pull-down menus. The Chart Expert will appear.

The Chart Expert is a tabbed dialog box that gives you tremendous flexibility for designing your charts. If you used a version of Crystal Reports prior to Version 7, you'll be pleasantly surprised by the vast increase in flexibility with the new Chart Expert. You specify chart options by progressing through the Chart Expert's five tabs: Type, Data, Axes, Options, and Text.

The Type Tab

When the Chart Expert first appears, the Type tab will be displayed. Figure 10-1 shows the Type tab.

First, choose the general type of chart (such as pie, bar, area, etc.) that you want to use from the list. When you make a general choice, you'll typically see a more specific set of choices shown as thumbnails on the right. To use the specific type of chart, click the thumbnail that best represents what you want to use. You'll see a description of the layout and uses of the chart in the scroll box below.

Certain chart types give you a choice of horizontal or vertical direction. If you choose vertical with a bar chart, for example, the bars will "grow" out of the bottom of the chart. If you choose horizontal, they will "spread" from the left of the chart towards the right.

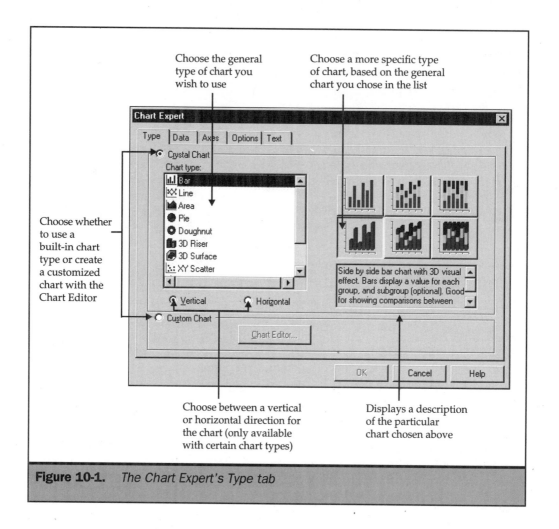

Choose the general type of chart you wish to use

Choose a more specific type of chart, based on the general chart you chose in the list

Choose whether to use a built-in chart type or create a customized chart with the Chart Editor

Choose between a vertical or horizontal direction for the chart (only available with certain chart types)

Displays a description of the particular chart chosen above

Figure 10-1. *The Chart Expert's Type tab*

If you click the Custom Chart radio button, followed by the Chart Editor button, a separate graphical application called the Chart Editor will appear. The Chart Editor lets you completely customize your chart with many useful tools. The Chart Editor is discussed in detail later in the chapter.

If you have used a version of Crystal Reports previous to Version 7, there are now many advanced features available right from the Chart Expert. You may not need to use the Chart Editor now where you would have had to in the past.

The Data Tab

The Data tab is where you choose the layout for the chart—whether it will be a Detail, Group, Cross-tab, or OLAP chart. You also use the Data tab to select the actual database or formula fields you want Crystal Reports to use when creating your chart, and to choose where you want the chart placed, and when you want the chart to "change" graphically (when you want a new bar or pie slice to be created, when you want a new point plotted on the line, etc.).

Begin by choosing the chart layout you want to use. The four buttons on the left side of the Data tab may or may not be enabled, based on other elements in your report.

- The Group button will only be available if at least one group has been created on your report.

- The Detail button will be available except when you've selected an OLAP grid before starting the Chart Expert.

- The Cross-Tab button will only be available if you've selected a cross-tab object on your report before starting the Chart Expert.

- The OLAP button will only be available if you've selected an OLAP grid object on your report before starting the Chart Expert.

The only parts of the Data tab that remain constant regardless of the button you choose are the Place Chart drop-down list and the Header and Footer radio buttons. The Place Chart drop-down list lets you choose where on the report you want Crystal Reports to initially place your chart. Again, depending on the chart type you use, the choices here will be different. Group charts can be placed in a higher-level group or in the report header and footer. Detail, Cross-tab, and OLAP charts can be placed in a group or report header or footer. Choose Once per Report or For Each <Group> from the drop-down list. Then click the radio button that corresponds to where in the report you want the chart placed: the header or footer.

The rest of the Data tab will change, based on the chart layout button you click.

Group

A Group chart will graph data based on fields in an existing report group. You will have to have at least one group defined, with at least one subtotal or summary field, before you can make use of this button.

Figure 10-2 shows the Data tab when the Group button is clicked.

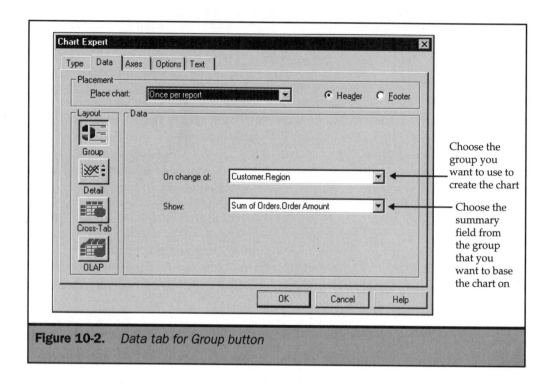

Figure 10-2.   *Data tab for Group button*

The On Change Of drop-down list lets you choose when you want the graph to start a new element. If, for example, you choose Customer.Country, then a new bar will show up in a bar chart for every country. On Change Of Orders.Sales Rep, for example, will create a new slice in a pie chart for every salesperson.

The On Change Of drop-down list's contents change in correlation with what you choose in the Place Chart drop-down list. In essence, the On Change Of drop-down list will show you one or two levels lower than where you're placing your chart. For example, if you choose to place the chart Once per Report, the On Change Of drop-down list will show the highest-level group on the report. If there is more than one group, it will also show an additional option of showing the highest-level group and the next-highest-level group. If you choose to place the report in a group, On Change Of will show the next two lower-level groups, and so on.

Here's an example of what shows up in the On Change Of drop-down list when the chart is placed Once per Report and there are country and region groups on the report.

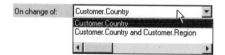

If you choose a single group, your chart will just summarize the values in that group, as shown here:

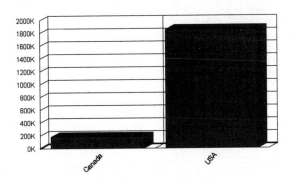

If you choose the two-group option, Crystal Reports actually creates two sections of the chart: the first section based on the first group, and a second section based on the second group, like this:

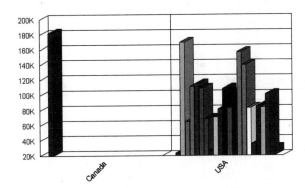

The Show drop-down list will let you choose what makes up the chart element. If, for example, you create a bar chart with On Change Of set to Customer.Country and Show set to Sum of Customer.Last Year's Sales, you'll see a new bar for every country. The bar's height or width (based on whether you chose a horizontal or vertical bar chart) will be based on the subtotal of Last Year's Sales for the group.

The Show drop-down list is populated based on what subtotal and summary fields you place in the group header or footer of the group chosen in On Change Of. For a group graph to work, you must have at least one summary or subtotal for the group. If you choose a group in On Change Of and nothing is available in the Show drop-down list, you'll need to cancel the Chart Expert and add at least one summary or subtotal to the group.

Detail

A Detail chart graphs data from the details section of your report. Although you can create a Detail chart even if you have groups defined, it won't be affected by the groups at all. Figure 10-3 shows the Data tab when the Detail button is clicked.

This rather busy dialog box lets you choose data from your detail section to create a chart. Because there can be several different fields in the detail section that can affect the chart's appearance, there's a little more forethought required when using this dialog box.

The Available Fields list shows report, formula, and database fields in the report. You can select any of these fields that you need for creating your chart. If you're unsure what kind of data is in a field, select it and click the Browse button to see a sample of database data. Once you're ready to use a field as either an On Change Of or Show Value(s) field, select the field and click the right arrow next to the box where you want the field placed. It will be copied to the box on the right.

The drop-down list in the upper right gives you two choices: On Change Of or For Each Record. The choice you make here determines how often a new chart element (bar, pie slice, etc.) will appear in the chart.

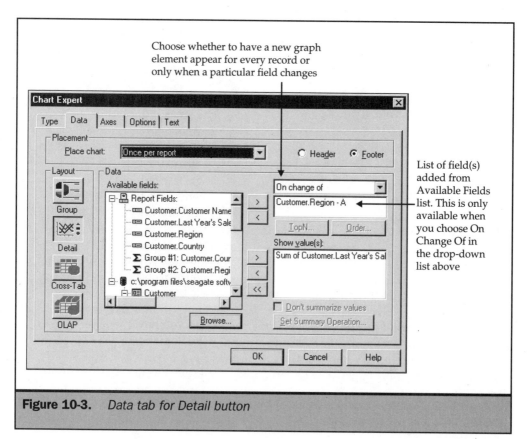

Figure 10-3.   *Data tab for Detail button*

If you choose For Each Record, a new element will appear in the chart for every record in your details section. This may be useful for very small tables that have only a few records in them. However, if your database has more than a few records, making this choice will probably render a chart that's too crowded to be of any real value. If you make this choice, the box below the drop-down list will remain empty—you won't be able to add any fields to it from the Available Fields list.

By choosing On Change Of in the drop-down list, and choosing one or more fields from the Available Fields list, you can create a chart that summarizes values in your details section. This option will basically create an invisible group on your report and create a new chart element every time the chosen field changes. For example, if your report contains no groups, but you choose On Change Of Customer.Country, your chart will have a new element appear for each unique country that appears in your details section. Whatever field you add to the Show Value(s) list will be summarized or subtotaled by country, and the result will be used as the value for the chart.

Tip *You can choose one or two fields to add to the On Change Of list. This works like the Group chart option described previously in which you could choose to show the highest-level group and the next-highest-level group. If you choose one field, the chart will only contain one section with all the elements located in it. If you choose two fields, the chart will be broken into two side-by-side sections, with individual elements for the second field in each section.*

Although there isn't an actual group on the report, Crystal Reports is creating an "invisible" group to base your chart on. You have control over the way the Chart Expert uses these groups. The TopN and Order buttons control this. If you click the TopN button, you'll see the Top N/Sort Group Expert dialog box. Here you can choose to include only the top *N* or bottom *N* groups in your chart, and you can choose which number to use for *N*. If you click the Order button, you'll see the Chart Sort Order dialog box with a drop-down list containing Ascending, Descending, and Specified Order options. You may choose to show the chart elements in A to Z order, Z to A order, or using specified grouping. Refer to Chapter 3 for information on Top N and Specified Order grouping.

Once you've chosen a field in the On Change Of box to determine when a new chart element will appear, you can add a field or fields to the Show Value(s) list to indicate which values Crystal Reports will use to size the chart element. If you add multiple fields to this list, the chart will contain multiple bars, lines, etc.—one for each field you add to the list.

If you add a number or currency field to this list (and you haven't chosen For Each Record in the top drop-down list), Crystal Reports will automatically use the Sum function to summarize the field for each invisible group. If you choose another type of field, Crystal Reports will automatically use the Count function. If you wish to change the summary function (for example, to graph the average sales amount instead of the total) you can select the field you want to change in the Show Value(s) list and click the

Set Summary Operation button. A dialog box will appear with a drop-down list containing the available summary functions for that type of field. Choose the summary function you want used to size the chart element.

If you choose For Each Record in the top drop-down list, Crystal Reports will display a new chart element for every record on the report—no invisible group will be created. In this case, any fields you add to the Show Value(s) list won't be summarized. If you choose On Change Of in the top drop-down list and the invisible groups are created, you can specify that one or more values in the Show Value(s) list *not* be summarized by selecting the field and checking Don't Summarize Values. Be careful if you do this—only the first occurrence of the field in the invisible group will be included in the chart. The rest will simply be ignored.

The following illustration shows the resulting chart for the Data tab shown in Figure 10-3.

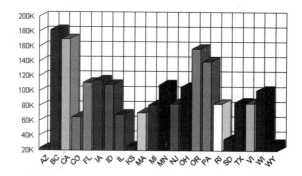

Cross-Tab

The Cross-Tab button will only be available if you have a cross-tab object on your report, and you have selected it before starting the Chart Expert (Chapter 9 discusses cross-tab objects).

Figure 10-4 shows the Data tab when the Cross-Tab button is clicked.

The Graph On drop-down list will show the summary field or fields you placed in your cross-tab. Choose the field that you want to use in your chart. This field will determine the size of the chart elements (height of a bar, size of a pie slice, etc.).

The By drop-down list will include the two outer fields you chose for your cross-tab row and column; if you used multiple row and column fields, only the first row or field can be used. Crystal Reports will create one chart element (bar, pie slice, etc.) for each occurrence of this field in the cross-tab.

The Subdivided By drop-down list is initially set to None. If you leave it this way, the chart will only create one series of chart elements, based on the field in the By drop-down list. If, however, you want to create two series of elements for side-by-side comparison, or if you're using a 3-D riser or 3-D area chart and want to see multiple elements three-dimensionally, choose the other row/column field in the Subdivided By drop-down list.

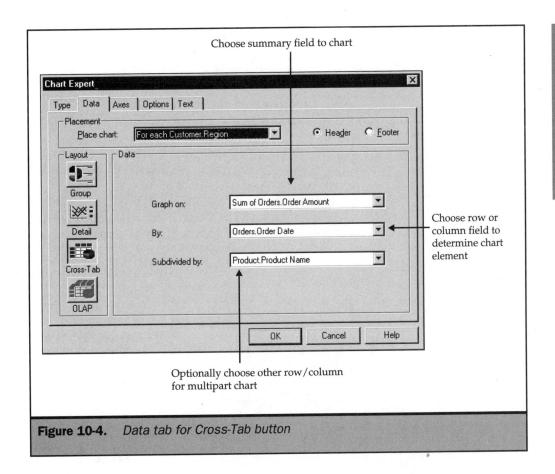

Figure 10-4. Data tab for Cross-Tab button

The following illustration shows the resulting 3-D riser chart for the Data tab shown in Figure 10-4.

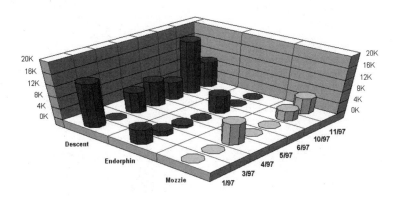

OLAP

The OLAP button will only be available if you have an OLAP grid on your report and you have selected it before starting the Chart Expert (Chapter 17 discusses OLAP reporting).

Figure 10-5 shows the Data tab when the OLAP button is clicked.

Creating a chart based on an OLAP grid is very similar to creating a chart based on a cross-tab. There are just a couple of differences between the two. There is no summary field to choose (OLAP grids only display one value, so there is no choice to make). Also, the dimension hierarchy of your OLAP grid may be a little different than the multiple row/column fields you added to a cross-tab object.

Choose a dimension on which to base the chart from the By drop-down list. A new chart element will be created for every occurrence of this dimension. As with cross-tab charts, only the outer or first dimension, if you've added multiple dimensions to your

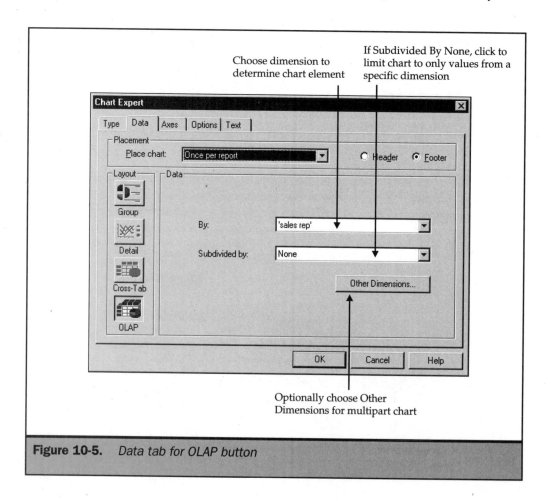

Figure 10-5. *Data tab for OLAP button*

OLAP grid, will be available. If you leave the Subdivided By drop-down list set to None, the chart will only create one series of chart elements, based on the dimension in the By drop-down list. If, however, you want to create two series of elements for side-by-side comparison, or if you're using a 3-D riser or 3-D area chart and want to see multiple elements three-dimensionally, choose another dimension in the Subdivided By drop-down list.

If you leave the Subdivided By drop-down list set to None, the OLAP chart will be limited to just one of the other outer dimensions. For example, consider the following OLAP grid fragment:

		Year 1995						
		Quarter 01 95				Quarter 02 95		
		Jan 95	Feb 95	Mar 95		Apr 95	May 95	
'All reps'	Nancy Davolic	29,231.39	22,142.27	32,315.55	83,689.21	46,109.24	26,050.09	
	Janet Leverling	34,738.99	31,537.33	13,326.14	79,602.46	26,799.92	41,946.57	
	Margaret Peacc	27,905.17	36,168.91	6,846.81	70,920.89	12,662.12	33,266.45	
	Michael Suyan	41,418.84	51,649.73	26,605.79	119,674.36	23,287.93	18,104.84	
	Robert King	27,464.18	23,052.19	36,689.93	87,206.30	24,424.72	28,650.16	
	Anne Dodswor	38,573.23	27,988.28	29,605.63	96,167.14	42,319.04	18,892.37	
		199,331.80	192,538.71	145,389.85	537,260.36	175,602.97	166,910.48	

If you chose to chart by the Sales Rep dimension and not subdivide, your chart will create just one element for All Reps, or an element for each individual rep (depending on what you choose in the By drop-down list). However, it's very important to know that by default your chart will only include data for Year 1995. Because Crystal Reports will not "roll up" dimension totals for you, you'll need to choose which dimension total you want to see if the default isn't sufficient.

To do this, click the Other Dimensions button. This will display the Other Dimensions dialog box, in which you can choose the particular subdimension of the OLAP grid that you want charted.

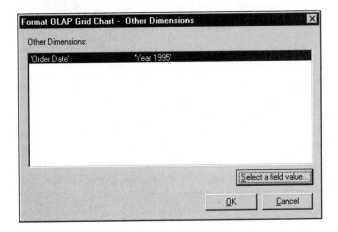

Click one of the available Other Dimensions and click the Select a Field Value button. The Select a Field for Dimension dialog box will appear, with the dimension hierarchy displayed in an Explorer-like fashion.

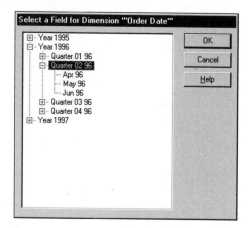

Navigate through the dimension hierarchy and choose a level that you want to limit the chart to. For example, if you navigate down from Year 1996 and choose Quarter 02 96, your OLAP chart will just contain totals for Quarter 02 96 in the OLAP grid.

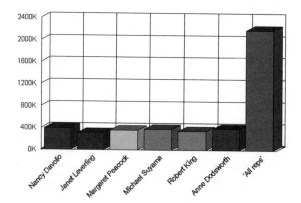

The Axes Tab

The Axes tab gives you complete control over how Crystal Reports displays the x, y, and z (if you're using a 3-D chart) axes of the chart. Figure 10-6 shows the Axes tab.

By making choices in the Axes tab, you can control how Crystal Reports will display axes on your charts. The *axes* are the areas of the chart that describe or depict the data values in the chart. If, for example, you have a bar chart in which each bar represents sales volume for a salesperson, the bottom of the chart where each

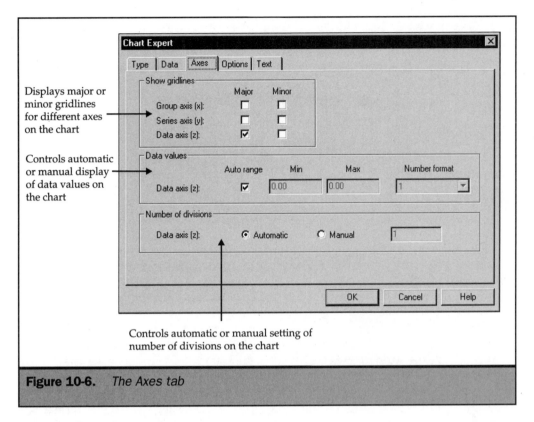

Displays major or minor gridlines for different axes on the chart

Controls automatic or manual display of data values on the chart

Controls automatic or manual setting of number of divisions on the chart

Figure 10-6. *The Axes tab*

salesperson is listed is called the *group axis* (also sometimes called the x-axis). The left side of the chart where the numbers representing the volume appear is called the *data axis* (sometimes called the y-axis), as shown here:

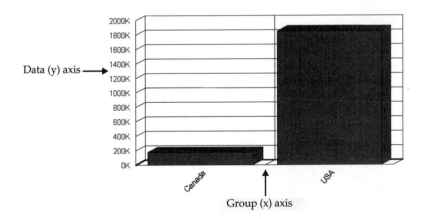

Data (y) axis

Group (x) axis

If you are using a three-dimensional chart, the data axis is the z-axis, and a new axis called the *series axis* is the y-axis, like this:

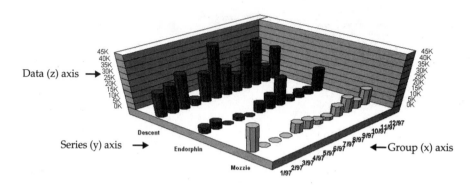

Click the Major or Minor check boxes to add gridlines to the chosen axes. *Major gridlines* fall directly in line with the axis labels that Crystal Reports assigns to the axis. *Minor gridlines* will appear in between the axis labels, and will only work for numeric labels. Depending on the type of chart you're using, you may not notice any difference between major and minor gridlines. Also, some charts will always have a group axis gridline, regardless of what you choose on the Axes tab.

If you leave the Auto Range check box for the Data values option on, Crystal Reports will automatically format the chart based on the number of elements it includes. If you wish to customize this, you can turn off the Auto Range option and add starting and ending values for the axes, as well as choosing the number format (decimals, currency symbols, etc.) to use for the labels. If you choose a certain number format, such as a currency symbol, and then recheck Auto Range, the axes will be automatically renumbered, but the number format you chose will stay in place.

If you leave the Number of Divisions set to Automatic, Crystal Reports will create a predefined number of labels and gridlines for the data axes. Clicking the Manual radio button and specifying a number in the text box will create your specified number of divisions, along with labels and gridlines, for the data axes.

 Not all of the options on the Axes tab will necessarily apply to the style of chart you are using. For example, a pie chart will make no use of any options on the Axes tab. If an option doesn't apply to the type of chart you've chosen, it will be dimmed.

The Options Tab

The Options tab allows you to customize general options for your chart, such as whether to display it in color or black and white, whether to show a legend and where to place it, and other options. The Options tab will change based on the type of chart you've chosen. Figure 10-7 shows the Options tab for a bar chart.

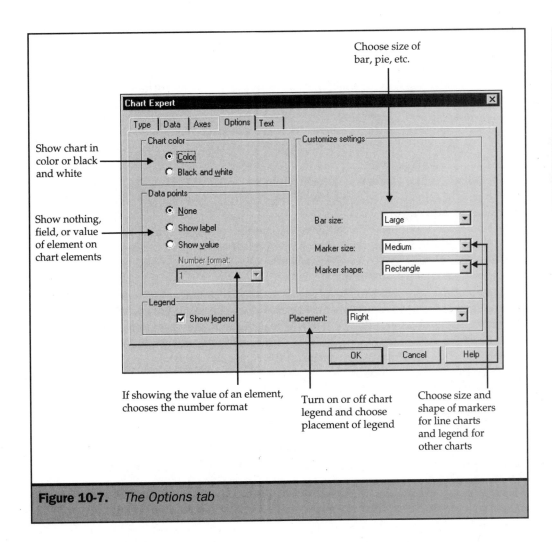

Figure 10-7. *The Options tab*

The most self-explanatory options on the Options tab are Chart Color and the Bar/Pie Size drop-down list. Make choices as you see fit for your particular chart.

Tip   *If you're printing your reports on a black and white printer, it may be preferable to leave the chart in color and let the printer assign gray tones to the chart elements. These may actually look better than the ones Crystal Reports assigns. Experiment to determine what works best with your particular printer.*

The Data Points section lets you choose whether you want labels or numbers to appear on your chart elements. If, for example, you choose Show Label with a pie chart, each of the slices of the pie will be labeled with the item that the slice refers to. If you choose Show Value with a bar chart and choose a number format of $1, you'll see the actual dollar amounts (with no decimal places) appearing above each bar.

The Marker Size and Marker Shape drop-down lists let you choose how markers look on a line chart. Markers are the points on the line chart that get connected with the lines. Even if your chart is not a line chart, the Marker Shape drop-down list will customize the display of the chart legend, if you show one.

The Show Legend check box will determine whether or not a legend appears on your chart. The legend is the color-coded key that indicates what the elements of your chart refer to. You can also choose where to place the legend with options in the Placement drop-down list. You might want legends for a pie chart with no labels, for example. However, if you are using a bar chart with labels already appearing along the bottom of the chart, a legend is redundant and should be turned off.

There are two additional features of the Options tab that apply to 3-D riser, 3-D area, pie, and doughnut charts. If you're using a three-dimensional chart, the Options tab will contain a Viewing Angle drop-down list. Choose a different viewing angle for the chart, such as From the Top or Bird's Eye to present the chart from a different angle. If you're using a single pie or doughnut chart (not multiple pies or doughnuts), a Detach Pie Slice option will appear that allows you to detach the smallest or largest slice from the rest of the slices.

The Text Tab

The Text tab, shown in Figure 10-8, allows you to assign text to different parts of your chart, and to change the appearance of these text items. You can add a chart title, subtitle, and footnote. And, you can place titles on the group, data, and series (or data2) axes of your chart.

Just type the material you want to appear on the chart in the text boxes on the Text tab (the Data2 Title box will only be available if you have multiple data ranges on your chart). If you leave a text box blank, that title won't appear on the chart.

To change the appearance of the different items, select the item you want to change in the list on the lower right of the Text tab. Then, click the Font button to choose the font face, size, and appearance for that item. A sample of the font you chose will appear in the shaded box above the Font button. If you choose Group Title or Data Title labels to format, the Staggered Text check box will be available. Checking this will alternate the labels instead of printing them side-by-side. This will enhance readability when the labels are long.

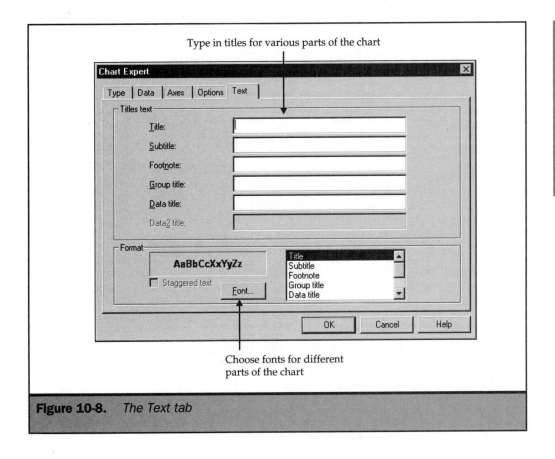

Type in titles for various parts of the chart

Choose fonts for different
parts of the chart

Figure 10-8.   *The Text tab*

Figure 10-9 shows a chart with all the labels set. You can see where each of the labels appears on a typical chart.

In the initial release of Crystal Reports 7 (7.0.1.192), most font options don't work consistently. You may set fonts and notice that they don't have any effect on the chart. If you save the report and reopen it, you'll notice that your font changes weren't saved. Hopefully this will be corrected in future versions of the product.

Placing and Sizing Charts

Once you complete all the information on the Chart Expert and click OK, Crystal Reports will place the chart in the upper-left corner of the header or footer section you

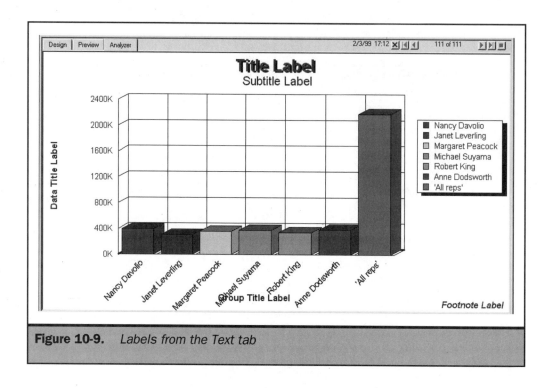

Figure 10-9.   *Labels from the Text tab*

chose. Unlike other objects you add, it won't be attached to a mouse cursor allowing you to drop it where you wish. If there are already other objects in the section, the chart will be placed on top of them.

When the chart is placed, it remains selected, however. You'll notice the shaded outline and sizing handles around the chart. You can now drag it to another location in the same section, or move it to another section on the report. You can also resize the chart by using the sizing handles, or move and resize the chart by choosing Format | Object Size and Position from the pull-down menus, or right-clicking the chart and choosing Object Size and Position from the pop-up menu.

Remember that where you place a chart determines the data that it displays. If you place a Detail or Group chart in the report header or footer, it will display data for the whole report. If you place the chart in a group header or footer, the chart will appear for every group, only showing data for that particular group. Cross-tab and OLAP charts display the data from the objects they're attached to. If you place a cross-tab object and matching chart in a group header or footer, the cross-tab and chart will only display data for the group they're in. Since OLAP grids don't change based on their location on the report, a matching OLAP chart will look the same no matter where you place it.

Depending on the type of chart you've chosen and whether or not you've displayed the chart in the Preview tab, you will see live data in the Design tab or just a dummy chart that represents what the chart will look like. Even though the dummy chart doesn't show actual report data, it will display properly when you click the Preview tab.

Placing Charts Alongside Text

When you first create a chart in a section, it's placed in the upper-left corner of the section by default. If the chart is in a report or group header, the chart will print before the rest of the report or the group, as the section containing the chart will print first. There may be times when you'd like a chart to appear *alongside* the data it's referring to. Typically, this might be a detail chart that you've placed in a group header. Instead of having the chart print by itself, followed by the details that belong to the group, you may want the chart to print alongside the details sections.

By using the Underlay option in the Section Expert, you can format the group header section to underlay the following details sections, thereby printing the chart alongside the other items. For this to work effectively, you need to size and move the details section objects so that they won't be overprinted by the chart. Then, move and size the chart so it will appear to the side of the details section objects. Format the section containing the chart to Underlay Following Sections. If there is a group name, column headings, or other information in the group header that you *don't* want to be underlaid, you'll need to create a second group header section for the chart that you underlay. Format it to use the Underlay feature and format the first group header containing the textual information with Underlay turned off. See Chapter 8 for more information on multiple sections and the Underlay feature.

Figure 10-10 shows a Detail chart placed in Group Header b with Underlay Following Sections turned on.

Modifying Existing Charts

Once you've created a chart, you may wish to change the chart. Perhaps you prefer to see a pie chart instead of a bar chart. Or, you may want to change the titles that appear on the chart. You may even want to change the chart from a Detail chart to a Group chart, or vice versa.

First, select the chart you want to change in either the Design or Preview tab. Then, choose Format | Chart Expert or Format | Graph | Chart from the pull-down menus, or right-click the selected chart and choose Chart Expert from the pop-up menu. The Chart Expert will reappear and you can make any desired changes before clicking OK.

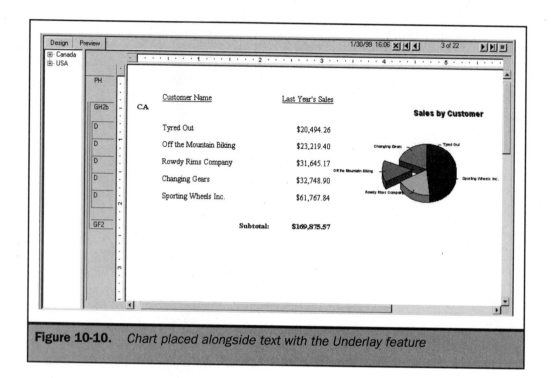

Figure 10-10. *Chart placed alongside text with the Underlay feature*

If you want to change the chart layout (from Detail to Group, Cross-tab to Detail, etc.) there are some restrictions you should keep in mind:

- You can change a Group chart to a Detail chart and vice versa.

- You can change a Cross-tab chart to a Group or Detail chart, but not an OLAP chart. You *cannot* change a Group or Detail chart to a Cross-tab chart.

- You can change an OLAP chart to a Group or Detail chart, but not to a Cross-tab chart. You *cannot* change a Group or Detail chart to an OLAP chart.

Customizing Charts with the Chart Editor

If you've created charts of any sophistication in a version of Crystal Reports prior to Version 7, you're probably familiar with the PG Editor. This was often required to customize charts to even the smallest degree. In Crystal Reports 7, the Chart Expert has been greatly expanded to provide much more flexibility when creating charts. However, there may still be times when you want to have even more control over how your charts appear, and the Chart Expert doesn't provide the necessary options.

The PG Editor has been renamed the Chart Editor in Crystal Reports 7 and is used to customize charts beyond the features found in the Chart Expert. You can use the

Chart Editor either when initially creating a chart, or after you've used the Chart Expert to create the chart. To use the Chart Editor, display the Chart Expert for a new or existing chart, as described earlier in this chapter. On the Type tab, click the Custom Chart radio button, then the Chart Editor button.

If you are creating a new chart for the first time, the Chart Editor will appear and display a dummy chart. You'll need to select options from the Chart Editor menus to create your chart. If you are editing an existing chart, it will appear in the Chart Editor where you can customize it to your liking.

Figure 10-11 shows the Chart Editor displaying an existing chart.

The Chart Editor is a completely separate program (the program is known as Seagate Charts) that passes chart information to and from Crystal Reports. It's a fairly sophisticated charting program that could easily fill several chapters on its own. It was originally developed for Seagate Software by a third party, and doesn't match Crystal Reports layout or terminology. Toolbars and dialog boxes, for example, are referred to as *palettes*. It's best to experiment with the different pull-down and pop-up menu options and read the online Help file to get a feel for the Chart Editor.

Once you've modified an existing chart or created a new chart in the Chart Editor, simply close the Chart Editor with the close button, or by choosing File | Exit from the pull-down menus. You'll be asked if you want to save your chart. If you reply Yes, the chart will be saved and placed on your report. If you want to modify the chart later, select the chart and display the Chart Expert from the Edit menu or pop-up menu.

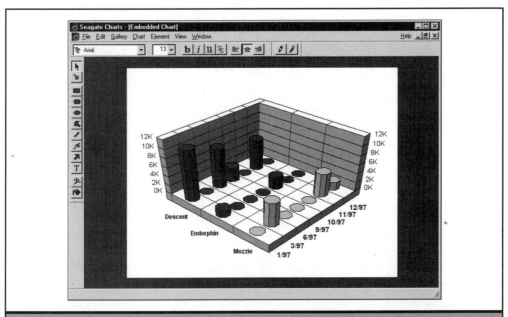

Figure 10-11. *The Chart Editor*

Then, click the Chart Editor button on the Type tab to redisplay the chart in the Chart Editor.

To get you started using the Chart Editor, here are a few simple features that will give you a taste of the flexibility of the tool.

Because the Chart Editor is a separate executable program (known as Seagate Charts), it opens in its own window. If you click back in the Crystal Reports window, you may cover up the open Chart Editor window. If you then return to the Chart Expert and click the Chart Editor button, nothing will happen. This is not because the Chart Editor isn't working, but because it's already open. Just use ALT-TAB to cycle through open programs until you come to Seagate Charts. You can also look for Seagate Charts in the Windows 95/98 or NT taskbar and select it there.

Changing Colors and Shades of Chart Elements

When you create a chart in the Chart Expert, your only choices on the Options tab for affecting chart colors are the Color/Black and White radio buttons. You have no control at all over what individual colors or shades the chart elements will have. The ability to completely customize element colors and shades is another feature available in the Chart Editor.

Begin by selecting the element you wish to color. This can be an individual bar, pie slice, or line. Note that it may look as though you've only selected a part of an element, for example, just one side or just the top of the bar. Whenever you change the color, however, it will apply to the entire element. If you want to color more than one element, you can select multiple elements with SHIFT-click.

Ensure that the Color Palette buttons are displayed in the Chart Editor. You'll see the two buttons toward the right of the top toolbar.

If you don't see them, make sure that Color Palette is turned on in the View pull-down menu. The Color Palette consists of two small buttons, one displaying a pencil and one displaying a paintbrush. The pencil button will change the color of lines or borders around the selected object. The paintbrush button will change the fill color of the selected object. Clicking either button will display a color palette.

You can click one of the colors in the palette to apply the fill or border color to the objects you've selected. You can click the RGB box in the palette (if your video settings are set to 16-bit or higher color resolution) to display the Windows Color Picker, in which you can pick or create your own color. If you click the large X box, the line or background of the object will become transparent, letting other objects show through the border or background of your selected objects.

 You can also apply a background pattern to an object. If, for example, you don't want slices in a pie chart to have solid color, but to have a gradient or cross-hatch pattern, you can apply existing patterns or create your own. Once you've selected the object you wish to apply a pattern to, click the Special Effect Palette button on the left side of the screen. The Fill Effect Palette will appear.

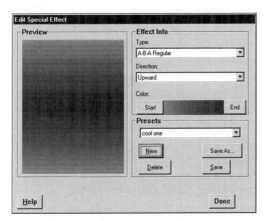

Click the Pattern, Gradient, or Texture buttons to choose the kind of fill effect you want to apply to your selected element. You'll see the first predefined effect for the chosen effect type in the sample window, along with its name in the drop-down list at the top of the dialog box. You can choose from any of the predefined effects by choosing them in the drop-down list or using the arrow buttons below the sample window to cycle through them. Once you've located an effect that you'd like to apply, click the Apply button to apply the effect.

If you want to create and save your own effects or edit the predefined effects, click the Edit button. The Edit Special Effect dialog box will appear.

You can modify the type and direction of the effect, choose starting and ending colors, and save the effect with its own name for future use. Click Done to return to the Fill Effect palette to apply your effect.

Customizing and Moving Chart Titles and the Legend

When you add a title, labels, and legend to your chart with the Options and Text tabs of the Chart Expert, Crystal Reports places them in specific locations, using specific colors and alignment. If you choose to display a legend on your chart, you only have a few predefined locations on the Options tab where you can place it. The Chart Editor gives you the flexibility to move, change, and format these objects as you see fit.

Chart titles, labels, and the legend are all objects that you can select by pointing and clicking. Once you've selected an object, you can use toolbar buttons, pull-down menu options, or right-click pop-up menus to change appearance and formatting. To move or resize an object, simply select it and drag it to a new location, or resize it with the sizing handles. To change alignment, choose the object and click one of the alignment buttons in the top toolbar. To change the color of an object, select it and click the Color Palette in the top toolbar. To change the font or point size of any of the labels or titles, select them and choose different font information from the top toolbar.

Using Additional Chart Types

While the Chart Expert contains many different types and variations of charts (bubble, scatter, etc.), the Chart Editor contains even more. Depending on the database you're using, you can create Gantt charts for project management, histograms, 3-D scatter charts, and more. The Gallery menu provides all the different types of charts that can be selected.

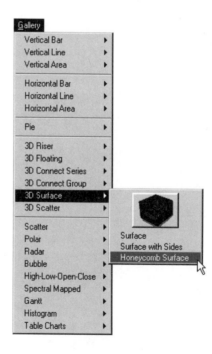

When you choose one of the main Gallery menu options, a submenu will appear with all the variations on the main option. When you point to submenu items with your mouse, a thumbnail of the chart type will appear in the submenu. This helps you determine how that particular type of chart will look.

Using Chart Editor Templates

If you have a particular set of Chart Editor settings you'd like to use on more than one chart, you can save the settings in a Chart Editor *template*. You can then apply the template to another chart that you create or edit.

To save a template, make any desired changes to your chart, such as changing label positions, element colors, and perhaps the legend position. Then choose File | Save As from the pull-down menus. The resulting dialog box will let you save the template in a file with the .3TF extension. Typical settings that are saved in the template file are title and label formatting, legend formatting, chart type, and element colors and shading.

To apply the saved template to a new chart, create a new chart or open an existing chart from the Chart Expert. Choose File | Apply Template from the pull-down menus and choose the correct .3TF template file you want to apply. When you click OK, the template settings will be applied to the existing chart.

Figure 10-12 shows two charts. The first is created using settings right in the Chart Expert. The second shows the chart after customizing with some of the Chart Editor features just discussed.

Drilling Down on Charts

If you create a Group chart, you'll notice the mouse cursor change to a magnifying glass when you point to a chart element. This drill-down cursor indicates that you can double-click a chart element that you're interested in to drill down on the chart. When you drill down on a chart element, another tab appears next to the Preview tab for the particular group you drilled down on. Drill-down allows your report viewer to interact with charts, much as they interact with group footer and group header subtotal and summary fields.

By creative use of Group charts and hiding of details and group header/footer sections, you can create a very visually appealing, interactive report for use in online reporting environments. You could, for example, create a large Group pie chart and place it in the report header, along with grand totals and text objects. You might add a text object that directs the viewer to double-click a pie slice for more information. You may also set Tool Tip text for the chart, prompting the viewer to double-click the slice they're interested in. Select the chart and right-click, choosing Change Border from the pop-up menu. Click the Common tab and use the Conditional Formula button to add Tool Tip text.

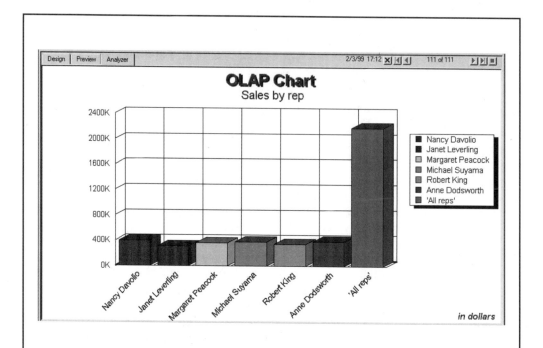

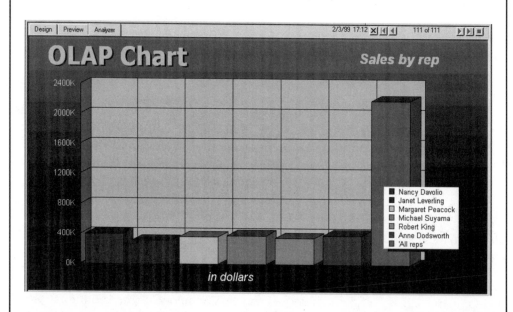

Figure 10-12. *Before and after the Chart Editor*

To add even more interactivity, you could add lower-level Group or Detail charts in the group headers or footers, hiding them with the Section Expert. When the user drills down on the higher-level chart in the report header, a drill-down tab showing a more detailed chart will open in a drill-down tab. You can continue to create drill-down levels until the viewer eventually reaches details sections to see low-level transaction data.

Get more information about creating multiple groups, drill-down, and hidden sections in Chapter 3 and Chapter 8.

Note   *Drill-down is only available and useful when viewing a report in its native format. Viewers can drill down on reports displayed right on the Preview tab of Crystal Reports by using a compiled report or by using a Crystal Smart Viewer and a Web browser. Drill-down doesn't work with exported reports or printed reports.*

Using the Analyzer with Charts

Crystal Reports 7 provides the new Analyzer tab to let you view and interact with individual charts on your report. Pick the specific chart instance that you want to analyze and choose Analyzer I Launch Analyzer from the pull-down menus, or right-click on the chart and choose Chart Analyzer from the pop-up menu. The chart you chose will be displayed in a new Analyzer tab next to the Preview tab.

Tip   *If you return to the Preview tab and analyze another chart, the Analyzer tab will be split in half, showing one chart on top of the other. If you try to analyze a third chart, you will be prompted to discard one of the existing charts, as the Analyzer can view a maximum of two charts.*

Once you've displayed the chart in the Analyzer tab, there are several options available for modifying the appearance of the chart. You can change the title of the chart, change the axes titles, and reverse the display of the series or group axes. Choose these options from the Analyzer pull-down menu or by right-clicking in the Analyzer tab and choosing options from the pop-up menu.

To change the report title or axes titles, choose the appropriate menu option and type in the new title. Reversing the group or series order will show the axis items in the opposite order. If you later uncheck the option, the axes will return to their original order. Other options will appear in the menu, depending on the type of chart being displayed. Options may include changing the size of elements or the angle at which the chart is displayed.

Note   *The Analyzer toolbar, available from View I Toolbars only contains items useful for analyzing maps. It will not be useful for analyzing charts. Right-click in the Analyzer tab and choose options from the pop-up menu or choose options from the Analyzer pull-down menus.*

Chapter 11

Using Subreports

A s you become more sophisticated in your report design, you will find times that it's difficult, if not impossible, to create certain kinds of reports. For example, you might want to create one of the following:

- A single-page Company Condition report that contains an accounts receivable summary in the upper left, an accounts payable summary in the upper right, a payroll expense summary in the lower left, and a sales summary in the lower right. At the bottom of the report, you'd like some grand totals for each of the summary reports.

- A listing of orders by customer for the month that also has a summary of the top five products sold during the month, regardless of customer.

- A sales report grouped by state, with a list of all credit granted in the same state in the group footer.

- A report based on a PC-style database that you can't properly link because of the lack of indexed fields.

- A report that contains a report title, logo, and company information from a separate Company Information table in the database that doesn't contain any field that can be linked to other fields in other tables.

In each of these cases, you can't create the report using traditional Crystal Reports methods. The first three instances are prohibitive because a report, by nature, can only make use of a single result set, or a single group of fields returned all at once, from the database. The fourth instance exhibits Crystal Reports' requirement that PC-style databases be linked using indexed fields. And the fifth instance (a fairly common situation), exhibits the problem encountered when there are no fields that can be linked between the two tables.

Crystal Reports provides an innovative way to deal with these types of reporting challenges. *Subreports* allow you to solve these problems by, in essence, placing one report inside another report. A subreport is simply another report that appears inside the original *main report* as an object. Even though both reports have separate layouts and separate Design tabs, they appear together in the same place. The main report is created initially, after which one or more subreports are added to the main report.

Each subreport is designed separately, based on its own database tables and fields. You can preview each subreport in its own Preview tab, format individual objects in each subreport, and create unique selection criteria for the subreport. However, when you return to the main report's Preview tab or print the main report, the subreports will be processed and printed at the same time, appearing inside the main report.

There are two main types of subreports: unlinked and linked. *Unlinked subreports* have no tie-in to the main report at all—they exist completely on their own and don't typically communicate with the main report. The Company Condition report mentioned previously falls into this category. Each of the unlinked subreports stands on its own and won't change based on any controlling field in the main report.

Linked subreports are controlled by the main report. The subreport will "follow" the main report, only returning a certain set of records based on the main report's controlling field. The subreport containing sales by state followed by matching credit, mentioned previously, is an example of a linked subreport. When the state group changes in the main report, the subreport will only return records for that particular state.

You can also choose when subreports are processed by the main report. *In-place* subreports process at the same time as the main report and return their results at the same time. *On-demand* subreports only appear in the Preview tab with a placeholder and don't process until a viewer double-clicks on them. This improves the performance of the main report, as it doesn't have to process all the subreports at the same time as the main report.

Unlinked Subreports

The most straightforward subreport is an unlinked subreport. An unlinked subreport can be thought of as a completely separate report that just shows up on the main report—there's no connection at all. The subreport has its own layout, its own database connection, and its own selection criteria. It is not affected at all by what appears on the main report.

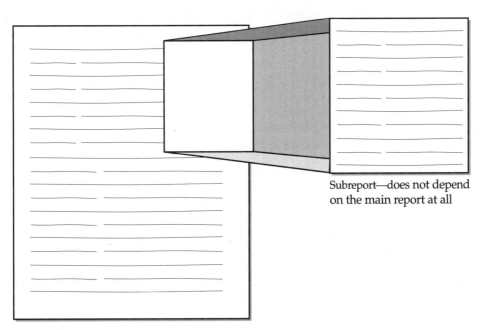

Subreport—does not depend on the main report at all

Main report

It's important to understand that Crystal Reports will not create another .RPT file when you create a subreport. Even though you will see another Design tab with separate tables and record selection, the subreport definitions are all contained in the main .RPT file.

To create an unlinked subreport, you must first create at least the skeleton for the main report, and then create the subreport. You can use the Subreport Expert from the Report Gallery, or create the main report using the Custom option and then add the subreport later.

To use the Subreport Expert, choose it from the Report Gallery when you create a new report. Create at least the basic components of your main report by choosing options in the Data and Fields tabs, at a minimum. When you click the Subreport tab, the Insert Subreport dialog box will appear inside the Report Expert.

If you use the Custom option to create a report, or you wish to add a subreport to an existing report, it's best to add a subreport in the Design tab. That way, you'll know exactly what section you will be placing the subreport in when you drop it on the main report. Start to create the subreport by clicking the Insert Subreport button on the Supplementary toolbar or by choosing Insert | Subreport from the pull-down menus. The Insert Subreport dialog box will appear.

Insert Subreport	☒
Subreport	Link
┌─ Insert Subreport ─────────────────────────────┐
C Choose a report
Report File name: [·] Browse...
● Create a subreport
Report Name: [ ] Report Expert...
OK Cancel

The Insert Subreport dialog box contains two tabs: Subreport and Link. The Link tab is used to create a linked subreport and will be discussed in "Linked Subreports" later in this chapter. The Subreport tab contains two radio buttons: Choose a Report, and Create a Subreport. If you've already created another report that you would like to import as a subreport now, you can click the Choose a Report radio button and type in the path and filename of the existing report, or use the Browse button to navigate to the existing report. If you use this option, another Design tab will show the report layout for the report you just imported.

Even if you choose an existing report to import as a subreport, Crystal Reports will not create a real-time link to the other report. It will simply copy the report design into this report, and then "forget" about the other report. If you later make changes to the original report that you imported, the changes won't be reflected here.

If you wish to create a new subreport from scratch, click the Create a Subreport radio button and give the subreport a descriptive name in the Report Name text box. Remember that you are not creating a new .RPT file when you create a subreport, so the subreport name doesn't have to conform to file-naming conventions. It should be descriptive of the subreport, as the name will appear on the main report Design tab wherever the subreport object is placed. Notice that once you enter a name, the only button that becomes enabled is the Report Expert button. The OK button at the bottom of the dialog box is still dimmed. This indicates that you must use a Report Expert to create at least a minimal portion of your subreport. Once you close the Report Expert and return to the Insert Subreport dialog box, the OK button will be enabled. When you click the Report Expert button, the Subreport Expert appears.

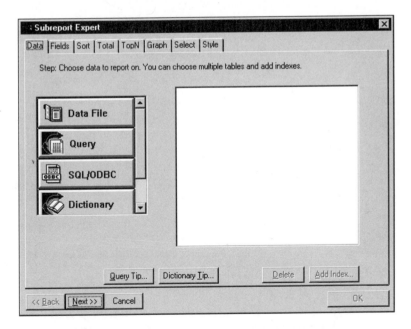

Don't forget that one of the powerful features of subreports is the ability to create reports based on entirely different databases and tables. You can select completely different databases, tables, and fields than are used on the main report. You must choose options on at least the Data and Fields tabs before you can click the OK button on the Subreport Expert. You can use the other tabs to refine your subreport before you click OK or wait and work in the subreport Design tab directly.

When you've selected your desired options in the Subreport Expert and clicked OK, you'll be returned to the Insert Subreport dialog box. Notice that the OK button is now enabled, because you have specified the necessary information with the Subreport Expert. When you click OK, you will be returned to the main report Design tab and a box-like subreport object will be attached to your mouse cursor. Drop the object by clicking in the report section of the main report where you want the subreport to appear. Choose this section carefully; it typically makes no sense for an unlinked subreport to appear more than once in the main report. For example, if you place the subreport in the details section, the same unlinked subreport will appear over and over again, once for each detail record. You'll typically place an unlinked subreport in a report header or footer, unless you want it to repeat on more than one page.

Don't forget the Underlay formatting option on the Section Expert (discussed in detail in Chapter 8). You can, for example, easily create a second page-header section for your subreport object and format the second page header to Underlay Following Sections. That way, your subreport will print alongside any data on the main report, not on top of it.

When you place your subreport in the main report Design tab, it simply shows up as a box with the subreport name centered inside it. Notice, however, that another Design tab labeled with the subreport name now appears alongside the main report Design tab. If you click the new tab, the subreport Design tab will appear.

Design	1997 Top 10 Products	
Report Header		**1997 Top 10 Products**
Group Header #1: Product.Product Name - A		Group #1 Name
Details		Product Name ... Order Amount
Group Footer #1: Product.Product Name - A		Group #1 Name ... ars.Order Amount
Report Footer		

You can now move, resize, reformat, and otherwise modify the subreport just as you would the main report. It will present its own Insert Fields dialog box, will allow a separate set of formulas to be created, and will allow you all the flexibility you have on the main report. However, there is one limitation in the subreport Design tab: you cannot add another subreport to it—subreports can only be created one level deep.

Caution *Since subreports can only be one level deep, an existing report that already contains subreports will not include the subreports when it is imported in the Insert Subreport dialog box. The main report will be imported into the subreport Design tab, but the lower-level subreports won't show up. You may need to modify the imported report to make up for the empty space that appears where the subreport used to be.*

You can even preview a subreport in its own Preview tab. With the subreport Design tab displayed, preview the report using the Preview toolbar button, the F5 key, or the pull-down menu options. A separate Preview tab for the subreport will appear next to the subreport Design tab.

When you now preview the main report, you'll see the subreport appearing where you placed it in the Design tab. By default, subreports are surrounded by a border, so you'll see a box appearing around the subreport. If the subreport is not entirely visible (it may be partly off the right side of the page, or it may be overwriting main report data if you set it to Underlay Following Sections), return to the main report Design tab and reposition or resize the subreport object. If you don't have sufficient room in the subreport Design tab to properly place objects, return to the main report Design tab and resize the subreport object. The subreport Design tab width is determined by the subreport object width in the main report.

Tip *You may save a subreport in its own .RPT file to use elsewhere or on its own. Select the subreport object in the main report Design or Preview tab and choose File | Save Subreport As from the pull-down menus, or right-click on the subreport object and choose Save Subreport As from the pop-up menu.*

Drilling Down on Subreports

You have the same flexibility for drill-down reporting in subreports as you do in the main report. If you design a subreport with grouping, hidden sections, or charts, you can drill down in the subreport too.

When you first preview the main report, the subreport will appear inside it. If you point to the subreport, you'll notice the mouse cursor will change to a magnifying glass, indicating drill-down capability. When you double-click the subreport, it will be displayed in its own Preview tab (but no actual subreport drill-down will occur). If you've designed the subreport to allow drill-down, you'll notice the mouse cursor displaying a drill-down cursor again in the subreport Preview tab. If you then double-click again, additional drill-down tabs will appear for groups you've created in the subreport.

If Crystal Reports runs out of room to display all the tabs, two small left-right arrows will appear to the right of the group of tabs. You can use the arrows to cycle through the tabs from the left or right. If you wish to close some of your drill-down tabs, click the red X next to the page navigation controls. This will close the tab you are currently viewing and display the tab to the left. Figure 11-1 shows an unlinked subreport with more tabs than can be displayed at once.

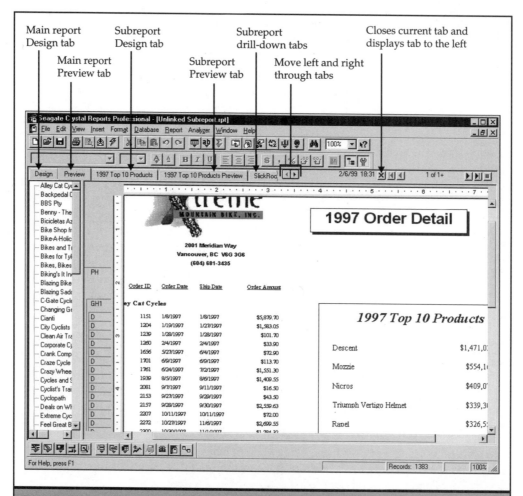

Figure 11-1. Unlinked subreport with drill-down tabs

Tip *When you add a subreport to the main report, a Design tab for the subreport is created automatically. You can close the subreport Design tab with the red X button. To redisplay a subreport Design tab, display the Design tab for the main report and double-click the subreport object, select the subreport and choose Edit | Subreport from the pull-down menus, or right-click on the subreport object and choose Edit Subreport from the pop-up menu.*

Linked Subreports

A linked subreport is handy when you want to have multiple records from one database appear after multiple related records from another database. The previous example of a report that shows all sales in a region, followed by all credits in a region, fits this category. The subreports follow along with the main report.

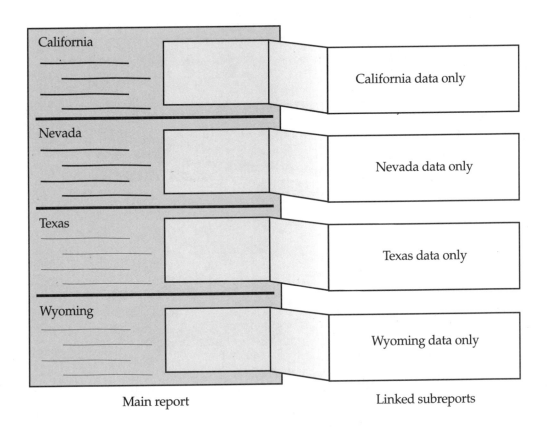

Main report   Linked subreports

A linked subreport is also required if you have a report based on a PC-style database that requires linking to a field that's not indexed. Since a linked subreport can show matching records based on a non-indexed field, you can create reports using a linked subreport that you would normally be unable to create.

The initial steps for creating a linked subreport are the same as creating an unlinked subreport. Use the Insert Subreport toolbar button or menu options to create a subreport. Then import an existing report or create a new subreport with the Subreport Expert. However, before you click OK in the Insert Subreport dialog box, click the Link tab. This will display the Subreport Links dialog box, shown in Figure 11-2, in which you can choose how to link the subreport with the main report.

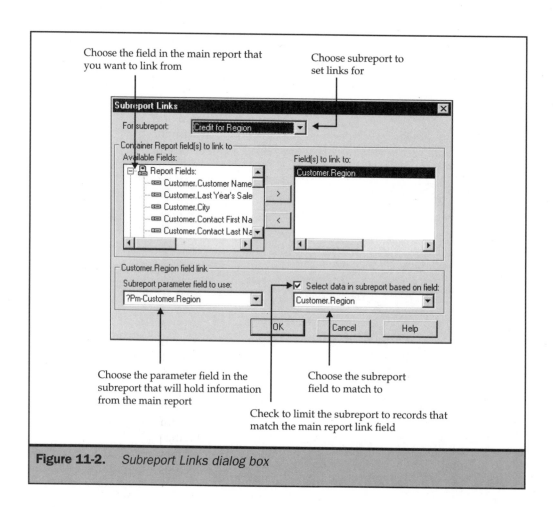

Figure 11-2.   *Subreport Links dialog box*

Tip	*If you inadvertently click OK in the Insert Subreport dialog box before linking, you can still link the subreport after you place it in the main report. You can also choose to change links for an existing linked subreport or to link a previously unlinked subreport. Select the subreport object you want to link and choose Edit	Subreport Links from the pull-down menus, or right-click on the subreport object and choose Change Subreport Links from the pop-up menu.*

If you are linking right from the Link tab on the Insert Subreport dialog box, the For Subreport drop-down list will be dimmed—you will be setting links for the subreport you are currently creating. If you are linking a subreport already on the main report, you can choose the subreport you want to set links for (don't forget—there can be more than one subreport on a main report).

The Available Fields list shows fields and formulas available in the main report. Select the field from the list you want to link from, and add it to the Field(s) To Link To list by clicking the right arrow button. If you later decide you don't want to link on that field, select it in the Field(s) To Link To list and remove it with the left arrow button.

Once you've added a main report field to link on, three additional options appear at the bottom of the Subreport Links dialog box. The Subreport Parameter Field To Use drop-down list will contain any parameter fields you have created in the subreport (see Chapter 12 for information on parameter fields). In addition to any that you have created, Crystal Reports will create a parameter field consisting of the main report field prefixed with Pm-. If you want to link the subreport so that it only shows matching records for the main report field, just leave this automatically created parameter field selected.

The general approach of linked subreports is to limit the subreport to records that match the linking field from the main report. If this is the behavior you want, make sure Select Data in Subreport Based on Field is checked. Then, use the drop-down list below the check box to choose the field in the subreport that you want to use to limit records (Crystal Reports will automatically show a subreport field that has the same field name as the main report linking field). If you want to use more than one field to link the main report to the subreport, just add additional fields to the Field(s) To Link To list, and match them up to the corresponding subreport fields.

Clicking OK will close the Subreport Links or Insert Subreport dialog box and create the links between the main report and subreport. A subreport link is based on two concepts: passing data from the main report into a subreport parameter field, and creating a record-selection formula in the subreport based on the parameter field. This way, every time the main report runs the subreport, it places the value of the main report linking field in the parameter field, which is used to select records for the subreport.

Because of this method of subreport linking, whenever you try to preview a linked subreport on its own, you'll see a prompt similar to this:

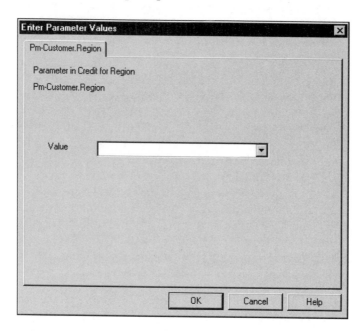

This indicates that the value for the parameter field is not being passed from the main report and you will need to provide it. Type in a valid value for the linked field (like a state abbreviation, customer number, department code—whatever value is appropriate for the linked field) and click OK. The subreport Preview tab will appear showing just the records that you specified.

When you preview the main report, it will pass data to the subreport via the parameter field every time the subreport is processed; the subreport will use the parameter field in its record selection formula and will return the limited set of resulting records to the main report. Figure 11-3 shows the customer/credit report mentioned previously, with the credit subreport appearing in the state group footer.

Linking on Formula Fields

If you use the Visual Linking Expert (discussed in Chapter 14) to link tables together in the main report, you can only link on database fields. This may be a problem if a field in one table doesn't exactly match the data type or organization in another table. For example, you may want to link two tables together on a First/Last Name because there is no other common number field or other linkable field. The problem, however, might

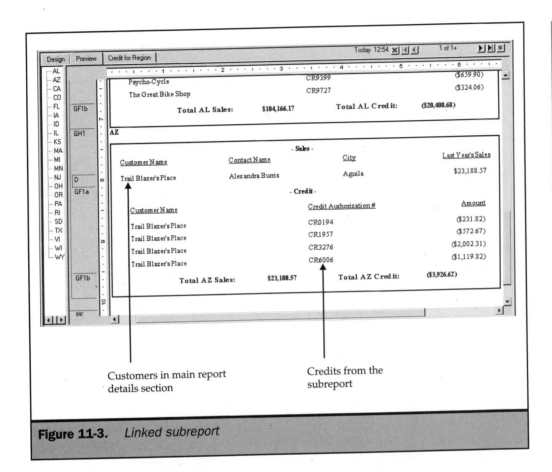

Figure 11-3.   *Linked subreport*

be that the fields are separated into individual First and Last Name fields in one table, and contained in a single Name field in the other table. The link will never work in the Visual Linking Expert because of the differences in the data layout.

One of the benefits of using subreports is their ability to link based on a formula field, instead of just using database fields. By creating a subreport, you can link the two tables together. The key is to use a formula to concatenate the individual First and Last Name fields together into one combined formula field. You can then use the formula field to link to the subreport that contains the single Name field. Once you've created the formula in the main report or subreport, it will appear in the Subreport Links dialog box and you can choose it as a from or to linking field.

Note   *Chapter 5 discusses concatenating string fields and other formula creation techniques.*

On-Demand Versus In-Place Subreports

By default, a subreport will process *in-place* as soon as Crystal Reports encounters it during main-report processing. Therefore, if you place a subreport in a group footer and preview the report, the subreport will process every time Crystal Reports comes to a group footer. If the report contains 75 groups and you click the last page navigation button (or you have a total page count special field on your report), 75 subreports will have to be processed before you see the page.

Depending on subreport size, database speed, or any of a number of other factors, this subreport processing may present a prohibitive performance problem. That's why Crystal Reports 7 introduces the concept of *on-demand* subreports. An on-demand subreport simply exists as a placeholder on the main report, but it doesn't process as the main report progresses. Only when you drill down (double-click) on the subreport placeholder, does the subreport actually process and appear in its own Preview tab.

There are no special steps to creating an on-demand versus an in-place subreport. The determination is actually made when you format the subreport. On the main report Design or Preview tab, select the subreport object that you wish to make on-demand. Then, display the Format Editor by clicking the Object Properties button in the Supplementary toolbar, choose Format | Format Subreport from the pull-down menus, or right-click the subreport object and choose Format Subreport from the pop-up menu. The Format Editor will appear with a Subreport tab.

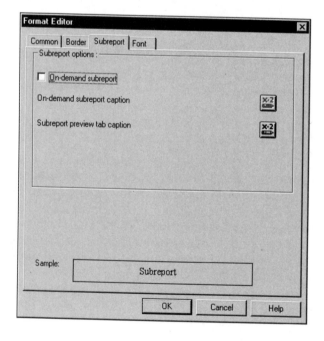

Check On-Demand Subreport to make the currently selected subreport on-demand. Now, when you preview the main report, only a placeholder outline will appear where the subreport would be. When the viewer double-clicks on the placeholder, the on-demand subreport will process and appear in its own Preview tab.

Caution
Since data is not saved in on-demand subreports, you may wish to avoid them if you distribute a report to a viewer who doesn't have access to the database. Even if a viewer opens a report with File | Save Data with Report checked, on-demand subreports will have to connect to the database to be shown.

There are two helpful text options that make on-demand subreports more intuitive and interactive. The On-Demand Subreport Caption and Subreport Preview Tab Caption properties also exist on the Format Editor's Subreport tab. Both these properties are set via Conditional Formula buttons, which allow you to create a conditional string formula that determines what appears inside the subreport placeholder in the main report and in the subreport Preview tab, respectively.

Since both are conditional formulas, you can use the complete Crystal Reports formula language to create a string formula to display. This gives you the flexibility to include actual database data in the formulas. For example, to prompt the user to double-click on a subreport placeholder to see credit information for a particular state, you could enter the following formula for the On-Demand Subreport Caption:

```
"Double-click to see Credit records for " + GroupName ({Customer.Region})
```

To show the state name in the Preview tab for the particular on-demand subreport a viewer chooses, you could use the following conditional formula for the Subreport Preview Tab Caption:

```
GroupName ({Customer.Region}) + " credits"
```

Tip
The Subreport Preview Tab Caption will work with either on-demand or in-place subreports (if in-place subreports are drilled down on). The On-Demand Subreport Caption will only be available if you check On-Demand Subreport.

You can use other options on the Format Editor to choose the font face, size, and color, border style, and background color that appear on the placeholder. By creative use of these formatting options, you can make an on-demand subreport placeholder look clickable.

Figure 11-4 shows the resulting main report Preview tab. Notice that several subreports have been double-clicked and their Preview tabs have been customized.

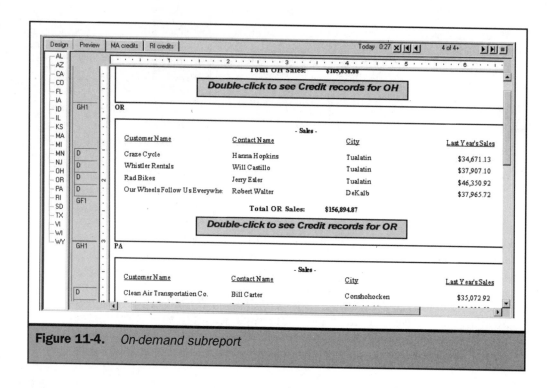

Figure 11-4.   *On-demand subreport*

If you are passing data back to the main report from a subreport, making the subreport on-demand will prevent the data from being passed back when the main report runs. Since the subreports aren't processing as the main report runs, there's nothing for them to pass back!

Making an On-Demand Subreport Look Like a Button or Graphic

If you'd like an on-demand subreport placeholder to look even more like a clickable image, you can place a bitmap graphic on the report and suppress the subreport placeholder. When the user double-clicks on the bitmap image, the on-demand subreport will be displayed in its own Preview tab.

To replace the on-demand subreport placeholder with a graphic image, perform the following steps:

1. Display the main report Design tab.

2. Select the subreport placeholder and format it with the Format Editor.

3. Click Suppress on the common tab to suppress the placeholder frame.

4. Insert the bitmap graphic you wish the viewer to double-click on with the Insert Picture button on the Supplementary toolbar or the Insert | Picture pull-down menu option. Position the bitmap on top of the dimmed subreport placeholder frame.

5. Select the graphic you just added and move it behind the subreport placeholder by choosing Format | Move to Back from the pull-down menus, or right-click the object and choose Move to Back from the pop-up menu. This step is very important, as the subreport placeholder frame must be on top of the graphic for the double-click to work. However, since the frame has been suppressed, the bitmap graphic will show through.

Figure 11-5 shows the resulting main report Preview tab.

When you suppress the subreport object to show the graphic, the subreport caption you specified in the Subreport Preview Tab Caption conditional formula won't appear on the subreport Preview tab.

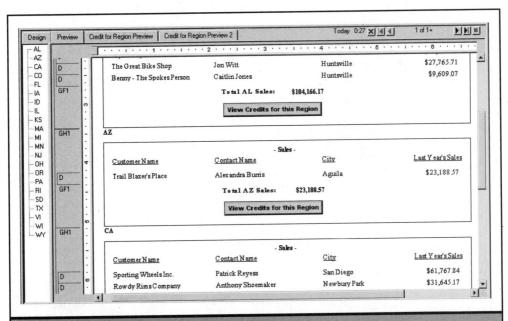

Figure 11-5. *On-demand subreport enhanced with a bitmap graphic*

Passing Data Between Main Reports and Subreports

In addition to passing a linking field to a subreport from a main report to limit the subreport's record selection, there may be other times you want to pass data from a main report to a subreport. Or, you may want to pass data from a subreport back to the main report to use in summary calculations or similar functions. You can pass data to a subreport from the main report using a parameter field. Crystal Reports Version 7 introduces the *shared variable*, which allows you to pass data back and forth between main reports and subreports.

Passing data to a subreport from the main report but not having the subreport use it in record selection is fairly straightforward. Display the Subreport Links dialog box as explained earlier in this chapter. Choose a linking field from the main report and add it to the Field(s) To Link To list. This will automatically add a parameter field prefixed with Pm- (all parameter fields automatically begin with a question mark) to the Subreport Parameter Field To Use drop-down list. Now, just uncheck Select Data in Subreport Based on Field.

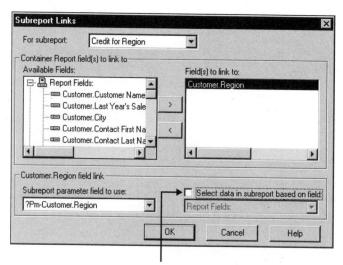

Uncheck to create a linked parameter field that
doesn't change subreport record selection

These steps will create the Pm- parameter field in the subreport and pass data to it, but won't use the parameter field for subreport record selection. Then, just use the parameter field in subreport formulas or place it on the subreport for display, as desired.

- Shared Variable has to print in both the subreport and main report. Cannot suppress.
- Shared Variable has to print before its used.
- Cannot sort or group on formula using Shared Var value.

Note *Chapter 12 discusses how to use parameter fields in your report.*

Using shared variables is a consistent way to pass data back and forth between the main report and one or more subreports, or even from subreport to subreport. You'll need to create formulas that declare the same shared variable in both the main report and subreport. You can assign the variable a value in the subreport, and then read the contents of the variable in the main report. Or, you can assign a value in the main report and read it in the subreport.

Here's an example of a formula in a subreport that places the sum of a currency field into a shared variable:

```
WhilePrintingRecords;
Shared CurrencyVar CreditTotal := Sum ({Credit.Amount})
```

And, here's the corresponding formula in the main report that retrieves the value of the shared variable:

```
WhilePrintingRecords;
Shared CurrencyVar CreditTotal ; CreditTotal
```

For more information on assigning and using variables, and other formula topics, refer to Chapter 5.

Caution *In versions of Crystal Reports prior to Version 7, there is no such thing as a shared variable. If you want to pass data to a subreport from the main report in those versions, use the parameter field method outlined earlier. If you want to pass data back to the main report from a subreport, you must use the UF5STORE.DLL (for 16-bit Crystal Reports) or U25STORE.DLL (for 32-bit Crystal Reports) User Function Libraries. These UFLs add Store and Fetch functions to the Formula Editor, which you can use to pass data back to the main report from a subreport. Check Crystal Reports online Help for assistance with these functions.*

Showing an Informational Message Instead of the Empty Subreport

When you link subreports, there may be situations in which the subreport won't retrieve any records that match the linking field from the main report. Typically, this will just result in a subreport showing up without any details sections. If there are column headings or other information in other sections, they will appear with zeros for subtotals. You may prefer to display an informational message instead, similar to what's shown in Figure 11-6.

This is accomplished by conditionally suppressing different sections of the subreport, based on a condition indicating the presence or absence of detail records. Look at the Design tab for the subreport.

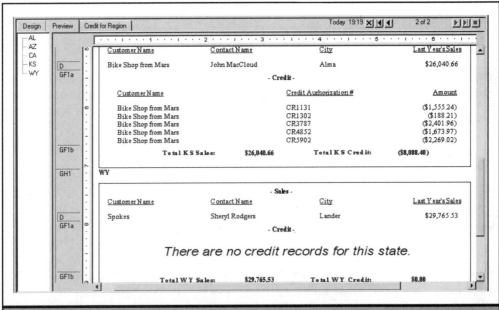

The report header and details sections contain objects that you want to appear if the subreport will return records. The report footer contains the object (the text message) that you want to appear if the subreport doesn't return records. This can be controlled by conditionally suppressing all sections using the Section Expert.

Figure 11-6.   *An empty subreport with an informational message*

Conditionally suppress the section containing the informational message by adding the following formula with the Conditional Formula button next to the Section Expert's Suppress property:

```
Not IsNull({Credit.Credit Authorization Number})
```

Then, conditionally suppress the sections that contain the actual subreport data with the following conditional formula applied to the Suppress property:

```
IsNull({Credit.Credit Authorization Number})
```

Don't forget—you are conditionally *suppressing* these sections, not displaying them, so you may need to think backwards. If the subreport is empty because no records were returned based on the linked field from the main report, the Credit Authorization Number will be null. You'll want to suppress the actual subreport data and not suppress the informational message in this case. If data is returned, then the Credit Authorization Number will contain data and will not be null. In this case, you want to suppress the informational message and not the actual subreport data.

Tip   *You can use this technique for all your Crystal Reports, not just subreports. If you might potentially have main reports that return no records, you can display an informational message in them. See Chapter 8 for more information on conditionally formatting sections.*

Performance Considerations

Subreports create potential performance problems for your reporting projects. Here are some tips to help maximize performance for your report viewer. Obviously, these considerations are more important if a viewer will be viewing a report online via a compiled report or on the Web. If a report is being printed or exported, subreports affect performance as well, but the user won't be staring at the screen waiting for them.

- Use on-demand subreports if you can. That way, a viewer won't have to wait for many subreports to process. Viewers can double-click on the individual subreports they want to see when they want to see them.

- If you are creating a linked subreport, try to base the link on an indexed field in the subreport. This will cause record selection in the subreport to occur substantially faster. If the subreport is based on an ODBC or SQL database, make sure you are keeping as much of the SQL query on the server as possible (see Chapter 14 for SQL database performance considerations).

- If you are linking subreports with formula fields, try to keep the formula field in the main report and use a database field in the subreport. Using formula fields in the subreport, particularly with subreports based on SQL databases, will move part or all of the subreport query off the server, impeding performance.

- If possible, limit the number of subreport occurrences to less than about 700 or 800. If, for example, you are putting a subreport in a group footer, do everything possible to avoid having more than 700 or 800 groups appear in the report. This is particularly important when using Windows NT 4 Service Pack 3, as there is an OLE incompatibility with it that causes problems with large numbers of subreports.

Chapter 12

Viewer Interaction with Parameter Fields

If you are designing reports to distribute to a viewer audience that may not be familiar with Crystal Reports or the Select Expert, you will soon have the need to prompt the viewer for values that affect record selection, conditional formatting, or some other ad hoc information. This becomes even more crucial when the viewer doesn't actually have a copy of Crystal Reports, but wants to view a compiled report (discussed in Chapter 13) or a report presented in a Web Smart Viewer (covered in Chapter 29). In these situations, the viewer won't have the ability to make changes with the Select Expert anyway.

The ideal solution for these types of ad hoc reporting requirements would be to present the viewer with a dialog box prompt, preferably including a choice of default values or a range of values, to help the user enter the correct values for the prompt. The response the viewer provides could then be passed to the Select Expert to customize record selection, and the values the viewer supplied could also be included on the report to indicate what data makes up the report.

This ideal solution is made possible by *parameter fields*. Parameter fields are prompts that are presented to the viewer when he or she refreshes the report. The value the viewer provides is then passed on to the Select Expert, the record selection formulas, or conditional formatting formulas to customize the way the report appears, based on the viewer's response. The viewer doesn't have to know how to enter selection criteria or conditional formulas to customize the way the report behaves.

Consider the following report:

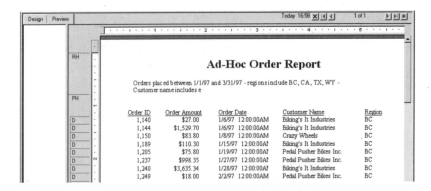

This report uses three fields in record selection: Order Date, Region, and Customer Name.

- The order date is filtered with a Between selection criteria to include orders that were placed in the first quarter of 1997 (between January 1 and March 31).

- The region is filtered with a One Of selection criteria to include orders placed from BC, CA, TX, and WY.

- The customer name is filtered with a Like selection criteria to include customer names that contain a lowercase *e*.

These criteria are hard coded into the Select Expert, and a text object appears in the report header to indicate the restrictions.

The difficulty comes when you want a report viewer to be able to easily change these criteria whenever they refresh the report. The way this report is currently designed, a report viewer must have their own copy of Crystal Reports and know enough about it to be able to use the Select Expert and edit text objects. Even in this case, it's time consuming to change this information every time the viewer wants to change these options. Parameter fields are the answer.

Using parameter fields is, at minimum, a two-step process. The third step is optional.

1. Create the parameter field.

2. Use the parameter field in record selection.

3. Place the parameter field on the report, perhaps embedded in a text object, to indicate what is included on the report.

Creating a Parameter Field

Parameter fields are created from the Insert Fields dialog box. You can display the dialog box when either the Design or Preview tabs are displayed. You can choose Insert | Parameter Field from the pull-down menus. This will simply display the Insert Fields dialog box and choose the Parameter tab. If the Insert Fields dialog box is already displayed, just click on the Parameter tab.

If there are parameter fields in the report already, you can edit them by selecting the desired parameter field and clicking Edit. You can also rename or delete existing parameter fields with the Rename and Delete buttons. If there are no existing parameter fields, or if you wish to create a new parameter field, click the New button. The Create Parameter Field dialog box appears, as shown in Figure 12-1, and the various fields and options are described in Table 12-1.

Field or Option	Description
Name	Name of the parameter field being created
Prompting Text	Descriptive text that will appear when the viewer is prompted for the parameter value
Value Type	Data type to assign to the parameter field
Allow Multiple Values	Check this box to allow more than one value to be assigned to the parameter field
Discrete Value(s) Range Value(s)	Choose between a single parameter field value or a beginning and ending value range

Table 12-1.   *Fields and Options in the Create Parameter Field Dialog Box*

Field or Option	Description
Browse Table	Choose a database table to help provide default values
Browse Field	Choose a database field to help provide default values
Select or Enter Value To Add	Type a value to be added to the Default Values list or select a value from the database with the scrolling list
Default Values	List of values that will appear in the parameter field's pick list. Use the up and down arrow keys to the right of this list to change the order the default values will appear in the pick list
Allow Editing of Default Values	Check this box to allow the viewer to type values into the parameter field, even if the values are not in the pick list
Length Limit	Check this box to limit the length of string parameter fields
Min Length Max Length	If Length Limit is selected, enter the minimum and maximum lengths for string parameter fields
Edit Mask	Control how information can be entered into string parameter fields

Table 12-1. *Fields and Options in the Create Parameter Field Dialog Box* (continued)

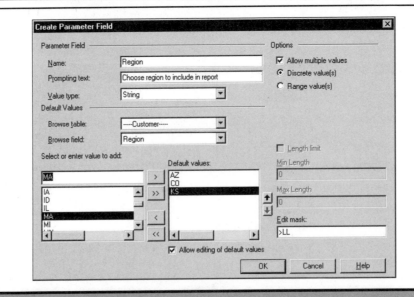

Figure 12-1. *The Create Parameter Field dialog box*

Choose a name for your parameter field. It can be the same name as other database or formula fields, as Crystal Reports distinguishes parameter fields by preceding the parameter field name with a question mark. Choose a descriptive, yet reasonably short name for your parameter field.

Although not absolutely required for parameter fields, you'll want to enter the message that will appear in the parameter field dialog box when a viewer is prompted to provide the value. The message is entered in the Prompting Text field and should be easy to understand and helpful to the user, such as "Enter the state code (2 characters only) for this report." The prompting text can be up to 254 characters long, although prompting text that long will probably look unsightly when the parameter value is prompted for. Crystal Reports will word-wrap the prompting text when the viewer is prompted, if the prompting text won't all fit on one line.

Choose a value or data type for the parameter field from the Value Type drop-down list. This is a crucial step, as it determines how your parameter field can be used in record selection, formulas, and conditional formatting. For example, if you are planning on using the parameter field to compare to a string database field in the Select Expert, choose a String value type. If you are going to limit the report to a certain date range, based on a date/time field in the database, choose a DateTime value type.

These are the only items that are actually required for using a parameter field. However, there are many new features in Crystal Reports 7 that enhance the flexibility of parameter fields. You can set up a *pick list* that provides one or more default values for a viewer to select. You can allow the viewer to select a from/to *range of values*, which is helpful for selecting beginning and ending date ranges. And, if you are using a string parameter field, you can set minimum and maximum lengths for the parameter field, or use an *edit mask* to force the viewer to enter the string in a certain way. These features are discussed later in this chapter.

Setting Up a Pick List

If you don't add any default values when you first create a parameter field, the viewer will have to type in the value for the parameter field. While this sometimes may be desirable, it requires that the viewer know enough about the parameter field and the way the report is designed so that they can type the value correctly. They may make a mistake in typing or enter lowercase letters when the field requires uppercase letters. By creating a pick list, you can let the viewer choose from a predefined list of default values.

The pick list presented to the viewer will be the set of values contained in the Default Values list (refer back to Figure 12-1). You can add items to this list by typing them in the text box under the Select or Enter Value To Add label and clicking the right arrow next to the text box.

Or, you can choose a database table and field to choose values from. To do this, choose a table and field in the Browse Table and Browse Field drop-down lists. This will fill the list under the Select or Enter Value To Add label with sample data from the database. You can then select an item in the list to place in the text box. Then, by clicking the right arrow, you can add the selected item to the Default Values list. If you want to add all the sample database values, click the double right arrow. If you decide you don't want some existing values to be included in the pick list, you can remove specific items by selecting them in the Default Values list with the left arrow, or you can remove all the values by clicking the double left arrow.

While it might be a nice feature for a future Crystal Reports release, choosing a Browse Table and Browse Field in the Insert Parameter Field dialog box will not automatically populate the parameter field's pick list with live database data whenever the viewer is prompted for the value. This table and field combination is only used to provide a list of sample values for you to manually add to the Default Values list. If the database later changes, the pick list won't reflect the changes unless you manually edit the parameter field and add new values to the Default Values list.

You can force the viewer to only choose values from the pick list by unchecking the Allow Editing of Default Values check box. If you leave this option checked, the viewer will be able to select an entry from the pick list or type in their own entry.

Responding to Parameter Field Prompts

Once you've created a parameter field, you will be prompted for it the first time you preview the report after the parameter field has been created. The Enter Parameter Values dialog box will be displayed.

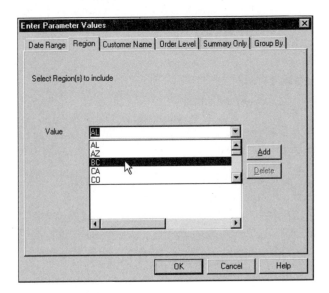

If you haven't entered any default values or created a pick list, the viewer will need to type in their response to the prompt. If you've created a pick list, the prompt will be a drop-down list where one of the predefined values can be selected. If you have created more than one parameter field for the report, only one Enter Parameter Values dialog box will appear, but each parameter field will have its own tab. Click the tab of the parameter field you want to select.

Typically, parameter fields will appear in the Enter Parameter Values dialog box in the order you created them. If you'd like to change the order in which they appear, return to the Parameter tab of the Insert Fields dialog box and reorder the parameter fields with the small up and down arrow buttons in the lower right of the box.

When you refresh the report, the Refresh Report Data will ask whether to use the currently set parameter field values or to prompt for new values. If you use the current values, the database will be reread with the current values in the parameter fields. If you choose to prompt for new values, the Enter Parameter Values dialog box will appear again, and you'll need to specify new values for all parameter fields.

When you refresh the report and select Prompt for New Parameter Values, you'll need to resupply all parameter values. The information you had placed in them previously won't be retained.

Value Type Considerations

The value type you choose for your parameter field determines how the parameter field can be used in the rest of the report. If, for example, you need to compare to a date database field, you'll need to use a date parameter field. The value type will also determine how the report viewer must respond to the parameter field prompt.

String and number/currency parameter fields are fairly straightforward. In the case of strings, a viewer can respond with any combination of letters, numbers, or special characters. For numbers, only the numbers 0 through 9 and a minus sign can be used—other characters will result in an error message. Using date, time, date/time, or Boolean parameter fields will introduce some new features and limitations.

Ranges and edit masks may limit what a viewer can enter into a parameter field. These special features are discussed later in this chapter.

Dates and Times

You'll often want to use date or time parameter fields to limit your report to certain date or time ranges. You can choose value types of Date, Time, or DateTime. You can build a pick list for these value types just like you can for number or string fields. And, if you leave Allow Editing of Default Values checked in the Create Parameter Field dialog box, you'll be able to choose dates or times other than those in the pick list.

When you are prompted for a date or time parameter field, there are a few special features available to you:

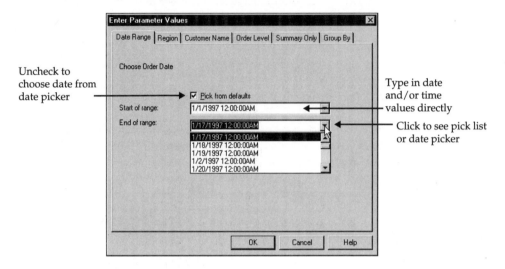

Uncheck to choose date from date picker

Type in date and/or time values directly

Click to see pick list or date picker

If you didn't allow editing of default values when you created the parameter field, then you'll only be able to click the drop-down list and choose from the pick list. If you did allow editing when you created the parameter field, you can just type a date and/or time value into the prompt.

Dates can be typed in the form *Date(yyyy,mm,dd)* or in the format of the Windows Short Date chosen in the Windows Control Panel. Times can be typed in the form *Time(hh,mm,ss)* or in the format of the Windows Short Time chosen in the Windows Control Panel. DateTime values can be typed in the form *DateTime(yyyy,mm,dd hh,mm,ss)* or in the combination of Short Date and Short Time format from the Control Panel. If no pick list or default has been specified, the current date and time will appear in the prompt. These can be left as they are or you can use them as a guide for typing in the correct values.

If a pick list is available, click the down arrow to see the available values in a drop-down list. There may also be a Pick from Defaults check box if Allow Editing of Default Values was checked when the parameter field was created. If you uncheck this option, the pick list will no longer be available.

If you are working with a time value, there will be increment and decrement arrows to the right of the time value. Use these to increment the selected hour, minute, or second up or down. If you are working with a date value, the down arrow will show the *date picker*, which is a small calendar from which you can choose the desired date.

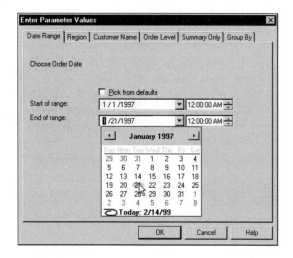

Boolean Parameter Fields

You may find a Boolean parameter field helpful when using record selection based on a Boolean database field or when conditionally formatting based on a parameter field value. A Boolean parameter field, like a Boolean formula (discussed in Chapter 5) can contain one of only two values: true or false.

When you choose a value type of Boolean in the Create Parameter Field dialog box, the dialog box changes to accommodate the special features of a Boolean parameter field. Figure 12-2 shows this altered dialog box. Specify the Name of the field and the Prompting Text for the parameter field just as you would for other parameter fields. You can also choose a True or False default value for the parameter field.

The Options section is different for a Boolean parameter field. If you check the Place in Parameter Group check box, you will add this parameter field to a grouping of one or more other Boolean parameter fields. Boolean parameter field groups allow you to simulate the "radio button" behavior you see in Crystal Reports and other Windows applications. Since you can have more than one group of parameter fields, use the Parameter Group Number text box to specify a group number for this parameter field. For example, you might create six Boolean parameter fields. The first won't be placed in a group, three of them will be assigned to group number 0, and the remaining two to group number 1.

The first parameter field will appear on its own tab when the prompting dialog box appears (described in the next section). There will be two other tabs on the dialog box, labeled Group #0 and Group #1. The Group #0 tab will contain a drop-down list containing the prompting text for the three parameter fields placed in the first group. The Group #1 tab will include the prompting text for the last two parameter fields.

If you check Group Is Exclusive, only one parameter field in a group can be chosen at a time in the drop-down list. The chosen field will return true, and all others will return false. If you don't check Group Is Exclusive, you will be able to click the Add

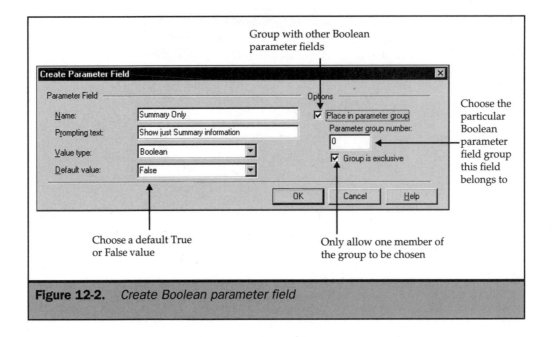

Figure 12-2.   *Create Boolean parameter field*

button to choose more than one member of the group. Each chosen parameter field will return true, while others not chosen will return false. The following illustration shows a prompt for a Boolean parameter field group.

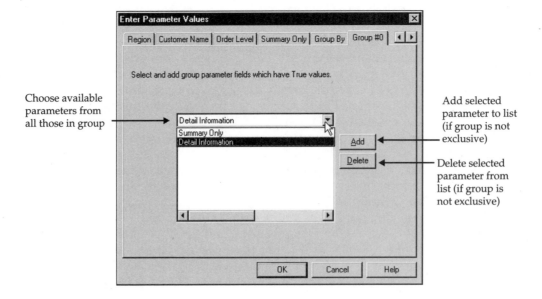

This group is not exclusive, so you can choose more than one of the Boolean parameter fields and add them to a list. Any parameters added to the list will return true when the report runs. If you create an exclusive group, the Add and Delete buttons, as well as the list box below the drop-down list, won't appear. You'll only be able to choose one of the parameter fields in the drop-down list. It will return true, while all others in the group will return false.

Using Parameter Fields in Record Selection

Probably the most common use for a parameter field is in report record selection. By creating a parameter field and using it with the Select Expert or a record-selection formula, you can prompt the viewer to provide variable information when the report runs, and have the report record selection reflect the viewer's choices.

After creating the desired parameter fields, use the toolbar button or pull-down menu option to start the Select Expert. Add a selection tab for the database field you want to compare to the value the viewer enters into the parameter field. When you choose the drop-down list to see sample database values, you'll see parameter fields of the same data type appearing in the list. Choose the correct parameter field.

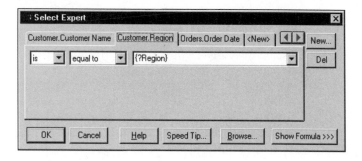

Caution *Only parameter fields of the same data type as the database field will show up in the Select Expert. If you don't see the parameter field you expect in the Select Expert, it wasn't created with the same data type as the database field you are using. Change the value type of the parameter field and rerun the Select Expert.*

If you use the Formula Editor to edit the record-selection formula, you'll see all parameter fields (regardless of data type) appearing in the Field Tree box. Choose the parameter field you want to use in the record-selection formula. The formula may look something like this:

```
{Customer.Region} = {?Region}
```

Make sure you choose a parameter field of the same data type, or use functions to convert the parameter field to the correct data type. If you try, for example, to compare a numeric parameter field to a string database field, you'll receive an error in the Formula Editor.

Displaying Parameter Fields on the Report

One of the other major benefits of using parameter fields is that you can place them on your report just like database or formula fields. Whatever value the viewer placed in them before the report ran will appear on the report. By creatively using parameter fields, you can have a customized report that changes record selection and shows the values used in record selection on the report.

To place a parameter field on the report, drag and drop it from the Insert Fields dialog box just like you would a database or formula field. Depending on the value type of the parameter field, you can format it using all the usual Format toolbar or Format Editor features discussed earlier in this book. You can also combine parameter fields with other fields and literal text inside text objects (as discussed in Chapter 2). A text object combining a parameter field that looks like this in the Design tab:

Orders over ?Order Level are highlighted

will use the value supplied by the viewer when the report runs.

Orders over $2,500.00 are highlighted

Special Parameter Field Features

If you are using a version of Crystal Reports prior to Version 7, you can still make use of many parameter field features. However, Version 7 introduced many enhancements to parameter fields. A viewer can choose multiple values for a single parameter field to allow One Of types of record selection. Parameter fields can be specified to include entire ranges of values, so a viewer can, for example, include all orders placed between January 1, 1998 and December 31, 1998. And, string parameter fields can be limited to certain lengths (for example, no less than 3 nor more than 6 characters) or limited to certain formats with edit masks.

Multiple Values

There are many times you may want to be able to choose more than one value for a parameter field and have the report recognize the multiple values in record selection.

You may, for example, want to initially specify only one region for a report, and later run the same report including ten different regions. If you're not using parameter fields, you'll need to change the Select Expert operator from Equal To to One Of and select the multiple regions.

By clicking the Allow Multiple Values check box in the Options section of the Create Parameter Field dialog box, you will allow multiple entries to be added to a parameter list. Even if you choose an Equal To operator in the Select Expert with a multiple-value parameter field, all the values will be included in record selection. When you are prompted for a multiple-value parameter field, you can use the Add and Delete buttons to add or remove multiple values. The values that are added to the list can be chosen from a pick list or typed in the text box and then added with the Add button (typing values is dependent upon the setting of the Allow Editing of Default Values check box in the Create Parameter Field dialog box).

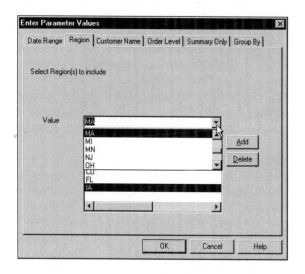

 If you add a multiple-value parameter field to your report to display selected values, only the first value will actually appear on the report, even though all values will be used by the Select Expert.

Range Values

In versions of Crystal Reports prior to Version 7, a from/to or high/low range of records can be chosen only by creating two different parameter fields and using them with the Between operator in the Select Expert. Crystal Reports 7 introduces the concept of *range-value* parameter fields. These allow you to create just one parameter field that can contain both the low and high values. When this parameter field is supplied to the Select Expert with the Equals operator, it effectively supplies both the low and high values and changes the operator to Between.

To create a range-value parameter field, click the Range Value(s) radio button on the Create Parameter Field dialog box (this is the opposite of a discrete-value parameter field, which doesn't contain high/low values). This will change the way the parameter field prompt appears when the report is refreshed.

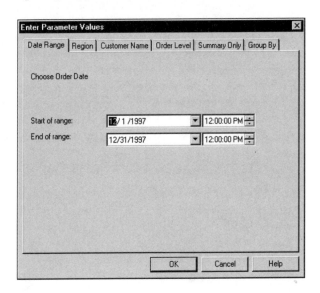

There are now two prompts to choose or enter values: the Start of Range prompt and the End of Range prompt. These two prompts behave the same way a single prompt would behave, being based on pick list creation, allowing editing of default values, etc. However, when the viewer clicks OK, both prompts will be supplied to the Select Expert or record-selection formula, and all records between and including the selected values will be returned.

If you add a range-value parameter field directly to your report to display selected values, the parameter field will not show anything. This is because the parameter field is actually an array value. An *array* is a single object (in this case, the parameter field) that can contain multiple values. If you just put the object on the report by itself, Crystal Reports won't return a value because it's not sure which value you want to return. You can use array functions in the Formula Editor to return an individual *element*, or entry, in the array, or the first or last entries in the array. For example, the following formula will display the starting and ending dates of a date-range parameter field:

```
"Orders between " + ToText(Minimum({?Date Range}),"M/d/yyyy") + " and " +
ToText(Maximum({?Date Range}),"M/d/yyyy")
```

The Minimum and Maximum functions return the first and last entry in the array, respectively. The ToText function turns the date values from the array into strings.

If, in addition to checking the Range Value(s) check box, you click the Allow Multiple Values check box in the Create Parameter Field dialog box, the parameter field will allow entry of *multiple* range values. For example, you could choose to see orders placed between January 1, 1998 and January 31, 1998; March 1, 1998 and March 31, 1998; and December 1, 1998 and December 31, 1998. When you are prompted for a range-value parameter field that allows multiple values, a list will appear where you can add multiple ranges.

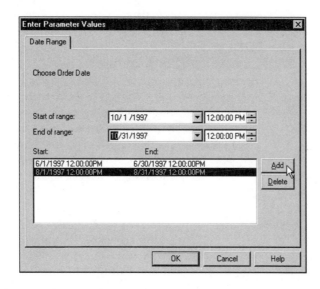

Different values can be specified in the Start of Range and End of Range areas and added to the list with the Add button. If you want to delete an existing range, select it in the list and click the Delete button.

This single parameter field, when supplied to the Select Expert or record-selection formula, will effectively change the selection operator to Between *and* One Of at the same time.

Don't try to apply the same Minimum and Maximum array functions demonstrated earlier to a range parameter field that accepts multiple values. The formula editor will fail with an unexpected error.

Controlling Parameter Field Data Entry

One of the limitations of Crystal Reports versions prior to 7 is the lack of control for parameter field entry. Crystal Reports would provide little, if any, *entry validation*. This lack of validation means that Crystal Reports would simply return an error message if you tried to, for example, enter a string value into a numeric parameter field. If you wanted to somehow limit or control the way the viewer supplied information (such as requiring two-letter uppercase responses to a prompt for State), your only choice was to develop a separate reporting application front end in a Windows development tool, and integrate the report. In Crystal Reports 7, parameter fields have been enhanced dramatically to allow more flexibility in validating viewer responses to parameter prompts.

Limiting Entry to Certain Ranges of Values

For parameter field types, except string and Boolean, you can limit the range of entries that a viewer can supply. By checking Range Limited Field on the Create Parameter Field dialog box, you can specify a Beginning and Ending value for the range in the controls that become enabled below the check box. When the viewer is prompted for the parameter field, they will be unable to enter values that are below the beginning range or above the ending range.

An extra added feature of range limiting is the group of default values that can be added to the parameter field. When you range limit a parameter field and choose a database table and field to help populate the Default Values list, only database items that fall within the specified range can be added to the Default Values list. If you use the double right arrow to add all browsed database values to the list, only those that fall within the beginning and ending ranges will be added.

When a viewer is prompted to supply a range-limited number or currency parameter field, they will receive an error message if they type in a value outside the range. If the range-limited parameter field is a date, time, or date/time field, the viewer will not be able to even type dates or times outside the range. The date picker will only display dates that fall within the range.

Minimum and Maximum Lengths

If you create a string parameter field, the Length Limit check box appears in the Create Parameter Field dialog box. By checking this option, a Min Length and a Max Length text box appear below the check box. You can specify the minimum and maximum number of characters that must be supplied when responding to the parameter field's prompt. If you enter too few or too many characters, an error message will appear.

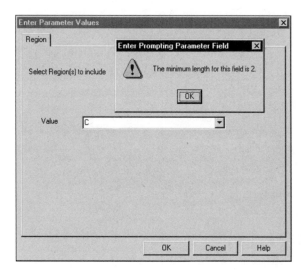

If you supply a length limit, you are also restricted from adding any default values to the pick list that fall outside the minimum and maximum lengths.

Edit Masks

The most flexibility for controlling string parameter field entry comes from *edit masks*. An edit mask is a string of characters that controls many different aspects of data entry. One example might be an edit mask that allows only 2 uppercase characters to be entered (perhaps for a state abbreviation). Another example would be an edit mask that sets up the parameter field to accept data in a social security number format, only accepting number characters, and automatically adding in hyphens between characters 3 and 4 and characters 5 and 6.

The key to using edit masks is learning the correct use of masking characters. These are listed in Table 12-2. Note that not only is the character you use significant, but so is

Character	Usage
A	Requires entry of an alphanumeric character
a	Allows an alphanumeric character to be entered, but doesn't require it

Table 12-2.   *Parameter-Field Masking Characters*

Character	Usage
0 (zero)	Requires a digit between 0 and 9 to be entered
9	Allows a digit between 0 and 9 or a space to be entered, but doesn't require it
#	Allows a digit, space, or plus or minus sign to be entered, but doesn't require it
L	Requires entry of a letter between A and Z to be entered
?	Allows a letter between A and Z to be entered, but doesn't require it
&	Requires entry of any character or space
C	Allows entry of any character or space, but doesn't require it
<	Automatically converts any subsequent characters to uppercase
>	Automatically converts any subsequent characters to lowercase
\	Causes the next character to be included in the parameter field as a literal—helpful if you want to actually include masking characters in the parameter field
. , : ; - / or any character not listed in this table	These characters will be included in the parameter field as literals—they will just appear in the parameter field exactly as typed
Password	Causes characters typed in to the parameter field to be displayed with asterisks instead of their actual characters; the actual characters are passed to the report

Table 12-2.   *Parameter-Field Masking Characters* (continued)

the *case* of the character—uppercase and lowercase versions of the same character perform different masking functions.

So, an edit mask of (000) 000-0000 when used with a phone number parameter field will require entry of the area code and phone number portions, and will include the parentheses and hyphen in the parameter field as literals. An edit mask of Password will replace characters typed in the parameter field with asterisks. This is commonly used for entry of passwords or other sensitive information to prevent the information from being learned by someone looking at the screen. When the viewer clicks OK, the actual characters typed will be passed to the report.

Conditional Formatting with Parameter Fields

Parameter fields can be used to customize other parts of the report, not just record selection. If a viewer wishes to highlight orders over a certain amount, they can specify the amount in a parameter field and use the parameter field to set conditional formatting. If they wish to see summary data instead of detail data, they can respond to a Boolean parameter field that is used to suppress the details section. Basically, any place you can do conditional formatting, you can base it on parameter fields just as easily as you can on database or formula fields.

Highlighting Data Based on Parameter Fields

Once a parameter field has been created, it can be used for conditional formatting just as easily as any database or formula field. As with any parameter field, you'll need to consider the value type used to create the parameter field. For example, you might wish to prompt the viewer for an order amount threshold, so that you can highlight orders over that amount in red. If the Order Amount field in the database is contained in a currency data type, you'll need to either create the parameter field with the currency data type, or do some data type conversion in the conditional formula.

A currency parameter field will prompt the viewer to enter an order amount threshold. Then, you can use two conditional formulas: one for the background color of the details section and one for the font color of the order amount and customer name fields. The details section background color can be formatted to show in silver if the order exceeds the parameter field, as follows:

```
If {Orders.Order Amount} > {?Order Level} Then Silver Else NoColor
```

The following conditional formula, when applied to the font color of both the order amount and customer name, will display the fields in red if the order amount exceeds the threshold.

```
If {Orders.Order Amount} > {?Order Level} Then Red Else Black
```

Figure 14-3 shows the result when a threshold of $2,500 is supplied to the parameter field prompt.

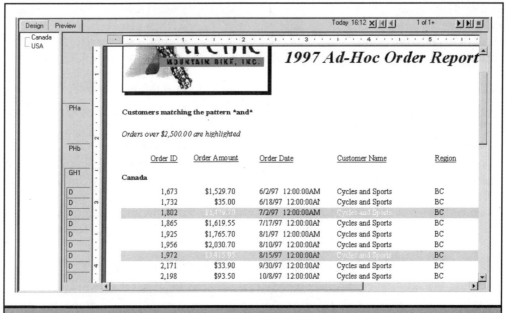

Figure 12-3. *Conditional formatting using parameter fields*

 Since the Highlighting Expert only allows you to compare to actual database values to set formatting conditionally, the Highlighting Expert will not work with parameter fields. You must use the Conditional Formula buttons that appear in the Format Editor if you wish to conditionally format with parameter fields.

Conditionally Suppressing Based on Parameter Fields

Use a parameter field just like a database or formula field to conditionally suppress individual objects or sections. Since the Suppress property requires a Boolean formula when being set conditionally, you can create a Boolean parameter field and supply it as the sole part of the Boolean formula, or you can create a Boolean formula by using a comparison operator with another type of parameter field.

You could, for example, create a Boolean parameter field called Summary Only that returns a true or false value based on the viewer's choice. By simply supplying the Boolean parameter field as the only item in a section or object's Suppress conditional formula, you could control whether the details section or a page header section containing column headings for the details section appears or doesn't appear.

When prompted for this parameter field, the viewer could select a True or False option for the Summary Only parameter field. You could then place this parameter field directly in the Suppress conditional formula for the details section. If the Summary Only parameter were true (indicating that the viewer wants a summary-only report), the details section would be suppressed. You could also suppress the page header section that contains column headings for the detail fields.

Using Parameter Fields with Formulas

There will be many situations in which you need to prompt for a parameter field in a certain way or need to choose a particular value type for a parameter field so it will work properly with record selection. However, you might want to display the parameter field on the report in a different way, perform some calculation based on the parameter field, or otherwise manipulate the parameter field in a formula.

When you create a parameter field, it will appear in the Formula Editor's Field Tree box under Report Fields. It can be added to a formula just like a database field or another formula. Just remember the value type you chose when creating the parameter field—you must use it correctly inside the formula to avoid type-mismatch errors. You may need to use ToText, ToNumber, or other conversion functions.

Using a Parameter Field for Partial Text Matches

A handy capability of the Select Expert is the Like operator that can be used when selecting records based on string database fields. Like allows you to supply *wildcard characters*, such as the question mark (?) and asterisk (*) to indicate single-character and whole-field matches, respectively. For example, supplying a Select Expert operator of Like with the literal *?eor?e* would return George, Jeorge, Jeorje, or Georje. Using the Like operator with an asterisk in the literal *Je** would return Jean, Jenny, Jennifer, and Jerry.

Note *A more complete discussion of record selection is contained in Chapter 6.*

By allowing question marks and asterisks to be included in parameter fields, and by using the Like operator in the Select Expert, you give your report viewer great flexibility in choosing only the records they want to see. However, if you want a meaningful message to appear on the report indicating what the user has chosen, you'll need to use a formula to display different information than the parameter field actually supplies to the Select Expert.

Consider a parameter field called Customer Name that will prompt the viewer to add question marks or asterisks for partial-match searches:

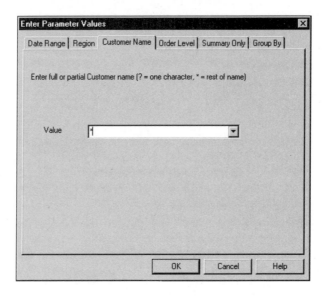

If you wish to place a descriptive message in the page header indicating which customers have been chosen, you can create the following formula:

```
If {?Customer Name} = "*" Then
   "All Customers"
Else
   If Instr({?Customer Name},"?") > 0 or
      Instr({?Customer Name},"*") > 0 Then
      "Customers matching the pattern " + {?Customer Name}
   Else
      "Customer: " + {?Customer Name}
```

This formula simply uses the Customer Name parameter field as you would another database or formula field in an If-Then-Else statement. If the parameter field only contains an asterisk, it will return all records, so the formula returns "All Customers." Otherwise, if the parameter field contains at least one asterisk or question mark (the Instr function will return the location of the first occurrence of the character, or zero if there isn't any occurrence), the formula indicates that the report is based on a partial pattern. Finally, if there are no asterisks or question marks at all, then the report will be returning an exact text match to the parameter field, and this formula indicates that.

Using a Parameter Field to Change Sorting or Grouping

You may often wish to have a report viewer choose the report sorting or grouping on the fly. Since a parameter field can't actually return a database or formula-field name itself, you'll need to create a formula based on the parameter field, and use that formula as the sort or group field in the report.

You could, for example, create a parameter field called Group By that prompts for grouping by Customer or Region. These would be the only two options, as the viewer will not be allowed to edit the default values. The prompt for this parameter field would look like this:

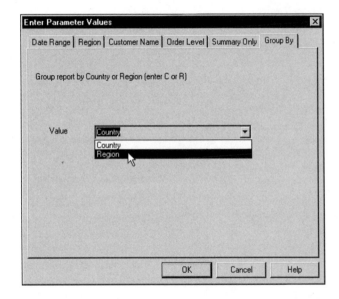

Because the parameter field will only contain the string Region or Country, you can't use the parameter field directly as a sort or group field. You'll need to create a formula based on the parameter field and supply it as the sort or group field. Look at this formula:

```
If {?Group By} = "Country" Then {Customer.Country} Else {Customer.Region}
```

This will actually return a different database field based on the parameter field's value. Then, this formula can be supplied as the grouping or sorting field, and the group or sort will change based on the viewer's response to the parameter field.

You may pay a slight performance penalty when you use this method with SQL or ODBC databases. Since the sorting or grouping will be done with a formula field and not directly with a database field, the ORDER BY clause won't use this formula, requiring Crystal Reports to actually sort the data once it arrives from the database server.

Chapter 13

Distributing and Compiling Reports

W hen you save a Crystal Report, your report file is saved on disk with an .RPT extension. This Crystal Reports native format can only be used with another copy of Crystal Reports or with the Crystal Web Reports Server (discussed in Chapter 29). Since everyone who might ever need to view a report probably won't have their own copies of Crystal Reports, there are many ways to *export* a report to a different file format for use with such products as Microsoft Word, Microsoft Excel, Lotus 1-2-3, and others. You can also export your reports to HTML format for viewing in a Web browser. You can also attach these differently formatted files to e-mail messages or place them in a Lotus Notes database or a Microsoft Exchange public folder.

Although exporting is a handy way of distributing reports to non-Crystal Reports viewers, your exported reports are *static*. That is, they contain a picture of the database as it existed when the report was exported. As soon as the database changes (perhaps the second after the report was exported), the report becomes outdated. If your viewers have their own copies of Crystal Reports, they could solve this problem by opening and refreshing the report. This means, however, that they could also *change* the report, and they would also have to know enough about Crystal Reports to be able to open and refresh a report.

For this situation, Crystal Reports allows reports to be *compiled*, creating a stand-alone, royalty-free Windows program that runs a report in "real time." With compiled reports, users can run reports directly against the database whenever they want, eliminating the static reporting problem mentioned previously.

The examples in this chapter are based on a report containing both text and a chart placed beside the text with the Underlay feature. In addition, some of the text contains special formatting, such as drop shadows. The report also contains additional graphical elements, such as line and box drawing. The report is shown in Figure 13-1.

Exporting Reports to Office Applications

You'll often wish to convert or export a report you've designed to a popular office file format, such as Excel, Word, WordPerfect, or Lotus 1-2-3. With Crystal Reports, this is as simple as choosing an option from the File menu. You can also export the file to a temporary location and immediately launch the application you want to view the file in, provided it's installed on your PC.

Exporting to Different File Formats

To export a file, first open the report you wish to export. Refresh and preview the report, if necessary, to ensure that it contains the most up-to-date data from the database. Then, click the Export button on the Standard toolbar or choose File | Print | Export from the pull-down menus. The Export dialog box will appear:

You have two simple choices to make for your export: the file format of the export and the destination of the export. The Format drop-down list lets you choose from the large number of file formats that Crystal Reports will export to. You can choose from several different ASCII or "straight-text" formats, several versions of Microsoft Excel, Microsoft Word, Lotus 1-2-3, and others.

The Destination drop-down list lets you choose how you want the report exported: to a disk file, attached to an e-mail message, sent to a Lotus Notes database, or placed in a Microsoft Exchange public folder. If you choose Disk File, the Choose Export File dialog box will prompt you for the folder and filename to export to. Choose a folder and type a filename, if the default folder and filename aren't sufficient.

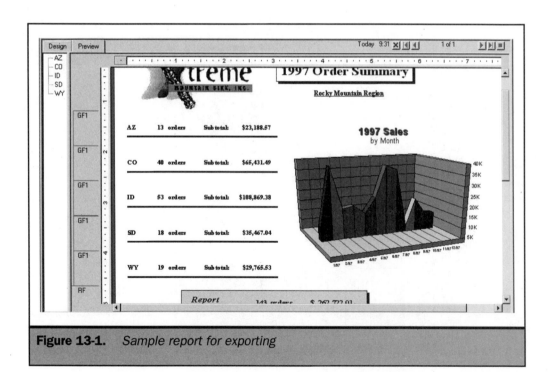

Figure 13-1. *Sample report for exporting*

If your report contains several drill-down tabs or subreport Preview tabs, ensure that the tab you want exported is selected before you begin exporting. Whatever appears in the current tab (and all pages generated by that tab) is what will be exported by Crystal Reports.

Figure 13-2 shows the sample report from Figure 13-1 after it has been exported to a Microsoft Word document.

If you drill down on a report, a different report "view" will appear inside the drill-down tab. Only the material inside this drill-down tab will be exported. The main

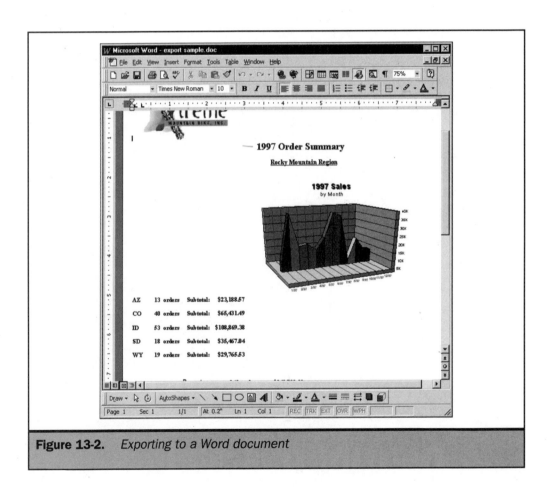

Figure 13-2. *Exporting to a Word document*

preview tab won't be included. Exporting the WY drill-down tab will result in a Microsoft Excel file, shown in Figure 13-3.

Note

Notice in the Word document example that the drop shadows around the report title and the title of the chart weren't converted, and the chart is not underlaid as the original was. You'll find that some of the Crystal Reports formatting doesn't translate to other file formats. You should export to your ultimate destination format throughout your report design process to make sure everything you want to include will be exported correctly.

Depending on the file format you choose, you may receive an additional dialog box prompting you for extended information about the export. If, for example, you choose

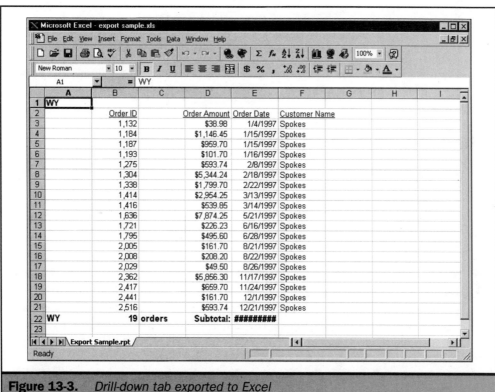

Figure 13-3. *Drill-down tab exported to Excel*

one of the Excel extended formats, a dialog box will allow you to choose more customized information when exporting to Excel.

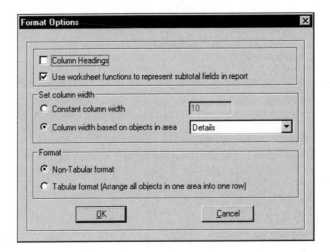

Exporting to various text file formats, such as Character Separated Values, will present additional dialog boxes prompting you for, among other things, the characters to surround and separate fields.

Exporting and Launching an Application

If you choose Application in the Destination drop-down list, Crystal Reports will export the file to a temporary folder and immediately open the file in the corresponding application. If you choose a file format for an application that isn't installed on your computer, you may be presented with a dialog box asking you to choose an application to open the file with. If there is an alternative application that will open that file type, choose it from the list.

The temporary files that Crystal Reports creates will be located in the Windows temporary folder (typically \WINDOWS\TEMP) and may not automatically be deleted when you close the application. If you wish to periodically "clean out" your Windows temporary folder, use Disk Cleanup or another appropriate utility or measure to remove temporary files.

Exporting to an ODBC Data Source

You can export a Crystal Report to an ODBC data source, such as a Microsoft SQL Server or Oracle database. Typically, you'll want to do this with a simple columnar

Creating a Report Definition File

When you create reports, you may want to keep documentation that details the report design, such as the tables that are included, what formulas you've created, and what objects are contained in the report sections.

Crystal Reports provides a Report Definition format in the Format drop-down list. When you choose this format, Crystal Reports will save a text file containing a great deal of helpful information about the makeup of the report. You may wish to create and keep these text files in a central location to document the design of your reports. You may also open the text files in a word processor and reformat them to look more appealing.

```
|       Crystal Report Professional v7.0 (32-bit) - Report Definition

1.0 File Information

        Report File:
        Version: 7.0

2.0 Record Sort Fields

3.0 Group Sort Fields

4.0 Formulas

4.1 Record Selection Formula
        {Customer.Region} in ["SD", "ID", "AZ", "WY", "CO"] and
{Orders.Order Date} in DateTime (1997, 01, 1,00, 00, 00) to DateTime (1997, 12,
31,00, 00, 00)

4.2 Group Selection Formula
```

detail report that you might be using to transport data from a PC database to a client/server database.

You cannot create a new ODBC data source inside Crystal Reports. Use the ODBC icon in the Windows Control Panel to modify or create ODBC data sources.

To export to an ODBC data source, choose the data source you want to export to in the Format drop-down list. You'll then be asked to supply a table name, which Crystal Reports will create in the database referred to by the data source. If the data source refers to a secure database, you will be asked to supply a database logon userid and password before the export starts. And, if the data source does not contain a specific database reference, you may be asked to choose a database in addition to the table name.

Crystal Reports will create a new table in the ODBC database and define fields to hold data from the exported report. If you want to change field names or the layout of the table, you'll need to use a utility specific to the ODBC database that you exported to.

 ODBC is "picky" about the organization of data you export. You may need to modify the report (perhaps removing groups or changing the formatting of parts of the report) to get the report to export without ODBC errors.

Exporting Reports to HTML Web Pages

One of the best ways to distribute Crystal Reports to a large audience is via a Web format through a company intranet or the Internet. In order to provide this capability, you will need to convert your report to hypertext markup language format, or HTML format—the "markup language" understood by Web browsers.

When you choose the Export command, there are three HTML format options available in the Format drop-down list. The different versions refer to the different extensions of the HTML language that Crystal Reports can use. If your viewing audience is using newer versions (4.0 or greater) of Netscape Navigator or Communicator or Microsoft Internet Explorer, you can safely use HTML 3.2 (Extended). If older versions of browsers may be in use, you might want to use HTML 3.2 (Standard) or HTML 3.0. It's a good rule to test your export to HTML as your report design progresses so you can be sure your reports will be exported in the desired manner.

No matter what destination you ultimately choose from the Destination drop-down list, Crystal Reports must write the HTML code and any associated graphics files (for charts, maps, and bitmaps) to a disk folder. You will be asked to choose a directory to place these files in.

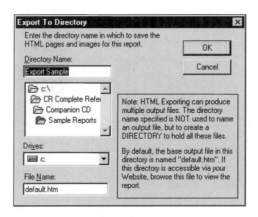

Choose a drive and directory or folder into which you would like the report to be exported in HTML format. The Export to Directory dialog box will automatically use the report name as the directory name. If you want to create a different directory, type a different name in the Directory Name text box. If you wish to place the HTML in a specific folder referred to by a Web "home" page, make sure you export to the predetermined folder on the Web server referred to by the page.

By default, Crystal Reports will export the report to one HTML file named DEFAULT.HTM. If your Web server uses a different default filename or the HTML page that calls the report uses a different filename as its link, type a new filename in the File Name text box.

If the folder you specified doesn't exist, Crystal Reports will automatically create it. If the folder already exists and contains an HTML file with the same name as you specified, the old file will be overwritten. In addition to the HTML report file, Crystal Reports will create sequentially numbered .JPG graphic files—one for each bitmap, chart, or map contained in the report.

When you point your browser to the folder and view the HTML file, you'll see the exported report in the browser window, as shown in Figure 13-4.

Again, notice that not all Crystal Reports formatting options can be converted to HTML. It's a good idea to try sample exports as you're developing your report to make sure you don't depend on any features that may not convert properly.

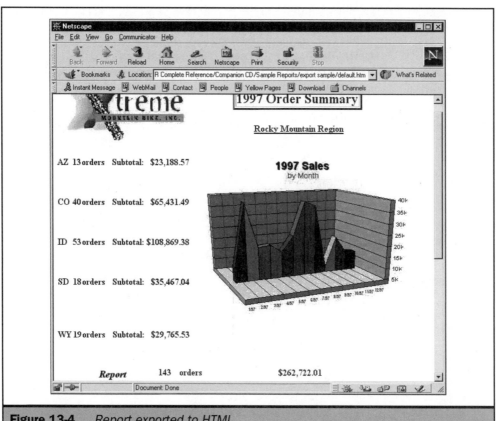

Figure 13-4.   *Report exported to HTML*

When you export reports to HTML, you are creating static Web pages. They will simply show database information as it existed when the report was exported. The only way to update the HTML reports is to refresh the report in Crystal Reports and export again. Also, drilling down and group trees don't work with exported HTML reports. If you want viewers to be able to refresh reports on their own, as well as interact with the report by drilling down and using the group tree, you'll need to set up the Crystal Web Reports Server. This is discussed in Chapter 29.

Sending Reports Electronically

In addition to exporting reports to office applications and Web pages, you may want to create an exported report and attach it to an e-mail message, place it in a Lotus Notes database, or put it in a Microsoft Exchange public folder. You might expect to have to do this in two steps: exporting to your chosen file format and then running a separate e-mail package to send the file. However, Crystal Reports lets you do it all in one step.

Display the Export dialog box, and in the Format drop-down list, choose the format you want the report exported to. From the Destination drop-down list, choose the e-mail system you wish to send the report with. Choosing Lotus Notes Database will place a report on the Lotus Notes Desktop, choosing Exchange Folder will add the report to a Microsoft Exchange or Outlook Folder, and choosing Microsoft Mail (MAPI) will use a Microsoft-compatible e-mail program, such as Microsoft Outlook, to attach the report to an e-mail message. Note that you'll need to have the appropriate "client" software installed on your PC for this to work.

Although you can choose File | Print | Mail from the pull-down menus, the same dialog box will be displayed as with the Export toolbar button or menu command. Just choose the correct e-mail type from the Destination drop-down list to electronically send your exported report.

If Microsoft Outlook is installed on your PC and you choose Microsoft Mail (MAPI) as the Destination, the following dialog box will appear:

Specify the e-mail addresses you want the message to go to, along with the message you want to appear in the e-mail body. The message will be sent with the report file attached (in the format you specified).

Compiling and Distributing Real-Time Reports

All the export and distribution methods mentioned previously in the chapter export the report with the data that was current when you went through the exporting process. If the report is based on a constantly changing database, such as a real-time transaction database, the reports you export or distribute may be out of date by the time that your recipient receives them. While you can just give viewers a copy of the .RPT file and require them to open and refresh it in their own copy of Crystal Reports, you may want a more cost-effective way of letting viewers run reports in real time.

Compiled reporting is a feature of the Professional Edition of Crystal Reports that lets you create a royalty-free, stand-alone version of a report that a user can run without having Crystal Reports. Once you have compiled the report, you can use the Report Distribution Expert to create a Windows setup program on diskettes or on a shared network drive. Any viewer who runs the setup program will have a copy of the report installed on their own PC and can run the report in real time without having a copy of Crystal Reports.

Compiling the Report

A compiled report will run on a viewer's PC without Crystal Reports being installed. This is accomplished by creating an *executable* version of the report file with an .EXE extension. Windows can run this file from the desktop or a Windows program group—Crystal Reports doesn't need to be running to use the report.

To compile a report, open the report that you wish to use. If the report is already open and you are ready to compile it, make sure you save it first—a report must be saved on disk before it can be compiled. Then, click the Compile button on the Supplementary toolbar, or choose Report I Compile Report from the pull-down menus. The Compile Report dialog box will appear, as shown in Figure 13-5.

By default, Crystal Reports will use the same name as the .RPT file for the compiled report .EXE file. If you wish to use a different name, choose it in the Compiled File Name text box. If you want to run the compiled report on your own computer, choose to Create a Program Item for the Report and choose the Program Group or Start-button group where you want the icon for the report placed. This will place the icon on your own computer so that you can run the compiled report yourself without having to open Crystal Reports. If you also want to distribute the report immediately after it has been compiled, choose Yes under Distribute the Report After.

Once you click OK, Crystal Reports will create the .EXE file you specified and, if you so chose, put an icon that points to the compiled report in a Windows program group or Start-button group. Double-click the icon to run the compiled report.

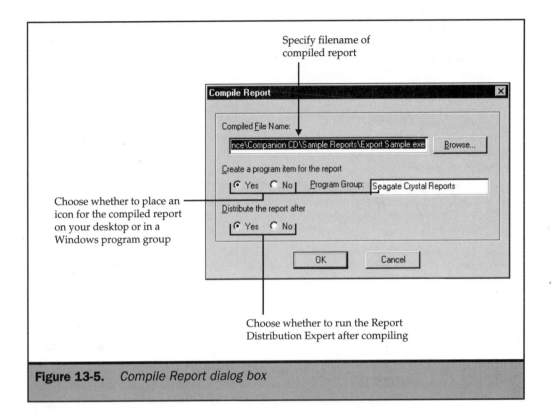

Specify filename of
compiled report

Choose whether to place an
icon for the compiled report
on your desktop or in a
Windows program group

Choose whether to run the Report
Distribution Expert after compiling

Figure 13-5.   *Compile Report dialog box*

Note

It's tempting for Windows developers to create compiled reports and then call them from within their custom Visual Basic programs. While this may work, it's much more efficient and flexible to use one of the Visual Basic programming interfaces to call a report directly.

If you just want to give a stand-alone report to a viewer, use compiled reports. However, if you want to include one or more Crystal Reports as part of a custom Windows application, refer to Part II of this book.

Using the Report Distribution Expert

It's important to remember that compiling a report won't create one large .EXE file that can stand completely on its own. In fact, the .EXE file is very small and simply points to many other files that are required to run a compiled report, such as the .RPT file itself, the CRRUN.EXE run-time file, and a .CRF file that contains initialization information about the report. In addition to these files, the compiled report will need to use any database access dynamic link library (.DLL) files that Crystal Reports uses. And, if your viewer wants to be able to export or e-mail reports in other file formats, another set of .DLL files will need to be available as well. The Report Distribution Expert is designed to easily "collect" all the necessary files and create an automatic setup package to install them on a viewer's PC.

The Report Distribution Expert will run immediately after you compile a report, if you choose the option in the Compile Report dialog box. Or, you can run the Report Distribution Expert directly by clicking the Distribution Expert button on the Supplementary toolbar or by choosing Report I Report Distribution Expert from the pull-down menus. The Report Distribution Expert dialog box will appear, consisting of four different tabs: Options, File List, Third Party DLLs, and Distribution.

Options Tab

The first tab in the Report Distribution Expert is Options, shown in Figure 13-6. Specify general information about your compiled report on this tab.

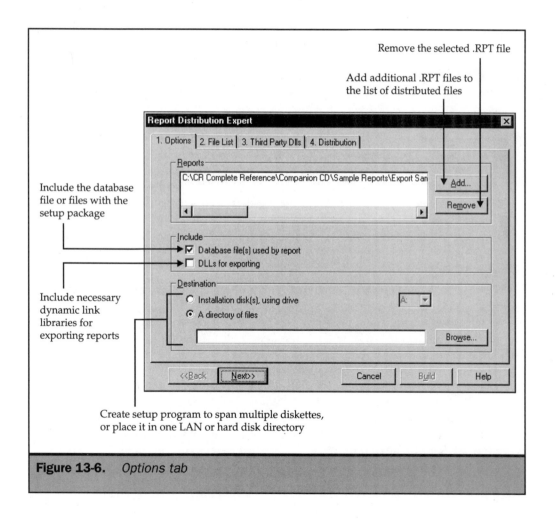

Figure 13-6. *Options tab*

By default, the report you are compiling will be included in the setup package. If you need to include other reports, you can click the Add button to select additional report files. If you need to distribute the database, as well as the report itself, check the Database File(s) Used by Report check box to set that option. If the compiled reports will be using a common database, perhaps located on a central LAN server, there will be no reason to distribute the database with the report. However, if you want the viewer to be able to export the compiled report to Microsoft Word or Excel, or to attach the report to an e-mail message, you'll need to check the DLLs for Exporting check box so that the proper dynamic link library files for export are included in the setup package. And, if any formulas you've included in the report use User Function Libraries, make sure you include the .DLL files for these as well (Chapter 28 discusses how to create these libraries in Visual Basic).

You can choose to have the setup package created on multiple diskettes or in a single directory of files. Choose the diskette option if you need to distribute the report to an audience that may not have access to a central installation directory (on a LAN server, perhaps). If your viewers do have access to a shared directory, it is preferable to create an installation directory for the setup package on the common directory. In either case, the Report Distribution Expert will compress all the associated files to save disk space and create a SETUP.EXE file to uncompress and properly install the files on the target computer.

If your report is based on a PC-style database (such as Microsoft Access), the Report Distribution Expert may present an error message indicating that you must set the report's database location to be "same as report." Use the Database | Set Location command to set this option. You'll also need to ensure that the database and the report share the same drive and directory. If the report is based on an ODBC data source, you'll need to ensure that the same data source is set up on each target machine. The Crystal Reports Setup program will not do this, so you'll need to ensure this with other means.

File List Tab

When you click the File List tab, the Report Distribution Expert may give you extra prompts to include database drivers, such as the Microsoft DAO driver. If you are unsure of whether or not the target machine has these necessary drivers, you should choose to include them in the setup package. Then the Report Distribution Expert will evaluate the report and create a list of support files that it believes may be required by the compiled report, as shown in Figure 13-7. Be patient—this analysis may take a little while.

When the list appears, you can scroll through the filenames to make sure all the support files that your report needs are included. If you want to see different information about the files, click the Description, Path, and Size radio buttons at the top of the screen. You can also add additional files or remove unnecessary files by using the Add and Remove buttons.

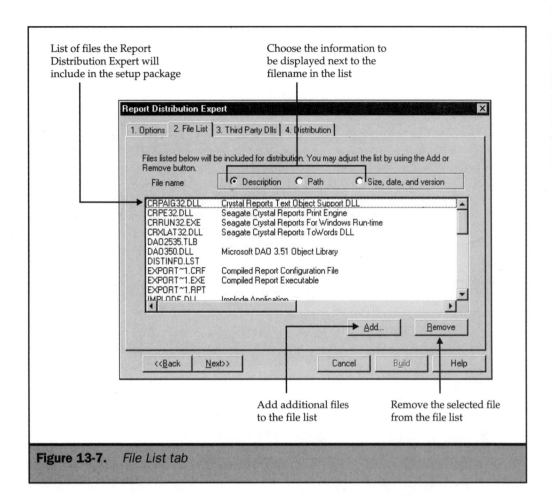

List of files the Report
Distribution Expert will
include in the setup package

Choose the information to
be displayed next to the
filename in the list

Add additional files
to the file list

Remove the selected file
from the file list

Figure 13-7. *File List tab*

Tip

For more information on which files you may need to include, choose Runtime File Requirements on the Seagate Crystal Reports program group to see the RUNTIME.HLP online Help file, or refer to Chapter 27.

Third Party DLLs Tab

If your report is using a particular DLL that was not included on the Crystal Reports CD (perhaps a third-party DLL required to connect to a proprietary database), you'll see a list of those DLLs on the Third Party DLLs tab, shown in Figure 13-8.

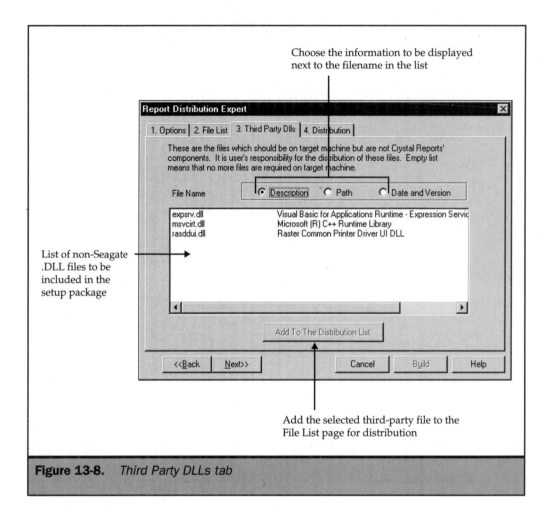

Choose the information to be displayed next to the filename in the list

List of non-Seagate .DLL files to be included in the setup package

Add the selected third-party file to the File List page for distribution

Figure 13-8. *Third Party DLLs tab*

If you want to include any or all of these third-party files in your setup package, select the files that you want to include and click the Add To The Distribution List button to add them. If this tab is empty and the Add To The Distribution List button is disabled, there are no third-party DLLs required for this report.

Distribution Tab

The final step in the Report Distribution Expert is the Distribution tab, shown in Figure 13-9. This tab simply displays a message indicating that the Report Distribution Expert is ready to prepare the setup package. Click the Build button when you're ready

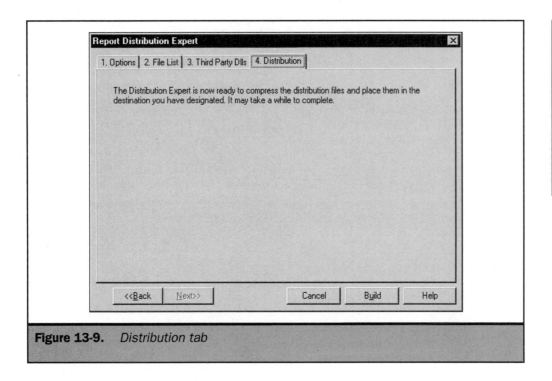

Figure 13-9. *Distribution tab*

to proceed. If you choose to distribute on diskettes, you'll be prompted to insert formatted, blank diskettes into the chosen diskette drive. If you chose to place the setup package in a single directory, the directory will be created. Then the Report Distribution Expert will compress all the included files to make them as compact as possible. It will also create a standard Windows SETUP.EXE program that can be run on the report viewer's PC to install the compiled report.

Using a Compiled Report

If the compiled report setup package was placed on diskettes or a common directory, the viewer will need to run the SETUP.EXE program to install the compiled report. This is a standard Windows setup program that copies files to their correct locations and creates a new program group to contain the compiled report's icon.

Once the setup program has been run (or if you just compiled a report on the same machine that Crystal Reports is installed on), you can start your compiled report by choosing the icon from the program group or Start-button group. The compiled report dialog box will appear, as shown in Figure 13-10.

Choose the report
destination

Choose when to run
the report

If you wish to run the report
in the future, select a date
and time

Choose whether to use the
saved data or to refresh data

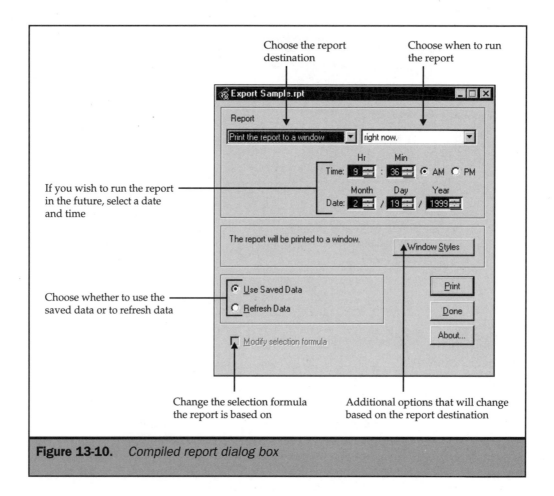

Change the selection formula
the report is based on

Additional options that will change
based on the report destination

Figure 13-10.   *Compiled report dialog box*

The first drop-down list lets you choose where you want the report output to go.
The report can be previewed in an onscreen window, printed on a printer, or exported
or e-mailed in another file format (provided you included the export DLLs when you
created the report setup package). You can also choose whether you want the report to
run immediately or at a later time by choosing options in the second drop-down list
and with the Time and Date options.

A button will appear in the middle of the dialog box that changes based on the
report destination. If you choose to print to a printer, the button will let you choose
different print options, such as which printer to use and what pages to print. If you
choose to export the report, the button will display the Export dialog box that lets you
choose the report format and destination. If you choose to preview the report in a
window, the button will let you change window styles by presenting this dialog box.

Window Style Options   ☒

☑ Has <u>N</u>avigation Controls

☑ Has <u>P</u>rint Button

☐ Has Print <u>S</u>etup Button

☑ Has <u>E</u>xport Button

☑ Has <u>Z</u>oom Box with Default Level   [75%   ▼]

☑ Has <u>C</u>ancel Button

☐ Has C<u>l</u>ose Button

☑ Has P<u>r</u>ogress Controls

☐ Has Re<u>f</u>resh Button

☐ Has Searc<u>h</u> Button

☐ Has <u>D</u>rill Down

☐ Has <u>G</u>roup Tree

[OK   ]   [Cancel   ]

Here you can choose many options for the preview window, such as whether to
display a group tree, whether to allow drill down, what the initial zoom level should
be, and much more.

If the compiled report has the Save Data with Report option chosen from the File
menu, you can choose whether to view the report with saved data or to refresh the
report data. Using saved data is faster and doesn't require you to connect to the
database the report is based on. However, the saved data is "static" and the report may
not represent the most current data in the database. Because this is little better than
having received the report in a Word or Excel document, the viewer will most probably
want to select Refresh Data. If the report was not saved with the Save Data option
chosen, the only option will be Refresh Data and the viewer will have to connect to the
database to run the report.

If the viewer chooses to Refresh Data, they can also check the Modify Selection
Formula check box. If this is checked, the viewer will be able to change record selection
before the report processes. A series of dialog boxes will prompt the viewer to enter
new selection options.

*A viewer can change the selection criteria only if you limit your Select Expert or
record-selection formula operators to those that take one value, such as Equal To or Less
Than. Those that can take more than one value, such as One Of, will prevent the viewer
from being prompted when they run the compiled report, even if they check Modify
Selection Formula.*

Once you are satisfied with these options, click the Print button to view, print, or
export the report. If the report contains parameter fields, the viewer will be prompted

to supply them before the report runs. If you choose to preview the report in a window, the preview window with the compiled report will appear, as shown in Figure 13-11.

Based on what was chosen with the Windows Styles button, you'll be able to print and export the report from the preview window, as well as drill down and navigate with the group tree. When you are finished viewing the report, simply close the preview window.

Note   *Because compiled reports can only be run by the viewer and not modified, make creative use of Parameter fields (discussed in Chapter 12) to allow the viewer as much flexibility as possible in customizing the report to their needs.*

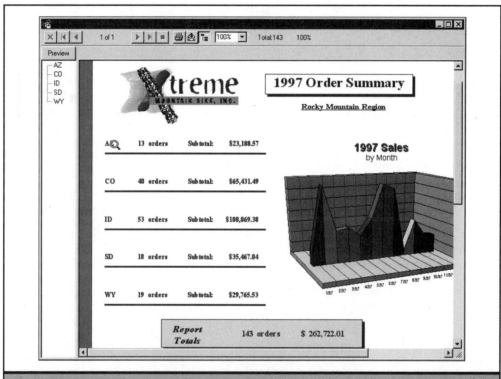

Figure 13-11.   *Compiled report in preview window*

The
Complete
Reference

Chapter 14

Reporting from SQL Databases

Although many companies and smaller software packages still rely on PC-style databases for their day-to-day functions, most "downsized" mainframe programs and many newer department or enterprise applications rely on *client/server database systems*. A client/server system includes two parts: a *client*, typically a PC running software such as Crystal Reports or a data-entry application, and a *server*, typically a larger, high-end PC running Windows NT/2000, or a midrange or even a mainframe Unix computer. The server maintains the database, and the client makes requests of the server for database access. There are many different client/server databases in existence, with Microsoft SQL Server, Oracle, Sybase, Informix, and IBM DB2 being among the more popular ones.

> **Caution** *SQL databases can only be used with the Professional Edition of Crystal Reports. The Standard Edition will only report on PC-style databases.*

It's important to understand and contrast the differences between a client/server database system and a PC-style database system that is installed on a shared local-area network (LAN). For reporting purposes, in particular, a LAN-based database system presents a much more serious performance hurdle than a client/server database. Figure 14-1 shows a PC reporting on two database environments. The first depicts a Microsoft Access database on a LAN server. The second depicts the same database on a SQL Server system.

The LAN-based scenario places heavy burdens on both the network and the PC making the reporting request. In this scenario, the PC must read the entire 100,000 record Access database across the network, picking and choosing the records that meet the report-selection criteria. This requires large amounts of data to be passed across the network, and the PC has to perform all the selection logic itself.

The client/server environment is much more efficient. The client PC simply makes a request to the database server via a structured query language (SQL) request. The database server, presumably a larger, high-powered PC, Unix computer, or mainframe, is running database software designed to process such queries very efficiently. It directly queries the 100,000 record database and sends only the required 1,000 records back across the network. This places less demand on the client and the network, and the whole process typically takes less time.

Logging On to SQL Databases

The first step to creating a Crystal Report is to select the SQL database that you want to base your report on. There are two general communication methods you can use to connect to a client/server database: direct database drivers and ODBC.

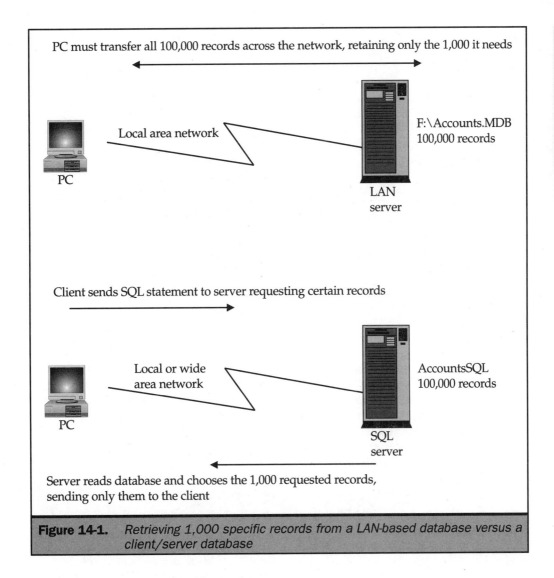

Figure 14-1. *Retrieving 1,000 specific records from a LAN-based database versus a client/server database*

Direct Database Drivers

Crystal Reports provides direct database drivers that work with many industry-standard client/server databases, including, among others, Microsoft SQL Server, Oracle, and IBM DB2. A direct database driver uses the native communication methods provided by the server vendor to communicate with the database server. This typically requires installing the specific client software provided by the database vendor on the PC. Examples of these packages include ISQL/W for Microsoft SQL Server and SQL + for Oracle.

Crystal Reports will recognize the existence of these packages and provide a direct database driver to connect to the database. In addition, Crystal Reports provides other direct drivers to allow you to report from Microsoft Outlook folders, Microsoft Exchange folders, Lotus Notes databases, Internet Web server activity logs, and the Windows NT event log. You can even write reports based on the *local file system*, which consists of the file and directory structure of your C drive or a network drive. More details on these specialized types of reports can be found in Chapter 21.

There are two general advantages of using direct database drivers to connect to the database server:

- Because there are fewer layers of communications protocols being used, there may be a slight performance improvement when reporting.

- The direct database driver may allow more flexibility for creating server-specific SQL statements or other query features for reporting.

ODBC

While many companies standardize on database servers that Crystal Reports provides direct database drivers for, there are many other database systems and specialized data systems that you may want to report on. Some standard method of communication is needed to connect standard PC clients with the myriad specialized servers and systems that exist. Microsoft designed open database connectivity (ODBC) to accomplish this communication.

Without too many exceptions, any server or proprietary data platform that is ODBC-compliant can be used with Crystal Reports. If the database or system vendor provides a Windows ODBC driver for their system, Crystal Reports should be able to report against that server or system. Because it has been accepted as an industry standard, ODBC is in widespread use.

Crystal Reports installs ODBC automatically. In addition, it installs some generic ODBC data sources for common database files and formats, including an ODBC data source for using the sample XTREME.MDB database. Before you can use Crystal Reports to report against other ODBC data systems, you must set up an ODBC data source. Use the ODBC Administrator from the Crystal Reports Program Group or Control Panel to set up the data source.

Choosing the Database

When you first start Crystal Reports, you can immediately choose and log on to a client/server database before you open an existing report or create a new report. If you don't log on, but open a report based on a client/server database, you will be prompted to log on as soon as you try to refresh the report or choose any other function that requires the database to be read.

If you want to create a new report based on a client/server database, there are different steps, depending on whether you create the report with a report expert or with the Custom option. If you use a report expert, the Data tab will automatically include a button for any direct database driver that Crystal Reports provides, and a button labeled SQL/ODBC to connect to any ODBC data source, as seen in the Standard Report Expert here:

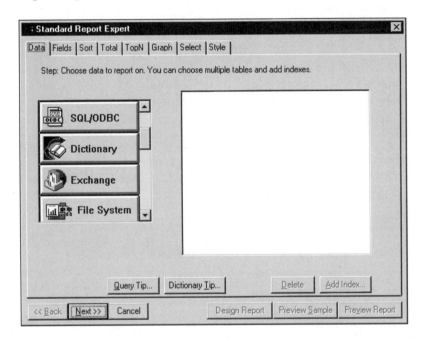

If you chose the Custom option to create a new report, click the SQL/ODBC button to begin your report. Choosing SQL/ODBC from either method will display the Log On Server dialog box.

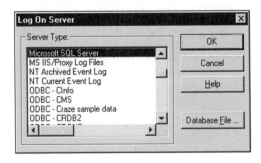

The Log On Server dialog box combines both direct database drivers and ODBC data sources in one place. It's easy to tell which is which: ODBC data sources are preceded by the letters "ODBC." Choose the data source or driver that you want to use in your report, and click OK. Based on the source you choose, another dialog box will appear and prompt for other information, such as a logon ID and password, the database you want to use, or other information that varies based on the driver or ODBC data source you choose. After you successfully log on, you'll see the Choose SQL Table dialog box, shown in Figure 14-2.

You'll see a list of all the available tables, stored procedures, and views in the database. Choose the table, stored procedure, or view that you want to include in your report. Click the OK button to continue with the report design process or Cancel to cancel your selections.

This dialog box is one of the rare Crystal Reports exceptions where you cannot choose multiple items by using CTRL-click or SHIFT-click—you can only choose one table at a time. If you've displayed this dialog box with the Custom option or by using Database | Add Database to Report from the pull-down menus, you will only be able to choose one table and click OK. If you've displayed this dialog box from within a report expert or the Visual Linking Expert (discussed later in this chapter), the OK and Cancel

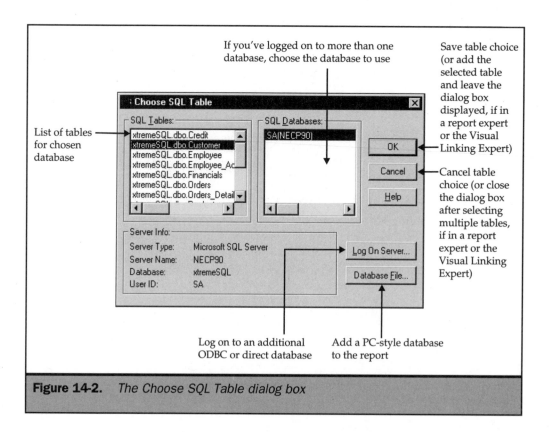

Figure 14-2.   *The Choose SQL Table dialog box*

buttons will change to Add and Done. In this case, you can select a single table, click the Add button, select another table, click Add, and so on.

Keep in mind that once you log on to a SQL database from the Log On Server dialog box, you remain connected to that database even if you close any reports that are based on that database connection. If you then begin a new report and attempt to choose a PC-style database or to log on to another SQL database, the Choose SQL Table dialog box with the original set of tables will immediately appear. If you don't want to use these tables in your report, you will need to log off the original server first. This is accomplished by either closing and restarting Crystal Reports, or by using the Log Off Server option. If you have a report open, choose Database l Log Off Server. If you don't have a report open, choose File l Log Off Server.

Changing SQL Options

Depending on the direct database driver or ODBC data source you choose, you may not see all the database elements you're looking for. In particular, if your database supports *SQL stored procedures* (precompiled SQL statements that may contain parameters) or *views* (virtual tables that may combine several actual database tables together into one group), you will want to make sure you can see these in the Choose SQL Table dialog box. You may also only want to use a particular ODBC data source or direct database driver on a regular basis. Or, you may want to limit the tables that you see in the Choose SQL Table dialog box to table names that match a certain pattern or that are owned by a certain database user.

These options can all be customized by choosing File l Options from the pull-down menus and clicking the SQL tab. Figure 14-3 shows these SQL options.

If you report on a specific data source more often than others, you can choose it in the Server Type drop-down list. It will automatically be chosen when the Log On Server dialog box appears. If you want to skip the Log On Server dialog box entirely and use the data source you chose in the drop-down list, check the Skip Server Type Dialog check box—the default data source will be automatically chosen.

You can also choose default server and database names, and a default userid. The Dict. Path and Data Path text boxes specify default paths if you're using NetWare SQL as your database system.

The Allow Reporting On section is where you choose what types of database objects to view in the Choose SQL Table dialog box. You can also limit available database objects based on their names and owners. If you'd like to be able to choose information in the Allow Reporting On section every time you open a database, check the Prompt On Every Table check box.

Converting a PC-Style Database Report to a Client/Server Database

You may initially create a report based on a PC-style database, such as Microsoft Access, and then desire to convert the report to use a similarly organized SQL

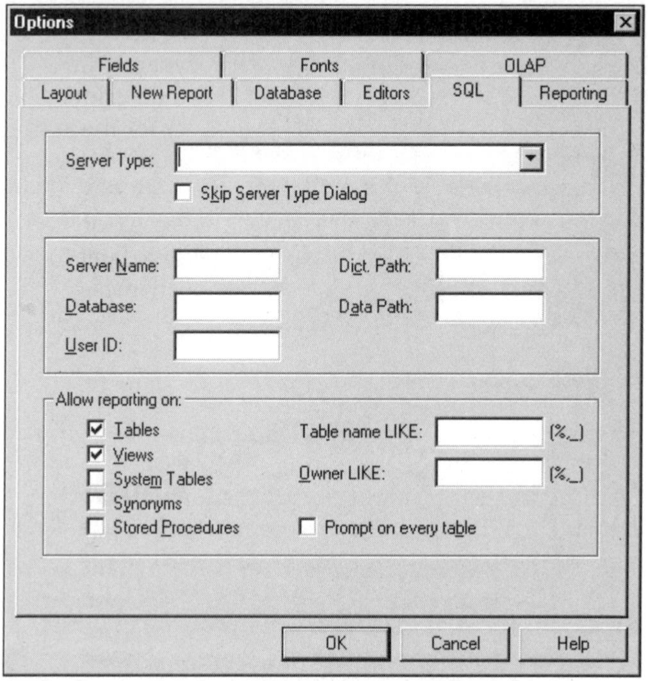

Figure 14-3. *SQL file options*

database. Perhaps the Access database has been upsized to SQL Server. Or, you may initially be developing reports against a test database in Btrieve, but the reports will eventually have to run against an identical Oracle database.

In each of these situations, you will need to choose a different database driver after the report has been initially created because you'll actually be changing the type of database you are using. Choose Database | Convert Database Driver from the pull-down menus. The Convert Database Driver dialog box will appear.

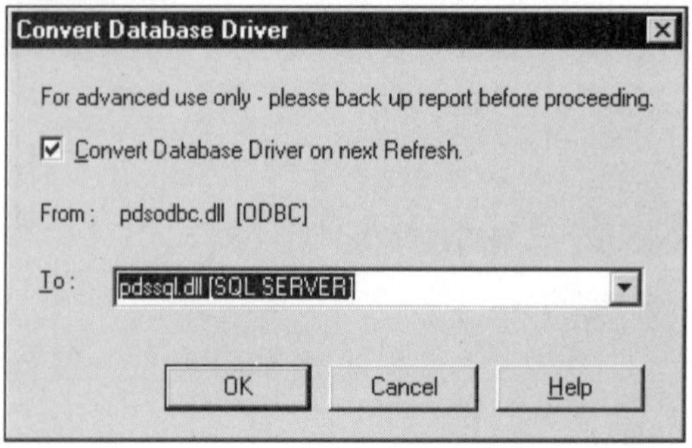

Check Convert Database Driver on Next Refresh. This will enable the To drop-down list. Next to the From label, you'll also see the driver that the report is currently based on. The drop-down list will show the dynamic-link library names of all installed Crystal Reports database drivers, followed by a description of the database that the driver connects to. Choose a new database driver for the report from the list, and click OK. If you chose a secure database, you'll be prompted to log on to the database.

If table or field names have changed in the new database (for example, spaces will probably have been replaced with underscores if an Access database was upsized to SQL Server), you'll have to remap old fields to their new names. This is explained in detail in Chapter 15.

 If you simply need to choose a different database of the same type, *use Database | Set Location instead of Convert Database Driver.*

Changing from One SQL Database to Another

You may have other situations where you initially develop a report against a particular database, perhaps a test ODBC database. You then need to point the report to another ODBC production database. Since both databases use ODBC connections, you can't use the Convert Database Driver dialog box to change to the production database. Instead, choose Database | Set Location from the pull-down menus. The Set Location dialog box will appear.

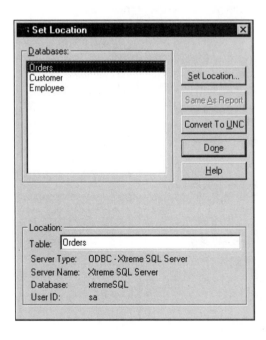

Select the first table you want to point to the production database and click the Set Location button. The Choose SQL Table dialog box will appear, showing all databases that you are currently logged on to in the SQL Databases list. If you are already logged on to the production database, simply choose it and then select the new table in the SQL Tables list.

If you aren't logged on to the production database, click the Log On Server button to display the Log On Server dialog box, in which you can choose the production database. Once you've logged on, the production database will appear in the SQL Databases list. Choose it, and then choose the corresponding table in the SQL Tables list. Once you click OK, you may see the Propagate Server and Database Changes Across Tables with the Same Original Information? question. If you choose Yes, any other table in the report that belonged to the original database will be pointed to the new database.

If table or field names have changed in the new database, you'll be prompted to remap old fields to their new names. This is covered in more detail in Chapter 15.

Linking Tables

Although there may be rare instances when you design a report based on just one database table, you will usually need to use at least two, and often more, tables in your report. This is because most modern relational databases are *normalized*. Database normalization refers to breaking out repetitive database information into separate tables in the database for efficiency and maintenance reasons. Consider the following employee table:

Employee Name	Department Name	Salary
Bill	Information Technology	50,000
Karen	Human Resources	32,500
Renee	Information Technology	37,500
John	Executive	85,000
Carl	Mail Room	24,000
Jim	Information Technology	48,000
Julie	Executive	87,000
Sally	Mail Room	23,500

While this makes for a simple reporting environment because you don't need to choose more than one table to print an employee roster or paycheck, it becomes more difficult to maintain. Notice that department names repeat several times throughout this small table. (Think about this same scenario for a 50,000 employee company!) This not only takes up a large amount of storage space, but should a department name change, there is much work to be done to make the change in this table. For example, if the Information Technology department changes its name to "Information Systems," a search and replace function must be performed through the entire employee table, replacing every occurrence of the old name with the new name.

Contrast this single table layout with the following database environment:

Employee Table:

Employee Name	Department Number	Salary
Bill	25	50,000
Karen	17	32,500
Renee	25	37,500
John	8	85,000
Carl	13	24,000
Jim	25	48,000
Julie	8	87,000
Sally	13	23,500

Department Table:

Department Number	Department Name
8	Executive
13	Mail Room
17	Human Resources
25	Information Technology

Here you can see that the database has been normalized by placing the department information in its own lookup table. In this environment, there is much less storage used by the employee table because only a department number is stored for each employee, not the entire department name. And, if the Information Technology department name changes, only one record in the Department table has to be changed in the entire database.

Visual Linking Expert

Using multiple tables complicates the reporting environment because you need more than just the employee table to print an employee roster or paycheck. In the preceding example, not only do you have to include the two tables in your report, but you must link them together with a common field. *Linking* tables (often also known as *joining* tables) consists of choosing the common field that will allow the second table to follow the main table as the main table is read record by record. You link tables in Crystal Reports with the Visual Linking Expert, illustrated in Figure 14-4.

The Visual Linking Expert will appear automatically if you initially choose two or more tables when you first create a report, or whenever you choose additional tables with Database | Add Database to Report from the pull-down menus. You can also display the Visual Linking Expert by clicking the Link Expert button in the Supplementary toolbar or by choosing Database | Visual Linking Expert from the pull-down menus.

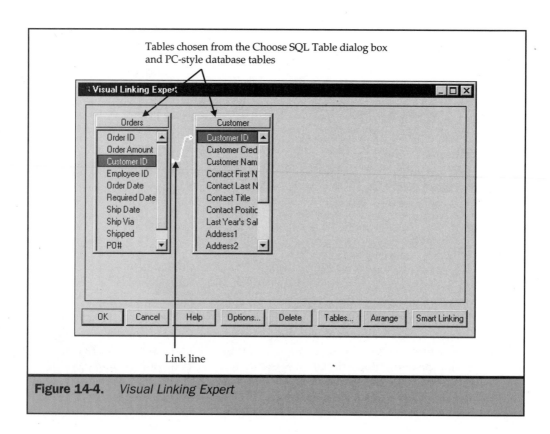

Figure 14-4.   *Visual Linking Expert*

The Visual Linking Expert will show all tables that have been included in your report, and it may have already chosen links between the tables. If you see lines with arrows connecting fields in the tables, the Visual Linking Expert has already applied Smart Linking to the tables (discussed later in the chapter). You may need to delete these existing links if they are incorrect, or add new links yourself.

To delete a link, click the line connecting the two tables. It, along with the fields it connects, will be highlighted. Click the Delete button or press the DEL key. If you want to change link options, such as the join type (discussed later in the chapter), the index used by the link, or multiple-table link behavior, click the Options button, or double-click the selected link.

To draw a link, click a field in the table you want to link from. Then *drag* your mouse to the other table you want to link and *drop* onto the field you want to link to. A link line will be drawn between the two tables. Note that the "from" side of the link line will display a small block and the "to" side of the link line will display an arrow.

Tip *A persistent bug in Crystal Reports involves dropping on the first field in the "to" table. If you drop much above the middle of the field, the link line won't be drawn. Drop on the lower part of the "to" field to ensure that the link line will be drawn. This problem only occurs if you're dropping on the very first field in the "to" table.*

If Crystal Reports detects no potential problems with the link you've drawn, the link line will simply appear and you'll see no messages. If, however, Crystal Reports detects a potential problem with the link, such as mismatched field types, you'll receive a warning message before the link line appears, or the link may not be created at all.

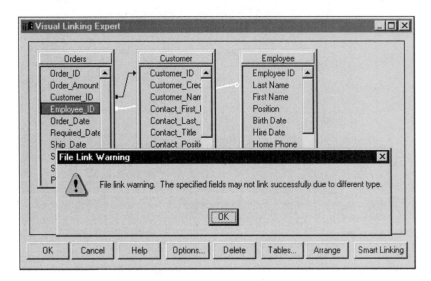

Adding New Tables to the Visual Linking Expert

You will often find that you need to add additional tables to your report as your report design progresses. To add one table, you can choose Database | Add Database to Report from the pull-down menus. It's often easier, though, to use the Visual Linking Expert to add additional tables. Click the Tables button to add additional tables to the report. The Choose Tables To Use In Visual Linking dialog box will appear, as shown in Figure 14-5.

Any tables that you've previously added to your report will already appear in the Linked Tables list. If you attempt to add one of these existing tables again, you'll be prompted to give the second occurrence of the table an *alias*, since each table used in the Visual Linking Expert must have a unique name. You can add additional PC-style databases or SQL/ODBC database tables by clicking the Add Data File or Add SQL/ODBC buttons (the Add Index and Table Description buttons don't apply to SQL databases). Once you've chosen the table or tables, they will appear in the Visible Tables list. These tables will be added to the Visual Linking Expert when you close this

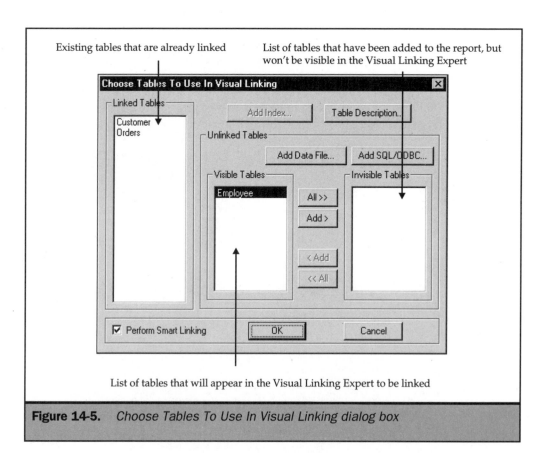

Figure 14-5. *Choose Tables To Use In Visual Linking dialog box*

dialog box. Use the Add and All arrow buttons to move tables between the Visible Tables and Invisible Tables lists depending on whether you want to add the tables to the Visual Linking Expert. If you want the Visual Linking Expert to link the tables automatically, check the Perform Smart Linking check box (Smart Linking is discussed in more detail later in the chapter). Once you click OK, the Choose Tables To Use In Visual Linking dialog box will close, and the additional tables will appear in the Visual Linking Expert. You can now add or delete links as necessary.

Removing Unused Tables from the Report

You may inadvertently add too many tables to your report, or you may no longer need tables that you used earlier in the report design process. While this might be a good future enhancement for Crystal Reports, you cannot currently remove any unused tables from the Visual Linking Expert. Close the Visual Linking Expert to return to the report Design tab or Report Expert.

To remove tables using the Report Expert, just remove any fields from the report that come from the table you want to remove. Then return to the Data tab, select the table you no longer want, and click the Delete button. If you used the Custom option and are working directly in the report Design tab, choose Database | Remove from Report from the pull-down menus. Choose the table you no longer want, and click Remove. If any fields remain on the report or are used in existing formulas, you'll receive a warning before the table is removed.

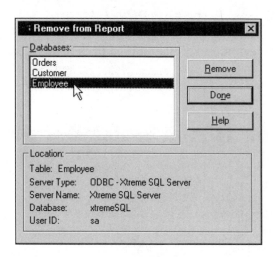

Make sure you really want to remove the table before you click Remove. You can't undo a table removal. Also, if you remove a table that is referenced in any formulas, the formulas will no longer work once the table is gone. If you remove a table by mistake, the best approach is to use the Visual Linking Expert or choose Database | Add Database to Report from the pull-down menus to add the table back in.

So, Which Tables and Fields Should I Link Anyway?

It won't take too long to figure out that you have to be very familiar with the database you are reporting against to accurately link tables and fields. You have to know the layout of the tables and the data that the common fields contain in order to successfully link them. This task is complicated even further by database designers who insist on protecting their jobs by creating confusing and cryptic table and field names.

Probably the most expeditious approach is to consult with someone who either designed the database or is familiar with its layout and contents. Barring that, you may be able to discern the proper tables and fields to link if they are named logically. If nothing else, you can browse individual fields in the Visual Linking Expert by right-clicking a field name and choosing Browse Field from the pop-up menu. By looking for similar data types and sample data that seems to match up in both tables, you can find good candidates for links.

Always make sure you test your report and verify that correct data is being returned, once you've linked tables. It's *very easy* to create an incorrect link that displays no error message, but doesn't return the correctly matched data to the report.

If you have a large group of report designers who are not familiar with the intricacies of the database, you may want to create a Crystal Dictionary for them to use in reporting. This feature is discussed in Chapter 20.

Linking Differences Between PC-Style and SQL Databases

While most concepts surrounding table linking apply equally to both PC-style and SQL databases, there are a few issues that you should keep in mind when dealing with PC-style databases.

First, notice the visual differences in the Visual Linking Expert when using a PC-style database.

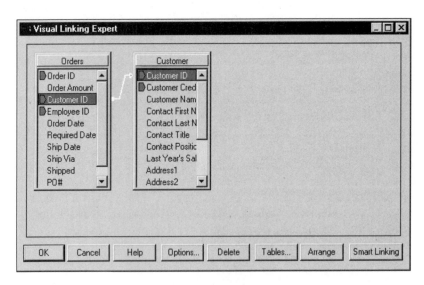

You'll notice the small "tent" arrows next to various fields that you don't see when using a SQL database. These arrows indicate that the field is indexed. An *index* is a special setting that the database designer creates to speed up access to a table. Searching for specific records from that table will be much faster when the search is based on an indexed field. Based on your video settings, you may also notice different colors for the index arrows. The different colors indicate Crystal Reports' best guess as to which fields may be the table's unique indexes for the fields. As a general rule, you needn't worry about the colors on the index arrows—just make sure that the field you're trying to link to has one.

In some cases, a single field in a table might be indexed more than once—perhaps once individually and also as part of another multiple-field index. In these situations, you may prefer to use one index instead of the other, based on the type of link you are trying to create. For example, if you are only linking on one field that's included in a multifield index, it will probably be preferable (and sometimes mandatory) to use the individual index for the field instead of the multifield index. You can choose an alternate index for a field by clicking the Add Index button in the Choose Tables for Visual Linking dialog box when you add a new table, or in the Link Options dialog box (illustrated later in the chapter).

Regardless of the visual differences you may see in the index arrows, PC-style databases impose one unavoidable requirement: *The "to" field on which you drop a link must be an indexed field.* The "from" field doesn't have this requirement, but you have no choice with the "to" field. If you try linking to a non-indexed field, the link won't stick and you'll see an error message.

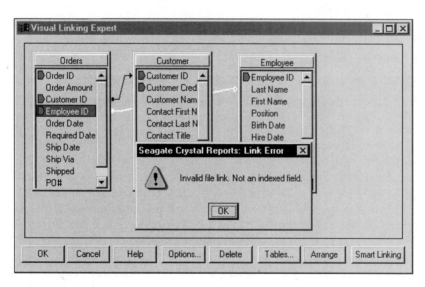

Choosing which fields to index when designing a database is a balancing act. The more indexed fields, the more choices you have as a report developer for linking.

However, creating too many indexes results in larger databases with potential performance problems. If you can't link to a table properly because the target field is not indexed, you may be able to contact the database designer or administrator and request that an index be added. If this isn't practical, you still may be able to create the same, or a very similar report, with the use of subreports. See Chapter 11 for more information.

Tip   *When using SQL databases via direct database drivers or ODBC, you won't see the colored tent arrows in the Visual Linking Expert, and the indexed "to" field requirement does not exist. However, you'll probably still want to link to indexed fields whenever and wherever possible. It's all too common for a viewer to chastise Crystal Reports for poor performance when the problem actually lies within the speed of the query (or lack thereof) on the server. In many cases this can be attributed to linking on non-indexed fields. Since there's no visual cue as to which fields are indexed, you should contact the database administrator or designer if you suspect performance problems are related to linking on non-indexed fields.*

Is Smart Linking Really That "Smart"?

When you first install Crystal Reports, Smart Linking is turned on by default. Smart Linking is a feature with good intentions, but it is often more trouble than it's worth. Smart Linking will automatically link fields in two adjacent tables if the fields meet these criteria:

- The field names are exactly the same
- The data types are identical
- In the case of string fields, the field lengths are the same
- In the case of PC-style databases, the "to" field is indexed

In an ideal setting (like the XTREME.MDB sample database provided with Crystal Reports), Smart Linking works perfectly. In the real world, however, things are usually quite different.

Consider, for example, a report that includes a vendor and customer table. Both tables contain fields named Address, City, State, and Zip_Code. It's perfectly conceivable that these fields have identical data types and field lengths. Smart Linking will dutifully link the two tables together on all four fields. But, these aren't the proper fields to link these two tables together.

Because Smart Linking can often result in you taking more time to delete incorrect links and then manually create the correct links, it can be turned off. Select File I Options from the pull-down menus, and uncheck Auto-SmartLinking on the Database tab.

Using Multiple Database Types in the Same Report

Crystal Reports doesn't limit you to using just one type of database per report. You may, for example, wish to get the main transaction table for your report from a client/server database using a direct access database driver, one smaller lookup table from a Microsoft Access database on a shared LAN drive, and another lookup table from a Microsoft Excel spreadsheet on your C drive via ODBC.

To accomplish this, simply choose the first table as you normally would. Then, display the Visual Linking Expert and click the Tables button. You'll notice both Add Data File and Add SQL/ODBC buttons. You can click either button to choose the desired type of database. Once you've chosen the tables, click OK to add them to the Visual Linking Expert and link them appropriately.

In general, this type of mixed reporting is perfectly acceptable, with a couple of caveats:

- If you are joining two tables from different ODBC data sources, such as a table from an Oracle database and another table from a SQL Server database, you can only link on *string fields*.

- If you use tables from different database types (such as one table from an ODBC data source and another from a PC-style database), you'll see a message indicating that the report is using more than one database driver. This message is usually informational, but may sometimes result in reports that won't run correctly.

Join Types

When you link two tables, you must consider carefully what records will be returned from both tables. Consider a slight modification to the normalized table structures illustrated earlier in this chapter:

Employee Table:

Employee Name	Department Number	Salary
Karen	17	32,500
Renee	25	37,500
John	8	85,000
Carl	13	24,000
Denise	32	125,000

Department Table:

Department Number	Department Name
8	Executive
13	Mail Room
17	Human Resources
4	Finance
25	Information Technology

A quick glance at these two tables reveals two inconsistencies: Denise has no matching record in the Department table, and the Finance department has no employees in the Employee table. These two tables are said to lack *referential integrity*—a fancy computer term that simply means, "the two tables don't completely match up." Fancy term or not, this will be *very* important to you as a report designer. You have to decide how you want to deal with a lack of referential integrity.

Many databases can enforce referential integrity, so the situation described previously will never happen. If the database designer chooses to enforce referential integrity between these two tables, an employee cannot be given a department number that doesn't exist in the Department table, and a department record can't be deleted from the Department table if there are any Employee table records that still contain that department.

However, enforcing referential integrity often introduces other complexities in the database, and there are many times when the basic function of the database will not allow referential integrity to be enforced. The database designer or administrator should be consulted if you have questions about the way your database is designed.

A situation where you would be very concerned about referential integrity is when you design a report to print paychecks for employees. Consider the tables previously shown as the basis for your paychecks. If you wish to have the employee's department printed on the check stub to help in check distribution, you'll need to link the Employee and Department tables together on the Department Number field. It's a fair assumption that your paycheck run would get at least this far:

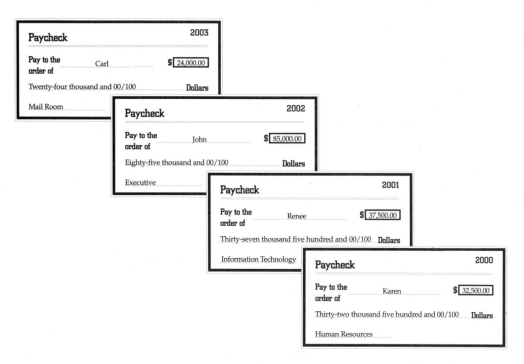

The big question for you, the report designer, is "What happens to Denise?" Considering that she's a highly paid employee (at least from most viewpoints), she will probably be very interested in being paid, regardless of referential integrity. Another interesting question is "Will any checks print for the Finance department?" The answer to your questions are dependent upon which *join type* you use when linking these two tables together.

There are two join types that you will be concerned with most of the time: equal join (often also referred to as an inner join), and left outer join (sometimes referred to as just as outer join).

- **Equal join**   Includes records from both tables *only when the joining fields are equal*
- **Left outer join**   Includes *all* records from the left table, and only records from the right table when the joining fields are equal

Even though Denise probably doesn't know what a left outer join is, she probably will be much happier if you choose it. This will result in her receiving a paycheck that will simply not have a department name printed on it. This is particularly important in Crystal Reports, as the default join type for SQL databases is an equal join. A third type of join that you may use less frequently is a right outer join.

- ■ **Right outer join** Includes *all* records from the right table, and only records from the left table when the joining fields are equal

Denise would be as displeased with this one as she would with an equal join. You would also get a wasted paycheck with the Finance department on the pay stub, but no employee or salary printed on it.

Choosing the Join Type in the Visual Linking Expert

Choose the join type in the Visual Linking Expert by double-clicking on the link line between the two tables you are concerned with. The Link Options dialog box, shown in Figure 14-6, will appear. Select the desired join type by clicking a radio button in the lower-right corner of the dialog box.

Note	*If tables are linked by more than one field, choosing a join type for any of the links will set the same join type for all the links. You cannot have different join types for multiple links between the same tables.*

Although most typical business reporting can be accomplished with equal and left outer joins, you may have occasion in specialized reporting situations to use the other join types.

- ■ **Greater join** Repeats records from the left table, matching records from the right table every time the joining field in the left table *is greater than* the joining field in the right table

- ■ **Less join** Repeats records from the left table, matching records from the right table every time the joining field in the left table *is less than* the joining field in the right table

- ■ **Greater or equal join** Repeats records from the left table, matching records from the right table every time the joining field in the left table *is greater than or equal to* the joining field in the right table

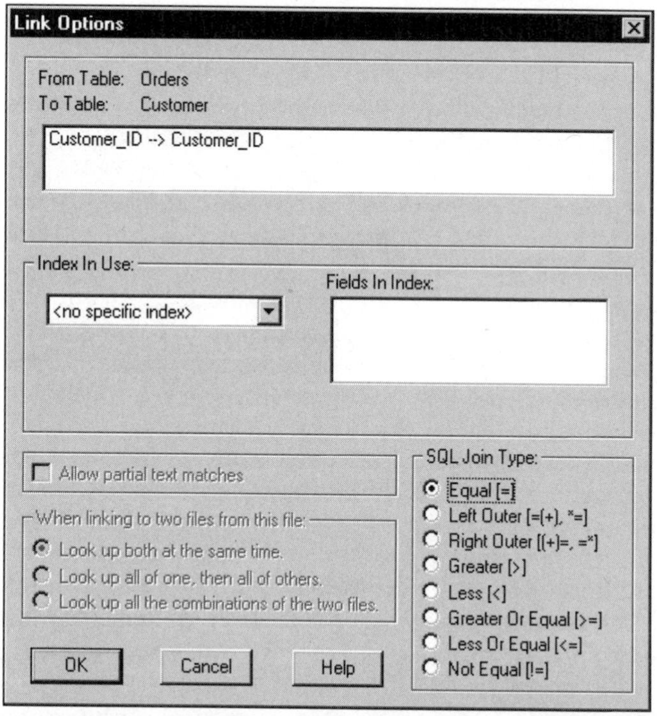

Figure 14-6.   *Link Options dialog box*

- **Less or equal join**   Repeat records from the left table, matching records from the right table every time the joining field in the left table *is less than or equal to* the joining field in the right table

- **Not equal join**   Returns all combinations of records from the two tables where the joining fields *are not equal*

Tip   *You can change the join type only for SQL databases. If you display link options for a PC-style database, the SQL Join Type radio buttons will be dimmed. The fixed join type for PC-style databases is a left outer join, even though the dimmed radio buttons indicate an equal join.*

Which Should Be the Left "From" Table and Which Should Be the Right "To" Table?

When you use the Visual Linking Expert, you begin to draw a link by clicking on a "from" table. You then drop the link onto the desired field in the "to" table. You can tell which table is the "from" and which is the "to" by looking at the direction of the link line, as well as the block and arrow. The link line will move *from* one table *to* the other, and the "from" side of the line will display a small block while the "to" side will display an arrow.

This begs the question, "Does it make any difference which is the 'from' and which is the 'to' table?" The answer, again, relates to the join type you choose. Generally speaking, if you select an equal join, it doesn't make a great deal of difference. However, if you use any other join type, then it makes a great deal of difference, as the "from" or "left" table and "to" or "right" table determine how records are returned.

A relationship between tables is often referred to as a *one-to-one relationship* or a *one-to-many relationship*. If there is always only one matching record in both tables, then it doesn't matter which table is the "from" and which is the "to"—it's a one-to-one relationship. However, if there are many matching records in one table for each record in another, then the direction of the link is significant. For example, if there is a table containing many orders placed by the same customer linked to a table containing only one matching customer record, you will want to link *from* the Orders table (the "many" table) *to* the Customer table (the "one" table).

If you're concerned that the link may be in "reverse" order, and you'd like to switch the "from" and "to" tables, you can simply delete and redraw the link, or right-click on the link and choose Reverse Link from the pop-up menu.

Linking One PC-Style Table to Multiple Tables

When you're using a PC-style database, you have some choices when you create certain types of links between multiple tables. These issues arise when you link a primary or "driving" table to two or more secondary lookup tables. The number and combination of records returned can vary, depending on how many matching records there are in the lookup table for each record in the primary table. These types of links are sometimes called "A to B, A to C" links. Because you can't change join types for PC-style databases, you may occasionally need to change the way Crystal Reports reads records in these situations.

Crystal Reports includes a small sample Microsoft Access database, ORDERCR.MDB, that demonstrates these concepts. This database contains three tables: Cust, containing a few customers; Orders, containing several orders for each customer; and Credits, containing credit memos for two customers, as shown in Figure 14-7.

If you are designing a report that lists customers, along with orders and credits for each customer, you will see that there are several ways the report could conceivably

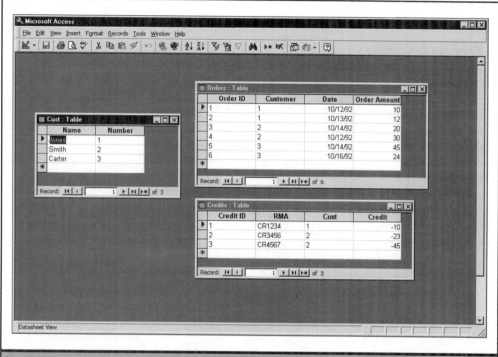

Figure 14-7.   *MS Access window showing three tables*

show these combinations of records. For this example, the tables have been linked as
follows in the Visual Linking Expert:

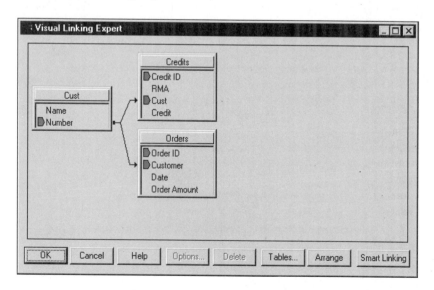

Notice that the Cust table is linked to both secondary tables on the Number field. Whenever you link multiple tables to a single table in this fashion, Crystal Reports will give you an extra choice—When Linking to Two Files from This File—on the Link Options dialog box, which will appear when you double-click on any link line. With these options, you can choose the lookup method for a multiple-table link:

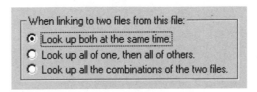

The When Linking to Two Files from This File radio buttons only apply to PC-style databases. They are dimmed whenever you use a SQL database. If you are concerned about the way your SQL database returns records in similar situations, try different join types or check with your database administrator.

The following three examples were created with ORDERCR.MDB, showing the Customer Name from the Cust table (we'll refer to it as Table A), the Order ID and Order Amount from the Orders table (we'll call it Table B), and the Credit ID and Credit Amount from the Credits table (Table C). Each example shows the results of one of the three choices under the When Linking to Two Files from This File area of the Link Options dialog box.

LOOK UP BOTH AT THE SAME TIME   This method begins by reading a record from Table A, along with the first matching record in Table B and the first matching record in Table C. The *same* record from Table A will then repeat (if there are additional matching records in Tables B or C), and the next matching Table B and Table C records will be included. If Crystal Reports runs out of matching records in Table B or C, while there are still some left in the other secondary table, null values will appear for that table. Here's the sample report with this option chosen:

Name	Order ID	Order Amount	Credit ID	Credit
Jones	1	10.00	1	-10.00
Jones	2	12.00	1	-10.00
Smith	3	20.00	2	-23.00
Smith	4	30.00	3	-45.00
Carter	5	45.00		
Carter	6	24.00		

LOOK UP ALL OF ONE, THEN ALL OF OTHERS   This option, in essence, completely separates the secondary tables from each other. Crystal Reports will read a record from Table A, and then read all matching records from Table B first, leaving fields for Table C blank. It will then continue repeating the same record from Table A and include all matching records from Table C, leaving Table B fields blank. Here's the sample report with this option chosen:

Name	Order ID	Order Amount	Credit ID	Credit
Jones	1	10.00		
Jones	2	12.00		
Jones			1	-10.00
Smith	3	20.00		
Smith	4	30.00		
Smith			2	-23.00
Smith			3	-45.00
Carter	5	45.00		
Carter	6	24.00		

Generally, this is the only one of the three options that will not repeat the same record from the secondary tables (although primary table records will repeat). For this reason, this method may be the most straightforward if you're calculating group subtotal or summary fields.

If the method you use does result in repeating records that skew group or report totals or summaries, search Crystal Reports online Help for "When linking to two files from this file." Then click the How to Subtotal True A to B, A to C Reports link below the Option 2 example.

LOOK UP ALL THE COMBINATIONS OF THE TWO FILES   This option can quickly turn records for a relatively small database into a monstrous report. It begins by reading the first Table A record and matching it to a Table B record. It then repeats both the Table A and B records for every matching Table C record. It then goes to the next matching Table B record (while *still* on the first Table A record) and repeats the A and B records for the next matching C record. When Crystal Reports runs out of Table B records, it then proceeds to the next Table A record and starts the whole process over again. Here's the sample report with this option chosen:

Name	Order ID	Order Amount	Credit ID	Credit
Jones	1	10.00	1	-10.00
Jones	2	12.00	1	-10.00
Smith	3	20.00	2	-23.00
Smith	3	20.00	3	-45.00
Smith	4	30.00	2	-23.00
Smith	4	30.00	3	-45.00
Carter	5	45.00		
Carter	6	24.00		

Working with the SQL Statement

You may remember from earlier in the chapter that SQL (the letters can be pronounced individually, or many people pronounce it as *sequel*) is an acronym for *structured query language*. This database query language has been established as a pseudo-standard method of querying databases. The term "pseudo" is used because although the American National Standard Institute (ANSI) settled on a standard SQL, virtually every database vendor adds their own personal touches, although they all appear to adhere to the ANSI standard.

Viewing the SQL Query

Because Crystal Reports works with SQL databases, it must eventually translate the tables, fields, links, sorting, and grouping that you've used to design your report into SQL. You can view the SQL statements Crystal Reports creates by choosing Database I Show SQL Query from the pull-down menus.

Consider the following report Design tab that uses data from the XTREME sample database, converted from Microsoft Access to Microsoft SQL Server, accessed via ODBC. This report uses the Orders and Customer tables, linked with a left outer join on Customer ID. The Select Expert is limiting the report to USA customers only. Notice the fields that have been placed in the Details section. Also, notice that a group based on Customer.Region has been created.

To view the SQL statement that Crystal Reports creates to query the database, select Database I Show SQL Query. You will see the dialog box illustrated in Figure 14-8.

Notice the different parts, or *clauses*, of the SQL statement. The SELECT clause matches the database fields that your report needs (for the details section, formulas, grouping, etc.). The FROM clause chooses the tables to use, as well as specifying the join type for table linking. The WHERE clause supplies record selection to the server. And, the ORDER BY clause requests that the SQL Server sort records in Customer.Region order (for the Region group) before sending them back to the client.

The SQL syntax may change, based on the type of database you are reporting against, and whether you're using ODBC or direct database drivers to communicate

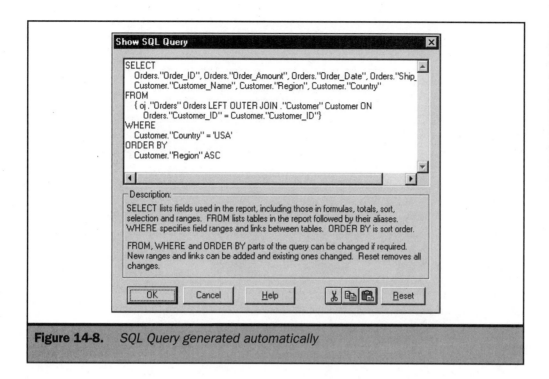

CRYSTAL REPORTS 7
INTRODUCED

Figure 14-8. *SQL Query generated automatically*

with it. You'll also see different syntax for joining tables. And, you may see the actual table join appear in either the FROM or WHERE clauses.

Here is the exact same Show SQL Query dialog box using the direct database driver to Microsoft SQL Server:

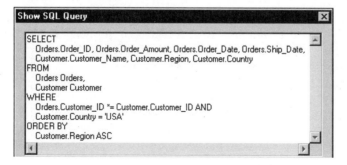

and, for the Microsoft Access version of the XTREME.MDB sample database via ODBC:

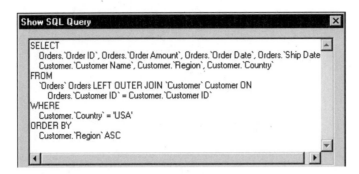

Although you may not consider yourself a database expert and you might not make a habit of writing huge SQL statements off the top of your head, there are two big advantages to being able to see and manipulate the SQL query:

- You can see what Crystal Reports is submitting to the database server, which can be useful if you are experiencing performance problems or other peculiarities.

- You can actually change most of the SQL query manually if you do have a basic understanding of SQL.

Modifying the SQL Query

There may be times where Crystal Reports won't take full advantage of your server's SQL language extensions and you would like to modify the SQL to include them. You may also want to paste SQL copied from another query tool into the Show SQL Query dialog box. You are completely free to modify the FROM, WHERE, and ORDER BY clauses of the SQL statement to your heart's content. The SELECT clause is off-limits, though. You can type over it, but any changes you make won't be saved. (Don't even bother to try changing the SELECT to a DELETE or UPDATE—your changes will never make it to the server!)

Make sure the modifications comply with the particular syntax of SQL that your report is based on. The three SQL statement examples shown previously give you an idea of the small syntax differences between different connection methods to the same data. If you enter SQL using incorrect syntax, you'll receive an error message when you refresh the report. If you change the SQL query manually and later think better of it, you can always click the Reset button at the bottom-right corner of the Show SQL Query dialog box. This will erase any changes you've made to the query and return it to the Crystal Reports default.

It's very import to understand how the Show SQL Query dialog box and report record selection interact with each other. They are, in effect, mutually exclusive: you can either use the Select Expert or record-selection formula to specify record selection, or the WHERE clause, but not both. When you first create a report using a SQL database and use record selection, either with the Select Expert or by entering a record-selection formula, Crystal Reports attempts to convert the record selection into a SQL WHERE clause. If you then change the WHERE clause manually in the Show SQL Query dialog box, the record selection you chose with a formula or the

Select Expert will disappear. Crystal Reports will then depend on your "custom" SQL to limit report records.

You can then return to the Select Expert or Record Selection Formula Editor and see that nothing is there. If you then re-enter Select Expert choices or a record-selection formula, you'll be presented with a message:

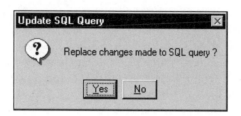

If you click Yes, any manual changes you made to the WHERE clause will be replaced by the Crystal Reports–generated WHERE clause.

Case Sensitivity

You may recall from Chapter 6 that PC-style databases are case sensitive when using record selection. An example of case sensitivity is that when comparing a country database field to the literal "USA", any data in the database stored as "usa" or "Usa" won't be retrieved for the report.

You may also recall that you have a choice when dealing with SQL databases. To change the option for the current report only, select File | Report Options and check Case-Insensitive SQL Data. If you want SQL queries to be case insensitive for any new report you create from this point forward, select File | Options and check Case-Insensitive SQL Data on the Database.

Remember that this option may still not work if the particular database server, ODBC driver, or direct database driver that you're using doesn't support case insensitivity. In these cases, you may be able to manually modify the SQL statement to ignore case. For example, the following Microsoft Access (via ODBC) WHERE clause is case sensitive:

```
WHERE
    Customer.'Country' = 'USA'
```

By using the specific "flavor" of Microsoft Access SQL, you can make the query case insensitive by changing it to:

```
WHERE
    UCASE(Customer.'Country') = 'USA'
```

This will use the built-in SQL UCASE function to force database records to all uppercase letters before the server compares them to the uppercase "USA" literal.

Using SQL Stored Procedures

Most SQL database systems include the capability to use stored procedures. A *stored procedure* is a SQL query that has been evaluated or "compiled" by the database server in advance, and is stored on the server along with regular database tables. Because the stored procedure is compiled in advance, it often performs faster than a SQL query submitted on the fly. Stored procedures can be created by the database designer or administrator for specific queries that will be run on a frequent basis.

To enhance flexibility, stored procedures can contain one or more *stored procedure parameters* that prompt the user to enter a value. The stored procedure then uses the value to run the query. For example, if you have a stored procedure that returns several fields from linked tables, based on Country and Order Date parameters, you'll be prompted to enter a particular country and order date when the stored procedure runs. The procedure will then return a result set containing only records matching the two parameter values you supplied.

Choosing Stored Procedures

As far as Crystal Reports is concerned, stored procedures appear in the Choose SQL Table dialog box and are used in a report just like regular database tables. The only difference is that the stored procedure may have parameters associated with it. However, you do have a choice of whether or not stored procedures will appear in the Choose SQL Table dialog box. Select File | Options from the pull-down menus, and click the SQL tab on the Options dialog box, shown in Figure 14-9.

The Allow Reporting On section of the dialog box includes the Stored Procedures check box. Only if this box is checked, will you see any stored procedures in the Choose SQL Table dialog box. (You can also check Prompt on Every Table in the lower right of the SQL tab and check Stored Procedures every time you open a new SQL or ODBC database.)

Now, when you open a SQL database, you'll see stored procedures appear in the Choose SQL Table dialog box, along with regular database tables. For Microsoft SQL Server, and most other databases, stored procedure names will be enclosed in parentheses following the word *Proc*.

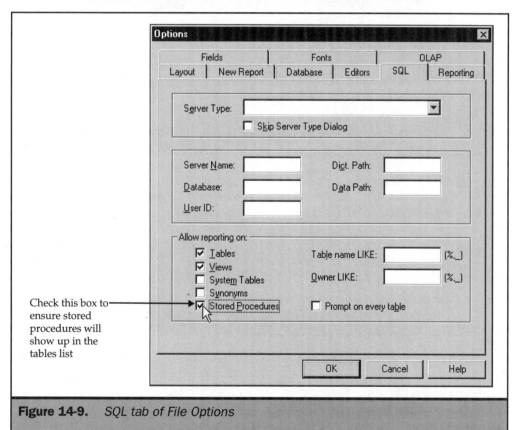

Check this box to ensure stored procedures will show up in the tables list

Figure 14-9. SQL tab of File Options

Your report can be based on a stored procedure or a combination of one or more database tables, but not both. You cannot link a stored procedure in the Visual Linking Expert, *so you will be unable to fully use a stored procedure in the same way you use a table. If the stored procedure does not include all the data you need, ask your database administrator to add additional fields to the stored procedure, or use a linked subreport (described in Chapter 11) to retrieve the necessary data.*

Working with Stored Procedure Parameters

Once you choose a stored procedure to report on, you'll be prompted to supply any values for any stored procedure parameters in the Enter Parameter Values dialog box. This tabbed dialog box is identical to the one that prompts for report parameter fields, discussed in Chapter 12.

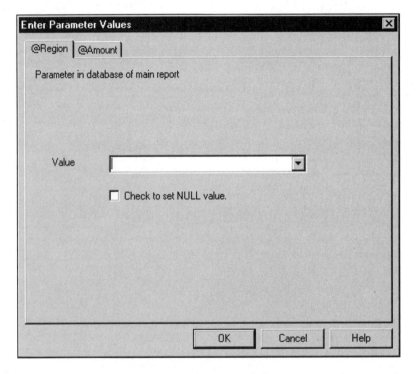

Type in your desired parameter values, and click OK. You can then simply continue your report design process normally. The stored procedure will supply a list of fields you can use in your report, just like a normal database table.

Stored procedure parameters behave almost identically to Crystal Reports parameter fields. The stored procedure parameters will appear on the Parameter tab of the Insert Fields dialog box.

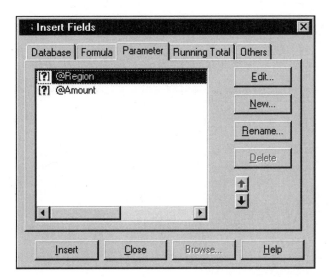

You can edit a stored procedure parameter by selecting it and clicking the Edit button. Although you can't change the value type or select Multiple or Range values, you can supply a pick list of default values, set length limits or an edit mask for string parameters, or range limits for number or date parameters. See Chapter 12 for more information on these options.

When you refresh the report, you'll receive the same prompt as when using parameter fields.

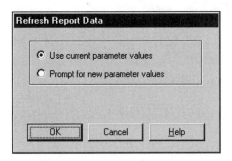

You can choose whether to use the existing values for the stored procedure parameters, or to prompt for new values. When you prompt for new values, the server will run the stored procedure with the new values and return a new result set to Crystal Reports.

Using SQL Expression Fields

New with Crystal Reports 7 is the ability to create SQL expression fields right from the Insert Fields dialog box. A *SQL expression* is like a formula, except that it's made up entirely of database fields and SQL functions that are supported by the language of the particular SQL server that you're working with. Sometimes there are advantages to using a SQL expression instead of a Crystal Reports Formula. The expression is evaluated on the server, not by the client, which often improves performance.

A particular advantage involves calculations or other specialized functions that are used in record selection. If you use a Crystal Reports formula in record selection, the database server won't be able to perform the selection, as it doesn't understand the Crystal Reports formula language. However, by creating a SQL expression and using that in record selection, the SQL server will fully understand the expression and the record selection will be performed by the database server.

Creating SQL Expressions

The first prerequisite for using SQL expressions is that you be using a SQL or ODBC database. If you're using a PC-style database, SQL expressions don't apply and you won't even see the SQL Expression tab on the Insert Fields dialog box. When you are using a SQL database, the Insert Fields dialog box will include an additional tab labeled SQL Expression. You may display the Insert Fields dialog box with this tab already selected by choosing Insert | SQL Expression Field from the pull-down menus.

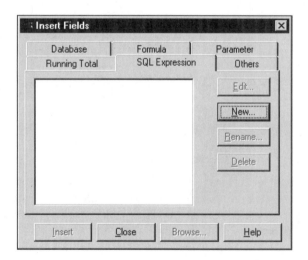

 You can't use SQL expression fields with stored procedures. If your report is based on a stored procedure, the SQL Expression tab won't even appear in the Insert Fields dialog box.

Creating a SQL expression is very similar to creating a Crystal Reports formula (discussed in detail in Chapter 5). You will be first asked to give the SQL expression a name. As with formula names, you should make the SQL expression name reasonably short and easy to understand. You may include spaces as well as upper- and lowercase letters in the name. The name you give the SQL expression will also be the column heading if you place the SQL expression in the report's Details section.

Once you've given the SQL expression a name and clicked OK, the SQL Expression Editor will appear, as shown in Figure 14-10.

Note the similarities between the SQL Expression Editor and the other Crystal Reports formula editors. Creating SQL expressions is essentially the same as creating other formulas: you can type the expression directly into the Formula text box, or double-click in the top three boxes to help build the expression. Notice that like

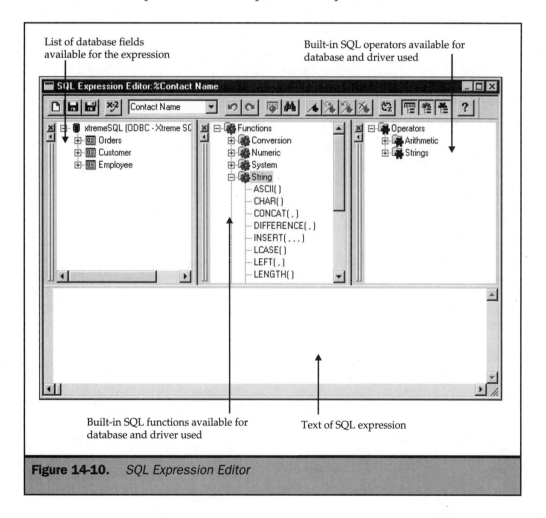

Figure 14-10.   *SQL Expression Editor*

formulas, parameter fields, and running total fields, Crystal Reports appends a special character to the beginning of the SQL expression's name. The percent symbol (%) is used to denote SQL expression fields.

The functions and operators available in the SQL Expression Editor will change, depending on the database and database driver in use. If you look at the Function Tree box in Figure 14-10, you'll notice a certain set of available SQL functions. This example is for a report using Microsoft SQL Server via ODBC. If you use the direct database driver to connect to the same database, however, the SQL Expression Editor will show a completely different set of SQL functions.

For this reason, you will probably have to edit or modify some SQL expressions if you change your report from one database to another using Set Location or Convert Database Driver, both available from the Database pull-down menu. To get detailed descriptions of the different built-in SQL functions for your particular database or driver, consult documentation for that database or driver.

For example, you may want a report viewer to be able to specify a full or partial contact name to search for with just one parameter field. If a customer exists whose contact matches what's entered, the customer will be included on the report. In the Customer table of the XTREME sample database that's included with Crystal Reports, the contact information is actually split into separate first and last name database fields. Without using a SQL expression, you have two choices for setting up this search.

- Create two parameter fields—one for first name and one for last name—and try to compare those to database fields.

- Create a Crystal Reports formula that combines the contact's first and last names, and compare the formula to the parameter field.

There are problems with both approaches. If you choose the first option, it's much harder for the viewer to just type in a full or partial contact name, like "Chris" (to find both Christopher and Christine, for example). This is because there will have to be some additional logic to ignore the last name parameter field if the viewer just wants to search for full or partial first names. Or, if the viewer wants to see everyone whose last name is "Jones," regardless of first name, then similar logic will have to apply for the first name parameter field. It would be much simpler for the viewer to be able to type in Chris* or *Jones to search for their desired customers.

If you choose the second option, the full or partial searches mentioned in the previous paragraph will work. But because the first and last names are combined in a formula, the record selection will not take place on the database server (remember that most Crystal formulas can't be converted to SQL, so the client will perform record selection).

By using a SQL expression, you can have the best of both worlds. The first and last names can be concatenated into one object and compared to the parameter field. But because the concatenation takes place on the database server, it will still perform the record selection, sending only the resulting customers back to the client, not all customers.

The SQL expression to accomplish this is surprisingly similar to a Crystal Reports formula:

```
Customer.Contact_First_Name + ' ' + Customer.Contact_Last_Name
```

Notice a couple of differences, however.

- There are no French or "curly" braces around the field names.
- The literal string that separates the first and last name fields must use apostrophes—quotation marks won't work.

Once this SQL expression has been created, it can be dropped onto the report just like a database field, formula field, or other object. It can also be used inside regular report formulas or in conditional formatting formulas. Notice the change to the SQL query (viewed with Database | Show SQL Query) after placing this SQL expression in the Details section:

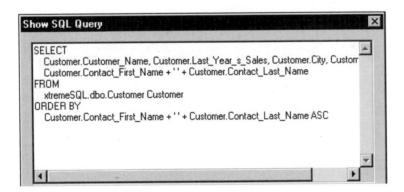

Even though the SQL expression field was given a name in the report, Crystal Reports just adds the SQL expression formula itself right into the SQL statement. The name is simply used by Crystal Reports in the Select Expert or elsewhere on the report.

To now use this SQL expression in record selection, you will use the Select Expert's Like operator to allow a wildcard search on the combined contact first and last name. If you have already created a string parameter field called {?Contact Prompt}, the Select Expert will look like this:

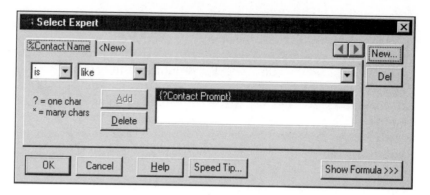

When you refresh the report and are prompted for the Contact Prompt parameter field, entering the Chris* wildcard will return the following records:

Customer Name	Contact Name	Last Year s Sales	City	Region
City Cyclists	Chris Christianson	$19,426.76	Sterling Heights	MI
Pathfinders	Christine Manley	$42,601.14	Allenspark	CO
The Bike Cellar	Christopher Carmine	$30,938.67	Winchester	VI

Now, look at the SQL query being sent to the database server:

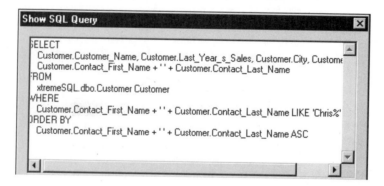

Notice that the WHERE clause includes the SQL expression formula text and a SQL comparison operator that allows wildcard searches. The end result: the flexibility of Crystal Reports formulas with the speed of server-based record selection.

Grouping on the Database Server

Another powerful feature of SQL database servers is server-side processing or server-based grouping. *Server-based grouping* refers to the ability of the SQL server to perform aggregate calculations on groups of records, only returning subtotals, summaries, and other aggregates to the client. If you are creating a summary report (very often the case), this server capability can significantly decrease the amount of data being passed over the network. Also, the summary calculations can be performed on the server rather than on the client.

Consider the following simple Sales by Region report:

Customer Name	Last Year s Sales	City
AL		
Psycho-Cycle	$66,791.39	Huntsville
The Great Bike Shop	$27,765.71	Huntsville
Benny - The Spokes Person	$9,609.07	Huntsville
3 customers	Subtotal: $104,166.17	
AZ		
Trail Blazer's Place	$23,188.57	Aguila
1 customers	Subtotal: $23,188.57	

This report simply shows all USA customers, grouped by region, with a customer count and sales subtotal for each group. Because the Details section is shown, the database server will need to send all customers in the USA to Crystal Reports. The client is actually calculating the subtotal and count for each group as the report processes. This is confirmed by looking at the SQL query for this report:

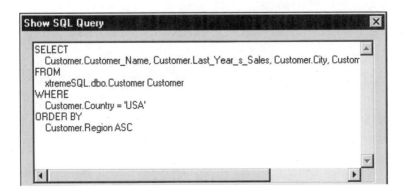

```
Show SQL Query                                          [X]

SELECT
    Customer.Customer_Name, Customer.Last_Year_s_Sales, Customer.City, Custom
FROM
    xtremeSQL.dbo.Customer Customer
WHERE
    Customer.Country = 'USA'
ORDER BY
    Customer.Region ASC
```

Notice that this fairly simple SQL statement just selects database fields and limits records to the USA. The only server feature used here that helps with grouping is the

ORDER BY clause, which presorts the result set into Region order before sending it to the client.

To create a summary report, simply hide the Details section by right-clicking in the gray section area in the left of the Design tab, and choose Hide (Drill-Down OK) from the pop-up menu. The report will now show just the summary data, with no individual customers appearing on the report.

AL

| | 3 customers | Subtotal: | $104,166.17 |

AZ

| | 1 customers | Subtotal: | $23,188.57 |

However, if you look at the SQL query, even after refreshing the report, you'll notice that it hasn't changed, since server-based grouping is turned off by default. The server is still sending all customers in the USA to Crystal Reports, and Crystal Reports still has to cycle through the individual customer records to calculate the customer count and sales subtotals.

Enabling Server-Based Grouping

There are several different ways to turn on server-based grouping:

■ To turn it on for the current report only, choose Database | Perform Grouping on Server from the pull-down menus. You can also choose File | Report Options from the pull-down menus and check Perform Grouping on Server.

■ To turn it on for all new reports you create from this point forward, choose File | Options from the pull-down menus and check Perform Grouping on Server on the Database tab.

Once this option is enabled, the report should look the same. There will be some significant changes to the SQL query, however.

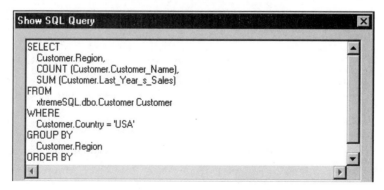

```
SELECT
    Customer.Region,
    COUNT (Customer.Customer_Name),
    SUM (Customer.Last_Year_s_Sales)
FROM
    xtremeSQL.dbo.Customer Customer
WHERE
    Customer.Country = 'USA'
GROUP BY
    Customer.Region
ORDER BY
```

You will see that the SELECT clause now only includes the group field (in this case, Region) and two *aggregate functions* that perform the sum and count functions right on the database server before data is sent to the client. You will also see a new GROUP BY clause that you have not seen before. This new SQL function tells the server to group database records and perform the summary calculations all on the server. Only the summary totals will be sent to the client.

What's Required to Use Server-Based Grouping

Your report must meet certain criteria and be designed in a certain way to use server-based grouping. When you think about the way the server groups and summarizes records, you'll begin to realize why your report must meet these requirements.

Requirement	Reasoning
There must be at least one group on the report.	For the GROUP BY clause to be added to the SQL query, there needs to be at least one group defined on the report.
The Details section must be hidden.	If the Details section is visible, no grouping will occur on the server, as the server must send down individual database records to show in the Details section.
Only include the group field or summary fields in group headers and footers.	If you include any other database fields (or formula fields that contain anything other than group fields or summary fields), the server will have to send detail data to the client to properly display the report.
Don't group on Crystal Reports formulas.	Because most Crystal Reports formulas can't be converted to SQL, they must be calculated on the client before the report can group on them. Because of this, the server will have to send detail records to the client. This is another reason you may want to use SQL expressions as an alternative to formulas, as SQL expressions can still be grouped on by the server.
Running totals must be based on summary fields.	If running totals (described in Chapter 5) are based on detail fields, Crystal Reports will need the detail data to calculate them as the report processes. This will prevent grouping from being done on the server.

Requirement	Reasoning
The report cannot contain Average or Distinct Count summaries or Top N values.	There are no SQL equivalents for these Crystal Reports summary capabilities. Therefore, the grouping will be performed by the client if these functions are used.
Report groups can only be sorted in ascending or descending order. Specified-order grouping won't work.	Since Crystal Reports bases specified-order grouping on its own internal logic, it needs detail records to properly evaluate what specified groups to place them in. This requires detail records to be sent by the server.
If grouping on date fields, you must choose "for each day." If grouping on time fields, you must choose "for each second."	There is no equivalent grouping logic available in SQL. The GROUP BY clause simply allows a database field or SQL expression to be applied to it.

Effects of Drill-Down

When Crystal Reports is performing its own grouping, the concept of report drill-down is fairly straightforward. Even though the Details section (or lower-level group headers and footers) aren't being shown, Crystal Reports is still processing them and storing the data they create. When a viewer double-clicks to drill down on a group, Crystal Reports simply opens a new drill-down tab and displays the data it had previously not displayed.

However, when you enable server-side grouping, there is no detail data to display when a viewer drills down—only the summary data has been sent to the client! Crystal Reports 7 still enables drill-down; however, it just sends another query to the SQL server whenever a viewer drills down. This second query requests just the detail data for the group that was drilled into by adding additional criteria to the WHERE clause. This method provides the benefits of server-based grouping, while still allowing the powerful interactivity of drill-down. The price a viewer pays is the additional time the SQL server may take to process the drill-down query.

Look at the example shown in Figure 14-11. Notice that a viewer has drilled down on a particular region. A new drill-down tab appears, showing detail data for that region. Notice the new SQL query that was created on the fly.

You can view drill-down SQL queries by choosing Database | Show SQL Query when viewing the drill-down tab. If you return to the main Preview tab and show the query, you'll once again notice the GROUP BY clause.

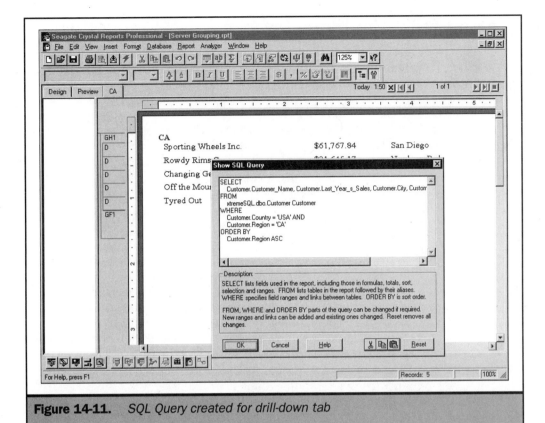

Figure 14-11.   *SQL Query created for drill-down tab*

Performance Considerations

SQL databases (or PC-style databases accessed via ODBC) present a very different set of performance considerations than PC-style databases. As has been discussed throughout the chapter, one of the main benefits of SQL databases over PC databases is the ability of the database server to perform record selection and grouping locally as soon as a SQL query is received from Crystal Reports. Only when the database server has performed record selection or grouping itself will it return the result set back to Crystal Reports.

Let the Server Do the Work

As a general reporting rule, you want to always have the database server perform as much of this processing as possible. Database server software is designed and tuned to perform just such operations, and server software is often placed on very high-end hardware platforms to enhance this performance even further. Any glitch that might cause the database server to send back every record in its database (million-plus record SQL databases are not at all uncommon) to be selected or summarized by Crystal Reports will often result in unsatisfactory performance.

To see how much (or if any) of the query is being evaluated on the database server, view the query by choosing Database | Show SQL Query from the pull-down menus. Look at the SQL statement for the WHERE clause. If you don't see one, then no selection at all will be done on the server—every record in the database will come down to the PC to be left to Crystal Reports to sort through. This can be *very* time consuming!

Look for an ORDER BY clause if you are sorting or grouping your report. If you see this clause, then the database server will presort your data before sending it to Crystal Reports. This can speed the formatting of your report. If you don't see an ORDER BY clause, but you specified grouping or sorting in your report, the server will send records to Crystal Reports unsorted, and the client will have to sort the records.

If you wish to use server-based grouping, make sure you see a GROUP BY clause in the query. This ensures that the server is grouping and aggregating data before sending it to Crystal Reports. If you don't see this clause, check back to the server-based grouping requirements earlier in this chapter.

To ensure record selection occurs on the server, Crystal Reports must convert your record-selection formula to a SQL WHERE clause. Several rules of thumb help ensure that as much record selection as possible is converted to SQL and is done on the server:

- Don't base record selection on formula fields. Crystal Reports usually can't convert formulas to SQL, so most record selection on formula fields will be passed on to Crystal Reports.

- Don't use Crystal Reports Formula language's built-in functions, such as ToText, in your selection criteria. Again, Crystal Reports usually can't convert these to SQL, so these parts of record selection won't be carried out on the server.

- Avoid using string subscript functions in record selection. For example, {Customer.Contact First Name}[1 to 5] = "Chris" cannot be converted to SQL, so record selection will be left to Crystal Reports. Create a SQL expression instead, perhaps using a SQL LEFT statement, such as LEFT(Customer.Contact_First_Name,5). Then use it in record selection.

Make Use of Indexed Fields

You may be lulled into a false sense of performance security because SQL databases don't have the indexed field linking requirement (remember, PC-style databases only allow you to link to an indexed field). Since you can't even see what fields are indexed in the Visual Linking Expert when using a SQL database, you may think that it really doesn't matter what fields you link to or select on.

Depending on the database system that you're using, linking to non-indexed fields or performing record selection on non-indexed fields can prove disastrous to the performance of your report. Most SQL database systems have indexing capabilities that the database designer probably considers when designing the database.

If at all possible, work with the database designer to ensure that indexes are created not only to solve your database application needs, but your reporting needs as well. Since you won't be able to tell what indexes exist, ask the database designer or administrator what database fields are indexed. Then, try to use those fields as much as possible as "to" fields in linking, and for record selection.

Also, it may improve performance to select records based on as many fields as possible from the main or driving table. For example, you may have a main transaction table that is linked to five lookup tables, and you want to use the descriptions from the lookup tables in record selection. Instead, consider using the fields in the *main* table for record selection (even if you have to use the codes in the main table, and not the descriptions from the lookup table). Again, if these fields in the main table are indexed, you'll probably see a performance improvement.

 Crystal Reports behaves oddly when tables are linked using date or date/time fields. Make sure the Use Indexes/Server for Speed option is turned off in File | Report Options if you are linking tables on date or date/time fields. Otherwise performance will suffer. In all other situations, this option should typically remain turned on for performance purposes.

Chapter 15

Accommodating Database Changes and Field Mapping

There are many situations where the database you initially developed a report against will change. Perhaps the database is in a state of flux and will be changing dynamically as your report design proceeds. Or, you may develop a report against a test database and then change the report to point to a production database later. For true flexibility you need to be able to accommodate these changes easily, so that you don't have to recreate any features or functions of your report just because the database has changed.

As part of these database changes, fields may be renamed by the database designer or administrator. When Crystal Reports detects these changes, it gives you the opportunity to change the field references inside your report, so the new field names can be automatically associated with the previous field names. This field mapping prevents you from having to add fields to the report again or modify formulas that refer to changed fields.

There are several ways to accommodate changes that have been made to the database:

- Verifying a database
- Changing database drivers
- Setting a location

These are all explained in this chapter.

Verifying or Changing the Database Location

If the database layout changes, if the database is moved to a new location, or if you want to point your report to a different database than it was originally designed with, you'll need to use Crystal Reports functions to recognize these changes.

Verifying a Database

If the database your report is based on changes (perhaps the database designer adds new fields, deletes old fields, or gives existing fields new names or data types), your report won't automatically recognize these changes when the report is opened. Even if you refresh the report, Crystal Reports won't detect the changes. In order to detect changes to the database the report is based on, you must verify the database.

Choose Database | Verify Database from the pull-down menus. If the database has not changed, you'll see a dialog box so indicating:

However, if the database has changed, you'll receive a message like this:

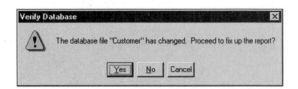

If you click Yes at this prompt, Crystal Reports will read the database structure and make any changes to table names, field names, and data types. When you display the Insert Fields dialog box, you'll notice the changes. And, if you have previously linked tables together and table structures have changed significantly, you may need to re-link tables in the Visual Linking Expert. If field names have changed, you will see the Map Fields dialog box (discussed later in the chapter).

Verify on Every Print

If the database changes and you don't verify the database thereafter, your report may show incorrect data if fields have been moved or renamed, or it may display an error message if tables have been removed or renamed. Be very careful when working with a database that may be changing. You'll want to verify the database often to catch any changes.

One way to accomplish this is to select Database | Verify on Every Print from the pull-down menus. When you check this menu option, Crystal Reports will verify the database every time a report is refreshed. The on/off state of Verify on Every Print will be saved with the report—if it was turned on when a particular report was saved, it will be turned on when that report is opened.

Changing the Database Driver

There will be times when you may not want to change the name of the database your report is based on, but the *type* of database. A fairly common situation occurs when a report is initially developed on a PC-style database, and is later upsized to some form of client/server or SQL Server database. In this situation, you must change the database driver the report is based on. A database driver is an underlying dynamic-link library (a special Windows data file with a .DLL extension) that Crystal Reports uses to communicate with the different layers of database communication on your PC. A unique driver exists for every type of database that Crystal Reports recognizes.

For example, if you've created a report based on a Microsoft Access test database using the Data File button, you are using the PDBDAO.DLL database driver to communicate with the Access database directly. If this Access database is upsized to a production Microsoft SQL Server, you'll need to change the report to use the

PDSSQL.DLL database driver (if you want to use a direct driver to get to SQL Server; see Chapter 14 for more information about direct database drivers). If you want to get to SQL Server (or any other ODBC-compliant database for that matter) using ODBC, you'll need to change the report to use the PDSODBC.DLL database driver.

Choose Database | Convert Database Driver from the pull-down menus. This will display the Convert Database Driver dialog box.

Once you check the Convert Database Driver on Next Refresh check box, you'll see the From name of the driver that your report is currently based on, followed by a To drop-down list showing all the available drivers that you can convert your report to. Choose the new driver you want to use, based on the type of database you want to convert to. When you click OK, you will be prompted to log on to a new database or choose a new ODBC data source (depending on the driver you are converting to).

As soon as you log on to the new database, your report will be connected to the new database and the database will be verified (as discussed previously in this chapter). When you display the Insert Fields dialog box, you'll notice the changes. If you have previously linked tables together and the table structures have changed significantly, you may need to re-link tables in the Visual Linking Expert. If field names have changed, you will see the Map Fields dialog box (discussed later in this chapter).

Using Set Location

There will be other situations in which the database your report is based on is physically moved to a new location on the network. Or, you may be developing a report against a test database using ODBC and then need to move the report to a production ODBC database. In these situations, the database type won't change (therefore you won't need to change to a different database driver), but you will need a method to point the report to the new database location. The Set Location option will accomplish this.

Choose Database | Set Location from the pull-down menus. The Set Location dialog box will appear.

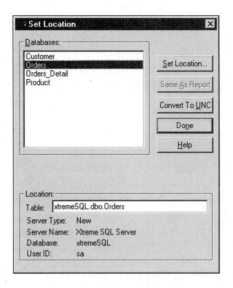

You'll see a list of all the tables in your report. Select the table that you wish to set the new location for. Then, click the Set Location button. If the table is from a PC-style database, a File Open dialog box will appear in which you can choose a different filename or path name for the database. If the table is from an ODBC or SQL database, the Choose SQL Table dialog box will appear so you can choose another table from a different server. If you need to log on to another database server, click the Log On Server button. Once you've logged on to the new server, you can choose the new table in the dialog box.

Once you've specified the new database location, you may be asked if you wish to propagate those changes to other tables with the same original information.

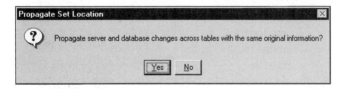

If you click Yes, any other tables in the report that originally were pointed to the same database as the one you just changed will be pointed to the new location automatically. If you click No, all other tables will point to their original locations.

Once you change the location of the database, Crystal Reports will verify the database. When you display the Insert Fields dialog box, you'll notice the changes. If you had previously linked tables together and table structures have changed significantly, you may need to re-link tables in the Visual Linking Expert. If field names have changed, you will see the Map Fields dialog box (discussed later in the chapter).

Same as Report Option

The Same as Report button on the Set Location dialog box only applies to reports based on PC-style databases. Same as Report will remove any drive letter and path name from the database location. From that point forward, Crystal Reports will look for the database on the same disk drive and in the same folder as the report.

This allows you to create and save a report for distribution to other report viewers. The other viewers can place the report on any drive and in any folder that they choose. As long as the database the report is based on is in the same folder as the report, the report will be able to find it.

Converting to a UNC Name

The Convert to UNC button on the Set Location dialog box only applies to reports based on PC-style databases. Convert to UNC will change the hard-coded drive letter and path name for the database to a Uniform Naming Convention (UNC) name that can easily be found by any computer on the network, regardless of its drive mapping. The Uniform Naming Convention is a way of pointing to a file on a network disk drive without using a drive letter. Consider the following scenario:

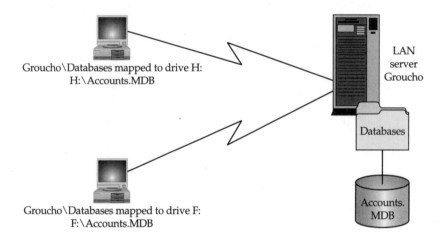

Groucho\Databases mapped to drive H:
H:\Accounts.MDB

Groucho\Databases mapped to drive F:
F:\Accounts.MDB

LAN server Groucho

Databases

Accounts. MDB

The two PCs are connected to the same LAN server, but are using different drive letters to reach the server. If the first PC creates a report based on Accounts.MDB, the report will have the drive letter and filename H:\Accounts.MDB hard-coded into it. When the second PC opens the report the report will fail—the database won't be found on drive H.

To avoid this kind of problem, you can use a UNC name to replace the drive letter. A UNC name appears in the following format:

\\<Server Name>\<Share Name>\<Path and Filename>

- The *Server Name* is the actual name of the computer or server where the file is located (in this case, Groucho). The server name is preceded by two backslash characters.

- The *Share Name* is a name that the LAN Administrator has given to a particular group of shared files and folders on the server. When a PC maps a drive letter to a LAN server, the drive letter is mapped to a particular share name (in this case, Databases). A single backslash character separates the *Server Name* from the *Share Name*.

- The *Path and Filename* are similar to path names and filenames used on a local PC hard drive, except they are located on the LAN server. In this case, the Accounts.MDB file is in the root of the Databases share name. A single backslash character separates the *Share Name* from the *Path and Filename* (and this path may contain additional backslash characters).

Based on these rules, the corresponding UNC name for the Accounts.MDB file will be:

\\Groucho\Databases\Accounts.MDB

Notice that the drive letter has been removed. Now, any PC on the network can find the file based on the UNC name—the PC doesn't have to have a drive letter mapped to the LAN server.

Using Set Alias

When you first create a new report based on certain database tables, you'll notice that the actual name of the table you originally chose shows up in the Insert Fields dialog box, the Visual Linking Expert, and other places in the report. Although it may appear that Crystal Reports must refer to a database table by its physical name, you have the flexibility to change the name Crystal Reports uses to refer to this table.

Crystal Reports can use an *alias* to refer to a table with a different name of your choice, regardless of what the physical file or table name for the table is. By default, Crystal Reports just assigns the physical name as the alias when the report is first created. To change the alias, choose Database | Set Alias from the pull-down menus. The Set Alias dialog box will appear.

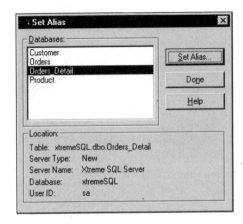

What To Do if Table Names Change

If a database designer or administrator changes the name of a table in the database, you will receive an error indicating that the table can't be found the next time you try to refresh your report. Unfortunately, refreshing the database or verifying the database will not solve this problem—the message will persist and the report will not print properly.

In order to solve this problem, perform the following simple steps:

1. Use the Set Location command. When the Set Location dialog box appears, choose the table whose name has changed. Then, just type the new table name directly in the text box at the bottom of the dialog box. (Make sure to leave the exclamation point that separates the table name from the database name if this is a PC-style database.) This will point the report to the new table name in the database.

2. If you want the new name to appear throughout the report, use the Set Alias command to change the alias of the old table to the new table name. Using Set Location will correctly point the report to the new table name, but won't change the name in the report—it will still be referred to by the old name. Set Alias will change the name of the table as well, avoiding confusion as to which physical table is actually being used.

Here you'll see a list of all the tables in your report. Select the table that you want to change the alias for, and click the Set Alias button. You'll be prompted to set a new alias for the table. Choose an alias name that's not already in use by another table (you'll be warned if you select an existing alias name) and click OK. Set aliases for as many tables as you'd like, and then click Done to close the Set Alias dialog box. You'll now see the new name applied to the table in all dialog boxes, formulas, and the Visual Linking Expert.

> **Tip** *There may be times when you need to add the same physical table to a report more than once. Perhaps you're using a lookup table with more than one primary table, or you need to use a self-join, in which a table needs to be added twice and joined to itself for a particular report. You may also need to add two tables with the same name from different databases. When this occurs, you'll be prompted to set the alias for the second occurrence of the table. Just give it a new alias name. You'll then see the two tables with different names throughout the report.*

Mapping Old Fields to New Names

Database changes can cause a mismatch of field names in your report. For example, your original report may be developed against a Microsoft Access database that includes a field named "Account Number" (note that the space between the words is significant to Crystal Reports). You may need to eventually have the same report work with a SQL Server database where the field is known as "Account_Number" (notice that the space has been replaced with an underscore).

Whenever Crystal Reports detects these kinds of database changes, it can't be sure what new database field the old report object should be associated with. By using Field Mapping, you can point the old object to the new database field. Field mapping simply allows you to change the field name that a report refers to, so that, for example, all objects that used to be associated with "Account Number" will now be associated with "Account_Number." No formulas have to be changed, no old objects have to be removed, and no new objects need to be added.

The Field Mapping function cannot be chosen from a menu. It is triggered when Crystal Reports detects any field name changes in the source database. Crystal Reports will check for these changes whenever you verify the database, change the database driver, or use the Set Location command. When Crystal Reports detects that fields in the report are no longer in the database, it displays the Map Fields dialog box, as shown in Figure 15-1.

The Map Fields dialog box is divided into four boxes or lists. The upper-left Unmapped Fields list shows report fields that don't match up to any field names in the new database. The upper-right list shows a choice of fields in the new database that you can map the report fields to. To map the report field to the new database field, select the report field you want to map in the upper-left box, then a matching database

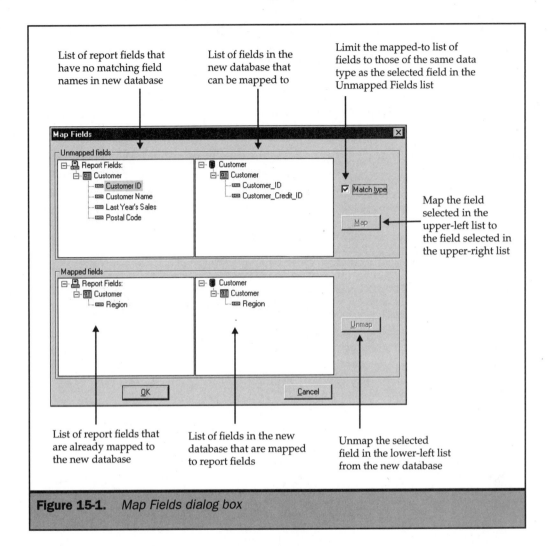

List of report fields that have no matching field names in new database

List of fields in the new database that can be mapped to

Limit the mapped-to list of fields to those of the same data type as the selected field in the Unmapped Fields list

Map the field selected in the upper-left list to the field selected in the upper-right list

List of report fields that are already mapped to the new database

List of fields in the new database that are mapped to report fields

Unmap the selected field in the lower-left list from the new database

Figure 15-1.   *Map Fields dialog box*

field in the upper-right box, and then click the Map button. The fields will be moved from the upper boxes to the lower boxes.

The list of database fields will change based on whether or not you click the Match Type check box on the right side of the dialog box. If the box is checked, only fields of the same data type (string, number, date, etc.) as that of the selected report field will show up. This helps to ensure that you're making the correct match of fields, by not inadvertently mapping a string field on the report to a number or date field in the new database (although you may want to do this sometimes). There may be times that you won't see the field you want to map to in the right list, however, because of data type mismatches. For example, if you're remapping fields originally from a Microsoft Access database to a SQL Server database, you may not find any SQL Server field that matches a currency field in the Access database. In this situation, uncheck Match Type and look for the field to map to.

When the Map Fields dialog box first appears, you will probably see some fields already showing up in the lower two Mapped Fields boxes. The lower-left list shows report fields that already have a matching field in the new database. And, once you've mapped fields from the upper lists, they will be moved to the lower lists, as well. If existing mapping was assumed by Crystal Reports (because of identical filenames), or you mistakenly mapped fields that don't belong together, you can select a field in the lower-left or lower-right list. The mapped field will appear highlighted in the other box. You can then click the Unmap button to unmap the fields and move them back to the top lists.

Once you have finished mapping fields, click the OK button to close the Map Fields dialog box. Crystal Reports will now associate the mapped fields with the new database. The Design tab, as well as any formulas, will reflect the new field names. If additional tables have mismatched fields, you'll be presented with the Map Fields dialog box for each subsequent table.

 Any fields that no longer exist in the source database must be remapped to new fields. If you don't map old field names to new fields, the old fields and objects they're based on will be deleted from your report!

Chapter 16

Importing Legacy Reports with the Document Import Tool

More and more companies are converting mainframe and minicomputer applications to Windows client/server platforms. This creates more and more demand to convert older "green bar" or *legacy* reports to new Windows-based reporting tools, such as Crystal Reports. In many cases, this involves completely redesigning reports from top to bottom. In versions of Crystal Reports prior to Version 7, this was the only option. Crystal Reports 7 introduces the Document Import Tool, which automatically converts text file representations of older reports to Crystal Reports without all the top-to-bottom design hassles.

By using the Document Import Tool, you can define the parts of the legacy report that make up report sections and objects and store the definitions in a *conversion interface file*, with a .CIF extension. Then, when you actually convert the report, the Document Import Tool will read the legacy report data into an intermediate database file in Microsoft Access format, and automatically design a Crystal Report based on the Access database.

Legacy File Requirements

Although legacy reports are typically printed on line printers, it's pretty tough to have Crystal Reports "read" a pile of green-bar paper. Therefore, you must be able to provide the Document Import Tool with a disk file representation of the legacy report. This is typically fairly easy, based on the system originally producing the report. Most mainframe or minicomputer systems store report output in a print "spool" on disk. With appropriate connectivity software, these report images can be downloaded to a PC disk drive. There are two main requirements for using a downloaded legacy report file with the Document Import Tool: file format and report organization.

The input file format required for the Document Import Tool is straight ASCII text. ASCII, an acronym for American Standard Code for Information Interchange, is a standard method used to represent letters and numbers in a series of 7-bit binary codes. Typically *ASCII text format* refers to data files that contain straight text—just letters and numbers. These files shouldn't contain any ASCII value above 128 (no special extended characters). Each line of text in the file should end with standard Carriage Return/Line Feed characters (ASCII 13/ASCII 10). If you can open a file with Windows Notepad or use the DOS TYPE command in a Windows command prompt and read the file without seeing any "smileys" or other extended characters, it meets the first Document Import Tool requirement.

The second requirement is how the report data is actually organized. In general, it must be organized like a report you would create from scratch in Crystal Reports. You must be able to identify the standard sections of the report, like the Report Header, Page Header, Group Headers and Footers, and Details. These sections must appear in a consistent manner throughout the report. Sections that appear sometimes and don't appear at other times may confuse the Document Import Tool.

Likewise, fields should be consistently placed. Individual fields in the report must be in *fixed locations*. In every detail record, the fields must appear in the same horizontal position. For example, a legacy report that shows a Part Number field starting in position one for one record type and in position five for another record type can't be imported—the Document Import Tool can't deal with multiple record types such as this.

Any nontabular report organizations, such as row/column layouts and cross-tabs, can't be imported by the Document Import Tool. Only reports that contain repetitive fixed lines of data are candidates for import.

Converting a legacy report to a Crystal Report involves several steps that must be performed in the following order:

1. Specify the legacy file to be converted.
2. Define the legacy report sections.
3. Define legacy report fields, text objects, and special fields.
4. Set the confidence level.
5. Convert the report.

These steps are explained in the rest of this chapter.

Layout of the Document Import Tool

To start the Document Import Tool, you must create a new report. When the Report Gallery appears, click the Document Import Tool button.

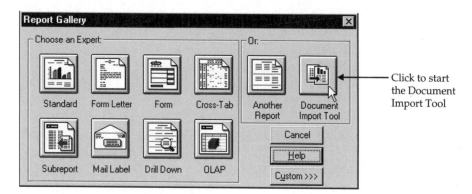

Click to start the Document Import Tool

The Document Import Tool appears, as shown in Figure 16-1.

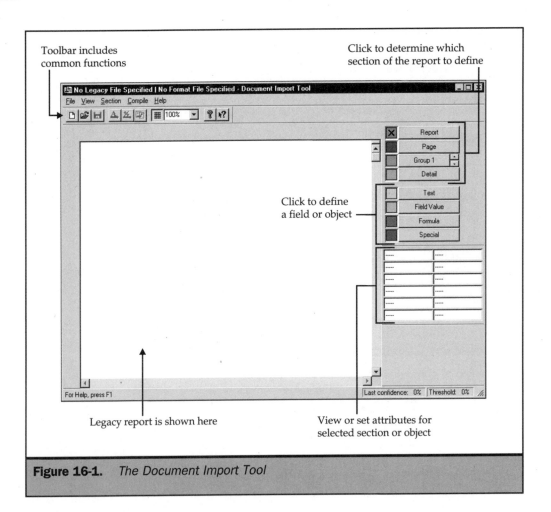

Toolbar includes common functions

Click to determine which section of the report to define

Click to define a field or object

Legacy report is shown here

View or set attributes for selected section or object

Figure 16-1. *The Document Import Tool*

Note   *The different colors and shades used in the Document Import Tool may be hard to discern in this black and white book. The colors are very distinct when actually using the tool, however.*

The first step in converting a legacy report to a Crystal Report is to choose the legacy report to convert. Click the New toolbar button or select File | New from the pull-down menus. You'll be prompted to specify the legacy file you wish to convert. Type in the path and filename directly, or use the Browse button to locate the ASCII file to convert. Once you've chosen the file, it will appear in the Document Import Tool window.

Because using the Document Import Tool requires selecting the *first* report and group header and the *last* report and group footer, it's often helpful to be able to split the legacy report view window so you can scroll through the top and bottom of the report separately. By choosing View | Split from the pull-down menus or clicking and dragging the small bar above the vertical scroll bar, you'll be able to split the legacy report window into top and bottom portions, each with its own scroll bars. You can then scroll the top half of the window to the first report and group headers of the legacy report, and the bottom half of the window to the last group and report footers.

Many legacy reports printed on green-bar paper can be up to 132 or more characters wide, requiring a lot of tedious scrolling back and forth to see all of the report. This problem can be solved by choosing a different zoom level for the legacy report window. Choose View | Zoom Level from the pull-down menus, choose a predefined zoom level

100% ▼   from the drop-down zoom control on the toolbar, or type a zoom percentage directly into the zoom-level control on the toolbar and press TAB or ENTER to set the new zoom level.

It also may sometimes be difficult to choose a width for a legacy report object. It may be helpful to see a small dashed line extend all the way down or across the legacy report to help delineate individual legacy records and fields. This can be accomplished by using *guidelines*, small dotted lines similar to those used in the Crystal Report designer. To toggle this option on or off, click the Guidelines button in the toolbar, or choose View | Guidelines from the pull-down menus.

Adding a guideline is as simple as clicking in the horizontal or vertical ruler of the Document Import Tool. A small guideline handle (looking like an upside-down tent) will appear in the ruler, indicating the placement of the guideline. You can move the guideline by dragging the guideline handle to another location in the ruler, or remove the guideline by dragging the guideline handle off the ruler.

Unlike in Crystal Reports, nothing is attached to the guidelines, and moving them won't change any aspects of the legacy report window. Guidelines are simply useful in the Document Import Tool to help see where the same columnar or record position is throughout the whole legacy report. Guidelines are illustrated in Figure 16-2.

Choosing Sections

Once you've set zoom levels and added guidelines to help you view the legacy report, it's time to define the sections that make up the legacy report. Since the Document Import Tool must convert the legacy report to a Crystal Report (with all of Crystal Report's sections and objects), you must determine what parts of the legacy report equate to the Crystal Reports Report Header and Footer, Group Headers and Footers, and Details section. Examine the legacy report closely to make this determination.

The Document Import Tool uses character patterns to determine that certain sets of lines in the legacy report constitute the various sections. By specifying the *first* occurrence

Guidelines help delineate columns
and records in the legacy report

Guideline handles
move guidelines

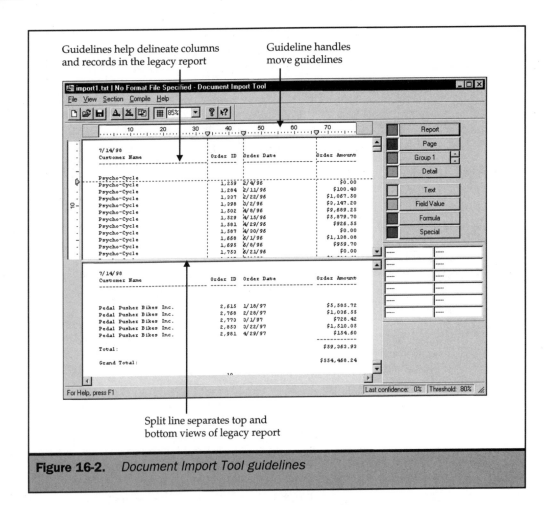

Split line separates top and
bottom views of legacy report

Figure 16-2.   *Document Import Tool guidelines*

of a header section, and the *last* occurrence of a footer section, the Document Import
Tool can use the character patterns to identify the rest of the sections throughout the
report. Although it's not absolutely required, it's probably less confusing to define
sections in the general order they will occur, starting with the report header and footer.
Then, you can choose the page headers and footers, one or more group headers and
footers, and finally the details section.

Defining Report and Page Headers and Footers

The *report header* is a section of the report that appears only once at the very beginning
of the report. This might consist of a title page, an opening disclaimer, or some
introductory information that appears only once at the beginning of the report. The

report footer is a section that appears only once at the very end of the report (but before the last page footer, described later). This section might contain grand totals, a closing statement or disclaimer, or some other information that appears only once at the end of the report.

To select the report header and footer in the legacy report, click the Report button in the upper-right corner of the Document Import Tool (this set of buttons is actually known as the *Section toolbar*). An × will appear in the colored box next to the button, indicating that you will be selecting these sections. Point to the legacy report window and click the row that begins the report header section. A colored box, with the same color as the box containing the × next to the Report button, will appear in the legacy report window. Note the sizing handles (the little blocks) that appear on the corners of the highlighted section. If the report header is actually more than one line tall, resize the colored box by dragging the top or bottom sizing handle up or down. Then, scroll down to the bottom of the report (or use the bottom part of the split-screen legacy report window) and find the report footer. With the Report button still showing the ×, click on the report footer to place the colored section around it. Again, use the sizing handles to size the section more than one line tall if necessary.

Tip *You don't have to define both header and footer sections if the legacy report doesn't have them. For example, if the legacy report contains grand totals (that constitute the report footer), but no introductory title page (that would constitute a report header), you need only define the report footer—no report header is required.*

When you define a page header or footer, you can choose settings or *attributes* for the section you just highlighted. By using the white boxes in the lower-right corner of the Document Import Tool (known as the *Attributes toolbar*), you can choose such options as New Page Before and New Page After the section.

Once you've defined the report headers and footers, you'll need to define page headers and footers as well. The *page header* is a section of the legacy report that will print at the top of each and every page. Examples of the page header might be the report title, the print date, or column headings that print at the top of every page. The *page footer* section prints at the bottom of every page. This might contain page numbers, the report name, or maybe the print date or time.

To define page headers and footers in the legacy report, click the Page button in the upper right of the Document Import Tool. An × will appear in the box next to the button. Then, find the part of the legacy report that constitutes the *first* page header (probably very close to the top, if not the top, of the first page of the report). Click on the line that begins the page header. A colored box, the same color as the box with the × next to the Page button, will appear around that line. As with the report header and footer sections, if the page header needs to be more than one line tall, click the bottom or top sizing handle and drag the section over all the legacy report lines that make up the page header. Then, move to the bottom of the report (probably in the lower half of the split legacy report window) and choose the line of the report that starts the *last* page footer. Again, the colored box will appear and can be resized to encompass more than one line by dragging the sizing handles. An example of section highlighting is shown in Figure 16-3.

You may have already defined a section and moved on, but later discover that you need to resize or move the previous section. By clicking on an existing defined section, you will automatically select it. Just use the sizing handles to resize it if necessary. If it needs to be moved, press the DEL key to remove the section, click the appropriate button in the Section toolbar, and replace the section in the correct location.

Defining Group Headers and Footers

After defining page headers and footers, you must define group headers and footers (if there are any). A *group* refers to a section of the report where related records are

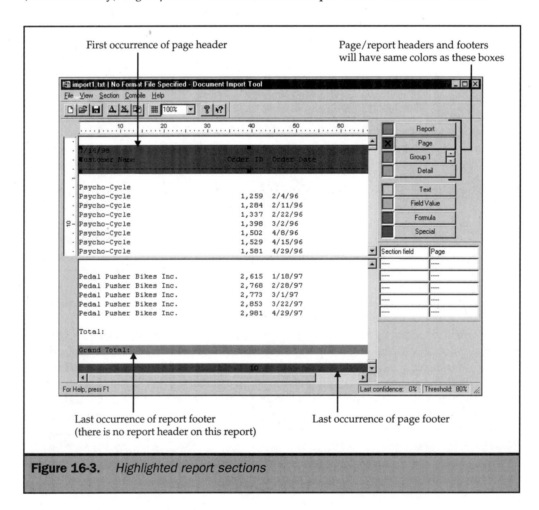

Figure 16-3. *Highlighted report sections*

grouped together. For example, if the legacy report shows orders by customer, you'll see all the orders for a particular customer placed together in a group. Once one customer's orders have printed, the next customer group prints, and so on. Typically, there are two sections that surround groups: the group header and group footer.

The *group header* prints at the beginning of a group, perhaps showing the name of the customer or some other information to introduce the group. The group header is followed by all the records that are included in that group. Then the group footer prints. The *group footer* is a section that wraps up a group by showing subtotal or summary numbers for that particular group, such as the number of orders that particular customer group placed and the total amount for all that customer group's orders.

A legacy report may very possibly contain more than one group. It might, for example, contain a Country group. Within the Country group, records might be grouped by State. Within the State group, records might be further grouped by Customer Name, and so on. Each group will probably have its own unique header and footer. To have the Document Import Tool correctly convert these multiple levels of grouping, you must make sure you can identify the different lines that make up the first group header and last group footer for each group in the legacy report.

> **Tip**   *There may not be any groups on the report at all (if it's just a straight listing with no subtotals). In this event, there's no need to define any groups. Also, there may be reports that just contain group footers, with subtotal or summary fields, and no group headers. Or, the report may contain just one or more group headers introducing the group (maybe even having subtotals located in the headers), but no group footers. In these situations, simply define the group header or footer by itself—there's no need to define the other section.*

To define group headers and footers, click the Group 1 button in the upper right of the Document Import Tool. An × will appear in the colored box next to the button. Navigate to the *first* occurrence of the group header toward the top of the report and click on it. As with previous sections that you've defined, a colored box will appear in the legacy report window. Use the sizing handles to resize the group header if it needs to be more than one line tall. Find the *last* group footer toward the bottom of the report and select it in a similar fashion.

If there is more than one group on the report, click the small arrows to the right of the Group 1 button to make it a Group 2 button. The colored box with the × will change to a new color. Now select the second group header and footer in the same fashion as the first. If there are yet other groups, increment the button as many times as necessary (resulting in additional colors) and select those group headers and footers.

Once you've selected the group, set attributes for the group in the Attributes toolbar in the lower right of the Document Import Tool. You can choose whether to have a new page before or after the section, whether to repeat the group header on a new page, and what detail field the group is based on. If you haven't yet defined detail fields (discussed in the following section), be sure to select the group after you've defined detail fields so you can choose which detail field the group is based on. Group definitions are illustrated in Figure 16-4.

When you define a section, the × will stay set in the colored box next to the just-clicked button. If you inadvertently click somewhere on the report before clicking another button, the Document Import Tool will attempt to define the line you clicked as a report section. Be careful that you don't mistakenly select a line that doesn't belong in that section. To click without defining a section, click the button with the × (or the × itself) again. This will turn off the ×, and you can click in the legacy window without fear of defining the wrong section. If you do create a section by mistake, just press DELETE to remove the wrong section.

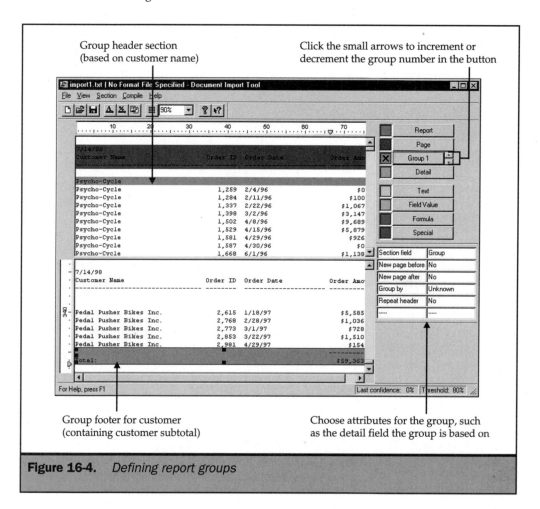

Figure 16-4.   *Defining report groups*

Defining the Details Section

You must always define a details section in the legacy report. The *details section* displays the lowest level of data in the report. For example, if a report shows individual orders placed by customers (perhaps grouped by customer name), the line or lines in the report that show the individual order information, such as order number, order date, and order amount, make up the details section.

Tip   *If you're familiar with Crystal Reports designing, you may be tempted to not define a details section if the report appears to just contain summary information by group, such as just a single order count and subtotal line for each customer. However, the Document Import Tool must always have a details section defined. So, in the case of the summary report, the customer subtotal lines will need to be defined as detail sections, and there may be no groups defined.*

Defining the details section is similar to defining other sections. Click the Detail button in the upper left of the Document Import Tool. An × will appear in the colored box beside the button. Then, click on the *first* occurrence of the details section in the legacy report window to place the colored box. Resize the colored box if the details section is more than one row tall. Once you've selected the details section, you can set New Page Before and New Page After attributes in the Attributes toolbar in the lower right of the Document Import Tool.

Caution   *Be very careful when defining report sections. Make sure you don't include too many lines, perhaps including the first details section in a group as part of the group header, or choosing two detail lines and defining them as one details section. These types of errors will result in an inaccurate conversion at best, and more likely, a failed conversion.*

Choosing Fields

You may notice that you cannot resize the colored box around a section horizontally; these sections all transcend the entire width of the legacy report window. It's important to remember that you have just defined report sections—the Document Import Tool has no idea yet as to what makes up the individual pieces of these sections. To define the individual fields in the sections, you use the lower set of buttons in the upper-right corner of the Document Import Tool (the Section toolbar). When you choose fields, the colored boxes can be sized both vertically and horizontally to indicate exactly where the fields begin and end.

Choosing Text Fields

Text fields are simply textual items that don't change as the report processes. Examples are column headings that appear in the page header (including the dashes that act as underlines), or the word "Page" that appears next to the page number in the page footer. These items will be created as Crystal Reports text objects when the report is converted.

To select text objects, click the Text button on the right side of the Document Import Tool. An × will appear in the colored box next to the button. Choose the first text field you want to define, and click on the first character of the field. A colored box one-character wide and tall will appear where you clicked. You can now click on any of the sizing handles and drag the colored box to the necessary height and width to encompass the entire text field. Continue to highlight every other text field in every other section in this same manner. Don't forget any—if you miss any text fields in any section, they won't be included in the new report. Text object definition is illustrated in Figure 16-5.

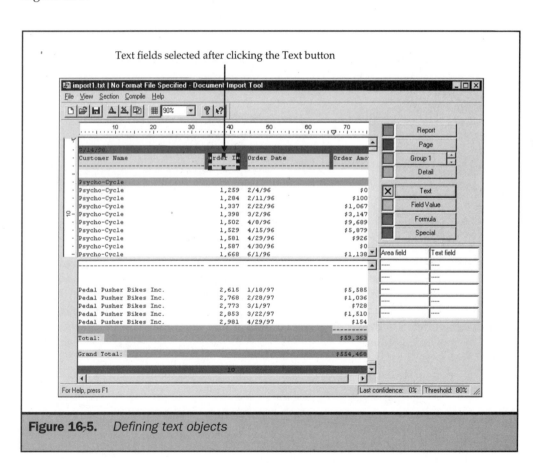

Figure 16-5. *Defining text objects*

Any text field (or any other type of field for that matter) can only be selected inside an existing section. If you try to select a text field in any part of the legacy report window that hasn't been included in a section, you'll receive a "must be bound within a section" error message.

Choosing Report Fields

You must indicate where individual fields begin and end inside the details section. Do this by clicking the Field Value button on the right side of the Document Import Tool. An × will appear in the colored box next to the button. As you have done in other sections, select and size colored boxes in the details section for each separate detail field. It's very important that you size the colored box to include the maximum size that the field might take up in *any* record. For example, even if the field in the details section you've highlighted only contains the value Joe, the field may contain the value Cassandra Jean later in the report. If you only highlight three characters to encompass Joe, the only data that will be included for the later record will be Cas. Using guidelines (which were discussed at the beginning of this chapter) may help avoid this problem by giving you a visual cue as to where one field ends and another begins.

Unlike with text fields, you can choose attributes for the report field in the Attributes toolbar in the lower right of the Document Import Tool. The Document Import Tool will choose default values for these attributes, based on its "best guess" of what the field contains.

For example, if the field just contains numbers (and perhaps commas or decimal points), the Document Import Tool will assume it's a numeric field. If it contains a dollar sign, it will assume currency. Other similar assumptions are made for date, time, and string fields. If the assumptions are incorrect, or if you want to customize the way the field will be converted, make your own choices in the Attributes toolbar. The name of the attribute appears on the left side of the display. When you click to the right of the attribute name, a drop-down list will appear where you can choose the value for the attribute. Attributes for a date field are shown in Figure 16-6 and described in the following table:

Attribute	Description
Area field	Choose the type of field (text, field, formula, or special), in case you miscategorized the field when you selected it
Type	Change the data type of the field
Field name	Give the field a name or leave the default
Default value	Supply a default value for the field, in case subsequent records have no value for the field
Suppress if same	Determine if duplicate field values should be suppressed
Date order (date fields only)	Choose the order in which the month, day, and year will appear

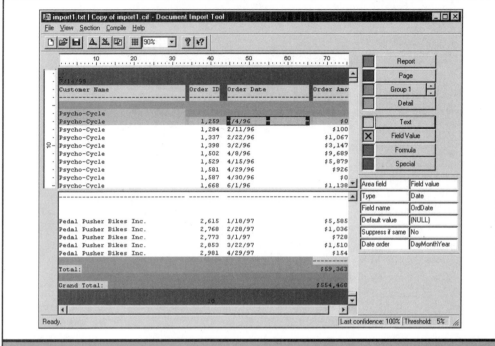

Figure 16-6. *Attributes toolbar options*

Choosing Formulas

Subtotals, summaries, or grand totals in the legacy report can conceivably just be converted as text (since the data that they are calculated against will be converted straight across with them). However, you want your converted report to be flexible should you wish to change the data source to a different database in the future. To accomplish this, you should define any subtotal or summary values located in group or report footers as formulas. This way, the converted Crystal Report will calculate the subtotal or summary based on the detail data—any change in data source will result in correctly calculated summaries.

To choose a formula, click the Formula button on the right side of the Document Import Tool. An × will appear in the colored box next to the button. Highlight, as you have done in previous sections, any subtotal, summary, or grand total fields in group footers or the report footer. As with report fields, the Attributes toolbar should be used to choose the type of summary (sum, average, count, etc.) and to choose the name of the field in the details section that the formula should summarize. This is illustrated in Figure 16-7.

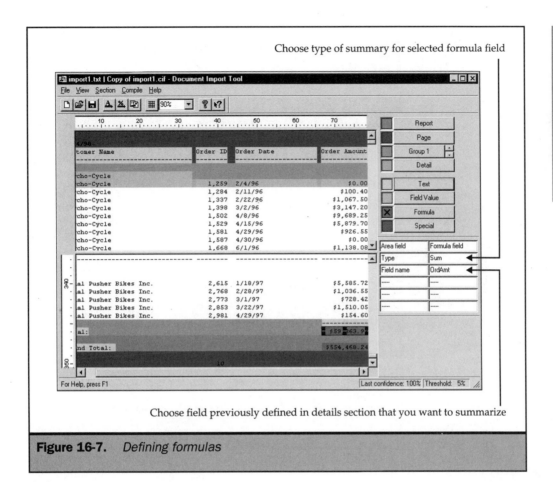

Choose type of summary for selected formula field

Choose field previously defined in details section that you want to summarize

Figure 16-7.   *Defining formulas*

Choosing Special Fields

As with a regularly designed Crystal Report, you will need to specify any legacy report fields that should be automatically generated by Crystal Reports when the converted file is run. The Document Import Tool will convert print date, print time, page number, and total page-count special fields.

To choose the legacy field that should be converted to a special field, click the Special button on the right side of the Document Import Tool. An × will appear in the colored box next to the button. Using the same techniques as for other fields, highlight the special field you want converted (make sure you make the selection wide enough to encompass any size of special field that may appear in the report). You can then choose the type of special field you want converted in the Type attribute on the Attributes toolbar. Special fields are illustrated in Figure 16-8.

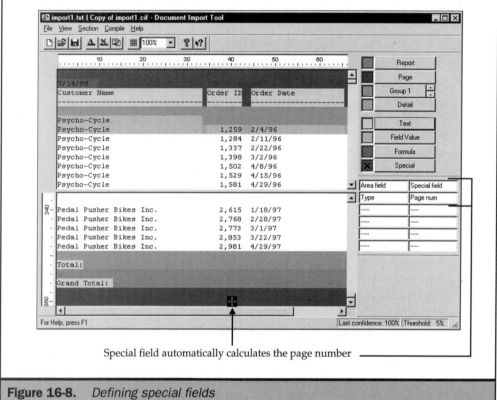

Special field automatically calculates the page number ————

Figure 16-8. *Defining special fields*

Caution *You must make sure that every bit of text, every field, every formula (such as subtotals, counts, and averages), and every special field (such as page number or print date) are defined in the report sections. If you don't define all these items, the conversion will be inaccurate or may fail.*

Creating the New Report

Once you've defined all report sections and highlighted all report fields, you're ready to actually convert the legacy text file to a Crystal Report. The conversion process actually involves several steps:

1. Saving the highlighting and attribute information to a conversion interface (.CIF) file

2. Setting the confidence threshold

3. Converting the legacy file

4. Checking for errors in the log file

Saving the .CIF File

The first time you try to convert the report, you'll be prompted to save certain Document Import Tool information to a .CIF (conversion interface) file. This file contains all the information about the fields and sections you highlighted, the attributes you set for them, and so on. Choose a location and filename for the .CIF file when prompted.

You will use the .CIF file whenever you need to convert the current legacy report to a Crystal Report. You can also use the same .CIF file for any other legacy reports you want to convert that have the same field and section layout of the current legacy report. If you open the .CIF file and then make changes to sections or fields that you've defined, make sure you save the updated .CIF file when you're finished. The Document Import Tool will prompt you if you close the program or try to open another .CIF file without first saving the current file.

Setting the Confidence Threshold

When the Document Import Tool converts a legacy report to a Crystal Report, it must match up legacy report sections and fields to your section and field specifications to properly convert the report. Every time the Document Import Tool can't successfully convert a defined field, it lowers its *confidence level*. When the confidence level falls below a predefined threshold, the conversion will stop, as the Document Import Tool will assume that the conversion will be of little use. You can set this threshold according to how accurate you want the conversion to be.

To set the confidence threshold, click the Set Confidence Threshold button on the toolbar or choose Compile | Set Confidence from the pull-down menus. Specify the confidence threshold that you feel comfortable with. When the legacy report is converted, if less than the percentage of fields you specify can be correctly converted, the conversion will fail. If you want to perform a trial conversion that won't stop if there are significant errors, try setting a low confidence level, such as 5 percent. Once you're more confident of your section and field specifications, increase the confidence level to ensure an accurate conversion.

Converting the Legacy Report

Once you've highlighted all your sections and fields and set the confidence threshold, you're ready to actually perform the conversion. When this occurs, the Document Import Tool will read the legacy report file and convert the data in the details section to a database file (in Microsoft Access format). A new Crystal Reports .RPT file will be created that reads the converted data from the Access database file and displays a report similar to the original legacy report.

To convert the report, click the Generate Report Locally toolbar button or choose Compile | Generate Report from the pull-down menus. You will be prompted to specify filenames for the report file and database file.

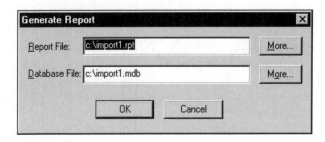

Specify the filenames you want to use for the report and database files. If the files already exist, you'll be prompted before they're overwritten. Once you click OK, the Document Import Tool will convert the report. You'll see a status window that shows the conversion progress, as well as the confidence level as the conversion proceeds. If you want to cancel the conversion, click the Cancel button.

Once the conversion is complete, you'll be asked whether or not you want to open the report inside Crystal Reports, and whether you want to close the Document Import Tool if you do open the report. When you open the report inside Crystal Reports, you'll be able to preview, format, and modify the report just as you would any other Crystal Report.

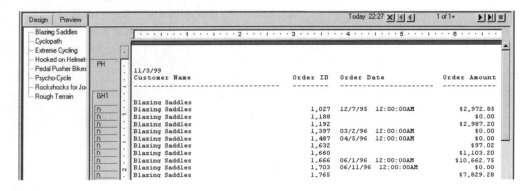

If you want to change the default font size that the Document Import Tool uses when creating the Crystal Report, click the Set Report Fontsize button in the toolbar, or choose Compile | Output Fontsize from the pull-down menus. Note that the Document Import Tool will always use the Courier font for the Crystal Report, regardless of the font size you specify.

If the conversion fails, you'll receive a message indicating so. Perform trouble-shooting steps described shortly in the chapter and try the conversion again, once you've made corrections to your legacy report section and field specifications.

Opening an Existing Report and .CIF File

Once you've created a conversion interface (.CIF) file, you can use it over and over again if the legacy report you wish to convert is generated by a mainframe or other system on a regular basis. For example, the legacy report may be automatically placed on a network drive every day with the same filename, overwriting the previous version. You will want to use the same .CIF file to convert the daily legacy report. Or, you can create one .CIF file that matches a particular legacy report file. Then, you can use the same .CIF to convert other legacy reports in different locations that have the same format and layout as the original legacy report file.

To open an existing legacy report text file and an existing .CIF file, click the Open toolbar button, choose File | Open from the pull-down menus, or use the CTRL-N shortcut key combination. Choose the legacy text file and .CIF file that you wish to load. The Document Import Tool will load the two files and attempt to match the .CIF file to the legacy text file. Be patient—this may take some time, depending on the size of the legacy file.

If the legacy file can be successfully read, you'll see the legacy report appear in the Document Import Tool with its sections and fields highlighted with the color boxes. If the Document Import Tool cannot successfully match the .CIF file to the legacy file, you'll be given an error message and the opportunity to show "absolute" highlighting (highlighting that the Document Import Tool cannot successfully resolve to the type of data contained in the legacy report file). If you choose to use absolute highlighting, you'll need to remove or change the highlighting to match the appropriate legacy report file sections and fields.

There are two sample legacy .TXT files and matching .CIF files included with Crystal Reports. Look in <program directory>\REPORTS\IMPORT for IMPORT1.TXT and IMPORT1.CIF, and IMPORT2.TXT and IMPORT2.CIF.

Troubleshooting the Document Import Tool

When you convert the legacy report to a Crystal Report, the Document Import Tool may be unable to match all (or any) sections and fields you defined to data in the legacy report file. The Document Import Tool will give you an error message and not create the report if the percentage of successfully converted fields falls below the confidence threshold you set prior to conversion. The Document Import Tool will perform the same process (but not create any Crystal Reports file) when you open a legacy text file and a .CIF file with the Open command.

If you receive an error message in either situation, the Document Import Tool will create a text file with the same filename as the .CIF file containing a .LOG extension.

This log file will be placed in the same directory as the .CIF file, and can be viewed with Notepad (if it's small enough), WordPad, or any word processor or text editor that can read an ASCII text file. The log file contains messages that may be helpful in determining why the Document Import Tool was unable to successfully convert or match up sections and fields to the legacy report.

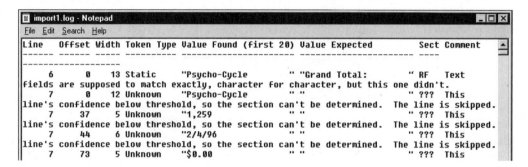

If these errors occur, you may be able to resolve them without even looking at the log file. Pay particular attention to the following suggestions:

- Make sure all fields inside a highlighted section are defined. Don't leave any text characters undefined.

- Make sure fields are defined to be wide enough. If you are defining report fields, make sure you stretch the fields to be wide enough to encompass the largest instance of the defined field.

- Don't forget that any subtotals, summaries, or grand totals should be defined as formulas in any group or report header or footer. Make sure you are using the correct summary function and have indicated the correct detail section field to summarize or total.

- Don't forget special fields, such as page numbers or print date. These need to be defined using the Special button.

- Make sure you define a group-name field in a group header as a field. If you forget to define it at all, or define it as text, the conversion will probably fail.

The
Complete
Reference

Chapter 17

Reporting from OLAP Cubes

R elational database systems provide the vast majority of data analysis and reporting that most organizations need. However, there is a smaller segment of many organizations that can benefit from more flexible and sophisticated analysis tools. In many cases, an organization's higher-level analysts are still using spreadsheet tools in combination with relational databases to make strategic company decisions.

OLAP (online analytical processing) is a newer analysis technique that provides much more flexibility in analyzing company data. Crystal Reports supports most standard OLAP tools and will allow you to create reports based on these database systems.

What Is OLAP?

Most typical company data is viewed in two dimensions, whether it is viewed by a reporting tool, such as Crystal Reports, or a spreadsheet program, such as Microsoft Excel. In the case of a spreadsheet, the rows and columns constitute the two-dimensional analysis. You may be viewing product sales by state, salesperson volume by product category, or customer totals by demographics. In each of these cases, you can typically only see two dimensions at any one time, even though you may prefer to actually analyze a combination of three or more of these factors.

	USA	CAN	UK
PROD 1	534	212	231
PROD 2	45	21	12
PROD 3	321	324	112
PROD 4	204	120	40
PROD 5	78	43	31
PROD 6	32	12	2
PROD 7	786	512	49
PROD 8	123	23	17

Region

Product

Online analytical processing, or OLAP, is a leading-edge analysis approach that allows data to be analyzed and viewed in multiple dimensions in real time. With a typical OLAP tool, you may initially be presented with a spreadsheet-like view that shows information using two dimensions, such as product sales dollars by state (or perhaps by country or region, allowing drill-down to the state level).

Even though only two dimensions are visible, additional dimensions are available "behind the scenes" to control the two dimensions you are viewing; you can limit dollars by state by using other dimensions. Perhaps you want to see dollars by state limited to just certain sales reps, certain customer demographics, or certain product categories—you still see the original dollars and state dimensions, but the numbers are *filtered* by the other dimensions. You may also want to quickly see sales by product category, demographics by state, or some other combinations of dimensions. Using an OLAP analysis tool, "slicing and dicing" through the different dimensions is typically as easy as dragging and dropping one dimension on top of another. Figure 17-1 shows Seagate Software's Worksheet analysis tool viewing a multidimensional "FoodMart" database included with Microsoft SQL Server 7.0 OLAP Services.

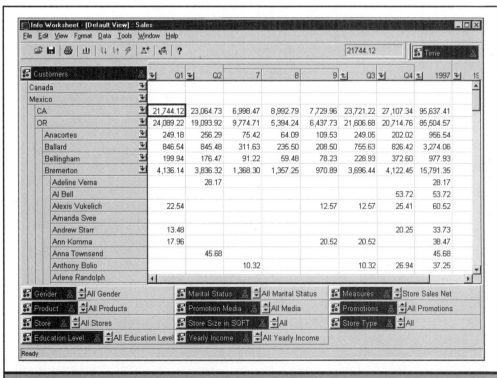

Figure 17-1.   *Seagate Worksheet OLAP analysis tool*

While relational databases represent data in a two-dimensional row and column (or field and record) structure, OLAP databases utilize a multidimensional structure known as a *cube* (which, despite its name, is capable of storing more than three dimensions of data). Often, cubes are built based on regular relational database systems—the relational database is populated using typical data entry or data import techniques, and a cube is built based on the relational database. Cubes can be refreshed or repopulated on a regular basis to allow multidimensional, real-time analysis of the data in the relational database.

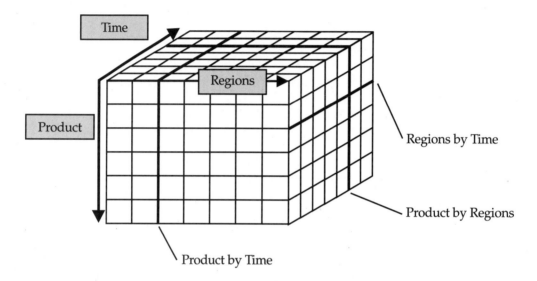

Crystal Reports OLAP Capabilities

You might ask, "Where does Crystal Reports fit into all this?" Crystal Reports, obviously, can report on the data stored in the two-dimensional relational database. However, Crystal Reports also allows reporting against many industry-leading OLAP cubes. In fact, your Crystal Reports can combine reports that are based on both relational databases and OLAP cubes, all in the same report. You have several choices:

- Create a standard report against the relational database the cube is based on.
- Create an OLAP-only report based solely on the cube.
- Create a standard report against a relational database (either the same database the cube is based on, or an entirely different database) *and* include an OLAP report based on a cube inside the standard report.
- Create several *different* OLAP reports based on the same, or different, cubes. These OLAP-based reports can exist individually, or be included together inside a standard report based on a relational database.

Supported OLAP Systems

While OLAP technology has been somewhat fragmented and proprietary until recently, industry standards are starting to emerge. Crystal Reports will work with leading proprietary OLAP databases, as well as the emerging *Open OLAP* standard. Thus, Crystal Reports 7 can create OLAP reports based on the following tools:

- Hyperion Essbase
- Seagate Holos and Seagate Info/Crystal Info
- IBM DB2 OLAP Server
- Informix MetaCube
- Microsoft SQL Server 7.0 OLAP Services
- OLEDB for OLAP sources (or other "Open OLAP" sources)

 Versions of Crystal Reports prior to 7 support a smaller set of OLAP data sources. In particular, Crystal Reports 6 only supports Hyperion Essbase and Seagate Holos/Crystal Info.

Types of OLAP Reports

Crystal Reports can create several different types of OLAP reports, depending on the OLAP cube that the report is based on. The common type of report is based on an OLAP grid object. An *OLAP grid* is very similar in appearance and functionality to a cross-tab object (discussed in detail in Chapter 9). An OLAP grid displays one or more cube dimensions in rows and columns on the report. As with a cross-tab, you may format individual rows and columns to appear as you wish. You may also easily swap, or *pivot*, the rows and columns to change the appearance of the OLAP grid.

If you're writing reports with Hyperion Essbase or DB2 OLAP Server, you can choose an additional reporting approach called the *Report Script Method*. This approach uses a specific "Members" tab contained in a report expert to choose the cube dimensions to include in the report. And, if you're using Informix MetaCube for reporting, Crystal Reports can use a method that is very similar to that of a standard relational database for reporting on OLAP data.

 Because the OLAP grid object is common to all supported OLAP tools, this book will concentrate on it as the OLAP reporting method. For specific information on the other methods, refer to Crystal Reports documentation or online help.

Creating OLAP Reports

Creating reports with OLAP cubes is straightforward and very similar to creating reports with regular relational databases. You may either use the OLAP Report Expert right from the Report Gallery, or choose the custom option. The OLAP Report Expert leads you step-by-step through choosing the cube and dimensions you want to use in the row and column of your report. The expert will then create a report containing an OLAP grid. If you choose the custom option, you can create one or more OLAP grid objects in your report manually. Creating an OLAP grid object is very similar to creating a cross-tab object.

Using the OLAP Report Expert

The OLAP Report Expert is available from the Report Gallery that appears whenever you create a new report. Just click the OLAP button to use the expert. A tabbed dialog box, similar to Crystal Reports' other report experts, will appear.

The first step is to choose the OLAP database you wish to base your OLAP report on. Click the Select button to choose from Crystal Reports–supported OLAP databases. A list of database types will appear.

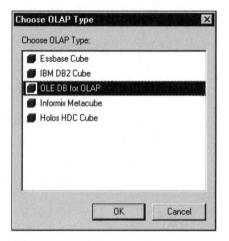

If your OLAP database type doesn't appear on the list, you may need to install client software specific to your particular OLAP system, such as a cube viewing application, on your PC. Once you've installed this software, restart Crystal Reports and try creating the report again.

Choose the type of OLAP database you wish to use. Depending on your choice, you'll need to log on to your OLAP server, or navigate to the proper folder and filename for the OLAP database you want to report on. Once you've made these choices, the fields on the Data tab of the expert will be filled. If the database you chose contains more than one cube, choose the cube you want to report on from the Cube drop-down list. If you are using a Seagate Holos or Seagate Crystal Info Cube and have

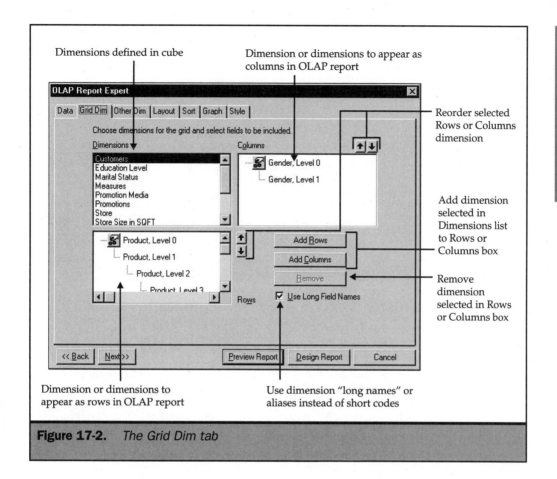

Dimensions defined in cube

Dimension or dimensions to appear as columns in OLAP report

Reorder selected Rows or Columns dimension

Add dimension selected in Dimensions list to Rows or Columns box

Remove dimension selected in Rows or Columns box

Dimension or dimensions to appear as rows in OLAP report

Use dimension "long names" or aliases instead of short codes

Figure 17-2. *The Grid Dim tab*

saved a cube view that you'd like to use for your OLAP report, click the Import Format button and choose the .WDF file that the view is saved in.

Once you've made these choices, click the Grid Dim tab to choose the dimension or dimensions you want to include in the rows and columns of your report. The Grid Dim tab is shown in Figure 17-2.

Choose the dimension from the Dimensions list that you want to appear as the row in your OLAP report. Then, simply drag and drop it into the Rows box, or click the Add Rows button. Use the same drag-and-drop method to add the dimension you want to appear as the column in your OLAP report to the Columns box. Or, select a dimension and click Add Columns.

You aren't limited to placing just one dimension in the Rows or Columns boxes. If you add multiple dimensions, Crystal Reports will "group" the dimensions in the OLAP report. For example, if you added a State dimension, followed by a Customer dimension, Crystal Reports will print states and show customers broken down within each state. If you place the dimensions in the Rows or Columns box in the wrong order, you can simply drag and drop the dimensions into the correct order within the Rows or Columns boxes. Or, you can select the dimension you want to move, and use the up and down arrows next to the Rows and Columns boxes.

If you wish to remove a dimension from the Rows or Columns box, select the dimension and press the DEL key. Or, you can select the desired dimension and click the Remove button.

Check Use Long Field Names if you want Crystal Reports to use the "long name" or "alias" in the OLAP report, instead of the short code contained in some cubes. For example, by checking this option, the OLAP report will show spelled-out state names instead of two-letter state codes.

 The behavior of the Use Long Field Names option is dependent on the OLAP database and cube you are using. If you see abbreviated code-like material in your OLAP report, ensure that this option is checked. However, if the OLAP database or cube isn't designed with long field names or aliases, selecting this option will have no effect.

Narrowing Down Dimensions with the Field Picker

Depending on the cube you choose for your report, you may find dimensions that contain many levels or generations. A *generation* is a lower level of information that breaks down the higher level above it. For example, a Products dimension could contain several generations: Product type, Product Name, and Size. Each generation further breaks down the information shown by the generation above it.

If the dimension you choose for your OLAP report contains generations, Crystal Reports will show all the generations in a group hierarchy when it displays the dimension. While this may be the way you want the report to appear, it may introduce too many levels of data to analyze efficiently. This can particularly become a problem when you wish to add more than one dimension to a row or column of the report. If you need to reduce the generations inside a dimension that appears on the report, you can use the Field Picker to select only the generations that you want to see.

 To display the Field Picker, click the button next to the dimension you want to work with. The Select Fields dialog box will appear, allowing you to pick the generations you want to use in this particular OLAP report.

The Select Fields dialog box shows the dimension generations in a hierarchy, with pluses and minuses to the left, much like the display of folders and files in Windows Explorer. You can expand the hierarchy to see lower generations by clicking the plus signs next to the generations. If you want to see just the higher-level generations, click the minus sign to collapse them.

Once you've expanded the dimension's generations sufficiently, you can simply click on individual generations to select or deselect them. Those that are highlighted will be included in the report—those that aren't won't. You can select or deselect all the generations by using the Select All or Unselect All buttons. These buttons will give you a good "starting point" if you want to include just a few, or almost all, of the generations in your report.

If you select a higher-level generation (a generation that has at least one level below it), you can use the Children or Descendents buttons to select specific levels of generations below the selected generation. Consider the following generations for a Products dimension:

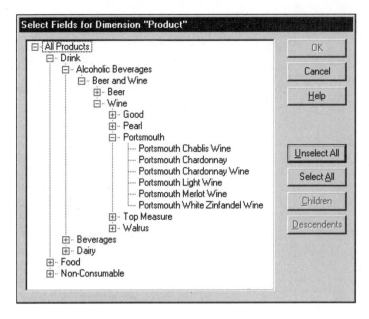

By selecting a higher-level generation and then clicking the Children button, only the *next lower* generation will be selected:

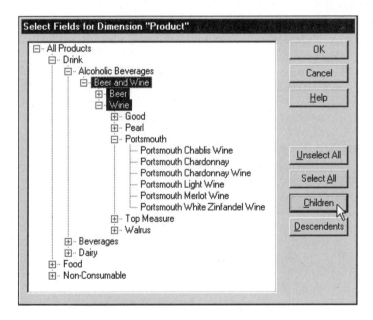

If you select a higher-level generation and then click the Descendents button, *all lower-level* generations will be selected, not just the next level:

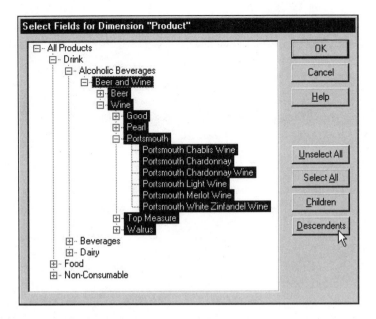

Once you've chosen the generations you want included in the report, click OK. The Field Picker will close and the Grid Dim tab will show only the generations (or levels) you chose. Click the Other Dim tab, shown in Figure 17-3, to determine how the remaining dimensions included in the cube will affect your OLAP report.

In the Other Dim tab you'll see all the other dimensions in the cube that you didn't include in the Rows or Columns boxes. You can use these dimensions to either filter or group your OLAP report. *Filtering* the OLAP report will limit the report to certain occurrences of data in these dimensions. *Grouping* the OLAP report, like the grouping of other reports discussed in Chapter 3, will create a new section of the OLAP report every time the value of the chosen dimension changes. Each resulting OLAP report section will contain data just for one group.

To *filter* the report based on a dimension, select the dimension in the Other Dimensions list at the top part of the dialog box. By default it will be set to a value defined when the cube was designed. Typically this default value will be "All" or a particular general value. Ensure that Is Equal To is selected in the drop-down list below the Other Dimensions box. Then, click the Field Picker button. The Select Fields dialog box, described earlier, will appear, where you can choose a particular value to limit the OLAP report. Once you've made your choice and clicked OK, the Other Dimensions list will change to indicate the single value you picked. The OLAP report will now be limited to only values that are included in the field you chose.

 You can only choose one value in the Select Fields box here. Selecting a new value will deselect the previous value.

CRYSTAL REPORTS 7 INTRODUCED

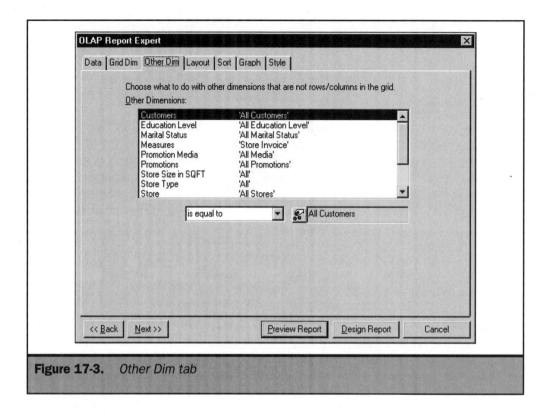

Figure 17-3.   *Other Dim tab*

To *group* the OLAP report based on a dimension, select the dimension in the Other Dimensions list. Then, change the drop-down list below the Other Dimensions box to Show Grid on Change Of. The dialog box will change to accommodate grouping. Click the Choose Fields button. Another dialog box will appear that allows you to choose the generation or generations of the field you want to group the OLAP report on. Click OK when you've made your choices. The fields you chose for grouping will appear in the list at the lower right of the Other Dim tab, shown next:

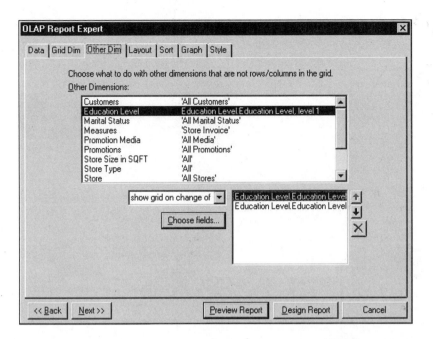

If you've chosen more than one field, you can change the order in which Crystal Reports will group the OLAP report by selecting a generation and clicking the up or down arrow. If you want to remove one of the grouping generations, select it and click the red ×. Once you've made any filtering and grouping choices, click the Layout tab, shown in Figure 17-4.

This tab allows you to make choices that affect the appearance of the OLAP report. If any OLAP report rows or columns don't contain data (an unlikely event with typical cubes), you can choose to suppress the rows or columns. You can make choices as to how Crystal Reports will format the OLAP report if it is too wide to fit on a single page. You can also change background colors in the OLAP report for specified dimensions. And, you can choose whether to "pad" the cells of the OLAP report with white space or draw a grid separating the cells.

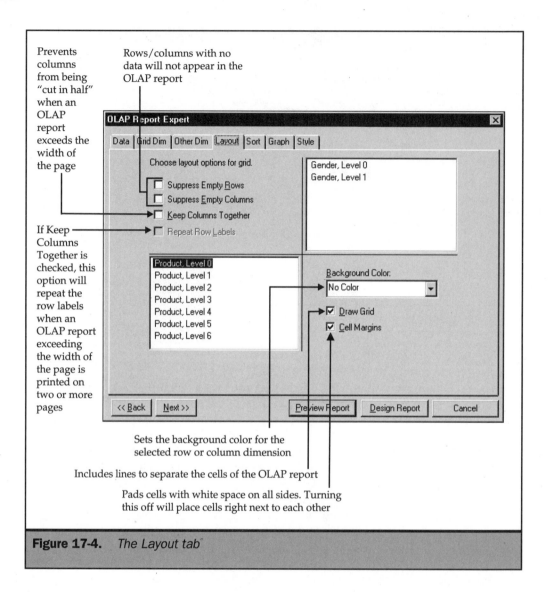

Prevents columns from being "cut in half" when an OLAP report exceeds the width of the page

Rows/columns with no data will not appear in the OLAP report

If Keep Columns Together is checked, this option will repeat the row labels when an OLAP report exceeding the width of the page is printed on two or more pages

Sets the background color for the selected row or column dimension

Includes lines to separate the cells of the OLAP report

Pads cells with white space on all sides. Turning this off will place cells right next to each other

Figure 17-4.   *The Layout tab*

Caution   *As the OLAP Report Expert has been designed to mimic the appearance of other report experts, you'll see the Sort, Graph, and Style tabs. The Sort and Graph tabs don't behave predictably with the OLAP Report Expert in the initial release of Crystal Reports 7 (version 7.0.1.192 as shown in Help | About), so don't make any selections on them. The only option on the Style tab that has any useful effect on an OLAP report is the report title.*

Once you've completed the OLAP Report Expert, you can click the Preview Report or Design Report buttons. If you choose Preview Report, the OLAP database will be read and the report will be shown in the Preview tab on the screen. If you choose Design Report, the Design tab will appear. You'll see a few simple objects on the report, such as the print date and the report title. The report will contain two Details sections: Details A and Details B.

Details A will contain the fields from the Other Dimensions tab to indicate how the report is filtered. Details B will contain an OLAP grid object. The *OLAP grid object* is very similar to a cross-tab object (discussed in Chapter 9). It represents the dimensions you chose in the Grid Dim tab as rows and columns.

If you need to make any changes to the OLAP report, you can rerun the OLAP Report Expert by clicking the Report Expert button in the Standard toolbar, or by choosing Report | Report Expert from the pull-down menus.

Alternatively, you can simply click in the upper-left corner of the OLAP grid object to select it. Then, click the Object Properties button in the Supplementary toolbar, right-click and choose Format OLAP Grid from the pop-up menu, or choose Format | OLAP Grid from the pull-down menus. The Format OLAP Grid Object tabbed dialog box will appear, and you can make changes to the dimensions and layout of the OLAP grid object.

Using the Custom Option

There will probably be situations when you want to create a standard database report that includes one or more OLAP grids. By choosing the custom option from the Report Expert, you have more flexibility in creating this type of report. Simply create a report using techniques discussed elsewhere in the book.

You may even find it useful to base the main report on some fields from your OLAP database. To use the OLAP database for the main report, choose SQL/ODBC as the data type, and look for your OLAP database type in the Log On Server dialog box. Once you've chosen, and successfully logged on to your OLAP database, you'll see a list of dimensions in the Choose SQL Table dialog box. You can add as many of these dimensions as necessary for the report. The Insert Fields dialog box will show the fields and levels of your chosen dimensions. You can add these fields to your main report as you would a regular database field. Once the main part of your report is finished, you can add the necessary OLAP grid objects.

Even though you can access the OLAP cube using the custom option, you won't be able to actually include any cube values in any report sections. You'll only be able to include and manipulate dimension names. The only way to actually include the numeric values from the cube is to create an OLAP grid object.

Adding an OLAP Grid Object

To create an OLAP grid on an existing report, choose Insert I OLAP Grid from the pull-down menus. The Insert OLAP Grid Object dialog box appears.

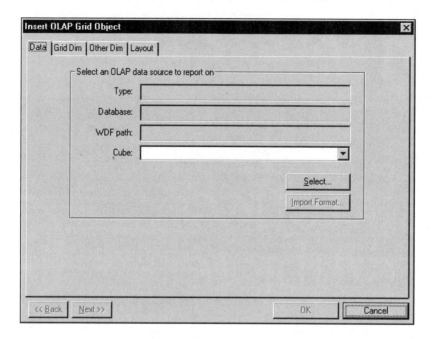

The four tabs, Data, Grid Dim, Other Dim, and Layout appear and behave identically to the same tabs on the OLAP Report Expert, described earlier in the chapter. Follow the same steps to choose the cube, dimensions, and formatting layout of the OLAP grid. Once you've made these choices, click OK. An outline of the OLAP grid object will be attached to the mouse cursor. Drop the object in the desired section of the report.

You may make changes or additions to the OLAP grid object by selecting it, and then formatting the OLAP grid by using pull-down menu options, the Object Properties button in the Supplementary toolbar, or format options from the right-click pop-up menu.

Changing the OLAP Database Location

An OLAP grid "points" to a specific OLAP cube location on a server. If that location changes, or if you want to report on a different cube without redesigning the entire OLAP grid, you'll need to change the location of the OLAP database that the grid refers to.

Select the OLAP grid you want to change by clicking on its upper-left corner. Right-click and choose Set OLAP Cube Location from the pop-up menu, or choose Database | Set OLAP Cube Location from the pull-down menus. The Set OLAP Database Location dialog box appears.

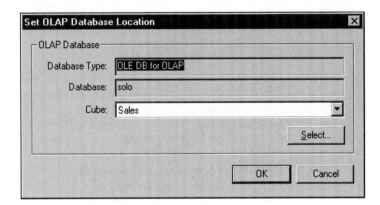

Choose the new OLAP cube or new server location for the associated OLAP database. Then click OK.

Controlling OLAP Grid Appearance

An OLAP grid organizes cube information in a row and column format, much as a cross-tab object does. In fact, formatting and changing OLAP grid appearance is essentially identical to formatting a cross-tab object.

- Make choices on the layout tab when formatting the OLAP grid. Here you can select background colors for rows or columns, control the appearance of grid lines, and choose whether or not to include white space around cell boundaries.

- Select individual fields that make up the OLAP grid, and resize or format them individually. When you resize an individual field, the row or column that the field is in will change accordingly. You can change field font face, font size, and color. And, if you're formatting numeric information, such as the OLAP grid value fields, you can choose rounding, decimal places, currency symbols, and other formatting that applies to the type of field you're formatting.

For more detailed information on formatting cross-tabs (which also applies to OLAP grids), refer to Chapter 9.

Interacting with OLAP Grids

Although you don't have quite the "slice and dice" flexibility with Crystal Reports that you may have with your particular OLAP analysis tool, you might be surprised by how easy it is to rearrange the appearance of an OLAP grid object. When you first create the OLAP grid, you choose which dimensions you want to use as rows and which you want to use as columns. If you choose multiple row or column dimensions, the order in which you add them determines the grouping order for the rows or columns.

You may want to change the order of the OLAP grid's row or column grouping, or you may want to swap or *pivot* the rows and columns. This is simple and straightforward, whether you're viewing the OLAP grid in the Preview tab or manipulating the report in the Design tab.

- To pivot the rows and columns, select the OLAP grid. Then, right-click and choose Pivot OLAP Grid from the pop-up menu. You can also choose Format | Pivot OLAP Grid from the pull-down menus.

- To reorder dimensions, simply click on the row or column heading of the dimension you want to reorder. As you hold the mouse button down, you will notice a little "piece of paper" icon appear on the mouse pointer. This indicates that the dimension can be dragged and dropped below or above another dimension to reorder the dimensions. You can even drag and drop a dimension from a row to a column or vice versa, provided there will be at least one dimension left in the row or column of the OLAP grid.

The
Complete
Reference

Chapter 18

Using Seagate Analysis

After Seagate released Crystal Reports 7, they released a separate query tool—Seagate Analysis—that they decided to give away for free. Seagate Analysis is an extension of the Seagate Crystal Query tool that shipped with the first version of Crystal Reports 7. Seagate Analysis is a query, reporting, and OLAP analysis tool that can operate completely on its own or can use existing Crystal Reports files. Seagate Analysis will not only run as a stand-alone application on Windows computers, but it can be run from a Web browser, as well, allowing the user to realize the power and flexibility of Crystal Reports without having to actually install the package.

Through Web browsers, users can now interactively build and view queries. Once they have a set of data that satisfies them, they can format it using functions and options similar to Crystal Reports to prepare a presentation-quality report for printing or exporting. Seagate Analysis also allows query results to be organized into a multidimensional worksheet for real-time drag-and-drop analysis, known as OLAP. Once the query, report, or worksheet is satisfactory, the file can be saved in a standard Crystal Reports .RPT file for later use by Seagate Analysis or Crystal Reports.

 Seagate Analysis is a 32-bit only program. You must have Windows 95/98 or Windows NT/2000 to use the tool. If you use Windows 3.1, Seagate Analysis won't be available.

What Is Seagate Analysis?

Seagate Analysis is a query, reporting, and multidimensional analysis tool that was released separately from Crystal Reports 7. It combines the functions of Seagate Crystal Query, which is included with Crystal Reports 7, and Seagate Worksheet, a multidimensional analysis tool that was previously available for free download from Seagate's Web site. Although Seagate Analysis stores its query files in standard Crystal Reports 7 .RPT format, it differs dramatically from Crystal Reports. Not only is it designed with a "thin client" architecture, but it adds real-time multidimensional analysis capability (discussed in detail later in this chapter). Seagate Analysis can connect directly to your corporate database for reporting and querying, and Analysis will also work with the middle-tier Crystal Analysis Server installed with the 32-bit version of Crystal Reports 7 to centralize connectivity between your corporate database and Seagate Analysis clients.

Because Seagate Analysis provides improved capabilities over both Seagate Worksheet and the Crystal Query product included with Crystal Reports 7, you'll probably want to upgrade any users of these tools in your organization to Seagate Analysis. There are more features in Analysis, and it's pretty hard to beat the price!

If you're upgrading Crystal Query to Seagate Analysis, there are several installation issues you'll need to be aware of. Refer to Appendix A for more details.

Seagate Analysis Components

Seagate Analysis can actually operate in two different modes: stand-alone mode and client/server mode. *Stand-alone* mode is more straightforward, operating similarly to Crystal Reports' method of connecting directly to a database. In *client/server* mode, an intermediate *Analysis Server* actually connects to your enterprise or local database, submitting database queries and accepting the result sets. It then passes the results of the queries back to the *Seagate Analysis client*, which the report viewer is using somewhere on the network. In client/server mode, the Analysis client looks and behaves almost identically to stand-alone Seagate Analysis (with more options for opening and saving locally or remotely), so the end-user will rarely even know the difference.

While stand-alone Seagate Analysis uses the same connection architecture as Crystal Reports, the client/server version's architecture introduces a new approach to reporting that's slightly different from that of standard Crystal Reports. Stand-alone Seagate Analysis requires a connection *directly* to your enterprise database. As you design your report in stand-alone Seagate Analysis, your PC makes a connection to the database. Analysis then creates a SQL query, submits it to the database, and displays the records the database sends back. Figure 18-1 shows this architecture.

The new Analysis Server/Analysis Client architecture introduces a new layer or "tier" into this model. An end user no longer requires a direct connection to the database—the Analysis Server is the only component that actually connects to the enterprise database. Any number of Analysis clients interact with the Analysis server to create queries. The Analysis server actually submits the SQL queries to the database and sends the result sets over the network to the Analysis clients. This approach can have yet another wrinkle added to it: the Analysis client can be run directly from your hard drive, or launched from a Web browser. This architecture is illustrated in Figure 18-2.

Starting Seagate Analysis

Because Seagate Analysis can run in either stand-alone or client/server mode, and because it can be launched directly from Windows or from a Web browser, you have lots of ways to start the tool. If you've installed Seagate Analysis directly from the CD or from the Seagate Software Web site download, you've installed the stand-alone

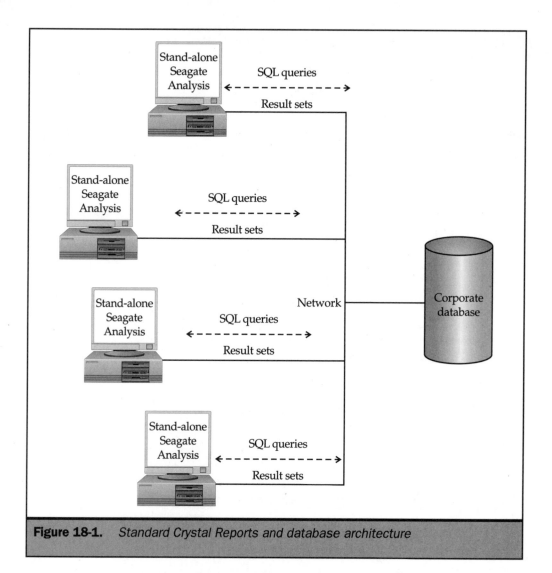

Figure 18-1.   *Standard Crystal Reports and database architecture*

version of Analysis by default. If you want to use client/server mode, you must set up an Analysis server somewhere on the network and then connect to it via a TCP/IP network connection. If you want to distribute Analysis via the Web, you'll need to make sure you install Analysis Server on the same computer that's running your Web server software. Discussions of the different methods follow.

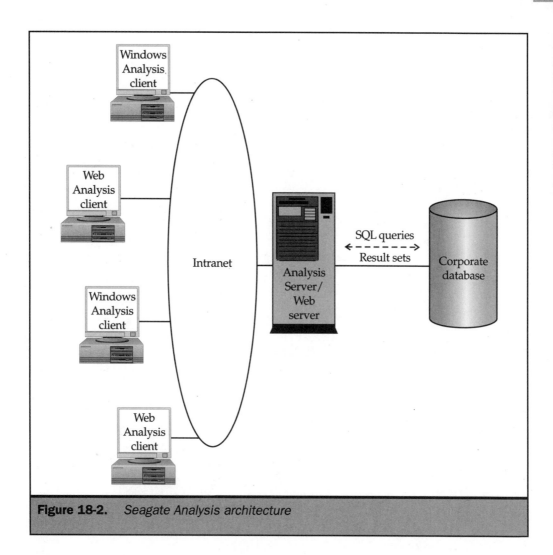

Figure 18-2.   *Seagate Analysis architecture*

Note   *There are several detailed steps for installing, upgrading, and configuring the Crystal Query Server that's included with the 32-bit version of Crystal Reports to support Seagate Analysis in client/server mode. Refer to Appendix A if you need information on this process.*

Why Use Seagate Analysis Instead of Crystal Reports or Seagate Query?

Seagate may have muddied the water a bit with the release of Seagate Analysis. You now potentially have four different ways to analyze data from a corporate database. In addition to the freely distributed Seagate Analysis, you can use Crystal Reports, Crystal Query Designer, and Crystal SQL Designer. You may wonder what benefit can be derived from Seagate Analysis if you already have Crystal Reports and its associated query tools.

First and foremost, Seagate Analysis is free. You can pass it out like candy and let a large number of users query your database. Because Analysis is an upgrade of the Crystal Query Designer, you'll want to use it instead of the tool included with Crystal Reports 7. Also, the Crystal Reports license agreement only allows a single use of Crystal Query or Crystal SQL Designer.

Using Seagate Analysis in client/server mode allows additional users who don't have direct database access to access your database, whereas stand-alone Analysis and Crystal Reports tools must reside on your Windows PC and connect directly to the database. This allows easy deployment of a query tool from within a Web browser without the tedium of manually installing software on each PC.

Seagate Analysis also adds multidimensional analysis capabilities that were previously available in Seagate Worksheet. This drag-and-drop worksheet allows real time "slice-and-dice" analysis of data in a row-and-column spreadsheet format. This allows much more sophisticated financial or statistical analysis than regular two-dimensional spreadsheets or reports can offer.

If you want absolute control over a report layout, however, you'll still want to use Crystal Reports. While Analysis does let you design simple reports for printing or displaying on the screen, it doesn't begin to approach the sophistication or flexibility of Crystal Reports. In particular, if you want a large number of Analysis users to be able to open and refresh reports, you'll still want to design the .RPT files in Crystal Reports for maximum flexibility. And, if you want to base a Crystal Report on an existing Crystal SQL Designer .QRY file, you'll still need to use the SQL Designer to create the .QRY files.

Running Analysis in Stand-alone Mode

When you install Seagate Analysis directly from the CD or by downloading from the Seagate Web site, your installation of Analysis will default to stand-alone mode. You'll find a desktop icon and program group for Seagate Analysis. Just double-click the icon on the Windows desktop or choose the Seagate Analysis option from the Seagate Analysis program group. Seagate Analysis will start and present the Welcome dialog box.

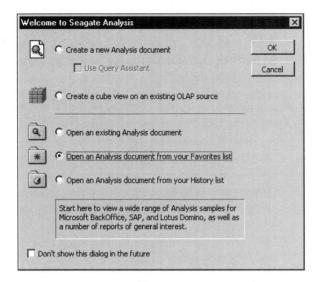

In this mode, you'll be able to connect to any databases that are configured on your local PC. This is similar to Crystal Reports, which also requires that databases be configured on your PC for you to report from them.

Running Analysis in Client/Server Mode

The initial requirement for running Seagate Analysis in client/server mode is that a Seagate Analysis Server is running somewhere on your TCP/IP network. Setting up the Analysis server requires installing the Crystal Analysis Server from the Crystal Reports 7 CD on an Analysis Server computer, and then installing Seagate Analysis on that machine to update the server to an Analysis Server (this is discussed in more detail in Appendix A).

Once the Analysis server is up and running, you must then connect the Analysis client to it. This is accomplished by starting Seagate Analysis directly from Windows Explorer so that you will be prompted to connect to an Analysis Server. If you start Analysis from the desktop icon or the Seagate Analysis program group, it will be started in stand-alone mode and you won't be prompted to connect to a server.

1. Start Windows Explorer by choosing Windows Explorer from Start | Programs, or right-click the My Computer icon and choose Explore from the pop-up menu.

2. Navigate to the drive and folder where you installed Seagate Analysis (C:\Program Files\Seagate Software\Seagate Analysis is the default location).

3. Double-click the QCLIENT.EXE program.

If you plan to use Seagate Analysis in client/server mode on a regular basis, you can set up an additional desktop shortcut or program group shortcut, or modify the existing desktop shortcut or program group shortcut. If you're changing the existing shortcuts, just change the "localhost" parameter that follows the QCLIENT.EXE command to the name of your Seagate Analysis server. If you're adding a new shortcut, just include QCLIENT.EXE, followed by a space, and then the name of your Seagate Analysis server as the command for the shortcut.

When you start the Analysis client, you'll be prompted to type the name of a Seagate Analysis server.

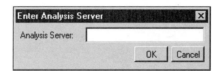

The default name for the Analysis server is "localhost." This is a reserved TCP/IP name for your own computer. If you leave this as is and click OK, you'll run Analysis in stand-alone mode, even if the Analysis server is running on your own computer. To run in client/server mode, replace the "localhost" entry with the name of the Analysis server you want to connect to, and click OK. If the server is running on your own computer, replace "localhost" with the actual machine name of your computer. Once you connect to the server, you'll be presented with the client/server Welcome dialog box, which differs slightly from the stand-alone Welcome dialog box.

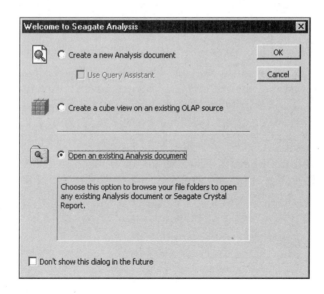

Starting the Web Browser Client

You may prefer to distribute Seagate Analysis over your intranet using a Web browser. This can simplify distribution by eliminating the need to run a setup program on each individual user workstation where you want to run Analysis. To do this, install the Seagate Analysis Server software on a Web browser (see Appendix A for more information on installing Seagate Analysis). Then, users can simply point their browsers to the Web server to install and run Seagate Analysis.

Start your browser and enter the URL:

```
http://<Analysis Server name>/ssquery
```

where <Analysis Server name> is the name of the particular Web server with the Seagate Analysis Server installed on it. The Web browser will indicate that Seagate Analysis is being launched.

When you first point to the Analysis Server from your Web browser, the Analysis Server will check to see if a current version of the Analysis Client software is installed on your computer. If not, you'll be prompted to install the client software. When you choose Yes, a setup program will be downloaded to your computer, and depending on your browser, you'll be given the choice to save the setup program to a disk file, or to just run it right away. If your only choice is to save the file, choose the folder where you'd like to place the QCLIENTUPGRADEALL.EXE setup program. Then, close your browser and use Windows Explorer to double-click on this program to run the Analysis Client setup. You can then restart your browser and type in the same URL as before to start Analysis.

If your browser gives you the choice, it's easier to run the installation program immediately. If you so choose, you'll be presented with a security warning dialog box, indicating that the setup program is "digitally signed" by Seagate software. Thereafter, the setup program behaves the same as it does when running directly from Windows. Simply respond to the few prompts that appear. When installation is complete, you'll be prompted to restart your browser. Close the browser, reopen it, and type in the same URL you used before.

Tip *Once you've installed the Seagate Analysis client, you can later remove the application by using Add/Remove Programs from the Control Panel.*

When you point your browser to the Analysis Server URL after installing the Analysis client, Seagate Analysis will start in client/server mode, automatically connecting to the Analysis server on the Web server you've pointed to. You'll receive a Welcome dialog box giving you several initial options for opening existing queries or creating new queries.

Opening an Existing Query, Report, or Cube

To open an existing query, report, or cube, select the Open an Existing Analysis Document radio button on the Welcome dialog box, and click OK. If you are using stand-alone mode, the Welcome dialog box will also include options to open documents from your Favorites or History list. These options allow you to open a document that you (or Seagate) have added to a list of "favorite" documents, or documents that you've recently opened.

If you've already closed the Welcome dialog box, you can use File I Open from the pull-down menus, or the same Open Folder toolbar button you use with Crystal Reports. If you are using stand-alone mode, you'll only have one option: to open existing files on your local or network drives and folders. If you are using client/server mode, the File I Open menu option will actually display a submenu allowing the choice of opening a local document or a remote document. Choosing the local option will allow you to open documents on drives or folders that are configured on your own PC. If you choose the remote option, an Open dialog box will appear, showing a document directory on the Seagate Analysis Server. In addition, you'll see a Favorite and History tab that lets you choose documents that have been organized in a favorites list or files that have been recently opened. Figure 18-3 shows the Open dialog box in client/server mode.

Seagate Analysis stores queries, reports, and Analysis cubes in the same .RPT file format as Crystal Reports. If there are any .RPT files in the default directory, you'll see them listed in the dialog box. If the desired .RPT file is located in another directory, you can navigate using the Windows Explorer–like path names until you find the file. You can also type the path and filename directly in the File Path text box, if you know it. Once you've selected the right filename, click Open. The query will be opened inside Analysis.

> **Note** *The Preview box will only show report "thumbnails" if you've checked Save Preview Picture in the Summary Info dialog box with a report displayed in the Report tab. Display this dialog box by choosing File I Summary Info from the pull-down menu.*

Whenever you open an Analysis document, there will be three tabs appearing at the bottom of the screen: Query, Report, and Cube. As a general rule, the tab that was last used to change the contents of the overall document will be displayed when the document is opened. If the query was modified, the query tab will be displayed; if a report object was formatted, the report tab will be displayed; and if a cube was modified, the cube tab will be displayed.

> **Note** *Queries, reports, and Analysis cubes are all stored in .RPT files. When you open an .RPT file, all three tabs will appear. If you want to simply open a Cube View on a Microsoft OLAP Services database, you'll need to open a .WDF file instead of an .RPT file. In that case, only the Cube tab will appear inside Analysis.*

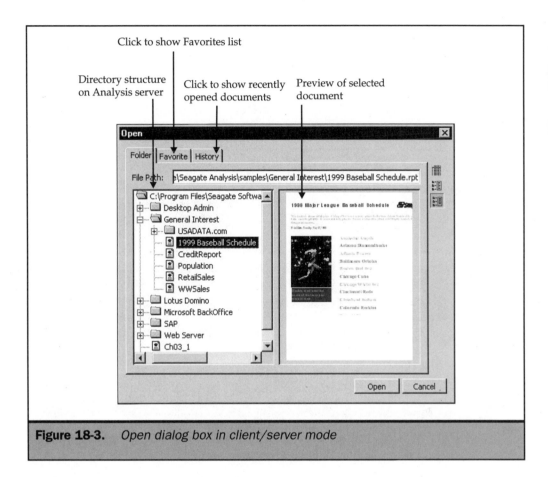

Figure 18-3.   *Open dialog box in client/server mode*

You choose the particular tab you wish to use, depending on what part of the document you want to change:

- **Query tab**   This tab is used to change the actual database data and customized data that is available for use in the document. Click this tab to change the tables, table links, and fields that are available. In addition, any filters (similar to Crystal Reports record selection), groups, and formulas are defined here. The end result in this tab is a row-and-column view of the selected data that can be viewed or copied to Microsoft Excel.

- **Report tab**   This tab is used to format a presentation-quality report, using data chosen and manipulated in the Query tab. You can change formatting, such as font size and color, of individual report fields. You can also add charts and change the overall appearance of the report. Once you've enhanced the report view, you can print the report to a printer or export it to several popular file formats.

■ **Cube tab** This tab is used to organize the data chosen in the Query tab and turn it into a multidimensional OLAP cube that can be analyzed in real time. Once you've created and organized your cube, you can print it on a printer or copy it to Microsoft Excel. Complete information on multidimensional data and OLAP is presented later in this chapter.

Parts of the Query Tab

Figure 18-4 shows Seagate Analysis displaying the Query tab of the Population.RPT sample file.

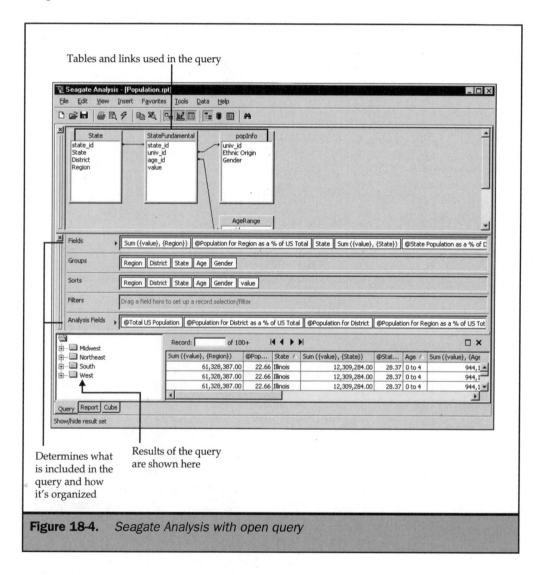

Figure 18-4. *Seagate Analysis with open query*

Seagate Analysis contains standard pull-down menus and a toolbar that you use to perform many query-design functions. You can also right-click almost any object or area of Analysis and choose options from pop-up menus. You make choices and view results in different sections of the Query tab.

The *Tables section* shows the tables that were chosen to be included in the query, as well as how they are linked together. The *Design section* is broken into multiple *panels* that indicate what fields, formulas, or special fields are included in the query, what selection criteria is applied to the query, how the query is sorted and grouped, and whether there are any group selection criteria applied. The *Results section* shows the actual results of the query in a row/column organization. If the query has been designed to group data, a subsection of the Results section called the group tree shows a Windows Explorer–like tree structure of the query groups. This is similar to the group tree in Crystal Reports.

Once a section has been used to create a particular part of the query, you may wish to hide it so that the other sections have more room in the Query tab. This is accomplished by selecting the section from the View pull-down menu, by using a toolbar button, or by right-clicking the desired section and choosing the appropriate option from the pop-up menu. For example, once you've chosen and linked tables for use in the query, you can hide the Table section by choosing View I Tables from the pull-down menus, by clicking the Show/Hide Tables button on the toolbar, or by right-clicking the actual Table section and choosing Hide Tables from the pop-up menu. The Tables section will then be hidden, and the other Query tab sections will fill the Analysis window.

You can use View menu options, toolbar buttons, or right-clicks to hide or display any other section of the Query tab.

Design Section Panels

The Design section is subdivided into several panels. By adding database fields, formulas, and parameter fields to these panels, you determine what the query includes and how it is organized. Seagate Analysis will create a SQL statement to submit to your database server, based on what fields you add to these panels. Of course, one of the main benefits of using Seagate Analysis is that it will create the SQL statement for you automatically; you don't have to know SQL to perform powerful data analysis. Table 18-1 identifies the various panels and their functions.

Viewing the Result Set

Once tables have been chosen and linked, fields have been placed in the proper panels, and selection criteria have been specified, you'll want to view the results of your query. This is accomplished by viewing the *result set*, the set of records returned by the database server when Analysis submits the automatically generated SQL statement. When you first open a query, you'll only see data in the Results section if File I Save with Data was checked on when the document was saved. This data may be old,

Panel	Usage
Fields	Fields placed in this panel will actually be included in the query or report, or will be available to add to the cube. These fields will appear in the Results section of the Query tab. This section creates the SELECT clause of the SQL statement.
Groups	Fields placed in this panel will control any grouping performed on the database server. This will instruct the database server to group records by this field and create any associated subtotal or summary fields by this field. This panel creates the GROUP BY clause of the SQL statement.
Sorts	Fields placed in this panel will control how the query results are sorted. Each field placed here will have an ascending or descending choice available. Also, the order in which the fields appear in this panel determines the levels of sorting for the query. This panel creates the ORDER BY clause of the SQL statement.
Filters	Fields in this panel will control record selection for the query. Each field placed here will have criteria assigned to it that limits records returned from the database. This panel creates the WHERE clause of the SQL statement.
Group Filters	Fields in this panel are used to create group-selection criteria. The only fields that can be placed in this panel are summary or subtotal fields that have already been created in the Fields panel. The Group Filters panel will use these summary or subtotal fields to limit the query to groups that are satisfied by the selection criteria applied to the summary or subtotal fields. This panel creates the HAVING clause of the SQL statement.
Analysis Fields	This panel shows all formula, parameter, and SQL expression fields that have been created for use with the query. If these fields are not also included in some other panel, they will not actually affect the contents of the query. This panel does not affect the SQL statement.

Table 18-1.   *Summary of Design Section Panels*

depending on when the document was saved with the data. To view the result set if there is no saved data, or to update the result set with current information, you need to *refresh* the query, which actually asks the database server to return the results of your query. To do this, choose Data | Refresh from the pull-down menus, or click the Refresh button in the toolbar.

The SQL statement created by Analysis will be submitted to the database server. Depending on the size and organization of the database, the results may be returned in just a few seconds, or it may take several minutes or more. Once the result set is returned by the server, it will be displayed in a row and column format in the Results section at the bottom of the window.

If you want to automatically refresh the result set any time you make changes to the panels, toggle on Data | Auto Refresh from the pull-down menus. This will automatically refresh the result set every time you make a change to a relevant panel. Be careful, though—this can be very tedious and slow with a large database.

An alternative to refreshing your data is previewing it. Previewing is similar to refreshing, but doesn't "hit" the database again. This can be used to display any changes to the query that don't require the database to be queried again, such as hiding a column. Choose View | Preview from the pull-down menus, or click the Preview button in the toolbar.

To view more of the result set than is initially displayed, you can hide the Table panel or any or all design panels.

Limiting Columns Shown in the Results Section

You can limit the fields that appear in the Results section by using the Edit Column Visibility dialog box. Choose Edit | Visible Columns from the pull-down menus. The Edit Column Visibility dialog box appears, as shown in Figure 18-5.

The Fields area shows all the fields that were added to the Fields panel and that are included in the result set by default. The Visible Columns area shows the fields that will actually show up in the result set. If you don't want to see all the fields that were placed in the Fields panel in the actual result set, select the field or fields in the Visible Columns area that you don't want to see, and click the Delete button. They will be removed from the result set when you click OK and refresh the query.

If you later decide that you wish to return a field to the result set that was removed earlier, you can simply drag it from the Fields area to the Visible Columns area. A red line will appear as you drag the mouse back and forth through the Visible Columns area. When the red line appears where you'd like the field to appear in the result set, release the mouse button to drop the field in that location. When you are finished with the Edit Column Visibility dialog box, click OK. You may need to refresh the query if you don't see the change immediately.

Searching for Specific Data

Even though the query may have record selection already chosen in the Filters panel, you might wish to search for just a few fields or a few records quickly. The Seagate Analysis Search Tool contains a complete subquery tool that allows you to search the

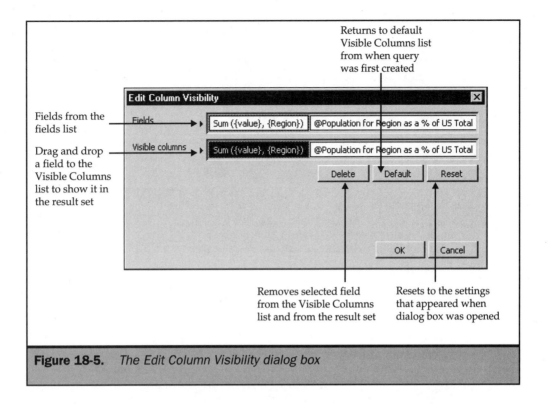

Returns to default Visible Columns list from when query was first created

Fields from the fields list

Drag and drop a field to the Visible Columns list to show it in the result set

Removes selected field from the Visible Columns list and from the result set

Resets to the settings that appeared when dialog box was opened

Figure 18-5. *The Edit Column Visibility dialog box*

existing result set easily and quickly. Choose Tools | Search from the pull-down menus, or click the Search button on the toolbar. The Search Tool appears, as shown in Figure 18-6.

To search your result set, follow these three quick steps:

1. Define your search criteria.

2. Choose the fields to view.

3. View the results of the search.

Define Your Search Criteria

From the list of fields on the Search Criteria tab, select the field you want to use to narrow your search, and drag it to the Expression box. You can then choose the individual search criteria for each field by selecting the field in the Expression box. When you select the field, drop-down lists will appear where you can choose the type of comparison you want to use and the value or values you want to compare to.

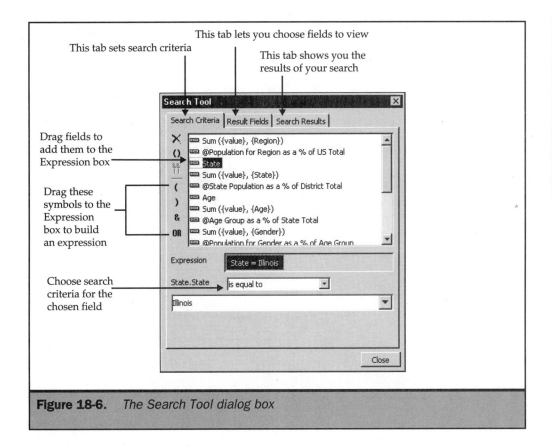

This tab lets you choose fields to view

This tab sets search criteria

This tab shows you the results of your search

Drag fields to add them to the Expression box

Drag these symbols to the Expression box to build an expression

Choose search criteria for the chosen field

Figure 18-6.   *The Search Tool dialog box*

Tip   *Choosing search criteria is very similar to using the Select Expert in Crystal Reports. For more information, refer to Chapter 6.*

If you add more than one field to the Expression box, Analysis will assume you want to use an AND operator to combine the two criteria. If you want to change the AND to an OR, select the AND operator in the Expression box, and click the Toggle AND/OR button on the left side of the search tool. You can also right-click the AND operator in the Expression box and choose Toggle AND/OR from the pop-up menu.

To add parentheses to the expression to force evaluation of certain parts of the expression before other parts, you can drag a left or right parenthesis from the left of the Search Tool to the Expression box. You can also select one or more parts of the expression (select multiple parts by using SHIFT-click or CTRL-click) and click the Enclose with Brackets button to surround the chosen objects with parentheses.

To delete one or more fields or operators from the Expression box, just select one or more items in the Expression box, and then press the DEL key, click the Remove Expression Item(s) button, or right-click the object and choose Remove from the pop-up menu.

Choose Fields to View

Once you've defined your search criteria, click the Result Fields tab. Here, you'll choose the fields you wish to view with this particular search.

You don't have to include all the result set fields. You can choose any combination of them to include in your search. Select one or more fields in the left side of the dialog box, and click the right-arrow button to add them as result fields. If you previously added any result fields that you no longer wish to see, select them on the right side of the dialog box, and click the left-arrow button.

View Results of the Search

Once you've chosen your search criteria and result fields, click the Search Results tab to see the results of your search. The dialog box will show a table-organized set of data that matches the search criteria and result fields you chose in the other two tabs.

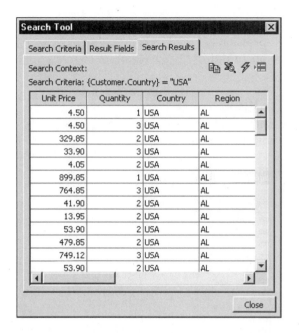

If you're satisfied with your search results, you can simply close the Search Tool with the Close button. You can also use the four toolbar buttons at the top of the Search Results tab to copy the results to the Windows clipboard, copy them to Microsoft Excel, refresh the underlying query and search again, or move to the row in the main result set that matches the row you've selected in the Search Results tab.

If the search doesn't return the data you are looking for, just click either of the other two tabs and respecify search criteria or result fields. Then, when you click the Search Results tab again, a new search will be performed, based on the new criteria.

Creating New Queries

Although Seagate Analysis can be used as a simple data-query tool to show rows and columns of data from your database, it also features the Report and Cube tabs for creating presentation-quality reports and multidimensional cubes. However, even if you eventually are interested in a report or cube, you must always create the underlying query first.

To create a new query, you can use the Welcome screen when you first start Analysis. If you have canceled the Welcome screen, or already have an existing query open, choose File | New from the pull-down menus, or click the New button on the toolbar.

If you made any changes to your existing query, you'll be asked whether you want to save them. Once you make your choice, the existing query will be closed and the Welcome screen will again appear (unlike Crystal Reports, the Seagate Analysis client only allows you to work with one query at a time). To create a new query, choose the Create a New Analysis Document radio button and click OK.

 If you click the Use Query Assistant check box, a separate window will open to guide you through the query-design process. The first few times you create queries from scratch, you may want to use the assistant. Thereafter, you should be familiar enough with the process to be able to perform the steps manually.

When you first start a new query, you'll notice that the different sections of the Query tab are empty and a smaller window appears on top. The smaller *Analysis Explorer* is where you begin all new queries.

Choosing a Data Source with the Analysis Explorer

The first step in creating a new query is choosing the data source for the query. The *data source* is the database or existing query that you want to base your new query on. You can choose from either of the two options on the Data Sources tab of the Analysis Explorer. By expanding the File Directory heading, you'll be able to search for an existing query or report .RPT file to use as the basis for your new query. Any tables contained in the existing query or report can be used in your new query. By expanding the Data Sources heading, you'll be able to choose from ODBC data sources or Seagate's direct database drivers for popular database systems.

 Entries in the Data Sources tab will be different depending on whether you're using Analysis in stand-alone mode or client/server mode. In stand-alone mode, the files and data sources are those defined on your own computer. In client/server mode, the entries are defined on the Analysis Server.

If the database you choose is a secure SQL database, you'll be asked to supply a userid and password to access the database. Once you've supplied a valid userid and password to log on to the database, the Analysis Explorer will expand to show the list of tables that are contained in the database.

Choosing and Linking Tables

In most cases, you'll probably want to choose at least two, and probably more, tables to use in your query. You can add a table to the query by selecting it in the Analysis Explorer and double-clicking it or dragging it to the Table panel (the top box) of the Query tab. If you need to add multiple tables, you can drag and drop them one at a time, or select multiple tables with CTRL-click or SHIFT-click and drag all the selected tables to the Table panel at once. When the table is added, a window containing the table name and all the fields it contains will appear in the Table panel. You can now drag the table windows to different locations or resize them, if necessary.

Once you've added tables, you must link them together on one or more common fields. In addition, you may want to change the default join type, depending on how your database is organized and what records you want included on your report. To link tables, simply choose the field you want to link from in the "from" table, and drag and drop the field onto the field you want to link to in the "to" table. A link line connecting the two tables on the linked fields will be drawn.

There are several options for the link that can be changed by right-clicking the link line and choosing Link Properties from the pop-up menu. You can choose a different join type instead of the default equal join. And, if you're using a PC-based connection object from another .RPT file that you opened, you can choose the order in which multiple table lookups take place. "Parallel" looks up combinations of both files at the same time. "Product" looks up all of one file, and then all of the other. And, "Series" looks up all combinations of the two files. If you add a link by mistake, or later wish to remove the link, select the link line and press the DEL key, or right-click the link and choose Delete from the pop-up menu.

The behavior of the Table panel closely mirrors the Crystal Reports Visual Linking Expert, detailed in Chapter 14. There are a couple of handy differences:

- You can remove a table directly from the Table panel by right-clicking the table and choosing Remove Table from the pop-up menu.

- You can browse all the fields in the table at once by right-clicking the table and choosing Browse Table from the pop-up menu.

Once you've added and linked tables correctly, you may no longer need to see the Table panel in the Query tab. You can hide it by choosing View | Tables from the pull-down menus, by clicking the Show/Hide Tables button, or by right-clicking the Table panel and choosing Hide Tables from the pop-up menu.

Adding Fields to Panels

Once you've chosen and linked tables, you now need to add the fields you want to include in your query to the various design panels. The panel to which you add the field or fields determines whether the fields appear in the query or not, or how the query behaves. The functions of the different panels are discussed earlier in the chapter.

You can use the Table panel (if you haven't hidden it) or the Query Contents tab of the Analysis Explorer to add fields to a panel. To add fields to the Fields panel for inclusion in the query, just double-click a field in either a table window in the Table panel or within a table in the Analysis Explorer. The field will be added to the Fields panel. To add a field to the Filters panel to set up selection criteria, drag and drop the field or fields to the Filters panel. The dialog box for specifying criteria will automatically appear. If you later want to modify the criteria, double-click the field in the Filters panel, or right-click the field and choose Edit from the pop-up menu. Figure 18-7 shows the various panels of the Analysis.

If you mistakenly add fields to a panel you don't want, or add fields in the wrong order, you can easily delete or reorder one or more fields. First, select the field or fields you want to delete or move (using click, CTRL-click, or SHIFT-click). To delete the field or fields, simply press the DEL key, or right-click the selected fields and choose Delete from the pop-up menu. To move the field or fields, just start to drag the fields. You'll notice a small vertical red line that moves throughout the panel as you drag the mouse. This red line indicates where the fields will be placed when you drop them. When you reach the desired location, just release the mouse button to drop the fields in their new location.

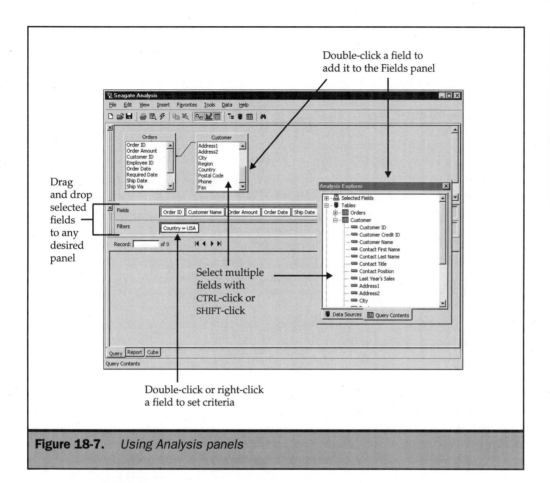

Figure 18-7.   *Using Analysis panels*

Creating Groups and Drilling Down

As with many reports you design, you may want to create groups, subtotals, or summaries for your queries. Seagate Analysis makes this very easy. There are two basic steps involved in creating a meaningful group:

1. Add the field or fields you want to group by to the Groups panel.
2. Choose one or more fields in the Fields panel as summary fields.

Grouping with the Groups Panel

If the Groups panel isn't already displayed, display it by choosing View I Design Panels I Groups Panel from the pull-down menus, or right-click in any of the currently visible design panels and choose Design Panels I Groups Panel from the pop-up menu.

Then, choose the field or fields you want to group the query by, and drag them to the Groups panel. You can choose preexisting fields from the Fields panel, or choose them from the Table panel or Query Contents tab of the Analysis Explorer. Once you've added the fields to the Groups panel, you may wish to set up Custom Groups (similar to Crystal Reports Specified Order grouping, discussed in Chapter 3). Just right-click the field you wish to use for the custom grouping, and choose Change to Specified Order Grouping from the pop-up menu.

You'll notice that the Sorts panel appears automatically when you add fields to the Groups panel. If you wish to change the order in which the groups appear (from ascending to descending order), double-click the field in the Sorts panel that corresponds to the group you wish to change. Then, choose the order in which you want the groups to appear.

If you preview the query after creating one or more groups, you'll see the group tree appear at the left of the Results section. The *group tree* is similar to the group tree in Crystal Reports (see Chapter 3). It shows the hierarchy of the query, with the groups you created appearing in a Windows Explorer–like tree. If you chose to group on more than one field, the outer groups will appear first with plus signs next to them. By clicking the plus signs, you'll be able to move down the hierarchy into lower-level groups. When you actually want to see query fields for a group, click the group itself. This will display the result set for just that particular group.

Click on lowest-level
group to see actual
data for the group

Result set for the
group appears here

Click on
plus sign
to look at
lower-level
groups

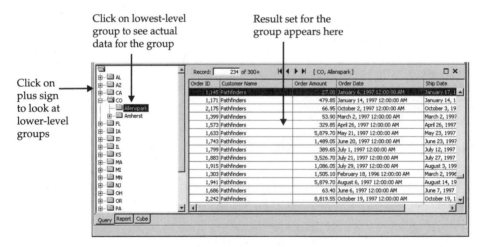

If the Data | Selected Group Only option is checked, only the group you have selected in the group tree will appear in the Results section. If this option is unchecked, the entire result set will appear, and selecting a group in the group tree will only move to the first record of that group in the result set.

Creating Summary Fields

Although grouping your query creates a meaningful hierarchy that may be helpful in your data analysis, it's often necessary to subtotal or summarize a database field for each group. For example, you may want to know what the total sales figure is for each state, or how many orders were placed for each country. This analysis is accomplished by creating subtotal or summary fields for your groups.

Once you've created groups by adding fields to the Groups panel, select the field in the Fields panel that you want to use for a subtotal or summary (if you need to add the field to the Fields panel, drag and drop it from the Table section or Analysis Explorer). Once the field is selected, right-click the field. The pop-up menu will give you two choices related to summarizing: Create Summary Field, and Create Summary Field on All Groups. There is only a subtle difference between the two:

- **Create Summary Field**   Allows you to choose an individual group or all groups that you want to create a summary field for.

- **Create Summary Field on All Groups**   Automatically creates multiple summary fields all at once: a grand summary for the entire query and an individual summary for each group in the query. If the selected field is numeric, the summary will be a total; otherwise it will be a count.

If you choose Create Summary Field, the Create Summary Field dialog box will appear.

Choose the group you want to create the summary for from the drop-down list. All Groups will create the summary field for all individual groups at one time. Grand Total will create a summary for the whole query, but not individual groups. You'll also be given a choice of summary functions that are available, based on the type of field you are summarizing. For example, numeric fields will contain a larger choice of summary functions than string fields. Choose the radio button that indicates the type of summary field you wish to create. Choose the group you want to create the summary for from the drop-down list. When you have made your choices, click OK. If necessary, refresh the query to see the results.

If you don't add the field you grouped on to the Fields panel, you won't see it in the result set next to the summary numbers, although you will be able to deduce what summaries you are seeing by navigating through the group tree. If you'd like to see the actual groups next to the summary numbers, add the field you're grouping on to the Fields panel.

Creating Formulas and SQL Expressions

As in reporting, there will be times when the database itself doesn't contain all the necessary data you need for your analysis, or it doesn't contain it in the desired form. In these situations, you can create formulas or SQL expressions to include in the query. *Formulas* make use of the Crystal Reports formula language used in Crystal Reports. They are very flexible and offer a wide variety of built-in capabilities. However, because they use functionality that isn't part of SQL, they are not processed or created on the database server. The Seagate Analysis tool itself must create these formula fields.

SQL expressions, however, are based on SQL. Depending on the database server that the Analysis Server is attached to, you may see different functions available when you create a SQL expression. These expressions are processed by the database server before they are sent to Analysis.

Creating Formulas and SQL Expressions

To create a new formula, choose Insert | Formula from the pull-down menus, or right-click in the Analysis Explorer's Query Contents tab and choose Insert | Formula from the pop-up menu. The New Name dialog box appears.

First, type in a unique name for the formula in the Name text box. If you want to create a formula that will be processed by Analysis locally, leave the Perform on Server check box blank. If you want to create a SQL expression that will be performed on the database server, check this box. Then, click OK to display the Formula Editor, as shown in Figure 18-8.

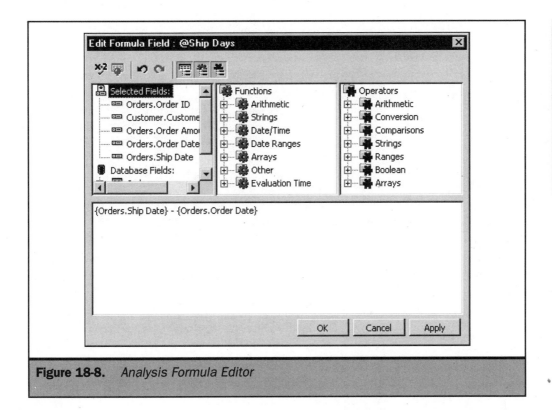

Figure 18-8. *Analysis Formula Editor*

If you are familiar with the Crystal Reports formula language or your particular database's version of SQL, you can just type the formula in the formula text box at the bottom of the editor. However, to help you build your formula with correct syntax, you may want to use the "trees" at the top of the editor (three trees if you're creating a formula, two if you're creating a SQL expression). If you double-click an object in the trees, it will be placed in the formula for you with correct syntax and punctuation. Use the toolbar buttons to check the formula for correct syntax, to browse field data, to undo or redo editing, or to show or hide individual object trees.

The Analysis formula editor differs slightly from the Crystal Reports formula editor. In particular, there aren't as many buttons available in the toolbar. Also, when you encounter a syntax error with a formula, you'll find the error messages to be less descriptive, and the cursor won't automatically appear at the location of the error. This requires a little more "sleuthing" on your part when an error occurs. Once you are satisfied with the formula, and it has passed syntax muster, click OK to save the formula or expression.

Creating formulas and SQL expressions in Seagate Analysis is almost identical to creating them in Crystal Reports. See Chapters 5 and 14 for more details.

Once you've created a formula or SQL expression field, the Analysis Fields panel will appear automatically with the fields in it. You'll also notice the fields appearing in their appropriate categories in the Query Contents tab of the Analysis Explorer. Simply double-click a single field in the Analysis Explorer to add it to the Fields panel. You can also select one or more formulas or SQL expressions in either the Analysis Fields panel or the Analysis Explorer, and drag and drop them to the desired panel.

To edit an existing formula or SQL expression, just double-click it in the Analysis Fields panel, or right-click it in the Analysis Explorer and choose Edit Field from the pop-up menu. To remove the field, select it in either the Analysis Fields panel or the Analysis Explorer and press the DEL key, or right-click it and choose Delete from the pop-up menu.

Make sure you really want to delete a formula or SQL expression field before you do so. You cannot undo a delete function. You may want to save the query before you delete an item, in case you want to retrieve the query with the item still in it.

Using Parameter Fields

It can be time consuming to change the Filters panel repeatedly when performing certain analyses. To minimize this effort, you may want to use a parameter field. A *parameter field* is a special field that will prompt you every time you refresh your query. Whatever response you give to the parameter field can then be substituted in the Filters panel or in a formula field. That way, you can base the record selection in the Filters panel on a parameter field and by just supplying different responses to the parameter prompt, easily retrieve a different set of records every time.

To create a parameter field, choose Insert | Parameter from the pull-down menus, or right-click the Analysis Explorer's Query Contents tab and choose Insert | Parameter from the pop-up menu. The Parameter Field dialog box appears, as illustrated in Figure 18-9.

First, type a unique name for the parameter field in the Parameter Name text box at the top of the dialog box. Then, from the Field Type drop-down list, choose the type of data the parameter field will contain. This should be the same data type as the database field you will be comparing to the parameter field in the Filters panel. If you only want the viewer to be able to enter or choose one value for the parameter field, make sure the Multiple Values check box is not checked. If you check Multiple Values, the viewer will be able to type or select more than one value for the parameter field. This will be handy if you want the viewer to be able to choose more than one state, or country, and so on, for their selection criteria.

You can supply default values that a viewer can select from a drop-down list when they are prompted for the parameter field values. Just type the values, one at a time, in

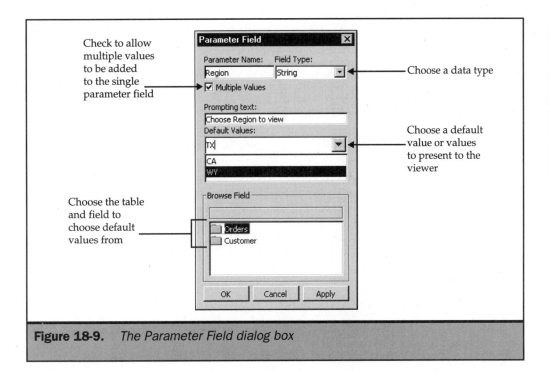

Check to allow
multiple values
to be added
to the single
parameter field

Choose a data type

Choose a default
value or values
to present to the
viewer

Choose the table
and field to
choose default
values from

Figure 18-9.   *The Parameter Field dialog box*

the Default Values drop-down box, pressing ENTER after each. The default values will
be added to the default value list below the drop-down list. If you want to delete a
value that you've already entered, just select it in the list and press DEL. If you'd like to
choose default values to add to the list from a database table and field, choose the table
and field from the Browse Field section of the dialog box. Then, when you expand the
Default Values drop-down list, you'll see sample data from the database that you can
choose for default values.

Caution   *Although it might be a nice feature for a future release of Seagate Analysis, the table and
field you choose will not automatically populate the parameter field when the viewer is
prompted for a value. The field is merely available for you to add default values when
you are initially creating the parameter field.*

Once you've finished creating your parameter field, click OK. The parameter field
will be added to the Analysis Fields panel, as well as to the correct category of the
Query Contents tab of the Analysis Explorer. You can now use the parameter field
inside the query just as you would a database field or a fixed value. There are two
ways you'll probably want to make use of parameter fields: in formulas and in the
Filters panel for record selection.

First, you can use a parameter field inside a formula. For example, if you wanted to calculate the total of the order amount, plus a sales tax amount, you could use a parameter field to specify the percentage of sales tax every time the query is run. If a formula had been hard coded to include 8 percent tax, the formula might look like this:

```
{Orders.Order Amount} + {Orders.Order Amount} * .08
```

The problem is, if you would like to run the query on an ad hoc basis and change the tax rate regularly for analysis, you would have to modify the formula every time. By using a parameter field, you can specify a different tax rate every time you refresh the query. By creating a parameter field called Tax Rate (which Analysis will automatically precede with a question mark), you can modify the formula as follows:

```
{Orders.Order Amount} + {Orders.Order Amount} * {?Tax Rate}
```

Now, whenever the query is refreshed, you'll be prompted to enter a number for the Tax Rate field. Analysis will automatically place the value you specified for the parameter field into the formula.

Using parameter fields for record selection in the Filters panel is even more commonplace, and very powerful. After you've added a parameter field, it will appear in the drop-down browse list when you are creating or modifying selection criteria with a field in the Filters panel.

Caution   *Only parameter fields with the same data type as the field you are using in the Filters panel will appear in the drop-down list. For example, if you've created a parameter field called Tax Rate that is numeric, but you are setting up the Filters panel for a string field, {?Tax Rate} won't appear in the drop-down list, because it doesn't match the string field data type.*

By selecting the parameter field, instead of typing in or choosing a literal value, you can force Seagate Analysis to use the contents of the parameter field in record selection. Every time you refresh the query, the parameter field will be prompted for and the results will be passed to the Filters panel. A particularly handy feature that's new to both Crystal Reports 7 and Seagate Analysis is multiple-value parameter fields. If you selected the Multiple Value check box when you created the parameter field, you'll be able to add multiple entries to the parameter field when it's prompted for. Even though you use an Equal To operator in the Filters panel, Analysis will effectively change the operator to One Of and supply all the multiple values you entered when responding to the parameter field prompt.

CRYSTAL REPORTS 7 INTRODUCED

Parameter Field Prompts

Parameter Fields ——— ?Region

?Region

Choose Region to view

WY

CA

TX

OK   Cancel

Tip

Parameter fields in Seagate Analysis don't have some features, such as edit masks and range values, that they do with Crystal Reports. However, you may find the chapter on Crystal Reports' parameter fields helpful. See Chapter 12 for more details.

Saving the Query

Once you've worked with the various panels and special features of Seagate Analysis and viewed the desired result set, you'll probably want to save the query so it can be reused in the future. There are several File menu options and a toolbar button to accomplish this. You can choose File | Save or File | Save As from the pull-down menus. The only difference is that Save As will always ask you to specify a filename, whereas Save will only ask for a filename the first time a new query is saved. Subsequent Save operations will use the same filename, overwriting any older version that may already exist. Save is also available from the toolbar.

There is also a difference in save options depending on whether you're running Analysis in stand-alone mode or client/server mode. In stand-alone mode, you'll be able to save your query to a local or network drive and folder. Simply navigate to the folder you want to save the query in, type the filename, and click Save.

In client/server mode, you'll have two options: Save Local and Save Remote. Save Local will enable you to save your query to a local or network drive and folder. Save Remote will display a directory tree on the Analysis Server. Navigate through the directory tree to find the directory on the Analysis Server where you want to save the query. Type a filename for the query in the Title text box. This will be used as the filename, with Analysis adding the .RPT extension automatically. Then, click Save As to save the query on the server.

Creating Simple Reports

In addition to viewing results from your queries as rows and columns of data in the Query tab, you'll notice a Report tab at the bottom of Seagate Analysis. With this tab, you can create simple reports that are more visually pleasing than rows and columns of data. Although the report-creation functions of Seagate Analysis are very limited when compared to the full Crystal Reports package, you can create simple presentation-quality reports right in Analysis to be printed or exported to several popular file formats. And, you can open any .RPT files created in Crystal Reports with Analysis, allowing many users to view more sophisticated reports without each having their own copy of Crystal Reports.

The very first point to consider if you want to create a report with Seagate Analysis is that it uses data from the Query tab as the source for its report—you won't have much luck if you try to start creating a report without first creating a query.

The Report Tab

Once you have created the query and viewed the result set, click the Report tab at the bottom of the Analysis window. You can also choose View | Report from the pull-down menus. Seagate Analysis will show a basic representation of the query data in the Report Preview tab, as illustrated in Figure 18-10.

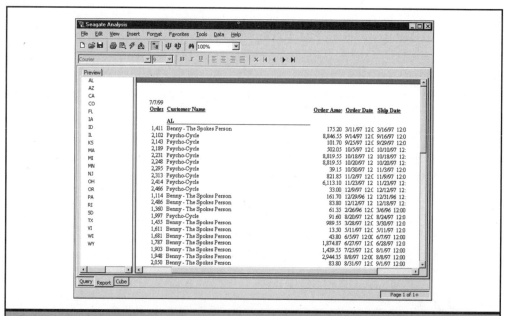

Figure 18-10. *Seagate Analysis Report tab*

Report Styles

When you first click the Report tab, the report you see will be very plain—there won't be any special formatting, color changes, graphic elements, or special fonts. Although you can format individual fields and sections of the report, Seagate Analysis includes several built-in report styles that you can choose from. A *report style* is a set of predefined formatting that is applied to the report. In particular, report styles set predefined colors and layouts for group sections of the report.

To apply a report style, choose Format | Report Styles from the pull-down menus. A choice of available styles will appear. Although the formatting each style applies is fairly self-explanatory, you may want to experiment with different styles to see what effect each has on your report. For example, the Shading style will apply drop shadows, boxes, and shading to certain report elements:

7/7/99				
Order] Customer Name		**Order Amount**	**Order Date**	**Ship Date**
AL				
	Huntsville			
1,411	Benny - The Spokes Person	175.20	3/11/97 12:00:[	3/16/97 12:00:[
2,102	Psycho-Cycle	8,846.55	9/14/97 12:00:[	9/16/97 12:00:[
2,143	Psycho-Cycle	101.70	9/25/97 12:00:[	9/29/97 12:00:[
2,189	Psycho-Cycle	502.05	10/5/97 12:00:[	10/10/97 12:00
2,231	Psycho-Cycle	8,819.55	10/18/97 12:00	10/18/97 12:00
2,248	Psycho-Cycle	8,819.55	10/20/97 12:00	10/20/97 12:00
2,295	Psycho-Cycle	39.15	10/30/97 12:00	11/3/97 12:00:[
2,313	Psycho-Cycle	821.85	11/2/97 12:00:[	11/9/97 12:00:[
2,414	Psycho-Cycle	6,113.10	11/23/97 12:00	11/23/97 12:00
2,466	Psycho-Cycle	33.00	12/9/97 12:00:[	12/12/97 12:00

By choosing one of the built-in styles, you can apply quick formatting to add impact to your report without any individual formatting requirements. If you wish to further format individual elements of the report, you are not prevented from doing so by using one of the built-in styles.

Report styles in Analysis are very similar to the report styles that are available in the Crystal Reports experts. And, as with Crystal Reports, you are limited to the available built-in styles. You cannot modify the existing styles or create your own.

Using the Group Tree and Drilling Down

The report will be displayed with any grouping hierarchy that you may have set up in the Query tab before showing the report. The left side of the Report tab will show a group tree, similar to that displayed on the Query tab. If you would rather see more of the actual report and not use the group tree, you can turn it off by toggling the Show/Hide the Group Tree button. Figure 18-11 shows a report with the group tree expanded.

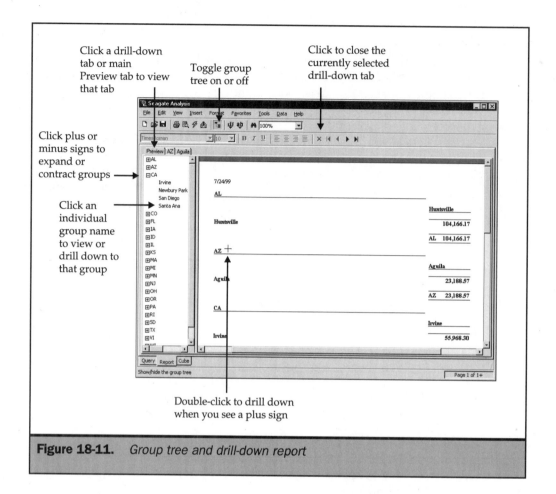

Click a drill-down tab or main Preview tab to view that tab

Toggle group tree on or off

Click to close the currently selected drill-down tab

Click plus or minus signs to expand or contract groups

Click an individual group name to view or drill down to that group

Double-click to drill down when you see a plus sign

Figure 18-11. *Group tree and drill-down report*

If you do leave the group tree turned on, you can use it to navigate through various parts of the report, just as you can with the group tree in the Query tab. Clicking the plus signs will navigate into the group hierarchy of the report. And, if you click directly on a group name, the report will display that group directly.

If the Data | Selected Group Only option was chosen in the Query tab, the report will automatically be designed to allow drill-down, and you'll notice a magnifying glass icon next to a group name in the group tree. When you click the group name, a *drill-down tab* will be created, showing just the detail data for that particular group. You can also drill down in the report by pointing the mouse cursor at any group names or summary fields that appear in the report. If drill-down is enabled, you'll see the mouse cursor change from an arrow to a plus sign. When you double-click with a plus-sign cursor showing, the group you were pointing to will open in its own drill-down tab.

You can navigate among the drill-down tabs and the main report Preview tab by just clicking the tabs. If you want to close a drill-down tab, click the tab you no longer want to see. Then, click the × button in the report toolbar to close the drill-down tab and display the tab just to the left of it. You can't close the main Preview tab—the × will be dimmed when the Preview tab is chosen.

Changing the Appearance of Individual Objects

Even if you use one of the built-in report styles to format the report, you may wish to format individual objects that make up the report. Perhaps a particular field needs to stand out from the rest. Or, maybe you want to change the font from Times Roman to Arial on other parts of the report. Also, the default location of the object may not be appropriate. Seagate Analysis may have actually placed objects so that one is printing right over the top of another. You can move, resize, and change the color or formatting of individual objects in the Report tab, much as you can with the Crystal Report Designer.

Moving and Sizing Objects

If you need to move or resize an object, the technique is similar to that used in Crystal Reports (see Chapter 1 for basic formatting and object-placement information). Begin by selecting the field or object that you wish to move or resize. Analysis will surround the object with an outline containing three small boxes or *sizing handles*. You'll also notice an outline around the entire report section that the object is placed in.

Once you have selected the object, you can move it to an alternative location by holding down the mouse button and dragging the object to another place on the report. As you drag, you'll see a crosshair-like display that indicates where the object will be placed when you release the mouse button. Once you've placed the object in the desired location, release the mouse button to drop the object.

If you wish to resize an object to be taller, shorter, wider, or narrower, use a similar technique. Select the object to be resized. Then, point the mouse cursor to one of the three sizing handles (small blocks) on the sides or bottom of the object. When you've properly placed the mouse cursor on a sizing handle, you'll see the cursor change to a two-way arrow. This *sizing cursor* indicates that when you hold down the mouse button and drag, you will be resizing the object, rather than moving it. Resize the object to the desired dimensions, and then release the mouse button.

Benny - The Spokes Person   ◄─►

Formatting Objects

You can also change the font or color of an object, add borders to the object, or set specific formatting options based on the data type of the object. Again, the first step is selecting the object by clicking on it. You then have several options for formatting. You can select items in the formatting toolbar, right below the standard toolbar. Here you can change font face and size, alignment, and whether the object is bold, italicized, or underlined.

Similar formatting options, plus additional options, are also available from the Format Editor. Display this dialog box by selecting the object you wish to format. Then, right-click and choose either Format Field, Change Border, or Change Font from the pop-up menu. You can also choose similar options from the Format pull-down menu after selecting the object. In all cases, the Format Editor dialog box appears. Depending on the object's data type (date, number, string), different tabs will appear in the Format Editor.

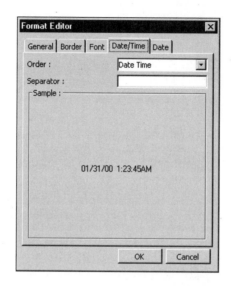

Here, you can choose a limited set of formatting options, such as alignment, fonts, borders, drop shadows, as well as formatting options specific to date and numeric data types. These objects generally follow the same options in Crystal Reports, although there is a much smaller number of formatting options available in Analysis.

Caution *You can also choose Delete from the pop-up menu when right-clicking a report object. If you delete an object, and respond Yes to the confirm prompt, the object will be removed from the report and cannot be placed back on the report again. This may also expose a bug back on the Query tab—you'll receive an error message if you try to remove and then re-add that field in the Fields panel.*

One unique formatting feature in Seagate Analysis is the Color Chooser. You can change the color of an object by selecting predefined colors from the drop-down list in the Font tab. Or, you can click the ellipsis button to display the Color Chooser.

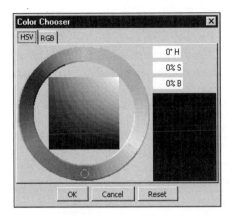

You can use the HSV or RGB tabs to specify an exact color value. You can either drag the small pointers in the HSV tab to select a color, or use the Red, Green, and Blue sliders in the RGB tab to select a color. A sample of the chosen color will appear in the dialog box. When you've chosen your desired color, click OK. The word "Custom" will appear in the color drop-down list. When you click OK to close the Format Editor dialog box, the custom color will be applied to the object.

Formatting Sections

When you create a report in the Report tab, Analysis actually creates several report sections in which to place different report objects. This is particularly true if your query contains one or more levels of grouping (Chapter 8 discusses different report sections and their functions in more detail). You may wish to hide certain report sections so that you don't see repetitive information. Or, you may wish to have every group start on its own page. These types of formatting options are available from pop-up menus in the Report tab.

Select the section of the report you wish to format by clicking anywhere in the section. Even if you don't select an individual object inside the section, you'll still know the section is selected by the outline that surrounds it. Then, right-click. A pop-up menu appears that displays section formatting options. Choose from one of the section formatting options:

- **Hide Section**   Causes the currently selected section to disappear. This may be helpful if you are seeing group information repeated twice for each group.

- **Show All Sections**   Shows every section on the report. This may give undesirable results if you have created a report with several groups. However, it is a way of showing everything at once.

- **Format Section**   Displays the Section Expert dialog box. Here, you can choose from several section formatting options, based on your particular needs. You can also display the Section Expert by selecting Format I Section from the pull-down menus.

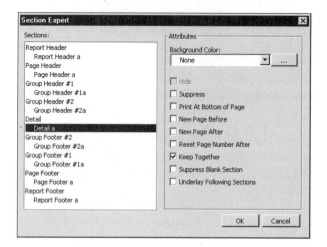

 Note   *You won't find all the features and flexibility of the whole Crystal Reports product when you try to format objects or sections in Seagate Analysis. If you find that you can't achieve the formatting or object placement that you need, save the report .RPT file. Then, start the regular Crystal Reports package, open the .RPT file you just saved, and make the changes with Crystal Reports. If you are using Analysis in client/server mode, you'll need to have sufficient permissions on the Analysis Server to edit the .RPT file there.*

Creating Charts

Seagate Analysis contains a complete charting option to create colorful bar, pie, and line charts, as well as other types of meaningful charts and graphs. These charts and graphs can depict data in the Report tab in a visually appealing manner anywhere on your report.

To create a new chart, click the Insert Chart button on the standard toolbar or choose Insert | Chart from the pull-down menus. The Chart Expert dialog box will appear, as shown in Figure 18-12.

After choosing options for your chart, click OK to close the Chart Expert and place the chart on the report. It will appear in the report section you chose (Group or Report Header or Footer), containing the graphical information you indicated.

You can select the chart, as you can other report objects, by clicking it. You'll notice an outline with sizing handles. Drag the chart object to move it to a different position on the report. Point to the sizing handles and look for a sizing cursor. You can then resize the chart to the desired size. You can delete or modify the chart in the Chart Expert by selecting the chart, right-clicking, and choosing Delete or Format Chart from the pop-up menu. You can also format the chart by selecting it and choosing Format | Chart from the pull-down menus.

Click tabs to
show different
main parts of the
Chart Expert

Choose the
particular subtype
of chart to use

Choose the
main type of
chart to use

Choose chart
options

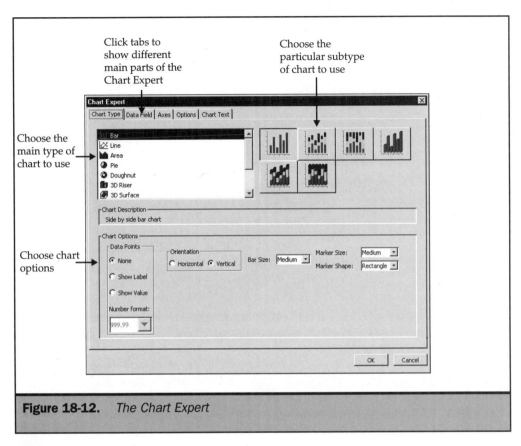

Figure 18-12.   *The Chart Expert*

    The Seagate Analysis Chart Expert is very similar to that used in Crystal Reports. Detailed information about chart types, Chart Expert options, and charting techniques can be found in Chapter 10.

Output Choices

Not only can the Report tab display your query in a more pleasing form, but it also allows you to print the results of the report to your locally attached printer. Or, if you want to share the report with another viewer who doesn't have access to Seagate Analysis, you can export the report to a separate Crystal Reports/Seagate Analysis .RPT file, a Word .DOC document, an Excel .XLS spreadsheet, or a Rich Text format .RTF file.

Printing the Report

    Printing the report is as simple as clicking the Print button in the standard toolbar or choosing File | Print from the pull-down menus.

This will display the standard Print Options dialog box, where you can select the particular printer and number of copies, as well as other printing options. When you click OK, the report will print on the printer.

Exporting to Other Formats

To export the report to another file format, click the Export button in the toolbar, or choose File | Export from the pull-down menus. The Export dialog box appears.

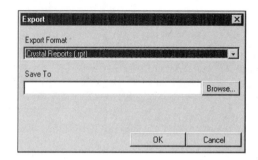

Choose the type of file you wish to export by selecting an option from the Export Format drop-down list. Then, either type a path and filename directly in the Save To text box, or click the Browse button to navigate to the desired directory and choose an existing filename or type in a new filename. Once you've made these choices, click OK.

The file will be exported to the chosen place in the chosen format on your own computer (*not* the Analysis Server if you are running in client/server mode). You can attach the file to an e-mail message, place it elsewhere on the network, or do whatever else you want with the file.

When you export to different file formats, some of the formatting options you've used in the report may not export in the same fashion, or at all. For example, drop shadows generally don't export to Excel or Word formats. If you are concerned about these formatting issues, perform sample exports during your report-design process to ensure the ultimate output destination displays the data in the desired fashion.

Creating and Analyzing Cubes

When Seagate Software released Seagate Analysis, they combined the capabilities of two previously existing products: Crystal Query and Seagate Worksheet. Crystal Query, which is included with Crystal Reports 7, creates database queries and simple reports. Seagate Worksheet is a viewer application for looking at predesigned OLAP cubes from Microsoft-standard multidimensional databases. Seagate Analysis not only includes the multidimensional viewer capability of Seagate Worksheet, but also the ability to actually design, process, and analyze your own OLAP cubes, as well.

What Is OLAP?

OLAP, which stands for *online analytical processing*, is a leading-edge analysis approach that allows data to be analyzed and viewed in multiple dimensions in real time. However, since it's difficult to effectively visualize more than two dimensions on screen at a time, OLAP analysis still depends on the tried and true "row and column" worksheet for its user presentation. However, OLAP has the unique ability to "slice and dice" data by changing the row or column with a simple drag and drop operation. Because the data can be contained in more than two dimensions, OLAP data is organized in what's called a *cube* (for lack of a better word—there typically are more than three dimensions in any OLAP cube).

Where the visible dimensions intersect (similar to the ubiquitous spreadsheet "cell"), the cube's measures are displayed. A *measure* is the actual numeric data value or values that you need to analyze. These typically would be sales figures, an inventory quantity, population figures, or the cost of goods sold. When a cube is designed, one or more measures are defined to be included in the worksheet cells. These measures are taken from database values stored in your regular relational database. When the cube is actually built, the measures are calculated for every possible combination of dimensions and all the values are saved in the cube data file.

In addition to just showing data in a row and column format, OLAP allows data to be organized in hierarchies. A *hierarchy* is a data organization that groups items in progressive levels of detail. A time hierarchy, for example, might start with Year. Within Year, data would be broken down by calendar Quarter, then by Month, then by Week, and finally by Day. The worksheet will initially just show the highest level of the hierarchy (in this case, Year) with a plus sign next to each year. If you click the plus sign, you *drill down* into the next level of the hierarchy (Quarter), which will also show a plus sign next to each quarter. You can drill down as far as necessary to see the level of detail that will identify the data trend you are looking for.

Whereas standard two-dimensional worksheets force you to analyze data in the prechosen row and column formats, OLAP cubes allow a great deal of flexibility in analyzing data from all different perspectives. A cube might contain product, product type, color, size, country, region, state, sales rep, time, and many other dimensions that can all be used to analyze data from different perspectives. Not only are there many dimensions available, but they can be organized in hierarchies to allow initial high-level analysis and drill-down to lower levels, if necessary. The beauty of OLAP is that this analysis can all be done in real time—when you drag and drop dimensions to see a different slice of data, the worksheet recalculates the measures and displays the new information instantaneously.

For more information on OLAP concepts, look at Chapter 17.

Creating the Cube

The most challenging portion of OLAP analysis is actually designing the cube. This is sometimes particularly difficult for a person who has an ingrained thought process revolving around the two-dimensional row-and-column or field-and-record metaphor of the standard spreadsheet or relational database. Trying to determine which, and even if, database fields are candidates for cube dimensions or measures can be a little tricky at first. Because cubes based on large corporate databases can be so large and take so long to build, it's a very good idea to think carefully about how you want to organize your cubes before you actually begin the design process.

You may find it beneficial to create a small sample of your regular corporate database and experiment with different cubes based on it. That way, you can see just how various combinations of dimensions and measures will behave without waiting for an exorbitant amount of time for each cube to be built. Once you've developed some meaningful cubes on the small database, you can replicate the cube-design process to the larger database, knowing that you'll have good data to analyze at the end of the cube-building process.

Although there is no inherent limitation as to the type of database that a cube can be built from, certain database layouts, or *database schemas*, lend themselves to cube design more than others. Standard relational database layouts that contain master tables, transaction tables, and lookup tables may be useful for certain types of cube design. However, databases that consist of a central *fact table* that contains the numeric data to make up measures, and one or more *dimension tables* that contain the dimension and hierarchy data, are more suitable for cube design. These databases are organized into what's known as a *star schema*. If the dimension tables actually refer to other dimension tables to fully define dimensions or hierarchies, then the database is organized into what's known as a *snowflake schema*. Check with your database administrator to see if the data you want to use for OLAP analysis exists in a star or snowflake schema.

There are three general steps to creating a new cube with Seagate Analysis:

1. Designing the query to populate the cube
2. Defining the cube in the Cube Builder
3. Actually building the cube

Once these three steps have been accomplished, the cube will appear in the Cube tab of Seagate Analysis, where it can be analyzed. When you are satisfied with the design and results of the cube, saving the Analysis .RPT file will save the view and design of the cube for later use.

Designing the Query to Populate the Cube

Design a query using the Analysis Query tab as described earlier in this chapter. Pay particular attention to the fields that you include in the query and the groups that you specify. The Cube Builder will make default use of these fields and groups to make a best guess on how you want your cube designed. In particular, any numeric fields that you place in the Fields panel will be chosen as measures and summed. If you don't add any numeric fields to the Fields panel, the first nonnumeric field will be added as a measure, except the field will be counted instead of summed. And, if you add fields to the Groups panel, they will all be automatically added as dimensions. Any nonnumeric fields in the Fields panel will be available in the Cube Builder, but won't be added as default measures or dimensions.

Date fields are treated specially by the Cube Builder. If you use a date field as a dimension field, the Cube Builder will automatically create a time dimension hierarchy for it. Typically, this dimension will start with year, then quarter, month, week, and day. You'll be able to choose which levels of this hierarchy (or any hierarchy) will actually be visible when you design the cube in the Cube Builder.

Also, if you want your cube to display nondate dimensions with a hierarchy, make sure to include all the related fields in your query (country, state, city, and so on) that can be used in a cube dimension. The way your result set is sorted will also affect the way the cube appears. If you want dimensions sorted in a particular order, make sure you add the necessary fields to the Sorts panel in the order you want the dimensions sorted.

Although you can change the way the Cube Builder makes use of the query result set, you'll save time if you consider the default Cube Builder behavior when designing your query.

Defining the Cube in the Cube Builder

Once you've designed your query (you can preview it if you wish, but it's not necessary), click the Cube tab at the bottom of the Analysis window. If no cube has been built previously, an empty window will appear, but the Cube Builder will automatically be displayed. If a cube already exists, but you want to modify it with the Cube Builder, you can display the Cube Builder by clicking the Cube Builder button in the standard toolbar or by choosing Tools | Cube Builder from the pull-down menus. The Cube Builder is illustrated in Figure 18-13.

As described earlier, the Cube Builder will automatically add certain query fields as measures and dimensions. You are not required to keep these settings, however. If the

Add selected source
field as measure

Add selected source
field as dimension

Fields from
query result
set available
for dimensions
and measures

Hierarchy
levels in
dimension

Build cube and
display worksheet

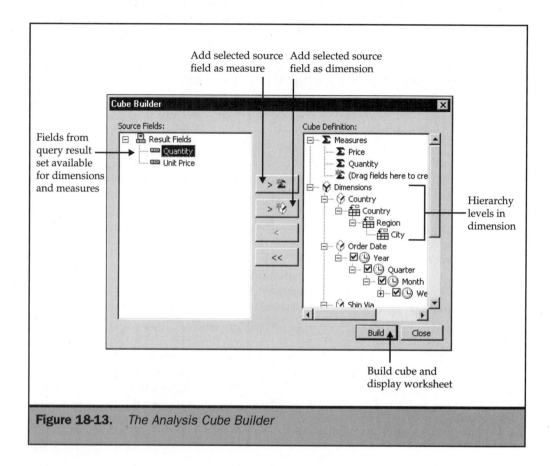

Figure 18-13.   *The Analysis Cube Builder*

fields chosen as measures or dimensions are incorrect, you can select the incorrect fields and click the left arrow to move them back to the Source Fields box. You can then select them there and move them to another part of the Cube Definition box by either dragging and dropping them, or selecting them and clicking the Add New Measure or Add New Dimension buttons.

The field or fields you choose as your cube measures are very important—these will determine what data appears at the cell intersection of your visible row and column dimensions. If you add a numeric field, the Cube Builder will automatically sum the fields. If you add a nonnumeric field, the Cube Builder will automatically count the fields. If you wish to change a sum to a count for a numeric field, select the desired measure in the Cube Definition box and right-click. Choose Edit from the pop-up menu, and the Edit Measure dialog box will appear.

You can change the summary by clicking the appropriate Sum or Count radio buttons. You can also change the name of the measure that will appear on the worksheet. It may also be preferable to change the name—for example, to name the measure "Sales" instead of "Sum of Sales."

After you've added dimensions, you may want to modify the way the Cube Builder creates grand totals, or you may want to create a dimension hierarchy. By default, Seagate Analysis creates a grand total for all fields in the dimension and gives the total the name "All." You may desire to either give the grand total a more meaningful name or eliminate the dimension grand total entirely. Select the dimension you wish to change, and right-click. Choose Edit from the pop-up menu. The Edit Dimension dialog box will appear.

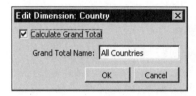

If you don't want to show the dimension grand total, uncheck Calculate Grand Total. If you leave this checked, you can rename the default name for the total by typing a new name in the Grand Total Name text box.

Your initial cube view will be more "high level" if you create meaningful hierarchies for related fields. Rather than having, say, separate country, region, and city dimensions, you may wish to create a hierarchy where country will be a top-level dimension, with region and city falling underneath it. When the worksheet is viewed, the analyst can then drill down on certain countries that are of interest, revealing all the regions within that country. If a certain region is of interest, it can be drilled down on to show cities within it.

To set up the hierarchy, simply add the top-level field as a new dimension by dragging and dropping the field or by selecting it and clicking the Add Dimension button. Then, create the lower levels of the hierarchy by dragging the lower-level fields on top of the *field name* (not the dimension name) of the higher-level field. The Cube Builder will automatically create a lower-level field in the existing dimension. These lower-level fields can be hidden or displayed in the Cube Definition box by clicking the plus or minus signs next to them.

If you create a dimension based on a date field, a time hierarchy will be created automatically—you won't have to take any special steps to create it. The lower levels will be named Year, Quarter, Month, Week, and Day. Each lower level in this time dimension will be indicated with a small clock icon and a check box. If you don't wish to include a certain level of the hierarchy in the cube, uncheck the box.

Building the Cube

Once you've created all your measures, dimensions, and hierarchies, the fun begins! Click the Build button in the Cube Builder dialog box. Analysis will read the database and cross-tabulate the measures for all combinations of dimensions. Be patient—the more dimensions and measures you've created and the larger the database, the longer the process will take. Once it is complete, you'll see the worksheet appear with two default dimensions appearing. You now have many flexible ways of slicing and dicing your cube data.

If you need to modify the measures, dimensions, or hierarchies of the cube (perhaps after changing the underlying query), redisplay the Cube Builder by clicking the toolbar button or by choosing Tools | Cube Builder from the pull-down menus. Make your changes to the cube design and click the Build button to rebuild the cube.

> **Tip**   *You can actually choose from two different OLAP engines to process your cubes. By choosing Tools | Options from the pull-down menus, you'll display the Options dialog box. The Seagate Cube Builder is chosen by default. If you have Microsoft OLAP Services installed somewhere on your network, you can select the Microsoft Pivot Table Service option. If you choose the Microsoft option, there are some differences in the way your cube will be built. Also, you'll need to add the name of the Microsoft OLAP server using OLAP Server Configuration from the Seagate Analysis program group. Consult Analysis online Help for more information.*

Analyzing the Cube

Once the cube has been built, the Cube Builder dialog box will disappear and the cube data will be displayed in the worksheet, as illustrated in Figure 18-14.

You'll notice that two initial dimensions are displayed as rows and columns (typically, the measure or measures you chose will appear as the columns). Any additional dimensions you chose will appear on the worksheet as rows or columns, but will appear at the bottom of the worksheet. You now have many choices for interactively analyzing the data in the worksheet, as described in the following sections.

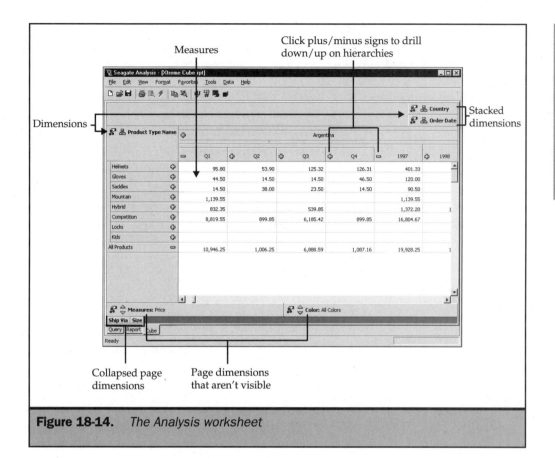

Figure 18-14.   *The Analysis worksheet*

SWAPPING DIMENSIONS   You certainly aren't stuck with the two default
dimensions that are displayed in the row or column of the worksheet. You can simply
swap one dimension with another by performing a quick drag and drop with your
mouse. Point to the dimension that you want to move. You'll notice the mouse cursor
change to a hand symbol. Drag the dimension overtop another dimension (either the
opposite row/column dimension if you want to swap the row and column, or a *page*
dimension at the bottom of the screen) until you see an arrow symbol appear next to
the dimension name. Then, release the mouse button. The dimensions will swap and
the worksheet will recalculate the measures.

PAGE DIMENSIONS   Even though only two dimensions are typically viewed at a
time, additional dimensions can be used to "slice" the data shown by the two visible
dimensions. These *page dimensions* don't actually appear as rows or columns, but
appear at the bottom of the screen. They are used behind the scenes to limit data in the
visible dimensions. If you'd like to see the page dimension as a row or column, you can

simply swap a row or column dimension with a page dimension as described previously. The worksheet immediately recalculates the subtotals for the new row and column organization and moves the previous row or column dimension down to the bottom of the screen as a page dimension.

You can also use the page dimensions to "slice" the data shown in the cube to just a piece of the page dimension. Referring to Figure 18-14, you may be viewing Product Type Name as the row dimension and Country and Order Date as stacked column dimensions. However, if you'd like to see the resulting measures only for a particular color, you can use the Color page dimension to limit what the worksheet is showing. Do this by clicking on the up or down spin arrows that appear on the Color page dimension at the bottom of the screen. Each click will cycle to the next field in the Color dimension—from all to black, then to champagne, and so on. Every time you choose a new color in the page dimension, the measures in the cube will be restricted to just that color.

COLLAPSED PAGES   If your cube contains lots of dimensions and many of them are appearing at the bottom of the screen as page dimensions, you may want to reduce the clutter. You can actually drag a page dimension down below its current location and make it a *collapsed page*. In this situation, its name will only appear at the very bottom of the worksheet, and it won't be available for slicing because its spin buttons won't be visible.

Simply drag the page dimension down to the very bottom of the worksheet (above the tabs). Only the name of the dimension will now appear. If you want to swap a collapsed page, or return it to a regular paged dimension, simply drag and drop the collapsed page out of the bottom area of the worksheet.

If you've sliced a page dimension so the cube is being limited, that limit will remain in effect when you collapse a page dimension. Don't be misled by the numbers—you won't be able to see what limit the dimension is placing on the cube unless you drag the collapsed page back to become a regular paged dimension.

STACKING DIMENSIONS   You aren't limited to viewing just one dimension as a column and one dimension as a row. Even if your row or column dimension contains a hierarchy, you may want to "nest" another dimension below it to further analyze the relationship between the two dimensions. For example, you may want to see Product as the single row dimension. But you would like both Country and Order Date to appear as column dimensions, with Country being the higher-level dimension and Order Date appearing within Country. That way, you can look at country totals, but also see how products were selling within each country by year, quarter, month, or week.

You can set up this nested relationship by *stacking* dimensions. Do this by dragging the page dimension that you want to stack below or above an existing row or column dimension to the row or column. Look carefully at the symbol that appears when you drag the page dimension over the existing row or column dimension. A double-arrow symbol will indicate that the dimensions will be swapped. A single arrow will indicate that the dimension will be stacked. The direction of the arrow will indicate whether the dimension you're dragging will be stacked before or after the current row or column dimension.

DRILLING DOWN AND DRILLING THROUGH   As discussed earlier, you can set up a dimension hierarchy to present a natural progression of data from highest level to lowest level. This hierarchy dimension might show, for example, just countries. You could then look deeper at a certain country to see totals for regions. If a particular region became of interest, you could look at the cities within it, and so on. This is accomplished by *drilling down* on the region hierarchy.

You'll notice plus signs appearing next to members of the hierarchy dimension. Simply clicking a particular plus sign will drill down to the next level of that hierarchy. You'll notice that additional rows or columns will become visible, showing the lower-level information. Then, a minus sign will appear where the plus sign used to be. If you want to drill up to close the lower level, just click the minus sign to hide the lower-level data.

If your cube is based on a Seagate Analysis query (not on a Microsoft OLAP Services cube, as will be discussed later in the chapter), you can *drill through* to see the actual portion of the query result set that's being summarized to create the particular measure you're interested in. Just select the cell of the worksheet that contains the measure you're curious about. Right-click and choose Drill Through from the pop-up menu. You'll see the Drill Through dialog box, as illustrated in Figure 18-15. Notice that the records that are shown in the Search Results tab add up to the summary measure shown on the worksheet.

This dialog box is a derivative of the Search dialog box discussed earlier in the Query section of this chapter. Look for information on "Searching for Specific Data" for available options for this dialog box.

Formatting the Worksheet

By default, the worksheet shows all its cells with black text on a white background. While you can identify trends by simply comparing the numbers to one another, Seagate Analysis offers rich formatting capabilities to highlight numbers that may be of particular interest to you. This is done by formatting cells on the worksheet.

You can change the number format of all or certain cells on the worksheet, modifying the number of decimal places shown, adding plus signs or parentheses to indicate positive or negative numbers, or showing numbers as percentages. You can also change both the foreground and background color of cells.

The first step in changing either the worksheet's number format or cell colors is to select the cells on the worksheet you want the formatting to apply to. You can have the formatting apply to just specific rows and columns that you choose, or to the whole worksheet. To select specific rows or columns, click on the field at the top of the row or

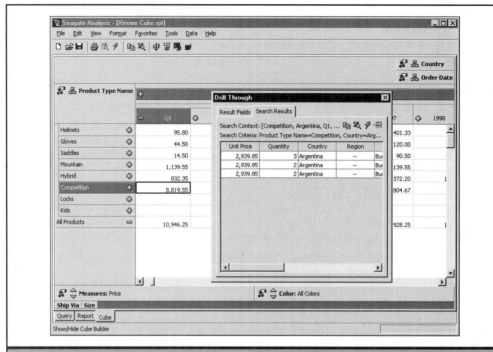

Figure 18-15. *The records shown in the Drill Through dialog box equal the summary measure shown in the worksheet*

left of the column that you want to select. The whole row or column will be highlighted. If you selected a row, selecting a column will highlight it while the row remains highlighted, and vice versa. To select multiple rows or columns, you can drag across them to select more than one, CTRL-click to select more than one row or column, or SHIFT-click to select a range of rows or columns. Selecting an individual cell will actually select both the row and column it intersects. If you wish to deselect any already-selected row or column, just click on it again to deselect it. To have formatting apply to all cells on the worksheet, you actually want to ensure that *nothing* is selected. Make sure you've clicked on any selected rows or columns to deselect them.

Once the rows and columns you want formatted are selected (or none are selected, for the whole worksheet), you can change number formatting by clicking the Number button on the toolbar or choose Format | Number from the pull-down menus. The Number Format dialog box will appear.

Number Format

Number Settings	Samples
☐ Use scientific notation	-0.77
	0.77
☑ Fix decimal places 2	
	-5.56
	5.56
Decimal point character .	
	-784.00
☑ Use thousands separator ,	784.00
☐ Use + for positive numbers	-32,567,201.01
	32,567,201.01
☐ Use () for negative numbers	
☐ Show as percentage	

OK   Cancel

Check the various check boxes and choose other options to customize the number format the values will have in the worksheet. You'll see samples of how the values will look. When you're finished, click OK to display the formatting options in the worksheet.

Once you've selected the rows and columns you want to format, you can also change the foreground and background colors of the cells—either *absolutely* (regardless of the cell contents) or *conditionally* (depending on what the cell value is). To change cell colors, click the Highlighting button in the toolbar or choose Format | Highlighting from the pull-down menus. The Highlighting dialog box will appear, as illustrated in Figure 18-16.

You now have several options for changing the colors of cells. For absolute formatting, simply select the Value Is Anything condition at the bottom of the Highlighting Items list. Then, choose the Number Color and Background Color you want cells to have from the drop-down lists on the right of the dialog box.

If you want to set up conditional formatting, select the built-in Value Is Uninitialized, Value Is Invalid, or Value Is Null conditions, and set colors for those cells (more information on exactly what constitutes these conditions can be found in Analysis online Help). You can also set up your own conditional formatting where you color cells based on criteria you specify. Click New Item at the top of the Highlighting Items list. Then, choose a comparison operator from the Value Is drop-down list, and

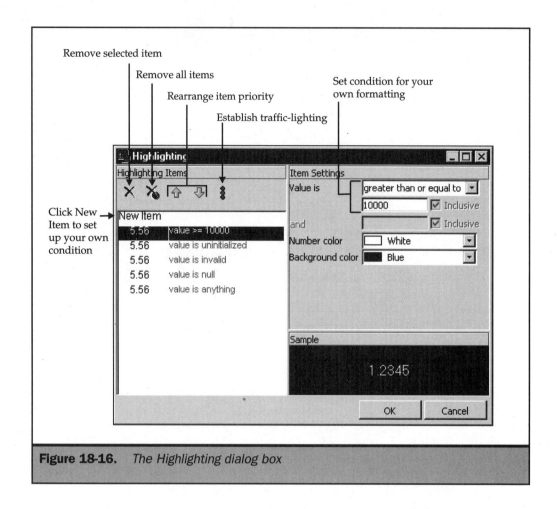

Figure 18-16. The Highlighting dialog box

supply the value or values that you want to compare the cell contents to. Then, set the appropriate background colors.

For example, if you have a $10,000 sales goal and you'd like any values that meet or exceed it to show up in white text on a blue background:

1. Select New Item.

2. Choose Greater Than or Equal To in the Value Is drop-down list.

3. Type 10000 in the value box.

4. Choose White and Blue, respectively, in the Number Color and Background Color drop-down lists.

You'll notice the item now appears at the top of the item list, above the other built-in items. This indicates that it has the highest *priority*. Even if the conditions below it have any colors set, the higher priority item will color the cells. If you'd like to change the priority, choose an item to move up or down in the list and click the up or down arrow button above the list. Once you click OK, the colors will be applied to the worksheet.

2,631.81	22,452.61	7,056.72	32,141.14
769.68	5,447.51	1,715.48	7,932.67
407.28	4,685.66	1,304.27	6,397.21
30,933.93	229,015.38	75,322.08	335,271.39
14,083.02	115,907.38	38,831.22	168,821.62
71,397.69	894,983.75	322,859.45	1,289,240.89
201.19	2,648.32	958.58	3,808.09
4,373.31	22,348.16	7,146.26	33,867.73
124,797.91	1,297,488.77	455,194.06	1,877,480.74

Traffic Lighting

Although you can set several user-defined color conditions to indicate numbers that may be above, below, or in between desired levels, Analysis includes a built-in function to simplify this type of color formatting. Using the *traffic lighting* feature, you can specify high and low values that will then be used to add three user-defined conditions to the Highlighting Items list. Based on these values, cells below the lower threshold will be one color (red by default), cells above the higher threshold will be another color (green by default) and cells in between will be a third color (yellow by default). With the Highlighting dialog box still displayed, click the Traffic Lighting button in the toolbar (the button that looks like a red-yellow-green traffic light). The Traffic Lighting dialog box will appear.

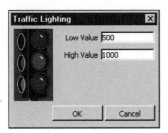

Specify the Low Value and High Value you want to set, and click OK. You'll notice that three new items have been added to the Highlighting Items list with green, yellow, and red colors specified by default. You can now change the colors for the individual items, if the default green, yellow, and red colors aren't appropriate. Also, notice that the traffic lighting colors appear at the top of the list, indicating that they have highest priority. Since every value will fall within their range, any other items you specified earlier (like the white/blue if over $10,000 condition) will be superceded. If you still want to see these conditions, move them higher in the list to take priority over the traffic-lighting items.

Displaying Charts

The flexibility of the worksheet allows you to view data in a wide variety of ways. But, they're still all just numbers. It might be beneficial in certain situations to display worksheet data graphically, say in a pie chart or bar chart. Seagate Analysis not only provides this capability for reports in the Report tab, but also allows you to graph data in the Cube tab.

The first step is choosing the cells you want to use to create the chart. If you want to include all cells in the chart, make sure every row and column is *deselected*, as described earlier in the formatting section. If you only want to include certain rows and columns in the chart, select just the rows and columns you want included. Then, click the Chart button in the toolbar or choose View | Chart from the pull-down menus. The Analysis screen will be reorganized, displaying a chart on the right side of the worksheet and reorganizing the cube on the left side. Figure 18-17 displays this.

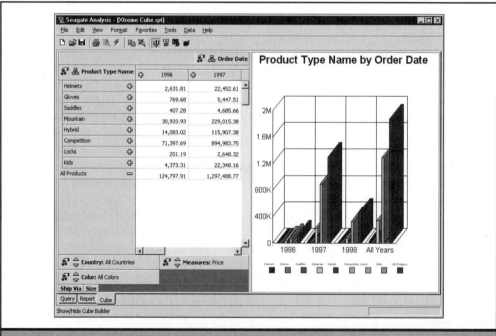

Figure 18-17. *Chart added to the worksheet*

The chart button and View | Chart option are toggles. If you select either of them again, the chart will disappear.

The chart is very interactive. While the chart is displayed, you can select or deselect rows or columns in the worksheet and the chart will be updated to reflect the newly chosen rows and columns immediately.

If you'd like to change the position of the chart, right-click the chart, itself, and choose options from the pop-up menu. You can choose to display the chart at the bottom of the worksheet instead of on the right, in its own free-floating window, or in the data grid. If you choose the data grid, the chart will appear inside the worksheet *in place of* the cells—you won't actually be able to see the numbers that the chart is representing, but you will be able to interactively change the chart by selecting and deselecting rows and columns.

To change the type of chart (from bar to pie, for example) or change other chart behavior, right-click the chart and choose Modify Chart from the pop-up menu. You can also choose Edit | Modify Chart from the pull-down menus. The Modify Chart dialog box will appear, as illustrated in Figure 18-18. Make selections from this dialog box to customize the chart's appearance.

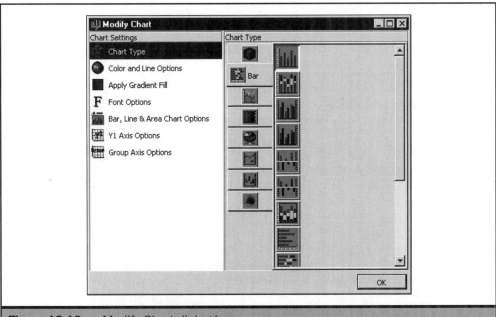

Figure 18-18.   *Modify Chart dialog box*

Saving the Cube

Once you've manipulated the cube in the worksheet, formatted cells, or added and modified a chart, you can save your Analysis document with File | Save or by clicking the Save button in the toolbar. The document will be saved, including the view settings you've made in the Cube tab. The next time you open the document, the Cube tab will be displayed with all the same formatting and settings you previously gave it.

Viewing Microsoft OLAP Services Cubes

Seagate Analysis features its own self-contained cube builder and OLAP engine. With it, you can create your own simple cubes very easily and quickly. However, if your organization is implementing an OLAP solution on a department or enterprise-wide scale, you may need a shared OLAP solution to accommodate many users. Seagate Software offers several enterprise OLAP solutions, including Seagate Info (which includes Seagate Analysis) and Seagate Holos. Other vendors, including Microsoft, also offer OLAP solutions.

While OLAP standards are still "shaking out," one standard that is evolving is that of Microsoft's OLAP Services or *open OLAP*. Microsoft first introduced this standard with SQL Server 7.0, and some other vendors are also complying with this standard. Seagate Analysis offers the ability to view cubes that have been created with Microsoft OLAP Services or another open OLAP database.

There are two general steps to viewing a Microsoft OLAP Services cube:

1. Adding the OLAP Server
2. Creating the Cube View

Adding OLAP Servers

Seagate Analysis is not set up by default to work with any particular Microsoft OLAP Services server—these are specific to your organization. Before you create your first cube view with your server, you need to add the name of the server to the OLAP Servers list that Analysis will refer to. This is accomplished with the OLAP Server Configuration utility that is installed in the Seagate Analysis program group when Analysis is installed. When you select that option, the OLAP Server Configuration dialog box appears, as illustrated in Figure 18-19.

Click the Add button to add a new OLAP server. A network explorer dialog box will appear. Navigate through the dialog box until you find the computer name of the Microsoft OLAP Services computer on your network (ask your network or database administrator if you're unsure of the name for this computer). Select the computer name, and click OK. The computer will be added to the list of OLAP servers. If you want to use the Microsoft OLAP Services computer to build your Seagate Analysis cube instead of using Analysis' own internal OLAP engine, check the appropriate box

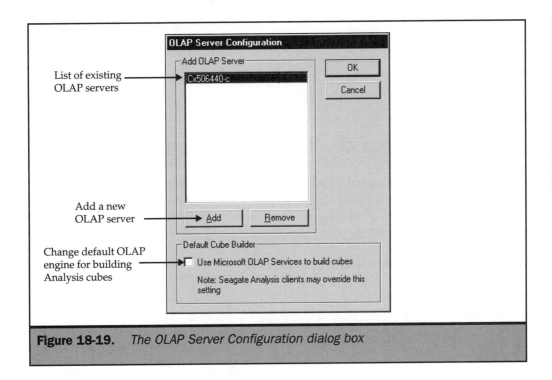

Figure 18-19.   *The OLAP Server Configuration dialog box*

(this option can be overridden in Analysis if you choose). Click OK to save your choices and close the OLAP Server Configuration program. If you were running Analysis when you made this choice, the new OLAP server won't be available to you until you exit and restart Analysis.

If you are using Seagate Analysis in client/server mode via the Web, the proper OLAP server must be added on the Analysis server computer. Run the OLAP Server Configuration utility on that machine to make Microsoft OLAP Services available to everyone who uses Analysis via the Web.

Creating a Cube View

Once you have an OLAP server available, you can create a view of an existing cube on that server with Seagate Analysis. A *cube view* is simply a worksheet view of an existing cube on the OLAP server—you won't be able to use Analysis to build any cubes on the server. The worksheet will behave just as it would if you created the cube yourself. You'll be able to view dimensions, drag and drop dimensions to swap them, format the worksheet, and create charts.

To create a cube view, create a new Analysis document by clicking the New button or choosing File I New from the pull-down menus. If a document is already open, it will be closed before the Welcome screen for the new document appears. Choose the Create a Cube View on an Existing OLAP Source radio button and click OK. The Choose a Data Source dialog box will appear with a list of your predefined OLAP servers in it.

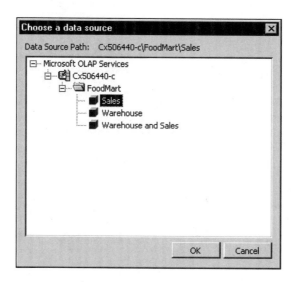

Find the desired OLAP server. Click the plus sign next to the server to see a list of available OLAP databases on the server. Click the plus sign next to the desired database to see a list of cubes defined in that database. Then, select the desired cube, and click OK. Analysis will show the Cube tab only, with the worksheet showing the default view of the cube on the OLAP server.

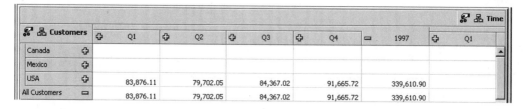

You can now drag and drop dimensions, select rows or columns, format the worksheet cells, or create charts as described earlier in the chapter. If you want to save your cube view for future access, just use the Save button in the toolbar or File I Save to save the document like any other Analysis document.

When you save the Analysis document, you are simply saving the "view" to the cube stored on the OLAP server. There will be no Query or Report tab saved with the document, and the document will be saved with a .WDF extension instead of an .RPT extension.

Exporting the Cube to Excel

Whether you are working with an internal Analysis cube that you designed yourself, or viewing a cube on an OLAP server, you may wish to transfer the cube values on the worksheet to Microsoft Excel for further analysis and manipulation. The Seagate Analysis worksheet makes this very easy for you.

 Simply choose the rows and columns you want to copy to Excel by selecting or deselecting them as described previously in the Formatting the Worksheet section. If you want to copy the entire worksheet to Excel, make sure no rows or columns are selected. Then, click the Copy to Excel button on the toolbar or choose Edit | Copy to Excel from the pull-down menus. Microsoft Excel will start, and the contents of the worksheet will be added to Excel automatically. You can now manipulate the data in Excel and save a separate Excel worksheet for further analysis or manipulation.

The Complete Reference

Chapter 19

Querying SQL Databases with the Crystal SQL Designer

S eagate Crystal Reports is an excellent tool for organizing and manipulating data coming from corporate databases. However, there are times when a tool for quick and simple database queries is needed. If you just want an easy way to look at your database without having to worry about formatting, fonts, and such, you'll want to look at the Crystal SQL Designer.

Its easy "expert" user interface makes querying SQL databases very straightforward. And, if you have several Crystal Reports that will be based on the same set of data, you can save the data returned from your SQL Designer query and base several reports on the saved data.

In versions of Crystal Reports prior to 7, this tool is known as the Crystal Query Designer.

Defining the Crystal SQL Designer

Most popular corporate database systems, such as Microsoft SQL Server, Oracle, Sybase, and Informix, use the common structured query language (SQL) as a means of submitting queries. Once the database server has processed the SQL query, it will return a *result set*, or a set of rows and columns of data, that comprises the results of the SQL query.

Although there are trained database professionals who can effectively submit queries to the database by typing in the "raw" SQL query, there are a vast number of database users who would prefer not to have to learn "SQL as a Second Language" in order to get meaningful data from their database. The Crystal SQL Designer is Seagate Software's original query tool for just such users. By choosing database tables and fields, choosing selection criteria, and supplying sorting requirements with a simple "tabbed" dialog box approach, users will be able to glean data from their corporate databases without having to learn SQL.

With Crystal Reports 7, Seagate has released Crystal Query (and even later, Seagate Analysis), which may prompt you to ask: "What should I use to query the database—Crystal Reports, Seagate Analysis, Crystal Query, or the SQL Designer?" The answer depends largely on how quickly you want to be able to query the database, and whether you need to prepare the results of your query in a fancy formatted presentation.

Crystal SQL Designer Versus Seagate Analysis or Crystal Query

The choice of query tools was complicated a bit with the introduction of the Seagate Analysis query, reporting, and OLAP tool. This new tool is an attempt by Seagate to merge the functions of a direct database-query tool, a simplified report designer, and an OLAP analysis worksheet. Although Seagate Analysis doesn't provide the vast array of reporting capabilities of Crystal Reports, it does largely duplicate (and in many cases, improve) the querying capabilities of the Crystal SQL Designer.

Whether you choose the new Seagate Analysis, Crystal Query, or the original Crystal SQL Designer is mostly a matter of personal choice. There are few technical reasons to choose one over the other, with the possible exception of Crystal Query's requirement that an intermediate query "server" be in place. This is not required with Seagate Analysis or the SQL Designer. However, the absence of this intermediary does add the requirement that the PC on which you run Analysis or SQL Designer have direct connectivity to your corporate database.

Note   *For detailed information on the new Seagate Analysis tool, see Chapter 18.*

Crystal SQL Designer Versus Crystal Reports

It's often asked, "Why bother using the SQL Designer when I can just create a report in Crystal Reports that gets the same data?" While there is some validity to this point, there are definitely times when a simpler query tool without the object-manipulation and formatting capabilities of Crystal Reports is a better choice. The SQL Designer is a good tool for simpler row-and-column data viewing.

Also, you may occasionally have situations where several reports need to access the exact same result set from the database, and you would prefer that each not have to query the database separately. You may create the single query in the SQL Designer, save the result set in the query's .QRY file, and then base the reports on the .QRY file rather than directly on the database.

Creating SQL Queries

The Crystal SQL Designer is a separate program on the Seagate Crystal Reports program group. Choosing this option will launch the SQL Designer, as shown in Figure 19-1.

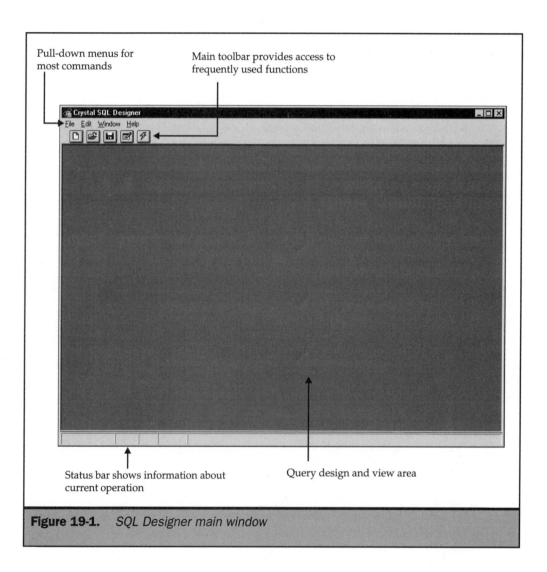

Pull-down menus for most commands

Main toolbar provides access to frequently used functions

Status bar shows information about current operation

Query design and view area

Figure 19-1. *SQL Designer main window*

Begin creating a new query by choosing File | New from the pull-down menus, or click the New button in the toolbar. The New Query dialog box appears, giving you three options: using the Query Expert, entering SQL directly, or starting from an existing query.

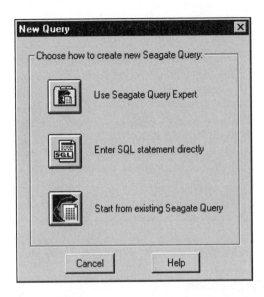

If you are not familiar with SQL, you'll want to choose the first option. The Query Expert leads you step by step through the query-design process. If you are familiar with SQL and just want to enter a SELECT statement directly, click the second button. Or, if you wish to open an existing .QRY file containing an already-created query, click the third button. This will simply open the query in the designer, but not "save" the filename that was used—when you save the query, it will ask for a new filename.

Entering SQL Directly

If you choose the second option from the New Query dialog box, the Log On Server dialog box will appear, allowing you to choose the ODBC data source you wish to use for your query.

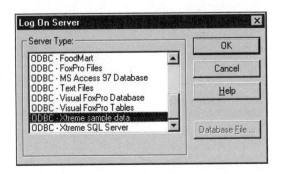

If the database you wish to query is not included in the list of data sources, use the ODBC Administrator application from the Windows Control Panel to add it. If you're unsure of how to set up an ODBC data source, contact your database administrator.

The Crystal SQL Designer only operates with databases via Microsoft's open database connectivity (ODBC) communications standard. If you're not sure whether your database is reachable via ODBC, contact your database administrator.

Once you've chosen the ODBC data source, you'll be prompted to log in to the database (if the database is secure). Depending on the database you chose, you will be required to supply a userid, password, and perhaps other information, such as the name of the database you wish to use. Once you've made these entries, a message will appear indicating that you've successfully logged on to the database. Once you click OK, the Enter SQL Statement dialog box appears, as shown in Figure 19-2.

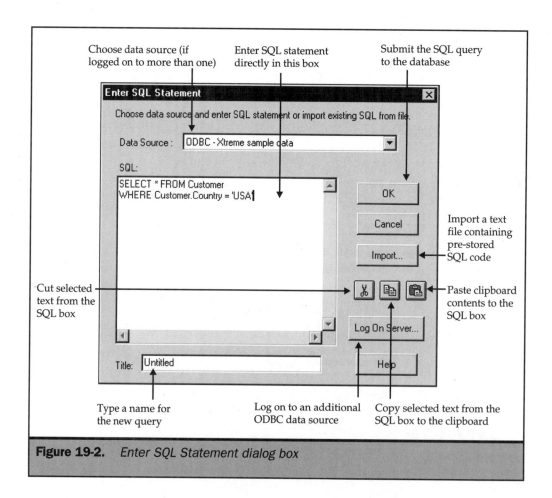

Figure 19-2. *Enter SQL Statement dialog box*

If you prefer to log on to one or more databases before beginning to create a new query, you can choose File | Log On Server from the pull-down menu. This will display the Log On Server dialog box, where you can choose a data source and proceed through the log on process. If you are already logged on to a database when you start a query, the Log On Server dialog box will be skipped, and you'll proceed directly to the next step.

You can now type a SQL statement directly into the SQL box. Use the SQL syntax that is particular to the ODBC data source that appears in the drop-down list at the top of the dialog box. To make your statement more readable, you may press ENTER to go to the next line, or CTRL-TAB to add a tab stop in the current line. If you've created a SQL statement in another tool and saved the query as an ASCII text file, you can import it directly into the SQL box by clicking the Import button.

Once you've either imported or typed the SQL query you want to use, click OK to send the query to the server. You'll be prompted if you want to run the query. If you click Yes, the query will be submitted to the server for processing. If there are any errors in the query, or other ODBC-related problems that prevent the query from running to completion, you'll see an ODBC error message.

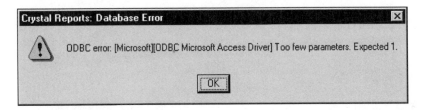

If the query is accepted by the server without any errors, you may have to wait anywhere from a few seconds to many minutes for the server to process the query. While this is happening, you'll simply see an hourglass while you wait. Once the query has completed and the server has returned a result set to the SQL Designer, you'll see the query appear in a simple row and column format for online viewing, as shown in Figure 19-3.

You have very limited options once the result set has been returned—the SQL Designer is a simple query viewer by design. You can only scroll through the query using the vertical and horizontal scroll bars or navigate directly to a certain record by typing a record number into the Record text box. If you wish, you can submit the same query to the server again to see if any data has changed. Just click the Refresh button in the toolbar, press the F5 key, or choose Edit | Refresh Data from the pull-down menus. The query will be resubmitted to the server. If any data has changed, been deleted, or been added since the last time the query was run, you'll see the changes in the result set.

If you want to modify the SQL statement, click the Edit Query button in the toolbar, or choose Edit | Query from the pull-down menus. The Enter SQL Statement dialog box will reappear, where you can make changes to the SQL statement and submit it again.

Using the Expert

Although the SQL Designer may be helpful for SQL-savvy programmers or analysts, its general purpose is to allow casual users who need to query the database to avoid

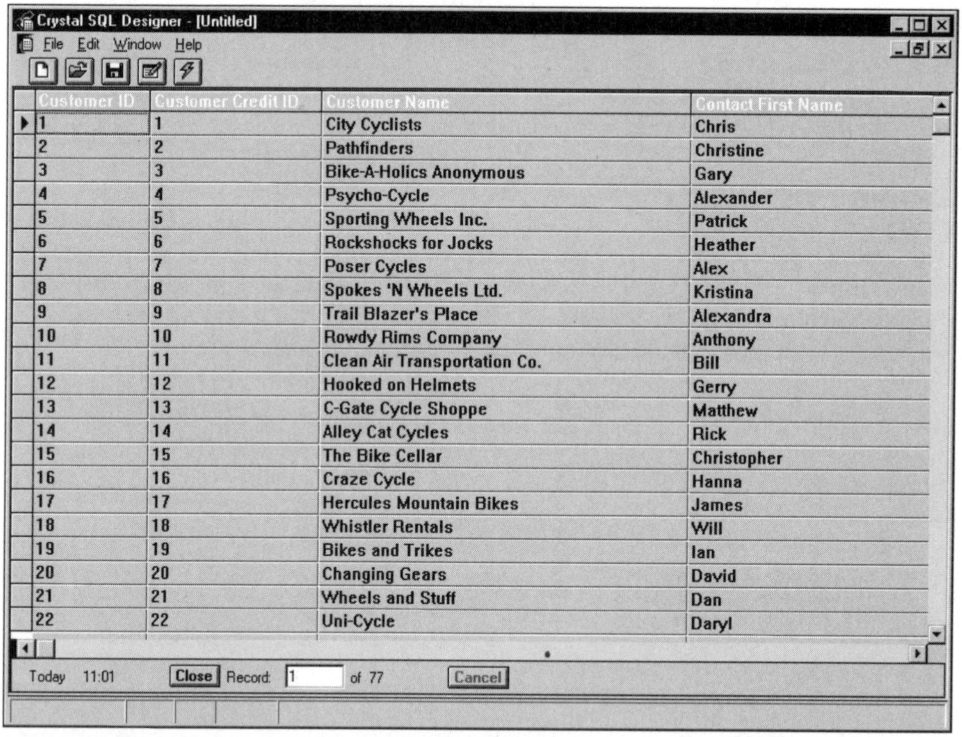

Figure 19-3. *Query results*

the use of SQL. The Crystal SQL Designer features the Query Expert for just such users. Using the expert, a user merely needs to progress through a familiar tabbed interface to create and view a database query.

To use the expert, click the Use Seagate Query Expert button on the New Query dialog box when you first create a new query.

The SQL Query Expert dialog box will appear, with the Tables tab showing.

The Tables Tab

Choose the data source for your query on the Tables tab, shown in Figure 19-4. You have two choices: Dictionary and SQL/ODBC. A dictionary is a predefined group of database fields that have been set up in advance. Using dictionaries makes it easy for a casual user to work with a database without knowing all the intricate details of table and field structure. When you click this button, a file dialog box appears, asking you to specify the dictionary file you want to use for your query. Navigate to the correct dictionary file, and click OK.

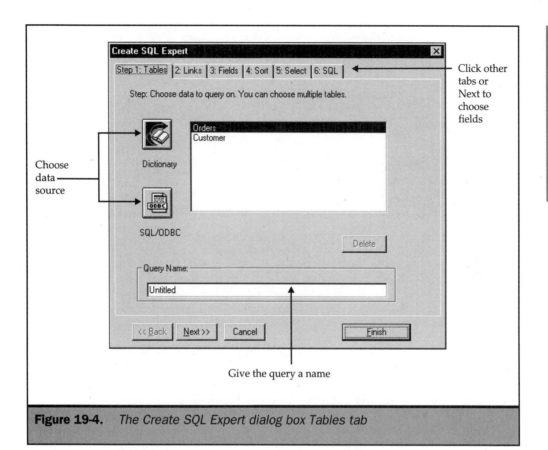

Figure 19-4. *The Create SQL Expert dialog box Tables tab*

> **Note**
>
> *Since the SQL Designer only works with SQL/ODBC databases, the dictionary must refer to this type of database. You'll receive an error message if you open a dictionary that refers to another style of database. The Crystal Dictionaries tool, used to define dictionaries, is discussed in Chapter 20.*

If a dictionary has not been created, and you need to connect directly to the database, click the SQL/ODBC button. If you aren't already logged on to an ODBC database, the Log On Server dialog box will appear.

Choose the database you wish to use for your query. If the database does not appear, you'll need to use the ODBC Administrator in Windows Control Panel to add it. Contact your database administrator if you need assistance. If your database is secure, you'll be prompted to log on to the database with a valid userid and password. Once you've done this, the Choose SQL Table dialog box appears, as shown in Figure 19-5.

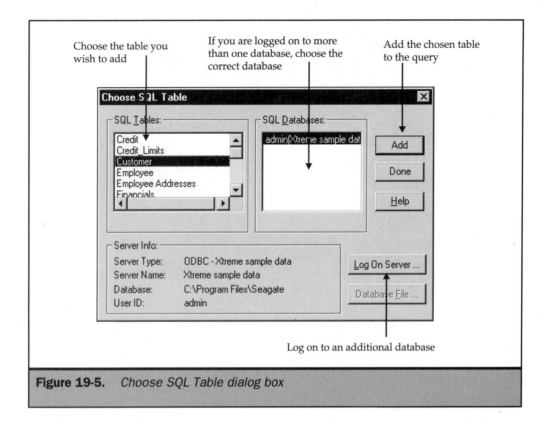

Choose the table you wish to add

If you are logged on to more than one database, choose the correct database

Add the chosen table to the query

Log on to an additional database

Figure 19-5. *Choose SQL Table dialog box*

Choose the tables you wish to use in your query. Since you can only choose one table at a time in the list (CTRL-click and SHIFT-click don't work in this dialog box), you must choose each table individually, by either double-clicking it, or selecting it and clicking the Add button. Once you've finished choosing tables, click Done. If you've chosen more than one table, a new Links tab will appear, as described next.

The Links Tab

If you choose more than one table to include in your query, you must link or join the tables together so they can follow each other properly when returning records. A table *link* must be on a common field. For example, if you want an employee table to follow a payroll table properly in your report, you need to link the two tables on a common field or fields.

Note *The Links tab works almost identically to the Visual Linking Expert in Crystal Reports. This Visual Linking Expert is discussed in detail in Chapter 14.*

You'll notice that the tables you chose are displayed at the top of the Links tab, shown in Figure 19-6. You can drag the windows to a new location, or resize them, if that helps. (The Arrange button will move them for you, but not always the way you want them moved.) Once you've positioned the table windows, you need to choose the common field or fields to link the tables together. To draw a link, simply drag from the "from" field to the "to" field and release the mouse button. A link line will be drawn connecting the two fields. If you need to link tables on several fields, you can drag and drop as many times as necessary.

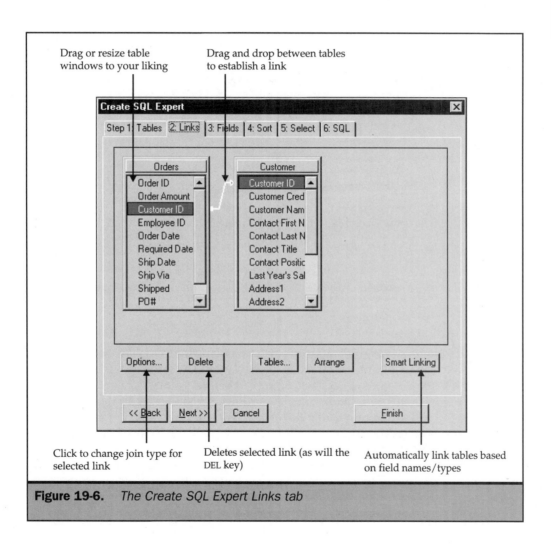

Figure 19-6.   *The Create SQL Expert Links tab*

There is a confusing bug in the SQL Designer. If you try to link to the first field in the "to" table, and you drop the link too high on the field, the link will not "stick." If this happens, simply drag and drop again, this time dropping on the very bottom of the first field in the "to" table.

If you link on fields that may create an unsuccessful link (perhaps they are different data types), you'll receive a warning message. Double-check to ensure that this is in fact the correct link. If so, just ignore the message. If not, draw the correct link. If you need to delete a link, select the link line and click the Delete button or press the DEL key.

The SQL Designer uses an equal join type by default. This may not be the type of join you need for your particular query. To change the join type, select the link you wish to modify. Then, click the Options button or right-click the link and choose Options from the pop-up menu. (Join types are discussed in Chapter 14.)

The default behavior of the SQL Designer is to link tables automatically, using Smart Linking. *Smart Linking* will automatically link fields if their field names and data types are identical. In addition, if the fields are string fields, they both must be the same length. If you deleted links and wish to Smart Link again, or if Smart Linking is turned off, just click the Smart Linking button to automatically link tables in the query.

Smart Linking works correctly only in specific cases. In many situations, you'll spend more time removing incorrect links and adding correct links than you would spend creating the links on your own. You can turn it off by starting Crystal Reports, selecting File | Options, and clearing the Auto-SmartLinking check box on the Database tab. This setting also affects the Crystal SQL Designer.

Once tables have been properly linked, click the Next button or click the Fields tab. You'll now be able to choose the fields to include in your query, as described next.

The Fields Tab

The Fields tab, shown in Figure 19-7, is where you choose the fields you actually want to appear in the query. You'll see all the fields in the tables you chose in the left Database Fields box. You can select one or more fields (using SHIFT-click or CTRL-click to select multiple fields) to add to the query. Add fields to the query by double-clicking them, dragging and dropping them to the Query Fields box, or using the Add or All buttons. If you accidentally add too many fields, select any fields you wish to remove from the Query Fields box and click the Remove button.

If you wish to build a SQL expression to add to your query, click the Expression button. A SQL expression is similar to a formula: you specify a calculation using operators or functions built in to SQL. You'll be asked to give the expression a name. Once you do so, the SQL Expression dialog box will appear, as shown next.

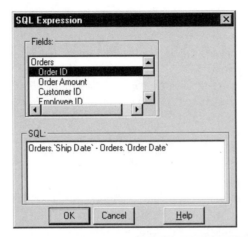

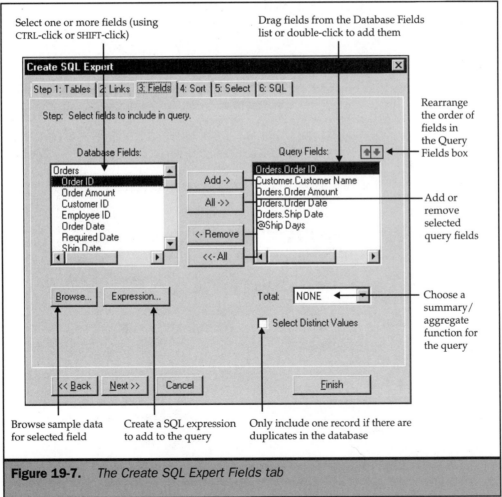

Figure 19-7.   The Create SQL Expert Fields tab

You can double-click on fields in the Fields list to add them to the SQL box (and even then, it may not place proper SQL punctuation around the fields). Other than that, you'll need to manually enter the SQL to make the expression work properly for your database. Once you've created the SQL expression, it will appear (preceded by an @ sign) under the SQL Expressions category in the Database Fields list. You can add it to the Query Fields list like any other database field.

> *You must have some knowledge of SQL and your database server to effectively create SQL expression fields. Check with your database administrator or a colleague who's knowledgeable about SQL if you need help.*

You may want to perform a summary or aggregate calculation, such as a sum or average. In this situation, the database server will create data "groups" (similar to Crystal Reports groups discussed in Chapter 3) and return only one database record for each group. The record will contain the summary or aggregate value for all the records in that group.

Choose the field in the Query Fields box that you want to aggregate, and then choose a function in the Total drop-down list. You'll notice the aggregate function is added to the field in the Query Fields list. Then, limit any other fields in the Query Fields list to those that will create the groups that you want to base your aggregate function on.

For example, if you wanted to see a total of all order amounts for each customer, you would choose the Order Amount field and choose Sum in the Total drop-down list. The only other field you would add to the query would be Customer Name. Even though there may be many records in the database, the server will group the records by customer, returning just one record per customer. Instead of individual order amounts, the server will total the order amounts for each customer and include the sum in the one-customer group record.

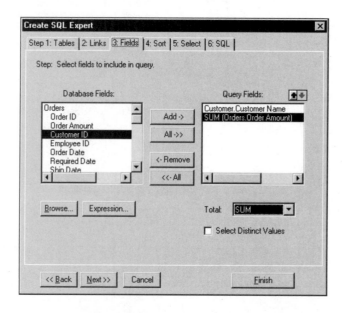

Once you've chosen all the fields, as well as any aggregate functions and SQL expressions you want to include in your query, you needn't specify any more information in the expert if you don't need to. You can click the Finish button to submit the query to the database server and view the results. Figure 19-8 shows the results of a sum aggregate function with Customer chosen as the group field.

If, however, you wish to sort the query in a specific order, or restrict the query to certain records, you'll need to complete either or both the Sort and Select tabs. You can click Next to choose the Sort tab, or click directly on the tab.

The Sort Tab

On the Sort tab, shown in Figure 19-9, you choose the field or fields you want the query sorted by. As with the Fields tab, you can add these selected fields to the Group Fields list by double-clicking, dragging and dropping, or clicking the Add button. Once you've chosen the field or fields you want to sort by, you can choose the order you want the query sorted in by selecting a field in the Group Fields list and choosing an

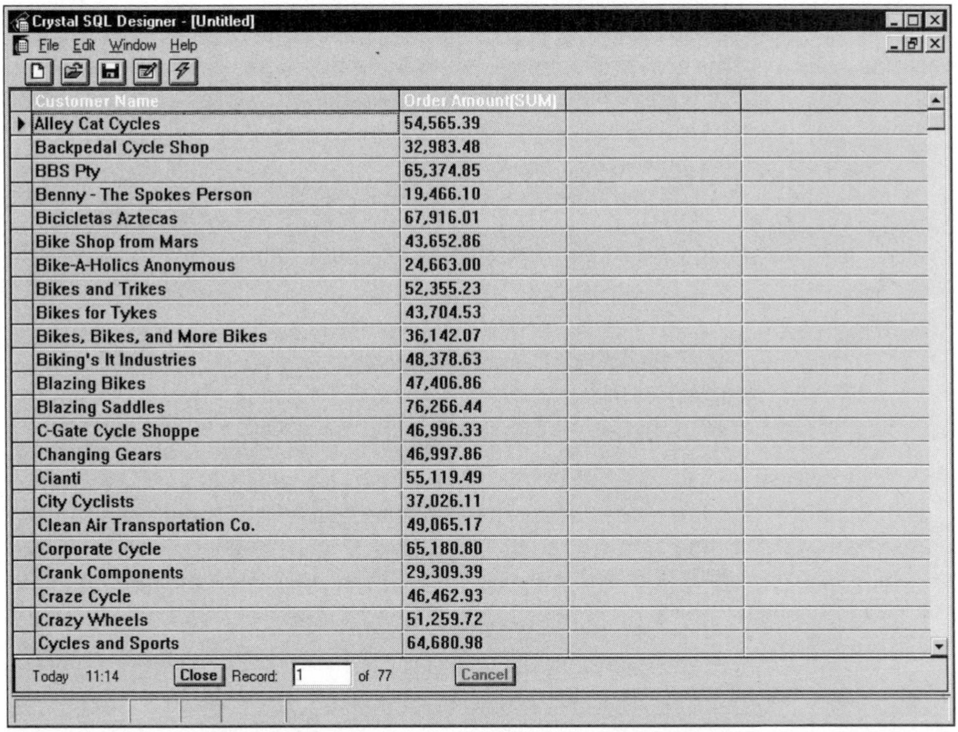

Figure 19-8. *Results of aggregate query*

Select query field or
fields to sort by

Click to add selected fields to Group Fields box

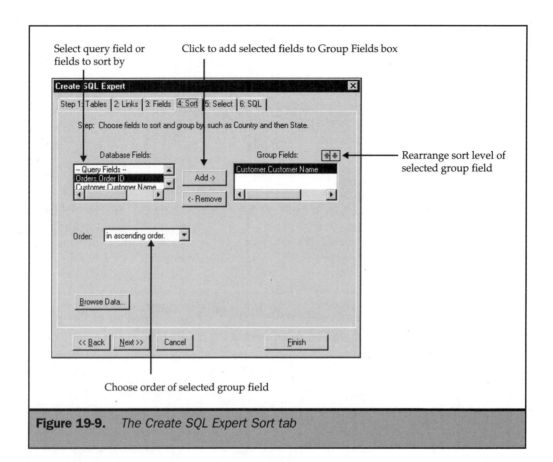

Rearrange sort level of
selected group field

Choose order of selected group field

Figure 19-9. *The Create SQL Expert Sort tab*

option from the Order drop-down list. Ascending order will sort from low to high
alphabetically, while descending order will sort from high to low. The Original order
option will simply not sort the records, leaving them in the original database order (if
you choose this option, there's actually no reason to even add the field to the Sort tab).

The order in which the fields appear in the Group Fields list is significant. If, for
example, you want the query sorted first by Country, then by Region, you'll want to
make sure the Country field is at the top of the list, followed by the Region field. If you
have the fields reversed, the query will be sorted first by Region, and then by Country
if there happens to be more than one country with the same regions. You can reorder
the fields with the two small arrow buttons above the list.

Once you've chosen how to sort records in the query, you'll probably want to limit
the query to only certain records. Click Next or the Select tab directly.

The Select Tab

One of the main reasons you'll probably be using the SQL Designer in the first place is to perform some real-time analysis on your database. This necessarily dictates that you probably won't want to be viewing every record in the database every time you run the query. To narrow down your query to only a desired set of data, you'll use the Select tab, shown in Figure 19-10.

Select one or more fields in the Database Fields list that you want to use to limit the query results. Add them to the Select Fields list by double clicking, dragging and dropping, or clicking the Add button. Then, select each field in the Select Fields list. A set of drop-down lists will appear below the lists in the expert. Choose options in these drop-down lists to compare the fields to a fixed value to limit the query.

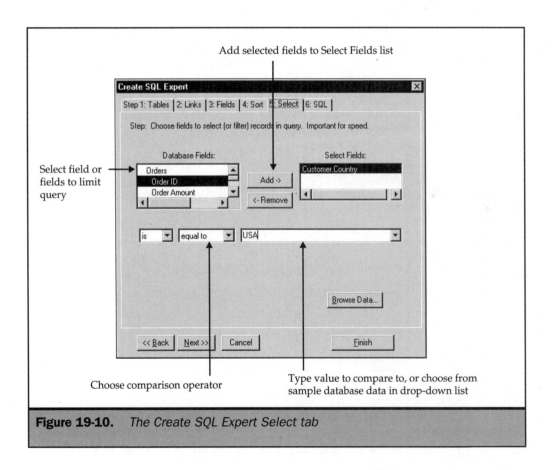

Figure 19-10.   *The Create SQL Expert Select tab*

The first drop-down list simply contains Is by default. Once you have chosen something other than Any Value in the second drop-down list, you can return to the first list and change the Is to Is Not, if necessary for your query. The second drop-down list contains a variety of comparison options, such as Equal To, One Of, Less Than, and Greater Than. Depending on which comparison you choose, there will be one or more additional drop-down lists, text boxes, and buttons that appear. Choose the comparison and fixed values to use for your query.

The Select tab behaves almost identically to the Select Expert in Crystal Reports. For more information, consult Chapter 6.

Once you've chosen selection criteria, you're ready to submit the query to the server and see the results of your query. However, if you'd like to see what the SQL Designer is actually submitting to the database server, or if you're knowledgeable about SQL and want to make manual modifications to the SQL query, you can click the SQL tab. The SQL that is automatically generated by the SQL Designer is displayed.

The SQL Tab

On the SQL tab, shown in Figure 19-11, you'll see the actual SQL statement that you've designed by selecting options on the previous tabs. You'll see the fields you chose in the SELECT clause, the tables you chose in the FROM clause, how they're linked together in the FROM or WHERE clauses, any sorting, grouping, and aggregate functions that you chose in the GROUP BY or ORDER BY clauses, and your selection criteria in the WHERE clause.

If you're not familiar with SQL, this is merely informational (perhaps it looks simple enough to you that you might teach it to yourself and consider a career change!). If you are knowledgeable, you are free to manually change any aspect of the SQL statement that you wish. You are restricted to the legal syntax of your database server and the ODBC driver that's being used. Also, since the SQL Designer is a *read-only* tool, you won't be able to successfully change the SELECT clause to an UPDATE or DELETE clause—this will result in an ODBC error.

If you make any manual changes to the SQL statement in the SQL tab, you won't be able to return to the other tabs in the expert to make changes there. Make sure you are familiar with SQL before making changes to the query. Once you take the SQL plunge, the other tabs won't even appear when you edit the query.

When you're finished specifying your query, click Finish in the expert to send the query to the server. You'll be asked if you want to run the query. If you click Yes, the query will be submitted to the server for processing. If there are any errors in the query, or other ODBC-related problems that prevent the query from running to completion, you'll see an ODBC error message.

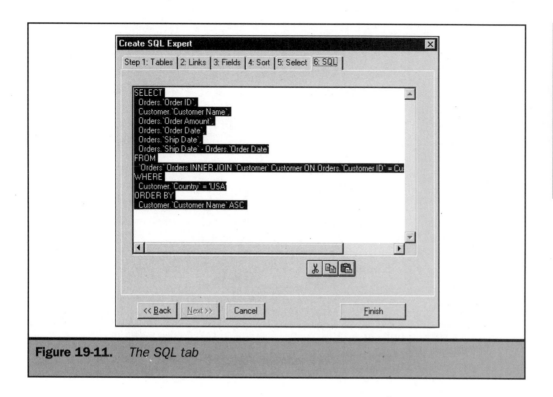

Figure 19-11.   *The SQL tab*

While the query is processing, you'll see an hourglass cursor pointer. Once the query has completed and the server returns a result set to the SQL Designer, you'll see the query appear in a simple row and column format for online viewing. Refer to Figure 19-3 earlier in the chapter to see an example of the query result set.

Since the SQL Designer is a view-only tool, you will only be able to scroll through the query using the vertical and horizontal scroll bars or navigate directly to a certain record by typing a record number into the Record text box. You won't be able to change any data. If you wish, you can submit the same query to the server again to see if any data has changed. Just click the Refresh button in the toolbar, press the F5 key, or choose Edit | Refresh Data from the pull-down menus. If you want to modify the query, click the Change Query button in the toolbar, or choose Edit | Query from the pull-down menus. The Query Expert with all tabs will reappear (unless you manually modified the SQL statement—then you'll only see the SQL tab). You can make changes to any tab and resubmit the updated query to the server.

Using Parameter Fields in Queries

If you are performing ad hoc, real-time queries on a database, you may find yourself running the same query over and over with only a few changes to the Select tab in the expert, or the WHERE clause if you're entering SQL directly. It may be simpler to create a parameter field to prompt you for a value whenever the query is refreshed, and just supply the results of the parameter field to the query's selection criteria.

You must be viewing the result set from a query before you set up a parameter field. The option is not available when you are working with the Query Expert or SQL Statement dialog box. Choose Edit | Parameter Field from the pull-down menus. If this is the first parameter field you are creating, you'll be prompted to give the new parameter field a name. Type in a meaningful name, and click OK. The Parameter Field dialog box will appear, as shown in Figure 19-12.

Enter a helpful message in the Prompting Text box to guide the viewer (or yourself) when the parameter field is prompted for. You may want to include entry requirements, such as "all capital letters," "two-character state abbreviations," or other helpful information. Although you can enter a fairly large prompt, only the first 20 characters or so will appear when the prompt is presented.

Choose a data type for the parameter field in the Value Type drop-down list. Make this determination based on the type of field in the query you will be comparing the

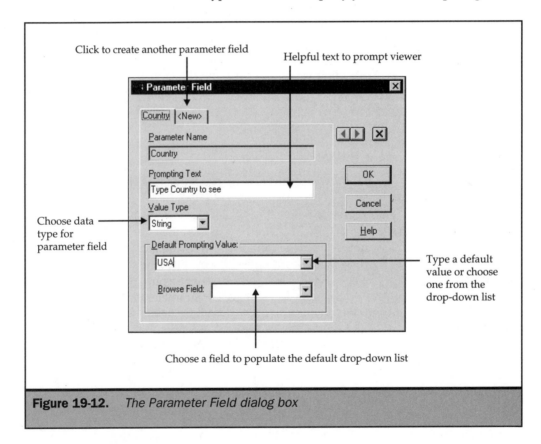

Figure 19-12.   *The Parameter Field dialog box*

parameter field to. If you are going to use the parameter field to select a number field, choose a numeric data type, for a string field choose string, and so forth.

The Default Prompting Value section consists of two drop-down lists. You can just type a default value for the parameter field in the first drop-down list. The value you type will appear in the parameter field when you are prompted. If you want some help in choosing the default value, you can choose a database field in the Browse Field drop-down list to populate the Default Prompting Value drop-down list. Then, when you click the down-arrow, a list of sample database data from the field you chose will appear. You can pick one of the values as the default.

The Browse Field drop-down list may be somewhat misleading. Although it's a good feature request for a future version of the tool, the choice you make in the Browse Field drop-down list won't populate a drop-down list when the parameter field is actually prompted for. It only populates the list so you can choose an existing value for the default.

When you've specified all the parameter field items, click OK. This will save the parameter field. It can now be used in either the SQL Expert or directly in the SQL statement that you created earlier. For either situation, click the Edit Query button from the toolbar or choose Edit | Query from the pull-down menus.

If you created the query by entering a SQL statement directly, the SQL statement will reappear. Simply modify the WHERE clause to refer to the parameter field instead of a literal value. For example, if the SQL statement previously read:

```
WHERE Customer.Country = 'USA'
```

you would change it to the following for a parameter field named Country:

```
WHERE Customer.Country = '{?Country}'
```

Make sure to leave any necessary punctuation, such as quotation marks or apostrophes, around the parameter field—remember that the parameter field just returns what you type when prompted. There is no automatic punctuation or other necessary SQL syntax. Also, make sure to surround the parameter field name by "curly" or French braces, as well as preceding the parameter field name with a question mark.

If you are using the expert, choosing the parameter field in the Select tab is simple. Just display the database browse drop-down list, where you typed the fixed value to compare to. You'll notice that all parameter fields that match the same data type as the database field will now appear in the list. Just choose the parameter field that you want to use. If you don't see the parameter field, it's probably because you used a data type for the parameter field that doesn't match the database field.

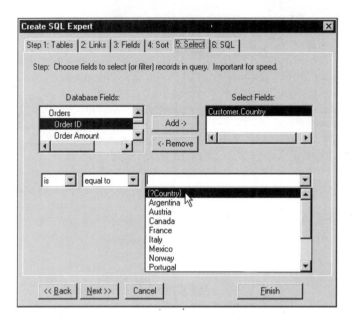

Once you've made these changes, refresh the query. You'll now be prompted for the parameter field or fields you added to the query. Type in an appropriate literal value, and click OK. The SQL Designer will substitute what you typed for the literal value in the query. You can now refresh the query over and over with different values, without having to go back and change the query manually.

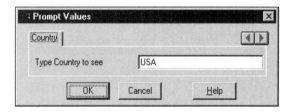

Query parameter fields are similar to Crystal Reports parameter fields, but they don't have as many features. Crystal Reports parameter fields are discussed in Chapter 12.

Saving the Query

Once you've created and viewed the results of your query, you'll probably want to save the query for future use, either for more direct data analysis in the SQL Designer, or for use with Crystal Reports.

First, determine whether you want the result set currently being viewed in the SQL Designer to be saved along with the query definition. If so, make sure Save Data with Query is checked on the File menu. If you don't save the data with the query, the size of the .QRY file will be smaller, but you will have to refresh the query when you later open it in the SQL Designer.

 Then, save the query using either the Save button from the toolbar, or choose Save or Save As from the File menu. Save saves the query with the same filename that currently belongs to the query, overwriting any existing file, while Save As will always ask for a new filename. SQL Designer files are saved with a .QRY extension.

Using Existing SQL Queries

Once you've created and saved queries, you'll want to make use of them again in the future for additional real-time data analysis. You may also use a .QRY file as the data source for a Crystal Report.

Opening Existing Queries

 Opening an existing query in the SQL Designer is as simple as clicking the Open button in the toolbar, or choosing File | Open from the pull-down menus. A file dialog box will appear showing all .QRY files in the default folder. Navigate to a different drive or folder and choose the .QRY file that contains the query you want to open. Then, click OK. The query will open with the result set showing (if you saved your query without saved data, the query will be refreshed as soon as it's opened). You can now change the query as described previously in the chapter.

Using Queries with Crystal Reports

One of the main benefits of the Crystal SQL Designer is the ability to use its .QRY files as a data source for a Crystal Report. But, you may ask, "Why use a query as a data source for the report, instead of just reporting against the database directly?" There are two main reasons why a query might be preferable:

- A query consists of only the tables (already linked) and fields that you might want a report designer to have access to. The report designer won't need to choose and link tables before being able to choose fields.

- If the query contains saved data, the report will use the saved data. This is helpful if you want to run a query to "hit" the database one time, and then save the data with the .QRY file. You can then create multiple similar reports against the .QRY file with saved data, thereby printing several reports that need to be based on the same data source, without having to hit the database multiple times. An additional benefit of a query with saved data is "point in time" reporting. Queries can be run against the database at various times and saved with data to indicate what the state of the database was at that time.

The steps involved in using a query as a data source for a report vary, depending on whether you use a report expert or the Custom option when creating a new report. If you use any of the report experts, Query will be one of the buttons available on the Data tab. Simply click it, and then choose the desired query from the file list.

If you use the Custom option to create your report, you'll notice that there is no Query data type button at the bottom of the Report Gallery. The undocumented trick here is to click the Dictionary button. A file dialog box will appear showing only .DCT and .DC5 file types (used with Crystal Dictionaries, discussed in Chapter 20). You must *change* the file type being searched for to *.QRY or list several file types, separated with semicolons, like *.DCT;*.DC5;*.QRY, to show both dictionaries and queries. Then navigate to the drive and folder where your query files are, and choose the desired query.

Once you've chosen the desired query, you will proceed directly to the rest of your report design with the query's fields available to you. There will be no need to choose or link tables.

Chapter 20

Simplifying Databases with Crystal Dictionaries

In many cases, once you've learned Crystal Reports, the easy part of your report design process is complete! Often, you'll discover that wading through the intricacies of your corporate database is a much more daunting task than learning the tools to report on it. It's not uncommon for larger databases to contain hundreds of tables, each containing a large number of cryptically named fields. It sometimes seems that some database administrators may be trying to ensure job security by creating a database that only they can understand.

Also, you'll probably run into fairly common situations where some parts of the database are off-limits to certain report viewers and designers. Payroll and accounting applications come immediately to mind. Certain tables in the database may be necessary for some users, while not necessary for others. And, there are often times where even individual fields need to be made available only to certain users.

And, last but not least, databases often don't contain all the data you need for your report, or don't contain it in the form that your company commonly needs it to be presented in. While each individual report designer can conceivably create the same formulas over and over to manipulate data in the necessary fashion, a common predesigned template that already contains these formulas would be immensely helpful.

So, is the only solution to take a week-long course on your database layout, set up elaborate security models to restrict tables and fields to authorized users, and make sure every user adheres to the same formulas? Of course not! Included with Crystal Reports Professional is the Crystal Dictionaries tool. This tool can be used to create a dictionary, or "meta-layer" that insulates a report designer from the actual database layout. By using a dictionary instead of tying a report directly to the database, a report developer can be given a simple set of predefined fields to work with.

What Exactly Is a Crystal Dictionary?

The organization of a database, such as the layout of tables and fields and how they all relate to each other (known as the database *schema*), can be very complex. Because of this, there has always been a need for a tool that could present a simplified view of the database to a report or query designer who didn't want to know all the little details of the database. And, there are many situations where a limited set of fields and predefined formulas, often renamed so they are easier to understand, are in order.

This, in essence, is what a Crystal Dictionary is. Using a dictionary, a user who would normally be intimidated by the complexity of the database can now be given a simplified view of the database, and can use this view to write reports or queries. By using a dictionary, the department responsible for the database can present different views of the database to different users, based on each user's level of database knowledge, "need to know" level, and area of concern. The dictionary can look entirely different from the database it's based on: fields and tables can be renamed, formulas can be predefined and included as if they were just other database fields, and even sample data for browsing, and bitmap images, can be preloaded inside the dictionary.

Consider the following two illustrations of the Insert Fields dialog box from Crystal Reports. Figure 20-1 appears when the report is based on several actual tables in a database. Figure 20-2 appears when the report is based on a dictionary (a PC-based file with a .DC5 extension). Notice the reduced set of fields, the better organization of field hierarchies, easy-to-understand field names (some of which are formulas that have been predefined), and the Dictionary Graphic tab that contains preloaded company logos and watermark graphics. The second example is much preferable for a report or query designer who isn't familiar with the layout of the huge database, the common fields required to join tables, and the cryptic field names.

The Crystal Dictionaries tool is a separate executable program that's run directly from the Crystal Reports program group. Crystal Reports doesn't need to be running to use Crystal Dictionaries. Once it's started, the main Crystal Dictionaries window will appear, as shown in Figure 20-3.

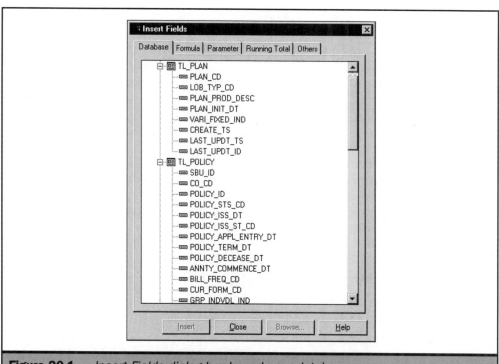

Figure 20-1.   *Insert Fields dialog box based on a database*

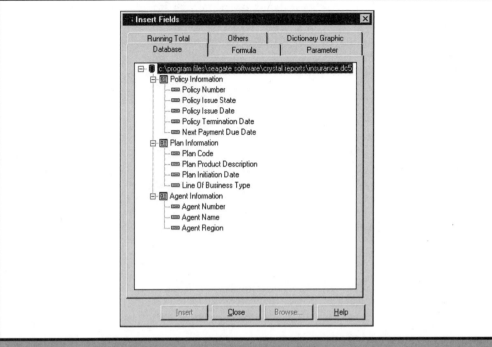

Figure 20-2. *Insert Fields dialog box based on a dictionary*

If you aren't intimately familiar with the table and field structure of your database, you should probably get someone who has this familiarity to create the dictionary, or to help you create it. The whole idea of Crystal Dictionaries is to simplify database access for those who aren't familiar with the actual database layout. The person who creates the dictionary in the first place must obviously have good knowledge of its structure.

Creating a Crystal Dictionary

When you first start Crystal Dictionaries, you have two main choices: open an existing dictionary, or create a new dictionary. To create a new dictionary, click the New button in the toolbar, or choose File | New from the pull-down menus. The Dictionary Expert will appear in the design area of Crystal Dictionaries. This tabbed dialog box is used for the entire dictionary-design process.

The expert consists of four main tabs (an additional tab, Links, appears as the second tab if you choose more than one table for the dictionary). Creating a dictionary is somewhat similar to creating a Crystal Report using the report experts (see Chapter 1

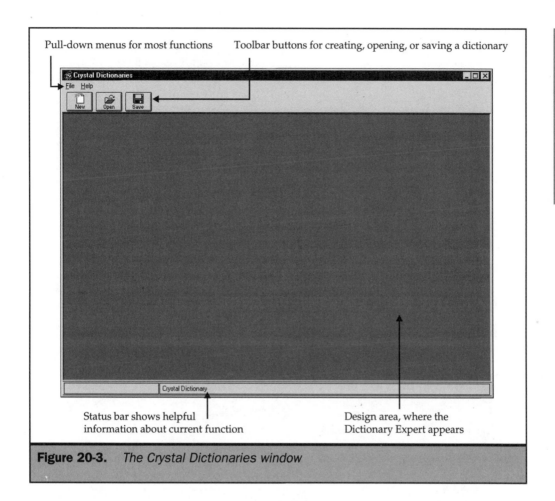

Pull-down menus for most functions   Toolbar buttons for creating, opening, or saving a dictionary

Status bar shows helpful
information about current function

Design area, where the
Dictionary Expert appears

Figure 20-3.   *The Crystal Dictionaries window*

for more information on report experts). Information is supplied on each tab and then the Next button, or the next tab in the sequence, is clicked. When the process is complete, the dictionary file is saved. It can then be used in Crystal Reports or the Crystal SQL Designer to create a report or query.

The Tables Tab

The Tables tab is the first tab in the Dictionary Expert, as shown in Figure 20-4. Here you choose the database and tables you want to use in your dictionary. Your dictionary can contain tables from more than one database, as well as more than one database type. For example, you might add a table from a Microsoft Access database and a dBASE for Windows database by clicking the Data File button, as well as including tables from an Oracle database and an Informix database by clicking the SQL/ODBC button.

Click to add a table from a PC-style database

Click to change the index associated with the selected table

Click to change the name the dictionary uses to refer to the original table

Click to point to a different location for the selected table

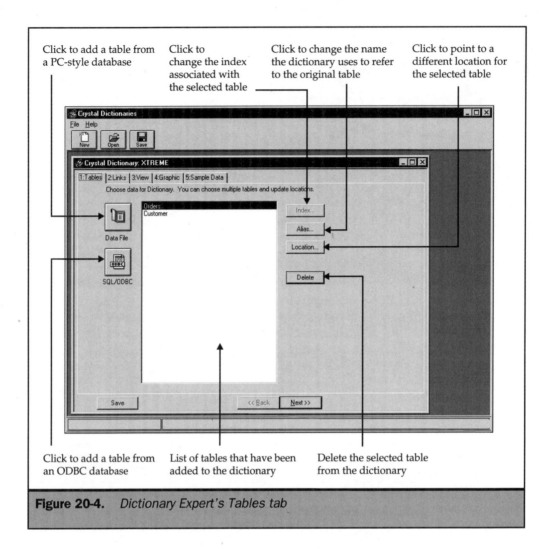

Click to add a table from an ODBC database

List of tables that have been added to the dictionary

Delete the selected table from the dictionary

Figure 20-4. *Dictionary Expert's Tables tab*

If you click the Data File button, a file dialog box will appear where you can navigate to the correct drive or folder until you find the PC-style database you want to use. Then, select the database filename. If the database contains multiple tables (such as a Microsoft Access database), you'll be presented with a Choose Tables dialog box where you can choose the tables you want to include in the dictionary.

To add tables from ODBC databases, click the SQL/ODBC button. If you are not currently logged in to any ODBC databases, the Log On Server dialog box will appear.

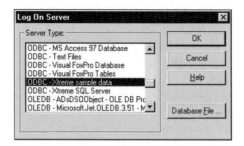

Choose the database you want to use. If the database is secure, you'll need to provide a valid login ID and password to use the database. Once you successfully log on (or if you're already logged on to an ODBC database), the Choose SQL Table dialog box will appear.

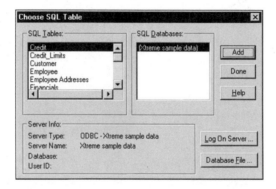

Add tables to the Tables tab by double-clicking on each table you wish to add, or selecting the table and clicking the Add button (selecting multiple tables with SHIFT-click or CTRL-click doesn't work in the Choose SQL Table dialog box). If you need to add tables from a different ODBC database, click the Log On Server button in the Choose SQL Table dialog box and log on to another database. Then, choose the table or tables you want to use from the new database that will be available in the dialog box. Once you've finished choosing tables, click Done.

If you add too many tables to the Dictionary Expert's Tables tab by mistake, select the table you no longer need and either click the Delete button or press the DEL key on your keyboard. You can also choose alternative index files for a particular table by selecting the table and clicking the Index button. The Alias and Location buttons are helpful if the location of the database or table or field names in the database change after you save the dictionary. These buttons are described in more detail later in the chapter.

Note   *The Index button will only be enabled when you've chosen a table in the list that supports external indexes.*

The Links Tab

If you choose more than one table (almost a certainty if you are creating any sort of even moderately sophisticated dictionary), a Links tab will appear after the Tables tab. You'll use this tab to link the tables together on common fields. You can position and resize the table windows and create links by dragging and dropping fields between tables. If you need to delete incorrect links, just select a link line and click the Delete button or press the DEL key. To change the join type for a particular link, select it and click Options.

Tables added to a dictionary are always smart-linked, regardless of the Auto SmartLinking setting in File | Options in Crystal Reports. Since "real world" smart-linking often creates more incorrect links than correct ones, you'll probably spend a bit of time deleting incorrect links and adding correct ones in the Links tab.

The Links tab works almost identically to the Visual Linking Expert in Crystal Reports. Review Chapter 14 for details on linking issues, join types, and specific details on how to link tables together in the Links tab. Once you've correctly linked tables, click Next or directly on the View tab to add fields to the dictionary.

The View Tab

The View tab is the heart of Crystal Dictionaries—this is where the real work happens. Figure 20-5 shows the View tab.

The general idea in the View tab is to add only the fields from the left "database" list that you want the report designer to see. The fields you add to the right "view" list will be the only fields that will be available when a report or query based on the dictionary is designed. In addition to limiting fields in this fashion, you can create formulas that manipulate database data and add these predefined formulas to the dictionary. And, to make the dictionary more readable and easy to understand, you can rename fields you add to the dictionary, as well as create your own "pseudo table names" using field headings.

Adding Fields

To add a database field to the dictionary view, select one or more fields in the database list. You can select multiple fields by using CTRL-click and SHIFT-click. Then, just drag and drop the selected fields to the view list, or click the Add button to add them. The fields will appear in the dictionary view in the same order as they appear in the view list. If you want to reorder the fields in a more logical order, just select the field you want to move and drag it to a new location in the view list. Or, you can select the field and click the small up or down arrow above the view list to move the selected field.

List of actual database fields and tables

Add database fields to, or remove them from, the dictionary view

List of fields included in the dictionary view

Reorder fields in the view

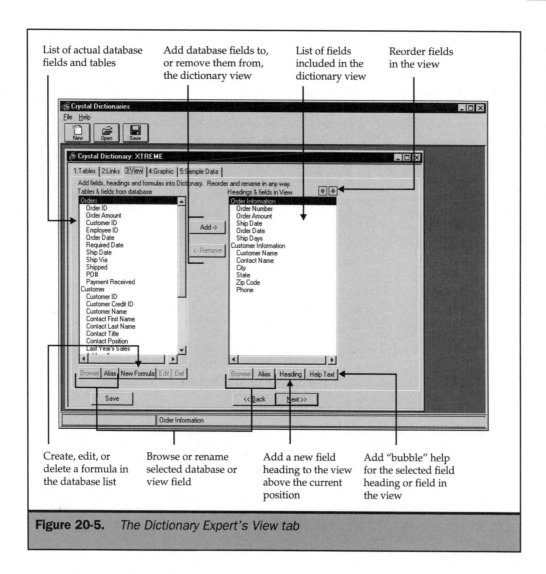

Create, edit, or delete a formula in the database list

Browse or rename selected database or view field

Add a new field heading to the view above the current position

Add "bubble" help for the selected field heading or field in the view

Figure 20-5. *The Dictionary Expert's View tab*

Creating and Adding Formulas

One of the many benefits of using Crystal Dictionaries is the ability to create predefined formulas and include them as though they were regular database fields. The person designing the report has no indication that the data from the formula isn't just coming directly from the database. This allows often-used formulas to be created in advance, freeing each individual report designer from having to create them.

To create a new formula, click the New Formula button. Give the formula a meaningful name (though you can still rename it in the view list, if you want to) and click OK. The Edit Formula dialog box will appear, where you can use the same set of database fields and built-in functions.

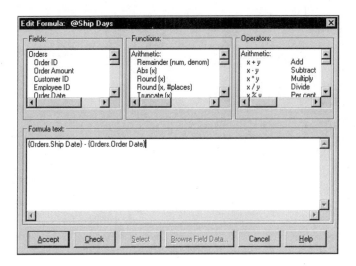

 The Edit Formula dialog box used in Crystal Dictionaries has the older layout style of Crystal Reports 6. You'll notice that the newer Version 7 features, such as toolbars and undockable windows, don't appear in this dialog box.

Create the formula as you would in Crystal Reports, and click Accept when you are finished. This will add the formula you created to a separate section labeled Formulas at the bottom of the database list. You can then select the formula in the database list and add it to the view window the same way you would add a database field. If you wish to edit or delete an existing formula, select it in the database list and click the Edit or Del buttons under the database list.

Adding Field Headings

Another benefit for the report designer when creating a report based on a dictionary is that they won't have to manually choose any specific database or tables. These are already defined in the dictionary. However, the Insert Fields dialog box in Crystal Reports can still show fields as though they were contained in individual tables. This *field hierarchy* can be completely controlled by the creator of the dictionary with Field

Headings. A field heading will appear in the dictionary as though it is a table name, even though it has no relationship at all to actual tables in the database. You can use as few or as many field headings as you choose (you have to retain at least the one that's created by default).

To create a field heading, select the field in the view list that you want to place the field heading *above*. Then, click the Heading button. A dialog box will prompt you for the name of the field heading. Type in a meaningful heading, such as "Customer Information," and click OK. The heading will be added to the view list above the field you had selected. To later delete the heading, select it and press the DEL key.

> **Note** *The Remove button won't work for any field heading—you have to use the DEL key. And, you won't be able to delete the very first field heading that's created by default when you first add a field to the view list. You can, however, rename it to whatever you want.*

Renaming Fields and Headings

Another big benefit of using a dictionary is that you can give database fields more meaningful names. Very often, database fields are originally given somewhat cryptic names, oftentimes containing strange abbreviations, all uppercase letters and underscores. By using the Alias button, you can give the fields more meaningful names containing spaces and mixed case characters.

Select the field or field heading in the view list that you want to rename. Then, click the Alias button. A dialog box will appear with the current field name listed. Just type a new name into the dialog box, and click OK. You'll notice the new name now appears in the view list.

You can actually rename fields or column headings without even using the Alias button. Just select the field or heading you want to rename and start typing (or start by backspacing). As you type, you'll notice the object name changing.

> **Tip** *You may wonder how you can tell what the original field name is, once you've changed the name with the Alias button. Simply select the field in the view list and look in the Crystal Dictionaries status bar. You'll see the original database field name appear.*

Adding Help Text

You can add pop-up help or *bubble* help to field headings or individual view fields. If you then click on the field and wait for a second or two, the help text you entered will pop up, right over the field. This is helpful if you want to add meaningful information to the field or field heading to assist report designers when they are creating reports with the dictionary.

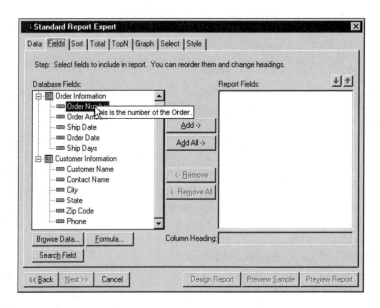

Select the field in the view list that you want to create bubble help for, and click the Help Text button. A dialog box will appear, in which you can type the help text you want to use, and then click OK when you are finished. If you later want to change the bubble help, simply select the field again and click the Help Text button. The existing text will appear, and you can make any necessary changes and click OK.

 The bubble help you add with the Help Text button will only appear in a Crystal Reports Report Expert or the Crystal SQL Designer Expert. If you are using the Custom option in Crystal Reports, the help text won't be visible in the Insert Fields dialog box.

When you're finished with the View tab, you can save the dictionary file by clicking the Save button. Or, you can add bitmap graphics to the dictionary file by clicking Next, or by clicking directly on the Graphic tab.

The Graphic Tab

If you have a standard company logo or other bitmap graphics files that you want to be easily available to report designers, you can add these to the dictionary in the Graphic tab, shown in Figure 20-6.

To add a bitmap image reference to the dictionary, click the Add button. A file dialog box will appear, in which you can navigate to the folder that contains the bitmap image. You'll see a list of supported graphics files in the folder. Select the bitmap image you wish to add to the dictionary, and click OK. The filename for the graphic will appear in the dictionary pictures list. You then can use the Alias button to give the graphic a more meaningful name, if you want.

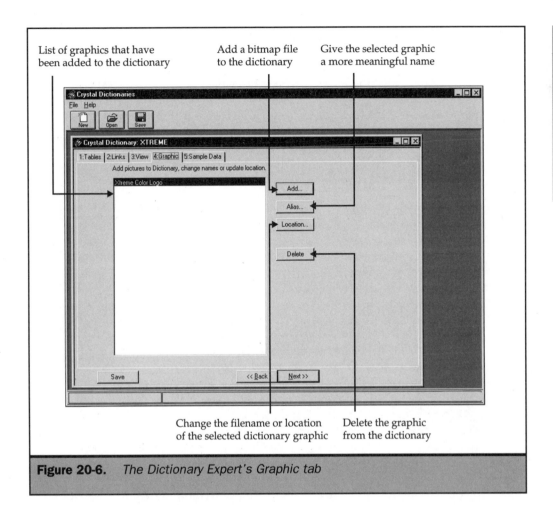

List of graphics that have been added to the dictionary

Add a bitmap file to the dictionary

Give the selected graphic a more meaningful name

Change the filename or location of the selected dictionary graphic

Delete the graphic from the dictionary

Figure 20-6.   *The Dictionary Expert's Graphic tab*

Note   *Crystal Reports will read Windows bitmap files (.BMP), PC Paintbrush files (.PCX), JPEG images typically found in Web pages (.JPG), TIFF files (.TIF), and Targa files (.TGA). If you have a graphic in another format, such as a CorelDRAW vector format, or an Adobe Photoshop .PSD file, you'll need to use a graphics program to convert them to a supported format before they can be used in a dictionary or in Crystal Reports.*

If you want to remove the graphic from the dictionary, select it in the list and click the Delete button. This will only delete the reference to the graphic in the dictionary—the original bitmap image will remain in its original location.

If you later move or rename an original graphic file, the dictionary will no longer point to the right location—a report designer will get a File Not Found message if they try to use the dictionary graphic. To remedy this situation, click the Location button on the Graphic tab and choose the new location or filename for the bitmap image.

 Since the dictionary merely points to the actual bitmap file, make sure that any PC that might be making use of the dictionary will have access to the original graphic files that were used when the dictionary was created. You may want to use a UNC (Uniform Naming Convention) name or to place the graphic files on a shared network drive that is mapped to the same drive letter on all PCs.

The Sample Data Tab

When you create a report or query based directly on the database, there is typically a Browse function available in dialog boxes and from pop-up menus. If you select a database field and then choose this function, Crystal Reports or the SQL Designer will query the database and return a short list of sample data for that field. The Sample Data tab, shown in Figure 20-7, allows you to control the data that is browsed when a dictionary is being used. This is helpful if the person designing a report or query may not have actual connectivity to the database when the report is being designed, or if the connection may be on a slow modem or WAN link, which would make browsing live database data tedious.

Sample browse data can be stored right inside the dictionary for selected fields in the view. If you choose not to store sample data for a field, and a user browses it, Crystal Reports or the SQL Designer will go ahead and query the database directly.

To store sample data in the dictionary, you must first collect it from the actual database. Select the field you wish to gather sample data for, and click the Collect button. The database will be queried, and unique sample data will be collected and placed in the Browsed Data list on the right side of the Sample Data tab. You can then scroll through the sample data and delete any pieces you don't wish to keep. You can also select a piece of sample data and click the Edit button. A dialog box will appear, in which you can change the value of the sample data. You cannot add new sample data—just delete or edit existing data.

Once you've collected and edited sample data, you'll see that the same data appear in the Browsed Data list every time you select that particular field in the field list. If you want to reread the database and refresh the sample data, click the Refresh button. The database will be re-queried and any old sample data (including any that you modified) will be discarded and replaced with new data from the database. If you select a field that hasn't had any sample data collected, the Browsed Data list will be empty and the Collect button will be enabled. You can then click Collect to add sample data for that field.

 Remember that the sample data you specify here will only appear when you Browse from the Insert Fields dialog box. If you create a report based on a dictionary, even though you don't have database connectivity, the sample data will not appear if you try to preview the report.

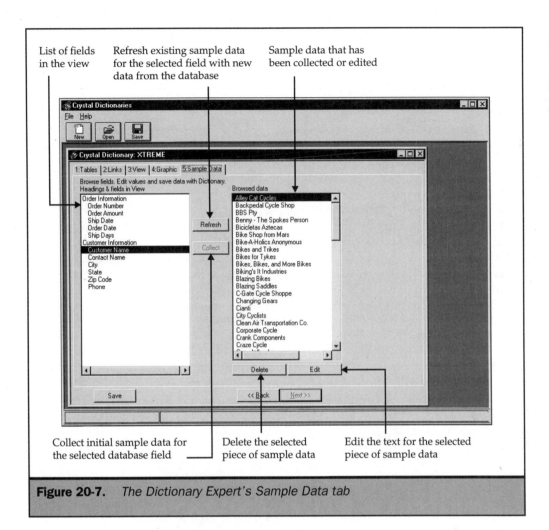

List of fields in the view

Refresh existing sample data for the selected field with new data from the database

Sample data that has been collected or edited

Collect initial sample data for the selected database field

Delete the selected piece of sample data

Edit the text for the selected piece of sample data

Figure 20-7. *The Dictionary Expert's Sample Data tab*

Saving the Dictionary

Once you've completed at least the Tables and View tabs, you can save the dictionary to a disk file. Just click the Save button in the Dictionary Expert, the Save button from the toolbar, or choose File | Save or File | Save As from the pull-down menus. If you've saved the dictionary previously, the buttons and File | Save option will overwrite the older version of the dictionary with the newer version. If this is the first time you're saving the dictionary, or if you use the File | Save As option, a file dialog will appear asking you to supply a filename. Choose a drive and folder where you want to save the file. The file will be saved with a .DC5 extension, indicating it's a Crystal Dictionary.

You may want to set up a shared network directory where you can save Crystal dictionaries. That way, many report designers will have ready access to the dictionaries for creating new reports and queries.

Setting Crystal Dictionaries Options

You can choose some default behavior for Crystal Dictionaries by specifying locations for dictionary files that you open or save, as well as default locations for PC-style databases and graphic files. You may also set options for logging in to SQL databases. Choose File | Options from the drop-down menu, and the Options dialog box will appear, as shown in Figure 20-8.

You can specify default drive and path names for three types of files used by Crystal Dictionaries. The Directory Location default is used when you open or save .DC5 files. The Table Location default is used when you add new tables from a PC-style database. And, the Graphic Location default is used when you add a bitmap graphic file to the dictionary. You can type drive and path names in directly, or click the Browse buttons to navigate to the desired locations.

The SQL Options button will display the SQL Options dialog box, shown in Figure 20-9. Here, you can specify default behavior for SQL and ODBC databases that you add to your dictionary. Specific information about this dialog box can be found in Chapter 14.

Finally, the two check boxes at the bottom of the Options dialog box let you choose whether or not to display the toolbar (referred to as the button bar here) and the status

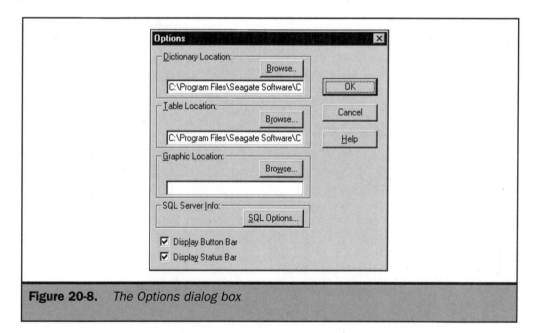

Figure 20-8. *The Options dialog box*

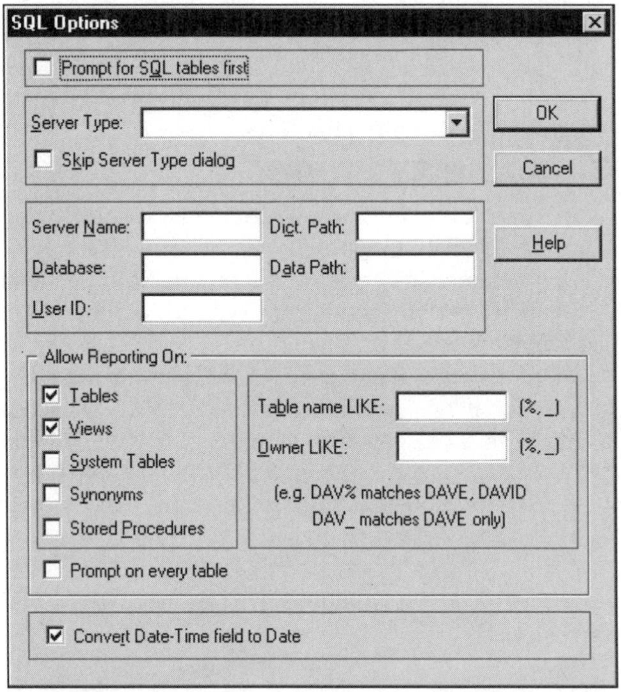

Figure 20-9. *Crystal Dictionaries SQL Options*

bar. When you are finished choosing options, click OK. The options will be saved for
the next time you start Crystal Dictionaries.

Opening an Existing Dictionary

Opening an existing dictionary is as simple as clicking the Open button in the toolbar,
or choosing File | Open from the pull-down menus. A file dialog box will appear,
showing any existing dictionary files in the Crystal Reports program folder. Navigate
to another drive or folder to locate your existing dictionary. Once you've located it,
simply select it and click OK. It will be opened in the Dictionary Expert for you to
modify as you see fit. Once you've made any necessary changes, click the Save button
in the toolbar, or choose File | Save from the pull-down menus to save your updated
dictionary file.

Note *You may notice that Crystal Dictionaries recognizes both .DC5 and .DCT dictionary files. The .DCT extension was used for dictionary files prior to Crystal Reports Version 5. Versions 5 and later (including Version 7) use the .DC5 file extension. While Crystal Dictionaries Version 7 can read .DCT files, it will only save .DC5 files.*

Updating the Database Location

When you create a dictionary, the .DC5 file "points" to a specific database name at a specific database location. The tables the dictionary uses are also referenced by name. Should the location of the database or names of tables or fields in the database change, any dictionaries based on them will need to be modified to point to the new database location or renamed tables.

To simply verify that the database still exists at the location and with the same table and field names it was originally created with, choose File | Verify Dictionary from the pull-down menus. If there have been no changes to the database that affect the dictionary, you'll simply receive a message that the dictionary is up to date. If, however, tables can no longer be found at the same location, you'll receive a message indicating that a table can't be found at its original location.

You'll need to then change the location that the table in the Table tab points to. Click the Location button inside the table tab. The previous location of the table will then appear. This location will either be displayed in the Choose SQL Table dialog box if the dictionary table is from an ODBC database, or a Windows file dialog if the table is from a PC-style database. Simply choose the new filename or table name that contains the new table location (use the Log On Server button on the Choose SQL Table dialog box, if necessary), and click OK. Data for the table will now be retrieved from the new location.

If you wish to change the name that the dictionary uses to refer to the original database table, select the table you wish to change. Then click the Alias button. You'll be given the opportunity to change the name, or *alias*, that Crystal Dictionaries uses to refer to the table. Remember that this has no relation to what table names ultimately appear in the dictionary view. Any field headings you create in the View tab will determine the pseudo table names that create a field hierarchy in the actual dictionary view.

If the table location is the same, but fields that were used in the dictionary have been deleted, added, or renamed, you'll receive a message indicating that the table layout has changed. If you click Yes, to "fix up the dictionary," the field names on the left side of the View tab will be updated to reflect the changes to the original database.

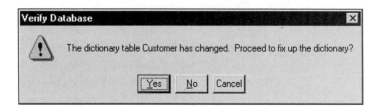

There is no tool in Crystal Dictionaries similar to the Remap Fields dialog box, which is new in Crystal Reports 7. If database field names change, you'll need to re-add them to your dictionary. You might then give the tables alias names that match the original table names so any reports based on the dictionary will still work without changes.

Basing a Report or Query on a Dictionary

The true power of Crystal Dictionaries is apparent when it comes time to design a new report in Crystal Reports or a new query in the Crystal SQL Designer. When you create a new report, using either a Report Expert or the Custom option, or when you create a query using the Create SQL Expert, there is a button that allows you to choose a Dictionary as the data source for your report. When you click the Dictionary button, a File Open dialog box appears in which you can choose an existing dictionary file.

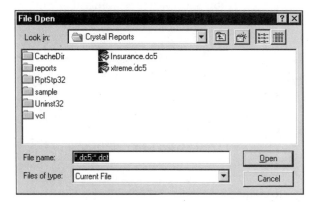

Navigate to the drive and folder where the desired dictionary resides, select it, and click OK. The report or query design process will now proceed as though you had logged on to a database, chosen tables, and properly linked them. You will be able to immediately choose fields.

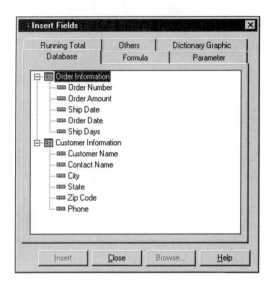

If the dictionary contains any bitmap graphics and you're using the Insert Fields dialog box inside Crystal Reports, you'll see a Dictionary Graphic tab, as well. Select the tab and add any graphics you need directly to the report by dragging and dropping or clicking the Insert button. There's no need to use the Insert Graphic button or menu option to insert dictionary graphics.

Here are some tips you'll want to keep in mind when setting up Crystal dictionaries for use within your organization:

- If you are using the Crystal SQL Designer, remember that the dictionary you use must be based only on SQL/ODBC databases. If you choose a dictionary based on a PC-style database, an error message will appear.

- If the dictionary you choose is based on one or more secure databases, you'll be required to provide a valid login ID and password for each database before you can begin to use the dictionary.

- You'll need to ensure that the same ODBC data source used to create the dictionary is located on the computer that the dictionary is being used on. If the dictionary is based on a PC-style database, the original database must be found in the same path as is contained in the dictionary file. Otherwise, the dictionary won't be able to ultimately resolve dictionary names back to the original database.

- If you created formulas that use any functions from the Additional Functions list in the formula editor, ensure that the User Function Library .DLL file that the functions come from is installed on any computers that will be using the formulas. Otherwise the formula will fail when the report designer tries to use a dictionary field that's based on the formula.

Chapter 21

Reporting from Proprietary Data Types

S eagate Crystal Reports is best known as the "reporting tool of choice" for use with any standard corporate database. "Standard" databases might generally be thought to include Microsoft Access or SQL Server, Sybase, Oracle, Informix, IBM DB2, and others that are well known in the mainstream of corporate database technology.

But, what do you do if your data is contained in some other form of database or data file? Well, if the database or data file system is *very* proprietary and out of the mainstream, and the vendor doesn't provide an ODBC (open database connectivity) driver for the database, then you may be, quite simply, out of luck. However, many proprietary databases can be accessed via ODBC, which Crystal Reports will work with. And Crystal Reports 7 supports other data types directly, without even requiring an ODBC driver. You can create reports based on Microsoft Exchange Server and Systems Management Server databases, Symantec's ACT! contact manager, Microsoft Outlook, Windows NT event logs, and Web server activity logs. You can also create reports against regular ASCII-delimited text files, but you'll need to use a supplied ODBC driver to accomplish this.

The general approach for creating reports against these types of data sources is similar, regardless of the data source:

1. Ensure that the software you want to report from (such as Microsoft Outlook), or the vendor's "client" application to access a database (such as ISQL/W for Microsoft SQL Server) is installed on the same PC as Crystal Reports. Crystal Reports automatically detects these software packages and will list them when you choose a data source.

2. Create a new report using either the report experts or the Custom option. If you use an expert, you'll see various buttons in the Data tab that correspond to the type of data you want to report on. If you use the Custom option, choose the SQL/ODBC data type. In addition to ODBC data sources that were set up with the ODBC Administrator application in the Windows Control Panel, you'll see the additional "direct" data sources in the list. So, if you want to write reports against a Microsoft Exchange server, you can click the Exchange button in the expert, or choose SQL/ODBC in the custom option. Then choose one of the Exchange data types, such as Exchange Folders/Address Book, Message Tracking Log, or Public Folder Admin from the Log On Server dialog box.

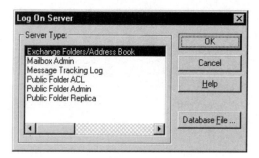

3. Follow any prompts specific to the data source, such as choosing an Exchange server and profile. You'll then see a list of tables and/or fields that are specific to that data type. Use them in your report just as you would use other database tables and fields.

Although Crystal Reports supports many popular data types, the rest of this chapter will focus on four of the most often used: Microsoft Outlook, the local file system (basically the disk directory on a PC or network disk drive), the Windows NT event log, and standard Web-server activity logs.

Reporting from Microsoft Outlook

Microsoft Outlook has become a popular standard on office desktops, as it smoothly integrates e-mail, contact management, and calendar maintenance in one package. Outlook's folder metaphor is handy for organizing your office affairs, and it's also handy for reporting.

The first requirement for creating a Crystal Report based on your Outlook folders is rather obvious—you must have Outlook installed on your PC. More specifically, you must have Outlook installed on the same computer on which you will be running Crystal Reports. Crystal Reports won't report on any other Outlook systems on the network, just your own.

To report on your Outlook data, start a new report just as you would for a standard database. You can use the report experts or the Custom option. If you use an expert, you'll see Outlook appear as a data-source button in the Data tab.

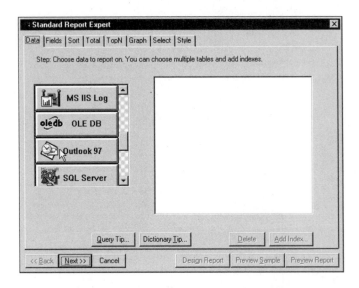

If you use the Custom option, you must choose SQL/ODBC as the data type. Then, when the Log On Server dialog box appears, choose Outlook from the list of servers.

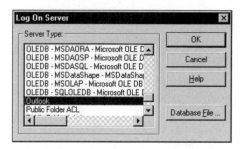

In either case, you'll be presented with the Choose Folder dialog box, showing the folder hierarchy of your Outlook data. Choose the folder that you want to report on, and click OK.

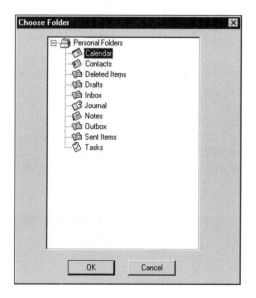

Note   *You cannot report on the Notes folder. You'll receive an error message if you try to select it.*

Once you've chosen the folder and clicked OK, the list of Outlook fields you can report from will appear in the expert or in the Insert Fields dialog box.

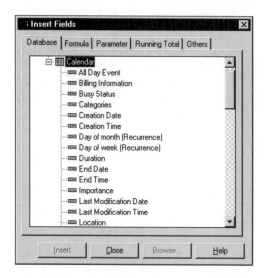

Use the Outlook fields just like other database fields to create your report. You can sort, group and format the report as you normally would. You can also create formulas, if necessary, to calculate or modify the way Outlook material appears in the report. Figure 21-1 shows a sample report based on the Calendar folder from Outlook.

Note   *The field names you see in the Crystal Reports Insert Fields dialog box may not always match the field names you see in Outlook. For example, you may see a Priority field in Outlook, but see an Importance field in Crystal Reports. If you don't see the field you expect, look for a reasonable alternative field name. Also, you may need to add other Outlook folders, (such as the Contact folder and the Inbox folder) and link the two together to get all the data you expect. Make sure you link on correct fields—Smart Linking will typically not pick the correct fields to perform an Outlook link.*

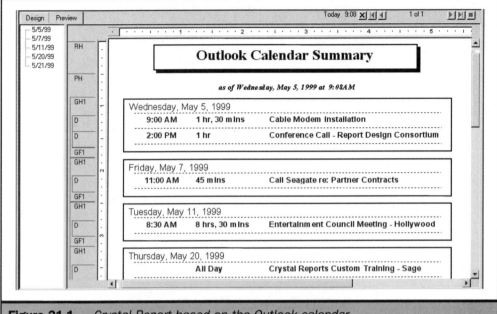

Figure 21-1. *Crystal Report based on the Outlook calendar*

Reporting from the Local File System

You are probably familiar with Explorer, the Windows 95/98 and Windows NT 4 application that helps you view the hierarchy and layout of your local and network drives, as well as locate one or more particular files you may be looking for. However, if you want a more powerful reporting-type tool to search or report on drive contents, you need another software solution.

Crystal Reports 7 includes the *local file system* as a data source, allowing you to write powerful reports against any local or network drive on your PC. By choosing a drive and folder or directory, as well as specifying some detailed criteria if you choose, you can create reports that select and sort files and folders with the complete power and flexibility of Crystal Reports.

To report on your local file-system data, start a new report just as you would for a standard database. You can use the report experts or the Custom option. If you use an expert, you'll see File System appear as a data-source button in the Data tab.

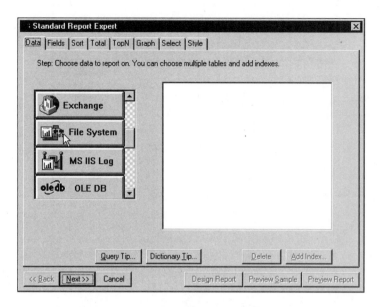

If you use the Custom option, you must choose SQL/ODBC as the data type. Then, when the Log On Server dialog box appears, choose Local File System from the list of servers.

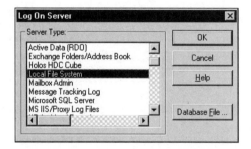

In either case, you'll be presented with the Select a Directory dialog box. If you simply want to supply a drive or path name, you can just type it in or click the Browse button to navigate to the desired drive and directory. If you click the Advanced button, you can narrow down the files and directories you want to see with some additional criteria. Figure 21-2 shows the Select a Directory dialog box.

Make your choices, and click OK. The Choose SQL Table dialog box will appear, starting with the directory you chose, as well as all directories underneath (subject to any limits you may have chosen).

You can choose any directory from the dialog box. Files in that directory, as well as directories below, will be included in your report. Once you've made the directory

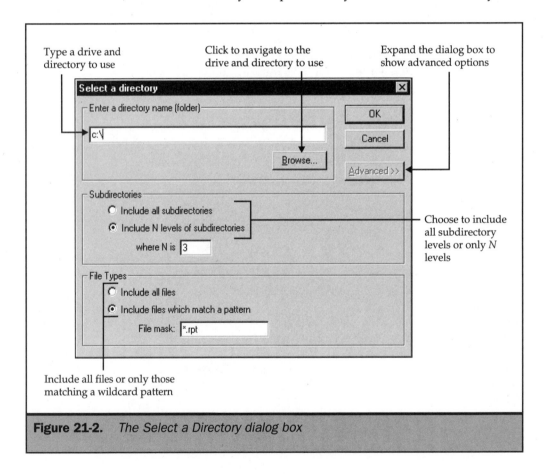

Figure 21-2.   *The Select a Directory dialog box*

choice, the list of file-system fields you can report from will appear in the expert or in the Insert Fields dialog box.

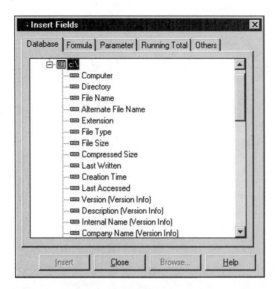

You'll notice many different fields containing information you might not have previously been familiar with. Some fields only apply to certain types of files, such as .EXE or .DLL files. Others only apply to files that belong to certain applications (for example, Number of Words generally only applies to Word or other word processing documents). Use these file-system fields just like other database fields to create your report. You can sort, group, and format the report as you normally would. You can use the fields to create flexible selection criteria to narrow down your report. You can also create formulas, if necessary, to calculate or modify the way file-system material appears in the report. Figure 21-3 shows a sample report based on a local C: disk drive.

Reporting from the Windows NT Event Log

Windows NT has traditionally been the powerful big brother of desktop operating systems, such as Windows 95 and Windows 98. However, with the advent of more powerful computer hardware for ever-falling prices, Windows NT is finding its way to more and more desktops. And Windows 2000, Microsoft's latest entry into the operating system arena, will build even further on Windows NT technology.

An integrated part of the Windows NT operating system is the *event log*, a series of files kept by Windows NT that document events that occur during the general operation of Windows. There are several different types of event logs available, and different types of entries are placed in the event logs as users log on and off, and programs start, stop, and operate. Crystal Reports includes the capability to create flexible reports on the Windows NT event logs.

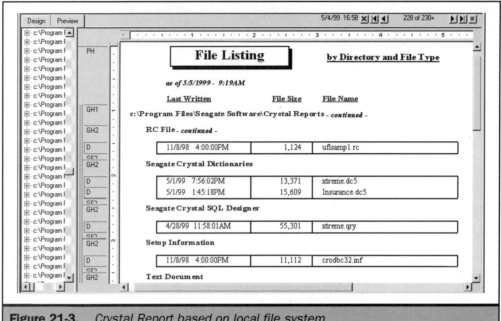

Figure 21-3.   *Crystal Report based on local file system*

Although designing reports against the Windows NT event logs won't harm the computer containing the log, you probably won't find the information returned to be of much use if you're not generally familiar with Windows NT and its components. This Crystal Reports capability will probably be most useful to NT administrators and other technical personnel.

To report on NT event logs, start a new report just as you would for a standard database. You can use the report experts or the Custom option. If you use an expert, you'll see NT Event Log appear as a data-source button in the Data tab. Once you choose this button, an additional dialog box will appear, giving you the choice of the NT Archived Event Log or the NT Current Event Log. Choose the log you wish to report on.

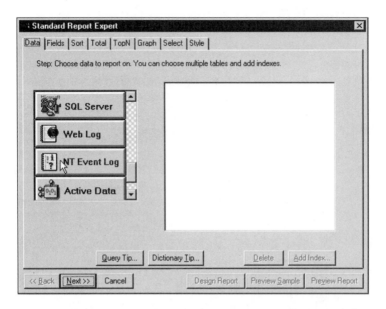

If you use the Custom option, you must choose SQL/ODBC as the data type. Then, when the Log On Server dialog box appears, choose either NT Archived Event Log or NT Current Event Log from the list of servers, depending on which event log you wish to report on.

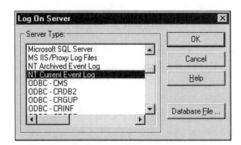

In either the expert or the Custom option, you'll be presented with the Select Current Event Log dialog box, shown in Figure 21-4. This allows you to select an event log on a remote computer—it doesn't have to reside on the computer that you are running Crystal Reports on. You can include event logs from more than one computer in your report, if you choose.

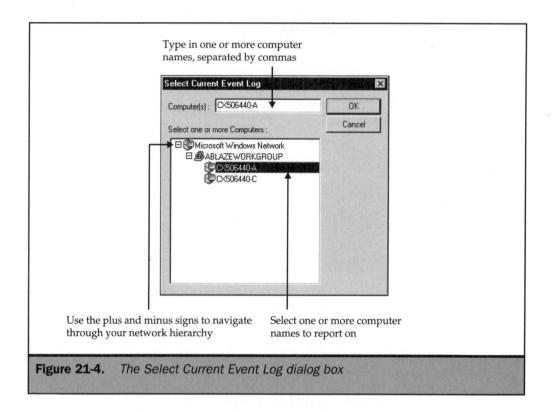

Type in one or more computer names, separated by commas

Use the plus and minus signs to navigate through your network hierarchy

Select one or more computer names to report on

Figure 21-4. *The Select Current Event Log dialog box*

If you know the domain and computer name, you can simply type it in the Computer(s) text box at the top of the dialog box. If you include more than one computer name, separate the names with commas. If you're not sure which computers to include, you can use the Explorer-like hierarchy to select the computers you wish to use. When you see the computer list, you can select one or more computers.

Make your choices and click OK. The Choose SQL Table dialog box will appear, showing the three NT event logs that are available: Application, Security, and System.

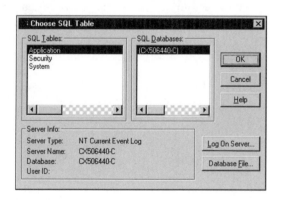

Depending on the types of events you want your report to be based on, choose the appropriate log. If you'd like a better idea of what types of events are contained in each log, use the Event Viewer application from the Administrative Tools program group to view the different event-log entries. Once you've made your log choice, the list of event-log fields you can report on will appear in the expert or in the Insert Fields dialog box.

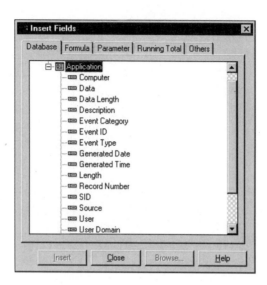

Use these NT Event Log fields just like other database fields to create your report. You can sort, group, and format the report as you normally would. The Event View application can help you identify what some of the available fields contain. You can use the fields to create flexible selection criteria to narrow down your report, and you can also create formulas, if necessary, to calculate or modify the way event-log material appears in the report. Figure 21-5 shows a sample report based on a Windows NT application event log.

Reporting from Web-Server Logs

With the ever-increasing proliferation of both the Internet and corporate intranets, there is an equally ever-increasing need to document what pages Web users are pointing their browsers to, when, and from where. Most Web servers, such as those from Microsoft, Netscape, and others, keep various amounts and levels of data about Web-site visits. What better tool to create Web activity reports than Crystal Reports 7?

There are several types of Web-server logs that you may encounter, depending mostly on the Web server that you are using. All Web-server logs are standard delimited ASCII files (a term you don't necessarily need to be familiar with, but it is a common

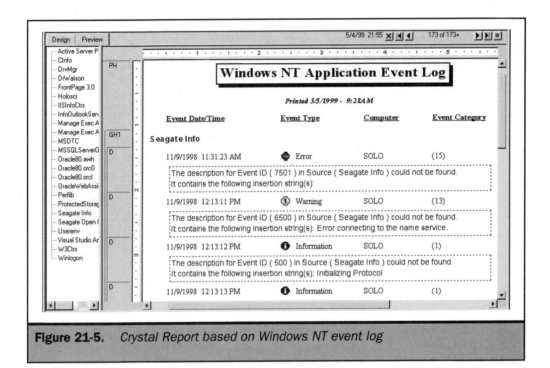

Figure 21-5.   *Crystal Report based on Windows NT event log*

denominator for data-file formats). However, the layout of fields in the files and the information they contain can vary from server to server. There are several "standard" types of log files, including a file type simply known as Standard, and another known as the NCSA Standard, defined by the National Center for Supercomputing Applications for its original Web server. Other Web server developers have adopted both standards. In addition, if you are using Microsoft Internet Information Server (IIS) you'll find additional types of log files available, such as Microsoft's extended log format. When you configure IIS, you can choose the type of log file that is generated, as well as the fields that are kept in the log file.

As a general rule, Web servers will create a new log file every day, adding hit statistics to the daily log file as they occur. The filenames consist of variations of the date on which they were created, with a standard file extension. For example, you may see a file named EX990719.LOG, indicating a Microsoft extended-format log for July 19, 1999. These files will be located in a standard directory, such as \WinNT\System32\ LogFiles\W3Csvc1 (this is the default location for Microsoft Personal Web Server 4 running on Windows NT Workstation).

To report on Web-server logs, start a new report just as you would for a standard database. You can use the report experts or the Custom option. If you use an expert, you'll see two Web-server buttons appear in the Data tab: MS IIS Log and Web Log.

MS IIS Log will report on both "standard" formats, the various Microsoft IIS formats, and Web proxy and Winsock Proxy formats. The Web Log button will simply report on "standard" and NCSA formatted logs.

If you use the Custom option, you must choose SQL/ODBC as the data type. Then, when the Log On Server dialog box appears, choose MS IIS/Proxy Log Files if you want to report on the IIS log types (including Standard and NCSA), or Web/IIS Log Files to report on just Standard or NCSA log files.

Regardless of whether you're using an expert or the Custom option, the rest of the prompts will be consistent. If you choose the more generic Web Log option, you'll simply be prompted to choose a drive and directory where the standard or NCSA Web logs are located. You can type or browse to select a local or network drive and directory. If you choose the IIS option, you'll see the Select Log Files and Dates dialog box, as illustrated in Figure 21-6.

Choose the type of log file your Web server uses (look for files in a standard location with the .LOG extension to help determine this). You can also choose the format your Web server uses when writing log files, based on how often it creates a new log file. And, if you prefer to limit Crystal Reports to only using log files within a certain date range, make that selection, as well.

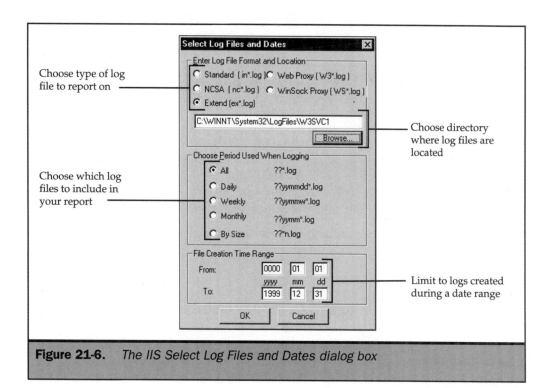

Figure 21-6. *The IIS Select Log Files and Dates dialog box*

When you're finished with your choices, click OK. The Choose SQL Table dialog box will appear, showing a somewhat-cryptic entry for the log files you just chose. Simply click OK, and the list of Web-server log fields you can report from will appear in the expert or in the Insert Fields dialog box.

 This illustration shows the limited set of log fields available with Microsoft Personal Web Server 4 for NT Workstation. If you're using IIS with NT Server, or another server, you may see a larger selection of fields. With IIS, you can configure the server to include a variety of helpful statistical fields.

Use these Web server log fields just like other database fields when creating your report. You can sort, group, and format the report as you normally would. You can use the fields to create flexible selection criteria to narrow down your report. You can also create formulas, if necessary, to calculate or modify the way Web-server log material appears in the report. Figure 21-7 shows a sample report based on an NT Workstation Personal Web Server log.

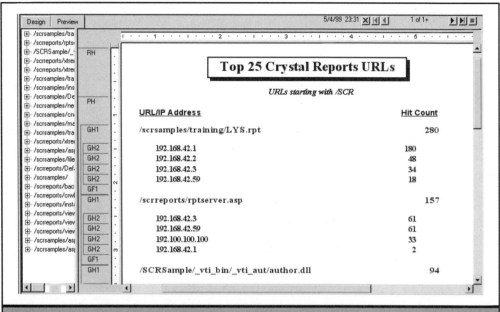

Figure 21-7. *Crystal Report based on Windows NT event log*

The Complete Reference

Part II

Developing Custom Window Applications

Chapter 22

Creating Your First Visual Basic/Crystal Reports Application

If you've read even a bit of Part I of this book, you've seen some of the power and flexibility of Seagate Crystal Reports. By making the vast array of corporate databases accessible with its simple, straightforward user interface, Crystal Reports has established itself as a valuable tool simply by virtue of its reporting and querying capabilities. But there's a whole other side of Crystal Reports that has yet to be explored.

As database reporting and querying is a large part of many standard business applications, there will often be a need to include these features in custom applications you create for your own use. If you develop custom applications for Microsoft Windows in any of the popular Windows languages, you'll probably soon need some type of database reporting inside the application. While you can develop your own routines to step through the database record by record to generate your own internal reporting mechanism, all the intricacies of formatting, font management, graphics, and other Windows-related printing issues can create a significant, if not impossible, coding challenge.

Crystal Reports has featured developer interfaces for virtually all of its Windows versions. Version 7 features some new developer integration features that make it an even better choice for inclusion in custom Windows applications. In particular, Microsoft Visual Basic (VB) developers will appreciate the new Report Designer component (RDC). This interface, new with Crystal Reports Version 7, allows both report design, and flexible report integration, to occur entirely in the Visual Basic Integrated Development Environment (VB IDE). You'll never have to leave Visual Basic to perform any report development or integration tasks! Even if you're using a version earlier than 7, you'll find a rich development environment included with the tool.

Furthermore, Seagate Software is very generous when it comes to distributing your custom applications. With the exception of the Crystal Reports design components (such as the Crystal Reports design program itself), you receive a royalty-free license to distribute the Crystal Reports Print Engine and associated files, such as .OCX, .VBX, and .DLL files. You may purchase a single copy of Crystal Reports, develop your custom application, and distribute the run-time files with as many copies of your application as you like, at no additional charge.

Some of the developer features discussed in this chapter are only available with the Professional version of Crystal Reports, or, to a limited extent, with a version that may be bundled with your development tool. For a complete set of features that are not "crippled" in any way, you'll probably want to upgrade to the full Professional version.

Development-Language Options

Crystal Reports developer interfaces have been designed to work with most popular Windows development tools. The most basic interface is the Crystal Reports Print Engine API. This is simply a Windows dynamic link library (DLL) file that can be called from any Windows language to support calls to external DLLs. This interface can be used with Microsoft Visual Basic and Visual C++, Inprise Delphi, and PowerBuilder, among others.

These, as well as other languages and development tools, may also support additional interface options that Crystal Reports supplies. If your development language can use automation servers compatible with Microsoft's Component Object Model (COM), Crystal Reports provides the Report Engine Automation Server. The Crystal ActiveX control (or OCX control as it's sometimes known) supplies a simple, object-oriented interface to Visual Basic and other languages that support OCX controls. If you're using an older version of Visual Basic, or another development language that supports Visual Basic extension VBX controls, a somewhat less-capable 16-bit-only interface is provided for these tools.

In addition to the multitool interfaces, there are several Crystal Reports interfaces available for specific development tools. If you're using Inprise Delphi, the Crystal Visual Component library (VCL) interface makes it easy to create custom Delphi applications using Crystal Reports. If you are using Informix NewEra, you'll appreciate the Crystal NewEra Class library which "wraps" itself around the Report Engine API to make NewEra report programming much simpler. And, if you're using a C++ development environment, you'll want to investigate the Crystal Report Engine Class library. This library, based on Microsoft's Foundation Class (MFC) library, provides an object-oriented reporting interface to Crystal Reports for C++ programmers.

And finally, Seagate Software has introduced its first Java-capable interface with Crystal Reports 7. The Crystal Reports Java Bean Viewer allows you to integrate a report into your Java applet or application. The Java Bean Viewer exposes a similar set of properties and methods as the Crystal ActiveX Control for non-Java development tools.

Which Development Language Should I Use?

This is a question that cannot be answered simply in this book. It obviously depends largely on your experience level with particular developer tools. Also, your company may standardize on certain development tools that limit your choices. However, if your project will depend heavily on built-in reporting, you may want to consider an alternate tool if the tool you are familiar with doesn't support Crystal Reports' more flexible interfaces.

Ultimately, the most flexible developer interface to Crystal Reports is the Report Engine API. Since many of the other developer interfaces are merely wrappers around this API, you'll find this the most straightforward route to working with Crystal Reports. Most common Windows languages support calls to Windows DLLs, so chances are good that you'll be able to program Crystal Reports applications using this method. However, this also tends to be the most complex and cryptic method of programming Crystal Reports applications. So, if you're not familiar with direct calls to Windows APIs and your language of choice supports another, simpler interface, such as ActiveX controls or COM automation servers, you'll probably want to make use of these simpler options.

DEVELOPING CUSTOM WINDOW APPLICATIONS

Also, the demands of your application will, to a certain degree, determine the language and developer interface that you choose. Almost all of the Crystal Reports functionality can be controlled from within your application. You can customize virtually every part of your report on the fly from within your application. You can even trap user events, such as drilling-down and mouse clicks. However, not all developer interfaces offer the same level of flexibility for all these functions. For example, event trapping is only supported by the Report Engine API, the Report Engine Automation Server, and the Report Designer Component. So, if your application will need to support this level of functionality, you may be somewhat more limited in your development-language choices.

Overall, you'll need to balance your corporate standards, your knowledge level, the size and speed you want your application to maintain, and the reporting demands of your application when making a development-tool choice. The comforting part is that Crystal Reports gives you many interfaces for many environments. By providing many different approaches for interfacing with the reporting engine, Seagate has given the developer more choice in selecting a custom development tool.

Why Is This Book Focusing on Visual Basic?

The remainder of this section will concentrate on Microsoft Visual Basic as the development tool for your custom reporting applications. There are a couple of reasons for this choice:

- Visual Basic is a wildly popular development environment. Microsoft estimates that there are upwards of three million Visual Basic developers in the world. Although one might not initially trust these estimates, it should be remembered that Microsoft also provides many other popular development tools, as well, so inflating Visual Basic figures would not appear to be particularly beneficial to them. In any case, it's hard to argue with the popularity of Visual Basic.

- Seagate Software estimates that a large number of Crystal Reports developers are using Visual Basic. Although other interfaces are provided with the tool, the large corporate and business penetration of Crystal Reports lends itself to Visual Basic usage.

Many of the methods and approaches discussed in the following chapters can easily be converted to other languages. If your language uses the same interface (ActiveX control, Automation Server, and so on) as those used in the Visual Basic examples in the chapter, very little effort will be required to convert to the syntax of your development tool.

The best source of developer-related information from Seagate is a Windows Help file that ships with Crystal Reports. Either choose Crystal Reports Developer's Help from the Crystal Reports program group, or use Windows Explorer to navigate to the Crystal Reports program directory, and open the DEVELOPR.HLP Windows Help file. You'll find information relating to most common development languages, sample code that you can copy from the Help file, and references to sample applications that are installed along with Crystal Reports.

Different VB Reporting Options

One of the big reasons for Crystal Reports' popularity is that it seems to automatically show up whenever you install a great number of other applications. It has been bundled with Visual Basic since VB Version 2. Crystal Reports is also included with other Microsoft development tools, the BackOffice suite of tools, and over 150 other general and specific off-the-shelf applications. This, combined with the introduction of Microsoft's Data Report Designer in Visual Basic 6 may beg the question: "Why should I upgrade to the full Professional version of Crystal Reports if I can use the Data Report Designer or already have a bundled version of Crystal Reports with Visual Basic?"

Crystal Reports Versus the Microsoft Data Report Designer

In VB versions prior to 6, the only reporting options you had "out of the box" were excruciatingly painful record-by-record coding options, or the various bundled versions of Crystal Reports. Visual Basic 6 introduced the Microsoft Data Report Designer, as well as continuing to include a bundled version of Crystal Reports. Whereas Crystal Reports was typically installed automatically with Visual Basic in versions prior to 6, you'll have to dig for it with VB 6. Microsoft automatically installs its own Data Report Designer instead.

However, a peek at the Microsoft offering will quickly give you an idea of where you may want to turn for report design. While the Data Report Designer is fairly well integrated with Visual Basic (using the new VB Data Environment), it quickly runs out of steam. For really powerful, sophisticated reports, you'll need to turn to another tool.

Bundled Crystal Reports Versus the Stand-Alone Version

Even with Microsoft's new Data Report Designer included in VB 6, Crystal Reports is *still* bundled in the VB package—you just have to install it separately. And, Visual Basic 4 and 5 also included bundled copies of Crystal Reports. The versions that are included with VB differ dramatically from off-the-shelf Crystal Reports 7 Professional, however.

DEVELOPING CUSTOM WINDOW APPLICATIONS

In VB 5 and VB 6, Seagate bundles a version of Crystal Reports known as Version 4.6. This is interesting, as Seagate never released an off-the-shelf version 4.6 of Crystal Reports—standalone Crystal Reports versions progressed from 4.5 to 5.0, then 6.0, and now 7.0. Why the version of Crystal Reports that's bundled with VB goes so far back is a question for someone who understands software company marketing and upgrade strategies. But for you, the developer, the differences between the 4.6 bundled version and off-the-shelf Crystal Reports 7 are vast and significant:

- Bundled Crystal Reports was brought to market before Microsoft's Component Object Model became a standard. It doesn't contain any of the newer programming interfaces, such as the Automation Server or Report Designer component.

- Crystal Reports Versions 5 and later introduced many new usability enhancements, such as conditional formatting, multiple sections, and subreports. There are so many of these critical features missing from the 4.6 version that your report-design capabilities will be severely limited if you choose to use it.

- The bundled version contains virtually no Web-reporting capabilities. If your VB apps will ever get *near* the Web, you'll appreciate the standalone version's Web-reporting features.

These are major reasons to purchase a standalone version of Crystal Reports 7. Typical upgrade pricing is available if you already have the bundled version with Visual Basic. The greatly enhanced features of Crystal Reports 7 should make the outlay well worth the price.

Visual Basic Developer Interfaces

Seagate Software provides several methods for you to use Visual Basic to create a custom reporting application. Your choice of a programming interface will depend on several factors, such as your experience level and the particular functions that you need to include in your application. Table 22-1 discusses the different methods and their advantages and disadvantages.

As a general rule of thumb, the Report Engine Automation Server tends provides a good mix of functionality and ease-of-use. With this object-oriented interface, you can accomplish most of the sophisticated report customization that you require without having to get down-and-dirty with Windows API calls. The Report Designer Component provides a similar level of flexibility as the Automation Server, but adds report design capabilities right inside VB. And, while the ActiveX control is a great way to integrate a report in simpler applications, you may find that it doesn't offer sophisticated features that you may need later on, when your application grows.

Method	Advantages	Disadvantages
Report Engine API	The API completely exposes every Crystal Reports function that can be changed programmatically. If it can be done at all, it can be done with the Report Engine API.	This interface is the most cryptic and code-intensive. If you haven't programmed using Windows DLL interfaces in the past, this is a somewhat challenging place to start. Some of the more advanced functions exposed by the API (such as trapping mouse and drill-down events) require CALLBACK programming, which is difficult to implement in Visual Basic. And, some functions, such as report exporting, require the use of a wrapper interface because of some VB limitations in handling data structures.
Report Engine Automation Server	This is the standard COM automation server method. It exposes Crystal Reports functions in a typical object model of properties, methods, and events. The Automation Server exposes almost all of Crystal Reports' functionality, including event trapping. This is also a method of integrating Crystal Reports in Active Server Pages on Microsoft Web servers. Once you learn the Automation Server with Visual Basic, you can apply many of the concepts to Active Server Pages, as well.	If you're not familiar with object-oriented programming, the Automation Server object model can be somewhat daunting. Some newer Crystal Reports 7 features are not exposed by the Automation Server. Also, you must be using Visual Basic 4 or greater, as automation servers are not supported in earlier versions. (However, if you're still using VB 3, you probably should consider an upgrade, anyway!)

Table 22-1. *Visual Basic Programming Interface Comparison*

Method	Advantages	Disadvantages
Report Designer Component	This new interface, introduced in Crystal Reports 7, combines both report design and integration completely inside Visual Basic. You can accomplish much of your report-design work right inside VB, without having to design reports in the Crystal Reports design environment first. In addition, the Report Designer component includes its own automation server (slightly different from the Report Engine Automation Server) that exposes Crystal Reports' functionality in a property-method-event object model.	ActiveX designers, like the Report Designer component, are only supported in Visual Basic 5 or later. Since these versions of VB produce only 32-bit code for Windows 95 or greater, you won't be able to use the Report Designer component to develop 16-bit applications for earlier versions of Windows. Also, the Report Designer component doesn't quite include the same level of functionality as the full Report Engine Automation Server. You may need to use it for certain application features.
ActiveX Control	This ActiveX control (also known as an OLE control or OCX control) is a very simple interface to Crystal Reports. If you are a relatively new VB programmer who hasn't gotten to automation server or Windows API programming yet, this is a great way to create some fairly sophisticated reporting applications very quickly and easily.	The ActiveX control's simplicity comes at a price—functionality. The ActiveX control doesn't provide the complete Crystal Reports capabilities of the other interfaces. In particular, Seagate Software did not update the ActiveX control to include new Version 7 Crystal Reports features. This will limit your ability to create sophisticated reporting applications with the ActiveX control.
VBX Control	This is the Visual Basic 3 holdover custom control. If you are using older versions of Visual Basic or other 16-bit programming environments that support the Visual Basic extension (VBX) interface, this tool is still available.	As this interface has not been updated to use new features introduced in recent versions of Crystal Reports, you'll have much more limited functionality with this tool. Only consider this approach if your development environment doesn't support any of the other developer interfaces.

Table 22-1.   *Visual Basic Programming Interface Comparison* (continued)

One thing to keep in mind when making your choice of a VB interface: you must choose one option for each individual application. You can't use more than one approach in the same application. For example, if you add the ActiveX control to your application and then try to make direct API calls, errors will result. Evaluate your needs and skills. Then, choose a method and stick with it. Changing an interface in mid-stream will require you to do significant recoding.

Sample Application Overview

Ultimately, you'll probably choose one Crystal Reports integration option as your favorite. However, you may want to experiment with the various options before making your choice. And, as your knowledge of the different methods (as well as your programming expertise) expands, you may very possibly graduate from one method to another. The rest of this section, then, will give you a good compare-and-contrast view of the different methods of report integration and of how you can accomplish the same things using the different methods. The book examines the following Crystal Reports programming methods, in the following order:

- The ActiveX control (Chapter 23)
- The Report Designer component (Chapter 24)
- The Report Engine Automation Server (Chapter 25)
- The Report Engine API (Chapter 26)

These approaches generally progress from simplest to most complex, so you'll be able to learn new skills as you progress from chapter to chapter. The same initial VB application will be used in each instance. The reporting functions will be progressively added in the same sequence in each chapter. You'll be able to follow the application from start to finish step-by-step using each integration method.

The Xtreme Mountain Bikes Orders Report

The sample application that will be used throughout the rest of this section is a sample orders report for the Xtreme Mountain Bike Company, a fictional company used throughout this book. The data for the report comes from the XTREME.MDB Microsoft Access sample database that's included with Crystal Reports 7. The application will present a user-friendly, graphical user interface for end-users who want to print an Xtreme order report.

This report contains several special features you'll want to enable for your end-users in the VB application:

- A user-specified sales-tax rate that is used in the "Order + Tax" formula.
- The ability to group by Calendar Quarter or Customer Name, based on user selection.

- A parameter field that will prompt for a highlight value to highlight orders over a certain amount.

- An order-date range that will limit the report's record selection.

- A label in the Page Header of the report indicating the choices the user has made.

- The choice to show detail data, or to just group subtotals and summaries for drill-down. The report contains two different Page Header sections and two different Group Header sections containing column headings that are suppressed and shown according to the summary/detail choice.

- Destination options to preview the report in a window, print the report to a printer, or send the report as a Word document, attached to an e-mail message.

If the report is grouped by quarter, given a 5 percent tax rate, restricted to orders from January 1 through December 31, 1997, and the parameter field to highlight orders is given a value of $5,000, the report will appear as illustrated in Figure 22-1.

The Visual Basic application that will be used to integrate this report is a simple, single-form dialog box that gathers data from the user via text boxes, a combo box, radio buttons, and a check box. When the user clicks OK, the report is previewed, printed, or e-mailed, based on the selections made. The main form from the application is shown in Figure 22-2.

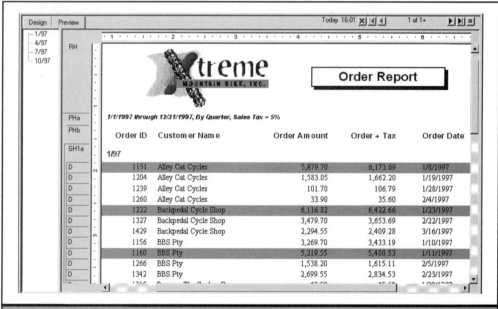

Figure 22-1. Sample Xtreme order report

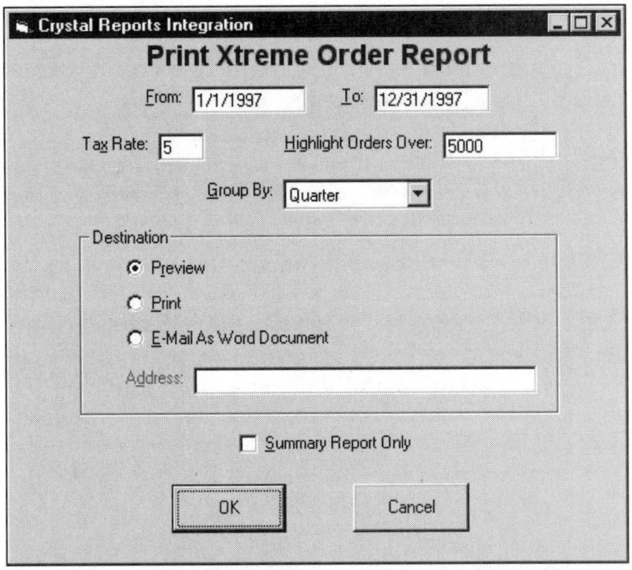

Figure 22-2. *Sample Visual Basic main form*

Beginning versions of both the report and Visual Basic project (created in Visual Basic 6) can be found in the Visual Basic folder on the CD that comes with this book. You are encouraged to copy these files to your hard disk and practice through the next few chapters. Completed applications for each integration method are included on the CD in their own folders within the Visual Basic folder.

In order to correctly accomplish the integration, you'll need to programmatically modify the following report properties from within your Visual Basic application:

- Record Selection Formula
- Report Formula
- Parameter Field
- Output Destination
- Report Section Formatting (Suppress and Show)

Part II Does Not Teach You Visual Basic!

The rest of Part II assumes you have a beginning to intermediate working knowledge of Visual Basic. It's not practical to try to teach you VB at the same time you're learning how to integrate reports. You'll need to have a fundamental knowledge of how to create Visual Basic forms and how to respond to events. There are many good texts (including several from Osborne/McGraw-Hill, such as *Visual Basic 6 from the Ground Up* by Gary Cornell), training programs, and interactive tutorials available to teach you these fundamental skills.

Also, this section assumes that you have gleaned report-design knowledge from Part I of this book. Crystal Reports features, such as selection criteria, parameter fields, and object and section formatting will be covered. If necessary, refer back to Part I to brush-up on these report-design topics.

The
Complete
Reference

Chapter 23

The ActiveX Control

The simplest Visual Basic (VB) programming interface to Crystal Reports is the Crystal ActiveX control. The ActiveX control is similar to Visual Basic extension (.VBX) controls found in earlier versions of Visual Basic (in fact, Seagate still includes an old-style VBX control in case you are using Visual Basic 3). When added to your project, the Crystal ActiveX control will appear on the Visual Basic toolbox, along with other icons for command buttons, forms, radio buttons, and other Windows controls. By simply adding the control to a form in your VB project, you will be able to control report behavior using properties and methods, the same way you control other object behavior on the form.

Procedures and illustrations in this chapter assume you are using Visual Basic 6. Some screens and procedures may differ slightly if you are using another version of Visual Basic.

Adding the ActiveX Control

The first step to using the Crystal ActiveX control is adding it to your VB project. This is similar to adding any other ActiveX control (also known as OLE Custom control) to your project.

1. Open an existing project or create a new VB project.

2. Choose Project | Components from the VB pull-down menus, or press CTRL-T. The Components dialog box will appear.

3. Scroll through the list on the Controls tab until you locate the Crystal Report Control item. Make sure you choose the Crystal Report Control, not other Crystal controls that may be registered on your system. If you don't find the Crystal Report Control, click the Browse button and locate and select the CRYSTL32.OCX file in the Windows system directory.

4. Click OK in the Components dialog box to add the Crystal ActiveX control to the VB toolbox.

Figure 23-1 shows the Crystal ActiveX control in the toolbox and the Components dialog box.

Note   *If you're using the 16-bit version of Visual Basic 4, the filename for the Crystal ActiveX control is CRYSTL16.OCX. If you are using Visual Basic 3, the Crystal Custom Control filename is CRYSTAL.VBX. Remember that the .VBX version doesn't contain the same flexibility as the .OCX version.*

Now you need to add the ActiveX control to a form in your project. Simply open the form you want to add the control to, and double-click on the report icon in the

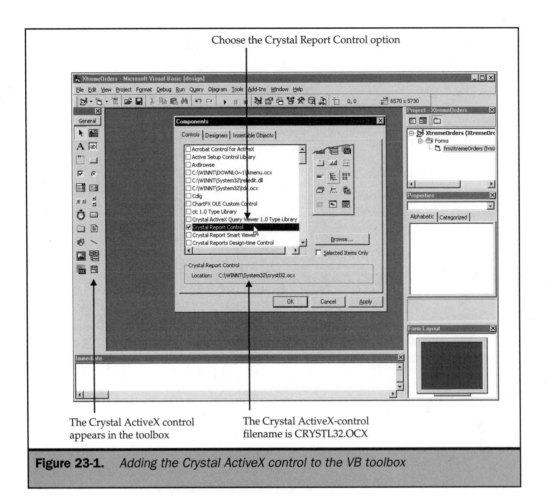

Choose the Crystal Report Control option

The Crystal ActiveX control appears in the toolbox

The Crystal ActiveX-control filename is CRYSTL32.OCX

Figure 23-1.   *Adding the Crystal ActiveX control to the VB toolbox*

toolbox. The icon will be added to the center of the form. You can drag the icon to an out-of-the-way place on the form if you wish. Remember that the icon is a design-time icon only—it won't appear on the form at application run time.

Typically, you'll want to add the control only once to one form. You can use the control from other forms and from module-level code by preceding the control with the form name, so you won't need to add the control to all forms in your project where you may want to display a report (see Figure 23-2).

Once you've added the control to a form, select the control to display and change design-time properties in the VB Properties box. You'll notice that many features of Crystal Reports are available in the Properties box. You can modify report object properties in this Properties box the same way you do for other VB objects at design time.

In addition, the ActiveX control includes a Property Pages dialog box that organizes many ActiveX-control design-time properties in a simplified tabbed dialog

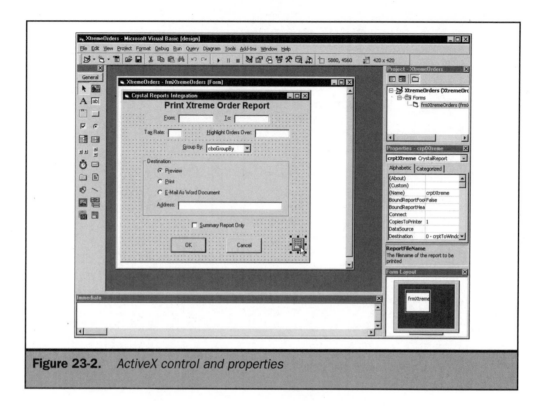

Figure 23-2.   *ActiveX control and properties*

box. To display it, select the (Custom) property in the Properties box and click the ellipsis (...) button next to it. The Property Pages dialog box will appear.

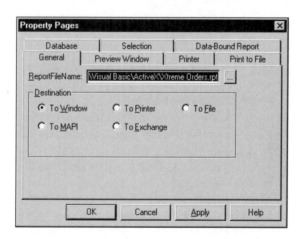

You'll notice many properties on the Property Pages dialog box that duplicate those in the VB Properties box. You can set these values in either place—it's entirely up to you.

The initial setting you may want to make with the new report object you've just added is the object name. Use the (Name) property in the Properties box to make this choice. Although the default name of "CrystalReport1" will probably suffice, you might want to give the object a more meaningful name, including a standard object prefix for a Crystal Report object. You'll notice the object is named crptXtreme in the sample application.

At its most basic level, the ActiveX control can display a report in a preview window by just setting a few properties and adding one line of code to a VB form, menu option, or other control. Initially, you'll only need to specify the name of the Crystal Report .RPT file to use. This name is set with the ReportFileName property in either the Properties box or Property Pages dialog box.

Once you've set the name of the report file, you can display the report by merely executing the control's PrintReport method:

```
intResult = crptXtreme.PrintReport
```

or by setting the control's Action property to 1:

```
crptXtreme.Action = 1
```

If the report can be found and run without any errors, it will be displayed in its own separate preview window.

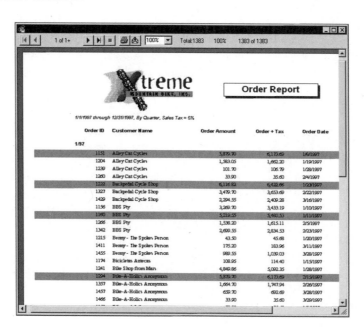

The difference between the two approaches is the way errors are handled. By using the PrintReport method, a result code is returned indicating whether the report processed or not. A result code of 0 indicates that the report processed properly. If the method results in an error, the result code will return an error in the 20*XXX* range.

However, setting the Action property to 1 doesn't return a result code. Should an error occur, a VB error in the 20*XXX* range will be "thrown," and it must be trapped by an On Error Goto routine. Crystal ActiveX-control error handling is discussed in more detail later in the chapter.

All of the ActiveX-control properties and methods discussed in this chapter are well documented in Crystal Reports Developer's Help. You may just want to open it in a separate Help window and minimize it for use while designing your Crystal Reports applications.

Customizing the Preview Window

When the preview window first appears, you may notice some default behavior that doesn't please you. For example, you may not see a group tree appear, even though you created groups on your report. And, if you specifically designed your report to facilitate drilling down by double-clicking on group names or summary fields, you may be frustrated to discover that drilling down won't work.

This is simply the default behavior of the ActiveX-control preview window, and it can be changed at design time or run time. Most properties that affect the behavior of the preview window begin with the word Window. For example, WindowTitle will set the text that appears in the title bar of the preview window. WindowShowGroupTree determines whether or not the group tree will appear. And, WindowAllowDrillDown will determine whether or not you can drill down on the report. These properties can be set in the Properties box, Property Pages dialog box, or at run time. The following code sets these properties at run time:

```
'Customize preview window
crptXtreme.WindowShowGroupTree = True
crptXtreme.WindowTitle = "Xtreme Orders Report"
crptXtreme.WindowAllowDrillDown = chkSummary
```

This will customize the preview window to show the group tree, provide a title to the preview window, and allow drilling down based on the true/false state of a check box on the form.

There are many other properties that you can set to further customize preview-window behavior, such as hiding preview-window buttons and presetting the size and location of the preview window.

Passing Parameter Field Values

Of the many features of Seagate Crystal Reports, parameter fields are one of the most flexible (see Chapter 12 for complete details). They allow a report viewer to select certain options when the report is run, such as choosing only certain records or affecting the way the report appears by using conditional formatting. Whatever value the viewer enters at the parameter-field prompt is passed into the report for use in formulas or record selection.

When you integrate a report containing parameter fields into a VB application, you have several choices as to how you want parameter fields to be handled by the application. By default, the ActiveX control will display the parameter field prompts in a separate window and use the results in the preview window. In simple report applications, this may be sufficient.

However, one of the main reasons you'll probably be using Visual Basic to integrate the report is to provide much more control over how information is supplied to the report. You'll most likely want to gather information from the user with your own user interface and pass that information on to the report at run time. Since you can control both the report record selection and report formulas at run time from within your VB application, using parameter fields isn't as necessary with an integrated report as it might be for a stand-alone report running directly out of Crystal Reports.

However, if your report may be run in a stand-alone environment by some report viewers, as well as inside an integrated VB application by others, you still may need to pass values to parameter fields from within your code. Do this by setting the ParameterFields property at run time. The syntax for setting this property is:

```
[form.]Report.ParameterFields(ArrayIndex)[=ParameterName;NewValue;
SetCurrentValue]
```

This is the first of several property arrays exposed by the ActiveX control. A *property array* is used when more than one item's property can be set inside the report. In the case of parameter fields, a report can contain more than one. By using a property array, you can set multiple parameter-field values in your code. This property array, as with all Crystal ActiveX-control property arrays is *zero-based*. That is, the first occurrence or *element* of the array is numbered 0, not 1. If your report contains four parameter fields that you want to change in the code, you'll set the ParameterFields property four times, using array indexes 0 through 3.

The property looks for a string value containing three arguments, separated by semicolons. The first, *ParameterName*, indicates the name of the parameter field you wish to change. The *NewValue* argument provides the actual value you wish to pass to the parameter field. The *SetCurrentValue* argument determines whether the parameter field will be prompted for a value, displaying as the default the value you pass.

DEVELOPING CUSTOM
WINDOW APPLICATIONS

Even if you pass parameter-field values, your report may not reflect the new values or may otherwise behave unpredictably if it contains saved data (that is, if Save Data with Report is checked on the Crystal Reports File menu). Since the overall purpose of a VB application is to run the report in real time after a user makes selections from the user interface, saving data with the report makes little sense anyway. If you are going to integrate a report with a Visual Basic application, turn this option off before saving your final version of the .RPT file.

The following code from the sample Xtreme Orders application uses the value of a text box to determine what is passed to the Highlight parameter field in the report. This parameter field is used in conditional formatting to add a light blue background to orders that exceed the parameter-field value.

```
'Supply "Highlight" parameter field
If txtHighlight = "" Then
    crptXtreme.ParameterFields(0) = "Highlight;0;TRUE"
Else
    crptXtreme.ParameterFields(0) = "Highlight;" & txtHighlight & ";TRUE"
End If  'txtHighlight = ""
```

Here, the parameter-field value will be passed, and the usual Crystal Reports prompt will not be displayed.

In this case, the value is set to 0 if the text box is empty. This is important to note, as the actual parameter field in the report is numeric. Passing it an empty string will cause a run-time error when the report runs. Also, if you are passing a value to a date parameter field from your application, make sure it conforms to the Crystal Reports date syntax. You must pass "Date(yyyy,mm,dd)," not "mm/dd/yyyy" for the parameter field to work properly. Always pass a value to a parameter field in the exact same format that you would use when typing in the value when prompted.

 This is the first of several ActiveX-control capabilities that haven't been updated for Crystal Reports Version 7. Although Version 7's parameter fields are much improved (multiple values, range values, and so on), none of these new features are exposed by the ActiveX control. You'll need to use another integration method to take full advantage of the Crystal Reports 7 parameter fields.

Controlling Record Selection

One of the most obvious benefits of integrating a Crystal Report into a VB program is controlling report record selection "on the fly," based on your user's interactions with the VB application. Your application can present any type of user interface you desire, including controls populated by databases. Crystal Reports parameter fields are very limited in their editing and validation capabilities (even though Version 7 is a vast improvement over previous versions), but text boxes and other VB controls can contain edit masks and other sophisticated validation features, such as the new VB date picker, to help users choose correct options. You can then use the results of user actions to build a new Crystal Reports record-selection formula before the report is printed.

If you are used to using the Crystal Reports Select Expert for record selection, you'll need to familiarize yourself with the actual Crystal Reports formula that it creates before you create a selection formula in your VB application. A Crystal Reports record-selection formula is a Boolean formula that narrows down the database records that will be included in the report. For example, the following record-selection formula will limit a report to orders placed in the first quarter of 1997 from customers in Wyoming:

```
{Orders.Order Date} In Date(1997,1,1) To Date(1997,3,31) And
{Customer.Region} = "WY"
```

> **Tip** *For a complete discussion of Crystal Reports record selection and how to create Boolean formulas, consult Chapters 5 and 6.*

There are two ActiveX-control approaches to changing record selection: the ReplaceSelectionFormula method and the SelectionFormula property. There is a *very* important distinction between the two. The ReplaceSelectionFormula method will completely replace any existing selection formula in the report with the one you pass. However, setting the SelectionFormula property will *append* the selection formula you pass to any formula that already exists in the report. Be careful—only set the SelectionFormula property if you're sure you want to keep what's already saved with the report. Otherwise, the ReplaceSelectionFormula method will ensure your report uses only the selection formula you supply in your application.

The syntax for these options is:

```
[form.]Report.SelectionFormula[= SelectionFormulaString$]
```

```
[form.]Report.ReplaceSelectionFormula [(SelectionFormulaString$)]
```

In each case, *SelectionFormulaString$* is either a string expression or string variable containing the Crystal record-selection formula. Thus, to pass a date-range record-selection formula to the Xtreme Orders report, based on the contents of the From Date and To Date text boxes, use the following code:

```
'Supply record selection based on dates
strSelectionFormula = "{Orders.Order Date} in Date(" & _
   Format(txtFromDate, "yyyy,m,d") & ") to Date(" & _
   Format(txtToDate, "yyyy,m,d") & ")"
crptXtreme.ReplaceSelectionFormula (strSelectionFormula)
'Note: parentheses around strSelectionFormula are optional
```

Record-Selection Formula Tips

There are several important points to keep in mind when building a Crystal record-selection formula within your application. Specifically, there are some tricks to making sure that your string values are formatted properly, and to making sure that as much of the SQL selection work is done on the server, rather than on the PC.

The string value you pass in your selection formula must adhere *exactly* to the Crystal Reports formula syntax. This includes using correct Crystal reserved words and punctuation. The previous example showed the necessity of building a Date(yyyy,mm,dd) string to pass to the selection formula.

It's also easy to forget the required quotation marks or apostrophes around literals that are used in comparisons. For example, you may want to pass the following selection formula:

```
{Customer.Region} = 'WY' And {Orders.Ship Via} = 'UPS'
```

If the characters WY and UPS are coming from controls, such as a text box and combo box, you might consider using the following VB code to place the selection formula in a string variable:

```
strSelectionFormula = "{Customer.Region} = " & txtRegion & _
" And {Orders.Ship Via} = " & cboShipper
```

At first glance, this appears to create a correctly formatted Crystal record-selection formula. However, if you submit this string with the ReplaceSelectionFormula method, the report will fail when it runs. Why? The best way to troubleshoot this issue is to look at the contents of strSelectionFormula in the VB Immediate window, by setting a breakpoint, or by using other VB debugging features. This will show the contents of the string variable after the preceding code has executed:

```
{Customer.Region} = WY And {Orders.Ship Via} = UPS
```

Notice that there are no quotation marks or apostrophes around the literals that are being compared in the record-selection formula, a basic requirement of the Crystal Reports formula language. The following VB code will create a syntactically correct selection formula:

```
strSelectionFormula = "{Customer.Region} = '" & txtRegion & _
"' And {Orders.Ship Via} = '" & cboShipper & "'"
```

The other major point to keep in mind is that if your report will be using a SQL database, remember that Crystal Reports will attempt to convert as much of your record-selection formula as possible to SQL when it runs the report. The same caveats apply to the record-selection formula you pass from your VB application as apply to a record-selection formula you create directly in Crystal Reports. In particular, using built-in Crystal Reports formula functions, such as UpperCase or IsNull, and using OR operators instead of AND operators, will typically cause record selection to be moved to the client (the PC) instead of the database server. The result is very slow report performance. To avoid this situation, take the same care in creating record-selection formulas that you pass from your application as you would in Crystal Reports. Look for detailed discussions on record-selection performance in both Chapters 6 and 14.

You may also choose to create the SQL statement the report will use right in your VB application, and submit it to the report by setting the SQLQuery property. More information on this approach can be found by searching for "SQLQuery property (ActiveX control)" in Developer's Help.

Setting Formulas

Another powerful feature of Crystal Reports/Visual Basic integration is the ability to change report formulas from within your application at run time. As you might imagine, this opens up tremendous opportunities for a VB program to control the appearance and behavior of a report. This can be useful for changing formulas that are related to groups that may also be changed from within your code, or formulas that show text on the report, or formulas that control math calculations or conditional formatting on the report.

Setting formulas at run time is similar to setting the record-selection formula at run time (described in the previous section). You'll need a good understanding of the Crystal Reports formula language to adequately modify formulas inside your VB code. If you need a refresher on Crystal Reports formulas, look back at Chapter 5.

The ActiveX control provides a property array that allows you to change one or more formulas in the report. The syntax for the Formulas property is:

```
[form.]Report.Formulas(ArrayIndex)[= FormulaName= FormulaText]
```

As with parameter fields, formulas are available in a zero-based property array. You should begin using array element 0 for the first formula you are going to change, 1 for the second, and so on. You needn't change the Formulas property for all formulas in the report—just the ones you want to modify at run time. When you modify the Formulas property, you must specify the exact formula name you wish to change, *without* the preceding @ sign, and then supply a string expression or variable that contains the new text you want the formula to contain.

In the Xtreme Orders sample application, two formulas are changed at run time, based on user-specified criteria on the Print Report form. First, the Order + Tax formula is modified, based on the user's entry in the Tax Rate text box. The formula is changed by the following code:

```
'Set @Order + Tax formula
If txtTaxRate = "" Then
    crptXtreme.Formulas(0) = "Order + Tax={Orders.Order Amount}"
Else
    crptXtreme.Formulas(0) = "Order + Tax={Orders.Order Amount} *"_
    & Str(txtTaxRate / 100 + 1)
End If   'txtTaxRate = ""
```

As in previous examples for parameter fields, note that you must take care when assigning a value to the formula. The Order + Tax formula is defined in Crystal Reports as a numeric formula. Therefore, you should pass it a formula that will evaluate to a number. If the user leaves the text box on the form empty, the program assumes there is no additional sales tax and simply places the Order Amount database field in the formula—the formula will show the same amount as the database field.

If, however, the user has specified a tax rate, the VB code manipulates the value by dividing it by 100, then adding 1. This will create the proper type of number to multiply against the Order Amount field to correctly calculate tax. For example, if the user specifies a tax rate of 5 (for 5 percent tax), the VB code will change the value to 1.05 before combining it with the multiply operator and the Order Amount field in the formula. Notice also that the formula name *does not* contain the leading @ sign. This should be left off when supplying formula names to the Formulas property.

Another helpful use of formulas is to change text that appears on the report at run time, as the ActiveX control does not allow you to change the contents of text objects from within your code (this capability exists in the Report Designer component, covered in Chapter 24). Changing text that appears at run time is helpful if you want to display criteria that the user has specified for the report, fields that the report is grouped or sorted on, or other useful information.

Consider the following code that modifies the Sub Heading formula on the Xtreme Order report. This formula, located in the page header, identifies the date range, grouping, and tax rates specified by the user.

```
'Set @Sub Heading formula
strSubHeading = "'" & txtFromDate & " through " & txtToDate
strSubHeading = strSubHeading & ", By " & cboGroupBy
If txtTaxRate = "" Then
    strSubHeading = strSubHeading & ", No Tax'"
Else
    strSubHeading = strSubHeading & ", Sales Tax = " & txtTaxRate & "%'"
End If   'txtTaxRate = ""
crptXtreme.Formulas(1) = "Sub Heading=" & strSubHeading
```

In this example, a string variable is used to build the correct formula syntax for the Crystal Reports string formula. Notice that the ultimate contents of the string variable must adhere to Crystal Reports syntax before the variable is passed to the report. In particular, this string formula begins and ends with an apostrophe. By using a string variable that is ultimately supplied to the Formulas property, you have more flexibility to examine the contents of the variable at a breakpoint in your code if you're unsure whether the correct syntax is being passed to the property.

Manipulating Report Groups

One of the requirements for the Xtreme Orders report is that the user be able to specify how the report is grouped. A combo box exists on the Print Report form that lets the user choose between Quarter and Customer grouping. In the Crystal Reports designer, this is normally accomplished by using the Change Group option to change the field a group is based on, as well as the order (ascending or descending) that you want the groups to appear in. If the group is based on a date field, such as Order Date, you can also specify the range of dates (week, month, quarter, and so on) that make up the group. To familiarize yourself with various grouping options, refer to Chapter 3.

By being able to change these options from within an application at run time, you can provide great reporting flexibility to your end-users. In many cases, you can make it appear that several different reports are available based on user input. In fact, the user will be calling the same report, but the grouping will be changed at run time, based on user input.

Grouping is modified at run time by setting the GroupCondition property. This property allows you to change most of the group specification (with the exception of Specified Order grouping) that you can set in the Change Group dialog box in Crystal Reports. GroupCondition, as with other previously discussed properties, is a zero-based property array. And, as with other similar properties, you needn't specify a GroupCondition property for every group on your report, only those that you want to change from within your application.

The syntax for the GroupCondition property is:

```
[form.]Report.GroupCondition(ArrayIndex%)
[= group; field; condition; sortDirection]
```

The arguments for changing this property are as follows:

group	A reserved word for each group contained on your report. The first group is referred to by the reserved word GROUP1, the second group GROUP2, and so on.
field	The database field or report formula (including curly braces) that you want to base the group on.

condition	A reserved word indicating the frequency of group creation. This is used for date field and Boolean field grouping to indicate how often a new group should be created. Allowed values for date fields are DAILY, WEEKLY, BIWEEKLY, SEMIMONTHLY, MONTHLY, QUARTERLY, SEMIANNUALLY, and ANNUALLY. Allowed values for Boolean fields are TOYES, TONO, EVERYYES, EVERYNO, NEXTISYES, and NEXTISNO. For nondate and non-Boolean fields, there is only one option you may supply for this argument, ANYCHANGE. Even though the ANYCHANGE argument doesn't truly affect grouping, you must still supply it.
sortdirection	The letters A or D. A specifies that groups will appear in ascending order, D specifies descending order.

All four arguments must always be supplied and must be separated by semicolons. The value may be supplied either as a string expression or string variable.

Based on this syntax, the following code from the Xtreme Orders sample application will change the field the report group is based on, depending on the selection the user makes from the Group By combo box.

```
'Change grouping
Select Case cboGroupBy
   Case "Quarter"
      crptXtreme.GroupCondition(0) = "GROUP1;_
      {Orders.Order Date};QUARTERLY;A"
   Case "Customer"
      crptXtreme.GroupCondition(0) = "GROUP1;_
      {Customer.Customer Name};ANYCHANGE;A"
End Select  'Case cboGroupBy
```

Caution *Although this example should correctly create quarterly or customer grouping, the ActiveX control suffers from a serious bug when performing date grouping. In the version of the ActiveX control that ships with Crystal Reports 7, the condition argument does not correctly affect date grouping. Even though the word QUARTERLY is supplied, the report will create a new group for every day. Thus, you'll note that the logic to create quarterly grouping is remarked-out in the sample application. If the user specifies quarterly grouping, the group is not changed, as quarterly grouping is specified in the .RPT file already.*

Changing Section Formatting

As Visual Basic applications often want to present reports to viewers in an online environment instead of just printing them on paper, interactive reporting features, such as drill-down, are invaluable to the application designer. Having control over these capabilities at run time provides for great flexibility.

The Xtreme Orders sample application gives the user the opportunity to specify whether or not to see the report as a summary report only. When this check box is selected, the VB application will need to hide the report's Details section so that only group subtotals appear on the report.

In addition, you'll need to control the appearance of the Xtreme Orders.RPT file's two-page header sections (*Page Header a* and *Page Header b*), as well as two Group Header #1 sections (*Group Header #1a* and *Group Header #1b*). This is to accommodate two different sections of field titles that will appear differently if the report is presented as a summary report instead of a detail report. If the report is being displayed as a detail report, the field titles should appear at the top of every page of the report, along with the subheading and smaller report title. If the report is displayed as a summary report, however, you will only want the field titles to appear in the Group Header section of a drill-down tab when the user double-clicks a group. Since no detail information will be visible in the main report window, field titles there won't be meaningful.

Finally, you'll want to show Group Header #1a, which contains the group name field, if the report is showing detail data. This will indicate what group the following set of orders applies to. However, if the report is only showing summary data, showing both the group header and group footer will be repetitive—the group footer already contains the group name, so showing the group header, as well, looks odd.

Therefore, you'll need to control the appearance of four sections when a user chooses the summary report option. Table 23-1 outlines how you'll want to conditionally set these sections at run time.

Now you must look at the available ActiveX-control properties to find one that allows control of section formatting at run time. The only property the ActiveX control offers is the SectionFormat property. As with many other properties, SectionFormat is a

Section	Detail Report	Summary Report
Page Header b (field titles)	Shown	Suppressed (no drill-down)
Group Header #1a (group-name field)	Shown	Hidden (drill-down okay)
Group Header #1b (field titles)	Suppressed (no drill-down)	Hidden (drill-down okay)
Details (detail order data)	Shown	Hidden (drill-down okay)

Table 23-1. *Section Formatting for Different Report Types*

zero-based property array that can be set as many times as necessary to format multiple sections of the report. The syntax is as follows:

```
[form.]Report.SectionFormat(SectionArrayIndex%)[= sectionCode; visible;
newPageBefore; newPageAfter; keepTogether; suppressBlankSection;
resetPageNAfter; printAtBottomOfPage; underlaySection; backgroundColor]
```

The best place to look for a detailed breakdown of all the SectionFormat property's arguments is Crystal Reports Developer's Help. Search for "SectionFormat property (ActiveX control)."

The arguments roughly equate to the check box properties you see when using the Format Section option in the Crystal Reports design environment (refer to Chapter 8 for more details). In a nutshell, arguments are broken down into three types: the section name, on-off properties, and a background color. The section-name argument is a reserved word (again, look at Developer's Help for details) that indicates the exact section of the report you want to format. The on-off (true-false) properties can all be supplied the letter T to turn the property on, the letter F to turn the property off, or the letter X to leave the property setting as it was when the report was created. The background-color property requires an RGB (red-green-blue) number consisting of three numerals from 0 to 255 inclusive, separated by periods (for example, 255.0.0 would set pure red as the background color for the section).

The following sample code will change a Crystal Reports ActiveX control named CrystalReport1. The code will show a second Group Header #2 section (Group Header #2b) that was suppressed when the report was created, set the New Page Before option on, and set the background color to pure blue.

```
CrystalReport1.SectionFormat(0) = GROUPHDR.1.1;T;T;X;X;X;X;X;X;0.0.255
```

Now that you've been given a fairly detailed overview of this property, how can it be used with the Xtreme Orders report to correctly format the report for summary viewing? If you refer back to Table 23-1, you'll notice an immediate need to hide several sections while still allowing drill-down functionality. In particular, the details section must be hidden, not suppressed. If the details section is suppressed, there's little sense in even creating a drill-down report in the first place.

Now, if you look at Developer's Help for available on-off arguments, you'll notice only the Visible argument. This equates to the Suppress (No Drill-Down) option from the Format Section dialog box in Crystal Reports. *There is no Hide (Drill-Down OK) argument available with the ActiveX control!* You cannot format a visible section to be hidden, still allowing drill-down. As mentioned in Chapter 22, the ActiveX control is limited in its capabilities—you might not always be able to complete all the report customization you desire with this particular developer interface. So, then, how do you still accomplish your goal of providing the user a summary report versus detail report choice?

A second .RPT file must be created to complete the ActiveX-control integration example. This .RPT file will have the report sections preformatted as described in Table 23-1, so that the report will already display in a summary fashion. In addition, the regular .RPT file showing the detail report will also be used. Based on the choice made in the Summary check box, the appropriate .RPT file will be assigned to the ActiveX control before any other properties are set. Here's the code from the sample application to accomplish this:

```
'Set report filename based on summary check box
'(because ActiveX control can't set Hide section property)
If chkSummary Then
    crptXtreme.ReportFileName = _
    "C:\Visual Basic\ActiveX\Xtreme Orders Summary.rpt"
Else
    crptXtreme.ReportFileName = _
    "C:\Visual Basic\ActiveX\Xtreme Orders.rpt"
End If   'chkSummary
```

Although this may not seem the most elegant method of accomplishing your ultimate goal, it is an acceptable method to deal with the inherent limitation of the Crystal ActiveX control. Subsequent chapters will illustrate that this limitation does not apply to other integration methods.

Choosing Output Destinations

Although viewing a report online in the preview window is a good way to interact with a report, you'll probably have situations where you want the report printed to a printer, exported to another file format, or attached to an e-mail message. These options are available from buttons in the preview window (if you haven't turned the options off with available ActiveX-control properties). However, you may want tighter control over these capabilities from within your Visual Basic application. If you want to always send the output to a specific destination, properties can be set in either the Properties box or the Property Pages dialog box at design time to choose the output destination. Or, you may want to make this choice at run time based on user input.

In the Xtreme Orders sample application, radio buttons and a text box allow the user to choose whether to view the report in the preview window, print the report to a printer, or attach the report as a Word document to an e-mail message. If the user chooses e-mail as the output destination, an e-mail address can be typed into a text box.

Once the viewer has made a selection, you will need to set the output destination automatically in your VB code.

There are several properties that you can use to control output destination: Destination, various EMail properties, and PrintFileType. The Destination property lets you make a general choice of output destination. The syntax is:

```
[form.]Report.Destination[= Destination%]
```

Destination% is an integer number or predefined constant that determines the output destination. The integers and associated available constants are listed in Table 23-2.

If you choose MAPI as the destination, the user's PC will need to have a MAPI-compliant e-mail client, such as Microsoft Outlook or Eudora Pro, installed. Also, you'll be able to set other options for the e-mail message, such as the To list, CC list, subject, and message text using the ActiveX control's EMailToList, EMailCCList, EMailSubject, and EMailMessage properties. If you choose a destination of file or e-mail, choose the format of the exported or attached report (such as Excel, Word, Lotus 1-2-3, and so on) with the PrintFileType property. And, if you choose to export to a file, specify the filename with the PrintFileName property.

There are additional properties that are used to specify the field separator character, as well as number and date formats used for reports exported to ASCII text files. Look at Developer's Help for more information.

Value	Constant	Description
0	crptToWindow	Sends the report to the preview window.
1	crptToPrinter	Sends the report to a printer.
2	crptToFile	Exports the report to a disk file. Specify the file format, such as Excel, Word, and so on, with the PrintFileType property and the filename with the PrintFileName property.
3	crptToMapi	Attaches the report to an e-mail message using any MAPI-compliant e-mail client installed on the user's PC. Specify the file format for the attachment with the PrintFileType property.
6	crptToExchange	Exports the report to a Microsoft Exchange folder.

Table 23-2.   *Constants Used with the Destination Property*

In the sample Xtreme Orders application, the following code is used to choose an output destination, as well as to specify a file type and e-mail information, based on user selection.

```
'Set output destination
If optPreview Then crptXtreme.Destination = crptToWindow
If OptPrint Then crptXtreme.Destination = crptToPrinter
If OptEmail Then
    With crptXtreme
        .Destination = crptMapi
        .EMailToList = txtAddress
        .EMailSubject = "Here's the Xtreme Orders Report"
        .EMailMessage = "Attached is a Word document showing
the latest Xtreme Orders Report."
        .PrintFileType = crptWinWord
    End With 'cprtXtreme
End If   'optEmail
```

Displaying Print Options

By default, setting the destination to Printer and setting Action = 1 will print the report to the default printer without any further prompts. If, however, you'd like the user to be able to change printers, choose the number of copies to print, or print only a certain range of report pages, you can display the Print Options dialog box with the PrinterSelect method. Examine the following code from the sample application:

```
'Let user change print options
If OptPrint Then crptXtreme.PrinterSelect
'WARNING: if a user cancels the Printer Select dialog box,
'the code has no way of knowing.
'The Action property will still be set!
```

As the remarks indicate, the one caveat to using the PrinterSelect method is that it doesn't return any result code. If the user happens to click the Cancel button on the dialog box, the VB code will continue merrily on its way, presumably to the Action property or PrintReport method, printing the report anyway.

If you prefer to design your own dialog box to gather print-related options from the user, you can use ActiveX-control properties, such as PrinterDriver, PrinterName, and CopiesToPrint to control printing. Look at Developer's Help for information on these, and other, print-related properties.

Error Handling

As with any Visual Basic program, you'll want to prepare for the possibility of errors that may occur. Integrating Crystal Reports with VB requires that you anticipate errors that the ActiveX control might encounter, in addition to other errors that the rest of your program may produce.

If you recall from earlier in the chapter, there are two ways of actually processing the report once the ActiveX properties have all been set: the PrintReport method and the Action property. You'll also recall that the main difference between these two approaches is the way errors are handled. The PrintReport method returns a result code indicating 0 if the report ran correctly, or a code in the 20XXX range containing an error code if it didn't. Conversely, setting the Action property to 1 doesn't return a result code, but does result in a VB run-time error being thrown if the report doesn't print properly. In either case, you'll want to be prepared to intercept the potential error.

The choice of error method is really up to you. However, if you've already developed an On Error Goto routine to handle routine VB errors, it may be easier for you to simply add additional code to handle reporting errors. The error codes returned by either report-processing method will be in the 20XXX range. Using members of the Errors collection, such as Err.Number and Err.Description, you can handle errors or present meaningful error messages to the user. The XXX three-digit codes are specific to the Crystal Reports Print Engine, which is actually called by the ActiveX control. For a complete breakdown of these error codes, search Developer's Help for "Error codes, Crystal Report Engine." There are a few additional error codes that only apply to the ActiveX control, and these can be found in Developer's Help by searching for "Error messages (ActiveX control)." Examine the following code from the Xtreme Orders sample application. Notice that this code doesn't trap any particular reporting errors, except when the user cancels report printing or exporting (which throws a 20545 error). Should another error occur, this routine will simply display the error code and text in a message box.

```
Private Sub cmdOK_Click()
   On Error GoTo cmdOK_Click_Error

. . .


cmdOK_Click_Error:
   If Err.Number = 20545 Then
      MsgBox "Report cancelled", vbOKOnly + vbInformation, _
            "Print Xtreme Orders Report"
      Exit Sub
   End If    'Err.Number = 20545
   MsgBox "Error " + CStr(Err.Number) + " - " + Err.Description, _
         vbOKOnly + vbCritical, "Print Xtreme Orders Report"
End Sub
```

Often you'll introduce errors before *processing the report with the PrintReport method or the Action property, such as by submitting a syntactically incorrect formula or using an incorrect section name when formatting sections. However, these statements won't result in an error. Typically no error will be detected until you actually process the report with PrintReport or Action = 1.*

Other ActiveX Properties and Methods

This chapter has covered many of the typical Crystal ActiveX-control properties and methods required for basic to intermediate report integration. The ActiveX control offers many additional features, however. To get an overview of other capabilities, search Developer's Help for "ActiveX control properties index" or "ActiveX controls methods index." In particular, you may want to explore additional features that are specific to SQL-database handling or working with Crystal Reports subreport objects.

The Reset Method

The Reset method is handy if your VB program can be designed to print a report several times within the same code loop. In the Xtreme Orders sample application, for example, when the OK button is clicked, the dialog box is queried to set several properties for the ActiveX control, culminating in processing the report with Action = 1. However, when the report is finished printing or being e-mailed, or when the viewer closes the preview window, the Print dialog box remains displayed. The user can change options and click OK again.

But what about previous property settings that were made from the last pass through the OK command button code? While your code may always set properties one way or another, regardless of the user interface, you may occasionally depend on the report's default behavior being in place.

For example, since the ActiveX control doesn't adequately handle quarterly date grouping, the sample application assumes this to be set when the report is initially loaded. If the user changes the grouping to Customer, it will remain that way for the next time the report prints, unless it is set back to Order Date grouping. Because date grouping can't be set to QUARTERLY, though, this won't work the next time a user wants quarterly grouping—you want the report to automatically return to its default setting of quarterly grouping.

By using the Reset method, you can have most report properties return to their default .RPT file settings before properties are again set in code. This ensures that all properties are set to their defaults, in case your code cannot modify all properties that were previously changed. Here's the example from the Xtreme Orders application:

```
'Reset properties in case they were set in a previous instance
crptXtreme.Reset
```

DEVELOPING CUSTOM WINDOW APPLICATIONS

SQL Database Control

Many corporate databases are kept on client/server SQL database systems, such as Microsoft SQL Server, Oracle, and Informix. Many Visual Basic applications provide front-end interfaces to these database systems, and they need to handle SQL reporting, as well. The Crystal ActiveX control contains several properties and methods that help when integrating reports based on SQL databases.

Logging On to SQL Databases

Because the VB application probably already handles SQL database security, and thus ensures that the application user has been validated by the database, you don't want the ActiveX control to require the user to log on to the database again when it comes time to print a report. By using the Connect or LogOnInfo properties, or the LogOnServer method, you can provide a valid database ID and password for a report from within the VB code. Search Developer's Help for information on these properties and methods.

Retrieving or Setting the SQL Query

When you submit a record-selection formula, as discussed earlier in the chapter, the Crystal ActiveX control will generate a SQL statement to submit to the database server automatically. However, if the record-selection formula contains Crystal formulas, an OR operator, or other characteristics that prevent Crystal Reports from including a WHERE clause in the SQL statement, report performance can be dramatically affected for the worse. You may, therefore, want to create the SQL statement the report uses directly in your VB application. As part of this process, you may find it helpful to retrieve the SQL statement that Crystal Reports is generating automatically.

To retrieve the contents of the existing SQL statement, use the RetrieveSQLQuery method. This populates the control's SQLQuery property, which can be examined inside your code. The SQLQuery property is a read/write property, so you can make changes to the query that the report will submit to the server by modifying this property. Search Developer's Help for specific syntax requirements for this method and property.

As with Crystal Reports, you cannot modify the SELECT clause in the SQL query. Only FROM, WHERE, and ORDER BY clauses can be modified. Don't forget that you must still include the SELECT clause, however, and that it must not be changed from the original clause Crystal Reports created.

Also, if you create an ORDER BY clause, you must separate it from the end of the WHERE clause with a carriage return/line feed (CR/LF) character sequence. Use CHR$(13) & CHR$(10) VB functions to add the CR/LF sequence inside the SQL query.

Reading or Setting Stored-Procedure Parameters

If your report is based on a parameterized SQL stored procedure, you will probably want to supply parameter values to the stored procedure from within your code, much as you will want to respond to any Crystal Reports parameter fields that appear in other reports.

To retrieve existing stored-procedure parameters, use the RetrieveStoredProcParams method, as illustrated here:

```
NumberofParams% = CrystalReport1.RetrieveStoredProcParams
```

Notice that this method returns an integer result indicating the number of parameters that the report contains. This method also populates the zero-based StoredProcParam property array with the contents of the parameters. You can then read the existing values if necessary. When you need to populate the parameters before running the report, set the StoredProcParam property with the new value, as illustrated here:

```
[form.]Report.StoredProcParam(ParameterArrayIndex%)[= newParameter$]
```

The *newParameter$* argument is a string expression or variable, regardless of the actual data type of the parameter. Just make sure to provide the proper type of data, such as only numeric information for a numeric parameter. Crystal Reports will automatically convert the string to the proper data type when it submits the parameter to the database server.

Subreport Control

If you've added subreports to your main Crystal report, you may want a degree of control over how they behave from within your VB application, as well. The ActiveX control uses an interesting approach to let you customize many aspects of subreports the same way you manipulate the main report.

If you already know the name of the subreport you want to change, simply modify the SubreportToChange property. The syntax follows:

```
[form.]Report.SubreportToChange(= SubreportName$)
```

The *SubreportName$* argument is a string expression or variable that contains the name of the subreport you want to manipulate. Be careful—this argument is case-sensitive. Once you've set the subreport name, many properties that you set thereafter will apply to the subreport instead of the main report. A list of the properties that will now apply to the subreport can be found by searching Developer's Help for "SubreportToChange property (ActiveX control)." To again manipulate the main report, simply change the property again, supplying an empty string (" ") for the subreport name.

If your code needs to query the main report for the number and names of subreports it contains, use the GetNSubreports and GetNthSubreportName methods to make this determination.

```
[form.]Report.GetNSubreports
```

The preceding statement returns a zero-indexed number indicating the number of subreports in the main report.

```
[form.]Report.GetNthSubreportName (SubreportNum%)
```

This statement returns a string containing the name of the subreport that matches the SubreportNum index (zero-based). Make sure you pass an index between zero and what was returned with GetNSubreports.

Developer's Help contains complete information on these methods.

Complete information on using subreports in Crystal Reports is available in Chapter 11.

Chapter 24

The Report Designer Component

The newest, and without argument the most innovative, Visual Basic integration method is the Report Designer component (RDC). The RDC is new to Seagate Crystal Reports Version 7—it's not included with any previous versions (although a somewhat less-capable version is available as a free download from Seagate's Web site and is included in the accompanying CD). The RDC's main advantage over other integration methods is the fact that it's entirely self-contained. You can create a complete VB-based reporting application from start to finish entirely inside the Visual Basic integrated development environment (IDE).

Whereas the other Crystal Reports integration methods require you to develop the report's .RPT file in the Crystal Reports design tool and *then* integrate it into your VB application, the RDC allows you to actually design the report right inside VB. Not only will you find most of the same design capabilities available from within the RDC, but virtually all the fields, formulas, text objects, sections, and other parts of the report will be exposed to VB as objects. Like VB forms and controls, report objects have properties and methods that can be set at both design time and run time. And, the RDC exposes several Component Object Model (COM) automation server interfaces to allow sophisticated object-oriented report integration.

The RDC is only available with the 32-bit version of Crystal Reports Professional. It will only work with Visual Basic 5 or later (which is a 32-bit-only environment), and it isn't included with the Standard version of Crystal Reports.

The RDC Explained

The entire RDC actually consists of several parts that work together. The designer itself allows you to actually create and modify reports inside the Visual Basic IDE.

Once you've created the report, the RDC exposes a set of powerful properties, methods, and events via a COM Automation Server (very similar, but not identical to, the Report Engine Automation Server discussed in Chapter 25). And, because the RDC doesn't include its own built-in preview window as the ActiveX control does, you use another ActiveX component, the *Smart Viewer*, to view reports on the screen. The Smart Viewer also exposes a large set of properties, methods, and events to allow you complete control over how your application user can interact with your report in the viewer window.

The ActiveX Designer

The RDC is an *ActiveX designer*, a relatively new interface that works with Visual Basic 5 and 6. Whereas other ActiveX controls and automation servers generally extend the capabilities of the Visual Basic language, an ActiveX designer actually extends the capabilities of the Visual Basic IDE. Some common examples are the User Connection Designer and the Data Environment Designer, both ActiveX designers for connecting to remote databases that are available with Visual Basic 6.

The designer portion of the RDC allows you to create a complete report right inside Visual Basic. There's no longer a need to use the iterative process of creating or editing a Crystal Reports .RPT file, working with it inside your VB code, going back to Crystal Reports to make changes to the .RPT file, and going back to VB to make changes in the code. The RDC looks similar to the Crystal Reports design screen, with multiple report sections, lists of database fields, formulas, parameter fields, and so on. You interact with the RDC via toolbar buttons and pop-up menus.

What the RDC Designer features that Crystal Reports doesn't is a complete object model for every report section and every object you place in any report section. Every field, text object, formula, parameter field, or any other type of object, has its own set of properties that appear in the property sheet, and many of those properties can be set at run time. With the RDC, you can customize formulas, text objects, section formatting, and most other aspects of report behavior and formatting by using VB coding. By creatively using text objects, you can even create report formulas using the Visual Basic language instead of the Crystal formula language, so that the text objects will be under complete VB control at run time. Of course, any Crystal formulas you create will still work, and they can still be modified on the fly from within your application, just as with other integration methods.

The Crystal Reports Smart Viewer

The RDC is the only Visual Basic integration method that doesn't include its own built-in preview window for previewing reports on the screen. While this may initially sound like a serious limitation, report previewing is provided by yet another ActiveX component that is available with the RDC, the Smart Viewer. This ActiveX control is added to a form, where it exposes a large number of properties in the Properties box displayed in the VB IDE that can be set at design time. When your program is run, the viewer is supplied with a report object from the RDC Automation Server, which it then displays in its window, based on the selections you made at design time.

Not only can many of these properties also be set at run time, but the viewer contains its own COM Automation Server, which exposes a large number of other properties, methods, and events that let you completely control report behavior and interaction. You can open drill-down tabs right from within your code, trap a button click in the viewer toolbar, or respond to a drill-down click on a group footer or header. The viewer is versatile enough that you can conceivably design your own container for the Smart Viewer window, creating all your own controls and logic for report interaction.

RDC Version 7 Versus "The Freebie"

Crystal Reports 7 is the first version of Crystal Reports to include the RDC as part of the off-the-shelf Crystal Reports package. However, between the release of Crystal Reports 6 and Crystal Reports 7, Seagate Software placed a free downloadable RDC on its Web site. That freebie is also available on the CD that accompanies this book.

Known by the code word "Baja," the RDC Version 6 provides a similar set of functions as that described in this chapter. With it, you can completely design and integrate reports inside the Visual Basic IDE without having to purchase a copy of Crystal Reports off the shelf. So, you might ask, "What do I gain by buying Crystal Reports 7 instead of just downloading the older RDC from the Web?"

The main benefit of the RDC bundled with Crystal Reports 7 is that it supports many new Crystal Reports 7 features, such as field mapping, SQL expression fields, running-total fields, and the enhanced Chart Expert. In addition, the Version 7 RDC will work with Visual Basic 6 Data Environments, whereas the previous version will not. If you are strictly interfacing reports with VB applications and have no other conceivable use for the Report Designer or other bundled tools, the decision of whether or not to purchase Crystal Reports 7 comes down to the features you need. If you need the additional functionality available with Version 7 of the RDC, your money will be well invested. If you don't immediately need these new features, try the RDC "freebie." If you later need the additional functionality, you can make the Crystal Reports 7 "upgrade from Visual Basic" purchase.

Adding the RDC to Your Project

The first step in using the RDC is to add it to your project. After installing Crystal Reports 7, or the free standalone RDC product, it should be properly registered on your system and ready for use.

1. Start Visual Basic and create a new project, or open the existing project with which you wish to use the RDC.

2. Choose Project | Components from the pull-down menus, or press CTRL-T. The Components dialog box will appear.

3. Click the Designers tab. You'll see a list of ActiveX designers registered on your system. Ensure that the Crystal Reports designer is selected, and then click OK.

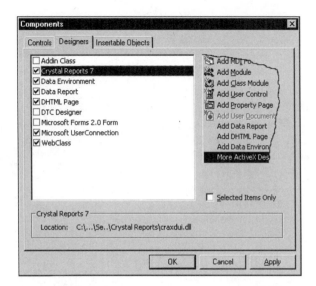

4. Using the Project pull-down menu, choose the Add Crystal Reports option (it may appear on the More ActiveX Designers submenu in VB 5). The RDC will be added to Visual Basic, and the Report Gallery dialog box will appear, as shown in Figure 24-1.

Once you've checked the Crystal Designer on the Designers tab of the Components dialog box, it will stay checked the next time you start Visual Basic. You'll only need to use the Project menu to add additional RDC objects in the future.

The RDC begins by displaying its own version of the Report Gallery. The RDC Report Gallery is very similar to the Report Gallery that appears when you create a new report in the Crystal Reports program, with a few changes. For example, there's no document import tool option, the Custom option has been replaced with an Empty Report button, and the Cross-Tab and Multiple Column report options aren't visible (you can just format the report for multiple columns or add a cross-tab once you've started the report). Your initial choices in the report gallery determine how your main report is designed inside the RDC.

Importing an Existing Report

If you've created an .RPT file in Crystal Reports 7 or an earlier version, and you want to use that report in the RDC, click the Import Report button. A File Open dialog box

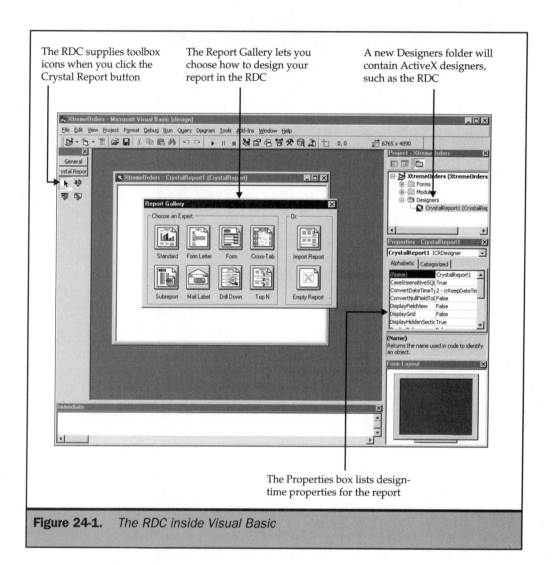

The RDC supplies toolbox icons when you click the Crystal Report button

The Report Gallery lets you choose how to design your report in the RDC

A new Designers folder will contain ActiveX designers, such as the RDC

The Properties box lists design-time properties for the report

Figure 24-1. *The RDC inside Visual Basic*

will appear, in which you can choose the .RPT file that you wish to import. Once you've chosen the report file, you are prompted to add the Crystal Reports Smart Viewer to your project.

Here you can determine whether you want the Smart Viewer added to a new form in your project, and if so, whether you want the Smart Viewer form to be set as the startup form. If you need to preview the report in a window from within your VB application, you'll need to add the Smart Viewer. Although you can do it later if you need to, the Report Expert will add it automatically, along with some simple code to tie the report to the viewer. If your report will be strictly used for exporting, e-mailing, or printing to a printer, there's no need to add the Smart Viewer control, as it won't be used.

If you import the Xtreme Orders sample report from the accompanying CD and add the Smart Viewer to a new form, your screen will look something like the one shown in Figure 24-2.

You'll notice that the RDC design window looks quite similar to the regular Crystal Reports design window—many of the features and report-design steps apply equally to both environments. There are several ways of carrying out functions in the RDC design window: by using toolbox and toolbar buttons, by choosing items from the field-view tree at the left of the report, and by right-clicking in the design window and choosing options from the pop-up menus. As with the regular Crystal Reports designer, you can select objects in the RDC design window and then move, resize, format, or delete them. Steps for these functions are basically the same as they are for regular Crystal Reports (with the exception that all RDC functions must be chosen with toolbar buttons and right-clicks—there are no pull-down menus here, as there are in regular Crystal Reports).

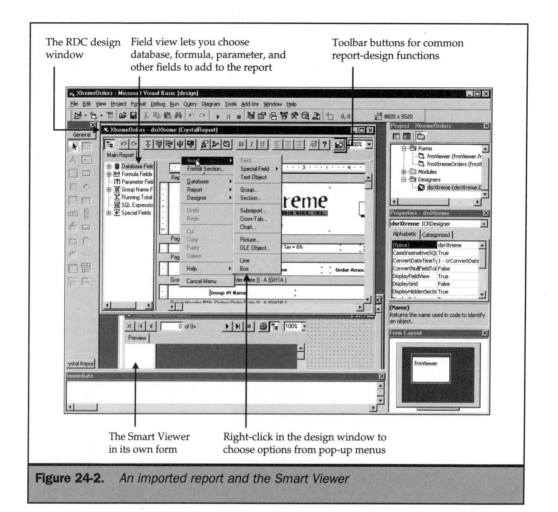

The RDC design window

Field view lets you choose database, formula, parameter, and other fields to add to the report

Toolbar buttons for common report-design functions

The Smart Viewer in its own form

Right-click in the design window to choose options from pop-up menus

Figure 24-2. *An imported report and the Smart Viewer*

Note   *Remember that when you import an .RPT file into the RDC, the RDC will simply copy the contents of the .RPT file into the design window and then completely disregard any changes that may later be made to the original .RPT file. Also, if you make any changes to the report inside the RDC, there will be no effect on the original .RPT file. You are not creating a real-time link to the .RPT file.*

While the RDC design window may not provide any particular functional advantage over the regular Crystal Reports designer (except that you don't have to exit VB to use it), the real benefit is the object model that it opens up for report contents. When you select an individual report object, such as a database field or text object, or a report section, such as the report header or details section, you'll see design-time properties in the Properties box.

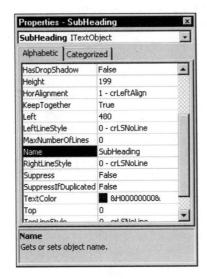

As you can with properties for a combo box, radio button, form, or other regular VB controls, you can set properties at design time for any of these report elements as well. The Properties box and pop-up menu options, such as the Format Editor, interact with each other. For example, you can select a date field, right-click it, and choose Format from the pop-up menu. On the Date tab of the Format Editor you might choose a four-digit year. When you click OK to close the Format Editor and then look in the Properties box, you'll notice that the Year Type property has changed to "1 – crLongYear." The opposite behavior is also true—changes you make in the Properties box will be reflected elsewhere in the RDC dialog boxes.

Tip   *Depending on how you plan to integrate your report and how much customization you want to perform at run time, you may want to rename some of the default names given to objects by the RDC. It's probably easier to understand what the SubHeading object is rather than the Text25 object when you begin looking through report objects in your VB code.*

When you've modified your report as necessary, save the report design the same way you save changes to a form, module, or project file from within VB. Just click the Save button in the toolbar, right-click the designer object in the Project Explorer window and choose Save from the pop-up menu, or just close the project or VB. You'll be prompted to choose a filename for the RDC designer, just as you would for a form or module. Choose a path and filename for the designer file—the default file extension for ActiveX designers is .DSR. When you next open the VB project, the .DSR file will load with the rest of the project files, and all properties and characteristics of the report design window will reappear.

Creating a New Report

Although the ability to import an existing .RPT file into the RDC is an excellent way to integrate an existing .RPT file into a Visual Basic application, you may prefer to maximize the power of the RDC and design the report entirely inside the Visual Basic IDE from scratch. The RDC allows you to do this with one of the Report Gallery choices that appear when you first add the RDC to your project.

If you choose one of the report experts, you'll be led through a tabbed dialog box, much as you are when you use the report experts inside regular Crystal Reports (refer to Chapter 1 for more information). If you choose the Empty Report option, you'll simply be presented with an empty report-design window, where you'll need to choose database connections, tables, and fields individually to add to the report. Do this by right-clicking in the window and choosing Database | Add Database to Report from the pop-up menu.

Choosing a Report Data Source

When you import an existing .RPT file into the RDC, the report inside your VB application will use the same data source as the imported report did (such as ODBC or a native database driver, perhaps using Btrieve). These data sources are all provided by Crystal Reports functionality, separate from any database-connectivity features within Visual Basic.

However, when you create a new report from scratch using a report expert in the RDC, you have several choices of how your report will "connect" to a database. Because the RDC is so tightly integrated with Visual Basic, it provides additional options for database connectivity. In particular, the RDC can connect to data using various Microsoft data-access methods provided by Visual Basic. These include Data Access Objects (DAO), Remote Data Objects (RDO), and ActiveX Data Objects (ADO). In addition, if you're using the RDC bundled with Crystal Reports 7, you'll be able to connect directly to an existing Data Environment that you may have already defined in your VB application (consult the VB documentation for more information on the Data Environment). And, if you installed the full version of Crystal Reports along with the RDC, you'll also be able to use Crystal Reports data connectivity to reach the database.

When you choose one of the report expert options, the expert's tabbed dialog box will appear. The first tab in the dialog box is the Data tab, as shown in Figure 24-3.

The Data Environment button will only be available if you've already added and defined a Visual Basic 6 Data Environment (which is another example of an ActiveX designer) in your project. When you click this button, the set of connections and commands in the Data Environment will be available to be chosen for your report.

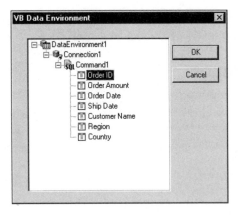

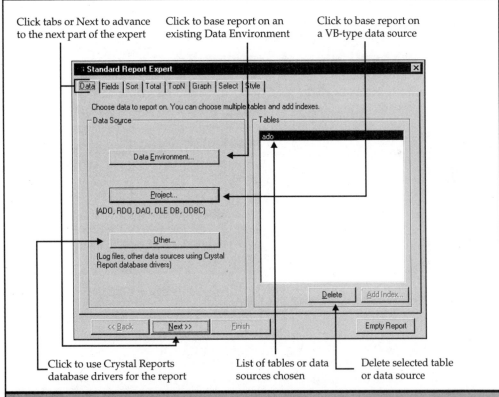

Figure 24-3.   *Data tab of the report expert dialog box*

If you want to use Microsoft's "intrinsic" connectivity methods, click the Project button to use DAO, RDO, or ADO to connect your report to the database. The Select Data Source dialog box will appear, as shown in Figure 24-4.

Choose the main connection method you wish to use by clicking the appropriate radio button.

- **ODBC**   Will connect to an ODBC (open database connectivity) data source that has already been set up on your PC. By clicking the Advanced button, you'll be able to choose whether to connect to the data source through the RDO or ADO connection method.

- **ADO and OLE DB**   Will connect to a data source using the newest Microsoft connection method. This will allow you to connect to varied data sources, such as OLAP cubes, Web server logs, and e-mail systems. You will need to supply a

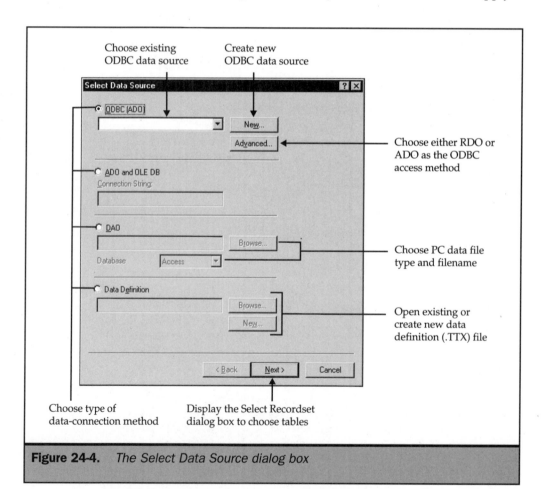

Figure 24-4.   *The Select Data Source dialog box*

syntactically correct connection string when prompted (more information about ADO connection strings can be found in the VB documentation).

- **DAO**   Will connect to a local database (typically Microsoft Access, dBASE, and so on). Specify the type of database you want to use, and use the Browse button if you need to search for the proper path and filename for the database.

- **Data Definition**   Will base the report on an existing data definition file or allow you to create a new data-definition file and base the report on that. A data definition file simply defines a set of field names and data types without actually connecting to any specific database.

Once you've selected the data-source type, filename, ODBC data-source name, or other necessary information, click the Next button on the Select Data Source dialog box to choose one or more tables from the data source to use in your report. The Select Recordset dialog box appears, as shown in Figure 24-5.

If the database you're connecting to is secure, provide the necessary login information in this dialog box. Also, you can choose to use just a single table from the

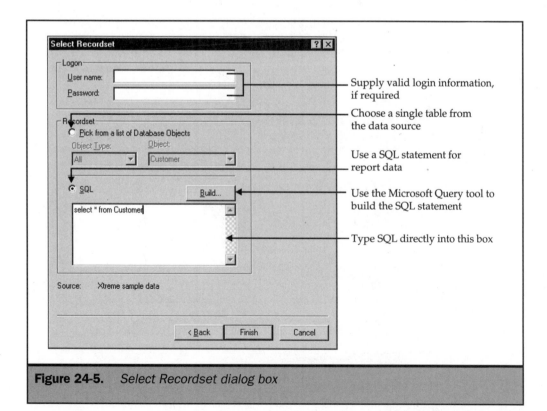

Figure 24-5.   *Select Recordset dialog box*

database by selecting the Pick From a List of Database Objects radio button and making your desired choices in the Object Type and Object drop-down lists.

If, however, you need to include and link more than one table, you wish to limit the result set to certain records with a WHERE clause, or you want to perform some other SQL function, click the SQL radio button to create a SQL statement to provide report data. If you are familiar with the SQL used by your data source, you can type a SELECT statement into the text box directly. If you'd prefer to be guided interactively through choosing and linking tables, choosing fields, and other steps necessary for creating a SQL statement, click the Build button to launch Microsoft Query. Click Finish when you've chosen and linked the necessary tables and fields.

Adding Objects

If you are using the report expert, you'll design the report using the simple tabbed interface. Since this approach is virtually identical to the technique discussed in Chapter 1, you should refer to that chapter if you're unfamiliar with designing a report with an expert.

If you chose the Empty Report option (or if you've already closed the report expert but want to add additional objects to the report), use the field-view tree on the left side of the RDC design window to add objects to the report. For example, to add a field from the database, click the plus sign next to the database fields category to display the data source or data sources the report is based on. Click the plus sign next to the data source to see the fields contained in it. Then, just drag and drop the fields you want to the desired section of the report design window.

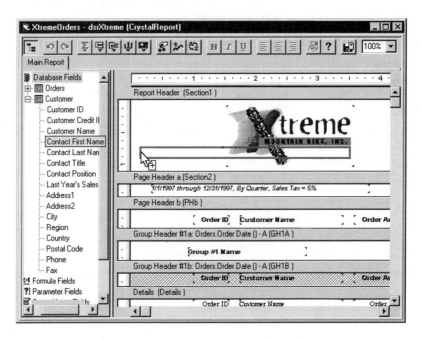

To create new formulas, parameter fields, or SQL expression fields, right-click their category in the field-view tree and choose New from the pop-up menu. When the new object has been added, you can drag and drop it on the report. Special fields can also be added to the report by dragging and dropping them from their area of the field-view tree.

Once objects have been added, you can select them and move or resize them just as you would in regular Crystal Reports. You can format an object that you've selected by right-clicking and choosing the appropriate choice from the pop-up menu. And, don't forget that you also have Visual Basic properties for every object or report section in the report. Select the object or report section and make design-time property choices in the Properties box—that's the power of a VB-integrated RDC.

 There are many capabilities and design techniques that you can apply to the RDC as you do with regular Crystal Reports. Look at the chapters in Part I of this book for ideas and techniques for designing sophisticated reports.

The RDC Object Model

The RDC actually consists of several different "pieces" that exist in your Visual Basic application. Two that have already been discussed, at least in general, are the RDC design window and the Smart Viewer. The design window is an ActiveX designer while the Smart Viewer is a more typical ActiveX control. When you actually process a report in VB, the two are tied together with a common report object.

The first step is to assign the design-window report definition to a Visual Basic object variable, as demonstrated in the following sample code:

```
Public Report As New dsrXtreme
```

In this code, from the modXtreme module in the sample application, dsrXtreme is the name given to the report designer in the Property Pages dialog box. *Report* is the name of the object that will "point" to the report. Because this object is declared to be Public in a module, it will remain in scope and be accessible throughout the entire application. Then, when the report is to be viewed in the Smart Viewer, the report object is passed to the Smart Viewer's ReportSource property. The following code is from the sample application's frmViewer Form_Load event:

```
CRViewer1.ReportSource = Report
```

In this code, CRViewer1 is the default name of the Smart Viewer (and it hasn't been changed to another name). The Report object is given to the ReportSource property so the Smart Viewer knows which report to show.

What happens in between these two lines of code is the "meat" of RDC integration programming. Once you've assigned the designer to the Report object variable, an entire object model becomes available to you for modifying and customizing the report. This object model is actually provided by an automation server that conforms to Microsoft's Component Object Model (COM). By using the RDC Automation Server's object model, consisting of objects, collections, properties, methods, and events, you have extensive control over your report behavior at run time.

When you add the RDC to your report, the CRAXDRT Automation Server is added to your project automatically. This COM interface provides a complete set of properties and methods that you can set at run time. To see the objects, collections, properties, and methods that are exposed by this automation server, use Visual Basic's *Object Browser*. The Object Browser can be viewed in Visual Basic any time your program isn't running. Press F2, or choose View | Object Browser from the pull-down menus. Then, choose CRAXDRT in the first drop-down list to see the object library exposed by the RDC Automation Server.

Although an extensive explanation of COM and its general approach to an object model and object hierarchy is better left to Microsoft documentation, changing a report formula will show you the RDC object hierarchy and how you can navigate through it. The highest level in the object hierarchy is the Application object—everything eventually falls below it. In general throughout the RDC, the Application object is assumed by default, so there's no need to explicitly refer to it (unless you use the

RDC Automation Server without the RDC ActiveX Designer report-design window). The highest level of object you'll need to be concerned about is the Report object.

While the Report object has many properties of its own (such as the RecordSelectionFormula property), it contains many objects and collections of objects that fall below it. One available Report object collection is FormulaFields, which contains a set of FormulaFieldDefinition objects, one for each formula defined in the report. Each of these objects contains all the properties for that particular formula, such as the formula name, the text of the formula, the data type that it returns, and other properties.

When you're dealing with a collection of objects, you'll need to identify which member of the collection you wish to manipulate by using an index pointer to the appropriate member. In the RDC, indexes are "one-based." That is, the first member is numbered 1, the second is numbered 2, and so on. This is in contrast to the ActiveX control and other VB object models which often expose "zero-based" indexes. The RDC typically numbers the collection members in the order in which they were added to the report.

For example, to print the formula text from the first (and only) formula in the Xtreme Orders sample application, you can type the following code into the Immediate window while the program is in break mode:

```
? Report.FormulaFields(1).Text
```

Here, the object hierarchy is being "navigated" to reveal the Text property of the first member of the FormulaFieldDefinitions collection (referred to just as FormulaFields) of the Report object.

Note *Some indexes (but very few as of the first version of the Crystal Reports 7 RDC), can use the actual name of the member passed as a string, instead of just the index number. Hopefully Seagate will enhance the RDC in a future release with this capability. This would allow you to view the text of the Order + Tax formula by using the name of the formula for the collection index instead of the number, so that you could use code such as Report.Formulas("Order + Tax").Text.*

Because the RDC and its Automation Server are tightly integrated COM components, you will benefit from *automatic code completion* when you use them. When you begin to enter code into the VB code window for the Report object, the properties, methods, and built-in constant values will become available to you from automatically appearing drop-down lists. If you've used Visual Basic 5 or 6, you're probably familiar with this feature. You'll enjoy the benefit it provides with the RDC.

In addition to the Object Browser and automatic code completion, there is comprehensive online Help for the RDC and its object model. You can either use Developer's Help from the Crystal Reports program menu, or a specific RDC Help file that is installed with either the stand-alone RDC 6, or the RDC bundled with Crystal Reports 7. Look in the Crystal Reports program directory for CRRDC.HLP.

  More information on automation-server concepts and COM is available from Visual Basic documentation.

Controlling Record Selection

One of the main benefits of Visual Basic's integration with Crystal Reports is the ability to control report record selection "on the fly," based on your user's interactions with the VB application. You can design the exact user interface you need for your application, and build the report record-selection formula based on how your user interacts with it. Because VB has such powerful user-interface features (such as the VB date picker and other custom controls), you will have much more flexibility using VB controls than you will with Crystal Reports parameter fields.

Because the record-selection formula you pass to the RDC must still conform to Crystal Reports syntax, you'll need to be familiar with how to create a Crystal Reports formula. If you are used to using the Crystal Reports Select Expert for record selection, you'll need to familiarize yourself with the actual Crystal Reports formula that it creates before you create a selection formula in your VB application. A Crystal Reports record-selection formula is a Boolean formula that narrows down the database records that will be included in the report. For example, the following record-selection formula will limit a report to orders placed in the first quarter of 1997 from customers in Wyoming:

```
{Orders.Order Date} In Date(1997,1,1) To Date(1997,3,31)
And {Customer.Region} = "WY"
```

> **Tip**
> *For complete discussions of Crystal Reports record selection and how to create Boolean formulas, consult Chapters 5 and 6.*

Use the RecordSelectionFormula property of the Report object to set the record-selection formula for the report. You can set the property to either a string expression or a variable. Here's the code from the sample application to set record selection, based on the contents of the user-supplied From Date and To Date text boxes:

```
'Supply record selection based on dates
strSelectionFormula = "{Orders.Order Date} in Date(" & _
    Format(txtFromDate, "yyyy,m,d") & ") to Date(" & _
    Format(txtToDate, "yyyy,m,d") & ")"
Report.RecordSelectionFormula = strSelectionFormula
```

Record-Selection Formula Tips

There are several important points to keep in mind when building a Crystal record selection formula within your application. Specifically, there are some tricks to making sure that your string values are formatted properly, and to making sure that as much of the SQL selection work is done on the server, rather than on the PC.

The string value you pass must adhere *exactly* to the Crystal Reports formula syntax. This includes using correct Crystal reserved words and punctuation. The previous example shows the necessity of building a Date (yyyy,mm,dd) string to pass to the selection formula.

Also, it's easy to forget the required quotation marks or apostrophes around literals that are used in comparisons. For example, you may want to pass the following selection formula:

```
{Customer.Region} = 'WY' And {Orders.Ship Via} = 'UPS'
```

If the characters WY and UPS are coming from controls, such as a text box or combo box, consider using the following VB code to place the selection formula in a string variable:

```
strSelectionFormula = "{Customer.Region} = " & txtRegion & _
" And {Orders.Ship Via} = " & cboShipper
```

At first glance, this appears to create a correctly formatted Crystal Reports record-selection formula. However, if you submit this string with the ReplaceSelectionFormula method, the report will fail when it runs. Why? The best way to troubleshoot this issue is to look at the contents of strSelectionFormula in the VB Immediate window, by setting a breakpoint or by using other VB debugging features. This will show that the contents of the string variable after the preceding code executes is as follows:

```
{Customer.Region} = WY And {Orders.Ship Via} = UPS
```

Notice that there are no quotation marks or apostrophes around the literals that are being compared in the record-selection formula, a basic requirement of the Crystal Reports formula language. The following VB code will create a syntactically correct selection formula:

```
strSelectionFormula = " {Customer.Region} = '" & txtRegion & _
"' And {Orders.Ship Via} = '" & cboShipper & "'"
```

If your report will be using a SQL database, remember also that RDC will attempt to convert as much of your record-selection formula as possible to SQL when it runs the report. The same caveats apply to the record-selection formula you pass from your VB application as apply to a record-selection formula you create directly in Crystal Reports. In particular, using built-in Crystal Reports formula functions, such as UpperCase or IsNull, and using OR operators instead of AND operators, will typically cause record selection to be moved to the client (the PC) instead of the database server. The result is very slow report performance. To avoid this situation, take the same care in creating record-selection formulas that you pass from your application as you would in Crystal Reports. Look for detailed discussions on record-selection performance in both Chapters 6 and 14.

You may also choose to create the SQL statement that the report will use right in your VB application, and submit it to the report by setting the report object's SQLQueryString property.

Setting Formulas

The RDC gives you an extra level of flexibility by allowing you to control the contents of report objects as each record is processed by the report (see the sections "Changing Text Objects at Run Time" and "Conditional Formatting and Formatting Sections," later in the chapter). Using these techniques, you can actually have objects on your report show the results of Visual Basic calculations and procedures. However, it still may be more straightforward to simply modify the contents of Crystal Reports formulas dynamically at run time. This will be useful for changing formulas related to groups that can also be changed from within your code, for changing a formula that shows text on the report, or for changing a formula that relates to math calculations or conditional formatting on the report.

Setting formulas at run time is similar to setting the record-selection formula at run time (described in the previous section). You'll need a good understanding of the Crystal Reports formula language to adequately modify formulas inside your VB code. If you need a refresher on Crystal Reports formulas, look back at Chapter 5.

The RDC provides a FormulaFields collection in the Report object that can be read or written to at run time. This collection returns multiple FormulaFieldDefinition objects, one for each formula defined in the report. Although there is a great deal of information that may be gleaned from the FormulaFieldDefinition object, the simplest way to change the contents of a formula is simply to set the Text property for the particular member of the collection that you want to change. The collection is one-based, with each member corresponding to its position in the list of formula fields.

In the Xtreme Orders sample application, the Order + Tax formula is modified based on the user's completion of the Tax Rate text box. The formula is changed using the following code:

```
'Set @Order + Tax formula
If txtTaxRate = "" Then
    Report.FormulaFields(1).Text = "{Orders.Order Amount}"
Else
    Report.FormulaFields(1).Text = "{Orders.Order Amount} *" &_
    Str(txtTaxRate / 100 + 1)
End If  'txtTaxRate = ""
```

You needn't change the property for all formulas in the report—just the ones you want to modify at run time. Remember that you can't specify the formula name as the collection index argument—you must use a one-based index number. This is determined by where the formula is in the formula list in the RDC design window—the first formula will have an index of 1, the fifth, 5, and so on. If you're unsure of which index matches to which formula, you can use the Count property in a For-Next loop to move through the entire collection, querying the Name property for each member.

The Text property requires a string expression or variable, correctly conforming to Crystal Reports' formula syntax, that contains the new text you want the formula to contain. Take care when assigning a value to the formula. The Order + Tax formula is defined in Crystal Reports as a numeric formula. Therefore, you should pass it a formula that will evaluate to a number. If the user leaves the text box on the form empty, the VB code assumes no additional sales tax and simply places the Order Amount database field in the formula—the formula will show the same amount as the database field.

If, however, the user has specified a tax rate, the VB code manipulates the value by dividing it by 100, and then adding 1. This will create the proper type of number to multiply against the Order Amount field to correctly calculate tax. For example, if the user specifies a tax rate of 5 (for 5 percent tax), the VB code will change the value to 1.05 before combining it with the multiply operator and the Order Amount field in the formula.

If you've examined other integration methods in this book, such as the ActiveX control or the Report Engine API, you'll see that one additional formula is modified at run time to show the report criteria that have been supplied by the user. While this can also be accomplished with a formula here, the RDC's capability of manipulating text objects at run time gives you the opportunity to approach this from another angle. Therefore, this second formula is not used in the Xtreme Orders sample application with the RDC. The following section explains how this is accomplished by using a text object.

Changing Text Objects at Run Time

With other integration approaches, changing textual information on the report, such as a company name or a description of the report's selection criteria, must be done with a formula. Typically the formula will simply contain a text literal (a text string surrounded by quotation marks or apostrophes) that is then changed at run time. While this will still work with the RDC, the RDC permits a new approach that can potentially give you much more flexibility.

Remember that when you add any object to the report (a field, formula, text object, or other object), it can be manipulated by VB. It has properties that can be set on the Property Pages dialog box at design time, as well as being modified at run time. If you add a text object to the report, a TextObject object becomes available from within the overall Report object. The TextObject object exposes many properties (you can see most of them in the Properties dialog box) that can be set at run time.

You can access the actual contents of the text object with a property and method. The Text property can be read during code execution to see what the text object contains. To change the contents of a text object, you'll need to use the TextObject SetText method at run time.

In the Xtreme Orders sample application, the Sub Heading formula that was originally created in the .RPT file has been removed in the RDC design window. In its place, a text object has been added and given the name SubHeading. The following code indicates how to set the contents of the text object to indicate what choices the user has made on the Print Xtreme Orders form. This code assumes the strSubHeading string variable has been declared elsewhere in the application. You'll also notice references to the text object and combo box controls on the form.

```
'Set SubHeading text object
strSubHeading = txtFromDate & " through " & txtToDate
strSubHeading = strSubHeading & ", By " & cboGroupBy
If txtTaxRate = "" Then
    strSubHeading = strSubHeading & ", No Tax"
Else
    strSubHeading = strSubHeading & ", Sales Tax = " & txtTaxRate & "%"
End If   'txtTaxRate = ""
Report.SubHeading.SetText (strSubHeading)
'Note: parentheses around argument to SetText method are optional
```

If you have used other integration methods in the past, you may want to change the general approach that you have used for custom formulas. Because you can change the contents of a text object from your VB code, you can essentially create "VB formulas" in your report by using the RDC. Each section of the report will fire a Format event when it is processed at report run time. You can use the SetText method inside this Format event to change the contents of text objects for each report record (in the Details section Format event) or for Group or Report Headers or Footers (in their respective Format events). More information on the Format event and conditional section formatting is contained later in this chapter.

Passing Parameter-Field Values

If you are importing an existing .RPT file into the RDC, the file may contain parameter fields that were designed to prompt the user for information whenever the report was refreshed. If you simply leave the parameter fields as they were, the application will automatically prompt the user for them when the report runs. Obviously, one of the main reasons to integrate the report into a VB application is to more closely control the user interface of the report. You'll probably want to alter the mechanism for gathering this data from the user and then have the application supply the appropriate values to the parameter fields from within the application code.

Since you can control both report record selection and report formulas at run time from within your VB application, there isn't as much necessity to use parameter fields with an integrated report as there might be for a stand-alone report running with regular Crystal Reports. And because the RDC does not actually use an external .RPT file for its integration, you won't be "sharing" an integrated report with other Crystal Reports users. So, there is probably little benefit to using parameter fields if you are creating a new report from scratch inside the RDC.

However, if you've imported a report that contains a large number of parameter fields and has them fairly tightly interwoven throughout the report logic, it may be simpler to just respond to them from within your code than to redesign the report to use some other method of customization. In this situation, use the Report object's ParameterFieldDefinitions collection to manipulate the parameters. As with formulas, there is one ParameterFieldDefinition object in the collection for each parameter field defined in the report. And, like formulas, the proper member of the collection is retrieved with a one-based index determined by the order in which the parameter fields were added to the report. You can't retrieve a parameter field by using its name as the index.

The RDC approach for setting the value of a parameter field being passed to a report is to use the ParameterFieldDefinition object's AddCurrentValue method. This passes a single value to the report parameter field. As Crystal Reports 7 allows multiple-value parameter fields, you can execute the AddCurrentValue method as many times as necessary (for example, in a loop that looks through a list box for selected items) to populate a parameter field with several values.

In the Xtreme Orders .RPT file that is used with other integration methods, there is a parameter field used to conditionally format the Details sections when the order amount exceeds a parameter supplied by the viewer. In this RDC example, this logic has been replaced by a direct format of the Details section during its Format event (discussed later in the chapter). However, if the original method of supplying the parameter field a value based on the VB user interface had been used, the following code would correctly pass the value to the parameter field.

```
'Set parameter value
'Alternative method is to format Details section within VB
If txtHighlight = "" Then
    Report.ParameterFields(1).AddCurrentValue (0)
Else
    Report.ParameterFields(1).AddCurrentValue (Val(txtHighlight))
End If  'txtHighlight = ""
```

Here, the value is set to zero if the text box is empty. This is important to note, as the actual parameter field in the report is numeric. Passing it an empty string might cause a run-time error when the report runs. Also, because the AddCurrentValue method is executed at least once, and a value has been passed to the parameter field, the user will no longer be prompted for it when the report is run.

Note   *The RDC object model exposes all the new features of Crystal Reports 7 parameter fields, such as range values, multiple values, and edit masks. Search the online Help for "ParameterFieldDefinition object (RDC)" for a complete description of the object, as well as all the new methods available for manipulating parameter fields.*

Manipulating Report Groups

One of the requirements for the Xtreme Orders report is that the user be able to specify how the report is grouped. A combo box exists on the Print Report form that lets the user choose between Quarter and Customer grouping. In the RDC design window, this is normally accomplished by using the Change Group option from a pop-up menu to change the field a group is based on, as well as the sequence (ascending or descending) that you want the groups to appear in. If the group is based on a date field, such as Order Date, you may also specify the range of dates (week, month, quarter, and so on) that make up the group. To familiarize yourself with various grouping options, refer to Chapter 3.

By being able to change these options from within an application at run time, you can provide great reporting flexibility to your end users. In many cases, you can make it appear that several different reports are available, based on user input. In fact, the application will be using the same report object, but grouping will be changed at run time, based on user input.

Manipulating groups in the RDC object model requires a bit of navigation "down the object hierarchy." Ultimately, the database or formula field a group is based on is specified by the GroupConditionField property of the Area object. A report contains an Areas collection containing an Area object for each area in a report. Consider an area of the report to be each individual main section of the report, such as the Page Header, Details section, Group Footer, and so on. If there are multiple sections on the report, such as *Details a* and *Details b* sections, they are still part of the overall details *area*, and there is only one member of the Areas collection for them. There is one advantage of the Areas collection not shared by most other collections exposed by the RDC—the index used to refer to an individual member of the collection can be a string value or a numeric value. This allows you to specify "RH", "PH", "GH*n*", "D", "GF*n*", "PF", or "RF" as index values, or to use the one-based index number. Using the string values makes your code much easier to understand when working with the Areas collection.

However, once you navigate to the specific Area object to specify the GroupConditionField property, you are faced with another peculiarity of the RDC object model. With other integration methods (the ActiveX control, in particular), you supply a string value containing the actual field name (such as {Orders.Order Date} or {Customer.Customer Name}) to indicate which field you wish to base a group on. The RDC doesn't make life this simple. You must specify a DatabaseFieldDefinition object to the GroupConditionField property—you can't just pass a string containing the field name.

The DatabaseFieldDefinition object is found quite "deep" in the object hierarchy—there is one of these objects for each field contained in the DatabaseFieldDefinitions collection in a DatabaseTable object. And, there are multiple DatabaseTable objects contained in the DatabaseTables collection of the Database object, contained inside the overall Report object. To make things even more complex, none of the collections just mentioned will accept a string index value—you must specify a one-based index value.

Although this sounds confusing and hard to navigate, you'll eventually be able to travel through the object hierarchy fairly quickly to find the database table and field you want to provide to the GroupConditionField property. Look at the following code from the Xtreme Orders sample application:

```
'Set grouping
If cboGroupBy = "Quarter" Then
    'The quarterly grouping will only work if the report is set
    'to "Convert Date/Time Fields to Date"
    'known bug w/initial SCR 7 release
    Report.Areas("GH").GroupConditionField = _
        Report.Database.Tables(1).Fields(5) 'Orders.Order Date
    Report.Areas("GH").GroupCondition = crGCQuarterly
Else
    Report.Areas("GH").GroupConditionField = _
        Report.Database.Tables(2).Fields(3) 'Customer.Customer Name
    Report.Areas("GH").GroupCondition = crGCAnyValue
End If  'cboGroupBy = "Quarter"
```

Caution *Notice the comments in the code relating to quarterly grouping. There is a bug in the initial version of the RDC that will ignore quarterly grouping and create a new group for every day. This is a known problem slated for repair in an RDC maintenance release. However, if you display Report Options (by deselecting any object in the RDC design window, right-clicking, and choosing Report | Report Options from the pop-up menu), and choose To Date as the Convert Date-Time Field option, quarterly grouping will work properly. The trade-off is that true date/time data types won't be available for use in the report—they will be converted to date-only fields.*

In this example, notice that the grouping is based on the user choice for the cboGroupBy combo box. In either case, the GroupConditionField property of the "GH" member of the Areas collection (the Group Header) is being set. If the user chooses to group by Order Date, the property is set to the fifth member of the Fields collection in the first member of the Tables collection. This indicates that the fifth field (Order Date) in the first table (Orders) will be used for grouping. If the user chooses to group by Customer, the third field (Customer Name) in the second table (Customer) will be used for grouping. As with other collections that don't allow string indexes, you can use quick Print statements in the Immediate window to search through different members of the collection. You can also look at the Database section of the Field Tree view in the RDC design window to determine which index numbers to use to point to the correct tables and fields.

In addition to choosing the database field you want to use for the group, you may have to choose how the grouping occurs, particularly if you use a date or Boolean field as the group field. This is accomplished by setting the Area object's GroupCondition property. The property can be set to an integer value, or an RDC-supplied constant (see the explanation for the Area object in the online Help for specific constants and integer values). In the sample code shown previously, the group is set to break for every calendar quarter if Order Date grouping is set (hence the crGCQuarterly constant that is provided). If Customer Name grouping is chosen, the crGCAnyValue constant is supplied, indicating that a new group will be created whenever the value of the Group field changes.

Note   *If you supply constants to some RDC properties, such as crGCQuarterly and crGCAnyValue discussed previously, you may receive a message inside VB indicating that the library containing the constants is not loaded, and if so, you'll be given the opportunity to load this library. If you choose "Yes," an additional library will appear in the Object Browser that resolves the constants to their proper integer values.*

Conditional Formatting and Formatting Sections

You'll often want to present your RDC reports in the Smart Viewer to allow report interaction in an online environment instead of having them printed on paper. The Smart Viewer provides complete interactive reporting features, such as drill-down, that are invaluable to the application designer. Having control over these capabilities at run time provides for great flexibility.

The Xtreme Orders sample application gives the user the opportunity to specify whether or not to see the report as a summary report only. When this check box is selected, the VB application will need to hide the report Details section so that only group subtotals appear on the report. In addition, you'll need to control the appearance of the report's two Page Header sections (*Page Header a* and *Page Header b*), as well as two Group Header #1 sections (*Group Header #1a* and *Group Header #1b*).

This is to accommodate two different sections of field titles that you wish to appear differently if the report is presented as a summary report instead of a detail report. If the report is being displayed as a detail report, the field titles should appear at the top of every page of the report, along with the subheading and smaller report title. If the report is displayed as a summary report, you only want the field titles to appear in the Group Header section of a drill-down tab when the user double-clicks on a group. Since no detail information will be visible in the main report window, field titles there won't be meaningful.

And finally, you'll want to show Group Header #1a, which contains the Group Name field, if the report is showing detail data. This will indicate which group the following set of orders applies to. However, if the report is only showing summary data, showing both the Group Header and Group Footer would be repetitive—the Group Footer already contains the group name, so showing the Group Header as well will look odd. However, you will want the Group Header with the group name to appear in a drill-down tab.

Therefore, you'll need to control the appearance of four sections when a user chooses the Summary Report option. Look at Table 24-1 to get a better idea of how you'll want to conditionally set these sections at run time.

You'll notice that in some cases, sections need to be completely suppressed (so they don't show up, even in a drill-down tab) as opposed to hidden (they will show up in a drill-down tab, but not in the main Preview tab). There is a somewhat obscure relationship among areas and sections that make this determination. Specifically, only complete areas (such as the entire Group Header #1) can be hidden, not individual sections (for example, Group Header #1a). However, both areas and sections can be suppressed. To further this concept, if you look in the Properties dialog box when you've selected a section in the design window, you'll see a Suppress property but no Hide property.

This presents a bit of a coding challenge for the Xtreme Orders sample application. First, you'll need to determine the correct combination of area hiding and section suppressing that sets what appears in the Preview window and in a drill-down tab. If an area is set to Hide, none of the sections in it will appear in the main Preview window. But, when the user drills down into that section, you will want to control

Section	Detail Report	Summary Report
Page Header b (field titles)	Shown	Suppressed (no drill-down)
Group Header #1a (group name field)	Shown	Hidden (drill-down okay)
Group Header #1b (field titles)	Suppressed (no drill-down)	Hidden (drill-down okay)
Details (detail order data)	Shown	Hidden (drill-down okay)

Table 24-1.   *Section Formatting for Different Report Types*

which sections inside the drilled-down area appear in the drill-down tab. Then, you must find where to set the Hide property for a particular area. You must also find where to set the Suppress property for sections inside the hidden area, or other sections that aren't hidden.

Since the Hide property is only available for an entire area, you'll need to set the HideForDrillDown property for the appropriate member of the Areas collection. Since the Suppress property needs to be set for individual sections, you can just refer to the individual sections in the RDC design window by name, setting the Suppress property for them as needed. Consider that the Page Header b section has been given the name PHb in the Properties dialog box (it was named Section 3 when the report was imported). Other sections have been given more descriptive names in the RDC design window, as well. Group Header #1a is named GH1A and Group Header #1b is named GH1B.

Keeping in mind the previous discussion and the hide and suppress requirements outlined in Table 24-1, look at the code from the sample application that follows.

```
'Hide/show sections
With Report
    If chkSummary Then
        .Areas("D").HideForDrillDown = True
        .PHb.Suppress = True
        .Areas("GH1").HideForDrillDown = True
        .GH1A.Suppress = False
        .GH1B.Suppress = False
    Else
        .Areas("D").HideForDrillDown = False
        .PHb.Suppress = False
        .Areas("GH1").HideForDrillDown = False
        .GH1A.Suppress = False
        .GH1B.Suppress = True
    End If  'chkSummary
End With  'Report
```

Note *You can navigate deeper into the object hierarchy and actually set the Suppress property for members of the Sections collection inside the Area object. Although this is a little more code-intensive, it will create code that is compatible with the Report Engine Automation Server (covered in Chapter 25).*

Notice that both Area objects for the details and Group Header #1 areas are being formatted, as well as individual sections. The areas must be formatted from their collection, whereas sections can be manipulated directly below the Report object by name.

The Format Event

Another benefit that only the RDC provides to developers is the Format event. This event is "fired" every time the processing of an individual report section begins. Consider the way the first page of a report might be processed. First, the overall report is "prepared," then the page header prints, then the report header (since this is the first page of the report), then the first group header, then all the details sections in that group, then the first group footer, and so on. Each time any of these sections begins to print (including when the report is "prepared"), its respective Format event fires.

You can intercept these formatting events and change the behavior of the section, or of objects within the section. This allows you complete Visual Basic functionality when it comes to conditional formatting or section formatting. In other integration methods that use .RPT files, you must use Crystal Reports conditional formulas or the Highlighting Expert to set background colors for sections, highlight fields over a certain value, and perform other formatting based on certain conditions. While the RDC continues to support that flexibility, you can now base individual section- and object-formatting on VB code.

To add code for any Format event, simply double-click a section in the RDC design window. This will display the Format event in the code window for the particular section you double-clicked. You can also right-click the designer in the Project Explorer and choose View Code from the pop-up menu. In either case, each report section will appear in the Object drop-down list in the upper left of the code window. The only available procedure for each report section is Format, which will appear in the Procedure drop-down list in the upper-right corner.

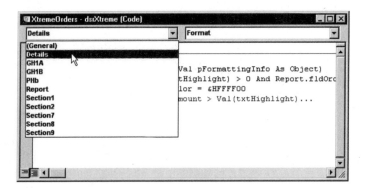

You have all the power of VB at your disposal to control the appearance and formatting of sections and objects, or the content of text objects, while the report is being formatted. This will allow you to write VB code to determine how to format a field in the current section being formatted (perhaps to set the background or font color of an object based on some VB code). You can also change the formatting of the entire section, as demonstrated in the following code from the Xtreme Orders sample application.

```
Private Sub Details_Format (ByVal pFormattingInfo As Object)
    If Val(frmXtremeOrders.txtHighlight) > 0 And _
    Report.fldOrderAmount.Value > Val(frmXtremeOrders.txtHighlight) Then
        Report.Details.BackColor = &HFFFF00
    End If   'Report.fldOrderAmount > Val(txtHighlight)...
End Sub
```

> **Tip**
>
> *The pFormattingInfo argument that is passed into the module is an object that exposes three read-only properties that return true or false: IsEndOfGroup, IsStartOfGroup, IsRepeatedGroupHeader. You can read the contents of these properties to help determine how to handle logic in the Format event.*

This code is contained in the Format event for the Details section (notice that the report section has been renamed Details from its default name of Section 6). Every time the Details section begins to format, this event fires. At that time, the contents of the Highlight text box on the Print Xtreme Orders form is checked for a value. If the user has supplied a value and the fldOrderAmount database field from the report is greater than the value the user supplied, the background color of the Details section is set. This logic replaces the parameter field and conditional formatting used in the original Xtreme Orders .RPT file.

Obviously, there are many other flexible and complex types of formatting and manipulation that can occur during the Format event. A common use of this manipulation is to replace formula fields on the report with text objects, and use the SetText method to change the contents of the text objects from within the Format event. This will, in essence, extend the complete power of the Visual Basic language to objects you place on your report.

> **Caution**
>
> *Certain object properties can only be set during certain times when the report is processing. This is mostly significant when writing code in the Format event. If you attempt to set a property that can't be set during that particular report-processing time, you'll receive either error messages or unexpected results. Look for a discussion of formatting modes by searching the online Help for "Format event (RDC)."*

Choosing Output Destinations

If your users will have a choice of output destinations (as the user does in the Xtreme Orders sample application), you'll need to create appropriate code to handle the user's choice. In the Xtreme Orders sample application, radio buttons and a text box allow the user to choose to view the report in the preview window, print the report to a printer, or attach the report as a Word document to an e-mail message. If the user chooses e-mail as the output destination, an e-mail address can be entered into a text box. Based on the user's selection, you will need to set the output destination automatically in your VB code.

If the user chooses to view the report on the screen, you'll need to activate the Smart Viewer. In the sample application, this simply entails displaying the form that contains the Smart Viewer control by executing the form's Show method. The Form_Load event of this form will pass the Report object to the Smart Viewer and execute the Smart Viewer's ViewReport method.

As mentioned earlier, use of the Crystal Reports Smart Viewer is completely optional—you are free to answer No when you are prompted about whether or not to add it when first adding the RDC to your project. However, if one of the output options will be to the screen (as in the Xtreme Orders sample application), make sure that the Smart Viewer is eventually added to your project.

If you respond Yes to the RDC's "Do you want to add the Smart Viewer" prompt, the RDC automatically adds the Smart Viewer for you. It will create a new form, place the Smart Viewer in the form, and automatically add rudimentary code to supply the Report object to the Smart Viewer and resize the Smart Viewer to be the same size as the form. If the RDC adds the Smart Viewer automatically, you can leave this default behavior as is, move the Smart Viewer object to another form, or build additional elements into the form that the RDC created automatically. You can also manually add the Smart Viewer to your project later and supply code to pass the Report object to the Smart Viewer.

If you wish to print the Report object to a printer, execute the Report object's PrintOut method. The syntax is as follows:

```
object.PrintOut Prompt, Copies, Collated, StartPage, StopPage
```

In this statement, *Prompt* is a Boolean value indicating whether or not to prompt the user for report options, *Copies* is a numeric value indicating how many copies of the report to print, *Collated* is a Boolean value indicating whether or not to collate the pages, and *StartPage* and *StopPage* are numeric values indicating which page numbers to start and stop printing on. The parameters are optional—if you want to skip any in the middle, just add commas in the correct positions, but don't include the parameter.

If you wish to export the report to a disk file or attach the report to an e-mail message as a file, use the Report object's Export method. The syntax is as follows:

```
object.Export PromptUser
```

In this statement, *PromptUser* is a Boolean value indicating whether or not you want to prompt the user for export options. If you choose not to prompt the user for export options, you'll need to set properties of the report's ExportOptions object. The ExportOptions object contains many properties that determine the output destination (file or e-mail), the file format (Word, Excel, and so on), the filename, the e-mail address, and many more properties. Many of these properties accept integer values or RDC-supplied descriptive constants. If you choose MAPI as the destination, the user's PC will need to have a MAPI-compliant e-mail client, such as Microsoft Outlook or Eudora Pro, installed. Look for all the available ExportOptions properties by searching the online Help for "ExportOptions object (RDC)."

In the Xtreme Orders sample application, the following code is used to choose an output destination, as well as to specify a file type and e-mail information, based on user selection.

```
'Set output destination
If optPreview Then frmViewer.Show
If OptPrint Then Report.PrintOut (True)
If OptEmail Then
    With Report
        .ExportOptions.DestinationType = crEDTEMailMAPI
        .ExportOptions.MailToList = txtAddress
        .ExportOptions.MailSubject = "Here's the Xtreme Orders Report"
        .ExportOptions.MailMessage = _
"Attached is a Word document with the latest Xtreme Orders Report."
        .ExportOptions.FormatType = crEFTWordForWindows
        .Export (False)
    End With   'crptXtreme
End If   'optEmail
```

> **Caution**
> *If you use the Report object's Export method to export or send the report attached to an e-mail message, make sure you specify all the necessary ExportOptions object properties. If you fail to specify necessary properties, or specify them incorrectly, an error may be thrown. Or, the user may be prompted to specify export options, even though you specifically add a False argument to the Export method. If the export takes place at an unattended machine, this will cause your application to wait for a response when no user is available to respond.*

Changing the Data Source at Run Time

Obviously, one of the main benefits of integrating a Crystal Report in a Visual Basic program is the ability to tie the report contents to a data set or result set that the program is manipulating. This allows a user to interact with your application and then run a report that contains the same set of data that the user has selected.

One way to accomplish this is to create a Crystal Reports record-selection formula or a SQL statement based on your user interface. The formula or SQL statement can then be passed to the report as discussed later in this chapter. This will allow the user to interact with a data grid, form, or other visual interface in the application and create a report based on its contents.

However, there may be situations where you prefer to have the contents of an actual Visual Basic record set from one of Visual Basic's intrinsic data models act as the data source for a report. The RDC provides for this with the SetDataSource method. Using SetDataSource, you can initially design the report using a particular database or data source, or using a field-definition file (discussed in the online Help). Then, you can pass a Visual Basic DAO, RDO, or ADO record set, snapshot, or result set to the report at run time. The RDC will use the current contents of the VB data set to populate the report.

The syntax for SetDataSource is as follows:

```
[form]Object.SetDataSource data, DataTag, tableIndex
```

In this statement, "*Object*" is the RDC Report object that you want to supply data to, "*data*" is the DAO, ADO, or RDO data set that you want to supply data to the report, and "*DataTag*" and "*tableIndex*" are parameters indicating the type of data and the index of the table that you want to change the data source for. The *DataTag* parameters should always be specified as 3, with *tableIndex* being set based on the table you wish to "point" to the new data source.

SetDataSource applies to the RDC's Database object, not just to the Report object itself. Thus, if you have created an RDC report and named the Report object "Report," and you have identified an ADO Resultset object elsewhere in your VB application with the name "ADOrs," the following code will pass the contents of the result set to the report. When the report is printed, exported, or passed to the Smart Viewer, the contents of the result set will be used by the report's Database object to populate the report.

```
Report.Database.SetDataSource ADOrs,3,1
```

Notice that the last two parameters to the SetDataSource method are 3 and 1, indicating the only allowable data tag (3), and the first table in the database (1).

There are actually two forms of the SetDataSource method available with the RDC. The method described previously applies to the entire Database object, requiring the third argument indicating a table index. There is also a SetDataSource method available for the DatabaseTable object. The syntax is almost the same—the only difference is that a table-index parameter is not required, as the method is only applying to a single Table object.

| Caution | *If you use SetDataSource to change the data source for a database table, make sure the data source you pass to the report remains in scope whenever the report runs. For example, you may define a Report object that's global to your application (by declaring it at the module level). But if you pass it a data source that was declared at the form level and then try to run the report in another form, the data source will be out of scope, and the report will fail. The ReadRecords method is available for reading the contents of the data source into the Report object, if maintaining scope for the data source isn't practical. Search the Developer's Help for information on ReadRecords.* |

Customizing the Smart Viewer

If you've added the Smart Viewer ActiveX component to your project, you have a great deal of flexibility in customizing the way the Smart Viewer appears and behaves. By default, the RDC will add the Smart Viewer to its own form and add a small amount of code to supply the Report object to the Smart Viewer and resize the Smart Viewer whenever the form is resized.

This default behavior just uses a fraction of the Smart Viewer's capabilities. It has many options, exposed by its own automation server, which will meld it more tightly into your application. You can customize how the Smart Viewer looks, what controls and toolbar buttons are available, what the Smart Viewer's size is, and even perform all the functions from within code that the built-in toolbar buttons would accomplish. If you prefer, this will allow you to make the Smart Viewer show virtually no controls but the report itself. You can design a completely separate user interface for page control, zoom levels, printing, exporting, and more.

In addition, the Smart Viewer contains a flexible event model that will "fire" events as the Smart Viewer performs various functions, or as a user interacts with it. You can trap button clicks, drill-down selections, changes in the zoom level, and other events. You can execute extra code when any of these events occur, or intercept the events and cancel them if you wish to not have the Smart Viewer complete them.

When you add the Smart Viewer to a form (or when it's added automatically by the RDC), you'll see the outline of the Smart Viewer appearing as an object inside the form. When you select the Smart Viewer object, you'll see a large number of design-time properties appear in the Properties box in VB. This is illustrated in Figure 24-6.

If you want the Smart Viewer to exhibit consistent behavior during the entire application, you can change properties for the Smart Viewer at design time, such as

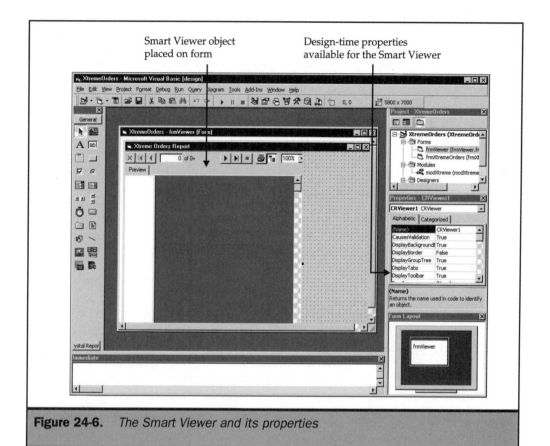

Smart Viewer object
placed on form

Design-time properties
available for the Smart Viewer

Figure 24-6. *The Smart Viewer and its properties*

which toolbar buttons will be shown, whether a report group tree will be displayed, whether a user can drill down, and so on.

Some of these properties (but not as many as you might like) can also be set at run time by supplying the appropriate values to the Smart Viewer object's properties. Because the Smart Viewer object actually adds its own COM Automation Server to your project, you can get an idea of the object model, properties, methods, and events that are available by looking at the Object Browser. Press F2, or choose View | Object Browser from the Visual Basic pull-down menus. Then, choose CRVIEWERLibCtl in the library drop-down list to see the object model exposed by the Smart Viewer's Automation Server.

In addition to the Object Browser, the online Help contains thorough information about the Smart Viewer object model. Consult either Developer's Help or the stand-alone CRRDC.HLP file and search for "CRViewer Object."

Despite the fact that many of the EnableToolbar properties are documented as read/write at run time, most of them can only be set at design time (with the exception of EnableDrillDown). Attempts to set them at run time will result in an error. This is a shortcoming of the initial version of the Smart Viewer that has been identified by Seagate for enhancement in a future release.

Here's some code from the Xtreme Orders sample application that controls the ability of the Smart Viewer to drill down on a report. The EnableDrillDown setting is based on the contents of the Summary check box. If Summary is checked, the report will only show group footers and the user will be able to drill down on the report. If the box is cleared, the report will show detail sections as well as group headers and footers. Even though you can still drill down on group headers and footers in a detail report, it makes little sense. Therefore, drill down is disabled if the Summary option is not checked. As this code is contained in the form that also contains the Smart Viewer, the print dialog form name is appended to the chkSummary object.

```
If frmXtremeOrders.chkSummary Then
    CRViewer1.EnableDrillDown = True
Else
    CRViewer1.EnableDrillDown = False
End If  'frmXtremeOrders.chkSummary
```

Trapping Smart-Viewer Events

The Smart Viewer's Automation Server, in addition to offering a good selection of properties and methods, also exposes a large number of events that allow you to trap button clicks, report-processing cycles, and drill-down attempts. These events can be used to modify the behavior of the Smart Viewer, to execute some additional supplementary code when a certain event occurs, or to potentially modify report contents while it is being viewed.

You can see which events are available for custom coding by searching the online Help for "CRViewer Object Events" or by looking at the Object Browser. You can also simply open the code window for the Smart Viewer object and look at the procedure drop-down list in the upper-right corner of the Code window.

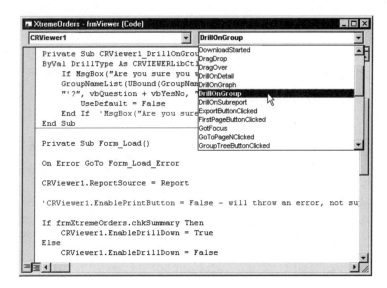

Because you can trap many events that occur during report-processing and user interaction with the Smart Viewer, you have tremendous power to customize your reporting application. In the Xtreme Orders sample application, there are only two simple examples of these capabilities. When the user drills down on a group, a confirmation message box appears, asking them to confirm the drill-down. If they answer Yes, the drill-down will occur. If not, the drill-down will be canceled. After a user has drilled down, and they click the Close View button (the red ×) in the Smart Viewer, another confirmation message box will appear, asking them to confirm the closure. As with the original drill-down, the drill-down tab will only be closed if the user answers Yes. Otherwise, the event will be canceled.

One of the more complex parts of these examples is actually determining which group will be affected when the drill-down or drill-down tab closure occurs. Understanding this is crucial for fully exploiting the power of the event model—trapping these events is probably of little use if you can't determine which group is actually being manipulated. The Smart Viewer DrillOnGroup event makes this task easier by passing the GroupNameList parameter into the event function. This zero-based array contains an element for each group that has been drilled into previously, with the current group that is now being drilled into being the last element of the array.

If your report only contains one level of grouping (as does the Xtreme Orders sample report), the GroupNameList will always contain just element 0, the group that was drilled down to. However, if your report contains multiple levels of grouping, you'll have the extra benefit of determining how deep and which groups are included in the group that is currently being drilled down to. For example, if your report is grouped on three levels, Country, State, and City, a user may first drill down on Canada. This will fire the DrillOnGroup event and the GroupNameList array will contain only element 0, "Canada." Then, in the Canada drill-down tab, the user might double-click on BC. This will again fire the DrillOnGroup event and the GroupNameList array will now contain two elements, "Canada" in element 0 and "BC" in element 1. Then, if in the BC drill-down tab the user double-clicks on Vancouver, yet another DrillOnGroup event will fire. Inside this event, the GroupNameList array will contain elements 0 through 2, "Canada," "BC," and "Vancouver."

If you are only concerned about the lowest level of grouping, just query the last element of the GroupNameList array using the VB UBound function. Even though the Xtreme Orders report only contains one level of grouping (thereby always allowing GroupNameList(0) to be used to determine the group), the UBound function has been used for upward compatibility.

The other argument passed to the DrillOnGroup event is UseDefault. This Boolean value can be set to true or false inside the event to determine whether the drill-down actually occurs. If UseDefault is set to true (or left as is), the drill-down will occur. If it is set to false inside the DrillOnGroup event, the drill-down will be canceled and no drill-down tab will appear for the group in the Smart Viewer.

Here's the sample code from the Xtreme Orders application. Note that the actual group being drilled on is included in the message box and that the results of the message box determine whether the drill-down occurs or not.

```
Private Sub CRViewer1_DrillOnGroup(GroupNameList As Variant, _
ByVal DrillType As CRVIEWERLibCtl.CRDrillType, UseDefault As Boolean)
   If MsgBox("Are you sure you want to drill down on '" & _
   GroupNameList(UBound(GroupNameList)) & _
   "'?", vbQuestion + vbYesNo, "Xtreme Orders Report") = vbNo Then
      UseDefault = False
   End If  'MsgBox("Are you sure you want to drill down...
End Sub
```

The other Smart Viewer event that is used in the Xtreme Orders sample application is CloseButtonClicked. This event fires whenever a user clicks the red × in the Smart Viewer to close the current drill-down tab (known in the Smart Viewer object model as the current view). Again, the sample application simply displays a confirming message box asking whether or not the user really wants to close the drill-down tab. By setting the UseDefault parameter inside the event code, the drill-down tab is closed or not, based on the user's choice.

As when drilling down, the actual drill-down tab that's being closed needs to be known inside the event (it's just being included in the message box in this example). Because the CloseButtonClicked event doesn't pass a GroupNameList or similar parameter into the event, a little more sleuthing has to be done to determine what the current view is. This is where both the Smart Viewer's GetViewPath method and ActiveViewIndex property come into play.

The ActiveViewIndex property simply returns an integer (one-based) indicating which drill-down tab is the currently selected tab. While this is helpful, it doesn't return the actual string containing the group name of the tab being viewed. This must be accomplished by using the GetViewPath method of the Smart Viewer object. This method accepts one argument, a numeric index indicating the tab in the Smart Viewer window for which you want to see the view path. The method returns a one-based string array that includes the actual views (or group names) that are included in the drill-down tab whose index is provided as the argument to GetViewPath. As with GroupNameList, you can then determine the actual name of the current tab being closed by accessing the last element (using the UBound function) of the array.

Examine the following code closely:

```
Private Sub CRViewer1_CloseButtonClicked(UseDefault As Boolean)
    If MsgBox("Close '" & _
CRViewer1.GetViewPath(CRViewer1.ActiveViewIndex)
UBound(CRViewer1.GetViewPath(CRViewer1.ActiveViewIndex))) _
    & "' Drill-Down tab?", vbQuestion + vbYesNo, _
       "Xtreme Order Report") = vbNo Then
       UseDefault = False
    End If  'MsgBox("Close...
End Sub
```

Due to width restrictions in the book, the line of sample code in the previous example that demonstrates the CRViewer1.GetViewPath command is broken after the first right parenthesis. If you look at the sample application, you'll notice that this is a continuous line, which is required for proper VB interpretation of the line.

Notice that GetViewPath is supplied with the ActiveViewIndex property. This will return a string array containing all the groups that are included in the current drill-down tab. Even though the Xtreme Orders report only contains one level of grouping, the UBound function is still used to retrieve the last element of the array returned by GetViewPath. This provides upward compatibility if you ever choose to add multiple groups to the report.

Error Handling

You will need to set up error-handling code for all aspects of RDC programming. As you manipulate the Report object itself (setting properties and executing methods), the possibility that errors may occur needs to be planned for. And, if you use the Smart Viewer in your application, it can also throw errors for any number of reasons. Add error-handling logic accordingly.

All Report and Smart Viewer errors will appear as regular Visual Basic run-time errors. These need to be trapped with an On Error Goto routine. The hard part is trying to figure out what error codes to trap. Unlike other integration methods, such as the ActiveX control and Report Engine Automation Server, the RDC is not a wrap-around tool for the Crystal Report Print Engine. Therefore, the errors it throws are not the same three-digit codes as those returned by the Print Engine (preceded with 20, to return 20*XXX* in the ActiveX control and Report Engine Automation Server).

To complicate things further, Seagate has yet to provide any comprehensive documentation for the errors that either the Report or Smart Viewer objects might throw. In many situations, you'll see typical VB-type error codes for report-related errors. For example, supplying a string index argument to a Report object collection that only accepts integer arguments won't generate an RDC-specific error. "Subscript Out of Range" will be returned, instead. However, certain error messages that are Report- or Smart Viewer–specific will generally throw errors that start with –2147, and are followed by six other numbers.

You'll simply have to test your application thoroughly and create error-handling code appropriately. Try intentionally creating any Report- or Smart Viewer–related errors that have even a remote chance of occurring. You can then determine what corresponding error codes the Report or Smart Viewer objects throw and add code to trap those specific errors. Here's sample code from the Xtreme Orders application that traps potential errors when setting Report properties at run time.

```
cmdOK_Click_Error:
Screen.MousePointer = vbDefault
Select Case Err.Number
    Case -2147190889
        MsgBox "Report Cancelled", vbInformation, "Xtreme Order Report"
    Case -2147190908
        MsgBox "Invalid E-Mail address or other e-mail problem", _
                vbCritical, "Xtreme Order Report"
        txtAddress.SetFocus
    Case Else
        MsgBox "Error " & Err.Number & " - " & Err.Description, _
                vbCritical, "Xtreme Order Report"
End Select   'Case Err.Number
```

Other RDC Properties and Methods

This chapter has covered many RDC procedures for handling most common report-customization requirements, but there are several other areas of RDC functionality that deserve some discussion. In particular, RDC functions that pertain to handling SQL database reporting, as well as dealing with subreports, should be addressed. In addition, the RDC DiscardSavedData method for "resetting" or clearing the contents of properties that may have been set in previous VB code should be explored.

The DiscardSavedData Method

A straightforward feature of the Crystal ActiveX control discussed in Chapter 23 is the Reset method. This method comes in handy when you may run a report more than once inside the application without explicitly closing and redeclaring the report. The ActiveX Reset method returns all properties to the values they originally had in the .RPT file that is being printed. Although there is no similar method for the RDC, you will still want to use the report object's DiscardSavedData method if you will be running a report multiple times without setting the Report object to "Nothing" and redeclaring it.

The Xtreme Orders sample application provides a good example of where this is helpful. The Report object is declared in a global module, and the Print Xtreme Orders form stays loaded during the entire scope of the application. Every time the OK button is clicked, the application sets Report properties based on the controls on the form, and then either prints or exports the report, or displays the form containing the Smart Viewer.

The issue of clearing previous settings comes into play when a user runs the report more than once without ending and restarting the application. Because the Report object is never released and redeclared, all of its property settings remain intact when the user clicks OK subsequent times. If the Visual Basic code doesn't explicitly set some of these previously set properties, the report may exhibit behavior from the previous time it was run that you don't expect. Executing the Report object's DiscardSavedData method clears many properties of settings from any previous activity, returning them to the state they were in when designed in the RDC design window.

Simply execute the DiscardSavedData method for any Report objects that you want to "clean up," as shown in the following sample from the Xtreme Orders sample application:

```
Report.DiscardSavedData 'required for consistent results
```

An equivalent to DiscardSavedData exists in the other integration methods, as well. However, in all those cases it seems to make a little more sense, since they all integrate an existing Crystal Reports .RPT file. If that .RPT file has been saved with File | Save Data with Report turned on, you'll probably want Visual Basic to discard the saved data at run time and refresh the report with new data from the database. Since the RDC is integrating a report that is contained entirely within the VB IDE (even if an .RPT file was imported, its saved data is not imported with it), you may be confused as to how DiscardSavedData applies. The RDC, in essence, "saves" data in the Report object when it is viewed in the Smart Viewer, printed, or exported (or when the ReadRecords method is executed). That saved data remains a part of the Report object until it's discarded or the object reference is destroyed.

SQL Database Control

Many corporate databases are kept on client/server SQL database systems, such as Microsoft SQL Server, Oracle, and Informix. Many Visual Basic applications provide front-end interfaces to these database systems and need to handle SQL reporting, as well. The RDC contains several properties and methods that help when integrating reports based on SQL databases.

Logging On to SQL Databases

It's probable that your VB application already handles SQL database security, requiring the user to provide a valid logon ID and password at the beginning of the application. The user will be frustrated if the RDC asks for yet another logon when it comes time to open the report. By using RDC methods and properties to pass logon info to the report, you can pass the valid ID and password the user has already provided, thereby allowing the report to print without prompting again.

One approach to passing logon information to a report is the LogOnServer method, available for both the Application and Database objects. This method logs on to a secure database and remains logged on until LogOffServer is executed, or until the Report object reference is destroyed. Search the online Help for "LogOnServer method (RDC)."

The other way to provide logon information from within your application is by executing the SetLogOnInfo method for the Report object's DatabaseTable object. If you have tables in your report that originate from different databases, this approach allows individual logon information to be provided for each table in the report. Search the online Help for "SetLogOnInfo method (RDC)."

Retrieving or Setting the SQL Query

When you submit a record-selection formula, as discussed earlier in the chapter, the RDC will generate a SQL statement to submit to the database server automatically. However, if the record-selection formula contains a Crystal Reports formula, an OR operator, or other characteristics that prevent the RDC from including a WHERE clause in the SQL statement, report performance can be dramatically and negatively affected. You may, therefore, want to create the SQL statement the report uses directly in your VB application. As part of this process, you may find it helpful to retrieve the SQL statement that the RDC is generating automatically.

The Report object provides a read/write SQLQueryString property that can be read or written at run time. By examining the contents of this property, you can see what the SQL query is that the RDC is generating. You can then make necessary modifications to the query, depending on the state of your application and the database on which the report is based. Then, pass the modified query to the SQLQueryString property to be submitted to the server when the report runs.

As with Crystal Reports, you cannot modify the SELECT clause in the SQL query. Only FROM, WHERE, and ORDER BY can be modified. Don't forget that you must still include the SELECT clause, however, and that it must not be changed from the original clause the RDC created.

Also, if you create an ORDER BY clause, you must separate it from the end of the WHERE clause with a carriage return/line feed character sequence. Use CHR$(13) & CHR$(10) VB functions to add the CR/LF sequence inside the SQL query.

Reading or Setting Stored-Procedure Parameters

If your report is based on a parameterized SQL stored procedure, you will probably want to supply parameter values to the stored procedure from within your code, much as you will want to respond to any RDC parameter fields that may have been created.

With the RDC, SQL stored-procedure parameters are treated identically to Report parameter fields. The Report object contains the ParameterFieldDefinitions collection, containing one ParameterFieldDefinition object for each Report parameter field *or* stored-procedure parameter contained in the report. The ParameterFieldDefinition object's ParameterType property will indicate whether the parameter is a Report parameter or a stored-procedure parameter.

By executing the ParameterFieldDefinition object's AddCurrentValue method, you can pass a value to a stored-procedure parameter from within your code. More detailed information on interacting with parameter fields can be found earlier in this chapter.

RDC Subreports

The RDC brings all the flexibility of Crystal Reports subreports to Visual Basic. If you import an .RPT file that contains subreports into the RDC, the subreports will be imported along with the main report. And, you can add your own subreports to the RDC design window at any time by right-clicking a blank area of the report and choosing Insert | Subreport from the pop-up menu (see Chapter 11 for more information on creating subreports).

The unique part of the RDC is the way a subreport fits into the object model. When you are displaying the main report in the RDC design window, a subreport will appear as an object outline, just as it does in regular Crystal Reports. However, if you click the subreport object, notice that it has a set of properties that appears in the Properties box, just like other objects on the report. Figure 24-7 illustrates this.

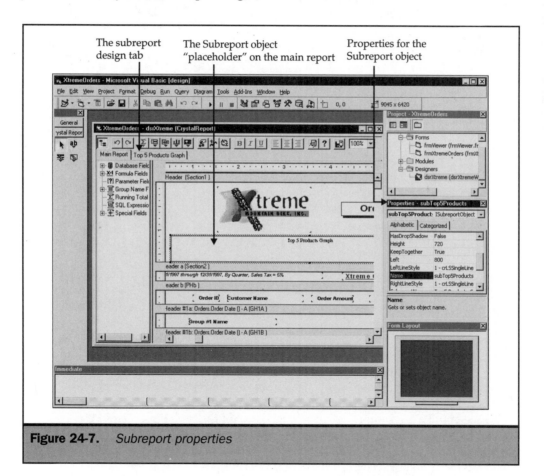

Figure 24-7. *Subreport properties*

You can set several design-time properties for the Subreport object, the same way you can for other objects on the report. One of the properties you may want to set as a matter of habit is the subreport name. By giving it a descriptive name, you'll be able to more easily identify and work with it as you write code for your application.

Once the Subreport object has been added to the main report, it's treated just like a text object, field, line, box, or other object that appears on the main report in the main Report object model. But because the subreport contains its own set of fields and objects that are separate from the main report, the object model can expose them in a number of ways. Subreport objects (fields, formulas, sections, lines, and others) actually appear as part of the main Report object. The RDC precedes the object names with the name of the subreport and an underscore.

Consider a main report that contains several database fields that haven't been renamed since the report was created (Field1, Field2, and so on). The main report also contains a subreport that you've named subTop5Products. The subreport objects actually become part of the main report. You can now set properties for the Report object named Field1, which will refer to the first field on the main report. If you then set Report properties for an object named subTop5Products_Field1, you are setting properties for the first field on the subreport.

Also, the main report exposes a SubreportObject object for every subreport "placeholder" contained on the main report. This object exposes a variety of properties that can be read and written at run time to control the appearance and behavior of the placeholder (although not the actual subreport itself). Look at the following code:

```
'Set subreport object borders to blank
Report.subTop5Products.TopLineStyle = 0
Report.subTop5Products.LeftLineStyle = 0
Report.subTop5Products.BottomLineStyle = 0
Report.subTop5Products.RightLineStyle = 0
```

Here, you see the SubreportObject object being manipulated from the Report object (referred to with the subreport name "subTop5Products"). The four line-style properties are all being set to 0, indicating that the border around the Subreport object will be invisible at run time.

Despite this tricky way of sharing objects and setting properties for the Subreport placeholder, not all Subreport properties, methods, and events are available from the main Report object. Since the subreport is, in essence, an additional report just appearing on the main report, you'll need a way to control the behavior of the subreport using the same object model as the main report.

To accomplish this, you must declare an object of the type Report from the CRAXDRT Automation Server (the automation server the RDC exposes). You then use the main report's OpenSubreport method to create another Report object variable to contain the subreport. You can then set properties, execute methods, and trap events for the main report using its original object variable, and for the subreport using its own object variable. The following code fragment demonstrates this approach:

```
Dim Subreport as CRAXDRT.Report
...
...
'Put subreport in its own object
Set Subreport = Report.subTop5Products.OpenSubreport

'Set record selection formula for subreport
Subreport.RecordSelectionFormula = "{ado.Unit Price} > 1000"
```

 More information on declaring and assigning object variables can be found in Visual Basic Help. To learn more about how Crystal Reports works with COM Automation Server, see Chapter 25.

Chapter 25

The Report Engine
Automation Server

Seagate Crystal Reports Versions 6 and 7 feature the Report Engine Automation Server (known simply as the "Automation Server") for integrating reports with Windows development tools. The Automation Server provides a richer set of capabilities than the ActiveX control, but is easier to interact with than the Report Engine API (discussed in Chapter 26). In fact, the Automation Server is known as a "wrapper" interface—it "wraps" itself around the Report Engine API, making it easier to program by not requiring direct API calls from Visual Basic or other languages.

The Automation Server is similar to the ActiveX control (discussed in Chapter 23) in that it exposes properties, methods, and events for report integration. It differs, however, in the larger "object model" that it exposes. Automation Server integration methods are much closer to those of the Report Designer component (the RDC, covered in Chapter 24). In fact, the report-processing portion of the RDC is simply an alternative automation server with a slightly different object model that was designed after Seagate created the original Report Engine Automation Server covered in this chapter.

Overview of the Automation Server

The Automation Server conforms to Microsoft's Component Object Model (COM). As such, it can be used in any COM-compatible development environment that supports a COM automation server (formerly known as an "OLE server"), such as Visual Basic, Visual C++, Delphi, and Microsoft Visual InterDev for Web page development (covered in more detail in Chapter 29). While an in-depth discussion of COM is better left to Microsoft documentation, you can consider COM to be a set of standards that allows one software environment to utilize the functions of another software environment by way of objects, properties, methods, and events.

COM development falls under the category of object-oriented programming. An *object hierarchy* is exposed by the COM-compatible automation server. This hierarchy begins with high-level objects that contain lower levels of objects. These second-level objects can contain lower levels of objects, and so on. If it sounds like the levels of objects can get "deep," they sometimes do. Some objects in the Automation Server are four or five layers deep in the object hierarchy.

Objects can not only contain additional single objects below them, but can also contain collections of objects. A *collection* is a group of related objects contained inside the parent object. For example, a Report object will contain a collection of Section objects (an object for the Report Header, Page Header, and so on). Each of these Section objects itself contains its own collection of Report objects, such as fields, text objects, formulas, lines, boxes, and so on. If the Details section of a report has ten database fields, four formulas, and a line-drawing, the Details Section object will contain an object collection consisting of 15 *members*—one member for each of the Report objects in the section. And, if a report simply contains the five default sections that are created with a new report, the report's Sections collection will contain five members—one for each section.

The highest level in the object hierarchy is the Application object—everything eventually "trickles down" from it. Although you do need to declare the Application object in your VB code, you will rarely (if ever) refer to it again, or set any properties for it, once it's declared. As a general rule, the highest level of object you'll regularly be concerned with is the *Report* object, created by executing the Application object's OpenReport method. You will then manipulate many of the Report object's properties (such as the RecordSelectionFormula property), as well as working with many objects below the Report object (such as report sections, as were just discussed).

Because the Automation Server is a tightly integrated COM component, you will benefit from Visual Basic's *automatic code completion* when you use it. When you begin to enter code into the VB code window for the Report object, the properties, methods, and built-in constant values will become available to you from automatically appearing drop-down lists. If you've used Visual Basic 5 or 6, you're probably already familiar with this feature. You'll enjoy the benefit it provides with the Automation Server, as well.

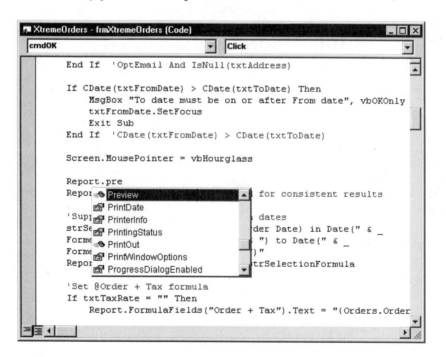

> **Caution** *Unlike the RDC (discussed in Chapter 24), the Automation Server will only automatically complete code to one level in the object hierarchy. When you type the period to go to the next level, you'll just hear a beep, and nothing else will display in the code window. If you want to proceed further down the hierarchy, you'll need to ensure you type the correct syntax for the deeper objects and properties. Check the Object Browser (discussed later in this chapter) or online Help for information on correct syntax.*

Adding the Automation Server to Your Project

The first step in using the Automation Server is to add it to your project. After installing Crystal Reports 7 (and including Developer Tools as part of the installation), Automation Server should be properly registered on your system and ready for use. There are two versions of the Automation Server available: CPEAUT32.DLL is the 32-bit version for use with Visual Basic 5 and 6; CPEAUT16.DLL is the 16-bit version for use with the 16-bit version of Visual Basic 4.

To add the Automation Server to your project, follow these steps:

1. Start Visual Basic and create a new project or open the existing project that you wish to use with the Automation Server.

2. Choose Project | References from the pull-down menus. The References dialog box will appear.

3. Select the Crystal Report Engine 7 Object Library check box. If you don't see this option, click the Browse button and locate the correct version of the Automation Server .DLL file (CPEAUT32.DLL or CPEAUT16.DLL) in the Windows System directory.

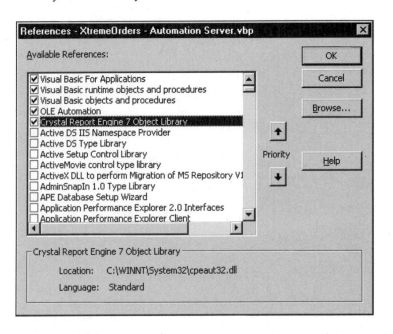

 These instructions apply to Visual Basic 5 and 6. Check Microsoft documentation for information on adding COM automation servers to a VB 4 project.

When you add the Automation Server to your project, there are several ways of viewing the various objects, collections, properties, methods, and events that are exposed. The first is simply by using the online Developer's Help provided with Crystal Reports. This is available from the Crystal Reports program group or by navigating directly to the Crystal Reports program directory and viewing DEVELOPR.HLP.

You can also use Visual Basic's *Object Browser*. The Object Browser can be viewed in Visual Basic any time your program isn't running. Press F2, or choose View | Object Browser from the pull-down menus. Then, choose CRPEAuto in the first drop-down list to see the object library exposed by the Automation Server.

And finally, Seagate Software provides a handy CrystalExplorer "object-model explorer" utility, shown in Figure 25-1, that you may prefer to the Object Browser. When Crystal Reports is installed, this utility is installed by default. Using Windows Explorer, navigate to <Crystal Reports program folder>\sample\Xtreme\browser. Double-click CrystalExplorer.EXE to launch the utility.

Note   *The CrystalExplorer application has not been updated with new Automation Server features for Crystal Reports Version 7; it is only current for Version 6. If you're concerned about seeing the most current reference, refer to Developer's Help or use the VB Object Browser.*

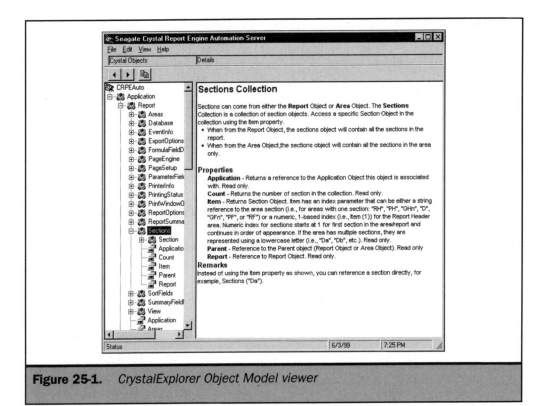

Figure 25-1. *CrystalExplorer Object Model viewer*

Declaring the Application and Report Objects

Once you've actually added the Automation Server library to your project, the first step is to declare Application and Report objects. These are the upper-level objects in the object hierarchy and must be declared for every project. There generally should only be one Application object per VB project. If you will be manipulating more than one report at a time, you can declare multiple report objects within the Application object (or, just reuse a single Report object if you are using multiple reports, but only need to use one particular report at a time).

Both objects are initially declared with the Dim statement in an appropriate declarations section of a form or Sub Main. In the Xtreme Orders sample application, these are declared in the declarations section of the form.

```
Dim Application As CRPEAuto.Application
Dim Report As CRPEAuto.Report
```

Note that the object types have been *fully qualified*. That is, they are not declared with the simple generic "Object" type. Instead, the Automation Server Application and Report object types are used. To take this a step further, the Automation Server CRPEAuto library name is added to the object types, separated by a period, to explicitly indicate that they are to refer to the Crystal Reports Automation Server. Using this specific class ID avoids confusion with other objects of the same type that may also be added to the VB project (such as the DAO library or another library with identical object types). This full qualification facilitates Visual Basic's "early binding," which improves application performance, as well as allowing automatic code completion.

Once the object variables have been declared, you must specifically assign the application variable to the Crystal Reports Automation Server and choose a particular .RPT report file for the report variable. This is accomplished by using the Set statement. For the Application object, use the VB CreateObject method, passing the class argument "Crystal.CRPE.Application". You can then use the Application object's OpenReport method to assign a specific .RPT file to the Report object. The Set statements should appear in Form_Load, Sub Main, or another appropriate location, depending on the scope you want the object variables to have throughout the project. In the Xtreme Orders sample application, these objects are assigned in Form_Load.

```
'Assign application object
Set Application = CreateObject("Crystal.CRPE.Application")
'Open the report
Set Report = Application.OpenReport(App.Path & "\Xtreme
Orders.rpt")
```

At the end of your application (in Form_Unload, for example), it is recommended that you set the object variables to "Nothing" to release memory.

```
Set Report = Nothing
Set Application = Nothing
```

Controlling the Preview Window

Once the Report object has been assigned to an .RPT file, then the "fun" can begin. In its simplest form, you simply display the report in a preview window with one call. Execute the Report object's Preview method to show the report in a preview window.

```
Report.Preview("Xtreme Orders Report")
```

The Preview method accepts several arguments, including the "Xtreme Orders Report" string that appears in the preview window's title bar.

If you compare the Automation Server with the RDC, discussed in Chapter 24, you'll notice you aren't dealing with a separate Smart Viewer ActiveX object—the Automation Server includes its own built-in preview window. However, you'll still probably want to be able to customize the behavior of the preview window. In addition to extra arguments that can be provided to the Preview method to control the window title, size, and position, there is a whole other set of properties that control which elements of the preview window appear or can be interacted with.

The PrintWindowOptions object resides below the Report object and contains a set of properties that controls the preview window's appearance and behavior. You can control which buttons appear and whether or not drilling down is enabled. In the Xtreme Orders sample application, two of these properties are set to control drilling down and the display of the group tree. Look at this sample code:

```
Report.PrintWindowOptions.HasGroupTree = True
Report.PrintWindowOptions.CanDrillDown = True
```

There are other properties of the PrintWindowOptions object that you can set, as well. Look at the Object Browser or Developer's Help for more information.

Controlling Record Selection

One of the obvious reasons to integrate Crystal Reports with Visual Basic in the first place is to completely control the user interface. You'll no doubt want to control report record selection, based on a user's selections made using your own user interface. Because VB has such powerful user-interface features (such as the VB date picker and other custom controls), you will have much more flexibility using VB controls than you will with Crystal Reports parameter fields.

As the record-selection formula you pass to the Automation Server must still conform to Crystal Reports syntax, you'll need to know how to create a Crystal Reports formula. If you are used to using the Crystal Reports Select Expert for record selection, you'll need to familiarize yourself with the actual Crystal Reports formula that it creates, before you create a selection formula in your VB application. A Crystal Reports record-selection formula is a Boolean formula that narrows down the database records that will be included in the report. For example, the following record-selection formula will limit a report to orders placed in the first quarter of 1997 from customers in Wyoming:

```
{Orders.Order Date} In Date(1997,1,1) To Date(1997,3,31)
And {Customer.Region} = "WY"
```

Tip   *For complete discussions of Crystal Reports record selection and how to create Boolean formulas, consult Chapters 5 and 6.*

Use the RecordSelectionFormula property of the Report object to set the record-selection formula for the report. You can set the property to either a string expression or a variable. Here's the code from the sample application that sets record selection, based on the contents of the user-supplied From Date and To Date text boxes:

```
'Supply record selection based on dates
strSelectionFormula = "{Orders.Order Date} in Date(" & _
Format(txtFromDate, "yyyy,m,d") & ") to Date(" & _
Format(txtToDate, "yyyy,m,d") & ")"
Report.RecordSelectionFormula = strSelectionFormula
```

Record-Selection Formula Tips

There are several important points to keep in mind when building a Crystal Reports record-selection formula within your application. Specifically, there are some tricks to making sure that your string values are formatted properly, and to making sure that as much of the SQL selection work is done on the server, rather than on the PC.

The string value you pass must adhere *exactly* to the Crystal Reports formula syntax. This includes using correct Crystal Reports reserved words and punctuation. The example from the sample application shows the necessity of building a Date(yyyy,mm,dd) string to pass to the selection formula.

Also, it's easy to forget the required quotation marks or apostrophes around literals that are used in comparisons. For example, you may want to pass the following selection formula:

```
{Customer.Region} = 'WY' And {Orders.Ship Via} = 'UPS'
```

If the characters WY and UPS are coming from controls, such as a text box or combo box, consider using the following VB code to place the selection formula in a string variable:

```
strSelectionFormula = "{Customer.Region} = " & txtRegion & _
" And {Orders.Ship Via} = " & cboShipper
```

At first glance, this appears to create a correctly formatted Crystal Reports record-selection formula. However, if you pass this string to the RecordSelectionFormula property, the report will fail when it runs. Why? The best way to troubleshoot this issue is to look at the contents of strSelectionFormula in the VB Immediate window, by setting a breakpoint, or by using other VB debugging features. Doing so will show that the contents of the string variable after the preceding code executes as follows:

```
{Customer.Region} = WY And {Orders.Ship Via} = UPS
```

Notice that there are no quotation marks or apostrophes around the literals that are being compared in the record-selection formula—a basic requirement of the Crystal Reports formula language. The following VB code will create a syntactically correct selection formula:

```
strSelectionFormula = "{Customer.Region} = '" & txtRegion & _
"' And {Orders.Ship Via} = '" & cboShipper & "'"
```

If your report will be using a SQL database, remember also that the Automation Server will attempt to convert as much of your record-selection formula as possible to SQL when it runs the report. The same caveats apply to the record-selection formula you pass from your VB application as apply to a record-selection formula you create directly in Crystal Reports. In particular, using built-in Crystal Reports formula functions, such as UpperCase or IsNull, and using OR operators instead of AND operators, will typically cause record selection to be moved to the client (the PC) instead of the database server. The result is very slow report performance. To avoid this situation, take the same care in creating record-selection formulas that you pass from your application as you would in Crystal Reports. Look for detailed discussions on record-selection performance in both Chapters 6 and 14.

You can also choose to create the SQL statement that the report will use right in your VB application. You can then submit it to the report by setting the Report object's SQLQueryString property.

Setting Formulas

Another major benefit of report integration with Visual Basic is that you can change Crystal Report formulas at run time. This is useful for changing formulas related to groups that might also be changed from within your code, formulas that show text on the report, or formulas that relate to math calculations or conditional formatting on the report.

Setting formulas at run time is similar to setting the record-selection formula at run time (as described in the previous section). You'll need a good understanding of the Crystal Reports formula language to adequately modify formulas inside your VB code. If you need a refresher on Crystal Reports formulas, look back at Chapter 5.

The Automation Server exposes a FormulaFields collection in the Report object that can be read from or written to at run time. This collection returns multiple FormulaFieldDefinition objects, one for each formula defined in the report. Although there is a great deal of information that can be gleaned from the FormulaFieldDefinition object, the simplest way to change the contents of a formula is simply to set the Text property for the particular member of the collection that you want to change. The collection is one-based, with each member corresponding to its position in the list of formula fields. Unlike the RDC, the Automation Server lets you pass a string value as the index to the FormulaFields collection. This is more convenient, letting you call the formula field you want to change by name, instead of by number.

In the Xtreme Orders sample application, the Order + Tax formula is modified based on the user's input in the Tax Rate text box. The formula is changed using the following code:

```
'Set @Order + Tax formula
If txtTaxRate = "" Then
   Report.FormulaFields("Order + Tax").Text = _
   "{Orders.Order Amount}"
Else
   Report.FormulaFields("Order + Tax").Text = _
   "{Orders.Order Amount} *" & Str(txtTaxRate / 100 + 1)
End If  'txtTaxRate = ""
```

Notice that the particular member of the collection that you want to change can be specified by the string "Order + Tax". Make sure you don't include the @ sign when specifying the formula name. Since Order + Tax is the first formula in the formula list, you could also change the formulas by using an index number, as in the following code:

```
Report.FormulaFields(1).Text = "{Orders.Order Amount}"
```

The Text property requires a string expression or variable, correctly conforming to the Crystal Report's formula syntax, that contains the new text you want the formula to contain. Take care when assigning a value to the formula. The Order + Tax formula is defined in Crystal Reports as a numeric formula, so you should pass it a formula that will evaluate to a number.

If the user leaves the text box on the form empty, the VB code assumes there is no additional sales tax and simply places the Order Amount database field in the formula—the formula will show the same amount as the database field. If, however, the user has specified a tax rate, the VB code manipulates the value by dividing it by

100, and then adding 1. This will create the proper type of number to multiply against the Order Amount field to correctly calculate tax. For example, if the user specifies a tax rate of 5 (for 5 percent tax), the VB code will change the value to 1.05 before combining it with the multiply operator and the Order Amount field in the formula.

If you're contrasting the Automation Server with the RDC, you'll also become aware that you can't change the contents of Text objects with the Automation Server at run time. So, changing textual information, such as an information message that contains selection options the user made, must be done by modifying a string formula at run time.

In the Xtreme Orders sample application, the @Sub Heading string formula appears in the Page Header and contains a description of the report options that are chosen at run time. This formula is set in the sample application based on selections the user has made on the form. Here's the sample code:

```
'Set @Sub Heading formula
strSubHeading = "'" & txtFromDate & " through " & txtToDate
strSubHeading = strSubHeading & ", By " & cboGroupBy
If txtTaxRate = "" Then
    strSubHeading = strSubHeading & ", No Tax'"
Else
    strSubHeading = strSubHeading & ", Sales Tax = " & _
    txtTaxRate & "%'"
End If  'txtTaxRate = ""
Report.FormulaFields("Sub Heading").Text = strSubHeading
```

Here, the string variable strSubHeading has been declared earlier in the procedure and is used as a work string to build the formula contents. It's actually possible to just use the Text property from the FormulaFieldDefinition object in the same fashion, as it's both a read and write property.

 You needn't change the property for all formulas in the report—just the ones you want to modify at run time.

Passing Parameter Field Values

The .RPT file that the Report object is bound to may contain parameter fields that were designed to prompt the user for information whenever the report was refreshed. If you simply leave the parameter fields as is, the application will automatically prompt the user for those values when the report runs. However, you'll probably want to supply these parameter values through code, based on your own user interface.

Since you can control both report record selection and report formulas at run time from within your VB application, there isn't as much necessity to use parameter fields with an integrated report as there might be for a stand-alone report running with regular Crystal Reports. However, you may be "sharing" a report on a network or via another sharing mechanism. In this situation, you might want to maintain parameter fields in the .RPT file to accommodate report viewers who won't be using your front-end application to run the report. Or it may just be simpler to use existing parameter fields rather than designing extra code to accomplish the same thing.

In these situations, use the Report object's ParameterFieldDefinitions collection to manipulate the parameters. As with formulas, there is one ParameterFieldDefinition object in the collection for each parameter field defined in the report. And, as with formulas, the proper member of the collection is retrieved by either using the actual parameter field name as an index, or a one-based index determined by the order in which the parameter fields were added to the report. Unlike the RDC, you can retrieve a parameter field by using its name as the index (without the question mark). To set the value of a parameter field, use the ParameterFieldDefinition object's SetCurrentValue method. This passes a single value to the report parameter field.

In the Xtreme Orders sample application, the ?Highlight parameter field is used to conditionally format the Details section when the order amount exceeds a parameter supplied by the viewer. Here is the sample code to correctly pass the value to the parameter field:

```
'Set ?Highlight parameter value
If txtHighlight = "" Then
    Report.ParameterFields("Highlight").SetCurrentValue (0)
Else
    Report.ParameterFields("Highlight").SetCurrentValue _
    (Val(txtHighlight))
End If   'txtHighlight = ""
```

Here, the value is set to 0 if the text box is empty. This is important to note, as the actual parameter field in the report is numeric. Passing it an empty string might cause a run-time error when the report runs. Also, because the SetCurrentValue method is executed at least once, and a value has been passed to the parameter field, the user will no longer be prompted for it when the report is run.

Note *The initial release of the Crystal Reports 7 Automation Server Object Model does not expose many of the new features of Crystal Reports 7 parameter fields, such as range values, multiple values, and edit masks. If the .RPT file you are integrating depends on these features, you may need to redesign the report to accommodate the Automation Server, or consider using the RDC to integrate the report.*

Manipulating Report Groups

You'll often want to add flexibility to your application by allowing the user to choose how they want their report grouped. By being able to change these options from within an application at run time, you can provide great reporting flexibility to your end-users. In many cases, you can make it appear that several different reports can be chosen based on user input. In fact, the application will be using the same Report object, but grouping will be changed at run time, based on the user's input.

For example, part of the Xtreme Orders sample application is a combo box on the Print Report form that lets the user choose between Quarter and Customer grouping. Based on this setting, you'll want your application to choose the field on which the first (and only) report group is based, as well as choosing quarterly grouping if the Order Date field is chosen. To familiarize yourself with various grouping options, refer to Chapter 3.

Manipulating groups in the Automation Server requires you to navigate "down the object hierarchy." Ultimately, the database or formula field a group is based on is specified by the GroupConditionField property of the Area object. A report contains an Areas collection containing an Area object for each area in a report. Consider an area of the report to be each individual main section of the report, such as the Page Header, Details section, Group Footer, and so on. If there are multiple sections on the report, such as Details a and Details b sections, they are each sections in the overall Details *area*, and there is only one member of the Areas collection for all of those sections. The index that is used to refer to an individual member of the collection can be a string value or a numeric value. This allows you to specify "RH", "PH", "GH*n*", "D", "GF*n*", "PF", or "RF" as index values or a one-based index number. Using the string values makes your code much easier to understand when working with the Areas collection.

Once you navigate to the specific Area object to specify the GroupConditionField property, you are faced with a peculiarity of the Automation Server Object Model. With other integration methods (the ActiveX control, in particular), you supply the actual field name (such as {Orders.Order Date} or {Customer.Customer Name}) to indicate which field you wish to base a group on. The Automation Server doesn't make life this simple. You must specify a DatabaseFieldDefinition object to the GroupConditionField property—you can't just pass a field name.

DatabaseFieldDefinition is found "deep" in the object hierarchy—there is one of these objects for each field contained in the DatabaseFieldDefinitions collection in a DatabaseTable object. And, there are multiple DatabaseTable objects contained in the DatabaseTables collection of the Database object, contained inside the overall Report object. However, unlike the RDC, which shares a similar object hierarchy, the collections just mentioned will accept a string index value or a one-based number.

Although this sounds confusing and hard to navigate, you'll eventually be able to travel through the object hierarchy fairly quickly to find the database table and field you want to provide to the GroupConditionField property. Look at the following code from the Xtreme Orders sample application:

```
'Set grouping
If cboGroupBy = "Quarter" Then
    'The quarterly grouping will only work if the report is set
    'to "Convert Date/Time Fields to Date" - known bug
    'w/initial SCR 7 release
    Report.Areas("GH").GroupOptions.ConditionField = _
        Report.Database.Tables("Orders").Fields("Order Date")
    Report.Areas("GH").GroupOptions.Condition = crGCQuarterly
Else
    Report.Areas("GH").GroupOptions.ConditionField = _
    Report.Database.Tables("Customer").Fields("Customer Name")
    Report.Areas("GH").GroupOptions.Condition = crGCAnyValue
End If  'cboGroupBy = "Quarter"
```

Caution   *Notice the comments in the code relating to quarterly grouping. There is a bug in the initial version of Crystal Reports 7 that will ignore quarterly grouping and create a new group for every day. This is a known problem slated for repair in a maintenance release. However, if you open the report in the Crystal Reports designer and choose File | Report Options and choose To Date as the Convert Date/Time Field option, quarterly grouping will work properly. The trade-off is that true date/time data types won't be available for use in the report—they will be converted to date-only fields.*

In this example, notice that the grouping is based on the user choice for the cboGroupBy combo box. In either case, the GroupConditionField property of the "GH" member of the Areas collection (the group header) is being set. If the user chooses to group by Order Date, the property is set to the "Order Date" member of the Fields collection in the "Orders" member of the Tables collection. If the user chooses to group by Customer Name, the Customer Name field in the Customer table will be used for grouping. Instead of specifying string indexes for these collections, you can use one-based numbers if you choose.

In addition to choosing the database field you want to use for the group, you may have to choose how the grouping occurs, particularly if you use a date or Boolean field as the grouping field. This is accomplished by manipulating the GroupAreaOptions object below the Area object. This object contains a Condition property that can be set to an integer value or to an Automation Server–supplied constant (see the explanation for the GroupAreaOptions object in online Help for specific constants and integer values). In the sample code shown previously, the group is set to break for every calendar quarter if Order Date grouping is set (hence the crGCQuarterly constant that is provided). If Customer Name grouping is chosen, the crGCAnyValue constant is supplied, indicating that a new group will be created whenever the value of the group field changes.

> | Caution | *Automatic code completion won't work when you navigate deep in the object hierarchy, as demonstrated in the code shown earlier in the chapter. The Automation Server will only help you complete code one level deep, so keep Developer's Help or the Object Browser handy to help you navigate through objects this deep in the hierarchy.*
>
> *An alternative mentioned in the online Developer's Help is using Dim statements to create additional object variables for each of the objects that are below the first level in the hierarchy, and then using multiple Set statements to assign them values. While this will let you use automatic code completion, it also creates monstrous amounts of extra code.*

Conditional Formatting and Formatting Sections

If you'll be presented reports in the Automation Server preview window, you'll want to take advantage of as many of Crystal Reports' interactive reporting capabilities as possible. One particular benefit of online reporting is the drill-down capability. This allows a report to be initially presented at a very high summary level, showing just subtotals or grand totals, or perhaps just showing a pie chart or bar chart that graphs high-level numbers. The viewer can then double-click a number or chart element that interests them to "drill down" to more detailed numbers, eventually reaching the report's Details section. These levels of drilling down are limited only by the number of report groups you create on your report.

The Xtreme Orders sample application gives the user the opportunity to specify whether or not to see the report as a summary report only. When the "Summary Report Only" check box is selected, the VB application will need to hide the report's Details section so that only group subtotals appear on the report. In addition, you'll need to control the appearance of the report's two Page Header sections (Page Header a and Page Header b), as well as two Group Header #1 sections (Group Header #1a and Group Header #1b).

This is to accommodate two different sections of field titles that you wish to appear differently if the report is presented as a summary report instead of a detail report. If the report is being displayed as a detail report, the field titles should appear at the top of every page of the report, along with the subheading and smaller report title. If the report is displayed as a summary report, you only want the field titles to appear in the Group Header section of a drill-down tab when the user double-clicks a group. Since no detail information will be visible in the main report window, field titles there won't be meaningful.

And finally, you'll want to show Group Header #1a, which contains the group name field, if the report is showing detail data. This will indicate what group the following set of orders applies to. However, if the report is only showing summary data, showing both the group header and group footer will be repetitive—the group footer already contains the group name, so showing the group header, as well, will look odd. But, you will want the group header with the group name to appear in a drill-down tab.

Therefore, you'll need to control the appearance of four sections when a user chooses the summary report option. Table 25-1 will give you a better idea of how you'll want to conditionally set these sections at run time.

You'll notice that in some cases sections need to be completely suppressed (so they don't show up, even in a drill-down tab) as opposed to hidden (which means they will show up in a drill-down tab, but not in the main Preview tab). There is a somewhat obscure relationship among areas and sections that make this determination. Specifically, only complete areas (such as the entire Group Header #1) can be hidden, not individual sections (for example, Group Header #1a). However, both areas and sections can be suppressed individually.

This presents a bit of a coding challenge for the Xtreme Orders sample application. First, you'll need to determine the correct combination of area hiding and section suppressing that sets what appears in the Preview window and in a drill-down tab. If an area is hidden, none of the sections in it will appear in the main Preview window. But, when the user drills down into that section, you will want to control which sections inside the drilled-down area appear in the drill-down tab. Once you've determined which areas you want to hide, you must find the correct property to set for that particular area. You must also find the correct property to suppress sections inside the hidden area, or to show other sections that aren't hidden.

This functionality is controlled by manipulating two different, but similar, sets of objects below the Report object. First is the Areas collection, which contains an Area object for each area in the report. For example, the Page Header is considered an individual area. An *area* encompasses one or more related sections—both Group Header #1a and Group Header #1b sections are combined in one single Group Header 1 area.

Section	Detail Report	Summary Report
Page Header b (field titles)	Shown	Suppressed (no drill-down)
Group Header #1a (group-name field)	Shown	Hidden (drill-down okay)
Group Header #1b (field titles)	Suppressed (no drill-down)	Hidden (drill-down okay)
Details (detail order data)	Shown	Hidden (drill-down okay)

Table 25-1.   *Section Formatting for Different Report Types*

DEVELOPING CUSTOM WINDOW APPLICATIONS

The Report object also contains a Sections collection, which contains a Section object for each section in the report. A *section* encompasses each individual section of the report, regardless of how many there may be inside a single area. For example, the Page Header is considered an individual section. But even though Group Header #1a and Group Header #1b are considered a single area, they are separate sections.

Manipulating areas and sections can "send you deep" into the object hierarchy. However, choosing the right member of the collections is made easier by the option of providing a string value as the index. Online Help can help you determine which section and area abbreviations to use as indexes, or you can use the short section names that appear in the Crystal Reports designer when you have the "Short Section Names" option turned on in File | Options. For example, either the Details area or Details section member can be accessed by supplying an index of "D". The Group Header 1 area can be accessed by supplying an index of "GH1" to the Areas collection. Getting to the individual sections is possible by providing either "GH1a" or "GH1b" indexes to the Sections collection.

Once you've navigated to the correct section or area, you must set the options by manipulating the AreaOptions or SectionOptions object below each respective Area or Section object. These objects contain the actual properties you'll need to set, such as NotHideForDrillDown and Visible. Note that these two particular properties are "backwards" from what you might be used to in other integration methods or in the Crystal Reports designer. If you want an area hidden for drill-down, you can't set a property to true. You must actually set the NotHideForDrillDown property to false. Also, if you want an individual section suppressed, you will have to set the SectionOptions object's Visible property to false.

Keeping in mind the previous discussion and the hide/suppress requirements outlined in Table 25-1, consider the following code from the sample application:

```
'Hide/show areas and sections
With Report
    If chkSummary Then
        .Areas("D").Options.NotHideForDrillDown = False
        .Sections("PHb").Options.Visible = False
        .Areas("GH1").Options.NotHideForDrillDown = False
        .Sections("GH1a").Options.Visible = True
        .Sections("GH1b").Options.Visible = True
        'NOTE! multiple-section letters in sections collection index
        '(e.g., GH1a) must be lower case!
    Else
        .Areas("D").Options.NotHideForDrillDown = True
        .Sections("PHb").Options.Visible = True
        .Areas("GH1").Options.NotHideForDrillDown = True
        .Sections("GH1a").Options.Visible = True
```

```
      .Sections("GH1b").Options.Visible = False
      'NOTE! multiple-section letters in sections collection index
      '(e.g., GH1a) must be lower case!
   End If  'chkSummary
End With  'Report
```

Notice the comments in the sample code that warn about case sensitivity of indexes provided to the Sections collection. "GH1a" will be correctly interpreted, while "GH1A" will result in a run-time error.

Notice that both Area objects for the Details and Group Header #1 areas are being formatted, as well as individual sections. While you can navigate ever deeper into the Areas collection to eventually get to the sections inside, it's easier and less code-intensive to manipulate the Sections collection directly.

Choosing Output Destinations

By executing the Report object's Preview method, you can display the report contents in the Automation Server's built-in preview window. However, you'll certainly encounter other situations where you want the report sent to a different destination. The Automation Server supports all the same output destinations as the Crystal Report designer's File | Print | Export command, including the printer, various file formats, and e-mail.

In the Xtreme Orders sample application, radio buttons and a text box allow the user to choose to view the report in the preview window, print the report to a printer, or attach the report as a Word document to an e-mail message. If the user chooses e-mail as the output destination, an e-mail address can be entered into a text box. Once that is done, you'll need to set the output destination automatically in your VB code, based on the user's selection.

If the user chooses to view the report on the screen, you'll use the Report object's Preview method. If you wish to print the Report object to a printer, execute the Report object's PrintOut method. The syntax is as follows:

```
object.PrintOut Prompt, Copies, Collated, StartPage, StopPage
```

In this syntax statement, *Prompt* is a Boolean value specifying whether or not to prompt the user for report options, *Copies* is a numeric value specifying how many copies of the report to print, *Collated* is a Boolean value specifying whether or not to collate the pages, and *StartPage* and *StopPage* are numeric values identifying which page numbers to start and stop printing on. The parameters are optional. If you want to skip any that come before a parameter you want to specify, just add commas in the correct positions for the skipped parameter, and don't include a value.

If you wish to export the report to a disk file or attach the report to an e-mail message as a file, use the Report object's Export method. The syntax is as follows:

```
object.Export PromptUser
```

PromptUser is a Boolean value indicating whether or not you want to prompt the user for export options. If you choose not to prompt the user for export options, you'll need to set the properties of the report's ExportOptions object. The ExportOptions object contains many properties that determine the output destination (file or e-mail), the file format (Word, Excel, and so on), the filename, the e-mail address, and others. Many of these properties accept integer values or Automation Server-supplied descriptive constants. If you choose MAPI as the destination, the user's PC will need to have a MAPI-compliant e-mail client, such as Microsoft Outlook or Eudora Pro, installed. Look for all the available ExportOptions properties by searching the online Help for "ExportOptions Object (Crystal Report Engine Object Library)."

In the sample Xtreme Orders application, the following code is used to choose an output destination, as well as to specify a file type and e-mail information, based on user selections. (Note that this sample code directly utilizes the report's Preview method, while the actual sample application on the CD accompanying this book sets a View object to the contents of the report's Preview method. This is discussed later in the chapter under "Handling Preview Window and Report Events.")

```
'Set output destination
If optPreview Then Report.Preview("Xtreme Orders Report")
If OptPrint Then Report.PrintOut (True)
If OptEmail Then
    With Report
        .ExportOptions.DestinationType = crEDTEMailMAPI
        .ExportOptions.MailToList = txtAddress
        .ExportOptions.MailSubject = "Here's the Xtreme Orders Report"
        .ExportOptions.MailMessage = _
"Attached is a Word document with the latest Xtreme Orders Report."
        .ExportOptions.FormatType = crEFTWordForWindows
        .Export (False)
    End With  'Report
End If  'optEmail
```

If you use the Report object's Export method to export or send the report attached to an e-mail message, make sure you specify all the necessary ExportOptions object properties. If you fail to specify necessary properties, or specify them incorrectly, an error may be thrown. Or, the user may be prompted to specify export options, even though you specifically add a "false" argument to the Export method. If the export takes place at an unattended machine, this will cause your application to wait for a response when no user is available to respond.

Changing the Data Source at Run Time

Obviously, one of the main benefits of integrating a Crystal Report in a Visual Basic program is the ability to tie the report's contents to a data set or result set that the program is manipulating. This allows a user to interact with your application and then run a report that contains the same set of data that the user has selected.

One way to accomplish this is to create a Crystal Reports record-selection formula or a SQL statement based on your user interface. The formula or SQL statement can then be passed to the report (as discussed later in this chapter). This will allow the user to interact with a data grid, form, or other visual interface in the application, and then create a report based on its contents.

However, there may be situations where you prefer to have the contents of an actual Visual Basic record set from one of Visual Basic's intrinsic data models act as the data source for a report. The Automation Server SetPrivateData method allows you to change the data source that a table is based on at run time. Using SetPrivateData, you can initially design the report using a particular database or data source, or using a field definition file (discussed in Chapter 27). Then, you can pass a Visual Basic DAO, RDO, or ADO record set, snapshot, or result set to the report at run time. The Automation Server will use the current contents of the VB data set to populate the report.

The syntax for SetPrivateData is as follows:

```
object.SetPrivateData DataTag, Data
```

In this statement, *object* is a DatabaseTable object that you want to supply data to, *DataTag* indicates the type of data you are passing to the object (the only allowable value for *DataTag* is 3), and *Data* is the DAO, ADO, or RDO data set that you want to have supply data to the report.

SetPrivateData applies to the Automation Server's DatabaseTable object, several levels deep in the object hierarchy. This object is below the Database object, which falls below the Report object. The Database object contains a collection of DatabaseTable objects—one for each table used in the database. For example, suppose you have declared a Report object that contains a database with several tables, including a table named "Customer." You also have defined an ADO Resultset object elsewhere in your VB application with the name "ADOrs." The following code will pass the contents of the result set to the report. When the report is previewed, printed, or exported, the contents of the result set will be used by the report in place of the Customer table.

```
Report.Database.Tables("Customer").SetPrivateData 3, ADOrs
```

One important issue to remember is that of field names. Make sure the data source you pass to the report using SetPrivateData contains the same field names and data types as the original data source. Otherwise the report may fail or return unexpected results.

 If you use SetPrivateData to change the data source for a database table object, make sure the data source you pass to the report remains in scope whenever the report runs. For example, you may define a Report object that's global to your application (by declaring it at the module level). But if you pass it a data source that was declared at the form level and then try to run the report in another form, the data source will be out of scope and the report will fail. The ReadRecords method is available to read the contents of the data source into the Report object, if maintaining scope for the data source isn't practical. Search Developer's Help for information on ReadRecords.

Handling Preview Window and Report Events

One powerful feature that the Automation Server shares with the RDC (discussed in Chapter 24) is the ability to trap events that occur in the preview window, as well as trapping certain events that the Report object creates. This allows the developer to trap button clicks, report-processing cycles, and drill-down attempts. These events can be used to modify the behavior of the preview window or report, as well as to execute some additional supplementary code when a certain event occurs.

 Automation Server event handling is only available in the 32-bit version of the Automation Server when using Visual Basic 5 or 6. Visual Basic 4 will not recognize Automation Server events.

Report Object Event Handling

To enable Report object events, the Report object must be declared "Public" and "WithEvents." So, instead of using the following declaration:

```
Dim Report As CRPEAuto.Report
```

you would use:

```
Public WithEvents Report As CRPEAuto.Report
```

The WithEvents parameter will add the Report object name to the object drop-down list in the upper left of the Code window. When you choose the Report object, three events can be chosen in the procedure drop-down list in the upper right of the Code window.

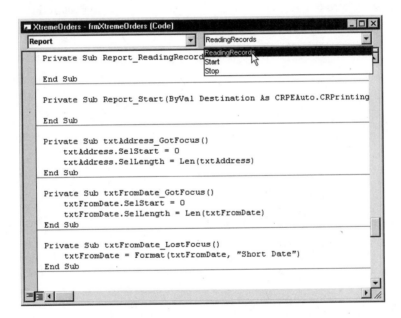

The Start event occurs when the report starts processing. The Stop event occurs when the report processing is finished. The ReadingRecords event occurs when the report begins reading database records. You can add code in these individual event modules to notify the user that processing has started or stopped, or to intervene when the report begins reading records.

Preview Window Event Handling

Although report event handling can be helpful, you'll probably get more use out of preview-window event handling. This allows your code to intercept button clicks, drill-downs, and other preview-window interactions. You can then modify aspects of the report or execute supplementary code based on the action.

Preview-window event handling is accomplished by declaring and using two new object types not previously discussed: the View object and the Window object. The *View* object is equivalent to a tab in the preview window. When the report is first previewed, the main Preview tab is considered a View object. If a viewer double-clicks a group and creates a new drill-down tab, that new tab is also considered to be a View object. While multiple View objects can exist at any one time, only one can actually be manipulated—the currently selected tab.

View objects are always contained inside the *Window* object. Generally, the entire preview window can be considered to be the single Window object, with the multiple View objects (the main Preview tab and drill-down tabs) all appearing inside it. The Window object cannot actually be declared directly. It must be declared using the Parent property of a View object after the View object has been assigned to a particular Report object.

Just as you have to declare a Report object to be "Public" and "WithEvents" to enable event trapping, the Window object must also be declared using these two options. As the actual View object doesn't "fire" any events, it doesn't have this requirement. Once the object variables have been declared, the View object must be assigned to the Preview method of a Report object. Then, the Window object is assigned as the parent of the View object. Look at the following sample code:

```
Dim View1 As CRPEAuto.View
Public WithEvents Window1 As CRPEAuto.Window

Set View1 = Report.Preview("Xtreme Orders Report")
Set Window1 = View1.Parent
```

Here, the object variable View1 is declared to be of the View class and Window1 is declared to be of the Window class (both are fully qualified to refer to the CRPEAuto Automation Server). Notice that Window1 is declared Public and WithEvents. Then, the View1 object variable is pointed to the main Preview tab of the report by assigning it to the Preview method of the Report object. Finally, the Window1 object variable is set to the whole preview window by assigning it to the Parent property of the View object.

As with the Report object, once the Window1 object has been declared "WithEvents," an additional object appears in the object drop-down list in the upper left of the Code window. When you choose the Window1 object, you'll notice several events available in the procedure drop-down list in the upper right of the Code window.

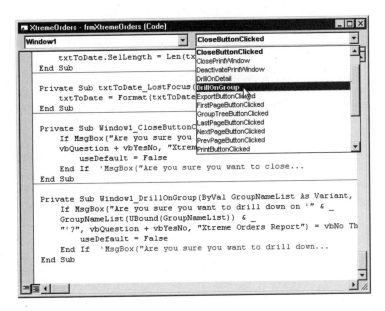

As you can see, there are a large number of preview-window events that can be trapped. In the Xtreme Orders sample application, there are only two simple examples of these capabilities. When the user drills down on a group, a confirmation message box appears asking the user to confirm the drill-down. If the answer is Yes, the drill-down will occur. If not, the drill-down will be canceled. And, after a user has drilled down and then clicks the close view button (the red ×) in the viewer, another confirmation message dialog box appears asking them to confirm the closure. As with the original drill-down, the drill-down tab will only be closed if the user answers Yes. Otherwise, the event will be canceled.

The initial drill-down is trapped by the window object's DrillOnGroup event. Every time a group name, summary, or subtotal is double-clicked, this event will "fire" before the actual drill-down occurs. Several parameters are passed into the event: GroupNameList contains an array of the group names that are being drilled into. DrillType indicates what type of drill-down is occurring (whether the view drilled down on a group or graph, or used the group tree). The useDefault parameter is a Boolean value that can be set to determine whether the drill-down actually occurs. And, ReportName is a parameter that is documented as "reserved for future use"—it currently serves no purpose.

One important part of the drill-down example is actually determining which group will be affected when the drill-down occurs. This ability may be important to fully exploit the power of the event model—trapping a drill-down may be of limited use if you can't determine which group is actually being manipulated. The Window object's DrillOnGroup event makes this task easier by passing the GroupNameList parameter into the event function. This zero-based array contains an element for each group prior to the group that is being drilled in to, as well as the current group just drilled in to. If your report only contains one level of grouping (as does the Xtreme Orders sample report), the GroupNameList will always contain just element 0, that of the group that was drilled in to.

However, if your report contains multiple levels of grouping, you'll be able to determine how many levels of drill down have occurred and which groups have been drilled down on to get to this point. For example, if your report is grouped on three levels, Country, State, and then City, a user can first drill down on Canada. This will fire the DrillOnGroup event and the GroupNameList array will contain only element 0, "Canada." Then, in the Canada drill-down tab, the user might double-click on BC. This will again fire the DrillOnGroup event and the GroupNameList array will now contain two elements, "Canada" in element 0 and "BC" in element 1. Then, if in the BC drill-down tab the user double-clicks on Vancouver, yet another DrillOnGroup event will fire. Inside this event the GroupNameList array will contain elements 0 through 2, "Canada," "BC," and "Vancouver."

If you are only concerned about the lowest level of grouping, just query the last element of the GroupNameList array using the VB UBound function. Even though the Xtreme Orders report only contains one level of grouping (thereby always allowing GroupNameList(0) to be used to determine the group), the UBound function has been used for upward compatibility.

The other argument of note passed to the event is useDefault. This Boolean value can be set to true or false inside the event to determine whether the drill-down actually occurs. If useDefault is set to true (or left as is) the drill-down will occur. If it is set to false inside the DrillOnGroup event, the drill-down will be canceled and no drill-down tab will appear for the group in the viewer.

Here's the sample code from the Xtreme Orders application. Note that the actual group being drilled on is included in the message box and that the results of the message box determine whether the drill-down occurs or not.

```
Private Sub Window1_DrillOnGroup(ByVal GroupNameList As Variant, _
ByVal DrillType As CRPEAuto.CRDrillType, useDefault As Boolean, _
ByVal ReportName As Variant)
    If MsgBox("Are you sure you want to drill down on '" & _
    GroupNameList(UBound(GroupNameList)) & _
    "'?", vbQuestion + vbYesNo, "Xtreme Orders Report") = vbNo Then
        useDefault = False
    End If   'MsgBox("Are you sure you want to drill down...
End Sub
```

The other Window event that is used in the Xtreme Orders sample application is CloseButtonClicked. This event fires whenever a user clicks the red × in the preview window to close the current drill-down tab. Again, the sample application simply displays a confirming message box asking whether or not the user really wants to close the drill-down tab. By setting the UseDefault parameter inside the event code, the drill-down tab is or is not closed, based on the user's choice.

Unlike the DrillOnGroup event, the Automation Server does not provide a string value indicating the drill-down tab that is being closed. The parameter being passed is ViewIndex, which returns an integer indicating the drill-down tab that is being closed (1 indicates the first drill-down tab, 3 the third, and so on). Unlike the RDC, there is no way for the Automation Server to determine the actual group name of the drill-down tab that's being closed.

Examine the following code from the Xtreme Orders sample application:

```
Private Sub Window1_CloseButtonClicked(ByVal ViewIndex As Integer, _
useDefault As Boolean)
    If MsgBox("Are you sure you want to close the drill down tab?", _
    vbQuestion + vbYesNo, "Xtreme Orders Report") = vbNo Then
        useDefault = False
    End If   'MsgBox("Are you sure you want to close...
End Sub
```

This event fires every time the close button in the preview window is clicked. If the viewer responds No to the message box, useDefault is set to false, thereby canceling the close event and still leaving the drill-down tab visible.

Enabling or Disabling Events with EventInfo

The Report object contains an EventInfo object below it. The EventInfo object contains several properties that you can set to true or false to control which report and preview-window events will fire. Even if you've declared a Window object to be "WithEvents," you may wish to occasionally restrict events from firing at certain times. EventInfo properties can be set to false to prevent the events from being trapped.

For example, to prevent the DrillOnGroup event from occurring, set the EventInfo GroupEventEnabled property to false. And, to disable the CloseButtonClicked event, set the EventInfo PrintWindowButtonEventEnabled property to false. Although this is not used in the Xtreme Orders sample application, the code would appear as follows:

```
Report.EventInfo.GroupEventEnabled = False
Report.EventInfo.PrintWindowButtonEventEnabled = False
```

In these situations, the events won't fire, but the actual action still occurs. In other words, if both these lines of code are added to the sample application, the drill-down will occur without ever firing the event and a new drill-down tab will appear without any user confirmation. When the close button is clicked, the drill-down tab will be closed, but the user won't ever be presented with the options to cancel the close operation.

Tip *Despite online Help that may indicate otherwise, the "enabled" properties of EventInfo are all read/write. They can be read or set at run time, not just read.*

Error Handling

As with any Visual Basic program, you'll want to prepare for the possibility that errors may occur. Integrating Crystal Reports with VB requires that you anticipate errors that the Automation Server might encounter, in addition to other errors that the rest of your program may produce.

Automation Server errors are trapped in an On Error Goto handler just like other VB errors. In many situations, you'll see typical VB-type error codes for report-related errors. For example, supplying an incorrect index argument to a Report object collection won't actually generate an Automation Server–specific error. "Subscript Out of Range" will be returned instead. Other error codes returned by the Automation Server will be in the 20XXX range. Using members of the Errors collection, such as Err.Number and Err.Description, you can handle errors or present meaningful error messages to the user. The *XXX* three-digit codes are specific to the Crystal Reports Print Engine, which is actually called by the Automation Server. For a complete breakdown of these error codes, search Developer's Help for "error codes, Crystal Report Engine."

Examine the following code from the Xtreme Orders sample application. Notice that this only traps two particular reporting errors; when an invalid e-mail address is provided, or when the viewer cancels report printing or exporting. Should another error occur, this routine will simply display the error code and text in a message box.

```
cmdOK_Click_Error:
Select Case Err.Number
   Case 20541
      MsgBox "Invalid e-mail address or other e-mail/export problem", _
            vbCritical, "Xtreme Orders Report"
      txtAddress.SetFocus
   Case 20545
      MsgBox "Process canceled", vbInformation, "Xtreme Orders Report"
   Case Else
      MsgBox "Error " & Err.Number & " - " & Err.Description, _
            vbCritical, "Xtreme Orders Report"
End Select    'Case Error.number
```

Caution *Often you'll introduce errors* before *processing the report with the Preview, Printout, or Export methods, such as submitting a syntactically incorrect formula or using an incorrect section name when formatting sections. However, these statements won't result in an error. Typically no error will be detected until you actually process the report with one of the three processing methods.*

Other Automation Server Properties and Methods

Although this chapter has covered most common Automation Server procedures for handling report-customization requirements, there are several other areas that warrant some discussion. In particular, Automation Server functions that handle SQL database reporting, and functions that deal with subreports should be addressed. In addition, there is the Automation Server DiscardSaveData method, which should be used to "reset" or clear the contents of properties that may have been set in previous VB code.

The DiscardSavedData Method

A straightforward feature of the Crystal ActiveX control discussed in Chapter 23 is the Reset method. This method comes in handy when you may run a report more than once inside the application without explicitly closing and redeclaring the report. The ActiveX Reset method returns all properties to the values they originally had in the .RPT file that is being printed. Although there is no similar method for the Automation Server, you will still want to use the Report object's DiscardSavedData method if you will be running a report multiple times without setting the Report object to "Nothing" and redeclaring it.

The Xtreme Orders sample application is a good example of where this is helpful. The Report object is declared in the Print Xtreme Orders form's Form_Load event. As such, the object stays loaded during the entire scope of the application. Every time the OK button is clicked, the application sets report properties based on the controls on the form and then either previews, prints, or exports the report.

The issue of clearing previous settings comes into play when a user runs the report more than once without ending and restarting the application. Because the Report object is never released and redeclared, all of its property settings remain intact when the user clicks OK subsequent times. If the Visual Basic code doesn't explicitly reset some of these previously set properties, the report may exhibit behavior from the previous time it was run that you don't expect. Executing the Report object's DiscardSavedData method clears many properties of settings from any previous activity, returning them to their state in the original .RPT file.

Simply execute the DiscardSavedData method for any Report objects that you want to "clean up," as shown in the following sample from the Xtreme Orders sample application:

```
Report.DiscardSavedData 'required for consistent results
```

This is particularly important if the .RPT file that you're integrating has been saved with File | Save Data with Report turned on. In this case, you'll probably want Visual Basic to discard the saved data at run time and refresh the report with new data from the database. In some cases, even if you do execute DiscardSavedData, a report with saved data will not behave as expected. As a general rule, you'll want to save reports that will be integrated with VB without any saved data, to avoid any unexpected problems.

SQL Database Control

Many corporate databases are kept on client/server SQL database systems, such as Microsoft SQL Server, Oracle, and Informix. Thus, your Visual Basic applications will probably provide front-end interfaces to these database systems, and will need to handle SQL reporting, as well. The Automation Server contains several properties and methods that help when integrating reports based on SQL databases.

Logging On to SQL Databases

It's probable that your VB application already handles SQL database security, requiring the user to provide a valid logon ID and password at the beginning of the application. The user will be frustrated if the Automation Server asks for yet another logon when it comes time to open the report. By using methods and properties to pass logon info to the report, you can pass the valid ID and password the user has already provided, thereby allowing the report to print without prompting again.

One approach to passing logon information to a report is the Application object's LogOnServer method (this is one of the few times you will manipulate the Application object directly). This method logs on to a secure database and remains logged on until LogOffServer is executed or the entire application ends. Search Developer's Help for "LogOnServer method (Application object), Crystal Report Engine object library."

The other way to provide logon information from within your application is by executing the SetLogOnInfo method for the Report object's DatabaseTable object. If you have tables in your report that originate from different databases, this approach allows individual logon information to be provided for each table in the report. Search the online Help for "SetLogOnInfo method (DatabaseTable object), Crystal Report Engine object library."

Retrieving or Setting the SQL Query

When you submit a record-selection formula as discussed earlier in the chapter, the Automation Server will generate a SQL statement to submit to the database server automatically. However, if the record-selection formula contains Crystal formulas, an OR operator, or other characteristics that prevent the Automation Server from including a WHERE clause in the SQL statement, report performance can be dramatically affected for the worse. You may, therefore, want to create the SQL statement the report uses directly in your VB application. As part of this process, you may find it helpful to retrieve the SQL statement that is being automatically generated.

The Report object provides a read/write SQLQueryString property that can be read or written at run time. By examining the contents of this property, you can see what the SQL query is that the Automation Server is creating. You can then make necessary modifications to the query, based on the state of your application and the database that the report is based on. Then, pass the modified query back to the SQLQueryString property to be submitted to the server when the report runs.

Note

As with Crystal Reports, you cannot modify the SELECT clause in the SQL query. Only FROM, WHERE, and ORDER BY clauses can be modified. Don't forget that you must still include the SELECT clause, however, and that it must not be changed from the original clause the Automation Server created.

Also, if you create an ORDER BY clause, you must separate it from the end of the WHERE clause with a carriage return/line feed character sequence. Use CHR$(13) & CHR$(10) VB functions to add the CR/LF sequence inside the SQL query.

Reading or Setting Stored-Procedure Parameters

If your report is based on a parameterized SQL stored procedure, you will probably want to supply parameter values to the stored procedure from within your code, much as you will want to respond to any parameter fields that exist in the .RPT file.

Unlike the RDC, the Automation Server treats stored-procedure parameters separately from report parameter fields. Stored-procedure parameters are contained in their own DatabaseParameters collection contained within the Database object, below the Report object. The DatabaseParameters collection contains one DatabaseParameter object for each stored-procedure parameter in the database. You can view or set the value of the parameter by manipulating the Value property of the DatabaseParameter object.

Note that you must always pass a string expression or variable to the Value property, even if the stored-procedure parameter is defined as another data type—just make sure to pass a string that can be properly converted. The Automation Server will convert the parameter when it passes it to the database. For more information, search Developer's Help for "DatabaseParameter object (Crystal Report Engine object library)."

Automation Server Subreports

Manipulating subreports with the Automation Server is a fairly straightforward process. To completely understand how subreports will interact with your VB code, consider that the main or *containing* report can contain a variable number of subreports. A subreport is actually considered to be a whole separate report, including its own sections, objects, record-selection formula, and other typical report properties. Manipulating each subreport piece is fairly easy.

To manipulate subreport properties, such as the record-selection formula, section or area formatting, or other settings discussed previously in the chapter, you'll need to assign the subreport to its own Report object variable. This is accomplished with the main Report object's OpenSubreport method. This method only takes one string argument, the name of the subreport to open. Consider the following sample code:

```
Dim mainReport as CRPEAuto.Report
Dim subReport as CRPEAuto.Report
...
Set mainReport = Application.OpenReport("C:\Samples\Subreport.RPT")
Set subReport = mainReport.OpenSubreport("Top 5 Products")
...
'Set selection formula for main report
mainReport.RecordSelectionFormula = "{Customer.Country} = 'USA'"
'Set selection formula for subreport
subReport.RecordSelectionFormula = "{Orders.Order Amount} < 1000"
```

You'll notice that two Report objects are declared: one for the main report and one for the subreport. The main Report object variable is assigned to the containing report with the Application object's OpenReport method. Once the main report has been assigned to an object variable, that object's OpenSubreport method will assign the subreport to the Subreport object variable. You can then manipulate the same properties and methods for the Subreport object that have been discussed earlier in the chapter.

The Complete Reference

Crystal Reports 7

Chapter 26

The Report Engine API

Of the different report integration options available to Visual Basic, both the Crystal ActiveX control and the Automation Server eventually pass their calls to a lower-level base component known as the Crystal Report Engine API (referred to as the REAPI throughout this chapter). In fact, the Report Designer component (RDC) is the only interface that doesn't ultimately pass calls to the REAPI. If your development tool doesn't support these other methods, or you have other reasons for preferring API-level coding, you can program directly to this REAPI.

API stands for application programming interface. Although this term is often used to refer to any number of ways of interfacing different software components, it originally referred to calling Windows DLL (dynamic link library) files from within a Windows programming language. Crystal Reports uses the term API in this fashion. The Crystal Report Engine API is comprised of one or more Windows DLL files. You can call functions from these DLL files from within your Visual Basic program.

There can be several advantages to using the REAPI directly. First, almost all Crystal Reports functionality is exposed by the REAPI. In particular, some newer Version 7 enhancements that have not been propagated to other integration methods are available in the REAPI. Second, because other methods eventually make REAPI calls themselves, you might see improved performance and a slightly smaller application "footprint" because of the reduced interface layers between your VB code and the actual REAPI.

There are some disadvantages to using the REAPI, as well. While Windows DLL programming is the most mature method of Windows integration, it also tends to be the most complex. As you work through the sample Xtreme Orders application, you'll notice that it is quite a bit more code-intensive than those created with other integration methods. Also, because the REAPI was originally designed with C programmers in mind, you'll find some functionality that is difficult, if not impossible, to implement in Visual Basic. Seagate includes a REAPI "wrapper" DLL to solve some of these problems. But others, such as the ability to trap preview-window events, aren't possible with Visual Basic because of inherent limitations, such as the lack of pointer handling and the inability to call structures from within other structures.

The REAPI is the most generic level of report integration. If your Windows development tool can make calls to either 16- or 32-bit Windows DLL files (most Windows programming tools can), you'll be able to integrate Crystal Reports with your tool, even if the tool doesn't work with newer technologies, such as ActiveX and COM. Because this text focuses on Visual Basic as the development tool, the REAPI is discussed only in the VB context in this chapter. However, the generic API calls and parameters are the same for any language, so the material presented here should be helpful to you even if you're using another Windows development tool.

Adding the Report Engine API to Your Project

The REAPI consists of two base-level DLL files. CRPE.DLL (which stands for Crystal Reports print engine) is the 16-bit version of the REAPI for Visual Basic 3 and 4 and other 16-bit development environments. CRPE32.DLL provides similar calls for 32-bit environments, such as Visual Basic 5 and 6. Also, don't forget that there are different versions of these DLL files for the Standard and Professional Editions of Crystal Reports. When referring to Developer's Help (available directly from the Crystal Reports program group or by opening DEVELOPR.HLP in the Crystal Reports program directory), you'll see that some REAPI calls are only supported in the Professional Edition of Crystal Reports. The examples used throughout this chapter assume the use of the 32-bit Professional Edition of the tool.

| Note | *As with other integration methods, Seagate Software grants you a license to redistribute CRPE.DLL or CRPE32.DLL, as well as other support DLLs, with your application royalty-free. You may copy these files along with your application files and distribute them to your customers or users at no additional charge. Chapter 27 discusses distribution issues in more detail.* |

You access REAPI features with VB function calls, much as you would your own Sub or Function calls. These calls are predefined to point to the CRPE32.DLL or CRPE.DLL with VB DECLARE statements. While you could write your own DECLARE statements to call only the REAPI functions you are particularly interested in, Seagate makes life much easier for you by predeclaring REAPI calls in an included .BAS module. By merely adding GLOBAL.BAS (for 16-bit calls) or GLOBAL32.BAS (for 32-bit calls) to your application, all REAPI calls will be available globally throughout your application.

How you add a .BAS file to your project varies by VB version. For VB 6, you can choose Project | Add Module or Project | Add File from the pull-down menus. You can also right-click in the Project Explorer and choose Add | Module or Add | Add File from the pop-up menu. Navigate to the Crystal Reports program directory and locate GLOBAL32.BAS or GLOBAL.BAS. When you add the module to your project, it will appear in the Project Explorer under the Modules folder. If you look at the file, you'll see the declaration of constants, structures, and functions that point to the REAPI DLL file.

You'll probably want to add additional modules to your project, as well, depending on the functions you're planning on using in your application. As you look through Developer's Help at various API calls, you'll notice many PE (for "Print Engine") constants that are used to provide various parameter values. These are defined in the GLOBAL module along with REAPI calls.

There are other constants that are not defined in this module, though. In particular, you'll soon find examples of CW_USEDEFAULT appearing in Developer's Help, as well as other generic Windows constants that are used in many API projects, not just those using Crystal Reports. These must be obtained from the Microsoft-provided WIN32API.TXT file that's installed with Visual Basic. You won't want to just add the entire file to your project. It's too large and contains many constants and procedures that you won't want. Just load the file into a text editor or word processor and copy selected constant declarations into your project. You can also use the API Viewer application to search WIN32API.TXT for just the constant declarations you need. Then, copy these constants to the clipboard and paste them into a module in your VB application. In the Xtreme Orders sample application, only the necessary constants have been added to the winCONST module.

Tip	*WIN32API.TXT is put in various locations, depending on the version of VB you're using. With VB 6, you'll find it in the \WINAPI subdirectory below the main Visual Basic directory. Launch the API Viewer by using the VB Add-In Manager from the Add-Ins menu.*

And finally, because of the inherent limitations of Visual Basic mentioned earlier in the chapter, Seagate has created "wrapper" .DLL and .BAS files that circumvent some of these limitations. In particular, the VB wrapper helps in setting parameter fields, exporting to e-mail and various file formats, and logging on to SQL databases. If you will need any of this functionality in your application, you'll want to add the wrapper to your project. However, you may not need to use the VB wrapper, depending on the functions you use in your VB application. If you begin your project without it and later need some of its functions, you can simply add it at that time.

The two wrapper DLLs are CRWRAP16.DLL (for 16-bit environments) and CRWRAP32.DLL (for 32-bit environments). Although there are two distinct DLLs, there is only one .BAS file that can be used to declare functions for either 16- or 32-bit VB. CRWRAP.BAS, located along with GLOBAL32.BAS in the Crystal Reports program folder, should be added to your project. This will declare additional constants and API calls specifically for Visual Basic.

Once all the necessary files have been added to your project, you're ready to begin coding. Figure 26-1 shows the VB IDE for the Xtreme Orders sample application. Notice the three different modules that have been added, along with some declarations in GLOBAL32.BAS.

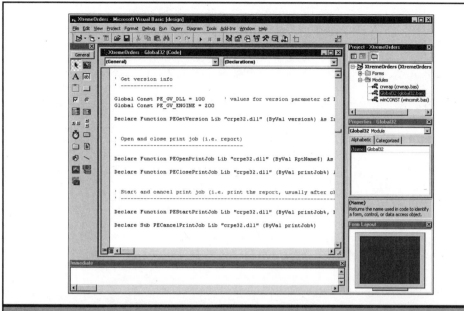

Figure 26-1.   *Modules added to Xtreme Orders application*

Creating a Simple Application with the REAPI

Once the REAPI has been added to your project, you're ready to begin coding your application. Coding with the REAPI is accomplished by calling the REAPI functions defined in the modules you just added. REAPI functions coming from GLOBAL32.BAS begin with the letters "PE" (indicating Print Engine). Functions coming from the CRWRAP.BAS wrapper module begin with the letters "crPE."

There are six basic steps to integrating a report with the REAPI:

1. Initialize the Crystal Report Engine (PEOpenEngine).

2. Open a specific report (PEOpenPrintJob).

3. Choose an output destination (PEOutputToWindow, PEOutputToPrinter, or various crPEExport calls).

4. Process the report (PEStartPrintJob).

5. Close the specific report that was opened earlier (PEClosePrintJob).

6. Close the Crystal Report Engine at the end of your application (PECloseEngine).

Based on program logic, you may repeat several of these steps multiple times, depending on how many reports you are integrating in your application at once, how many times they may be processed, and so on. Also, you'll probably make many additional calls between PEOpenPrintJob and PEStartPrintJob to customize report features, such as the preview window, record-selection criteria, formulas and parameter fields, and report-section formatting.

At the most basic level, you can create an application to preview a report in the preview window with no customization by using the following lines of code:

```
Dim intJob As Integer    'for report job number
Dim intResult As Integer    'to read results of PE calls
Private Sub Form_Load()
    'Open the print engine
    intResult = PEOpenEngine()
    'Open the report
    intJob = PEOpenPrintJob(App.Path & "\Xtreme Orders.RPT")
End Sub
...
...
Private Sub cmdOK_Click()
    'Send to preview window
    intResult = PEOutputToWindow(intJob, "Xtreme Orders Report", _
        0, 0, 0, 0, 0, 0)
    'Process the report
    intResult = PEStartPrintJob(intJob, True)
End Sub
...
...
Private Sub Form_Unload(Cancel As Integer)
    intResult = PEClosePrintJob(intJob)
    PECloseEngine
End Sub
```

Consider these points about this sample code:

- Most PE calls return integer results (with the exception of PECloseEngine). As a general rule, a result of 0 indicates that the call failed in some fashion. For most calls, a result of 1 indicates success. For PEOpenPrintJob, a 0 indicates failure and any other integer is the job number that is used in subsequent calls that relate to that particular print job. This sample code contains no error-handling logic. Error handling is discussed later in the chapter.

- You'll probably want to open and close the print engine as few times as possible during your application. In this case, there's only one form in the application, so the engine is opened in Form_Load and closed in Form_Unload. In other situations, you may want to do this in the load and unload events for the main form in your report, or perhaps in Sub Main().

- If you want to have more than one report open at one time, you may call PEOpenPrintJob as many times as necessary. Each open report will then have a unique job number to use in subsequent Print Engine calls. If you are simply going to have one report open at once, but perhaps use several different reports throughout the duration of your application, you can call PEOpenPrintJob and PEClosePrintJob every time you wish to change reports.

- PEStartPrintJob includes a second parameter that's set to true. This is the only value you can supply to this parameter, so always submit true to this call.

Controlling the Preview Window

In the sample code shown previously, there were very few customized options provided to the PEOutputToWindow call. The only customization done to the preview window at all was setting the window title. The remaining function parameters were set to zeros to specify default behavior. These other parameters relate to the size and position of the preview window. You'll probably want to further customize preview-window behavior, however. Perhaps you want to enable drill-down with a summary report, or eliminate the export or print buttons so a user can't print or export the report.

The REAPI allows you to customize all this preview window behavior by modifying members of the PEWindowOptions structure. This structure is one of several defined by GLOBAL32.BAS to control a series of related settings as a single group. These structures contain several elements that can be set to specific values or left unchanged by setting them to the predefined constant PE_UNCHANGED. Examine the following sample code:

```
'Set preview window options
Dim WindowOptions As PEWindowOptions
...
WindowOptions.StructSize = Len(WindowOptions)
' required to avoid error 538
With WindowOptions
    .hasGroupTree = 1
    .canDrillDown = 1
    .hasNavigationControls = PE_UNCHANGED
    .hasCancelButton = PE_UNCHANGED
    .hasPrintButton = PE_UNCHANGED
```

```
    .hasExportButton = PE_UNCHANGED
    .hasZoomControl = PE_UNCHANGED
    .hasCloseButton = PE_UNCHANGED
    .hasProgressControls = PE_UNCHANGED
    .hasSearchButton = PE_UNCHANGED
    .hasPrintSetupButton = PE_UNCHANGED
    .hasRefreshButton = PE_UNCHANGED
End With    'WindowOptions
intResult = PESetWindowOptions(intJob, WindowOptions)
```

Notice that you must declare a variable to hold the PEWindowOptions structure elements. The other requirement is to set the StructSize member to the size of the whole structure. This can be accomplished by just using Len of the structure variable itself. Then, set each of the structure elements to 1 to enable the option, 0 to disable the option. Make sure you specifically set each structure member that you want to use. If you don't set an option, the option will be disabled. By using PE_UNCHANGED, the option will exhibit default behavior or stay the same as it was set earlier in your program. Once you've assigned all the options, pass the structure variable, along with the job number, to the PESetWindowOptions call to actually set the preview-window options.

Although the REAPI facilitates trapping preview-window events, such as drill-down and button clicks, this requires complex Windows programming. Because of inherent Visual Basic limitations, you cannot develop these routines using the REAPI. If you need to trap these events, you'll need to use the Automation Server or Report Designer component to integrate your report.

Controlling Record Selection

Controlling report record selection is an integral part of VB report integration. You'll typically use your VB user interface to gather information from the user that will make up the record-selection criteria for the report. Then, you make the proper REAPI call to set the report's record-selection formula.

Because you must pass a valid Crystal Reports record-selection formula to the REAPI, you'll need to be familiar with the Crystal Reports formula language in general, and record-selection formula concepts in particular. If you are used to using the Crystal Reports Select Expert for record selection, you'll need to familiarize yourself with the actual Crystal Reports formula that it creates before you create a selection formula in your VB application. A Crystal Reports record-selection formula is a Boolean formula that narrows down the database records that will be included in the report. For example, the following record-selection formula will limit a report to orders placed in the first quarter of 1997 from customers in Wyoming:

```
{Orders.Order Date} In Date(1997,1,1) To Date(1997,3,31)
And {Customer.Region} = "WY"
```

> **Tip**   *For complete discussions of Crystal Reports record selection and how to create Boolean formulas, consult Chapters 5 and 6.*

Use the PESetSelectionFormula call to pass a record-selection formula to the report. The call takes two parameters: the job number of the report, and a string variable or expression that comprises the record-selection formula. The following code from the sample application sets record selection, based on the contents of the From Date and To Date text boxes. Notice that a work-string variable is being used to hold the formula before it's passed to the REAPI call. This allows you to stop program execution and look at the contents of the string to make sure it contains a syntactically correct formula.

```
'Supply record selection based on dates
strWork = "{Orders.Order Date} in Date(" & _
    Format(txtFromDate, "yyyy,m,d") & ") to Date(" & _
    Format(txtToDate, "yyyy,m,d") & ")"
intResult = PESetSelectionFormula(intJob, strWork)
```

Remember that the string value you pass must adhere *exactly* to the Crystal Reports formula syntax. This includes correct use of Crystal reserved words and punctuation. The example from the sample application shows the necessity of building a Date(yyyy,mm,dd) string to pass to the selection formula. Also, don't forget the required quotation marks or apostrophes around literals that are used in comparisons.

There are also important considerations if you are using a SQL database. The REAPI will attempt to convert as much of your record-selection formula as possible to SQL when it runs the report. The same caveats apply to the record-selection formula you pass from your VB application as apply to a record-selection formula you create directly in Crystal Reports. In particular, using built-in Crystal Reports formula functions, such as UpperCase or IsNull, and using OR operators instead of AND operators, will typically cause record selection to be moved to the client (the PC) instead of the database server, resulting in reduced performance.

To avoid this situation, take the same care in creating record-selection formulas that you pass from your application as you would in Crystal Reports. Look for detailed discussions on record-selection performance in both Chapters 6 and 14. You can also choose to create the SQL statement the report will use right in your VB application and submit it to the report by using the separate REAPI PESetSQLQuery call.

Setting Formulas

You'll also want to use Visual Basic to change the contents of Crystal Report formulas at run time. This is necessary for changing formulas that may be related to groups that are also being changed, for changing textual information on the report, or for using the VB user interface to change a report calculation.

Setting formulas at run time is similar to setting the record-selection formula at run time (described in the previous section). As with record-selection formulas, you'll need a good understanding of the Crystal Reports formula language to adequately modify formulas inside your VB code. If you need a refresher on Crystal Reports formulas, look back at Chapter 5.

Use the REAPI PESetFormula call to change an existing formula (you can't create new formulas that don't already exist in the report). The call accepts three parameters: the job number of the report you wish to modify, a string variable or expression that contains the name of the formula you want to change (without the @ sign), and a string variable or expression that contains the new text for the formula.

In the Xtreme Orders sample application, the Order + Tax formula is modified based on the user's input in the Tax Rate text box. The formula is changed using the following code:

```
'Set @Order + Tax formula
If txtTaxRate = "" Then
    strWork = "{Orders.Order Amount}"
Else
    strWork = "{Orders.Order Amount} *" & Str(txtTaxRate / 100 + 1)
End If   'txtTaxRate = ""
intResult = PESetFormula(intJob, "Order + Tax", strWork)
```

The string passed with the third parameter must correctly conform to the Crystal Reports formula syntax. Here, the Order + Tax formula is defined in Crystal Reports as a numeric formula. Therefore, you should pass it a formula that will evaluate to a number. If the user leaves the text box on the form empty, the VB code assumes no additional sales tax and simply places the Order Amount database field in the formula—the formula will show the same amount as the database field. If, however, the user has specified a tax rate, the VB code manipulates the value by dividing it by 100 and then adding 1. This will create the proper type of number to multiply against the Order Amount field to correctly calculate tax.

You may also need to change simple string formulas in your program. The sample application uses the @Sub Heading string formula in the Page Header to print a description of the report options that are chosen at run time. This formula is set in the sample application based on selections the user has made on the form. Here's the sample code:

```
'Set @Sub Heading formula
strWork = "'" & txtFromDate & " through " & txtToDate
strWork = strWork & ", By " & cboGroupBy
If txtTaxRate = "" Then
    strWork = strWork & ", No Tax'"
Else
    strWork = strWork & ", Sales Tax = " & txtTaxRate & "%'"
End If  'txtTaxRate = ""
intResult = PESetFormula(intJob, "Sub Heading", strWork)
```

Passing Parameter Field Values

Your report may contain parameter fields to prompt the user for information whenever the report is refreshed. If the parameter fields are ignored in the VB application, the REAPI will automatically prompt the user for them when the report runs. To take advantage of your VB user interface, you'll want to be able to supply these parameter field values from within your code. Setting parameter-field values in code is particularly helpful if you're integrating a predesigned report that is heavily based on parameter fields, or if you're sharing a report on a network with other non-VB users who will need to be prompted when they run the report directly in Crystal Reports.

There are two ways of setting parameter-field values with the REAPI. The PESetNthParameterField call (defined in GLOBAL32.BAS) accepts several parameters, including the PEParameterFieldInfo structure. Seagate has also provided the crPESetNthParameterField call in the REAPI wrapper (defined in CRWRAP.BAS), which doesn't require the structure definition. You may find this easier to use.

The crPESetNthParameterField accepts nine different parameters. The best place to get a complete description of all of them is Developer's Help. For the Xtreme Order report example, there are only a few that you need to be particularly concerned with. As with most REAPI calls, you'll need to submit the job number that was returned when you opened the report. Unlike some other REAPI calls, you don't supply the actual name of the parameter field that you wish to set. Instead, you use a zero-based index determined by the order in which the parameter fields were added to the report. If you wish to set the first parameter field, the value should be set to 0, 1 for the second parameter field, and so on. You must also use a predefined constant to indicate the data type of the parameter field. In the sample code that follows, the Highlight parameter field is numeric, so the constant PE_PF_NUMBER is supplied (again, the data type constants are documented in Developer's Help). The last parameter you supply to the call is the actual value you want the parameter field to contain in the report.

In the Xtreme Orders sample application, the Highlight parameter field is used to conditionally format the Details section when the order amount exceeds a parameter supplied by the viewer. Here is the sample code for correctly passing the value to the parameter field:

```
'Set ?Highlight parameter value
If txtHighlight = "" Then
    intResult = crPESetNthParameterField(intJob, 0, PE_PF_NUMBER, _
    0, 1, "", "", 0, 0)
Else
    intResult = crPESetNthParameterField(intJob, 0, PE_PF_NUMBER, _
    0, 1, "", "", 0, Val(txtHighlight))
End If  'txtHighlight = ""
```

Notice that if the user leaves the Highlight text box blank, you'll still need to pass a numeric value to the parameter field, even if it's just 0. Also, since the parameter field is being defined with a numeric data type, the Val function is being used to ensure that the contents of txtHighlight are submitted as a numeric value.

> **Note**   *New Crystal Reports 7 parameter-field features, such as range values and multiple values, are exposed by the REAPI, but not by the VB wrapper. Some of this new functionality may not be fully available because of Visual Basic limitations. If your application depends on this functionality, you may want to consider integrating the report with the Report Designer component.*

Manipulating Report Groups

You can add significant flexibility to your application by changing report grouping at run time. In many cases, you can actually make it appear that several different reports are available for users to choose from. In fact, the application will be using the same Report object, but grouping will be changed at run time from within your application.

The Xtreme Orders sample application features a combo box on the Print Report form that lets the user choose between Quarter and Customer grouping. Based on this setting, you'll want your application to change the field the first report group is based on, as well as choose quarterly grouping if the Order Date field is chosen. To familiarize yourself with various grouping options, refer to Chapter 3.

The REAPI provides the PESetGroupCondition call to change the grouping options for any group on your report. Although the call only requires you to supply five parameters, you need to use several other built-in REAPI calls within PESetGroupCondition to get the proper results. Look at the sample code from the Xtreme Orders report.

```
'Set grouping
If cboGroupBy = "Quarter" Then
    'The quarterly grouping will only work if the report is set
    'to "Convert Date/Time Fields to Date" -
    'known bug w/initial SCR 7 release
    intResult = PESetGroupCondition(intJob, _
    PE_SECTION_CODE(PE_SECT_GROUP_HEADER, 0, 0), _
    "{Orders.Order Date}", PE_GC_QUARTERLY, PE_SF_ASCENDING)
Else
    intResult = PESetGroupCondition(intJob, _
    PE_SECTION_CODE(PE_SECT_GROUP_HEADER, 0, 0), _
    "{Customer.Customer Name}", PE_GC_ANYCHANGE, PE_SF_ASCENDING)
End If  'cboGroupBy = "Quarter"
```

Caution   *Notice the comments in the code relating to quarterly grouping. There is a bug in the initial version of Crystal Reports 7 that will ignore quarterly grouping and create a new group for every day. This is a known problem slated for repair in a maintenance release. However, if you open the report in the Crystal Reports Designer and choose File | Report Options and choose To Date as the Convert Date-Time Field option, quarterly grouping will work properly. The trade-off is that true date/time data types won't be available for use in the report—they will be converted to date-only fields.*

You'll notice the first parameter is the now-familiar report job number. However, indicating which group you actually want to change with the second parameter requires some extra work. Ultimately, the REAPI expects a number indicating which section of the report contains the group you want to change. By using the built-in PE_SECTION_CODE function that's defined in GLOBAL32.BAS, you can supply section information in a more logical fashion and have the correct number returned.

The PE_SECTION_CODE function itself takes three numeric parameters: section type, group number, and section number. The section type number can be supplied with a predefined constant, such as PE_SECT_GROUP_HEADER, indicating the area you wish to modify. If this area is a group header or footer, you can indicate which group you wish to modify with the zero-based second parameter (0 is group one, 1 is group two, and so on). If the section is not a group, simply pass 0 to this argument. The third argument, also zero-based, is used if there is more than one section in the area. For example, if you have created Details sections a, b, and c, 0 refers to Details a, 1 to Details b, and 2 to Details c.

Caution   *If you follow the "Working with section codes" link in the Developer's Help PESetGroupCondition topic, you'll be shown incorrect section-code constants. To get a correct set of section-code constants, search Developer's Help for "Section codes, encoding (Crystal Report Engine)."*

The remaining three parameters in PESetGroupCondition are a string variable or expression indicating the database or formula field that you want the group based on, the condition that will cause a new group to appear (when using Date, Time, or Boolean grouping), and the order in which you wish groups to appear. The last two parameters are best supplied with predefined constants supplied by GLOBAL32.BAS. The PESetGroupCondition topic in Developer's Help provides the available constants.

Conditional Formatting and Formatting Sections

If your VB application displays a report in the preview window, you'll be able to take advantage of interactive reporting features, such as the group tree and drill-down. In particular, drill-down capabilities allow a report to be initially presented at a very high summary level, showing just subtotals or grand totals, or perhaps just showing a pie chart or bar chart that graphs high-level numbers. The viewer can then double-click a number or chart element that interests them to drill down to more detailed numbers, eventually reaching the report's Details section. These levels of drill-down are limited only by the number of report groups you create on your report.

The Xtreme Orders sample application Summary Report Only check box lets the user choose whether or not to see just a summary report. When this check box is selected, you'll need to hide the report's Details section with VB code so that only group subtotals appear on the report. In addition, the code will have to control the appearance of the report's two Page Header sections (Page Header a and Page Header b), as well as two Group Header #1 sections (Group Header #1a and Group Header #1b).

The Page Header and Group Header manipulation will accommodate two different sections of field titles that should appear differently if the report is presented as a summary report instead of a detail report. If the report is being displayed as a detail report, the field titles should appear at the top of every page of the report, along with the subheading and smaller report title. If the report is displayed as a summary report, you only want the field titles to appear in the Group Header section of a drill-down tab when the user double-clicks on a group. Since no detail information will be visible in the main report window, field titles there won't be meaningful.

And finally, you'll want to show Group Header #1a, which contains the Group Name field, if the report is showing detail data. This will indicate which group the following set of orders applies to. However, if the report is only showing summary data, showing both the Group Header and Group Footer will be repetitive—the Group Footer already contains the group name, so showing the Group Header as well will look odd. But, you will want the Group Header with the group name to appear in a drill-down tab.

Therefore, you'll need to control the appearance of four sections when a user chooses the summary report option. Look at Table 26-1 to get a better idea of how you'll want to conditionally set these sections at run time.

Section	Detail Report	Summary Report
Page Header b (field titles)	Shown	Suppressed (no drill-down)
Group Header #1a (group name field)	Shown	Hidden (drill-down okay)
Group Header #1b (field titles)	Suppressed (no drill-down)	Hidden (drill-down okay)
Details (detail order data)	Shown	Hidden (drill-down okay)

Table 26-1. *Section Formatting for Different Report Types*

You'll notice that, in some cases, sections need to be completely suppressed (so they don't show up, even in a drill-down tab) as opposed to hidden (which means they will show up in a drill-down tab but not in the main Preview tab). There is a somewhat obscure relationship among areas and sections that affect this determination. Specifically, only complete areas (such as the entire Group Header #1) can be hidden, not individual sections (for example, Group Header #1a). However, both areas and sections can be suppressed.

This presents a bit of a coding challenge for the Xtreme Orders sample application. First, you'll need to determine the correct combination of area hiding and section suppressing that sets what appears in the Preview window and in a drill-down tab. If an area is hidden, none of the sections in it will appear in the main Preview window. But, when the user drills down into that section, you will want to control which sections inside the drilled-down area appear in the drill-down tab. Once you've determined which areas you want to hide, you must find the correct property to set for that particular area. You must also find the correct property to suppress sections inside the hidden area, or to show other sections that aren't hidden.

There are two REAPI calls that accomplish this feat. First is PESetAreaFormat, which sets formatting options for an area in the report. An *area* encompasses one or more related sections. For example, the Page Header is considered an individual area. However, both Group Header #1a and Group Header #1b are combined in one single Group Header #1 area.

The REAPI also exposes PESetSectionFormat, which formats a section in the report. A *section* encompasses each individual section of the report, regardless of how many there may be inside a single area. For example, the Page Header is considered an individual section. But even though Group Header #1a and Group Header #1b are considered a single area, they are separate sections.

Both calls make use of the PESectionOptions structure defined in GLOBAL32.BAS. This structure contains members that allow you to control whether an area is shown or hidden for drill-down, whether a section is suppressed or visible, what the background color of the section is, and so forth. You must declare a variable that points to this structure and then set the individual options of the structure for the variable. Then, pass the variable to PESetAreaFormat and PESetSectionFormat. The complete syntax for these calls, as well as descriptions for all members of the structure can be found in Developer's Help.

Keeping in mind the previous discussion and the hide/suppress requirements outlined in Table 26-1, look at the code from the sample application that follows.

```
Dim SectionOptions As PESectionOptions 'report section options structure
...
'Hide/show areas and sections
SectionOptions.StructSize = Len(SectionOptions)
If chkSummary Then
    SectionOptions.showArea = 0 'Hide for drill down
    SectionOptions.Visible = 1 'Don't suppress
    SectionOptions.backgroundColor = PE_UNCHANGED
        'Set to avoid black bkgrnd

    'set for Details area
    intResult = PESetAreaFormat(intJob, _
    PE_SECTION_CODE(PE_SECT_DETAIL, 0, 0), SectionOptions)

    'set for all of Group Header 1 area
    intResult = PESetAreaFormat(intJob, _
    PE_SECTION_CODE(PE_SECT_GROUP_HEADER, 0, 0), SectionOptions)

    'set for Group Header 1b section
    intResult = PESetSectionFormat(intJob, _
    PE_SECTION_CODE(PE_SECT_GROUP_HEADER, 0, 1), SectionOptions)

    'set for Page Header b section
    SectionOptions.Visible = 0 'Suppress
    intResult = PESetSectionFormat(intJob, _
    PE_SECTION_CODE(PE_SECT_PAGE_HEADER, 0, 1), SectionOptions)
Else
```

```
   SectionOptions.showArea = 1 'Show
   SectionOptions.Visible = 1 'Show
   SectionOptions.backgroundColor = PE_UNCHANGED
      'Set to avoid black bkgrnd

   'set for Details area
   intResult = PESetAreaFormat(intJob, _
   PE_SECTION_CODE(PE_SECT_DETAIL, 0, 0), SectionOptions)

   'set for all of Group Header 1 area
   intResult = PESetAreaFormat(intJob, _
   PE_SECTION_CODE(PE_SECT_GROUP_HEADER, 0, 0), SectionOptions)

   'set for Page Header b section
   intResult = PESetSectionFormat(intJob, _
   PE_SECTION_CODE(PE_SECT_PAGE_HEADER, 0, 1), SectionOptions)

   'set for Group Header 1b section
   SectionOptions.Visible = 0
   intResult = PESetSectionFormat(intJob, _
   PE_SECTION_CODE(PE_SECT_GROUP_HEADER, 0, 1), SectionOptions)
End If   'chkSummary
```

Notice that several calls are made using the same SectionOptions structure variable. If the settings in the SectionOptions structure variable are the same for multiple sections or areas, you can simply call PESetAreaFormat or PESetSectionFormat multiple times with the same variable. If you need to change options between calls, only the structure members that require modification need to be changed—the others can be left alone. However, it's crucial to set as many members as necessary to ensure the correct report behavior. Even though the report sections have the default background color set in the .RPT file, you must specifically supply the PE_UNCHANGED constant to indicate no change. Otherwise, the background color will show up in black!

Notice also that the same PE_SECTION_CODE section- and area-encoding function that was described earlier in the chapter under "Manipulating Report Groups" is used here, as well. By supplying the three parameters to PE_SECTION_CODE, you can determine which areas and sections are to be formatted. Remember that the indexes for this function are zero-based: 0 indicates the first (or only) Details section, whereas 1 indicates the *second* Page Header section.

Caution   *Members of the two structures used in the Xtreme Orders sample application (PEWindowOptions and PESectionOptions) require only numeric values. Some REAPI structures accept string values, as well. The REAPI requires you to "null-terminate" any string values you pass to these structures. For example, if you're setting the fieldName member of a PEGroupOptions structure variable, you should terminate the value with a null character. Instead of*

```
GroupOptions.fieldName = "{Orders.Order Date}"
```

use

```
GroupOptions.fieldName = "{Orders.Order Date}" & Chr$(0)
```

Choosing Output Destinations

The first method of output, discussed at the beginning of the chapter, is the preview window. The REAPI also supports the same output destinations as the Crystal Report designer's File | Print | Export command, including the printer, various file formats, and e-mail.

In the Xtreme Orders sample application, radio buttons and a text box allow the user to choose to view the report in the preview window, print the report to a printer, or attach the report as a Word document to an e-mail message. If the user chooses e-mail as the output destination, an e-mail address can be typed into a text box. Once this selection has been made, you need to set the output destination automatically in your VB code, based on the user's selection.

The REAPI provides different calls for different report destinations. Make the correct call based on the user's choice, including setting options for the particular output method chosen. PEOutputToPrinter will send the report to a printer and PEExportTo will export the report to a data file or attach a file to an e-mail message. Once these options have been set, PEStartPrintJob will send the report to the selected output location.

Although you can use PEExportTo to choose any file or e-mail output destination, it requires setting up several different structures and options. Seagate has provided more intuitive calls in the CRWRAP.BAS wrapper definitions. In particular, crPEExportToMapi can attach a report to an e-mail message by just supplying parameters—no structure definitions are required.

In the sample Xtreme Orders application, the following code is used to choose an output destination, as well as to specify a file type and e-mail information, based on user selections.

```
'Set output destination
If optPreview Then
    intResult = PEOutputToWindow(intJob, "Xtreme Orders Report", _
    0, 0, 0, 0, 0, 0)
```

```
End If   'optPreview
If OptPrint Then
    intResult = PEOutputToPrinter(intJob, 1)
    'will print to printer assigned w/report or Windows default
End If  'OptPrint
If OptEmail Then
    intResult = crPEExportToMapi(intJob, txtAddress, "", _
    "Here's the Xtreme Orders Report", _
"Attached is a Word document showing the latest Xtreme Orders Report.", _
    "u2fwordw.dll", crUXFWordWinType, 0, 0, "", "")
End If  'optEmail
```

DEVELOPING CUSTOM
WINDOW APPLICATIONS

> **Note**   *For the sake of brevity, code to set preview window options has been eliminated from this sample. Look earlier in the chapter for details on setting preview-window options.*

If you wish to send the report to a printer, use PEOutputToPrinter. This call only accepts two parameters: the job number of the report to print and the number of copies of the report to print. The report will be sent to the printer that was chosen when the report was saved, or to the Windows default printer if there is no printer saved with the report.

Unlike other integration methods, the REAPI doesn't provide a simple option to display the Printer Options dialog box before printing. While the REAPI does provide the PESelectPrinter call to choose a print destination, it requires passing a Windows DEVMODE structure that contains print options. This structure, in combination with the Printer Options dialog box from Windows' common dialog functions, can be used to display a dialog box and pass printer options to PESelectPrinter.

As opposed to the REAPI's PEExportTo call, which exports to any destination with one call, the VB wrapper DLL exposes separate crPEExportTo calls for each destination. The crPEExportToMapi call is exposed by the wrapper to export to a MAPI e-mail system. The call requires no structure manipulation and allows all required options to be passed as parameters. While a description of all available parameters is best left to Developer's Help, there are several that deserve particular attention, such as the To and CC addresses, the e-mail subject line, and e-mail message text. These are all passed as simple string variables or expressions.

As Crystal Reports always sends e-mail reports as attached files, you'll need to specify the format of the file that will be attached. The Xtreme Orders sample application will attach a Word document to the e-mail message. Two parameters make this determination. FormatDLLName (the sixth parameter) supplies crPEExportToMAPI with the name of the Crystal Reports export .DLL file that will convert the report. Developer's Help contains a list of all available .DLL files. FormatType (the seventh parameter) accepts a predefined constant indicating the type of export that will be created. While this may seem redundant, considering the FormatDLLName parameter, a single format .DLL file can actually export to several different formats. For example, the U2FXLS.DLL format DLL can export to several versions of Excel.

> **Note**
>
> *If you use crPEExportToMAPI to attach the report to an e-mail message, the user's PC will need to have a MAPI-compliant e-mail client, such as Microsoft Outlook or Windows Messaging installed and configured.*

Error Handling

In normal report-integration programming, you may encounter unexpected errors from the REAPI, and the somewhat verbose coding requirements of this integration method may exacerbate this problem. Unlike other integration methods, however, the REAPI doesn't throw standard VB errors that can be trapped with On Error Goto. Instead each PE or crPE call returns an integer indicating whether the call succeeded or failed (1 means success, 0 means failure). You can check the return code to determine the success or failure of the call, as follows:

```
If intResult <> 1 Then
    HandleError
    Exit Sub
End If  'intResult <> 1
```

> **Note**
>
> *You'll notice that HandleError is not called with any parameters and does not actually return any results. Because it resides in the same form where intJob is declared, it can determine the report that caused the error. Typically, you will want to pass the job number so that it can be used in the error handling routine. You can also choose to have the routine return the error string.*

While you can obviously design your code to handle REAPI errors as you see fit, it may be easy to create a single point of error handling. The Xtreme Orders sample application simply contains the HandleError subroutine in the main application form to deal with REAPI errors. If your application contains more than a single form, you may wish to create a centralized error handler in a module, or different handlers for each form.

In any event, you will have to conduct some further coding "investigation" to determine what error actually resulted in a REAPI call failure, because the return code just indicates that the call *did* fail. There are several additional REAPI calls to help determine the cause. PEGetErrorCode is the simplest. It only needs one parameter: the report job number (just supply 0 if a job hasn't been opened yet). It will return an integer indicating the REAPI error code of the most recent error. (Search Developer's Help for a complete listing of REAPI error codes.)

While this may be sufficient for your application, you may want to provide more descriptive error messages to your users, instead of just numbers, should an unanticipated report error occur. While you could conceivably build your own lookup table and type in all the Crystal Reports error messages yourself, the REAPI provides several calls to retrieve a descriptive error message to be used along with, or in place of, the error code. PEGetErrorText will allow you to retrieve the actual error message of the most recent error, instead of just the error code. The complication is that PEGetErrorText doesn't return an actual string—it just returns a *handle* to a string. You then need to pass the string handle to another call that will actually get the error message in a string variable. Because the regular PEGetHandleString function is difficult to implement in Visual Basic, Seagate has defined the alternative crvbHandleToBStr call in CRWRAP.BAS to simplify retrieving the error text.

Examine the following sample code from the Xtreme Orders sample application:

```
Private Sub HandleError()
Dim lngHandle As Long 'gets string handle
Dim intLength As Integer ' gets string length
Dim strReturnText As String 'gets actual string
Dim intError As Integer 'keep error code

intError = PEGetErrorCode(intJob)
Select Case intError
    Case 541
        MsgBox "Invalid e-mail address or other e-mail/export error", _
        vbCritical, "Xtreme Orders Report"
        txtAddress.SetFocus
    Case 545
        MsgBox "Report Canceled", vbInformation, "Xtreme Orders Report"
    Case Else
        'get handle and length
        intResult = PEGetErrorText(intJob, lngHandle, intLength)
        strReturnText = String$(intLength, 0) 'stuff string with nulls
        'NOTE: Failure to stuff string may result in Invalid Page Faults
```

```
         'get the string
         intResult = crvbHandleToBStr(strReturnText, lngHandle, intLength)
         MsgBox "Report Error:" & vbCrLf & intError & " - " & _
         strReturnText, vbCritical, "Xtreme Orders Report"
End Select 'Case intError
End Sub
```

Note that the error code is simply placed in intError for use in the Case statement and a message box. Based on this error code, e-mail related errors or report cancellation is simply handled with appropriate message boxes.

If an unanticipated error occurs, extra steps are required to get the actual error string. You'll note that several variables have been declared to assist in this process. The lngHandle variable is used to actually contain the string handle returned by PEGetErrorText. The intLength variable is also used by PEGetErrorText to indicate the length of the error text. The actual error message, itself, is stored in strReturnText. Initially, PEGetErrorText is called with three parameters: the report job number, the handle variable, and the length variable. However, now you'll need to somehow turn the handle and the length into a meaningful string to be placed in strReturnText.

Before you actually make the call to fill the string, you should stuff the string variable with the same number of null characters as there are characters in the error message. The String$ function can be used with the intLength variable and 0 (to signify an ASCII zero, or null) to accomplish this. Seagate indicates in sample code that accompanies Crystal Reports that failure to do this may result in Invalid Page Fault errors.

Once the string has been stuffed, call the wrapper DLL's crvbHandleToBStr function to retrieve the actual contents of the error message. Supply three parameters: the string variable, the handle variable, and the length variable. The call will replace the nulls in the string variable with the actual error text, which can be used to display a meaningful error message.

This string-handling logic applies to many other REAPI calls that return strings. Keep it handy for future use!

Other REAPI Calls

While many of the most common REAPI calls necessary for report integration have been covered in this chapter, there are others that merit some discussion. Because many reports are based on client/server or other ODBC or SQL data sources, you'll need to know how to manipulate these types of databases with the REAPI. Also, if you will be integrating reports that contain subreports, you should know how to manipulate the subreports the same way that you work with the main report. And, to ensure that your integrated reports are displaying the most current data from the database, you'll want to know how to discard any saved data that may be stored in the .RPT file.

Discarding Saved Data

As a general rule, saving data with an .RPT file that you will be integrating is a waste of disk space. While there may be situations where your VB application will benefit from a Crystal Report with saved data, you'll most often want to have VB refresh the report with current database data. If the .RPT file is saved with File | Save Data with Report turned off, the .RPT file will be smaller in size and will always be refreshed with the most current data from the database.

If the .RPT file contains saved data, there is a REAPI call that will discard it and ensure that the report is displaying the most current set of data from the database. Use PEDiscardSavedData with one argument, the report job number.

```
intResult = PEDiscardSavedData(intJob)
```

SQL Database Control

Companies continue to convert mainframe or minicomputer applications to client/server platforms, as well as basing newer systems on this database technology. Your Visual Basic applications will probably provide front-end interfaces to these database systems, and will need to handle SQL reporting, as well. The REAPI exposes several calls that help when integrating reports based on SQL databases.

Logging On to SQL Databases

Because your VB application probably already handles SQL database security (requiring the user to provide a valid logon ID and password at the beginning of the application), you'll want to avoid requiring the user to log on to the report database separately. By using REAPI calls to pass logon info to the report, you can pass the valid ID and password the user has already provided, thereby allowing the report to print without prompting again.

While the REAPI exposes several SQL database functions, the VB wrapper provides functions that require no structure manipulation. These can be used to either provide logon information for a database that will apply throughout the VB application, or to set logon info for individual tables used in the report.

Both crPELogOnServer and crPESetNthTableLogonInfo are documented in Developer's Help. Parameters for the calls include the report job number, server name, user ID, password, and so forth. crPELogOnServer contains one argument that may require you to do a little research to properly provide it. The database .DLL name used to connect to the server must be provided as a string. These .DLL filenames follow the general format of PDB*.DLL for non-SQL databases and PDS*.DLL for SQL databases.

DEVELOPING CUSTOM
WINDOW APPLICATIONS

If you're unsure what database driver your report is using, open the report in Crystal Reports and choose Database | Convert Database Driver. The database driver being used by the report will appear after the word "From" in the dialog box.

Retrieving or Setting the SQL Query

If your report is based on a SQL database, the REAPI will convert as much as possible of your record-selection formula to SQL to submit to the database server. However, if the record-selection formula contains Crystal formulas, an OR operator, or other characteristics that prevent the REAPI from including a WHERE clause in the SQL statement, report performance can be dramatically affected for the worse. You may, therefore, want to create the SQL statement the report uses directly in your VB application. As part of this process, you may find it helpful to retrieve the SQL statement that is being automatically generated.

If you need to use the SQL query that the REAPI is automatically generating, use PEGetSQLQuery to get the query. As with PEGetErrorText described in the Error Handling section earlier in the chapter, you'll need to use a pointer to the SQL query string along with crvbHandleToBStr to get the actual SQL query in a string. You can then modify the WHERE clause or other parts as necessary, and resubmit the query using PESetSQLQuery. If you already know what SQL statement you want to create, you can simply submit it with PESetSQLQuery—you don't have to get anything first.

As with Crystal Reports, you cannot modify the SELECT clause in the SQL query. Only FROM, WHERE, and ORDER BY clauses can be modified. Don't forget that you must still include the SELECT clause, however, and that it must not be changed from the original clause the REAPI created.

Also, if you create an ORDER BY clause, you must separate it from the end of the WHERE clause with a carriage return/line feed character sequence. Use CHR$(13) & CHR$(10) VB functions to add the CR/LF sequence inside the SQL query.

Reading or Setting Stored-Procedure Parameters

If your report is based on a parameterized SQL stored procedure, you will probably want to supply parameter values to the stored procedure from within your code, much as you will want to respond to any parameter fields that exist in the .RPT file.

The REAPI exposes two calls for reading or setting stored-procedure parameters. PEGetNthParam will return any existing value from the parameter. Arguments include the report job number, the zero-based index of the parameter (the first is 0, the second 1, and so on), and a text handle and length. Use previously discussed text-handling routines to retrieve the value.

If you just want to set the value of the stored-procedure parameter, use PESetNthParam. Arguments include the report job number, the zero-based index of the parameter, and a string variable or expression containing the value you want to pass to the parameter.

DEVELOPING CUSTOM
WINDOW APPLICATIONS

> **Note**   *You must always pass a string expression or variable to the Value property, even if the stored-procedure parameter is defined as another data type (just make sure to pass a string that can be properly converted). The REAPI will convert the parameter when it passes it to the database.*

Report Engine API Subreports

Subreport handling in the REAPI is almost identical to handling manipulation of the main report. To completely understand how subreports will interact with your VB code, consider that the main or *containing* report can contain a variable number of subreports. A subreport is actually considered to be a whole separate report, including its own sections, objects, record-selection formula, and other typical report properties.

Manipulating each subreport piece is essentially identical to working with the main report, except that subreports have different report job numbers. You obtain a new job number for the subreport by issuing a PEOpenSubreport call after the main report has been assigned a job number. Consider the following sample code:

```
Dim intJob As Integer   'job number for main report
Dim intSubJob As Integer    'job number for sub report
...
intJob = PEOpenPrintJob("Xtreme Orders w-Subreport.RPT")
intSubJob = PEOpenSubreport(intJob, "Top 5 Products Subreport")
```

You now have two job numbers: intJob refers to the main report and intSubJob refers to the subreport named Top 5 Products Subreport contained in the main report. You can now make any number of necessary REAPI calls and pass the desired report job number to the call, depending on whether you want the call to change the main report or the subreport. For example, to set selection criteria for both the main and subreports, you might use the following code:

```
intResult = PESetSelectionFormula(intJob, _
   "{Customer.Country} = 'USA'") 'main report
intResult = PESetSelectionFormula(intSubJob, _
   "{Customer.Country} = 'USA'") 'subreport
```

Chapter 27

Distributing Visual Basic/Crystal Reports Applications

Once you've created your Visual Basic application including integrated Crystal Reports, you'll want to compile and test the application. Unless you're just using the application for yourself, you'll also need to set up a distribution mechanism to pass your application on to your intended audience: the application user.

Because you are distributing Crystal Reports features and components with your VB application, there are some distribution issues that come into play. This chapter discusses both the general points you'll want to keep in mind when creating your distribution package, as well as specific areas that concern certain reporting features you may want to include or exclude from your application.

Distribution Overview

The days of creating a single .EXE executable file that can be easily copied to a single floppy disk are long gone. Standard Visual Basic projects already consist of the main program executable file, run-time files, and a host of support files. Introducing Crystal Reports into the mix adds a fairly large burden to this process. Because Crystal Reports is designed in a very modular fashion, it's easy to add functionality and upgraded features to the tool. However, this modularity also complicates the distribution process because so many different files are involved in the overall Crystal Reports product.

When you design a Crystal Report, you're using the main report-designer executable (CRW32.EXE for 32-bit operating systems, CRW.EXE for 16-bit operating systems). The .RPT file that you create actually contains the report design, formulas, text objects, formatting, and all other report elements. Since there's no need to redistribute the actual report-designer executable (and you're prohibited from doing so anyway), you may think that the .RPT file is the only file you need to add to your VB project when it's distributed. Well, either stock up on floppy disks or buy a CD recorder, because you'll need the extra space for all the files that go along with the .RPT file to enable it to be fully integrated inside Visual Basic.

You must include .RPT files in your distribution package (with the exception of projects designed with the Report Designer component where the report design is stored in the project's .DSR files, which are automatically included). There are also a variety of support files that are required, depending on several issues, such as the database connections the report uses and the export capabilities that the project entails. The best part is that this is all handled pretty much automatically if you use Visual Basic distribution tools to create your distribution package.

In addition to available third-party distribution products, such as InstallShield, Visual Basic 6 includes the Package and Deployment Wizard and Visual Basic 5 includes the Application Setup Wizard. All these tools are designed to gather up all the necessary executable and support files required for a project, compress them into a smaller space, and add them to a setup program. When the setup program is run from floppies or a CD, a network share, or downloaded from a Web server, all the necessary files are decompressed and installed in the proper locations.

Specific instructions for using these distribution tools can be found in the documentation accompanying them—this chapter will not teach you how to distribute VB applications. Examples in the chapter are based on the Visual Basic 6 Package and Deployment Wizard.

Distribution tools, such as the Package and Deployment Wizard, look through your VB project file and attempt to determine all the necessary files that must be distributed with the project. Depending on the Crystal Reports integration method you choose, a different chain of events occurs to determine which files are automatically included in the distribution process. Having a fundamental understanding of this process will help you tailor your project's distribution, based on its individual needs.

Most tools make use of *dependency files* to determine what files to include in your distribution package. These files consist of the same base filename as the file used to provide Crystal Reports integration, but contain a .DEP extension. For example, the dependency file for the 32-bit Crystal ActiveX control (CRYSTL32.OCX) is CRYSTL32.DEP. There are also dependency files for each of the other integration methods, again based on the filenames for each integration method. The dependency file is a straight ASCII text file that you can open with Notepad, containing a list of all related DLLs or other files that may be required to use the integration method. The distribution package uses the dependency file to include all necessary files (and in most cases, several that are unnecessary) when the VB application is packaged. If you create VB projects on a regular basis, you may want to customize the appropriate .DEP files to include additional files or exclude files that your applications don't need.

Dependency files don't always catch every necessary file, however. First and foremost, most distribution tools *do not* detect the actual .RPT files that your project will be using. Make sure you take the necessary steps to manually include the .RPT files with your package.

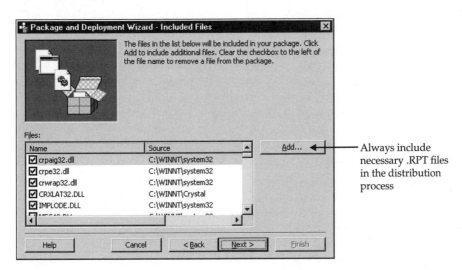

Always include necessary .RPT files in the distribution process

The only integration method that you don't need to add the .RPT files for is the Report Designer component (the RDC, discussed in Chapter 24). The RDC maintains its report-design information in the project's .DSR (designer) files. Since these are an integral part of the VB project, they are automatically compiled and included with the VB project—no .RPT files need to be included.

In many cases, once you've manually added any necessary .RPT files to the package, you can simply accept the remaining default settings and files that are automatically included. The project will operate as you expect when installed on your end-user's machine.

There are two potential disadvantages of just taking the remaining default options with your distribution tool, though: more files than you actually need are probably being included, or there may still be necessary files that aren't automatically detected. The first problem is probably a minor inconvenience, eating up a little more disk space than you really need to use. The second problem, though, means the application won't work correctly. By reading the following sections, you'll learn how to selectively remove unnecessary files that are included automatically. However, only by carefully considering your individual application, and the files that it ultimately requires, will you avoid the second problem. In all cases, the rule of thumb is test and then test again—always try installations on a "clean" machine (similar to what your end-users will have in place) to ensure that all files are being installed correctly.

Seagate includes an online Help file that contains a complete discussion of run-time file requirements. Look in the Crystal Reports program group for "Runtime File Requirements" or open the RUNTIME.HLP file directly from the Crystal Reports program directory.

ActiveX Control

If you're using the Crystal ActiveX control to integrate your report, the ActiveX control itself will cause several files to be automatically added to your package. In the case of the 32-bit control, the CRYSTL32.DEP file will indicate that CRPE32.DLL (the Crystal Report Engine API) also needs to be included in the package. Since CRPE32.DLL also includes its own .DEP file, several additional files will be included from it, as well.

You can look through the list of files that are automatically included and remove any that you're sure your application won't use. Some database drivers, as well as export support files, may not be required. While including them won't harm the application, they will take up additional disk space that you may wish to preserve. Also, don't forget to include the actual .RPT files your application uses, as well as any database files the report may require and that aren't already included by the VB application.

Note   *You may receive a message during Package and Deployment Wizard operation indicating that the file CRYSTAL cannot be found. You can safely ignore this message and proceed through the rest of the setup process.*

Report Designer Component

The Report Designer component is unique among integration methods in that it doesn't use external .RPT files. Report definitions are actually contained in the ActiveX designer (.DSR) files that are added to the project. As these are an integral part of your application, VB will compile the .DSR files and include them automatically in the project's executable. In addition, the other COM components that make up the RDC will be included in the project.

In particular, the CRAXDRT.DEP dependency file will include all necessary COM components for the RDC's automation server interface. If you are using the ActiveX Smart Viewer to view your reports in a form, CRVIEWER.DEP will be used to include its necessary components. While you don't have to worry about including external .RPT files, make sure any required database files are included in your package. You may also want to remove some unnecessary database or export-support files to save disk space.

Automation Server

If you are using the Report Engine Automation Server to integrate your report, the CPEAUT32.DEP dependency file (in 32-bit development environments) will include necessary COM components in your distribution package. Because the Automation Server ultimately calls the Report Engine API, CRPE32.DLL will also be included in your project, as well as any files contained in the CRPE32.DEP dependency file.

As with all other integration methods except the RDC, make sure you manually include all .RPT files that your project requires—they won't be included automatically. You'll also want to ensure that any necessary database files are included. And, you can choose to remove database or export-support files that aren't required for your particular application.

 You may receive a message during Package and Deployment Wizard operation indicating that the file CRYSTAL cannot be found. You can safely ignore this message and proceed through the rest of the setup process.

Report Engine API

If you use the Report Engine API (REAPI) to integrate your report, CRPE32.DEP (for the 32-bit REAPI) will determine what support files will be included in your distribution package. If you use the VB wrapper functionality by adding CRWRAP.BAS to your project, additional support files will be included. Don't forget to manually add all .RPT files that your project requires, as well as any databases that may not automatically be added by references in your project. You may also wish to save some disk space by removing unnecessary database driver or export-support files that your application doesn't need.

DEVELOPING CUSTOM WINDOW APPLICATIONS

You may receive a message during Package and Deployment Wizard operation indicating that the file CRYSTAL cannot be found. If you use CRWRAP.BAS in your project, you'll also find a wrapper .DLL listed as missing (if you're using 32-bit Visual Basic, CRWRAP16.DLL will be listed; if you're using 16-bit Visual Basic, CRWRAP32.DLL will be listed). Using CRWRAP.BAS will also cause a message to appear indicating that there is no dependency information for the CRWRAPxx.DLL file that is being used. You can safely ignore all these messages and proceed through the rest of the setup process.

Database Considerations

The databases that your reports use must be considered when you are deploying your VB application to end-users. Obviously, you'll need to ensure that each end-user will be able to connect to the database that the reports require. This may be a PC-style database distributed along with the application, a database shared on a common LAN drive, or a client/server database accessed through either a native Crystal Reports database driver or via ODBC. You'll also only need to include .DLL files specific to the database and access method being used by your reports. Although it won't hurt to include database driver DLLs for Microsoft Access in your project even if your reports all connect to an Informix database via ODBC, you can save disk space by eliminating any unnecessary database drivers.

Direct Access Databases

If your reports use a PC-style database, such as a Microsoft Access .MDB file or a dBASE for Windows .DBF file, you'll want to make sure that the reports will be able to locate the database when the application is installed. If these files were installed on the C drive when you designed the report, but will reside on a network F drive when the end-user runs the application, you'll need to make sure the reports can still find the file. You can either execute calls inside your VB application to change the data-source location of the reports, or use the Crystal Reports Database | Set Location command to point to a different database before distributing the .RPT files with the application. You may prefer using the Same as Report option in the Set Location dialog box to have the report look in the same drive and directory as the report for the database. In this scenario, you need only ensure that the database and reports reside in the same place, regardless of drive or directory, for the reports to be able to locate the database.

You may be able to save disk space by only including the necessary database drivers for your particular Direct Access database. If, for example, you are only using reports that connect directly to a Microsoft Access database, there is no reason to include all the other database drivers in your distribution package. Because the dependency files include references to all database drivers, they'll all be included by default. Look in the RUNTIME.HLP file to determine the core set of database drivers required for the particular method your reports use to connect to the database. Once you exclude other database drivers, make sure you test your installation on a machine similar to those found in your end-user environment to make sure all necessary drivers are being included.

ODBC Data Sources

As a general rule, ODBC will be used to connect to centralized client/server databases (although some desktop databases you distribute with your application still may use ODBC as the connection method). Therefore, you probably won't have to worry about distributing the actual database with your application. However, you'll need to make sure an ODBC data source is set up so that the report will be able to connect to the database from your end-user's machine. Your VB application may take care of this automatically if the application itself will be accessing the same ODBC data source. Also, if your report will be using the Active Data driver to connect to a DAO or ADO record set in the application, special provisions probably won't need to be made.

If your report is the only part of the application that will be using a particular ODBC data source, you'll want to make sure that the setup application creates the correct ODBC data source. You may even need to install ODBC as part of your setup program, if there's a possibility it won't already be installed on the end-user's machine.

You'll also save disk space if you eliminate other Crystal Reports database drivers that won't be used in your application. Look in the RUNTIME.HLP file to determine which ODBC drivers will be required for the particular ODBC data source and database your reports use. Once you exclude other database drivers, make sure you test your installation on a machine similar to those found in your end-user environment to make sure all necessary drivers are being included.

File Export Considerations

The Xtreme Orders sample application that is used throughout the book allows three output destinations to be used: the preview window, the printer, and a Word document attached to an e-mail message. Both exporting the report to a Word document and selecting e-mail as the output destination create additional file requirements when you distribute the application. Because Crystal Reports is designed with a modular framework, both the file type (Word, Excel, HTML, and so on) and output destination (disk file, MAPI e-mail, Exchange public folder, and so on) functions are provided in separate .DLL files. If you are using these export formats and methods, you'll want to make sure the correct files are included in your application.

Conversely, if you are only using a few output types and destinations, or perhaps using none at all, you'll save disk space by eliminating these DLLs from your distribution package. Crystal Reports output destinations are provided by UXD*.DLL files for 16-bit environments and U2D*.DLL files for 32-bit environments. Output formats are provided by UXF*.DLL files for 16-bit environments and U2F*.DLL files for 32-bit environments. There a few additional requirements for 16-bit Word and

WordPerfect exports, as well as additional file requirements for certain picture types when exporting to HTML. Look at RUNTIME.HLP for specifics. You'll only need to include the formats that you specifically call in your application or wish to be available to your end-users if they click the Export button in the preview window.

User Function Libraries

If you use formulas in your report that call external User Function Libraries (UFLs), don't forget to include the external UFL .DLL files when you distribute your application. An external .DLL file will be called any time a formula uses any functions in the Additional Functions list in the formula editor. If you fail to include the .DLL file with your application, the formula will fail when the report runs on the end-user's machine.

By default, Crystal Reports installs several UFLs with the rest of the Crystal Reports package. These are all included in the dependency files that Crystal Reports supplies, so you won't generally have to worry about manually including the UFL files in your distribution package. However, if you've created your own UFLs (Chapter 28 discusses how to create UFLs with Visual Basic), you'll want to either manually add them to your distribution package, or modify the .DEP files to include them in all future distributions. You'll also be able to save disk space by removing UFL files that aren't used in any of your formulas.

UFL files generally adhere to the file format UF*.DLL for 16-bit UFLs and U2*.DLL for 32-bit UFLs. RUNTIME.HLP contains a description of individual UFL .DLL files and the functions that they provide. If none of the formulas in your report use functions from the Additional Functions list, you can safely remove these UFL files from your distribution package. Again, you should test your installation on a target machine to ensure that your formulas will work properly without the extra UFL files.

The
Complete
Reference

Crystal
Reports
7

Chapter 28

Creating User Function Libraries with Visual Basic

The more sophisticated your reports get, the more sophisticated your use of Crystal Reports formulas will become. While you'll find the formula language's built-in functions satisfy a good deal of your sophisticated reporting requirements, you may eventually encounter situations where you need extra features that aren't available. This may mean needing something as simple as a square root function (Crystal Reports doesn't have one) or as complex as wanting to determine the number of days a problem ticket has been open, excluding weekends and company holidays. In some cases, you may be able to create these specialized formulas with a great deal of formula coding. In other cases, the capabilities of the built-in formula language just won't provide the necessary flexibility.

You have several approaches for solving this potential problem. If you're using the Report Designer component to integrate your report with a Visual Basic program (covered in Chapter 24), you can use all the power of Visual Basic to create a value and place it in a text object in the report. But, what if you want to be able to provide a company-specific calculation, such as the problem-ticket example mentioned previously, to anybody designing a Crystal Report, without having to integrate the report with a VB program? With a User Function Library (UFL) you can extend the capabilities of the Crystal Reports formula language with a Windows development language, which could be Visual Basic.

Note   *Chapter 5 discusses the finer points of using the Crystal Reports formula language.*

User Function Library Overview

In the Crystal Reports Formula Editor, the Function Tree box divides functions into logical groups. Arithmetic functions are combined in their own group, Date/Time functions are located together, and so forth. But, if you look at the bottom of the Function Tree box, you'll see an extra collection of functions listed in an Additional Functions category. You'll notice that these functions run the gamut from Year 2000 date conversions to date/time string manipulation to bar code printing.

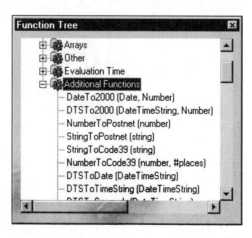

All functions in this Additional Functions category are considered UFLs and are provided to Crystal Reports by way of external dynamic link library (DLL) files. By creating a Windows DLL file using a Windows development language, you can extend the power of the Crystal Reports formula language by adding your own functions to the Additional Functions category. Each of these DLLs can expose one or more functions to the Crystal Reports formula language.

Crystal Reports installs several UFL DLLs by default. When you initially install Crystal Reports, all the functions in the Additional Functions list are supplied by these DLL files installed in the \CRYSTAL directory beneath the standard Windows installation directory (typically \WINDOWS or \WINNT). If you look in this directory, you'll recognize UFL filenames by the first few characters. All UFL filenames begin with the letter *U*. The second character is either *F* or *2*: 16-bit UFLs contain *F* as the second character, 32-bit UFLs contain *2* as the second character. In many (but not all) cases, the third character is the letter *L*, with the remaining characters describing the function of the UFL. All UFLs are dynamic link libraries having a file extension of .DLL.

If you wish to create your own UFLs, you have several Windows language choices. The original Crystal Reports language requirement for UFL design was the C language. However, starting with Crystal Reports 6, you have also been able to create UFLs with any language that can create automation servers that conform to Microsoft's Component Object Model (COM). These languages include Visual Basic and Delphi, among others.

UFLs in C

If you choose to use C to develop UFLs, the approach is dramatically different from the COM automation server approach with Visual Basic. There is plenty of helpful information in Developer's Help. Search for "User Function Library" and follow the various links to different parts of the C development process. You'll also find sample source code installed in the Crystal Reports program directory. Look at UFLSAMP1.C and UFLSAMP2.C for samples of C-developed UFLs.

UFLs in Visual Basic

A UFL that is installed by default with the 32-bit version of Crystal Reports is U2LCOM.DLL. This UFL doesn't actually expose any functions in the Formula Editor by itself. Instead, it acts as a gateway to COM automation servers that expose additional functions. By creating these automation servers in a COM-compatible language, you can expose external functions to the Crystal Reports formula language. Using Visual Basic 5 or 6, or the 32-bit version of Visual Basic 4, you can create automation servers that expose additional functions to Crystal Reports through U2LCOM.DLL.

While you can use C to develop 16-bit UFLs for use with Windows 3.1, Visual Basic UFLs are only recognized by the 32-bit version of Crystal Reports. As such, you must use a 32-bit Visual Basic environment to create them.

Creating a VB UFL requires a specific set of steps. You must start with an ActiveX DLL project to create the automation server. Project names must start with a certain set of characters for U2LCOM.DLL to recognize them. And, functions inside the project's class modules must be declared and created a certain way. When you compile the project into a .DLL file, Visual Basic will automatically register the automation server on your PC. Then, when you start Crystal Reports, U2LCOM.DLL will recognize the new automation server and expose its function in the Additional Functions list inside the Formula Editor. Once you've finished creating and testing the UFL, you'll need to use the Visual Basic 6 Package and Deployment Wizard, or another similar distribution mechanism, to install and register the automation server on the end-user's computer.

The remainder of this chapter will concentrate on developing UFLs with Visual Basic 5 and 6. The steps to create UFLs with 32-bit VB 4 are slightly different. Search Developer's Help for "Creating User Defined Functions using Visual Basic 4.0."

Creating the ActiveX DLL

Visual Basic refers to a COM-based automation server as an *ActiveX DLL*. When you create a new project in VB, choose this project type. A new project will be opened and a Class Module code window will immediately be displayed. Creating the functions to be exposed in the Formula Editor's Additional Functions section is now as simple as declaring public functions here in the class module.

Adding Functions to the Class Module

On the CD accompanying the book, there is a very simple sample UFL project that accepts a date value as its only argument and returns the next weekday after the date that is supplied. This might be used to determine when a product could next be shipped, or when a customer could next expect a return call from a sales representative. By adding a database lookup in the routine, you might also be able to include company holidays in the routine so Memorial Day or New Year's Day wouldn't be returned as the next weekday.

This function is simply added to the class module as it would be to a form or a .BAS module in a regular Visual Basic .EXE project. Examine the following sample code:

```
Public Function NextWeekDay(DateArg As Date) As Date
   Do
      DateArg = DateArg + 1
   Loop Until Weekday(DateArg) <> 1 And Weekday(DateArg) <> 7
   ' Could add logic here to look up date in database to
   ' see if it falls on a company holiday, etc.
   NextWeekDay = DateArg
End Function
```

Notice that the function is declared Public. This is a requirement for the function to be exposed to Crystal Reports. You'll also notice that the arguments to the function aren't specifically designated as ByRef or ByVal. It doesn't matter which method you use to pass arguments; either type of argument, or no type at all, is fine. This function simply uses a Do loop to add one day to the date until the day doesn't fall on a Saturday or Sunday. That date is then set as the function's return value.

You can create as many functions as you need inside the same class module. Just make sure that the functions are named with unique names that won't conflict with other Crystal Reports built-in functions. For example, if you create a UFL function named ToText, it will conflict with the existing Crystal Reports function of that name. Also, there are several reserved words and function names that you cannot use for your function names. In particular, U2LCOM.DLL makes special use of these function names:

UFInitialize
UFTerminate
UFStartJob
UFEndJob

And, COM itself makes use of the following reserved words, so you can't use any of these for your own function names:

QueryInterface
AddRef
Release
GetTypeInfoCount
GetTypeInfo
GetIDsOfNames
Invoke

> **Tip** *Function-name prefixing determines exactly how your UFL function names will appear in the Formula Editor. This is discussed in detail, later in the chapter.*

Your functions can accept as many arguments as necessary, and the arguments can be of any standard Crystal Reports data type. The actual names you give the arguments inside your VB function will be displayed in the Formula Editor as arguments for the Crystal Reports function. This requires you to think carefully about what argument names you want to use in your function. Although you'll notice straightforward argument names like *str* and *date* inside built-in Crystal Reports functions, you're limited to argument names that don't conflict with VB reserved words. With the sample application, an argument named *date* would be consistent with other Crystal Reports functions. But this conflicts with a VB reserved word and can't be used as a function argument. You'll notice that *DateArg* is used instead, and it will appear in the Formula Editor as the argument for this function.

When you return the function's value, Crystal Reports will automatically convert several VB data types into correct types for Crystal Reports formulas. In particular, functions that return VB's various numeric data types, regardless of precision (integer, long, and so on), will be converted to simple numbers in Crystal Reports. Date, String, and Boolean VB data types will be converted to the corresponding data type in Crystal Reports. You can also pass an array *to* Visual Basic from Crystal Reports. Visual Basic will recognize the array data type and allow you to manipulate the various array elements inside your function. However, the function *cannot* return an array to Crystal Reports—you can only return a single value.

 Testing your ActiveX DLL functions is made somewhat more complicated by the ActiveX DLL development environment. Microsoft recommends creating a project group and actually calling the automation server functions from another project that's loaded in the VB IDE at the same time. This may be one method of troubleshooting your UFL functions. You can also choose to create a regular .EXE project and create a simple form to test your UFL functions. You can then create the ActiveX DLL project and just copy your already-tested functions from the old project to the new one.

Special-Purpose Functions

As mentioned previously, several reserved words can't be used for your function names. Four of those names are reserved for special functions that your UFL can use for special UFL processing during your report, as discussed in the following sections.

UFINITIALIZE   This function is called just after the DLL is loaded into memory, before any functions are actually performed.

```
Public Function UFInitialize () As Long
```

One-time initialization of variables, opening of files, or other initialization code can be placed here. Return a value of zero (0) to indicate that the function completed properly. Should any errors or problems occur, return any non-zero value to indicate to Crystal Reports that initialization failed.

UFTERMINATE   This function is called just before the DLL is unloaded from memory, after any other functions are already completed.

```
Public Function UFTerminate () As Long
```

Use this function to de-allocate any variables or execute any other cleanup code that you'd like to perform. Return a value of zero (0) to indicate that the function completed properly. Should any errors or problems occur, return any non-zero value to indicate to Crystal Reports that UFTerminate failed.

UFSTARTJOB   This is similar to UFInitialize, except that it occurs once for every different report that may be processing.

```
Public Sub UFStartJob (job As Long)
```

You can determine the report that is being started by looking at the job argument that is passed to the function. Use this function for any per-job initialization. Notice that this is actually a subroutine, not a function. You cannot set any return code should errors occur in the routine.

UFENDJOB   This function is called when the current job finishes (when all report pages are finished processing, but before a new UFStartJob and before UFTerminate).

```
Public Sub UFEndJob (job As Long)
```

The actual job that is ending is passed with the job argument. Place any per-job clean up code here. Notice that this is actually a subroutine, not a function. You cannot set any return code should errors occur in the routine.

Naming and Saving the DLL

The combination of your function names, class module name, and ActiveX DLL project name all determine how (and if) your functions will appear in the Formula Editor. In particular, you *must* start your project name with the characters CRUFL. The remaining characters are up to you, allowing you to give the project a meaningful name. The CRUFL prefix indicates to U2LCOM.DLL that functions in this automation server will be exposed to Crystal Reports. If you don't prefix your project name with these characters, the functions won't appear in the Formula Editor. Name your project as you would any other VB project. Select the project in the Project Explorer window and give the project a name in the Properties window.

Once you've properly named the project, you need to actually create the automation server DLL file. Choose File | Make CRUFL*xxx*.DLL from the VB pull-down menus. You'll be prompted to choose a location for the actual DLL file. To be consistent with other UFL files, you can choose to save it in the \CRYSTAL directory below your regular Windows directory. This is not absolutely required, however, as the actual file location is not significant to U2LCOM.DLL. Instead, the DLL is *registered* by VB when the DLL is created. The registry setting contains the actual location of the DLL file, so it can be located in any drive or directory you choose.

Once the DLL is created and registered, start Crystal Reports. Open an existing report or create a new report. Open the Formula Editor and look at the functions that appear in the Additional Functions category. You'll see that your functions and their arguments now appear in the Formula Editor, as illustrated here:

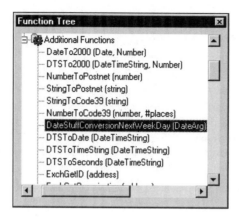

Error Handling

Crystal Reports will automatically handle certain error conditions that may occur. For example, if you declare a function argument as numeric in your VB UFL, but pass a string in the Formula Editor, Crystal Reports will automatically catch the error. You don't have to provide any special code to trap these kinds of errors.

Even though you design error-handling logic into your UFL functions, you may want to return function-specific error text to Crystal Reports from within your function. Declare and set the UFErrorText public string variable to accomplish this. Examine the following sample code:

```
Public UFErrorText As String
...
On Error GoTo NextWeekDay_Error
...
NextWeekDay_Error:
UFErrorText = Err.Description
```

Here, UFErrorText is declared in the general declarations section of the class module and is set if any error occurs inside the code. Whenever you set the value of this variable inside a function, Crystal Reports will stop the report, display the formula calling the function in the Formula Editor, and display the contents of UFErrorText in a dialog box. Because setting the value of this variable is what triggers the Crystal

Reports error, only use this for error handling. Attempting to use UFErrorText to store other values or attempting to read its contents may cause your report formulas to stop prematurely. Also, U2LCOM.DLL resets the value of the variable during report operations, so you can't reliably read its contents inside your code.

Function-Name Prefixing

If you look back at the preceeding illustration of the Function Tree, you'll notice that the function name added to Crystal Reports is quite long, and it differs from the actual name you gave the function in your VB code. By default, U2LCOM.DLL uses *function-name prefixing* to actually combine the project name (without the CRUFL characters), class module name, and then the function name to create the function that appears in the Formula Editor. For example, the sample UFL application on the CD is named as follows:

- Project Name: CRULFDateStuff
- Class Module Name: Conversion
- Function Name: NextWeekDay (with the DateArg argument)

The resulting function appears as DateStuffConversionNextWeekDay(DateArg) in the Formula Editor.

Function-name prefixing is designed to minimize the chance of duplicate function names appearing in the Formula Editor. Should you inadvertently use the same name for a UFL function as a preexisting Crystal Reports function (or another function created by a different UFL), errors or unpredictable formula behavior can result. By automatically adding the project and class module names to your function names, the chances of duplicate function names can be reduced. However, as you can see, report designers are also presented with rather large function names.

If you wish, you can turn function-name prefixing off, so only the function names themselves will be shown in the Formula Editor, without the project or class module names appended to them. Just be extra careful to make sure you don't use function names that already exist in the Formula Editor. To turn off function-name prefixing, declare the public Boolean variable UFPrefixFunctions in the general declaration section of the class module. Then, set the variable to false in the class's Initialize function. Here's some sample code:

```
Public UFPrefixFunctions As Boolean
...
Private Sub Class_Initialize()
   UFPrefixFunctions = False
End Sub
```

By setting the UFPrefixFunctions variable to false and then creating (or recreating) the DLL and restarting Crystal Reports, function names will appear in the Formula Editor without prefixing.

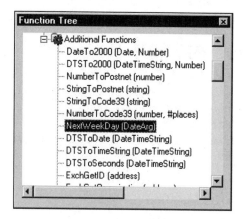

> **Caution** *Don't confuse the class's Initialize event with the UFInitialize function that's reserved for use by Crystal Reports. The class's Initialize event is accessed by choosing Class in the object drop-down list in the Code window and then choosing Initialize in the procedure drop-down list.*

Distributing the UFL

Although Visual Basic will automatically register your automation server DLL when you choose File | Make CRUFL*xxx*.DLL from the pull-down menus, you will need to distribute the DLL to any other report designer who will want to use the functions of the UFL. You also may want to distribute the UFL as part of a larger VB project that integrates reports using one of the integration methods discussed earlier.

To simply distribute the UFL to other report designers who will be using the Crystal Reports designer, it's probably best to use the Package and Deployment Wizard with VB 6, the Application Setup Wizard with VB 5, or another distribution tool. This will create a setup program that will install your UFL on the target system and register the automation server on the designer's computer. If you simply wish to pass the DLL file to a designer, they'll need to manually register the DLL so that U2LCOM.DLL will recognize it. VB provides the REGSVR32.EXE program to register an automation server from the command line.

Although it is typically installed automatically with 32-bit Crystal Reports, make sure that the target system has U2LCOM.DLL installed in the \CRYSTAL directory below the Windows program directory. Without this UFL file, no functions exposed by the automation server will appear in the Formula Editor.

If you want to include your UFL in reports that are integrated with a VB program, you'll want to make sure the DLL is distributed and registered when the whole VB application is installed by your end-user. This can be accomplished by simply adding the automation server you created to your project by using Project | References from the VB pull-down menus. You'll notice the name of your UFL appearing in the list of available references. Check the box next to the automation server name to add it to the project. When you later distribute the Visual Basic project, the distribution tool will automatically include the DLL file and register it on the target computer.

The Complete Reference

Part III

Crystal Reports 7 on the Web

The Complete Reference

Chapter 29

Crystal Reports and the Web

Earlier chapters in this book have discussed many techniques for creating sophisticated reports, as well as methods for integrating those reports into your custom Windows applications with Visual Basic. However, with Web-based technology making a huge impact on users of both internal corporate intranets and the Internet, providing a way to display your reports in a Web browser is crucial.

While you can easily export your reports to HTML format and place them on a Web server (Chapter 13 discusses these steps), those reports are *static*—that is, they can't be updated by the Web viewer to reflect the latest database information. Also, they're not interactive—the viewer can't use the group tree or drill down on charts or report groups. Seagate Software provides two real-time, interactive methods of putting your Crystal Reports on the Web: the Crystal Web Reports Server, and Crystal Reports with Microsoft Active Server Pages. This chapter discusses both options.

Both options allow Crystal Reports to be viewed and interacted with in a Web browser. No additional software needs to be installed on a user's computer—an industry-standard Web browser, such as Microsoft Internet Explorer or Netscape Communicator/Navigator is all that's required. In addition to allowing full real-time interactivity with a report, Crystal Web reporting options allow Web browser users to print the report on their local printer, or even export the report to a wide variety of export formats.

Note *Although you can use Seagate Analysis to provide report viewing through Windows-based Web browsers, it's a relatively large application that may not be appropriate for dial-up Internet environments. Also, if you are unsure of your end-user's browser platform, the Web options discussed in this chapter offer a more universal solution.*

Crystal Web Reports Server or Active Server Pages?

Because there are two methods of integrating "live" Web reports with Crystal Reports, you'll need to make a decision as to which method to use and under which conditions. The Crystal Web Reports Server can be installed on your Web server to allow .RPT files to be included in regular Web URLs, along with controlling command parameters. And, by using the Crystal Report Engine Automation Server with a Microsoft Web server running Active Server Pages, you can achieve a very high level of report control from a Web page. The question then becomes "Which method should I use, the Web Reports Server or Active Server Pages?"

There are several issues that will help you make this determination. The first question revolves around how sophisticated your Web pages will need to be and what level of report control you'll need to provide your viewers. By using the Automation Server with Active Server Pages, you can achieve the same level of report control as within a Visual Basic application (using the Automation Server with Visual Basic is discussed in Chapter 25). You can change report formulas at run time, hide and show individual report sections, and modify most report properties. While the Web Reports Server provides several command-line parameters that allow customization, you don't have nearly the flexibility as with the Automation Server and Active Server Pages.

However, the Crystal Web Reports Server can be set up very quickly, and implementing Web-based reports with it requires no programming. You'll be able to create a flexible report using parameter fields and pass values to these in your Web URL. In addition, the Web Reports Server is more streamlined for job caching and report sharing than is the Automation Server. If you anticipate having a large number of report viewers, particularly those who may be viewing the same reports, the Web Reports Server can probably offer overall better performance.

Consider whether you're a developer or a Web master. If you don't mind lots of VBScript or JScript coding and need maximum report flexibility, use the Automation Server with Active Server Pages (covered later in this chapter). If, however, you can create all the necessary flexibility by just using report parameter fields, and you want to be able to show reports by simply submitting Web URLs, then use the Crystal Web Reports Server.

Tip   *In addition to the sample Web Reports Server Web site included on the CD that comes with this book, Seagate provides both Web Reports Server and Active Server Pages example files when you install Crystal Reports. If the Web master has not removed the samples, you can point your browser to* http://<Web server name>/scrsamples *(where <Web server name> is the name of your particular Web server), and then click the Report Server Samples or Developer Active Server Page Samples links.*

Crystal Web Reports Server

The Crystal Web Reports Server is a Web server extension that you must install directly on your Web server (information on installing the Web Reports Server appears in Appendix A). Once the extension is installed and configured properly, your Web server will recognize and handle Crystal Reports .RPT files just like it recognizes .HTM, .GIF, and .JPG files (and other Internet file types). When you pass an .RPT filename as part of a Web Uniform Resource Locator (URL) in your Web browser, the Web server automatically intercepts the .RPT file and converts it to a format that the Web browser can display. Figure 29-1 displays a graphical overview of how the Crystal Web Reports Server interacts with the Web browser, Web server, and your database.

If you save your reports without saved data, they will be automatically run against the database whenever a viewer requests them, displaying the latest information directly from the database. If you wish to reduce database and network load, while still providing all the interactivity that isn't available with a simple HTML export, you can

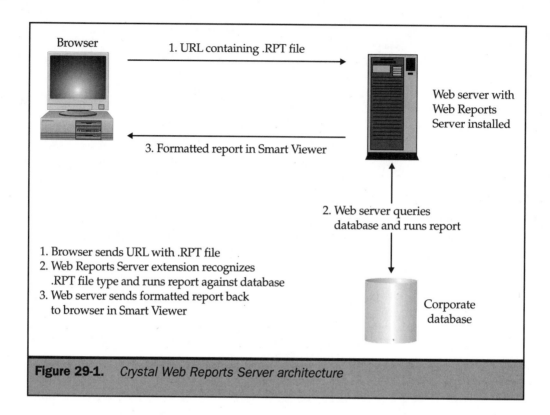

Figure 29-1.   *Crystal Web Reports Server architecture*

save your .RPT file with saved data and have the saved data appear in the Web browser. If you choose to offer the feature, you can allow your viewer to refresh the report if they wish to see the most current snapshot of the database.

Caution	*Because the Web Server will need to query databases for any reports that don't use saved data, make sure that any ODBC data sources or shared network drives that were used in the original .RPT files are configured on the Web server. Otherwise, the Web report will fail because the Web server won't be able to connect to the database.*

By using a *Smart Viewer* (discussed in the "Crystal Smart Viewers" section of this chapter), the Web Reports Server can display a report in its native format, including most fonts, special typographical effects, and formatting. In addition, the Smart Viewer allows complete report interactivity: the group tree, drill-down, and page navigation buttons that you're used to using in the Crystal Reports preview window are all available.

NSAPI/ISAPI and CGI Interfaces

Although a Web viewer probably won't be concerned about the Crystal Web Reports Server internal architecture, Web masters and developers will need to know some details about architecture choices. The first distinction you should be aware of is the Web server interface choice you'll need to make when you install the Web Reports Server. Prior to Version 7, the Crystal Web Reports Server would only operate on Netscape and Microsoft Windows-based Web servers using their native *NSAPI* (Netscape Server Application Programmer Interface) and *ISAPI* (Internet Server Application Programmer Interface). While Version 7 of the Web Reports Server still only runs under Windows, an additional *CGI* (Common Gateway Interface) version can be used with virtually any Windows Web server other than those from Netscape and Microsoft. Also, the Web Reports Server isn't limited to just Windows NT Web servers. You can use the server with Windows 95 and Windows 98 Web servers, as well (Microsoft's Personal Web Server, in particular).

Job Manager, Page Server, and Image Server Components

The Crystal Web Reports Server is modular, actually consisting of several different components. The three main components are the Image Server, the Page Server and the Job Manager. These components work together to maximize report throughput and to cache duplicate report requests.

The *Job Manager* is in charge of minimizing database and network traffic, wherever it can, by caching and organizing repeated report requests. If, for example, a report contains saved data, the Job Manager will cache the individual report pages and send them to a Web browser if they are repeatedly requested. If a viewer requests to refresh the report, the Job Manager will manage this process, and again cache certain pages of information before a specified refresh interval has passed—repeat refresh requests during this time will actually result in the cached pages being sent to the browser.

Tip	*A detailed description of Job Manager functionality can be found in Crystal Reports Developer's Help. Search for "Job Manager overview."*

The *Page Server* is the Web Reports Server component that actually intercepts .RPT report requests from the Web server. Based on the Web browser making the request or on parameters supplied with the report URL, the Page Server will also convert the report output to HTML or to a proprietary Seagate Software format (.EPF) to send back to the browser. If the report is to be presented in HTML, then the Page Server will also interact with the Image Server to convert any graphics to JPEG (.JPG) format for including in the HTML Web page.

The *Image Server* is called upon whenever a report needs to be viewed in HTML (hypertext markup language), the native language of the World Wide Web. Because

Crystal Reports doesn't store its reporting information in HTML, something must perform a conversion when the report is to be viewed in a Web browser. While the Page Server performs the conversion of text to HTML, the Image Server is used to convert any bitmap images, such as logos, charts, or geographic maps, to the JPEG (.JPG) format to be viewed in the Web browser. If the report is going to be viewed in either the Smart Viewer for ActiveX or Smart Viewer for Java (discussed in the "Crystal Smart Viewers" section of this chapter), the Image Server is not used, as the Smart Viewer component will read the Seagate Software proprietary file format directly.

The Page Server and Image Server components are actually separate Windows processes that need to be running whenever the Crystal Web Reports Server might receive report requests. If you are running a Windows NT Web server, these components can be run as with Windows NT services, or standard Windows programs. If you are using Windows 95 or 98, these components are standard Windows programs that are typically added to your Startup group so that they'll run as soon as you log on to Windows.

Note   *There are flexible configuration options for the Job Manager, Page Server, and Image Server components that can be set with the Crystal Web Reports Server Configuration program. See Appendix A for installation and configuration information.*

Using the Crystal Web Reports Server

In its simplest form, the Crystal Web Reports Server will display a report in your Web browser when you point the browser directly at the report file. By simply placing the desired .RPT files inside a Web server virtual directory and including the .RPT file in the URL, you'll see the report appear in the browser, as shown in Figure 29-2. If the report contains parameter fields or SQL stored procedures, or connects to a secured database that requires a user ID and password, you'll automatically be prompted to supply this information.

If you set up a Web server to allow directory browsing, and your Web viewers point to a directory that contains a selection of report files, this may provide all the flexibility you need. This will be sufficient if your reports require little customization and the automatic prompts provide sufficient interactivity.

Note   *To build complete interactive Web pages, you'll need a basic knowledge of HTML coding. Although you may be able to completely integrate your reports with an interactive Web editor, such as Microsoft FrontPage or Netobjects Fusion, you may need to edit the HTML pages manually in order to maximize flexibility. This chapter assumes you have a basic working knowledge of HTML. You may also need to work with your Web master to set up virtual directories or other specific permissions to create Web pages on your Web server.*

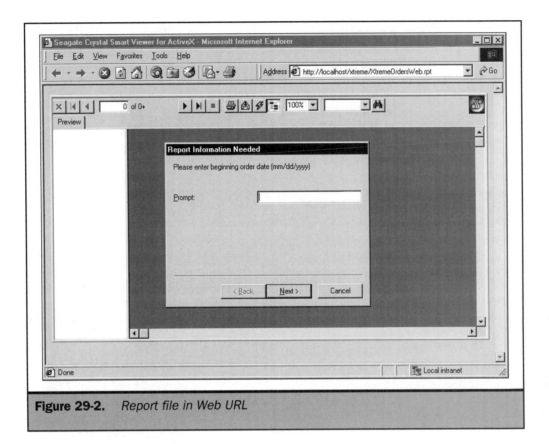

Figure 29-2.   *Report file in Web URL*

Linking to .RPT Files

Although simple directory browsing may be enough to satisfy your reporting needs, you'll most likely want to build a home page, or other complete Web pages that link to several reports. Just use the anchor tag in your HTML to link to the .RPT file that you wish to display. The following example will create a link to the sample Web report included on the CD that accompanies this book. This example assumes that an "xtreme" virtual directory has been set up on the Web server and that the XtremeOrdersWeb.rpt file is located in that directory.

```
<A HREF="http://localhost/xtreme/XtremeOrdersWeb.rpt">
   Xtreme Orders Report
</A>
```

This anchor tag, in combination with other graphical and textual elements of the Web page, will create a simple link that can be clicked to display the report in the viewer's browser.

 By default, the Crystal Web Reports Server requires URLs that contain the .RPT filename to use lowercase letters to specify the .rpt characters. Even if the filename appears uppercase (in a directory browse, for example), you must specify the file extension in lowercase letters, or the Web Reports Server will return an error message that it can't find the report.

Crystal Web Reports Server Commands

The link just demonstrated makes reporting easier for casual Web viewers, because they don't have to type in a long URL directly, or navigate through a list of files in a Web server directory to find the report they want. They simply click the desired link, and the report will display in their browser. However, if the report is based on a secure database that requires an ID and password, or the report contains SQL stored procedures or Crystal Reports parameter fields, you may prefer to supply these values to the report from within your HTML page, or based on an HTML form. This way, you gain more control over how the report is processed and customized.

This is accomplished by supplying commands to the report in the Web URL. By adding these commands after the .RPT filename, you can control how the Web Reports Server displays the report in the Web browser. Commands are available to supply userids and passwords for secure databases, to supply stored-procedure prompts and Crystal Reports parameter fields, to change the report's record-selection and group-selection formulas, and to control a viewer's ability to refresh report data.

Commands are appended to the .RPT filename in the URL in the following fashion:

```
<Report File Name>.rpt?<command1>=<value>&<command2>=<value>...
```

Note that the .RPT filename is separated from the first command with a question mark. Then, any subsequent commands are separated from the previous commands with an ampersand (&). Each command is typed, and the value for the command is provided after typing an equal sign (=).

Record and Group Selection

Using Crystal Web Reports Server commands, you can change the selection formula for the report on the fly by using the Web Reports Server SF command. Examine the following sample HTML:

```
<A HREF="http://localhost/xtreme/XtremeOrdersWeb.rpt?
   SF={Customer.Country}+%3d+'USA'">
   Xtreme Orders Report - USA Only
</A>
<br>
<A HREF="http://localhost/xtreme/XtremeOrdersWeb.rpt?
   SF={Customer.Country}+%3d+'Canada'">
   Xtreme Orders Report - Canada Only
</A>
```

In this example, there are two links appearing on the Web page: one to show customers in the USA and one to show customers in Canada. The distinction is made by supplying a different record-selection formula for each link with the Web Reports Server SF command. Type the letters SF and then the actual record-selection formula you want the report to use. Make sure your record-selection formula conforms to Crystal Reports formula language, as discussed in Chapter 6.

Tip *The +%3d+ characters used in the previous example are required to submit an equal sign as part of the UFL. Just typing an equal sign directly will cause an error, as the Web server will interpret it as a separator between a command and its value.*

You can also supply a group-selection formula to limit the groups displayed on your report. The command syntax is:

```
GF=<formula>
```

<Formula>, again, is a selection formula conforming exactly to Crystal Reports formula language syntax. This command will only display groups on your report that meet this criterion.

Parameter Fields and Stored Procedures

Because of the relative limitation of the Crystal Web Reports Server's flexibility as compared to the Automation Server with Active Server Pages (covered later in this chapter), you gain the most reporting flexibility in Web Reports Server by creative use of Crystal Reports parameter fields. Also, your report can be based on a SQL database parameterized stored procedure that prompts the viewer for a value before running the database query.

By supplying these values from an HTML link or HTML form, you can provide a good deal of flexibility to your report viewer without them having to know that

CRYSTAL REPORTS 7
ON THE WEB

parameters are being requested. Use the PROMPT# command to supply values for one or more parameter-field or stored-procedure-parameter prompts. Here's an example:

```
<A HREF="http://localhost/xtreme/XtremeOrdersWeb.rpt?
 PROMPT0=01/01/1995&PROMPT1=12/31/1995>
   Xtreme Orders Report - 1995 Orders
</A>
<br>
<A HREF="http://localhost/xtreme/XtremeOrdersWeb.rpt?
 PROMPT0=01/01/1996&PROMPT1=12/31/1996">
   Xtreme Orders Report - 1996 Orders
</A>
```

In this example, the first two parameter fields in the report are being supplied by the HTML code. These parameter fields are used inside the report to control record selection, as well as appearing on the report to indicate the date range. Notice that each prompt is sequentially numbered, and that prompts are *zero-based*, meaning that they start at zero (the first prompt is numbered 0, the second 1, and so on).

Just supply each prompt with a value, making sure that the type of material you're passing is appropriate for the type of parameter field that's being responded to. For example, if you try to pass alphabetic characters to a prompt that refers to a numeric parameter field, you'll get an error in the Web browser. There's no need to put quotation marks or apostrophes around the prompt values—if you do, the Web Reports Server will interpret them as part of the value you're passing.

Supply the prompts in the order they appear in the Parameters tab of the Insert Fields dialog box in the report—Prompt0 should respond to the first parameter in the tab, Prompt1 the second, and so on. If there are more parameter fields or stored procedure parameters in the report than you supply values for, only those that weren't supplied will be prompted for when the report runs.

   Get more information about parameter fields and how you can use them in both record selection and conditional formatting in Chapter 12.

Other Miscellaneous Commands

Although not discussed in the previous examples or used in the sample Web site included on the CD that comes with the book, there are additional Web Reports Server commands that you should know about.

USER#   If your report is based on one or more secured databases, you can use the USER# command to supply necessary userids. Because a report can contain more than one secure database, you may need to supply several USER# commands. Replace the # character with the zero-based index of the userid you wish to supply. For example, if there are two databases that require a userid, use USER0 and USER1 commands to supply them.

PASSWORD#   Along with the user ID that you supply with the USER# command, you may want to supply a password to the database from within your HTML to avoid having the user be prompted for the password. Use the PASSWORD# command to accomplish this. As with USER#, there can be more than one database that requires a password. Supply a zero-based index to PASSWORD# to indicate which database will receive the password.

Tip   *If your report contains one or more subreports that are based on secure databases, you'll need to add an at sign (@) and the name of the subreport after the USER# and PASSWORD# commands to indicate that the commands are to apply to the subreport. Make sure to refer to the subreport name exactly as it appears inside its main report container—if it was an imported .RPT file, don't forget to include the period and the characters RPT.*

Here is some sample HTML that supplies userids and passwords to a report that contains two secure databases; one in the main report and one in the subreport named Top 5 Products:

```
<A HREF="http://localhost/production/Sales.rpt?
 USER0=Administrator&USER0@Top 5 Products=Guest&
 PASSWORD0=Laurel&PASSWORD0@Top 5 Products=Hardy">
    Sales with Top 5 Product Summary
</A>
```

Caution   *Userids and passwords should appear in the URL in the same order in which the databases appear in the main report or subreports. If all userids and passwords are not provided in your HTML, the user will be prompted to supply them when the report runs.*

LOGDIR AND LOGS   If your report is based on a Web server log file, these two commands specify the directory of the Web server log file and the date range the Web server report should be limited to. The syntax for the LOGDIR and LOGS commands is as follows:

```
LOGDIR=<log_directory>
```

The *<log_directory>* is either the physical path or UNC path indicating the directory where the Web server log is located.

```
LOGS=<log_range>
```

The *<log_range>* is the date range of transactions to be included in the report, followed by your specification of the Standard or NCSA Web log. The following two examples illustrate correct formats for the *<log_range>* string:

```
logs=19970101-19970131<STD,ALL>
```

This will report on the Microsoft Internet Information Server standard activity log January 1, 1997, through January 31, 1997.

```
logs=19980601-19981231<NCSA,ALL>
```

This will report on NCSA standard activity-log transactions for June through December, 1998.

Note *For more information on designing reports against Web server logs, refer to Chapter 21.*

INIT The INIT command tells the Crystal Web Reports Server which Smart Viewer to use when it displays the report in the viewer's browser. The four options are *actx* for the Smart Viewer for ActiveX, *java* for the Smart Viewer for Java, *html_frame* to display the group tree and report in separate browser frames, and *html_page* to display the report in a single browser window without frames. More detailed information on Smart Viewers appears in the "Crystal Smart Viewers" section of this chapter.

PROMPTONREFRESH The PROMPTONREFRESH command indicates whether parameter fields should be prompted for if the viewer clicks the refresh button in the Smart Viewer. Available values are 1 for on and 0 for off. If this option is turned on, the parameter field prompts will be redisplayed whenever a user refreshes the report. If the option is turned off, then the existing values for any parameter fields will be passed to the database when the report is refreshed.

Caution *One improvement to Version 7 of the Web Reports Server is how the Job Manager and Page Server share documents. If you use any of the parameters described here (with the exception of INIT to choose a viewer), you will reduce the ability of the report to be shared among multiple users, which may result in increased network and database loads. This is required because of the possibility that each user can be submitting a unique record or group selection formula, unique parameter fields, or unique user and password information to the report.*

Supplying Commands from Within HTML Forms

The previous examples of coding commands in HTML are somewhat limited because the values of the Web Reports Server commands have to be hard coded right into the HTML. This requires that several links be created, each one supplying different fixed values to the commands. While this works fine if you have a limited set of choices you want to provide to your viewer, you may wish to allow the viewer to specify any number of options without having to type in the URL manually. You can provide this flexibility by using HTML forms.

An HTML form presents familiar user interface elements to a Web browser, such as text boxes, radio buttons, and drop-down lists. As long as you give these elements the names of the corresponding Crystal Web Reports Server commands, you can supply the values for the commands from the form elements. The sample Web site included on the CD accompanying this book uses this method to supply values for Web Reports Server commands without requiring the user to type in the URL manually, and without hard coding a limited set of commands in several links. If you choose either to view the report or export the report, another HTML page will appear containing a form. The ViewReport.HTM page for previewing the report in a viewer is shown in Figure 29-3.

You'll notice six user interface elements that gather customized information from the viewer, in addition to the View Report command button. Each of these elements corresponds to a different command that can be appended to the .RPT file URL to customize the way that the report behaves. An abbreviated set of the HTML code to create this form follows:

```
<form method="POST" action="XtremeOrdersWeb.rpt">
   <p>From: <input type="text" name="prompt0"
   <p>To: <input type="text" name="prompt1"></p>
   <p>Tax Rate: <input type="text" name="prompt2"></p>
   <p>Highlight Orders Over: <input type="text" name="prompt3"></p>
   <p>Group By: <select name="prompt4">
      <option selected value="Quarter">Quarter</option>
      <option value="Customer">Customer</option></select></p>
   <p>Viewer: <select name="init">
      <option selected value="actx">Active X</option>
      <option value="java">Java</option>
      <option value="html_frame">HTML Frames</option>
      <option value="html_page">HTML Standard</option></select></p>
   <p><input type="submit" value="View Report"></p>
</form>
```

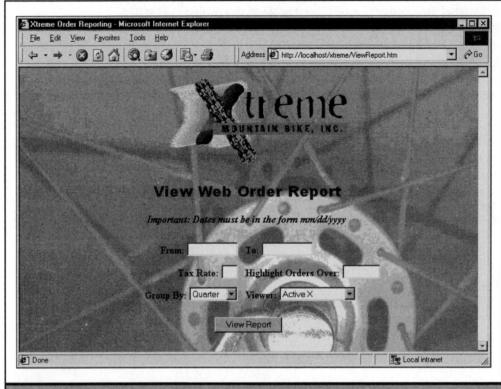

Figure 29-3.   *HTML form for Xtreme Orders report selection*

Note that with the single exception of the INIT command, which chooses a Smart Viewer to view the report, the remaining form elements refer to five parameter fields contained in the XtremeOrdersWeb.RPT report file. By creating the proper types of user interface elements (text boxes for the dates and number parameter fields and drop-down list boxes for grouping and viewer selection), you can create a very easy-to-use interface for the report. By using an HTML form, you can more tightly control the way commands are provided while still allowing the report viewer a great deal of flexibility.

The Web Reports Server Command Expert

Seagate provides a Web-based tool to help you interactively create the necessary command strings to use with the Crystal Web Reports Server. The Web Reports Server Command Expert is available, along with other Web Reports Server samples, in the SCRSAMPLES site that is installed on your Web server. Point your browser to http://<*Web server name*>/scrsamples where <*Web server name*> is the name of the

Web server where the Web Reports Server has been installed. Click on the Web Reports Server Command Expert link. Figure 29-4 shows how the expert will appear in your browser.

Begin by specifying the exact URL for the .RPT file you want to include in a Web page. Depending on other options you choose (the number of parameter fields, whether you want to view or export the report, and so on) the Command Expert will lead you through several other prompts. When you complete the prompts, the expert will show you the report in a viewer. It will also present a complete URL, including all Web Reports Server commands, that you can use in an anchor tag to display the report. If you are integrating your report with an HTML form, the Command Expert will also provide the necessary HTML to use. You'll just need to create the controls that match up to the command names that the Command Expert creates. Figure 29-5 shows the results of the Command Expert.

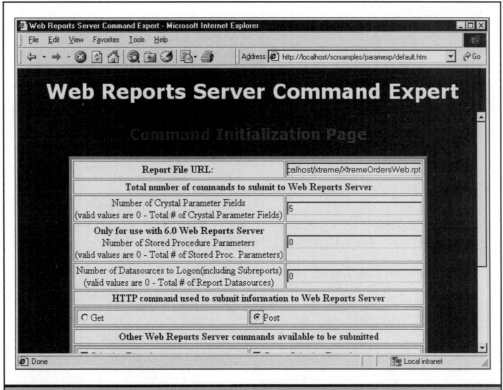

Figure 29-4.   *The Web Reports Server Command Expert*

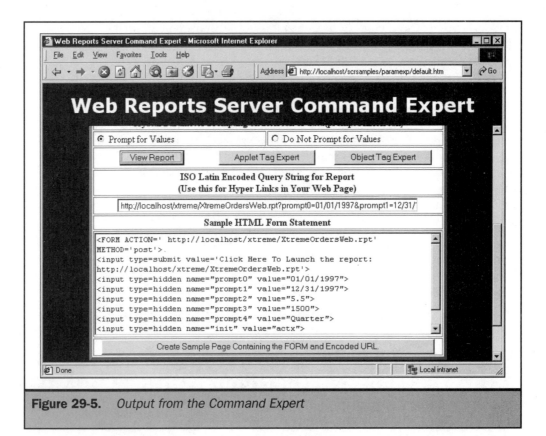

Figure 29-5.　*Output from the Command Expert*

Crystal Smart Viewers

As discussed earlier in the chapter, one of the main benefits of using the Crystal Web Reports Server instead of just exporting reports to HTML from the Crystal Reports Designer, is that it can offer full report interaction, such as drill-down and group-tree manipulation. The trick, though, is how to fully implement this interaction in a Web browser. While more flexibility and interactivity is added with each new revision of HTML, it has inherent limitations that make reproducing every element of a Crystal Report difficult, if not impossible.

To deal with this limitation, Seagate Software developed two Smart Viewer applications that can be used with most common Web browsers. The *Smart Viewer for ActiveX* is a Microsoft-compatible ActiveX control that can be viewed in Microsoft Internet Explorer Version 3.02 or greater. The *Smart Viewer for Java* is a Java applet that can be viewed in 32-bit versions of Netscape Navigator 2.0 or greater, Internet Explorer 3.02 or greater, or other Java-compatible browsers. Both viewers implement almost all the features and functionality of the regular Crystal Reports Preview tab, although there are some visual differences. Both allow you to drill down on group headers and footers, charts, and maps, as well as offering full interaction with the group tree. Both viewers maintain most font and object formatting, as well as allowing you to print reports in their "native" paginated format on an attached printer.

There are still situations, however, where an ActiveX control or Java applet cannot be used. Perhaps there are security restrictions in your company, maybe there are performance concerns about network traffic, or perhaps noncompatible browsers may be in use. For these situations, the Crystal Web Reports Server offers two HTML-based alternatives: the *Smart Viewer for HTML Frames*, and the *Smart Viewer for HTML Pages*. The Smart Viewer for HTML Frames requires a browser than can support JavaScript and frames. Frames allow more than one scrollable window to be displayed within the browser at one time, which is used to mimic the group tree as closely as possible in a separate frame on the left side of the browser. If your browser doesn't support frames, you can use the Smart Viewer for HTML Pages, which displays the entire report without a group tree in a single browser window.

 While an argument could be made that the HTML-based viewers aren't really "smart," Seagate still refers to them as such. Regardless, they do exhibit very creative use of HTML and JavaScript.

Smart Viewers Compared

The various Smart Viewers each have advantages and disadvantages, based on several factors. The ActiveX and Java viewers offer more features, but also place a higher burden on the Web server and network because of their size; they also have higher browser requirements. The HTML viewers have fewer browser requirements, but they make formatting compromises and limit functionality. Table 29-1 compares the different viewers and their advantages and disadvantages.

As a general rule, you should use the Smart Viewer that provides the highest level of user functionality for your particular browser and network environment. If your users are all on a 100-megabit intranet with fast PCs and the latest version of Microsoft Internet Explorer, there can't be too many arguments made against using the Smart Viewer for ActiveX. If you have a mix of Netscape and Microsoft browsers, the Smart Viewer for Java will work with both. But, if you are providing reports on your extranet that can potentially be accessed by any number of unknown browsers using 28.8Kbps modems, you may want to use either of the Smart Viewers for HTML to streamline performance and support the widest variety of browsers.

One thing should always be kept in mind: when you design reports to be distributed over the Web, take your target audience's Smart Viewer choices into serious consideration when you design your reports. If your ultimate goal is that reports look good on a printed page, you need to make serious changes to report formatting and layout if your audience will be using HTML-based viewers instead of the ActiveX or Java viewers. If your reports rely heavily on group tree and drill-down

Smart Viewer	Advantages	Disadvantages
ActiveX	Provides highest mirror-image level of original report and most flexibility, including full group tree and drill-down interactivity, and accurate printing of reports on your local printer.	Only works with 32-bit versions of Microsoft Internet Explorer 3.02 or later. Requires extra time and increases network strain when downloaded to browser.
Java	Provides good mirror-image level and high flexibility, such as group tree and drill-down interactivity and ability to print report on your local printer. Works with any Java-compatible browser.	Requires extra time and increases network strain when downloaded to browser. Will not work with earlier browsers that don't support Java.
HTML Frames	Will work with browsers that just support frames and JavaScript (such as earlier 16-bit browsers)—ActiveX and full Java capabilities aren't required. Mimics group tree with a browser frame. Faster initial response and no control or applet download is required.	Makes formatting compromises, sometimes significantly, because of HTML limitations. Only prints what's in the current browser window—original report pagination and layout are not preserved.
HTML Pages	Works with even the simplest browsers that don't support frames, while still allowing "pseudo" drill-down by creating links in group headers. Faster initial response and no control or applet download is required.	Makes formatting compromises, sometimes significantly, because of HTML limitations. Only prints what's in the current browser window—original report pagination and layout are not preserved.

Table 29-1.   *Smart Viewer Comparison*

interactivity (detail sections are hidden, lots of charts are included, and so on), don't realistically expect satisfactory results with the HTML-based viewers. And, don't forget that Crystal Reports includes many formatting options, such as drop shadows, underlaid sections, and object and section background shading, that won't convert properly to HTML when displayed in the HTML viewers. Always test your reports and make sure you're getting the results you expect in your target Smart Viewer.

If you are implementing reporting from a Java application, you may be able to make use of the Smart Viewer Java Bean. Similar to an ActiveX control that can be used in Visual Basic, the Java Bean Viewer can be added to a Java application and controlled with properties and methods.

Choosing and Customizing Smart Viewers

In its simplest implementation, the Crystal Web Reports Server will query the browser making a request for a report and automatically display the report in an appropriate Smart Viewer. If you make the request with Internet Explorer 3.02 or greater, the Web Reports Server will automatically send down the Smart Viewer for ActiveX. If you use a 32-bit version of a Netscape browser, you'll automatically see your report in the Smart Viewer for Java. Newer 16-bit versions of browsers will automatically display reports in HTML frames. And, older browsers (Netscape 2 or Internet Explorer 2 being examples) will display reports in HTML pages, by default.

Choosing a Specific Viewer

You may wish to specify a certain Smart Viewer for your audience, however, based on some of the earlier comparison points. The Crystal Web Reports Server allows you to override its default Smart Viewer choice with a specific viewer that you choose with the INIT command (as mentioned earlier in the chapter). By supplying *actx*, *java*, *html_frame*, or *html_page* values to the INIT command, you can choose which Smart Viewer you wish to send to the browser. If you would like to allow your audience a choice of viewers, you can add a control to an HTML form that allows them to make one of the four choices. By naming the control "INIT" and limiting its available choices to the four allowable INIT values, you allow the report viewer to make the choice. The sample Web Reports Server Web site on the CD that comes with this book demonstrates this capability with a drop-down list. Here's the portion of HTML code that accomplishes this:

```
<p>Viewer: <select name="init">
   <option selected value="actx">ActiveX</option>
   <option value="java">Java</option>
   <option value="html_frame">HTML Frames</option>
   <option value="html_page">HTML Standard</option></select></p>
```

Customizing Smart Viewer Behavior

When you view a report in either the ActiveX or Java viewers, certain characteristics of the viewers are enabled by default. For example, if the report was created with a group tree, the group tree will be visible. The user will be able to export the report to different file formats or print the report to a local printer. If the report contains group headers and footers with summary fields, the user will be able to drill down on the groups. You may wish to limit some of these features on a global basis, or just for certain chosen individual reports.

By using the Web Reports Server Configuration application from the Seagate Crystal Reports program group (discussed in more detail in Appendix A), you can control the availability of some of these Smart Viewer features on a global basis. However, if you wish to control these capabilities by individual report, you have a bit more work ahead of you. In order to specify individual properties of Smart Viewer for ActiveX or Smart Viewer for Java, you must add specific references to the ActiveX control or Java applet to your HTML. This complicates the integration process well beyond the simple INIT command added to your report URL, so you should only approach this technique if the benefit of Smart Viewer customization outweighs the complexity of implementing it.

SMART VIEWER FOR JAVA   To add a reference to the Smart Viewer for Java to your HTML code, use the Applet tag as demonstrated here:

```
<applet code=com.seagatesoftware.img.ReportViewer.ReportViewer
   codebase="/viewer/JavaViewer"
   id=ReportViewer
   width=100%
   height=95%
   archive="/viewer/JavaViewer/ReportViewer.jar">

   <param name=ReportName value="XtremeOrdersWeb.rpt">
   <param name=ReportParameter
   Value="prompt0=01/01/1997&prompt1=12/31/1997">
</applet>
```

This simply displays the Smart Viewer for Java right inside your Web page between any other text that may be surrounding the Applet tag. Notice that the ReportName and ReportParameter parameters, used to actually tell the viewer which report to display and provide values for the first two report parameter fields, are the only parameters being specified. To control viewer behavior more precisely, you can add additional parameters, such as:

```
<param name=ShowGroupTree value="false">
<param name=HasRefreshButton value="false">
<param name=HasPrintButton value="true">
<param name=CanDrillDown value="false">
```

Using these parameters (and others that aren't demonstrated here), you can fully customize the behavior of the Smart Viewer.

 The Web Reports Server Command Expert, discussed earlier in the chapter, can interactively create an Object tag and parameters for you, based on the responses you give it. Also, Developer's Help offers a complete description of all Java viewer parameters. Search for "Java, adding Crystal Smart Viewer to a Web page."

SMART VIEWER FOR ACTIVEX   A reference to the Smart Viewer for ActiveX can be added to your HTML code by using the Object tag, as demonstrated here:

```
<OBJECT ID="CRViewer"
    CLASSID="CLSID:C4847596-972C-11D0-9567-00A0C9273C2A"
    WIDTH=100% HEIGHT=95%
<PARAM NAME="DisplayGroupTree" VALUE=1>
<PARAM NAME="EnableRefreshButton" VALUE=1>
<PARAM NAME="EnablePrintButton" VALUE=1>
<PARAM NAME="EnableDrillDown" VALUE=1>
</OBJECT>
```

Notice that, as in the Smart Viewer for Java example presented earlier, you can control the behavior of individual elements of the viewer.

If you compare the two examples closely, though, you'll notice that there are no parameters here for choosing the actual report to be displayed in the viewer, or for setting report parameter fields. That's because the Smart Viewer for ActiveX (specifically the version included with Crystal Reports 7) doesn't have these parameters available. To specify this information, you must embed VBScript code to manipulate the Smart Viewer for ActiveX Object Model inside your HTML page, much like you control the viewer when using the Report Designer component in Visual Basic (discussed in Chapter 24). Because this method of viewer customization is so VBScript-intensive, the Web Reports Server Command Expert's Object Tag Expert button will create a section of VBScript, along with the Smart Viewer for ActiveX Object tag and parameters. It's highly recommended that you use this tool if you want to customize ActiveX viewer behavior.

 To see a complete list of available parameters, as well as sample VBScript code to fully implement a customized ActiveX viewer, search Developer's Help for "ActiveX, adding Crystal Smart Viewer to a Web page."

Exporting Files with the Web Reports Server

Not only will the Crystal Web Reports Server display Crystal Reports .RPT files in a Web browser, it will also export them to popular file formats, as well. When you set up the Web Reports Server to do this, it will actually download a file to the browser, as though you had exported the file from Crystal Reports (as discussed in Chapter 13).

The Web Reports Server will also include appropriate MIME-TYPE information with the file, including the appropriate file extension. If your Web browser is properly configured, this will launch the target application, such as Microsoft Word or Excel, right inside the Web browser to display the downloaded file. If your browser isn't so configured, you'll be given the opportunity to save the file on disk, where it can be opened later by the specified application. Figure 29-6 shows the results of the sample Web site choice of "Exporting to Excel" from the CD that comes with the book.

The Crystal Web Reports Server supports exporting to several versions of HTML, multiple versions of Microsoft Excel, Crystal Reports native .RPT file format, Rich Text format, and Microsoft Word. Two additional Web Reports Server commands are

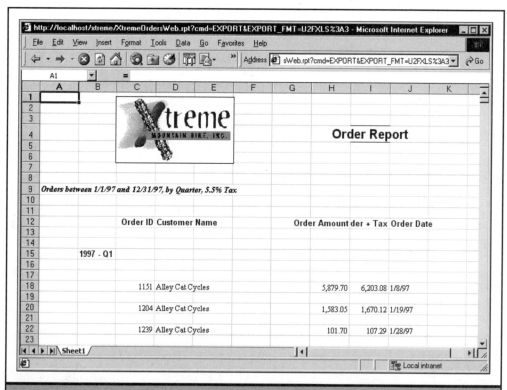

Figure 29-6.   *A Web Reports Server export to Excel*

available to control exporting: CMD and EXPORT_FMT. These are appended to the report UFL as follows:

```
cmd=EXPORT&EXPORT_FMT=<export format type>
```

The EXPORT_FMT command accepts a specific set of values that determine which format the file will be exported to:

File Format	Value
HTML 3.0 (Draft Standard)	U2FHTML:0
HTML 3.2 (Extended)	U2FHTML:1
HTML 3.2 (Standard)	U2FHTML:2
Seagate Crystal Reports (RPT)	U2FCR:0
Excel 2.1 (XLS)	U2FXLS:0
Excel 3.0 (XLS)	U2FXLS:1
Excel 4.0 (XLS)	U2FXLS:2
Excel 5.0 (XLS)	U2FXLS:3
Excel 5.0 (XLS) Extended	U2FXLS:4
Rich Text format (RTF)	U2FRTF:0
Word Document (DOC)	U2FWORDW:0

Therefore, to export a report to Microsoft Excel, you could simply provide the following URL:

```
http://localhost/xtreme/XtremeOrdersWeg.rpt?
cmd=EXPORT&EXPORT_FMT=U2FXLS%3A3
```

 Notice the characters %3A included in the EXPORT_FMT command value. This must be used to indicate the colon in the format type value. If you actually type a colon, the Web server will interpret it incorrectly and you'll receive an error message.

You can also easily develop an HTML form that contains a drop-down list control containing available format values. As long as you name the control EXPORT_FMT, the URL will use the item chosen from the drop-down list as the value for the export format. Although this is fairly easy to implement without much further assistance, you can use the Web Reports Server Command Expert to create a properly formatted URL to export a report to your chosen format.

While you can specify three different HTML file types when you export, one must question the benefit of doing so. Since the Web server will be downloading HTML, the browser will simply interpret it as a Web page and will display the report, much like using the Smart Viewer for HTML Pages.

Crystal Reports and Microsoft Active Server Pages

In addition to the Web Reports Server, you can integrate Crystal Reports into your Web pages using Microsoft Active Server Pages and the Report Engine Automation Server. Using this option is dramatically different from the Web Reports Server. The benefit is that you have complete control and flexibility for your reports, just as you do when using the Automation Server within Visual Basic. The downside is that the process is much more labor intensive than the Web Reports Server. There are copious amounts of code involved.

What Are Active Server Pages and What Is VBScript?

The original language of the Web, hypertext markup language (HTML), can be used to create attractive hyperlinked pages with graphics, various font sizes, and (with the advent of newer HTML extensions such as Dynamic HTML) more interactivity and multimedia features. However, being a "markup language" instead of a true procedural or event-driven development language, HTML falls far short of providing all the flexibility you may need to create full Web-based custom applications. To help fill this void, the industry has moved towards *scripting* languages that allow browsers to perform much more sophisticated and intricate procedures. Two scripting languages are leading the forefront: *JavaScript* is a scripting language based on Java, and *VBScript* is a scripting language based on Microsoft's Visual Basic for Applications (VBA). JavaScript is supported by both major browser vendors, Microsoft and Netscape. VBScript, generally, is limited to versions of Microsoft Internet Explorer.

JavaScript and VBScript are *client-side* scripting languages—both being interpreted by the browser after being downloaded in a Web page. The scripts are not compiled into machine-executable code and generally cannot make database connections to a corporate database. And, because they execute on a browser that can be affected by any number of client-side variables, a developer cannot always expect consistent results.

To provide more flexibility and to offer connectivity to corporate databases, Microsoft also implements *server-side* scripting on Internet Information Server, Personal Web Server, and the Peer Web Services Web servers. In this instance, the scripting language is interpreted by the Web server instead of the Web browser client. The results of the server-executed script are then sent to the Web browser as HTML. Because the script is executed on the server, you can create much more robust and flexible applications that are browser-independent—all that is sent to the browser is

HTML. Microsoft's implementation of server-side scripting is called *Active Server Pages*, or ASP for short. When a Web server has ASP support installed, pages scripted with ASP are given a file extension of .ASP instead of .HTM. The Web server will then scan the .ASP file for server-side script and execute any it finds, sending the results of the script to the browser.

To enhance ASP even more, Microsoft extends the Component Object Model (COM), which is discussed in the Visual Basic chapters in Part II of this book, to its Web server platform. Because of this, the Crystal Report Engine Automation Server can be integrated with server-side scripts to create extensive reporting flexibility in Web applications. By using the full VBA power of Active Server Pages, combined with the ability of the Crystal Reports Automation Server to control almost every aspect of a report at run time, you can create VB-like applications that integrate reports in a Web browser.

Although both VBScript and JScript (Microsoft's version of JavaScript) can be executed in Active Server Pages, VBScript is discussed in the book. Also, Seagate Software's example ASPs installed with Crystal Reports all utilize VBScript.

Visual InterDev as a Development Tool

Microsoft's Visual InterDev has established itself as the de facto standard for ASP development. It is designed to look very similar to Visual Basic and offers much of the same functionality for developing ASPs as Visual Basic does for Windows applications. In addition to providing a complete HTML page and forms designer, Visual InterDev's code window mimics that of Visual Basic, providing automatic code completion and different font coloring to indicate the syntax of VBScript or JScript. Visual InterDev can also debug server and client-side scripts with integrated debugging tools. Microsoft Front Page can also edit ASPs, but not with the same debugging features and database integration features of Visual InterDev. Since ASPs are straight ASCII files, you can even use a simple text editor, such as Notepad, to edit them.

While you'll derive a good deal of coding and debugging benefit from using Visual InterDev to develop your Web application's user interface, you won't enjoy the same level of integration and debugging with the Crystal Report Engine Automation Server that you do with Visual Basic. The Automation Server's object model is implemented in Visual InterDev in such a way that automatic code completion won't be available. Also, the Design-Time Control feature of Visual InterDev, which provides an easy, interactive method of generating ASP code by answering some simple prompts, has not been included in either the initial release or first maintenance release of Crystal Reports 7. Crystal Reports 6 does include a Visual InterDev Design-Time Control, but it only works with Visual InterDev Version 1, not the newer Version 6.

You must specifically indicate that you want to install Crystal Reports ASP support when you install Crystal Reports on your Web server. If this choice has not been made, you'll need to reinstall Crystal Reports and specify this option.

Seagate-Supplied Sample ASPs

Probably the best way to begin working with Crystal Reports integration inside Active Server Pages is to view and evaluate the sample ASPs that are installed automatically when you install Crystal Reports 7 on a Microsoft Web server. After installing Crystal Reports on a Web server, point your browser to http://<web server>/scrsamples. Click on the Developer Active Server Page Samples link to choose and run several ASP examples of different types of report integration. To evaluate the actual ASP code, you'll need read access to the Crystal Reports directory on your Web server. Use Visual InterDev or Notepad to look in <Crystal Reports Program Directory>\Sample\ ASPSamples for the different ASP files. They are well documented and give you many good examples of how to implement Automation Server coding inside Active Server Pages.

What Is RPTSERVER.ASP?

As you look through ASP example files supplied by Seagate Software, you'll notice that ASP Web reports are displayed in the Crystal Smart Viewers just as Web Reports Server reports are (as discussed earlier in the chapter). You'll note, however, that the actual .RPT report file is not being passed to the Smart Viewers. Instead, the Smart Viewers are always pointed to another file called RPTSERVER.ASP. This Seagate-supplied ASP is a very important integral part of Crystal Reports' integration with Active Server Pages.

When you integrate a report with the Automation Server and Visual Basic (as covered in Chapter 25), you use the Automation Server's own internal report viewer to execute the Report object's Preview method. However, because integrating with the Web means your eventual display target is a Web browser, the Automation Server's viewer can't be used with ASPs. This is left to one of the four Smart Viewers discussed earlier: ActiveX, Java, HTML Frames, or HTML Page. Because these viewers use Crystal Reports' page-on-demand architecture, they expect report pages to be fed to them by the Automation Server's PageEngine object. This rather complicated logic and interaction is handled by RPTSERVER.ASP. Although you might be able to write your own ASP code to replace the function of RPTSERVER.ASP, one look at the ASP code in this file will probably convince you that it won't be worth the effort.

The Automation Server Object Model in ASPs

Because Active Server Pages support COM automation servers, you can implement Crystal Reports integration in ASPs much the same way as you do in Visual Basic. The complete Report Engine Automation Server object model is available for you to use in your Active Server Pages. You can set properties and execute methods for different Automation Server objects to customize report behavior. Typically, you'll use controls your user has completed on a form, or perhaps values your ASP is retrieving from a database, to control report appearance at run time.

The Application and Report Objects

As with Visual Basic, there are two base-level objects that must be initially declared in your Web project: the Application object and the Report object. The Application object need only be declared once at the beginning of a project. The Application object is then used to declare a Report object and then is generally not used throughout the rest of the project. Because these objects must remain in scope throughout the project and all associated ASP files, they are declared as *session* variables, which retain their values and remain in scope throughout an entire ASP project. Here's sample ASP code to declare them:

```
' CREATE THE APPLICATION OBJECT
If Not IsObject (session("oApp")) Then
   Set session("oApp") = Server.CreateObject("Crystal.CRPE.Application")
End If

' CREATE THE REPORT OBJECT
reportname = Path & "Xtreme Orders.rpt"
'Path must be physical path, not virtual path
If IsObject(session("oRpt")) then
   Set session("oRpt") = nothing
End If
Set session("oRpt") = session("oApp").OpenReport(reportname, 1)

' Disable error messages on the Web server
Session("oRpt").Options.MorePrintEngineErrorMessages = 0
```

A few notes about this sample VBScript code:

- Variables don't need to be identified with DIM or declared before use. In Visual Basic terms, no Option Explicit statement has been executed. While this may seem to ease your coding requirements, you'll need to remember that this means that all variables used in this fashion are variants. Some Automation Server methods require that variables be passed with a specific data type, so in those cases, use VBScript variable-declaration functions, such as CStr and CDbl to correctly cast variables when passing them.

- The report file has been preceded with a Path variable. This variable is assigned in previous VBScript not shown here (look in the sample Seagate ASPs for the routine to generate this variable). The path must be the physical path to the report file (for example, C:\REPORTS) because the Automation Server can't resolve Web server virtual paths.

- The Application object is only declared once. Should this section of VBScript be executed again, the previous declaration of oApp will remain. However, if there is a previous declaration of the Report object (presumably for a different report that may have been processed in a previous pass through this code), it will be set to Nothing before being set to the new report with the Application object's OpenReport method.

- The MorePrintEngineErrorMessages property of the ReportOptions object (below the Report object) is set to 0. This will reduce the chances of any error messages or prompts appearing on the Web server if unexpected problems occur with a report request. If the Automation Server displays a message or prompt on the Web server screen while a browser is waiting for a report request, it's doubtful that the Web master will be sitting by, waiting to respond to the Web server message. The browser session will hang, or eventually time out, if this happens.

For complete information on the Report Engine Automation Server's object model, methods, and properties, refer to Chapter 25, or look in Crystal Reports Developer's Help.

Manipulating the Report Object

Once the Report object has been assigned to an .RPT file, you can use your user interface elements, such as controls on the calling form, to customize the way the report behaves. Use objects, collections, methods, and properties for the Report object to control report behavior.

Here are some examples:

```
session("oRpt").DiscardSavedData
session("oRpt").RecordSelectionFormula = _
   "{Orders.Order Amount} < " & CStr(Request.Form("value"))
```

This code first discards any saved data records that may exist within the .RPT file. It then sets the Report object's RecordSelectionFormula property to limit the report to orders over the amount supplied by the user in a control named "value" on the calling form. Notice that the CStr function is used just to make sure that the entire value being submitted to the RecordSelectionProperty is a string.

The following sample code is used to pass a value to a report parameter field:

```
Set session("ParamCollection") = Session("oRpt").Parameterfields
Set Param1 =  session("ParamCollection").Item("Report Title")
ParamValue = Request.Form("ParamValue")
Call Param1.SetCurrentValue CStr(ParamValue), 12
```

Again, this code is using the value from the calling form object "ParamValue" to pass to the SetCurrentValue method. This method applies to a member of the ParameterFields collection of the Report object.

Notice that in the previous parameter field code, an object variable is set to the ParameterFields collection, another object variable is set to the "Report Title" member of the collection, and a variant variable is assigned the value of the calling form "ParamValue" control. The SetCurrentValue method is then called using all of the previously declared variables. While this is perfectly acceptable and does allow your code to only delve one level deep in the Automation Server's object hierarchy, it does involve more object and variable declarations that can introduce more chances for errors. Examine the following alternative:

```
Session("oRpt").ParameterFields("Report Title").SetCurrentValue _
CStr(Request.Form("ParamValue")),12
```

Here, the same parameter field assignment is accomplished by navigating down through the Report object's hierarchy directly—no additional object variables need to be assigned. Also, notice that the calling form's "ParamValue" control is supplied directly to the SetCurrentValue method without being placed in an intermediate variable. Just remember that you should use a type declaration function (such as CStr) to ensure that the proper data type is being passed to the Automation Server.

Once you've set all necessary properties for the report object and are ready to process the report, you may need to execute the Report object's ReadRecords method to actually populate the report with data from the database. If the report is based on a PC-style database or an ODBC connection that the Web server can reach during the report process, this step may not be necessary. However, if you've used the SetPrivateData method to change the data source of the report to an ADO recordset or some other data source that's only in scope in the current VBScript procedure, you'll need to execute ReadRecords so that the report won't fail. If you don't, and the Report object is used in another VBScript procedure (such as RPTSERVER.ASP) when the recordset is no longer in scope, the report won't be able to read records from the recordset. Here's sample code to execute ReadRecords:

```
On Error Resume Next
session("oRpt").ReadRecords
If Err.Number <> 0 Then Response.Write _
   "A server error occurred when trying to access the data source"
```

The PageEngine Object

The Automation Server exposes a PageEngine object that you normally don't need to worry about in Visual Basic applications because of the Automation Server's internal report viewer. However, since you need to pass the Report object to RPTSERVER.ASP to page out to a Crystal Smart Viewer, you need to declare the PageEngine object so that RPTSERVER.ASP can use it to communicate with the Smart Viewers. If you look at RPTSERVER.ASP, you'll be able to get an idea (probably after a significant amount of poking around, though) of how the PageEngine works. Declare it with code similar to the following:

```
If IsObject(session("oPageEngine")) Then
    set session("oPageEngine") = Nothing
End If
Set session("oPageEngine") = session("oRpt").PageEngine
```

Caution   *Because RPTSERVER.ASP is the ultimate ASP that processes the report, you'll need to think about it when you declare session variables. It expects three session variables to be declared with specific names:* session("oApp") *which is the Application object,* session("oRpt") *which is the Report object, and* session("oPageEngine") *which is the PageEngine object. Don't use alternative variable names for these session variables, or RPTSERVER.ASP will fail.*

Using the Smart Viewers

As discussed previously, the Report Engine Automation Server's built-in preview window won't work with a Web browser—you have to use a Crystal Smart Viewer. To use the Smart Viewer for ActiveX or the Smart Viewer for Java, you can add the Object or Applet tags and parameters that were outlined in the "Customizing Smart Viewer Behavior" section of this chapter. Just make sure the report name you pass to the viewers is RPTSERVER.ASP, not the actual .RPT file that you assigned to the Report object.

Seagate also provides some intermediate ASPs that you can use to set up the Smart Viewers without explicitly coding the Applet or Object tags. You'll find SmartViewerActiveX.ASP, SmartViewerJava.ASP, SmartViewerHTMLFrame.ASP, and SmartViewerHTMLPage.ASP in the *<Crystal Reports Program>*\sample\ASPSamples folder. You can just copy and paste the code from one of the ASPs into your own file, or use the VBScript *#include file* statement to bring in the proper Smart Viewer code. If you've set up a control (perhaps a drop-down list) on your application form that allows the user to choose a Smart Viewer, you might use code similar to the following to set the chosen Smart Viewer:

```
viewer = Request.Form("Viewer")
If cstr(viewer) = "ActiveX (IE Only)" then
%>
<!-- #include file="SmartViewerActiveX.asp" -->
<%
```

```
ElseIf cstr(viewer) = "Java" then
%>
<!-- #include file="SmartViewerJava.asp" -->
<%
ElseIf cstr(viewer) = "HTML Frame" then
%>
<!-- #include file="SmartViewerHTMLFrame.asp" -->
<%
Else
%>
<!-- #include file="SmartViewerHTMLPage.asp" -->
<%
End If
```

The Seagate-supplied Smart Viewer ASPs for Java and ActiveX set certain viewer parameters to default settings. If you simply want to change these options, you can change the Seagate ASPs to use your new desired options (perhaps you don't want to offer a Print or Export button to your users at any time). If you only want to hard code a change for a particular application, while others still use the Seagate defaults, you'll need to copy the code from one of the Seagate files into your own ASP file and change the parameter in your own file.

And finally, if you have set up yet other user options to control Smart Viewer behavior, you can conditionally set the Smart Viewer parameters based on a control on a form. Look at the following sample code:

```
<% 'Set drill down parameter based on check box
If Request.Form("chkSummary") = ON Then %>
   <PARAM NAME="EnableDrillDown" VALUE=1>
<% Else %>
   <PARAM NAME="EnableDrillDown" VALUE=0>
<% End If %>
```

Note   *The <% and %> characters in the preceding code indicate separation of the server-side ASP script from the actual text to be submitted to the browser. Because the parameters are part of the Smart Viewer Object tag, they'll need to be returned to the browser, while the If-Then-Else statement will execute on the server. This separation of server-side script from client-side HTML is the basic premise of Active Server Pages.*

CRYSTAL REPORTS 7
ON THE WEB

The Complete Reference

Crystal Reports 7

Part IV

Appendixes

The Complete Reference

Appendix A

Installing and Configuring Crystal Reports Components

Installing Crystal Reports is a fairly straightforward process, especially if you are simply installing with a standard set of options on an end-user PC. If you wish to install Crystal Query Server (and presumably update it to the new Analysis server) or install the Crystal Web Server components on a Web server, there are a few more installation and configuration options that you'll want to pay special attention to.

The steps for installing the 32-bit version of Crystal Reports and 16-bit Crystal Reports are similar, but not entirely the same. In particular, some 32-bit components, such as the Crystal Web Reporting options and Crystal Query server and client, won't be available when you install 16-bit Crystal Reports. This chapter discusses the 32-bit installation.

Installing the Crystal Reports Designer

When you put the Crystal Reports program CD into a CD-ROM drive, the Setup program will start automatically in Windows 95/98 and Windows NT 4. If Setup doesn't start automatically (perhaps your CD-ROM drive has Auto-Insert notification turned off), you can start Setup manually by navigating to the root directory of the CD and double-clicking SETUP.EXE. The Installation Menu will appear. If you wish to see demos of Seagate products, you can click those options. When you're ready to install Crystal Reports, choose the 16-bit installation program (typically used if you're still using Windows 3.1) or the 32-bit installation program for Windows 95 or greater or for Windows NT 3.51 or greater.

Typical Setup prompts, including a prompt for the installation key on the back of the CD, will appear. Click the Next button after responding to a prompt to continue. Of particular note is the prompt giving you the option to choose a Typical or Custom setup. Typical setup includes almost all Crystal Reports components, including developer files, the Crystal Query Server and Client, and Web Server components (if you are running a Web server on the machine that Crystal Reports is being installed on). If you choose the Custom option, a Custom Installation Options dialog box will appear, as shown in Figure A-1.

Here you can choose to add the few additional components that aren't chosen by default, or remove some components that you don't want to install. For example, if you want to install just the Web Server components without actually installing the Crystal Reports Designer, you can make that choice here (although it's highly recommended that you install Crystal Reports on the Web server to help with troubleshooting of Web reports). Just make sure it still includes the Database Access and Developer's Files along with the Web Reports Server components.

As with most common setup programs, if a check box is checked, but is shaded gray, it means that some of that item's options are selected, but not all. Even if the

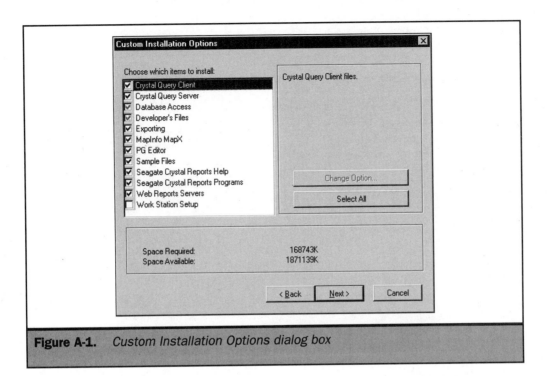

Figure A-1. *Custom Installation Options dialog box*

check box is not gray, there may be additional options available for that item—select the item next to the check box, and if there are additional options available for the item, the Change Option button will be enabled. Click it to see another set of check box options just for that topic. Once you've chosen all the custom options you want to use, click Next to proceed through the installation process.

Installing Web Components on Your Web Server

Setup will automatically detect a Web server running on the machine you are setting up. If you choose the Typical option, the Crystal Web Reports Server components will be installed automatically. If you choose the Custom option, you'll have a choice of whether or not to install the Web reporting options. If you are installing on a Microsoft Web server with Active Server Pages, you can select the Web Reports Servers option on the Custom dialog box and click Change Options. You'll then be presented with check boxes to choose one or both the Web Reports Server and Active Server Pages extensions. Once you've made this choice, Setup will then prompt you for a more detailed choice of which Web server components you wish to install, as shown here:

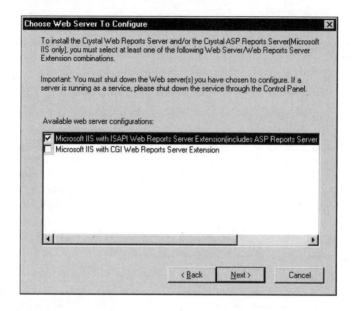

This dialog box is based on the Web servers that are detected on the PC that Setup is running on. If you are running Netscape or Microsoft Web servers, you'll be given two options: the ISAPI or NSAPI Web server extension and the CGI Web server. You can choose either or both. Generally, you can expect better results with Microsoft and Netscape servers if you use their native API interfaces. If you are running a Web server other than Netscape or Microsoft, you'll be given the option to install the CGI Web server. If you do so, you'll need to choose the directory on your Web server where the CGI program should be installed (typically CGI-BIN).

If the Web components are being installed on a Windows NT computer, you'll be asked whether you want to install the Web Image Server and Web Page Server as NT services. If you choose Yes, additional entries will be placed in the Windows NT Control Panel Services icon, which you can double-click later to configure the services. Because NT services will start as soon as the computer boots, regardless of who may or may not be logged on, it's highly recommended that you install these items as services. If you choose not to, you'll only be able to start them manually from the Crystal Reports program group.

Note *If you're installing the Web Reports Server to a Windows 95/98 computer running Personal Web Server, you'll be asked if you want to add the Image and Page Servers to the Startup group. Again, it's a good idea to let Setup do this so that these items will start when the machine boots.*

Web Reports Server Configuration Utility

Once the Crystal Reports Web software has been copied to the Web server's hard disk, the Crystal Web Reports Server Configuration dialog box will appear, as shown in Figure A-2. If you decide to just accept the default settings (which, in most cases, are perfectly acceptable), click OK. If you later decide to reconfigure the Web Reports Server, you choose the Web Reports Server Configuration option from the Crystal Reports program group.

If you click Help on the Crystal Web Reports Server Configuration dialog box, you'll be presented with detailed descriptions of each of the following options. General descriptions of the options are provided here.

THE PAGE SERVER TAB   The Page Server tab configures the Web Reports Server component that feeds page-on-demand information to the Crystal Smart Viewers. Specify the TCP/IP port used by the Page Server and the virtual directory where the ActiveX and Java viewers are located (typically /viewer by default). If you click the Advanced button, another dialog box appears where you can configure how many NT threads the Page Server can use, how often the Page Server will refresh reports that

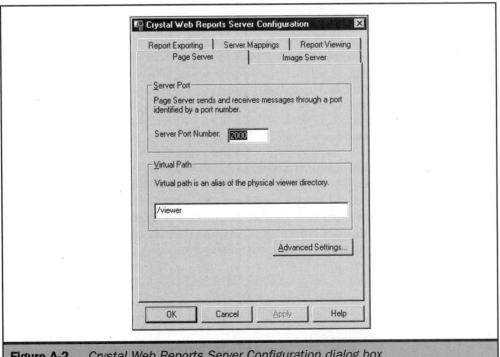

Figure A-2.   *Crystal Web Reports Server Configuration dialog box*

have been cached for repeat viewing, how many simultaneous jobs can be handled, and how long to wait before closing an idle job.

THE IMAGE SERVER TAB   The Image Server tab configures the Web Reports Server component that converts Crystal Reports graphics to JPEG files when reports are viewed in HTML Smart Viewers. Choose a TCP/IP port number and the number of threads you wish to assign to the Image Server component.

THE REPORT EXPORTING TAB   If your Web viewers use either the Smart Viewer for ActiveX or the Smart Viewer for Java, they'll be able to export reports to Crystal Reports, Microsoft Word, Excel, and Rich Text format by clicking the Export button in the viewer. This tab lets you turn the entire export function, or an individual export format, on or off globally. If you turn any of these options off, users won't be able to export Web reports. Don't forget, though, that you can leave these global options turned on and still control whether or not the Export button is enabled by customizing the Smart Viewers, as described in Chapter 29.

THE SERVER MAPPINGS TAB   The Web Reports Server adds two recognized file types to your Web server: .RPT for Crystal Reports files, and .CRI for Crystal Image Server files. Use this tab to map the TCP/IP ports used by the Page Server and Image Server to these specific file extensions. These ports must correspond to the ports specified on the Page Server and Image Server tabs. To change a setting, choose the file extension you wish to modify, and click Edit. You can then change the port number or Web server name if necessary.

THE REPORT VIEWING TAB   This tab allows you to choose whether or not users can actually view reports from the Web Reports Server, which options are available on Smart Viewers, and the Web Reports Server will generate a group tree, and if so, how large. If you only want to export reports to alternative file formats, turn off the View Report Allowed option. If you leave the option turned on, you can then set the buttons and options that you want displayed by default on the ActiveX or Java Smart Viewers. When these viewers are displayed in a Web browser, these controls and functions will only be available if the option has been enabled here. Note that if you place Applet or Object tags in your Web pages directly (as discussed in Chapter 29), the settings in the Web Configuration Utility can be overridden by the Object and Applet parameters.

If you click the Cache button on this tab, another dialog box appears where you can specify the maximum size, the location, and the interval to "clean up" the location where the Web Reports Server stores cached page-on-demand files for Smart Viewers.

Note   *Setup will stop your Web server to install Web components. If you don't immediately restart your computer after installing Crystal Reports, you'll need to manually restart your Web server.*

Installing Seagate Analysis

When you install the first release of Crystal Reports 7, you'll be installing an early version of a query tool known as Crystal Query. Since this version of Crystal Reports was released, Seagate has announced a free query tool called Seagate Analysis (see Chapter 18 for details). If you've already installed Crystal Query along with Crystal Reports 7, you'll want to upgrade it to Seagate Analysis, because Analysis provides more functionality and performs more reliably.

If you are installing Crystal Reports and Seagate Analysis at the same time, you'll want to install Crystal Reports first, so the Query Server will be installed. You can then install Seagate Analysis, which will update the Query Server to the newer Seagate Analysis Server configuration. When installing the 32-bit version of Crystal Reports with the Custom setup option, you'll be prompted to install the Crystal Query Server and Crystal Query Client components. These will be installed by default if you use the Typical option.

If you choose to install the Crystal Query Server, you'll be asked if you wish to install it as an NT service. If you choose Yes, an additional entry will be placed in the Windows NT Control Panel Services icon, which you can double-click later to configure the service. Because NT services will start as soon as the computer boots, regardless of who may or may not be logged on, it's highly recommended that you install this as a service. If you choose not to, you'll only be able to start it manually from the Crystal Reports program group. You'll then be presented with the Query Server configuration dialog box. Just leave these options as-is during Crystal Reports setup. You'll want to return to this dialog box once you've installed Seagate Analysis, which upgrades the Query Server, to make any necessary changes.

Running Seagate Analysis Setup

After you've completed installing Crystal Reports, particularly after you've installed the Crystal Query Server or Crystal Query Client, you'll want to install Seagate Analysis on the same machine to upgrade these components with newer Seagate Analysis capabilities. Insert the Seagate Analysis CD into your CD-ROM drive. If the Analysis Setup program doesn't start automatically, navigate to the CD and double-click SETUP.EXE. Once Setup starts, click the Install Seagate Analysis button to begin.

Seagate Analysis is developed in the Java programming language. In order to run Analysis with Windows 95, 98, or NT (Analysis doesn't run in a 16-bit Windows environment), your computer will need to have the Microsoft Java VM (Virtual Machine) installed. Analysis Setup detects the presence or absence of the Microsoft Java VM, and installs it automatically if necessary. If Setup needs to install the Java VM, you'll be notified and you will need to reboot your computer once the installation is complete. Once the machine reboots, Analysis Setup will continue automatically.

If Analysis Setup determines that an existing Crystal Reports 7 Query Server is installed on your computer, you'll be given a prompt indicating that it will be upgraded.

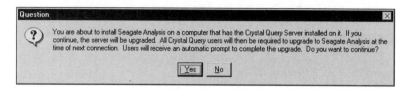

This is merely a notification that your Query Server will be upgraded from a Crystal Query Server to a Seagate Analysis Server. This will then require older Crystal Query Clients to also upgrade to Seagate Analysis. This process is totally automatic for end-users—when they next connect to the Analysis Server (typically through a Web browser), their Crystal Query Client will be automatically updated to Seagate Analysis.

  When you install Seagate Analysis on an existing Query Server computer, you'll need to have a shared folder that contains the Analysis Client upgrade program, which is used to automatically upgrade old Crystal Query Client software to Seagate Analysis. Setup may not automatically share this QclientInstall folder as QClient (the default share name for the update directory). When clients try to install Seagate Analysis from a Web browser, an error message will result. If this should happen, you'll need to use Windows Explorer to share the QclientInstall folder with the share name QClient.

Configuring the Query/Analysis Server

Once you've installed Seagate Analysis, and the Query Server has been upgraded to a Seagate Analysis Server, you may want to fine-tune the Analysis Server's performance, or set other configuration options. Regardless of whether you've set up the Analysis Server to run as an NT Service or are just running it from the Crystal Reports program group, you use the same steps to set its configuration. Just choose the Crystal Query Server item from the Seagate Crystal Reports program group. Even if the Analysis Server is already running as an NT service, the Analysis Server icon will still appear in the lower right of the Windows taskbar. Double-click the icon and the Analysis Server will appear. Choose File | Options to display the Seagate Analysis Server Options dialog box, as shown in Figure A-3.

  For a detailed description of the Analysis Server configuration options, look at README.HLP in the Crystal Reports program directory, or choose Crystal Reports Readme from the Crystal Reports program group. Search the Help file for "Configuring the Query Server."

You can set several configuration options on this screen, as well as the supplementary screens that appear when you click the Default Client Options and Local Manager Options buttons.

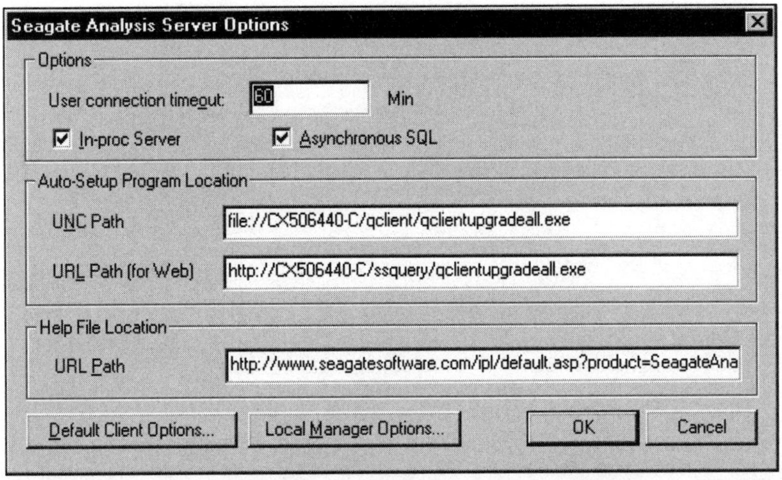

Seagate Analysis Server Options   ☒

┌─ Options ──┐
│   User connection timeout: [80]   Min   │
│   ☑ In-proc Server   ☑ Asynchronous SQL   │
└──┘
┌─ Auto-Setup Program Location ───┐
│   UNC Path   [file://CX506440-C/qclient/qclientupgradeall.exe] │
│   │
│   URL Path (for Web) [http://CX506440-C/ssquery/qclientupgradeall.exe] │
└──┘
┌─ Help File Location ──┐
│   URL Path   [http://www.seagatesoftware.com/ipl/default.asp?product=SeagateAna] │
└──┘

[Default Client Options...] [Local Manager Options...]   [OK   ] [Cancel]

Figure A-3.   *Analysis Server options*

The first panel in the initial Analysis Server Configuration dialog box contains options for controlling the length of time the Analysis Server will allow no activity from an Analysis Client before disconnecting it, as well as settings that control the way the Analysis Server interacts with the operating system and SQL databases. The Auto-Setup Program Location information is used to determine where the Analysis Client upgrade program is located, for both client/server and Web-connected Crystal Query clients. And, the Help File Location URL Path indicates where client/server and Web-connected Analysis clients will find online Help.

If your users are accessing Seagate Analysis from a Web server, or using Client/Server mode (discussed in Chapter 18), your network must have a persistent connection to the Internet. This is because the online documentation for client/server Seagate Analysis comes directly from the Seagate Web site. If you'd prefer to point your client/server Analysis users directly to documentation on your local Web server, change the Help File Location URL Path text box in Analysis Server configuration to http://<Web server>/ssquery/docs/.

If you click the Default Client Options button, the Default Client Options dialog box will appear, as illustrated in Figure A-4.

Most of the settings here can also be made on the Analysis Client. Many of the settings in this dialog box, however, will be sent to the client as the default settings when the client starts—if an option is checked here, it will be on by default when the client starts. The Data Options settings determine how many records, or how large the

APPENDIXES

Default Client Options

Data Options

Max DB Records: `0`   Browse Records: `100`

Rowset Batch: `100`

☐ Auto Refresh   ☑ Server Side Grouping   ☐ Save Data With Document

View Options:

Report Style: `Standard` ▾

☑ Allow editing links   ☑ Show link panel   ☐ Need to verify logon

☑ Show rowset panel   ☐ Show long field name   ☑ Show Analysis Explorer

☑ Group content view

[OK] [Cancel]

Figure A-4.   *Default Client options*

batches of records will be, when the Query Server communicates with a SQL Server. The View Options settings determine default behavior when the Query Client views result sets or reports. Once you've finished making changes to this dialog box, click OK to return to the main Query Server Configuration screen. There, you can click the Local Manager Options button to choose default directories for Query Server files.

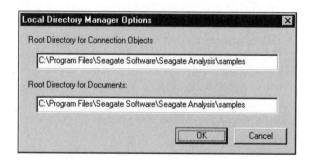

Local Directory Manager Options

Root Directory for Connection Objects

`C:\Program Files\Seagate Software\Seagate Analysis\samples`

Root Directory for Documents:

`C:\Program Files\Seagate Software\Seagate Analysis\samples`

[OK] [Cancel]

When you use a Web-connected or client/server Seagate Analysis client, these directories act as the root directory for the Analysis Explorer window. When you base a query on an existing Connection object, or choose to open or create an Analysis document, the contents of the directories you specify here will be displayed.

Configuring NT Service Startup Options

If you choose to install the Web Reports Server's Page Server, Image Server, or the Crystal Query Server as Windows NT services, you'll need to properly configure them to work with Windows NT security. If you leave them set to their default configurations, there may be potential security conflicts that prevent them from accessing all necessary files on the Web server machine or the network. If you have Administrative rights on the Web server or Analysis Server computer, you can change the default Windows NT userid and password that these services use.

From the Control Panel, double-click the Services icon. The list of all Windows NT services will appear. You'll find services named Crystal Web Image Server, Crystal Web Page Server, and Crystal Query Server. Select the first service that you want to configure, and click the Startup button. The Service dialog box will appear, as shown here:

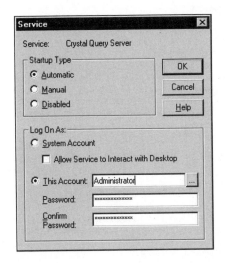

If you want to have the service start automatically when the system boots, choose Automatic as the startup method. No matter what startup method you choose, you will need to reassign these services to a Windows NT user account with Domain Administrator rights—the System account to which they're initially assigned may not give them sufficient rights on the network. The services will log in to Windows NT with the userid and password that you specify here whenever they start up. Once you've set these options, click OK to save your changes. Then, choose the remaining two services and make the same change. When you restart the services (or the next time you boot the machine), these services will start automatically, logging in to Windows NT with a userid with sufficient rights.

The Windows NT userid assigned to the Crystal Query service may affect the ODBC data sources that are available for Seagate Analysis clients that connect to the Server in client/server mode. Ensure that necessary ODBC data sources are available on the server machine for the userid being used by the Crystal Query service.

Appendix B

What's on the Accompanying CD

This book is accompanied by a CD that contains a wealth of free software and sample files. You'll find a complete, unrestricted copy of Seagate Analysis, Seagate Software's new query, reporting, and multidimensional OLAP tool. There's also Seagate Info 7, Seagate's report and OLAP scheduling and distribution system. And, Version 6 of the Report Designer component is included.

Most of the sample report, Visual Basic, and Web files referred to in the text are also on the CD. Use them to see examples of advanced reporting techniques and several methods of Crystal Reports/Visual Basic integration. You'll also find a complete sample Web site that uses the Crystal Web Reports Server to integrate a report on the Web.

Simply insert the CD into your CD-ROM drive. You should see the CD main menu appear, shown here:

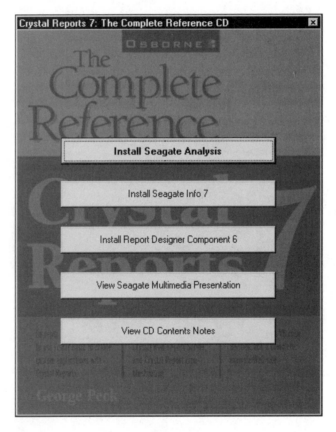

If you don't, double-click on the STARTUP.EXE file on the CD to display the CD menu.

Free Software

Use and enjoy the free software that Seagate Software has provided for the CD. Choose the package you wish to install from the CD main menu, or look in the following sections for more detailed installation instructions. If you'd like to learn more about these products, there's a Seagate multimedia demo right on the CD. Choose the option for this demo from the CD main menu, or just double-click SSMMEDIA.EXE in the root folder of the CD.

Seagate Analysis

Seagate Analysis, Seagate's newest query, reporting, and multidimensional OLAP tool is provided in the \SA folder on the CD. You can install it by:

- Choosing the option from the CD's main menu or,
- Navigating to the \SA folder and double-clicking SETUP.EXE to begin Seagate Analysis installation.

Once you start Seagate Analysis, complete online documentation is provided. Support for Seagate Analysis is available via e-mail, provided you register your copy of Analysis. This is a full, unrestricted copy of the software. Feel free to share it with others in your company, as well!

Seagate Info 7

You'll also find a copy of Seagate Info 7, Seagate's multi-tier report, query, and OLAP scheduling and distribution system. You can install it by:

- Choosing the option from the CD's main menu or,
- Navigating to the WIN32\X86 folder on the CD and double-clicking SETUP.EXE to install Seagate Info.

To explore most of Seagate Info's features on a stand-alone computer, just choose the Standard Seagate Info Client Components option when you run Setup. If you wish to explore more of Seagate Info's multi-tier component capabilities, you'll need to run Setup on multiple machines. This can be a little more complicated, so look at the Getting Started Guide (GETSTART.PDF) in the \SI\X86\Docs folder on the CD for more information. You may also install a free Computer Based Training module that discusses Seagate Info Administration. Navigate to the \CBT folder on the CD and run SETUP.EXE.

APPENDIXES

This copy of Seagate Info provides 50 client licenses and one developer license. It is not time-limited in any way. Additional licenses can be purchased from Seagate.

Report Designer Component 6

The Report Designer component (RDC) Version 6 (discussed in Chapter 24) is included, in case you haven't purchased Crystal Reports 7 Professional Edition. The Report Designer component allows you to design your reports from start to finish right in the Visual Basic Integrated Development Environment. Then, control all aspects of your report at run time with the RDC's rich object model. You can install the RDC by:

- Choosing the option from the CD main menu or,
- Navigating to the \RDC6 folder on the CD and double-click on the self-extracting CRVBSTP.EXE file.

If you've already installed Crystal Reports 7 Professional, use the included RDC Version 7. Additional features particular to Crystal Reports 7 are made available by this latest version.

Sample Files

The CD contains a selection of sample report files, sample Visual Basic applications, and a Web site that can be used with the Crystal Web Reports Server. Most of the samples are discussed in detail in the relevant chapters in the book.

Sample Reports

A good selection of reports can be found in the \Sample Reports folder on the CD. Most names of the sample reports are self-explanatory. Most are also saved with Save Data with Report turned on, so that you'll be able to view the report content as soon as you open the report. You'll see screen shots of many of these reports in their relevant chapters in the book. Also, many of the reports contain comments—either in text objects placed right in the report sections, or as comments placed in the report formulas.

All sample report files are created against the XTREME.MDB sample database that's installed with Crystal Reports 7. Depending on the concepts demonstrated in the report, it uses either a direct-access connection to Microsoft Access (the Data File button was used when the report was created), or the Xtreme Sample Data ODBC data source, which points to XTREME.MDB. In both cases, the expected location of the database is C:\Program Files\Seagate Software\Crystal Reports\XTREME.MDB. If your installation of XTREME.MDB is in a different path, you'll need to use the Set Location command (Database I Set Location) to point the report to the proper database.

Sample Visual Basic Applications

Part II of the book discusses several methods of integrating Crystal Reports into Visual Basic applications. There are completed sample applications for each of these integration methods on the CD. If you'd like to work through the applications on your own while you read the book, the report used in the integration, along with the Visual Basic project and form that are used to integrate the report, are located right in the \Visual Basic folder. Just copy the Visual Basic files and the .RPT file to your hard disk, and open the project in VB.

The completed applications are located in their own folders within the \Visual Basic folder. The subfolders are named according to the integration method that is demonstrated in the application. Again, just copy all the files from the desired folder to your hard disk, and open the project file in Visual Basic.

Sample Web Site

A complete Web site using the Crystal Web Reports Server is contained in the \Web Reports Server folder on the CD. You'll find the report that is integrated on the Web, along with several HTML and graphics files.

In order to view the sample Web site, you must have a working Web server with the Crystal Web Reports Server installed. Copy the files in the \Web Reports Server folder from the CD into a virtual directory on the Web server. Then point your browser to the Web server and the virtual directory. For example, if you create a virtual directory called XTREME and then copy the files from the CD to it, point your browser to http://<Web server>/XTREME to view the site. Just opening the DEFAULT.HTM file from the CD directly in your Web browser won't work, as there won't be a Web server to intercept the .RPT file and display it in a Smart Viewer.

APPENDIXES

Index

D

Q

U